AI Driven Tools for Sustainable Public Administration

Ulas Akkucuk
Bogazici University, Turkey

Murat Onder
Boğaziçi University, İstanbul, Turkey

IGI Global
Scientific Publishing
Publishing Tomorrow's Research Today

Published in the United States of America by
IGI Global Scientific Publishing
701 East Chocolate Avenue
Hershey, PA, 17033, USA
Tel: 717-533-8845
Fax: 717-533-8661
Website: https://www.igi-global.com E-mail: cust@igi-global.com

Library of Congress Cataloging-in-Publication Data

Names: Akkucuk, Ulas, 1975- editor. | Onder, Murat, editor.
Title: AI driven tools for sustainable public administration / Edited by Ulas Akkucuk, Murat Onder.
Description: Hershey, PA : IGI Global Scientific Publishing, [2025] | Includes bibliographical references and index. | Summary: "As artificial intelligence continues to transform various sectors, its potential to drive sustainability and efficiency in public administration is unparalleled. This book aims to explore innovative AI solutions that can enhance public services, optimize resource management, and foster transparent governance"-- Provided by publisher.
Identifiers: LCCN 2024054446 (print) | LCCN 2024054447 (ebook) | ISBN 9798369383728 (hardcover) | ISBN 9798369383735 (paperback) | ISBN 9798369383742 (ebook)
Subjects: LCSH: Public administration--Technological innovations. | Artificial intelligence. | Sustainable development.
Classification: LCC JF1525.A8 A42 2025 (print) | LCC JF1525.A8 (ebook) | DDC 351.0285/63--dc23/eng/20250214
LC record available at https://lccn.loc.gov/2024054446
LC ebook record available at https://lccn.loc.gov/2024054447

British Cataloguing in Publication Data
A Cataloguing in Publication record for this book is available from the British Library.

Table of Contents

Detailed Table of Contents

The chapter examines the complex ties among privacy, surveillance, and public safety in today's world of AI-driven governance. The chapter will further examine what happens when a data-driven decision-making process works without transparency in Nigeria. Historically, those in authority have had an easier time keeping power when the decision-making process is hidden from the citizens. It will outline compelling strategies for mitigating the privacy risks that come with using AI in law enforcement, such as strong democratic oversight, the use of AI in a "data minimized" way, and the design of AI systems that ensures privacy is maximized. The chapter concludes by arguing that these strategies—and the informed, equitable future they make possible—are better than the alternative: a society governed by AI systems that infringe on individual rights and are not safe or secure.

This chapter examines the technological, economical and societal obstacles that may prevent Artificial Intelligence from being widely used in public administration. In order to fully utilise AI's potential to improve public administration, obstacles must be addressed. Adoption of AI necessitates a large initial financial outlay, which is sometimes limited by financial constraints and conflicting goals in the public sector. Additional financial strains are incurred by long-term maintenance and training costs. Social resistance to AI originates from worries about data privacy, distrust of automated systems, and fears about job displacement. Furthermore, the acceptance of AI may be slowed down by public awareness of its ethical ramifications. In order to fully utilise AI's potential to improve public administration decision-making, efficiency, and transparency, it is imperative that these obstacles be addressed. This chapter gives a detailed analysis of these barriers, offering stakeholders and policymakers insights in advancing AI adoption.

This chapter provides a comprehensive framework for the implementation of Artificial Intelligence (AI) in public administration. It highlights the growing importance of AI technologies in improving public services, while emphasizing the need for a systematic approach to their deployment, also examines the literature on AI frameworks, outlines the basic benefits and risks of AI in public administration, and suggests guidelines for responsible implementation. It also seeks to provide a comprehensive understanding of the effective integration of AI tools in public management to enhance public value while upholding ethical standards.

This qualitative study examines the perspectives of 60 public authorities from six metropolitan areas: Copenhagen, Helsinki, Bucharest, Milan, Prague, and Berlin, regarding the use of AI technologies in public service provision. The research explores both the potential benefits and challenges associated with AI implementation. Many respondents expressed positive attitudes towards AI as a tool to improve public service delivery, while others voiced concerns about AI's developmental stage. A portion of the participants indicated that their lack of familiarity and technological literacy regarding AI was a barrier to its effective adoption. This highlights the need for training programs to equip local authorities with the skills to utilize AI in enhancing public services. The study also analyzes the data using MAXQDA software to categorize themes and provide structured insights. The findings emphasize the importance of preparing metropolitan managers for AI integration and offer strategic proposals for its successful implementation in public administration.

Technology with Artificial intelligence (AI) continues to evolve daily and transform public administrations. This study focuses on natural language processing (NLP), one of the effective AI technologies. Sustainability will be addressed within the

The Turkish judicial system is very fragmented and each unit has its own rules, it is more accurate to focus on the benefits of AI to the Turkish judicial system in general rather than examining the units in the Turkish judicial system one by one. In addition, preliminary preparations are vital for governmental duties, education and legal strategies in order to use AI more efficiently. The proposed ways for the application of AI-based tools for the utilization of the AI-based technology in Turkish courts will be analyzed. The problem of acceptability and serviceability of AI in the Turkish judiciary will be analyzed by the help of previous studies, legal reasonings, current examples and existing theories. Firstly, examples around the world regarding the usage of AI systems in law will be discussed. Secondly, examples from Türkiye regarding the usage of AI in law will be discussed. Finally, whether the decision-making mechanism in Turkish law is compatible with the AI systems will be discussed and recommendations will be made to increase the use of the AI systems.

Preface

In an age where technological innovation is reshaping society, artificial intelligence (AI) emerges as a pivotal force in advancing sustainable public administration. The capabilities of AI to optimize decision-making, streamline services, and foster sustainability hold profound implications for the future of governance. This edited volume, **"AI Tools for Sustainable Public Administration,"** aims to offer a comprehensive exploration of how AI is transforming public administration across the globe.

This book brings together contributions from experts across disciplines, showcasing the diverse applications of AI in addressing complex challenges. By examining both opportunities and barriers, it provides a holistic view of how AI tools can be integrated into public systems while maintaining a focus on sustainability and ethical governance.

CHAPTER OVERVIEW

The chapters are structured to guide readers through a detailed exploration of AI's potential and its practical implications:

1. **Introduction: AI Tools for Sustainable Public Administration** sets the stage by introducing the fundamental concepts and potential of AI in public administration. It provides a foundational understanding of how these technologies are driving sustainable governance.
2. **Steering the AI Revolution in Local Governments: Merits and Demerits** talks about the advantages and limitations of implementing AI at the local government level. It highlights lessons learned and offers insights for future adoption strategies.

3. **Balancing Public Safety and Individual Rights in AI-Driven Public Administration in Nigeria** provides a focused examination of the ethical dilemmas and trade-offs involved in leveraging AI for governance, with a specific case study on Nigeria.
4. **AI-Driven Tools for Sustainable Public Administration: Identification of Potential Barriers to AI Adoption** addresses the technological, organizational, and societal hurdles that impede the effective integration of AI in public systems.
5. **AI in Public Services: Analysing AI-Driven Tools in Healthcare, Education, Transportation, and Safety** explores the transformative role of AI across critical public service sectors, emphasizing its contributions to efficiency and inclusivity.
6. **Implementing Artificial Intelligence in Public Administration – Managing Challenges, Risks, and Opportunities** presents strategies for navigating the complexities of AI adoption, focusing on mitigating risks while leveraging opportunities.
7. **Innovative Intelligence: AI Tools Transforming Public Service Excellence** highlights cutting-edge AI tools and their applications in driving innovation and excellence in public service delivery.
8. **Metropolitan Managers' Perspectives on Artificial Intelligence (AI) Technologies** shares insights from metropolitan managers on the practical implementation and perceived benefits of AI technologies in urban governance.
9. **Natural Language Processing (NLP) for Sustainable Public Administration** examines the role of NLP in enhancing communication, automating administrative tasks, and fostering citizen engagement.
10. **Algorithmic Governance and Its Transformative Role in Decision-Making** explores how algorithmic systems are reshaping decision-making processes, emphasizing transparency and accountability.
11. **Cost-effective Sustainable Energy Solutions for Turkey: AI-Driven Renewables** provides a case study on Turkey, illustrating how AI is advancing renewable energy solutions and addressing energy challenges.
12. **Intentions and Premises: An Analysis of Sustainability in U.S. Security Institutions' AI Strategies** critically examines the integration of sustainability principles into AI strategies within U.S. security institutions.
13. **Mitigating Financial Anomalies: Dimensions, Vulnerability, and Stratagem in Service Organizations** explores policy and ethical considerations in addressing financial vulnerabilities in public administration.
14. **The Use of Artificial Intelligence in the Turkish Judiciary** analyzes the adoption of AI in judicial processes, highlighting its potential to enhance efficiency and justice delivery.

By offering diverse perspectives and in-depth analyses, this book serves as a resource for policymakers, researchers, and public administration professionals. It underscores the transformative potential of AI tools in achieving sustainable governance while fostering a thoughtful dialogue on the ethical, policy, and practical considerations of AI adoption.

As the editors, we hope this volume stimulates meaningful discussions and inspires innovative approaches to integrating AI into public administration for a sustainable future.

Ulas Akkucuk
Bogazici University, Turkey

Murat Onder
Boğaziçi University, İstanbul, Turkey

Chapter 1
Introduction:
AI Tools for Sustainable Public Administration

Murat Önder
Bogazici University, Turkey

Ulas Akkucuk
https://orcid.org/0000-0001-6731-0634
Bogazici University, Turkey

ABSTRACT

The integration of Artificial Intelligence (AI) tools into public administration presents transformative opportunities for enhancing sustainability and efficiency in governance. This edited volume explores how AI-driven solutions can address key challenges faced by public institutions, including resource management, decision-making, and citizen engagement. By leveraging artificial intelligence, machine learning, natural language processing, and predictive analytics, public administrators can make better decisions, optimize operations, reduce environmental impacts, and meet demands of citizens. The collection highlights successful case studies, identifies potential risks such as ethical concerns and data privacy issues, and outlines best practices for implementing AI in a transparent and equitable manner. Emphasizing the role of innovation in achieving sustainable development goals, this introduction to the edited volume serves as a roadmap for policymakers and practitioners aiming to harness the power of AI for a more sustainable and resilient public sector.

DOI: 10.4018/979-8-3693-8372-8.ch001

1. AI AND PUBLIC ADMINISTRATION

In contemporary governance, public authorities are called to face some transformation challenges such as the enhancement of public service efficiency and the conveyance of a sustainable public administration based on justice, solidarity, and equity. Both of these challenges can be met with the aid of artificial intelligence. AI tools are aimed at rationalizing how to solve complex issues and problems, integrating functional competencies that are hard to find in one single person, and facilitating a trust-based interaction. In fact, these tools are capable of combining a high cognitive observance of reality with human capabilities, providing auto-explanatory evidence, so people can understand "why" and "how" an output has been reached. The described evolution scenario presents AI as a useful solution to meet governance needs in a public administration moving towards providing services (Onder & Saygili, 2018) that can "think" and "interact" with people.

To acknowledge the potential of AI, in this introductory chapter to the edited volume, we will outline some significant technologies capable of redefining the way public services are offered and citizens are engaged (Van Noordt & Misuraca, 2022). AI is too often associated with "robo-administration" and, consequently, with probable several risks and dangers in terms of justice, lawfulness, and administration. This may be due to some public administration innovation inertia in acknowledging the effective role of AI tools as a resource rather than a menace. Reports of these studies aim at investigating how AI technologies can really redefine the way public services are offered and citizens are engaged, enhancing public governance sustainability by respecting human dignity and the values charters, empowering citizens and public workers with a new level of non-algorithmic transparency (Lahdili, Önder, & Nyadera, 2024).

Operational AI has a deep history of evolution since its early automatic reasoning conception in the 1950s and evolved into AI symbolic methods and the modern statistical methods used recently (Shao et al.2022). With the increasing demand for e-government, AI tools have gradually become more important, which is useful to support public administration. The existing orientation, the context of countries, and their administration and society will be well served by AI in-house development, in ways that support the open governance models to the people.

Artificial Intelligence has the potential to revolutionize the services provided by public administration, natively tending to be automated, more efficient, responsive, and user-tailored, contributing to the productivity gains necessary for governments to do "more with less." The recent evolution of Information and Communication Technology has transformed citizens more into customers, increasing their expectations in public service; they are looking for quality services provided quickly to serve their needs and cannot be patient for inefficient or non-transparent processes

(Osborne, 2020; Scupola & Mergel, 2022). On-demand and timely service delivery, as well as transparency in administration processes, have become key determinants for allowing citizens to feel like participants in the governance process. But citizens also want to be partners of the government and not just customers, and this is something that e-participation can strongly create—the so-desired page of e-democracy, where everybody is part of the decision process of the governance system of public institutions. The trends are clear in the sense that he global digital audience wants a government and the public sector created by them and run for them whenever, wherever, and however they desire.

Short-term implications for the reform agenda show that worldwide the decision is clear to modernize, to make efficient and effective the operations of public administration, to bring the government to the citizen, and to change the public official into a citizen servant (Rosenbloom et al., 2022). Here is point where AI comes into the focus of e-government. With potential customized, understandable, and widely diffused AI tools and services, we can add an extra dimension to processing efficiency, citizens' governance feeling, and transparency of the system (Onder & Saygili, 2018). Challenges are also enormous, and among them is not the least the introduction of these in-house intelligence tools to the existing AI enabled services and tools. Fully AI-open populations will make the transition of introducing AI systems seamless, as such communities are already open to ICT services. The question is to what extent AI is now appropriate in policy making and policy analysis, and to what degree we will let the traditional public administration govern and be governed by human society.

Specific objective of this introduction is to develop a solid understanding of how AI tools could be applied to advance the aims of sustainable public administration in support of the implementation of the 2030 Agenda (Wirtz et al. 2020). The beneficiaries targeted by this introduction are policymakers and other relevant stakeholders in governmental organizations and other relevant stakeholders.

The central task of this introduction is to investigate the potential consequences of AI for public administration through the decentralized delivery of, or participation in, public services using AI tools in the EU context. Drawing on the initial years of widespread experimentation and piloting of applications of AI-supported decentralized public services, the overarching objective of this introduction is therefore to identify these lessons learned with the view to explore models for the adoption of AI tools for public service delivery across the globe. The introduction will therefore strive to accomplish three specific objectives (Tan et al., 2022): First, to assess the impacts of the use of AI tools for the delivery of decentralized public services. Second, to identify best practice exemplar applications of AI tools for the decentralized delivery of public services. And third, is to develop a series of recommendations for the best practice implementation of AI tools for the delivery of decentralized public services.

The focus of this introduction will be on the potential as well as the limitations of AI tools and the conceptual implications. The investigation is determined by the topical relevance of digital transformation in the public sector. Both the problems and potential solutions identified to date indicate that AI tools are a complex challenge for different areas of public administration.

2. THE ROLE OF AI IN PUBLIC ADMINISTRATION

The role and value of AI tools in public administration are vital. Through the utilization of AI tools, governments can optimize internal administration processes, such as the management of resources and the streamlining of workflows. In the public service delivery aspect, AI tools can enhance administrative decision-making processes due to the unique collection, processing, and analyzing of different sets of data (Kommisetty, 2022). However, while the emphasis is on utilizing AI for administrative services, it is more focused on services within public administration and local governments to enhance the quality of social, economic, and technological services delivered to citizens. Citizens' identity is highly connected to their relationship with public services, which, in turn, reflects their relationship with public administration in general. AI applications have a direct impact on delivering or enhancing the quality of such services. Furthermore, AI tools can represent a competitive advantage and make public services more accessible and user-friendly by optimizing and delivering a new intermediary environment, driving down costs and ultimately optimizing internal operations or citizen and business services. However, for all the benefits and opportunities that AI offers, an equal amount of challenges and obstacles can limit and even prevent AI from being successfully integrated within public administration or public service delivery. These are indicative of ethical, institutional, availability of infrastructural, and AI-literate human capital, the threat of future and unknown technological changes, as well as changes in policy and legislation. Despite these significant challenges and obstacles, AI-driven solutions promoting public interest are already starting to emerge.

Desirable for public administration, digitalization suggests an integration of artificial intelligence (AI) tools. This is broadly expected to deliver sustainable benefits of improved efficiency and greater accuracy in service delivery (Gesk & Leyer, 2022). Examples include the application of AI-based algorithms in resource management. Faster response times are similarly noted as efficiencies gained from AI usage. Challenges, however, consist of the intensified administration risks like tracking and surveillance due to greater data usage. Concerns about privacy and data over-reliance, and the potential for human and environmental harm are evident in this respect. Where AI focuses on aspects of direct safety, reliability and ethical issues stand out. Administrations face concerns that automated decision-making might prolong systemic discrimination or include forms of prejudice as the AI system may lack transparency. Such challenges may slow or impede AI implementation into public services.

To deal with AI's potential for better and for worse, the responsible use of AI within public administration requires maturity in our understanding of the benefits of AI as well as its risks if not properly governed (Desouza et al., 2020). This understanding is at the core of considering the sustainability of AI usage in public administrations. This focus is aligned with calls for the development and enactment of policy and regulatory frameworks able to substantially respond to the unique questions and practical challenges associated with AI in practice. Implementation needs to blend the technical and social, organizational prerequisites for AI embedding into public administration. The intrinsic properties and potential of AI in Public Administration can create sustainable growth of public administrations. But to date, taking seriously both the opportunities and risks of AI in public administration remains underexplored (Kuziemski & Misuraca, 2020; Pencheva et al. 2020).

3. SUSTAINABLE DEVELOPMENT GOALS AND AI

As artificial intelligence (AI) technologies continue to develop, they are shown to be an enabler in the achievement of the Sustainable Development Goals (SDGs) outlined by the 2030 Agenda for Sustainable Development. There are several ways in which AI can enable the achievement of the SDGs (Van Noordt & Misuraca, 2022). First, the development and deployment of AI tools can serve as enablers for strengthening public service delivery and evidence-based decision-making in public administration, with substantial impacts on the governance and institutions connected to SDG 16. Second, AI could serve as a booster, enabling more efficient and effective public services and increasing transparency in administrative processes. Third, AI is a tool to address inequalities, opportunities, and participation through policies for digital inclusion to extend the possibility to access public services and data. Last but not least, AI also opens up possibilities for monitoring progress and producing data on outcomes in several sectors.

AI will add value to the public sector at the national level. Artificial intelligence can be developed, implemented, and deployed to create several measurable outcomes across diverse sectors. The fact that AI has the potential to affect multiple sectors suggests the need for policymakers to integrate AI into holistic or unified approaches to other public policies, especially in public administration (Zuiderwijk et al., 2021).

Experience indicates that SDGs need to impact different levels of governance and in different arenas that have a direct relationship with the citizens, and their impact will naturally vary accordingly. Public policies should align with the broader principles of sustainable development, truly reflecting broader constituencies, including public, private, and civil society actors. Developments in AI may or may not be in alignment with these goals, which means monitoring needs to be put in place to include these developments in the priorities of those commissioning or conducting monitoring. The impact of AI on public administration is one component of this, and efforts to enable the potentially just, equitable, inclusive, and sustainable social outcomes of AI could be bolstered by aligning them with the broader goals of the SDGs. By this, AI will turn out to be a support in implementing the 2030 Agenda. To help drive these efforts, collaborative and responsive mechanisms are essential.

Many AI applications, and indeed the ecosystem of AI are helpful if their purpose is to achieve the objectives of the 17 items in the 2030 UN Agenda for Sustainable Development (Di et al.2020). There is a natural alignment between AI applications that grow out of inputs in a wide range of public sectors. AI innovation in these sectors is helpful, for example, for health, education, cities, agriculture, the oceans, energy, climate, the environment, biodiversity, justice, decent work, and public spending and investments, if those are used with sustainability in mind. The tutorial makes contributions in relation to AI in health, in education, and for the effective execution of work carried out in national environmental management agencies.

Some of the applications considered in both single- and multi-country study examples align reasonably well with the functions of government. In those functions, and where AI applications are located, objectives to be met over orders of integrated data-rich bodies are just as relevant for less data-rich, focused, lower-level specialist bodies (Zuiderwijk et al., 2021). Public bodies beyond those at the center of government, such as local education or health services, sector-focused public bodies or criminal justice and environmental protection, are no less data-rich (Dunleavy & Margetts, 2023). To also contribute to achieving the multiple SDGs, what is needed are more and better applications, as this book will describe, of AI in these different specialist areas of public administration. It is necessary and desirable to use new kinds of data-rich knowledge and analytical systems if the big picture of a piece of society is whole and unrestrained, unchecked, and uncorrupted by insufficient bits from the shadows. Piloting an integrated approach to public data across government is one way, through ICT, to begin the systemic change (Stylos et al. 2021).

4. AI APPLICATIONS IN PUBLIC SERVICES

The use of AI is particularly popular in public service. In healthcare, AI forms the basis of predictive diagnostics and personalized treatment for patients and public health. Smart traffic management and predictive maintenance are useful in the transportation industry. With the exception of a few instances of targeted applications, AI has still not been widely adopted by public service.

In healthcare, AI enhances management and also expands personalized patient care. This results in a healthier overall public, which is an essential requirement for all states. A case was seen recently where AI helped overcome healthcare barriers by developing a platform that shortened the time to diagnose a form of dementia from about 8 months to 13 days (Sultan et al. 2020). Representing the development of smarter cities, AI also forms the basis of intelligent traffic systems that trigger smart lighting and maintenance in the transportation industry. For smarter parking options, municipalities in various cities also use AI. Furthermore, the application of AI has powerful teaching and learning potential, empowering more interactive and personalized learning practices. However, only a portion of respondents from the organization are aware of the various ways that we can be employed by AI to meet specific public needs, so that we can be delegated operational goods and outcome services to make a decisive difference (Aoki, 2020). Many technology experts do not yet possess the required expertise or capability to foster technology in short period of time. Its adverse effect can be decreased or eradicated by strong collaboration between countries in implementing AI solutions in their public service institutions. Therefore, engagement is an effective way of overcoming the perceived challenges posed by AI. These AI-driven solutions will lead to more sustainable and adaptive public services, benefiting both citizens and states (Valle-Cruz and García Contreras2023).

4.1. Healthcare

AI and blockchain are revolutionizing the healthcare field in an unimpaired way, right from research and development to later stages of patient care. Now, industries are strongly considering AI appointments at different levels, and soon there will be AI-enabled surgeons. The innovations and their implications are limitless in the field of healthcare. The following are some simple examples that help to streamline and improve healthcare administration processes:

1) Predictive analytics: Many healthcare and social care service systems are still in a very reactive cycle, dealing with problems mainly after they have arisen. New AI methods can use complex linked data from multiple sources to 'predict

and pre-empt' potential patient problems much earlier for any population group (Onder & Uzun, 2021). This can include anything from child protection and adult safeguarding to mental health crises, diabetes, and severe asthma. This greater insight into patient needs will not only mean that the most costly forms of care and/or harm can be avoided, but treatments can be more personalized and appropriate (Meskó & Topol, 2023).

2) Decision support systems: AI can use data that is constantly being updated to aid professionals in making evidence-based decisions. Many countries use these for matching children with educational resources and methods, for example, where and how to deploy pupil premium funding for the greatest effect.
3) Telemedicine: AI systems are being tested that can spot the early signs of diseases remotely, or even in the home environment. AI can autonomously review the data that wearable and medical devices produce, and alert healthcare professionals or the patient themselves if an anomaly is detected. In addition to the benefits of the appointment system, AI can have huge benefits in terms of diagnostic accuracy. However, predictive analytics and new treatment development are not things that are attractive to be holistic; rather, any one system: AI must be able to join data from multiple sources, for example, GP and hospital data, to provide a more complete picture (Lu et al.2020). Ethical sensitivities in healthcare are high, and AI linking different patient activities raises many concerns about privacy and patient consent. It is the role of the public administrator to navigate this terrain and make the best use of the technology, not only to bring widespread benefit but also to do so ethically.

Challenges that will be faced are highlighted, and aside from the need to maintain public trust, greater collaboration and a rethinking of existing business models are necessary. From an operational perspective, it is critical to ensure that healthcare professionals have the correct training and, in many cases, understand how these tools integrate into existing systems. Healthcare is inherently risk-averse, and fundamental change is typically difficult to realize. Major improvements in data science and probabilistic computational methods are likely to be required in order to convince healthcare stakeholders that AI solutions are reliable and trustworthy. Given the significant challenges, the need for ethical and responsible AI that is transparent and accountable is paramount. As with most of these applications or suggestions, there are ethical considerations that must be addressed, with privacy and consent being the two most obvious ones. Healthcare is naturally a private, consent-based economy at both the system level and individual level (Oskam et al., 2021). Group decision-making, where the various benefits and costs of a technology are taken into account, makes this less challenging but no less important to draw interest.

4.2. Transportation

Transportation is a key area of concern as it fundamentally determines the quality of urban life through enabling mobility. Reports estimate that AI technologies deployed in the transportation sector create wise cities by revolutionizing economically friendly urban mobility, fostering public transportation efficiency, and advancing traffic management. AI applications in public transportation cover an extensive range of areas including scheduling, demand management, asset maintenance, and security backup. Significantly, AI promotes data-driven methods that help in comparing options for meeting present and future transportation demand. AI tools that predict traffic benefit investments in congestion management, traveler information systems, and increased infrastructure capacity (Javed et al.2022). Accordingly, states and local communities are employing smart transportation technologies to use what they have more effectively, in addition to adding systems.

With regard to traffic management, the state-of-the-art solution based on actual behavior is the intelligent transportation systems application known as intelligent control. Intelligent control focuses directly on the underlying traffic carriers and formulates optimal control strategies to optimize the system performance regarding one or multiple well-defined performance measures. Furthermore, intelligent control is increasingly present in daily life given the automation of existing inductions, such as automated traffic light systems or collaborative adaptive traffic signal control systems that represent an intelligent traffic signal control strategy based on vehicle-to-infrastructure communications (Liu & Ke, 2023). By implementing an AI-driven transport system that works autonomously, it becomes possible to make progress toward traffic safety goals. Automating traffic light intersections can mitigate congestion caused by human factors and ultimately improve safety. Similarly, the integration of predictive maintenance algorithms can also improve the condition of vehicles and consequently support safe movement. In this way, AI can have a direct impact on Vision Zero goals in traffic safety.

4.3. Education

AI and digital technologies are reshaping the way students learn and the way they are assessed. AI-based education tools range from the development of intelligent tutoring systems to online learning platforms that deliver personalized instruction to students based on their performance on learning tasks. Empirical research has shown the potential of digital learning tools to engage and motivate students, resulting in significantly improved performance with the tools in math, reading comprehension, and natural science. Additionally, the tools may increase educators' ability to meet student learning needs by identifying learning gaps and then providing personalized content, which can benefit the majority of students (Kim & Kim, 2022). Evaluation of the AI technologies would require not only measuring their impact on learning gains, but also the extent to which they promote social and emotional learning, a critical component of 21st century skills. Consequently, potential negative effects of AI on data privacy and algorithmic bias need to be monitored, such as those mediated by virtual assistants in online tutoring systems. To address ethical issues, data literacy and transparency standards are urgently needed, as the adoption of these tools requires ongoing training and development for educational staff, including educators, pedagogical staff, and educational administrators. National and local government, educators, parents, students, researchers, policymakers, and IT professionals could work together to develop a robust national framework to govern the applications of AI technologies in education. In doing so, care should be taken to ensure equitable physical, mental, and cyber security measures are in place to provide access to innovative learning environments.

5. ETHICAL CONSIDERATIONS IN AI FOR PUBLIC ADMINISTRATION

AI tools carry great promise for stimulating innovation and technological progress in the public sector, driving more efficient public service delivery. At the same time, rapidly mounting evidence suggests that their implementation can also give rise to harmful consequences. Fostering the necessary trust of citizens, public employees, and political leaders to harness this promise necessitates the use of AI tools within a framework that safeguards against the inherent ethical risks. With the aim of identifying such risks and offering ways to align the deployment of AI with ethical use, this report seeks to support public authorities designing operational guidelines for responsible use of AI in public administration by providing a comprehensive overview of existing literature (Chen et al., 2021).

One of the major spheres of attention in discussions about the ethics of AI is the principle of transparency, because the operation of AI tools often appears opaque to stakeholders and the intent behind a given output is often difficult to ascertain. Intuitively, transparent AI decision-making processes are conceived of as necessary to facilitate other important ethical principles, such as inclusion, equity, non-discrimination, and respect for human agency. One particular concern is the identification of biases in algorithmic outputs, and consequently the implications of such biases on different measures of fairness in public service delivery. Another focus of debate has been on issues relating to the design and operation of AI governance and algorithmic accountability mechanisms (Ayling & Chapman, 2022). It is widely agreed that public oversight mechanisms, for review of specific

AI implementations or to provide oversight of regulatory guidelines, are necessary to alleviate these ethical and social problems.

A central issue of this debate is whether formal guidance is necessary to govern the development of AI tools in the public sector. Missing from much of this debate is actual community engagement with principles of AI governance and trust in public institutions. Some research clearly has been undertaken into how to involve communities in the discussion of the use of AI in the public sector and can offer insights to AI tool designers. Stakeholder engagement necessitates engaging early with the intentions and purposes that AI trust guidelines should serve, and accordingly also the actors that such guidelines are intended to protect. Both private and public actors agree about the necessity of these normative aims. For example, it is necessary to capture social preferences for norm compliance. Publicly engaging with communities can also reveal their normative expectations for public AI services, such as identifiable control and accountability, and provide feedback about how interventions are received from those that they affect. However, despite the overarching agreement about stakeholder engagement, there is less consensus about how to do this in practice and to what end. In particular, research highlights a strong perception that it is difficult to talk to or engage with users of public sector AI algorithms, which can be a challenge for regulators and developers (Kerr et al., 2020).

In sum, the existing literature reveals there are strong normative worries about the use of AI tools in the public sector, but limited attempts to offer formal guidance to navigate these ethical landmines. Social research on the perceptions of public sector AI tools suggests that there is a moral imperative, if not also a practical interest, in doing so.

5.1. Transparency and Accountability

Transparency and accountability are fundamentally important for the application of AI in the public domain. The use of any AI algorithm in public administration should be consistently open to the scrutiny of the affected individuals, the jurisdictions in which they live, and other stakeholders. By demonstrating that no more is hidden than necessary, public administrations will demonstrate their proactiveness in establishing public trust. As AI and machine learning evolve, it is important to communicate the distinction between "explainability" and "interpretability" as regards AI systems (Kim et al., 2020). In this context, an "interpretable" model is one for which a user has some understanding of how variables interact in a model and of relative feature importance, whereas an "explainable" model has additional information data scientists would require to troubleshoot the model. As only a small proportion of users will have the technical skill to do this, we therefore focus primarily on the former.

Transparency is an ethical concept which is closely related to governance and to the manner in which this is communicated. Any one of two types of governance flow occurs: either governance is by general consensus or is decided by law, the latter making true transparency a matter of law (Zhang & Zhang, 2023). For AI to be truly ethical, transparency must be true, i.e., not only in "spirit" but also in law. Also important are accountability frameworks which are implemented that hold an organization responsible for an outcome, accepting punishment if the decision made was not in the best interest of the organization and its constituents. AI is being used in various applications that impact lives and should be monitored in the same way that other professionals operate, advancing public education, managing professional responsibilities to society, accepting enhancements in the process, dealing with acquisition and loan applications, carrying out e-disclosure processing in litigation and reviewing documentation in response to regulatory investigations. Largely deployed in public administration, AI is gaining use in clinical diagnosis, primary justice systems and remote consultations. Given that performance is currently significantly below human levels and as mistakes are made using AI, AI should ideally be regulated. Policymakers should thus be focused on how AI can be reliably used and should have ethical commitments. Regulatory treatment of AI also focuses on ethics, setting universal guidelines regarding AI applications in addition to sector-specific rules. Supranational and international frameworks should ideally be congruent. Governments, not tech companies, should primarily be responsible for putting forward and enforcing such regulations.

In order for the public sector to be effective and fair, transparency and accountability should be relevant to their governance function. The public supports AI governance frameworks. A basis for transparency exists on the expectations of the public and in big data and AI principles.

5.2. Bias and Fairness

Training data reflects broader societal attitudes, stereotypes, and power dynamics. If an AI system is trained on biased data, it may reproduce functions and practices that entrench systemic inequality. Users of public services experiencing discrimination and prejudice are particularly vulnerable to an AI system that replicates these dynamics. Not only can these issues diminish the public value of AI by reducing access to service functionality, but service quality can also be lower for particular groups.

Research shows that AI systems are most likely to show accuracy differences between members of different racial and ethnic groups. In some circumstances, AI systems may refuse to work with any member of a protected group in an attempt to maintain a low false positive rate, which may have its own public value concerns. There are also cases now coming to light where AI systems identify Indigenous individuals' faces at much lower levels than would be expected. For example, one study looking at action recognition in videos found accuracy differences of up to 27 percent between different racial groups, with results being less accurate for 'dark-skinned' individuals (Daneshjou et al.2021). Microaggressions embedded in AI applications, such as the potential to misclassify transgender individuals and reveal their pre-transition names, may also cause harm.

There are a variety of methods for identifying and mitigating bias in AI, some of which we have outlined above. There are growing calls for AI systems to be trained on diverse data sets, with diverse applicants. There have been encouragements for public administrators to seek data on inequalities when designing public services and to conduct regular audits of AI systems once they are deployed. This involves examining the automated decision to ascertain whether it disadvantages any particular group and addressing the biases using policy responses, as well as updating the AI regime more broadly (Desouza et al., 2020; Busuioc, 2021). There are calls for public administrators to champion fairness at every stage of algorithm deployment, including development. It is also argued that software developers, public administrators, and community representatives should collaborate to create more inclusive AI systems, and that more research is required in this space to deepen understanding and marshal resources to create best practices.

6. SMART CITIES

One of the brightest examples of AI scope in urban governance is the notion of smart cities, which has garnered considerable attention and investment in recent years. This trend is led by the surging urban population, aggravating urban governance manifold, along with the rise of data for enhancing governance. Despite disagreements concerning the conceptual underpinnings of smart cities, what makes the buzzword interesting in the discussion on AI and sustainable public administration is the seamless integration of AI technologies in addressing urban issues efficiently. This is labeled as the use of 'smart technologies', also called AI systems or advanced analytics in practical use cases of city management for improving service delivery and the quality of life for citizens in a sustainable manner.

For example, traffic management utilizing IoT devices to detect, classify, track, and observe traffic, along with sounding alarms, automatic control of some devices, and results management for displaying information to the public. AI-enabled smart traffic management systems can improve travel times, reduce harmful emissions, optimize traffic flow, and maximize the safety of city roads (Uzun et al., 2022). 'Smart traffic management' systems' ability to boost the efficiency, effectiveness, and safety of urban transport and logistics increasingly denotes the effort of urban communities towards sustainability. Automated waste management is another feather in AI's city sustainability hat. Waste collection has been improved by sensory technologies that monitor bin volume data and create overfill alerts to the control room, allowing waste collectors to arrange collections before waste overflows, cutting carbon emissions, improving health and safety, and reducing vermin. Due to automated waste systems, significant fuel and operational savings have been made by reducing the frequency of refuse collections.

While considerable potential benefits can be gained from AI and smart technologies, there have also been manifold roadblocks encountered by early adopters, which deter the adoption and diffusion of AI and smart technologies across other local authorities—particularly those in the global South. At face value, the cost associated with AI and smart systems looms large when overhauling traffic, transport, public safety, and waste infrastructure and IT systems. The investment deficit, which would amount to hundreds of millions of dollars for a mid-sized town in developed countries, is surmountable due to numerous smart city funding, grants, business cases, loan finance, and cost recovery mechanisms. Efforts from local and central governments, borrowing and levies on residents, the tech industry, and other commercial interests and indeed residents and businesses themselves have been the primary financing vehicles implemented. More importantly, the success of AI and smart initiatives isn't a foregone conclusion, and without widespread citizen engagement and participation, the large-scale failure of smart cities is anticipated. Prosecuting a vision of smart cities requires meaningful collaboration between local authorities, citizens, industry, and other stakeholders. An inclusive, citizen-centered, and people-oriented approach to the development of sustainable smart cities is considered integral to a better urban future for the increasing proportion of humanity who call cities their home. Public decision-makers are advised to respect the authority, work with the strengths, and harness the ideas of a broader community of citizens, industry practitioners, associations, and experts to shape a collective vision for sustainable smart cities. The fruits of such developmental efforts with economic, social, and environmental value proliferate in smart projects. In sum, smart cities are a transformative multimodal governance shift, incorporating a pantheon of AI technologies, human-centered design, and forward-looking thinking to enhance urban governance, community well-being, and economic and social growth.

7. FUTURE TRENDS AND INNOVATIONS

AI-powered technologies are experiencing rapid advances and the development of new tools and algorithms. AI-as-a-service is a keen focus of startup companies and large corporations, while major technology firms are also now investing in AI research. Emerging AI technologies could reshape the way public service is conceived and delivered, favoring new forms of governance and public management. The most relevant trend seems to be represented by the growth of machine learning and predictive analytics over traditional rule-based AI applications. The most noticeable AI-based computing utility is likely to be an AI engine designed to predict future events in the pseudo-science of 'seen-unknowns.'

For this reason, public administrators need to be attentive to the new conditions and to the new governance technologies, which might disrupt the established ideas of democracy. These changes are often so rapid that public administrators scarcely have time to fully react before they need to evolve to another technology, other approaches, and the next policy (Wirtz et al.2020). Future public administration, therefore, becomes an 'evolving domain' that has to be sensitive to changes in relation to technology and policy, and these policy shifts often cannot afford the time to be underpinned with the relevant decision-making literature. Beyond the trends, this estimation exercise springs us into a growing need to build scenarios that might shape the ways governments and policymakers run public service organizations. In shaping possible futures, public administration scholars should not focus their attention solely on technologies and trends. Emerging issues in public administration frameworks and policies are also important. Secondly, very importantly, policymakers and governmental personnel are no longer asking questions only about how to use AI, but how to live with it as well. To what extent is a human being supposed to take into account smart systems in the exercising of their professional opinion? The question looms larger specifically in decision-making professions. Furthermore, we may only guess public inclination if AI should be assimilated into judicial or ministerial roles. Thirdly, this observation brings us to the matter of ethics and responsible AI, about which ample has been written. Fourthly, let's assume AI as the third in the marriage management decision of 'Technology X Ethics.' In the coming years, public managers and policymakers will be intellectually minced through the implications of such debates.

One way public administration is using AI is for predictions. Predictive analytics can be defined as a system that uses data and algorithms to forecast future trends, characteristics of interest, or events. Also called machine intelligence, such tools can learn from data and become more accurate over time (Van Noordt & Misuraca, 2022). More specifically, as a branch of AI, machine learning refers to a collection of algorithms and techniques that allow computers to learn from data.

These services are capable of enhancing data-driven decision-making, improving public service delivery, and increasing the efficiency and productivity of resource allocation. Public administrations seek to foresee issues and challenges before they become a problem. An analysis of statistical data is suitable for revealing trends and obtaining essential information, providing a solid foundation for subsequent action. Despite all advantages, there are also ethical implications to using machine learning and predictive analytics. This is mainly due to concerns regarding the privacy of data used to train algorithms or develop predictive models. Outsourcing predictive analytics to the business sector may raise additional concerns about trade secrets and long-term public sector dependency on these types of services. Moreover, the inherent sensitivity of predictions may give rise to calls for increased algorithmic accountability. Ensuring fairness and transparency in the use of machine learning is necessary. It is essential to continually evaluate the accuracy of AI models and ensure they are regularly audited, especially since the model parameters may drift over time as societal issues and understandings evolve. Public administrations should collaborate with other key stakeholders to ensure that the benefits of machine learning are realized and ethical implications are considered over time. Overall, there seems to be a need for a better understanding of the potential benefits and impacts that machine learning services could make to government as they become more mature, transparent, and well-managed. In the coming decade, a more sustainable approach to AI is likely to become a priority for public administrations. Product vendors and development teams will have to comply with a set of regulations and practices that would include the use of common interfaces and data standards in order to allow for different services to exchange information and feedback loops.

8. CONCLUSION

AI has the potential not only to change public services, but also to help us transform our approaches toward public services. Most see data-driven and AI-enabled public services as critical in addressing many facets of the Sustainable Development Goals. Stakeholders in public governance appreciate the transformative potential of AI, but fear a technological crisis similar to previous waves of modernization. In the forefront of stakeholders' minds are ethical considerations, transparency, and public accountability. Politicians and city leaders are extremely sensitive to citizen concerns regarding the ways technology companies obscured targeted political messages, resulting in more polarized election outcomes. Ultimately, citizens and residents may simply demand the right to opt out of being treated as data, or may require alternative services from the state that are non-automated, similar to the ways in which one can opt for a human call center operator over an automatic menu system.

Public administrators and academic researchers see the promise of AI tools but are operating within organizational norms and cultural logics that discourage risk. For public administration in the fourth Industrial Revolution, the challenge is not the development of improved methods or tools; it is the design and redesign of institutions to innovate and then deliver on the promise of computational thinking. This is the ambitious but reachable vision that we hope has allowed everyone to see for the public administration of the future. We need a shared investment in sustaining the practices that can make this future possible.

Artificial Intelligence has the potential to shape public administration for the benefit of society. This introduction underlines the need for an ethical approach to AI in public administration. Policymakers should: - Facilitate cooperation platforms between public administrations and the private sector to provide AI solutions; - Invest in training and education to develop the AI expertise for the public sector; and - Set up independent accountability and quality control mechanisms to evaluate AI applications in the public service. It should include people from government and business as well as civil society. The qualitative and quantitative analysis presented in this introduction has led to the following informed recommendations for European institutions and Member States. European affairs ministers and national administrations now need to make a decisive choice. Action should be taken on the following: - AI can promote sustainable public administration. Its use should therefore be encouraged. - However, public authorities should remain in control of AI for public management decisions and promote ethical public administration. AI, as used by public authorities, should take these values as a starting point. - Further reflection is needed on the ethical guidance and regulations that AI for public service delivery should be aligned with. Ministers should encourage the relevant public and private sectors to engage in this debate. - Public administrations should be equipped with the necessary expertise. European governments should invest in the education and training necessary to empower the public service to understand and manage the technologies it uses. Cooperation with the private sector could encourage knowledge sharing, as long as the public service remains in control of its training needs. - AI policy processing and monitoring cannot be left exclusively to public administrators or governments. AI systems should be implemented transparently and be open to continuous evaluation and public scrutiny, just as any other policy measure. Ministers should ensure that an independent body has the authority to interrogate the principles for using AI that were set by lawmakers. - Investments in AI should be kept under evaluation. Ministers should investigate which public policy measures are most suitable and effective, using AI as a way to improve service to the citizens.

REFERENCES

Aidonojie, P. A., Ikubanni, O. O., Okuonghae, N., & Oyedeji, A. I. (2021). The challenges and relevance of technology in administration of justice and human security in nigeria: Amidst the covid19 pandemic. *Cógito (Salvador)*, 13(3), 149–171.

Aoki, N. (2020). An experimental study of public trust in AI chatbots in the public sector. *Government Information Quarterly*, 37(4), 101490. DOI: 10.1016/j.giq.2020.101490

Ayling, J., & Chapman, A. (2022). Putting AI ethics to work: Are the tools fit for purpose? *AI and Ethics*, 2(3), 405–429. DOI: 10.1007/s43681-021-00084-x

Busuioc, M. (2021). Accountable artificial intelligence: Holding algorithms to account. *Public Administration Review*, 81(5), 825–836. DOI: 10.1111/puar.13293 PMID: 34690372

Chen, T., Guo, W., Gao, X., & Liang, Z. (2021). AI-based self-service technology in public service delivery: User experience and influencing factors. *Government Information Quarterly*, 38(4), 101520. DOI: 10.1016/j.giq.2020.101520

Daneshjou, R., Smith, M. P., Sun, M. D., Rotemberg, V., & Zou, J. (2021). Lack of transparency and potential bias in artificial intelligence data sets and algorithms: A scoping review. *JAMA Dermatology*, 157(11), 1362–1369. DOI: 10.1001/jamadermatol.2021.3129 PMID: 34550305

Desouza, K. C., Dawson, G. S., & Chenok, D. (2020). Designing, developing, and deploying artificial intelligence systems: Lessons from and for the public sector. *Business Horizons*, 63(2), 205–213. DOI: 10.1016/j.bushor.2019.11.004

Di Vaio, A., Palladino, R., Hassan, R., & Escobar, O. (2020). Artificial intelligence and business models in the sustainable development goals perspective: A systematic literature review. *Journal of Business Research*, 121, 283–314. DOI: 10.1016/j.jbusres.2020.08.019

Dunleavy, P. & Margetts, H. (2023). Data science, artificial intelligence and the third wave of digital era governance. *Public Policy and AdministrationSpecial Issue: Artificial Intelligence and Public Administration: Actors, Governance, and Policies*. 1-30.

Gesk, T. S., & Leyer, M. (2022). Artificial intelligence in public services: When and why citizens accept its usage. *Government Information Quarterly*, 39(3), 101704. DOI: 10.1016/j.giq.2022.101704

Javed, A. R., Shahzad, F., Rehman, S., Zikria, Y. B., Razzak, I., Jalil, Z., & Xu, G. (2022). Future smart cities: Requirements, emerging technologies, applications, challenges, and future aspects. *Cities (London, England)*, 129, 103794. DOI: 10.1016/j.cities.2022.103794

Kerr, A., Barry, M., & Kelleher, J. D. (2020). Expectations of artificial intelligence and the performativity of ethics: Implications for communication governance. *Big Data & Society*, 7(1), 2053951720915939. DOI: 10.1177/2053951720915939

Kim, B., Park, J., & Suh, J. (2020). Transparency and accountability in AI decision support: Explaining and visualizing convolutional neural networks for text information. *Decision Support Systems*, 134, 113302. DOI: 10.1016/j.dss.2020.113302

Kim, N. J., & Kim, M. K. (2022, March). Teacher's perceptions of using an artificial intelligence-based educational tool for scientific writing. [). Frontiers Media SA.]. *Frontiers in Education*, 7, 755914. DOI: 10.3389/feduc.2022.755914

Kommisetty, P. D. N. K. (2022). Leading the Future: Big Data Solutions, Cloud Migration, and AI-Driven Decision-Making in Modern Enterprises. *Educational Administration: Theory and Practice*, 28(03), 352–364.

Kuziemski, M., & Misuraca, G. (2020). AI governance in the public sector: Three tales from the frontiers of automated decision-making in democratic settings. *Telecommunications Policy*, 44(6), 101976. DOI: 10.1016/j.telpol.2020.101976 PMID: 32313360

Lahdili, N., Önder, M., & Nyadera, I. N. (2024). Artificial Intelligence and Citizen Participation in Governance: Opportunities and Threats. *Amme Idaresi Dergisi*, 57(3).

Liu, C., & Ke, L. (2023). Cloud assisted Internet of things intelligent transportation system and the traffic control system in the smart city. *Journal of Control and Decision*, 10(2), 174–187. DOI: 10.1080/23307706.2021.2024460

Lu, L., Zhang, J., Xie, Y., Gao, F., Xu, S., Wu, X., & Ye, Z. (2020). Wearable health devices in health care: Narrative systematic review. *JMIR mHealth and uHealth*, 8(11), e18907. DOI: 10.2196/18907 PMID: 33164904

Meskó, B., & Topol, E. J. (2023). The imperative for regulatory oversight of large language models (or generative AI) in healthcare. *NPJ Digital Medicine*, 6(1), 120. DOI: 10.1038/s41746-023-00873-0 PMID: 37414860

Onder, M., & Saygılı, H. (2018). Yapay Zekâ ve Kamu Yönetimine Yansımaları / Artificial Intelligence and the Reflections on Public Administration. *Türk İdare Dergisi*, 90(487), 629–668.

Onder, M., & Uzun, M. M. (2021). Roles of Artificial Intelligence (AI) on COVID-19 pandemic crisis management policies. [IJPADA]. *International Journal of Public Administration in the Digital Age*, 8(2), 1–13. DOI: 10.4018/IJPADA.294122

Osborne, S. (2020). *Public service logic: Creating value for public service users, citizens, and society through public service delivery*. Routledge. DOI: 10.4324/9781003009153

Oskam, I., Bossink, B., & de Man, A. P. (2021). Valuing value in innovation ecosystems: How cross-sector actors overcome tensions in collaborative sustainable business model development. *Business & Society*, 60(5), 1059–1091. DOI: 10.1177/0007650320907145

Pencheva, I., Esteve, M., & Mikhaylov, S. J. (2020). Big Data and AI–A transformational shift for government: So, what next for research? *Public Policy and Administration*, 35(1), 24–44. DOI: 10.1177/0952076718780537

Rosenbloom, D. H., Kravchuk, R. S., & Clerkin, R. M. (2022). *Public administration: Understanding management, politics, and law in the public sector*. Routledge.

Scupola, A., & Mergel, I. (2022). Co-production in digital transformation of public administration and public value creation: The case of Denmark. *Government Information Quarterly*, 39(1), 101650. DOI: 10.1016/j.giq.2021.101650

Shao, Z., Zhao, R., Yuan, S., Ding, M., & Wang, Y. (2022). Tracing the evolution of AI in the past decade and forecasting the emerging trends. *Expert Systems with Applications*, 209, 118221. DOI: 10.1016/j.eswa.2022.118221

Stylos, N., Zwiegelaar, J., & Buhalis, D. (2021). Big data empowered agility for dynamic, volatile, and time-sensitive service industries: The case of tourism sector. *International Journal of Contemporary Hospitality Management*, 33(3), 1015–1036. DOI: 10.1108/IJCHM-07-2020-0644

Sultan, S., Taimuri, U., Basnan, S. A., Ai-Orabi, W. K., Awadallah, A., Almowald, F., & Hazazi, A. (2020). Low vitamin D and its association with cognitive impairment and dementia. *Journal of Aging Research*, 2020(1), 6097820. DOI: 10.1155/2020/6097820 PMID: 32399297

Uzun, M. M., Yıldız, M., & Önder, M. (2022). Big Questions of AI in Public Administration and Policy. *Siyasal: Journal of Political Sciences*, 31(2), 423–442. DOI: 10.26650/siyasal.2022.31.1121900

Valle-Cruz, D., & García-Contreras, R. (2023). Towards AI-driven transformation and smart data management: Emerging technological change in the public sector value chain. *Public Policy and Administration*, 0(0), 09520767231188401. Advance online publication. DOI: 10.1177/09520767231188401

Van Noordt, C., & Misuraca, G. (2022). Artificial intelligence for the public sector: Results of landscaping the use of AI in government across the European Union. *Government Information Quarterly*, 39(3), 101714. DOI: 10.1016/j.giq.2022.101714

Wirtz, B. W., Weyerer, J. C., & Sturm, B. J. (2020). The dark sides of artificial intelligence: An integrated AI governance framework for public administration. *International Journal of Public Administration*, 43(9), 818–829. DOI: 10.1080/01900692.2020.1749851

Zhang, J., & Zhang, Z. M. (2023). Ethics and governance of trustworthy medical artificial intelligence. *BMC Medical Informatics and Decision Making*, 23(1), 7. DOI: 10.1186/s12911-023-02103-9 PMID: 36639799

Zuiderwijk, A., Chen, Y. C., & Salem, F. (2021). Implications of the use of artificial intelligence in public governance: A systematic literature review and a research agenda. *Government Information Quarterly*, 38(3), 101577. DOI: 10.1016/j.giq.2021.101577

Chapter 2
Steering the AI Revolution in Local Governments:
Merits and Demerits

Nadia Lahdili
https://orcid.org/0000-0002-2059-6118
Ankara Yıldırım Beyazıt University, Turkey

Israel Nyaburi Nyadera
https://orcid.org/0000-0002-0432-6935
National Defence University, Kenya

ABSTRACT

Local governments are transitioning from traditional systems to digital platforms, with artificial intelligence (AI) playing a transformative role in this shift. AI offers innovative solutions to manage administrative complexity, enhance service delivery, and promote inclusive governance and sustainability. As the most accessible tier of government, local administrations are uniquely positioned to address citizens' needs efficiently. By leveraging AI, they can decentralize services, improve resource management, and optimize infrastructure. AI applications, such as chatbots and data analysis tools, streamline citizen interactions, optimize resource allocation, and forecast public trends. However, financial constraints, data privacy concerns, and algorithmic biases challenge AI integration. Ensuring robust governance frameworks and compliance with regulations like GDPR is vital for public trust.

DOI: 10.4018/979-8-3693-8372-8.ch002

INTRODUCTION

In the dynamic and transitional realm of public administration, local governments are positioned at a pivotal juncture that requires strategic planning, resilient management, and careful consideration. Local government institutions continue to play an essential role in delivering public services and managing local affairs (Walker & Andrews, 2015; Lahdili, 2023). The Sustainable Development Goals (SDGs), formally adopted by the United Nations in 2015, have emerged as a foundational element in the ongoing discourse surrounding public administration in contemporary societies. These comprehensive and ambitious objectives address a wide range of global challenges, including poverty, hunger, inequality, and environmental degradation. At the same time, they emphasize the promotion of peace, accountability, inclusion, and prosperity, striving to benefit both individuals and nations alike.

Biermann et al. (2022) argue for a multi-level governance approach in which local, regional, and national governments collaborate to align their policies and programs with the broader global agenda. This alignment entails incorporating the SDGs and their specific objectives into the strategies, plans, and activities at all levels of government. This transforms global goals into concrete actions that serve local needs while also contributing to global progress. In other words, the realization of these SDGs necessitates substantial contributions and collaborative efforts from various levels of governance, with particular emphasis on the vital role played by local governments, which are uniquely positioned to foster sustainable development owing to their competencies, capacities, and direct and immediate proximity to the citizens they serve. Hence, local governments are at the heart of SDGs implementation (Saner et al., 2017).

Local governments possess the distinct advantage of being able to govern territories and communities with a high degree of effectiveness, as they can adapt solutions that specifically address the unique challenges and conditions faced by their localities, all while remaining committed to the overarching principles of sustainability (Guarini et al., 2022). They are responsible for managing critical areas such as urban planning, public transportation systems, and waste management practices, all of which are intricately aligned with the objectives set forth by the SDGs agenda. Furthermore, the active engagement of local governments with their citizens promotes a form of participatory governance, which is essential for ensuring that the public policies and programs are designed, developed, and implemented transparently, accountably, responsibly, and representatively, and reflect the actual needs and priorities of the community (Lahdili, 2023).

In order to successfully achieve the UN's SGDs agenda, local governments must focus on enhancing their administrative capacity (Haque et al., 2021; Farazmand, 2019; Santoro, 2019; Glemarec & Puppim de Oliveira, 2012) or the ability and approaches through which public services are planned, designed, implemented, and measured for efficacy and efficiency, and in this context, policies that are conducive to sustainable development. In light of this, administrative capacity is not limited to the simple allocation of resources such as workforce and public funding but also involves the critical integration of innovative technological tools, including AI-based technologies, which have the potential to transform local governance practices fundamentally. Therefore, sustainable development in the AI era entails using artificial intelligence technology in urban planning, governance, and services to achieve a balance between economic growth, social fairness, and environmental preservation (Vinuesa et al., 2020). It strives to build smart, resilient, and inclusive cities that will fulfill the requirements of current and future generations.

This chapter thoroughly examines the various and intricate implications of implementing AI in the realm of local governance, looking into both the significant transformative opportunities it provides and the multifaceted challenges and complexities that it poses for public administrators and the communities they serve. By critically evaluating these dynamics, the chapter attempts to shed light on the consequences of AI on local decision-making processes, service delivery, and the general governance environment in a way that is both informative and representative of the current challenges confronting local governments.

In framing AI within the realm of local governance, this chapter employs an extensive definition that incorporates a variety of technological capacities. AI is conceptualized as a set of software technologies distinguished by one or more of the following essential functions: perceptual processing (which includes auditory, visual, textual, and tactile inputs), decision-making processes, predictive modeling, automated knowledge extraction, pattern identification, interactive communication, and logical reasoning frameworks (Vinuesa et al., 2020). This broad definition encompasses various applications, ranging from facial recognition systems and medical diagnostic instruments to weather forecasting models and social media analytics platforms. Additionally, this conceptual framework includes machine learning as an integral subset of AI technology, wherein systems develop the capability to learn from and adjust to new data autonomously, without the necessity of explicit programming.

This comprehensive definition supports a deeper insight into the role of AI within present-day governance structures, acknowledging that AI applications commonly combine multiple capabilities to address intricate urban dilemmas (Allam & Dhunny, 2019). For example, a smart city infrastructure may utilize perceptual analytics for traffic surveillance, predictive analytics for resource distribution, and interactive communication channels for civic participation. Such a holistic perspective on defining AI permits a more refined examination of its applications and implications within urban governance structures.

Incorporating AI-driven technologies into governmental institutions' operations signifies a momentous enhancement of existing technological frameworks and a fundamental reconfiguration of their administrative capacity. In the era of globalization, it is imperative to enhance administrative capacity to address the global landscape that involves complexity, fierce competition, and uncertainty (Farazmand, 2019).

The fast expansion of information and communication technology has radically changed the face of public administration, posing both opportunities and challenges for digital governance. As AI-rooted technologies evolve unprecedentedly, local governments must negotiate complicated systemic risks while reinventing administrative processes. The digital transition necessitates a comprehensive strategy that balances technological optimization with serious ethical considerations. As Shvets et al. (2024: 511) put it, the major challenges go beyond technology implementation and include fundamental concerns about digital citizenship, institutional responsiveness, and societal equality. Public administration must deal with complex issues such as preserving digital identity, establishing complete digital literacy, and building strong measures to limit subsequent digital violations. These imperatives necessitate a thorough grasp of how AI technology may enhance decision-making processes while upholding fundamental principles of democracy and human liberties. The intersection of technology innovation and public administration exposes a complex landscape in which digital intelligence must be developed not just within governmental structures, but also across larger societal ecosystems. This calls for comprehensive methods for improving digital competencies, building institutional trust, and developing adaptive frameworks capable of adapting to fast technological change. The ultimate objective goes beyond technology implementation and focuses on developing inclusive, transparent, and ethically guided digital governance models that can bridge current social divides while preserving liberties and well-being.

This chapter explores diverse aspects of AI in local government administration. First, it presents the shifting paradigms of public governance and the transformative potential of AI technologies. The following section on AI applications in local governments, comprehensively examines the multifaceted deployment of AI across service optimization, urban planning, and administrative processes. Next, the chapter critically analyzes the merits of AI integration in local governments, exploring how intelligent technologies can revolutionize decision-making frameworks, enhance service delivery, and modernize operational efficiency. Counterbalancing this optimistic perspective, the limitations and challenges of adopting AI in local governments section provides a nuanced assessment of the barriers -technical, ethical, cultural, and financial- that local governments encounter during AI implementation. To ground the discussion in practical insights, the case studies and real-world applications section presents concrete examples of successful AI interventions in diverse local government contexts. The chapter concludes with lessons learned, best practices, key strategic insights, and recommendations for local governments seeking to meaningfully integrate AI-based technologies into their governance models.

AI APPLICATIONS IN LOCAL GOVERNMENTS

Although the potential of AI was acknowledged several decades ago, its pragmatic use and integration was previously hindered by a lack of sufficient data (Sanchez et al., 2022: 3). Nonetheless, recent progress in data collection technologies has revealed the transformative possibilities of AI, particularly within the realm of local governance. Shvets et al. (2024: 510) argue that the increasing volume of data collected within the public sector requires the development of innovative methods for its processing and analysis. This section discusses the transformative capacity of AI in local governance, scrutinizing the methodologies through which AI is reformulating public service delivery and policymaking. Based on recent empirical studies and case analyses, the authors conduct a thorough examination of the multifaceted areas of AI application, encompassing service optimization, infrastructure oversight, policy formulation, and citizen participation. The discourse critically assesses how AI technologies empower local governments to cultivate approaches that are more adaptive, effective, and informed by data in response to urban challenges.

In the context of local governance, AI can be described as a paradigm-shifting and evolutionary technology that significantly impacts policy-making, planning, and sustainable development. Sanchez et al. (2022) stress that AI is becoming increasingly essential to local government operations, with its main applications concentrated in two major areas: improving the efficiency and effectiveness of urban service delivery and advancing urban policy formulation, decision-making, and strategic planning (Table 1).

The rapid emergence of AI-based applications in local governments is astounding, providing unique opportunities to enhance planning, management, and monitoring processes. Local governments are progressively transitioning into interlinked data ecosystems, exemplified by comprehensive digital infrastructures, including sensor networks, CCTV systems, and sophisticated telecommunication frameworks. These technological innovations facilitate an unparalleled degree of data acquisition vis-à-vis urban dynamics, spatial configurations, policy shifts, and human behavior (Jha et al., 2021, p. 938). Such technological developments highlight the transformative capabilities of AI in the realm of local governance, enabling more adaptive and evidence-based methodologies in policy formulation.

Research supports the potential of AI to revolutionize various aspects of local governance, from optimizing land use and zoning regulations to streamlining permitting processes and enhancing transportation management and environmental planning

(Almukhalfi et al., 2024; Nasim et al., 2023; Sanchez et al., 2022; Mahendra, 2021; Jha et al., 2021; Cugurullo, 2020). Based on Sanchez et al.'s (2022) survey results, key areas such as transportation planning, demographic analysis, and urban design are particularly conducive to the application of AI-based solutions. Adding to this is the importance of sensor networks for monitoring complex urban systems such as land use dynamics, traffic patterns, real estate investments, and energy usage. These technical infrastructures provide a holistic, data-driven approach to local administration that transcends traditional administrative boundaries.

As local governments progressively embrace digital technologies and consequently produce large amounts of information, the significance of AI in the systematic processing and advanced data analysis becomes ever more vital and indispensable. AI and Big Data analytics have emerged as a disruptive force in urban administration, substantially transforming how local governments assess information to make policy choices. The advent of digital synthesis marks a paradigm shift in public administration, with data-driven decision-making becoming increasingly important for good governance. AI reveals a deeply intrinsic and multifaceted relationship with Big Data analytics, particularly within the realm of urban governance and management. The availability of near-real-time data, combined with the power of modern technologies, empowers urban governance to make timely, informed, and sustainable decisions that directly benefit citizens (Allam & Dhunny, 2019, p. 82).

Table 1. AI applications in local governments: Areas, examples, and utilization

AI application area	Specific domain	AI applications	Examples of utilization	Key benefits
Enhancing Service Delivery and Operations	Traffic Management	AI-powered Traffic Control Systems	Real-time traffic flow optimization; Adaptive traffic signal timing; Congestion prediction and reduction.	Optimize traffic flow; Reduce traffic congestion; Enhance transportation efficiency; Improve public safety.
	Waste Management	Intelligent Waste Collection Systems	Optimized waste collection routes; Predictive waste generation analysis; Recycling rate improvement.	Reduce cost; Enhance environmental sustainability; Resource optimization; Enhance recycling rates by leveraging data on waste patterns and collection schedules.
	Public Safety	AI Surveillance and Predictive Policing	Video surveillance analysis; Crime pattern detection; Predictive crime hotspot identification.	Enhance public security; Allocate resources efficiently; Detect and prevent crime using AI-powered video analytics; Identify potential crime hotspots for proactive interventions.
Improving Policy, Decision-Making, and Planning	Land Use Planning	Data-Driven Urban Development Analysis	Optimal land use pattern identification; Future land use need prediction; Development scenario impact assessment	Sustain urban growth; Develop evidence-based planning; Predict future land use requirements.
	Development Control	Automated Permit and Compliance Systems	Streamlined permit processing; Automated code compliance checks; Rapid development application review.	Reduce administrative burden; Fasten approval processes; Increase transparency.
	Urban Planning	Predictive Urban Development Modeling	Infrastructure investment prediction; Transportation planning; Urban renewal strategy development.	Enable long-term strategic planning; Enhance resource allocation optimization; Facilitate adaptive urban management.

Source: Adapted by the authors, 2024.

The role of AI in local governments goes well beyond simple data gathering. Local governments are using AI to scrutinize substantial aggregates of data, providing policymakers with the critical insights necessary for strategic decision-making and data-driven policy choices. Machine learning models can provide deep insights into resource allocation and urban environments, uncovering complex logistical patterns and systemic interactions that policymakers including local planners previously overlooked. Integrating Big Data collection technologies has significantly reshaped governance and planning approaches. Emerging technologies including AI, the Internet of Things (IoT), machine learning, deep learning, artificial neural networks, and advanced communication networks like 5G and 6G, have all transformed local governance systems. Specifically, autonomous vehicles, robotics, machine learning, IoT, blockchain, augmented reality, and virtual reality, have significantly altered urban spaces and planning approaches. The widespread emergence of technological advancements, encompassing the implementation of sensors and the increasing availability of AI resources, has instigated a fundamental transformation in governance. Through the examination of trends in mobility, land utilization, and energy consumption, AI equips local governments with the ability to optimize resource distribution, refine infrastructure planning, and, in turn, improve their citizens' overall quality of life.

By analyzing large datasets related to infrastructure, resource allocation, population movements, land use, and environmental factors, AI presents a groundbreaking approach to local governance and strategic planning. For instance, AI has fundamentally transformed the methodologies employed in revenue forecasting (Buzyali & Sanbigs, 2023; Chung et al., 2022). Local governments may accurately evaluate complex and large datasets by using machine learning algorithms, innovative predictive modeling approaches, and data analytics. AI-based technologies facilitate the discernment of latent patterns, trends, and correlations that would be exceedingly challenging to identify through conventional approaches. This is because AI possesses the capacity to integrate historical revenue data with external variables, including economic indicators, demographic shifts, and policy modifications, to yield predictions. This aspect not only assists in enhancing the precision of financial planning but also contributes to the strategic allocation of resources, budget formulation, and the mitigation of risks associated with potential revenue deficits. Additionally, AI-driven instruments can dynamically adjust to new data inputs, thereby ensuring that forecasts remain pertinent amidst fluctuating economic landscapes. When executed effectively, AI-enhanced revenue forecasting can promote fiscal sustainability and transparency, as well as empower local governments to engage in data-informed decision-making that optimizes public service delivery and citizen satisfaction.

Furthermore, AI is effecting a profound transformation in the mechanisms of service delivery and decision-making within local governmental frameworks by automating routine operational tasks, increasing operational efficiency, and providing significant support to personnel performing frontline duties (Vogl, 2021). Back-office automation optimizes monotonous administrative processes including but not limited to data entry, report generation, and document verification, allowing human capital to focus on more strategic activities. Predictive analytics further strengthens decision-makers by scrutinizing previous and real-time datasets to forecast patterns, discern potential obstacles, and prioritize necessary interventions.

For example, predictive methodologies can significantly support urban planning initiatives, such as identifying areas susceptible to traffic congestion or resource deficiencies, thereby facilitating proactive management.

Smart Cities technologies have sparked major changes. Transportation systems are a prime example of this evolution, with the emergence of autonomous vehicles and sustainable infrastructure such as dedicated bike lanes and pedestrian pathways, which help lower fossil fuel use (Barns et al., 2016). These innovations transcend technological interventions; they signify a fundamental rethinking of urban mobility and environmental responsibility. In the building sector, Smart City technologies have led to significant shifts in construction practices. These technological integrations demonstrate how urban infrastructures can become more attuned to environmental needs (Allam & Jones, 2018). Modern construction methods incorporate innovative solutions such as low-energy systems, vertical gardens, smart waste management, and more efficient land-use techniques. The construction industry's experience reveals that effective AI implementation requires a holistic approach. This approach mergers technological innovation with human-centered design, continuous learning, and adaptable strategies (Regona et al., 2022; Abioye et al., 2021). It involves closing technological gaps, resolving data interoperability challenges, and building comprehensive ecosystems that integrate diverse digital technologies such as IoT, blockchain, and augmented reality. Most importantly, these technological solutions enable alternative land use strategies by minimizing gentrification and developing more compact, resource-efficient urban fabrics.

AI-empowered chatbots and virtual assistants represent another innovative application for citizen-government dynamics, fundamentally altering how citizens engage with local governmental services (Lahdili et al., 2024). AI-driven applications, based on natural language processing (NLP), machine learning, and data mining, create interactive communication channels that enable more dynamic and efficient forms of interaction. Inspired by "success stories" or the effective implementation of AI-based technologies in the private sector, government agencies are increasingly adopting AI solutions to address multifaceted challenges across various sectors, including taxation, healthcare, and education (Millán-Vargas et al., 2024; Androutsopoulou et al., 2019). Virtual agents are operational 24/7, delivering immediate responses to frequently asked questions, streamlining service requests, and mitigating wait times for citizens. In addition to basic interactions, advanced AI algorithms can offer tailored recommendations, such as guiding citizens to the most related community programs or resources that align with their specific requirements. Hence, the capacity to engage in informed decision-making rooted in data and executed in real-time fundamentally amplifies the ability of local governments to effectively cater to the needs of their citizens while simultaneously addressing and mitigating the multifaceted challenges that local environments face proactively. This shift not only revolutionizes citizen engagement but also significantly improves the accessibility and responsiveness of public services.

Blockchain technology serves as a powerful complement to Big Data and AI, holding the potential to transform local governance which encompasses complex transactional processes across financial, contractual, and administrative areas, which are often obstructed by bureaucratic inefficiencies, complex policies, and privacy issues (Allam & Dhunny, 2019: 82). The main benefit of this technology is its use of smart contracts which signify a major shift in how transactions are conducted, removing traditional obstacles such as uncertainty, delays, and reliance on third parties. The unchangeable nature of blockchain guarantees that once contracts are set in motion, they cannot be modified or tampered with, offering unmatched transparency and security in governance systems. Moreover, blockchain's potential goes beyond just improving transaction efficiency. As noted by scholars like Tapscott and Tapscott (2015), this technology contributes to collaboration among machines, Big Data systems, and human participants. By establishing permanent, accessible data networks, blockchain enables citizens to engage directly in addressing local issues. This method promotes a more transparent and participatory approach to data management, paving the way for innovative local governance models. This technology also tackles important issues in data management and collaboration between institutions. With its secure, distributed ledger system, blockchain can greatly improve the integrity of local government data, lower administrative costs, and foster more agile governance structures. The opportunity to develop collaborative services based on integrated data ecosystems signifies a major shift in how local governments can handle complex administrative and civic tasks.

Local policymakers, including urban planners and designers, can leverage AI to develop more efficient, adaptable, and equitable communities (Farida et al., 2023). Advanced analytics and machine learning algorithms support the creation of optimized traffic networks, responsive public transit systems, and dynamic urban spaces that address evolving community needs (Almukhalfi et al., 2024; Nallaperuma et al., 2019). Additionally, AI applications such as machine learning have demonstrated effectiveness in detecting fraud and corruption in social security systems, enhancing transport network planning, optimizing route efficiency, and streamlining processes like document processing and citizen interactions (Shvets et al., 2024). Moreover, AI excels in environmental monitoring by predicting and analyzing critical urban parameters, including air quality, pollution levels, energy usage, fossil fuel emissions, and waste management (Mahendra, 2021). By harnessing AI-powered predictive modeling, policymakers can anticipate future urban trends, enabling proactive planning and adaptation to emerging societal challenges.

Allam and Dhunny (2019: 82) argue that the expansion of IoT technologies alongside the rise of Big Data has generated remarkable opportunities for the connectivity and analysis of data. In this context, AI functions as a pivotal enabler for the processing and understanding of these complex, multidimensional datasets, empowering local governments to quickly detect and tackle current urban challenges, emerging patterns, and potential future scenarios. AI utilizes advanced machine learning algorithms and innovative data processing techniques to analyze extensive and varied datasets produced by interconnected systems. This provides local policymakers with insights that surpass the constraints of conventional data analysis methods. Consequently, it facilitates the creation of proactive and predictive management strategies, enabling local governments to spot and tackle potential issues before they grow. As a result, AI not only improves operational efficiency but also reinforces the resilience of governance systems against complex and evolving challenges. These technologies are not separate instruments, but rather integrated systems that provide comprehensive frameworks for sustainable development (Berawi, 2019).

Beyond operational improvements, AI empowers urban administrations to shift from reactive to proactive governance. By providing real-time, data-driven insights into complex systems, AI enables local policymakers to make informed decisions that balance economic, social, and environmental considerations. This transition towards data-driven, strategic planning can lead to more sustainable and resilient communities.

With the rapid development of AI and the increasing availability of datasets, it is anticipated that AI will be essential in addressing the multifaceted challenges of local governments. While AI is often associated with personalized online experiences, its application in local governments' planning and sustainable development holds even greater promise. Hence, improved decision-making using AI-powered analytics has transformed how local governments, municipalities, and cities approach management and planning.

MERITS OF AI INTEGRATION IN LOCAL GOVERNMENTS

Employing AI signifies a profound shift in the operational competencies of local governments, marking a pivotal stage in the evolution of how governments, municipalities, and cities manage, use, and evaluate data. Research shows that AI is more than just a technological tool -it represents a comprehensive strategy for addressing systemic challenges, particularly in complex, data-intensive environments. Equally important, adopting AI isn't about completely replacing existing technologies, but about creating integrated, intelligent systems that enhance human capabilities and decision-making.

Enhanced Decision-making and Strategic Planning: The potential of AI in local governance goes beyond the simplistic idea of automating routine administrative tasks that have traditionally burdened municipal operations. This chapter argues that AI-based technologies have the potential to revolutionize the way local governments operate by significantly improving data analysis capabilities, enabling predictive policy planning and evidence-based decision-making, as well as optimizing the delivery of essential services to the community. By effectively applying AI, local governments can enhance resource allocation, streamline public service delivery, and foster greater responsiveness and citizen engagement through AI-driven interactive platforms (Lahdili et al., 2024; **Shvets et al., 2024;**Vrabie, 2023; Toll et al., 2020).

Moreover, AI can enhance decision-making frameworks by supplying data-driven insights that mitigate human biases and enhance objectivity. By scrutinizing complex datasets, AI systems empower policymakers to make informed, evidence-based decisions that align with the needs and preferences of various populations. These systems also reinforce responsiveness, enabling local governments to quickly adapt to evolving circumstances and community requirements.

Additionally, AI tools enable accurate monitoring of SDG performance metrics, ensuring alignment with the desired outcomes envisioned in these goals (Vinuesa et al., 2020). For instance, the integration of community participation in experimental urbanism can be enhanced through the application of AI, which can assess citizen behaviors and preferences (Mahendra, 2021). This analysis can significantly inform local planning decisions, leading to a more inclusive policy process that aligns better with local community needs. In light of these circumstances, applying AI-based technologies becomes even more critical and relevant in pursuing the SDGs (Vinuesa et al., 2020).

Efficient and Inclusive Governance: AI holds significant transformative potential within local governance by promoting inclusive and efficient administrative practices (Alhosani & Alhashmi, 2024; Millán-Vargas et al., 2024). Through the implementation of intelligent systems, local administrations can optimize the allocation of resources, thereby ensuring that limited resources are distributed equitably and effectively. For example, AI-driven predictive analytics can discern areas that are underrepresented and channel investments into those communities, consequently addressing systemic disparities and advancing social justice.

Implementing AI can provide invaluable support to local governments by offering predictive analytics that enable them to anticipate various challenges, such as rapid population growth or the potential impacts of climate change, thus facilitating more effective and sustainable urban planning initiatives. Moreover, AI can significantly enhance the allocation of resources across essential services, including those related to water supply, energy provision, and transportation systems, thereby contributing to their overall efficiency and equity. Recent empirical investigations have revealed that a growing number of municipalities that have begun to adopt AI-powered systems are witnessing remarkable enhancements in their operational efficiencies, as well as significant improvements in the way in which they deliver services to their citizens.

In addition to these benefits, AI-driven platforms can promote more robust and inclusive community engagement by establishing improved mechanisms for citizen feedback, which in turn strengthens the principles of participatory democracy. By integrating these advanced technologies into their operations, local governments can actively address the resource and capacity gaps that frequently obstruct their progress toward the achievement of the SDGs, thereby reaffirming their crucial and pivotal role in the broader framework of sustainable development efforts across the globe.

By integrating ethical tenets into AI-based applications, local governments can harmonize efficiency with responsibility, ensuring that technological progress contributes to a governance model that is not only effective but also inclusive and equitable. This ethical framework strengthens public trust and fortifies the social contract between citizens and their governments, thereby facilitating a sustainable and inclusive public administration.

Nonetheless, the incorporation of AI into governance requires the establishment of a public digital ethos to tackle ethical dilemmas on transparency, fairness, and accountability (Margetts, 2022). Transparency can be realized through the adoption of explainable AI models, which permit stakeholders to comprehend the decision-making processes and engender trust in the technology. The principle of fairness must be prioritized by conducting audits of algorithms for biases and ensuring inclusivity in the design and implementation of AI tools. Mechanisms for accountability, such as oversight committees and feedback circles, are imperative to guarantee that AI systems remain congruent with democratic principles and public expectations.

Personalized Public Services: AI has the potential to revolutionize how public services are delivered providing customized services that meet the specific needs and preferences of individuals (Ladislas, 2024; Liu et al., 2020; Alghamdi et al., 2020). By leveraging advanced data analytics and machine learning methods, local governments can analyze large amounts of citizen data to identify patterns, behaviors, and preferences. This approach allows them to create tailored solutions that align closely with the unique requirements of citizens, significantly improving their satisfaction and engagement with public services (Janssen et al., 2021). For instance, AI-driven systems can predict citizen needs by examining historical data and current trends, offering proactive recommendations for essential services like social support, education, or healthcare (Ali et al., 2023). AI draws on clustering and segmentation to categorize users based on similar traits, allowing for a better understanding of various demands and personalized service delivery (Shvets et al.,

2024). Local governments might use these insights to inform eligible citizens about upcoming public programs, subsidies, or community events that are relevant to their interests or circumstances. This approach not only improves the accessibility and effectiveness of public services but also demonstrates a government's attentiveness to individual concerns, thereby strengthening the relationship between citizens and their local authorities. Additionally, AI can facilitate real-time personalization through tools like chatbots and virtual assistants (Mullick & Patnaik, 2022; Prasad, 2021). These systems can regulate their responses based on user interactions, providing accurate and relevant information or assistance. For example, a citizen asking about construction permits could receive tailored guidance that considers local regulations, the type of construction, and previous interactions with the system.

Personalized strategies are also applicable in urban planning and infrastructure management. AI systems can analyze data from multiple sources, such as traffic patterns, utility usage, and demographic information, to create customized solutions for particular neighborhoods or areas. For example, traffic management plans could be developed based on the commuting habits of local residents, improving overall efficiency and reducing congestion.

This chapter argues that integrating AI in local government and public administration needs a thoughtful approach that focuses on human-centered goals rather than just technology itself. Drawing from Allam and Newman's (2018) critical framework, sustainable public administration should see technology as a strategic tool within a larger societal context, not an end goal. Their model highlights three key pillars: Culture, Metabolism, and Governance, which offer a comprehensive perspective for implementing AI-based technologies. By viewing technology as a facilitator rather than an isolated factor, local governments can ensure that AI and big data analytics primarily aim to enhance urban livability and the well-being of citizens. This perspective challenges the common technocratic view that often emphasizes efficiency and economic indicators over social inclusivity and quality of life. The framework indicates that local policymakers should first create strong governance structures, understand cultural contexts, and examine urban metabolic systems before thoughtfully integrating technological solutions. In practice, this means AI should be calibrated to promote human-centered outcomes, processing and interpreting data in ways that directly enhance public services, sustainability, and community resilience.

LIMITATIONS AND CHALLENGES OF ADOPTING AI IN LOCAL GOVERNMENTS

Implementing artificial intelligence in the local government setting has revolutionized public civil service. From the AI-based prediction of future trends to the automation of service delivery, AI solutions can increase the effectiveness and timeliness of the governance processes. However, the growing use of AI in municipal environments has raised severe challenges, such as algorithmic bias, lack of infrastructure, and widening the sociable divide (Yigitcanlar et al., 2022; Devlin & Coaffee, 2023). Nonetheless, its integration is full of numerous issues that bring ethical, technical, financial, and societal issues into focus. Such obstacles not only hamper the actualization of AI but also give rise to ethical and socio-political questions that need immediate academic and policy responses (Ahn & Chen, 2020).

It is thus appropriate to ask critical questions about the various forms of risk associated with AI in local governance and place these in the context of technology and public administration. This section will discuss the main risks of AI implementation in local governance, including ethical issues, resource disparities, organizational resistance, lack of public trust, and cybersecurity threats. To this end, the authors present the current empirical data and case studies and stress the importance of developing inclusive policies and ethical standards to address the described issues and promote the fair implementation of AI.

Ethical Issues in the Use of Artificial Intelligence: Unquestionably, one of the most discussed problems of AI adoption in local governments is the ethical question of algorithmicizing of decisions (Nassar & Kamal, 2021). Bias in AI systems arise from the data used and thus have implications on a large scale. For instance, a study conducted by ProPublica exposed that the COMPAS system was predicting African Americans as risky to re-offend than Whites when the fact was otherwise. Such biases erode the public's confidence in the justice system's fairness and maintain structural discrimination, especially in criminal justice domains (Akinrinola et al., 2024). Furthermore, another issue is the Introduction of other AI-based technologies, like facial recognition, to monitor people (Konidena et al., 2024). Facial recognition was banned in San Francisco in 2019 due to the public's concerns about misuse and threats to civil liberties. These cases make it necessary to discuss the ethical guidelines of AI use, especially in policing and urban planning.

Technical and Infrastructural Constraints: Sometimes, local governments suffer technical challenges that hinder the implementation of artificial intelligence. AI capability is contingent upon good data and sound digital support; however, as evident from the information presented, many municipalities have these inputs in scant measure (Gwagwa et al., 2020). India tried to introduce AI in the traffic system.

Still, the big problem was that the data needed to be more consistent and updated, a problem of infrastructure in developing countries.

Moreover, the incorporation of AI in traditional systems presents significant issues. European municipalities have noted that integration of AI has been a challenge due to technological limitations on compatibility between the AI tools and the e-governance platforms (Li, 2024). Such barriers not only put the cost up but also prolong the time to achieve the potential of AI. Solving these technical issues requires investing in digital technology development and cross-sectoral cooperation.

Financial Constraints and Digital Divide: AI encompasses considerable expenses in terms of capital investment, recurring costs, and security costs (He et al., 2020). These costs are expensive, especially for resource-limited local governments. For instance, New York City spent tens of millions of dollars on an AI-based waste management system that could have made more difference. It is also important to mention that the financial difference between developed and less-developed cities widens digital divides because while developed cities can buy perfect AI systems, less-developed ones cannot (Sinha & Lee, 2024). This situation is quite evident whenever we see only well-endowed cities in America developing AI-aided contact tracing during the COVID-19 pandemic. Crossing these divides, therefore, needs to be supported by fair funding models and context-sensitive training activities.

Organizational and Cultural Resistance: AI implementation requires organizational change, which is always a resisted process. Employees may be concerned about AI's threat to their jobs or may need more training to work effectively and integrate this technology. The AI use case in Nairobi County, Kenya, for planning cities was hampered by the absence of technical knowledge and personnel within the municipal staff and, therefore, the need for capacity building (Gwagwa et al., 2020). Implementation of AI is hindered by bureaucracy. In Mexico City, bureaucracy posed a challenge to implementing an artificial intelligence crime prediction system due to institutionalization. This situation means that overcoming these barriers requires leadership support, engagement of change management levers, and promoting an organizational culture of innovation.

The Erosion of Public Trust: Lack of trust in AI significantly affects local governments (Aoki, 2020). This paper discusses how surveillance, job losses, and unfair treatment foster distrust. The black box problem aggravates this problem since AI systems are complex to explain and make decision-making processes virtually impossible for the public to understand (Robles & Mallinson, 2023). The recent controversy around the UK using artificial intelligence to grade student's papers during the COVID-19 outbreak demonstrates it. The system gave lower grades to students from poor schools, fueling public outcry and loss of faith in the fairness of AI. Such examples indicate that it is paramount to include transparency and public participation in AI governance frameworks.

Cybersecurity Vulnerabilities: AI systems are highly vulnerable to cyberattacks because they deal with sensitive data. An Atlanta ransomware attack in 2022 affected the local government and disclosed the weak points in municipal networks (Ruggiero et al., 2022; Hossain et al., 2024). Likewise, manipulating data inputs in AI systems also presents a threat in adversarial attack situations. For example, some individuals can hack an AI traffic management system to create or cause an accident or bring about traffic jams. To address these threats, employing more rigorous security measures, periodic system checks, and cooperation between countries to set standards for AI security in public administration is necessary.

Environmental Considerations: The high-power consumption of AI systems is an environmental concern, mainly due to local governments' growing adoption of AI for monitoring and forecasting applications. The University of Massachusetts calculated that creating one AI model could generate as much carbon as the lifetime emissions of five cars. Such conclusions pose the need to investigate the environmental impacts of AI deployment and the emergence of green computing systems.

Exacerbation of Social Inequities: AI systems may perpetuate existing unfair practices if the AI is not developed and deployed with the proper methodologies. For example, studies show that predictive policing algorithms have amounted to increased policing of poor and black neighborhoods. This situation not only reinforces prejudices in communities and societies but also erodes the credibility of public authorities. Mitigating these disparities necessitates an intersectional approach to AI regulation that embraces equity and inclusiveness.

CASE STUDIES AND REAL-WORLD APPLICATIONS

AI is necessary to revamp local government administrative structures, reshape urban systems, and enhance public services. Alhosani and Alhashmi (2024) note that AI increases efficiency in both the public and the private domain. AI has been successful in the local governance system, indicating the system's ability to solve intricate issues, improve efficiency, and promote citizen participation (Toll et al., 2020; Lahdili et al., 2024). But these implementations also offer a wealth of information about what is required to get there - robust infrastructure, stakeholder engagement, and even ethical issues. In this section, we review selected case studies in detail to discover specific lessons from what has already been implemented by other local governments. Recommendations derived from this section shall provide a detailed guide on how AI can be integrated into local government administration in other jurisdictions, considering the sectors in which the technology is already operational.

Smart Traffic Management: The traffic management challenge continues to haunt many countries, with local government authorities, especially in developing countries, suffering losses and experiencing inefficient cities by commuters. Local governments have turned to various means and methods to address this challenge, such as employing traffic marshals and erecting roundabouts and traffic lights. However, these efforts must be more effective due to the lack of automation. However, local authorities have adopted innovative solutions to deal with traffic challenges. One example is the city of Los Angeles because it has been one of the first to use AI to solve one of the most common problems, namely traffic jams. The Automated Traffic Surveillance and Control (ATSAC) system is an excellent example of an application of AI in regulating efficient urban transport. ATSAC then used data from over 4,000 sensors and cameras to adapt the traffic signals in real time.

Through this, the system calculates the traffic patterns and corrects them before they occur. In fact, after the implementation of ATSAC, traffic congestion has been cut by 16%, hence cutting greenhouse emissions and time spent on the road. The system has also offered a way of enhancing road safety through timely response to occurrences such as an accident or a vehicle breakdown. The case of ATSAC is particularly relevant for local governments in the developing country context, where adequate and well-connected institutional infrastructure is a crucial precondition for effective action. A vital enabler was the investment Los Angeles had made in a large number of sensors; the data collected by these sensors was the raw material that the AI system needed to operate in real time. Further, the system exhibited the expansion requirement as ATSAC was gradually integrated to cover more intersections and newer technologies.

Predictive Policing: Public administration and local governance have increasingly become complex, and with predictable policies, it is easier to manage local governments effectively. Issues such as crime, waste management, urban planning, climate change, and education require officials to interact with vast amounts of data, which can sometimes take time to manage manually. Furthermore, keeping up with the rapidly changing contexts and situations related to the above issues requires forward-looking policies based on a detailed analysis of trends and patterns. The city of Santa Cruz was among the first to adopt predictive policing, whereby, using AI, historical crime data is analyzed to identify hot spots for criminal activity (Bachner, 2013). They were then posted to these zones to prevent possible crimes as a measure used by the police. Subsequently, the application of this system reduced property crimes in the city by 19% within its first year (Yen & Hung, 2021).

Besides optimizing the use of resources, the police department stated that there was an improvement in the rate of patrolling. One should note that the program, which brought down crime rates, suffered criticism for privacy invasion issues as well as concerns about bias in AI systems. Some opponents stated that reliance on predictive policing was not suitable for practice because it only generates bias against people of color. However, the experience of Santa Cruz demonstrates an urgent need for openness and people's involvement. To gain that trust, local governments need to explain how AI systems work and create some structure to respond to the issues of bias and accountability.

***Citizen Engagement Through Chatbots*:** Citizen engagement has become an essential indicator of good governance not only by the national government but also by the local administration. Policymakers have become conscious of public opinion and seek to incorporate their thoughts and ideas in decision-making processes. Despite its significance, engaging with members of the public can be challenging due to population size, geographical area, and inadequate personnel to handle public relations, among others. However, AI allows local governments to engage with citizens effectively and conveniently. For example, the regional administration of Bengaluru, India, released the Bruhat Bengaluru Mahanagara Palike (BBMP) "BBMP Sahaaya," which is an AI-driven chatbot aimed at enhancing citizens' communication with the municipality (Prasad, 2021). This outcome is actual because the chatbot operates through NLP to help residents by providing information, lodging complaints, and monitoring service requests. In its first year, the chatbot responded to more than half a million queries, which relieved government staff and shortened response time (Mullick & Patnaik, 2022). This innovation made the system available in different languages to fit the Bengaluru population in case of any issue. The effectiveness and acceptability of the BBMP Sahaaya prove that the user-centered design approach is appropriate. Thus, accommodating language differences and focusing on effective system navigation helped make these tools accessible to the public in linguistically diverse areas, which is always the potential of any system aimed at providing public services.

AI in Waste Management: Waste management is one of the most challenging tasks faced by local government authorities today (Guerrero et al., 2013). Traditional approaches to waste management cannot address the high level of waste disposal attributed to consumerism and rural urban migration. However, one local government is leveraging the merits of AI to transform waste management. Seoul, the capital and largest city in South Korea, has shown the world how using artificial intelligence can transform waste management. The city introduced an artificially intelligent recycling program with image recognition and IoT smart bins for waste segregation analysis. The initiative helped raise the recycling percentages by 24% and further decrease the waste disposed in landfills. Smart bins deliver real-time data, making waste management schedules easier, cutting operational costs, and reducing the negative impacts on the environment. This experience in Seoul shows that the development of such apps is not a one-time project but requires continuous evolution. Infrequent changes to the system could have been more effective in responding to changes in waste types or in implementing new recycling methods. This reason is why local governments must continuously make resource provisions for enhancement.

***Public Health Monitoring*:** Community health management has become a devolved function in many countries. This development means local government authorities are now mandated to deal with primary health issues in many places as part of decentralization. This task comes with a huge responsibility, especially in the wake of growing infectious diseases that require monitoring. However, some local governments have adopted new ways of monitoring public health. In the recent past, especially during the COVID-19 outbreak, the city of Toronto in Canada used AI to tackle some of its health challenges. In partnership with private tech companies such as BlueDot, the city leveraged big data and algorithms to follow infection patterns, identify possible hot spots, and distribute medical care. The AI system helped bring about timely decisions and ensured containments where required while optimally utilizing the hospitals. Hospitals and mobility patterns were used in real time and were critical to the project's success. Toronto case shows that implementing AI requires the support of both the government and the private sector. The partnership provided the city with modern equipment and professional assistance while emphasizing the population's needs.

AI-Driven Urban Planning: contemporary cities thrive on proper urban planning failure to which urban areas can be unlivable. This experience is synonymous with many local governments. Poor urban planning has negative consequences on the quality of life. Singapore has always been among the forefront adopters of innovative city solutions, applying AI to city planning. The use of AI in Virtual Singapore is to develop a virtual city environment where planners can rehearse their urban development plans and monitor its effect on factors such as transportation, accommodation, and environmental friendliness (Perdana & Mokhtar, 2022). The platform has enhanced efficiency in executing urban planning tasks, reduced the time it takes to complete projects, and enhanced the quality of decisions made. In this way, the government has pursued sustainable and efficient urban policies for development since it can visualize or predict the impacts of different policies once implemented (Ibid, 2022). Singapore's case reveals that incorporating AI into the strategic planning frameworks is mandatory. The same can be said about its success: the higher the quality of the data used, the higher the platform's effectiveness; besides, the work of multiple departments underlines the importance of interdepartmental cooperation.

LESSONS LEARNED AND BEST PRACTICES

From the case studies presented here, there are many applications of AI that local governments, including those in the least developed countries, can leverage. From the above case studies, there are several lessons that local government officials can draw as follows. These include:

Invest in Data Foundation: AI systems require good-quality data to produce good results. The elements that made Los Angeles' Advanced Traffic System Coordination, ATSAC, for example, include significant coverage of sensors and real-time data processing. Governments should consider investments in data gathering and guarantee the possibility of data exchange between databases and data preservation.

The necessity to promote Transparency and Trust: Social acceptance is a significant factor in any AI project. Santa Cruz's predictive policing program was an example of how the application of AI possesses inherent danger when a community is not sufficiently involved or made aware of the use of the technology. They should also set an ethical framework, explain how and why the decision, and engage in an outside audit.

Prioritize Inclusivity: The AI systems must ensure they can reasonably attend to the citizens' needs. The chatbot used in Bengaluru was successful because its design supported multiple languages to help the government deliver services to a population that was diverse in its language. Subordinate governments should prevent bias in AI algorithms to achieve fairness.

Build Technical Capacity: Skilled personnel can better manage and optimize AI systems. The halt of Nairobi's urban planning intervention underscores the dangers of lack of capacity development. Governments should support educational courses in artificial intelligence, promote partnerships with universities, and hire AI specialists to maintain AI projects.

Start Small and Scale Gradually: Begin with a small-scale adoption of a particular technology until you gain enough knowledge about it. Pilot projects are helpful to governments because they allow them to introduce AI systems, identify possible problems, and adjust solutions before large-scale applications. The phased plan of the waste management program implemented by Seoul provides the blueprint for the usefulness of incremental scaling to other municipalities.

Leverage Public-Private Partnerships: According to several studies, there are core principles that could help governments foster the adoption of AI and its uses for development purposes. Involving the private sector in this strategy is paramount as it increases efficiency and transparency. The cooperation between Toronto and BlueDot offers a perfect example of the local government's willingness and ability to engage private companies' expertise, which protects the population's interests by signing clear contracts.

***Continuous Monitoring and Updates*:** To meet the future needs of urban communities, seeking new AI systems and the ability to adapt to new challenges or new technologies is crucial. Seoul's waste management experience shows that evaluation and update are critical time-to-time activities.

***Engage Citizens Early*:** Public engagements and feedback processes that allow for the inclusion of the public are legitimized through AI. During the pandemic, Toronto implemented citizens' participation in AI decisions, enhancing trust and guaranteeing solutions' relevance to people's needs.

AI is an instrument that has shown the capabilities to revolutionize the operation of local governments due to the immense innovation that has been accomplished in implementing AI in successful endeavors across the globe. The above examples, ranging from the traffic control of Los Angeles to the integrated urban planning system of Singapore, show that AI can solve some of the most challenging problems and enhance human life. However, as the following challenges indicate, the road to effective implementation could be more complex and ridden with hurdles including ethical issues, data infrastructure, and public trust.

From the above cases, the following lessons emerge the need to put resources into constructing sound infrastructure, the need to embrace diversity, and the need for organizations to operate under high levels of transparency. This methodology calls for local governments to take appropriate measures to adopt such an AI, mainly through stakeholder engagement, scaling up progressively, and constant monitoring. Finally, AI can create better, more intelligent, and more adaptive societies if its application is based on a concept and involves adherence to ethical standards.

CONCLUSION

The digital transformation of local governments marks a paradigm shift in public administration, as traditional paper-based systems give way to AI-powered platforms that are reshaping how public services are planned, managed, and delivered. Local governments, as the closest governance entities to citizens and schools of democracy, are uniquely positioned to harness AI benefits. Their proximity to communities enables them to identify and address individual and collective needs effectively while promoting long-term development through decentralized governance.

This chapter explored the transformative potential of AI in local government operations, emphasizing its capacity to enhance service delivery, promote sustainability, and advance data-driven decision-making. AI's applications in local governance are wide-ranging, encompassing tools such as chatbots that improve citizen engagement, predictive analytics that shape informed policymaking, and smart city solutions that optimize infrastructure and emergency responses. Additionally, AI enhances cybersecurity measures and supports personalized, secure service delivery.

However, these opportunities come with significant challenges, including technical, infrastructural, and financial constraints, the need for specialized personnel, organizational and cultural resistance, and ethical considerations such as algorithmic bias, accountability, transparency, and data privacy. Adhering to robust governance frameworks and regulations like the GDPR is critical to overcoming these obstacles. While adopting AI remains a complex plan, these challenges also highlight areas that need reforms. Deliberate investments in digital infrastructure, support for public-private partnerships, and ethical frameworks can help local governments avoid the worst pitfalls of AI adoption.

Best practices from case studies of AI implementation provide valuable insights into stakeholder management, publicizing AI decision-making, and using policy feedback. Ethical issues, practical challenges, cost considerations, and public trust deficits are not insurmountable barriers; instead, they represent opportunities to rethink governance in the digital age. Local governments can adopt AI-inclusive policies and create an accountability culture to ensure the accessibility of its benefits while minimizing the adverse effects.

Looking ahead, AI integration will be increasingly essential for addressing the evolving needs of local communities. This chapter argues that success in this transformation requires strategic planning, inclusive stakeholder engagement, and a commitment to continuous learning and adaptability. By proactively and effectively addressing challenges and harnessing the transformative potential of AI, local governments can emerge as leaders in technological innovation, paving the way for the future of public service delivery. By prioritizing ethical implementation, ensuring digital equity, and addressing cybersecurity risks, they can position themselves at the forefront of the AI-driven transition in public administration, setting a global standard for smart governance in the 21st century.

As AI evolves, its role in predictive analytics, service and smart urban planning, and participatory governance has the potential to transform citizens' relationships with their local governments, paving the way for more equitable, efficient, and responsive governing models. Nonetheless, it is crucial to acknowledge the profound challenges many local governments face, including constraints on resources, limitations in technical expertise, and restricted autonomy in policy-making. These challenges significantly hinder their capacity to effectively meet targets such as those established by the SDGs. More studies are needed to formulate context-sensitive interventions to achieve fair AI implementation, especially in the developing world, where its impact is likely to be most significant.

Locality is a quintessential feature of the modern political scene, and applying AI in this sphere is not a hopeless dream. Through strategic frameworks that prioritize strong policies, capacity-building efforts, and inclusive stakeholder participation, local governments can realize the transformative potential of AI. Establishing a culture of innovation and adaptability will further enable municipalities to respond accurately and responsively to changing community demands.

REFERENCES

Abioye, S. O., Oyedele, L. O., Akanbi, L., Ajayi, A., Davila Delgado, J. M., Bilal, M., Akinade, O. O., & Ahmed, A. (2021). Artificial intelligence in the construction industry: A review of present status, opportunities and future challenges. *Journal of Building Engineering*, 44, 103299. DOI: 10.1016/j.jobe.2021.103299

Ahn, M. J., & Chen, Y. C. (2020, June). Artificial intelligence in government: Potentials, challenges, and the future. In *Proceedings of the 21st Annual International Conference on Digital Government Research* (pp. 243–252). DOI: 10.1145/3396956.3398260

Akinrinola, O., Okoye, C.C., Ofodile, O.C., & Ugochukwu, C.E. (2024). Navigating and reviewing ethical dilemmas in AI development: Strategies for transparency, fairness, and accountability. *GSC Advanced Research and Reviews, 18*(3), 050–058.

Alghamdi, M., Alsolami, R., Alghamdi, W., & Alnehmadi, Y. (2020). Personalizing government services through AI: Opportunities and challenges. In *2020 4th International Conference on Computer and Communication Systems (ICCCS)* (pp. 595–599). IEEE.

Alhosani, K., & Alhashmi, S. M. (2024). A review of the opportunities, challenges, and benefits of AI innovation in government services. *Discover Artificial Intelligence*, 4(1), 18. DOI: 10.1007/s44163-024-00111-w

Ali, O., Abdelbaki, W., Shrestha, A., Elbasi, E., Alryalat, M. A. A., & Dwivedi, Y. K. (2023). A systematic literature review of artificial intelligence in the healthcare sector: Benefits, challenges, methodologies, and functionalities. *Journal of Innovation & Knowledge*, 8(1), 100333. DOI: 10.1016/j.jik.2023.100333

Allam, Z., & Dhunny, Z. A. (2019). On big data, artificial intelligence, and smart cities. *Cities (London, England)*, 89, 80–91. DOI: 10.1016/j.cities.2019.01.032

Allam, Z., & Jones, D. (2018). Towards a circular economy: A case study of waste conversion into housing units in Cotonou, Benin. *Urban Science (Basel, Switzerland)*, 2(4), 118. DOI: 10.3390/urbansci2040118

Allam, Z., & Newman, P. (2018). Redefining the smart city: Culture, metabolism, and governance. *Smart Cities*, 1(1), 4–25. DOI: 10.3390/smartcities1010002

Bachner, J. (2013). *Predictive policing: Preventing crime with data and analytics.* IBM Center for the Business of Government.

Barns, S., Cosgrave, E., Acuto, M., & McNeill, D. (2016). Digital infrastructures and urban governance. *Urban Policy and Research*, 35(1), 20–31. DOI: 10.1080/08111146.2016.1235032

Berawi, M. (2019). The role of Industry 4.0 in achieving sustainable development goals. *International Journal of Technology*, 10(4), 644–647. DOI: 10.14716/ijtech.v10i4.3341

Biermann, F., Hickmann, T., & Sénit, C. A. (2022). *The political impact of the Sustainable Development Goals: Transforming governance through global goals?* Cambridge University Press. DOI: 10.1017/9781009082945

Chen, H.. (2023). Algorithmic fairness in municipal AI systems. *Government Information Quarterly*, 40(1), 101–115.

Chung, I. H., Williams, D. W., & Do, M. R. (2022). For better or worse? Revenue forecasting with machine learning approaches. *Public Performance & Management Review*, 45(5), 1133–1154. DOI: 10.1080/15309576.2022.2073551

Cugurullo, F. (2020). Urban artificial intelligence: From automation to autonomy in the smart city. *Frontiers in Sustainable Cities*, 2, 38. DOI: 10.3389/frsc.2020.00038

Devlin, C., & Coaffee, J. (2023). Planning and technological innovation: The governance challenges English local authorities face in adopting planning technologies. *International Journal of Urban Sciences, 27*(sup1), 149–163.

Farazmand, A. (2009). Building administrative capacity for an age of rapid globalization: A modest prescription for the twenty-first century. *Public Administration Review*, 69(6), 1007–1020. DOI: 10.1111/j.1540-6210.2009.02054.x

Farida, I., Ningsih, W., Lutfiani, N., Aini, Q., & Harahap, E. (2023). Responsible urban innovation working with local authorities: A framework for artificial intelligence (AI). *Scientific Journal of Informatics*, 10(2), 121–126. DOI: 10.15294/sji.v10i2.43818

Glemarec, Y., & Puppim de Oliveira, J. A. (2012). The role of the visible hand of public institutions in creating a sustainable future. *Public Administration and Development*, 32(3), 200–214. DOI: 10.1002/pad.1631

Guarini, E., Mori, E., & Zuffada, E. (2022). Localizing the sustainable development goals: A managerial perspective. *Journal of Public Budgeting, Accounting & Financial Management*, 34(5), 583–601. DOI: 10.1108/JPBAFM-02-2021-0031

Guerrero, L. A., Maas, G., & Hogland, W. (2013). Solid waste management challenges for cities in developing countries. *Waste Management (New York, N.Y.)*, 33(1), 220–232. DOI: 10.1016/j.wasman.2012.09.008 PMID: 23098815

Gwagwa, A., Kraemer-Mbula, E., Rizk, N., Rutenberg, I., & De Beer, J. (2020). Artificial intelligence (AI) deployments in Africa: Benefits, challenges, and policy dimensions. *The African Journal of Information and Communication*, 26(26), 1–28. DOI: 10.23962/10539/30361

Hao, K. (2019). Training a single AI model can emit as much carbon as five cars in their lifetimes. *MIT's Technology Review*, 75, 103.

Haque, M. S., Ramesh, M., Puppim de Oliveira, J. A., & Gomide, A. A. (2021). Building administrative capacity for development: Limits and prospects. *International Review of Administrative Sciences*, 87(2), 211–219. DOI: 10.1177/00208523211002605

He, M., Li, Z., Liu, C., Shi, D., & Tan, Z. (2020). Deployment of artificial intelligence in real-world practice: Opportunities and challenges. *Asia-Pacific Journal of Ophthalmology*, 9(4), 299–307. DOI: 10.1097/APO.0000000000000301 PMID: 32694344

Hossain, S. T., Yigitcanlar, T., Nguyen, K., & Xu, Y. (2024). Cybersecurity in local governments: A review and framework of key challenges. *SSRN*. DOI: 10.2139/ssrn.4631885

Janssen, M., Janowski, T., & Scholl, H. J. (2021). AI for personalized e-participation. *Government Information Quarterly*, 38(2), 101571.

Jha, A. K., Ghimire, A., ... (2021). A review of AI for urban planning: Towards building sustainable smart cities. In *2021 6th International Conference on Inventive Computation Technologies (ICICT)* (pp. 937-944). Coimbatore, India.

Konidena, B. K., Malaiyappan, J. N. A., & Tadimarri, A. (2024). Ethical considerations in the development and deployment of AI systems. *European Journal of Technology*, 8(2), 41–53. DOI: 10.47672/ejt.1890

Ladislas, E. S. (2024). Personalizing government services through artificial intelligence: Opportunities and challenges. *Indian Journal of Artificial Intelligence and Neural Networking (IJAINN, 3*(5), 13-18.

Lahdili, N. (2023). Citizen participation in local government: A case study of Safi [Doctoral dissertation, Ankara Yıldırım Beyazıt University]. *ResearchGate*. https://doi.org/DOI: 10.1234/researchgate.374477797

Lahdili, N., Önder, M., & Nyadera, I. N. (2024). Artificial intelligence and citizen participation in governance: Opportunities and threats. *Amme Idaresi Dergisi*, 57(3), 202–229.

Li, C. (2024). Future trends and technological innovations of private AI deployment. *Science. Technology and Social Development Proceedings Series*, 1, 1–14. DOI: 10.70088/6fmynz86

Liu, H., Shen, J., & Xu, Z. (2020). The integration of artificial intelligence and e-government: Opportunities and challenges. *International Journal of Information Management*, 50, 28–37.

Mahendra, S. (2021). Artificial intelligence and urban design. *AI Plus Info*. https://www.aiplusinfo.com/blog/artificial-intelligence-and-urban-design

Margetts, H. (2022). Rethinking AI for good governance. *Daedalus*, 151(2), 360–371. DOI: 10.1162/daed_a_01922

Millán-Vargas, A. O., Sandoval-Almazán, R., & Valle-Cruz, D. (2024). Impact and barriers to AI in the public sector: The case of the State of Mexico. *Proceedings of the 25th Annual International Conference on Digital Government Research,* 81- 89. DOI: 10.1145/3657054.3657249

Mullick, M., & Patnaik, A. (2022). Pandemic management, citizens, and the Indian smart cities: Reflections from the right to the smart city and the digital divide. *City. Cultura e Scuola*, 30, 100474. DOI: 10.1016/j.ccs.2022.100474

Nallaperuma, D., Nawaratne, R., Bandaragoda, T., Adikari, A., Nguyen, S., Kempitiya, T., De Silva, D., Alahakoon, D., & Pothuhera, D. (2019). Online incremental machine learning platform for big data-driven smart traffic management. *IEEE Transactions on Intelligent Transportation Systems*, 20(12), 4679–4690. DOI: 10.1109/TITS.2019.2924883

Nasim, S. F., Qaiser, A., Abrar, N., & Kulsoom, U. (2023). Implementation of AI in traffic management: Need, current techniques, and challenges. *Pakistan Journal of Scientific Research*, 3(1), 20–25. DOI: 10.57041/pjosr.v3i1.942

Nassar, A., & Kamal, M. (2021). Ethical dilemmas in AI-powered decision-making: A deep dive into big data-driven ethical considerations. *International Journal of Responsible Artificial Intelligence*, 11(8), 1–11.

Perdana, A., & Mokhtar, I. A. (2022). Seniors are adopting digital devices and virtual event platforms in Singapore during COVID-19. *Technology in Society*, 68, 101817. DOI: 10.1016/j.techsoc.2021.101817 PMID: 34785827

Prasad, A. (2021). *Examining bureaucratic responsiveness in India: A comparative study of municipal services* (Doctoral dissertation, The George Washington University).

Regona, M., Yigitcanlar, T., Xia, B., & Li, R. Y. (2022). Opportunities and adoption challenges of AI in the construction industry: A PRISMA review. *Journal of Open Innovation*, 8(1), 45. DOI: 10.3390/joitmc8010045

Robles, P., & Mallinson, D. J. (2023). Artificial intelligence technology, public trust, and effective governance. *The Review of Policy Research*, ropr.12555. DOI: 10.1111/ropr.12555

Ruggiero, A. F., Owusu, T. D., & Staley, J. J. (2022). Ransomware in local government: Risk factors, vulnerabilities, and exploitation during a global pandemic. *Issues in Information Systems*, 23(4).

Sanchez, T., Shumway, H., Gordner, T., & Lim, T. (2022). The prospects of artificial intelligence in urban planning. *International Journal of Urban Sciences*.

Saner, R., Saner-Yiu, N., & Gollub, L. (2017). Implementing the SDGs by subnational governments: Urgent need to strengthen administrative capacities. *Public Administration and Policy*, 20(2), 23–40.

Santoro, P. (2019). The sustainability of institutions: An unstable condition. *International Review of Administrative Sciences*, 85(4), 609–626. DOI: 10.1177/0020852317741533

Shvets, K., Onyshchenko, A., Kudin, V., Korchak, N., & Ivanii, O. (2024). Application of artificial intelligence in modern public administration: New opportunities and challenges. *International Journal of Informatics and Communication Technology (IJ-ICT), 13*(3), 509–518.

Sinha, S., & Lee, Y. M. (2024). Challenges with developing and deploying AI models and applications in industrial systems. *Discover Artificial Intelligence*, 4(1), 55. DOI: 10.1007/s44163-024-00151-2

Tapscott, D., & Tapscott, A. (2015). *Blockchain revolution: How the technology behind Bitcoin is changing money, business, and the world*. Penguin/Portfolio.

Toll, D., Lindgren, I., Melin, U., & Madsen, C. Ø. (2020). Values, benefits, considerations, and risks of AI in government: A study of AI policies in Sweden. *JeDEM: EJournal of EDemocracy and Open Government*, 12(1), 40–60. DOI: 10.29379/jedem.v12i1.593

Vinuesa, R., Azizpour, H., Leite, I., Balaam, M., Dignum, V., Domisch, S., Felländer, A., Langhans, S. D., Tegmark, M., & Fuso Nerini, F. (2020). The role of artificial intelligence in achieving the sustainable development goals. *Nature Communications*, 11(1), 233. DOI: 10.1038/s41467-019-14108-y PMID: 31932590

Vogl, T. M. (2021). Artificial intelligence in local government: Enabling artificial intelligence for good governance in UK local authorities.

Vrabie, C. (2023). E-Government 3.0: An AI model to use for enhanced local democracies. *Sustainability (Basel)*, 15(12), 9572. DOI: 10.3390/su15129572

Walker, R. M., & Andrews, R. (2015). Local government management and performance: A review of evidence. *Journal of Public Administration: Research and Theory*, 25(1), 101–133. DOI: 10.1093/jopart/mut038

Wilson, R., & Lee, J. (2023). Technical challenges in municipal AI implementation. *Digital Government: Research and Practice*, 4(2), 1–18.

Yen, C. P., & Hung, T. W. (2021). Achieving equity with predictive policing algorithms: A social safety net perspective. *Science and Engineering Ethics*, 27(3), 1–16. DOI: 10.1007/s11948-021-00312-x PMID: 34075448

Yigitcanlar, T., Li, R. Y., Inkinen, T., & Paz, A. (2022). Public perceptions on application areas and adoption challenges of AI in urban services. *Emerging Science Journal*, 6(6), 1199–1236. DOI: 10.28991/ESJ-2022-06-06-01

Chapter 3

Balancing Public Safety and Individual Rights in AI-Driven Public Administration in Nigeria

Dayo Akindipe
https://orcid.org/0009-0000-4884-0760
Afe Babalola University, Nigeria

Olalekan Moyosore Lalude
https://orcid.org/0000-0003-1603-163X
Wisconsin International University College, Ghana

ABSTRACT

The chapter examines the complex ties among privacy, surveillance, and public safety in today's world of AI-driven governance. The chapter will further examine what happens when a data-driven decision-making process works without transparency in Nigeria. Historically, those in authority have had an easier time keeping power when the decision-making process is hidden from the citizens. It will outline compelling strategies for mitigating the privacy risks that come with using AI in law enforcement, such as strong democratic oversight, the use of AI in a "data minimized" way, and the design of AI systems that ensures privacy is maximized. The chapter concludes by arguing that these strategies—and the informed, equitable future they make possible—are better than the alternative: a society governed by AI systems that infringe on individual rights and are not safe or secure.

DOI: 10.4018/979-8-3693-8372-8.ch003

INTRODUCTION

Across the world AI is becoming more and more popular within governments, in ways, such as to improve operational effectiveness or optimize services, such as the support of law enforcement agencies (Berryhill, Heang, Clogher, & McBride, 2019). But as governments transit to using AI systems for surveillance, privacy concerns are mounting, making it an important task to reconcile public safety with the rights of individual (Xia, Semirumi, & Rezaei, 2023).

Artificial Intelligence is being applied in numerous areas of public administration, ranging from law enforcement through healthcare and transportation to social services (Bignami, 2022). AI can be powered by mining personal data like biometric standards and online behavior. By using AI technologies, the way governments respond to emergencies or manage resources can be made more efficient and help in reducing criminal activity. Yet, the reasons for surveillance must be carefully examined. It is intended as a way to keep citizens safe, but might also become a tool for repression and persecution (Feldstein, 2019). Surveillance overreach is a concern and, if there are no safeguards in place, this becomes an ugly turn in the spirit of public safety; away from mere privacy invasions to potential zeroing-in on people, inhibiting dissent and violating personal freedoms. Balancing public safety and individual rights means establishing robust legal systems and ethical frameworks to govern the use of faces from AI in public administration. Strong data protection legislations should be put in place by governments which ensures transparency and no misuse of such data. The types of data collected, how they are stored and maintained, and who has access to these information should be something that citizens can know.

Public agencies also have a duty to embrace ethical AI principles that uphold accountability and fairness. This ensures continuous AI privacy impact assessment and bias identification and mitigation. Fair and just AI policies — those that fully respect fundamental rights yet help keep us safe — are built collaboratively by better-engaging stakeholders, such as civil society organizations, technology specialists, as well as community representatives. Civil society organizations are key stakeholders advocating for privacy rights and holding public institutions accountable. Through making the costs of AI and surveillance explicit, organizations can help generate public demand for stronger safeguards. They can also advocate for more public engagement around surveillance technologies in general so that people are more aware of how they are used today.

Open and transparent initiatives, public consultations, and educational efforts can contribute to de-mystifying AI technologies allowing citizens to be aware of their rights and advocate more effectively for a responsible governance. Because for an AI-impacted public administration, that fine line between public safety and individual rights can become more complicated. The promise of AI is so great, but not at the cost of privacy and civil liberties. In order to navigate this complex landscape responsibly, governments can create strong legal frameworks, promote transparency and mitigate risks by engaging with the public. Most importantly, to implement AI in public administration may help ensure the proper compliance with democratic values and the balance between security and fundamental rights of individuals.

As next-generation artificial intelligence becomes integrated into the public sector, it brings new opportunities to use these powerful tools to maintain the public's safety. But at what cost? “Governance by Artificial Intelligence (AI),” as it might be called, offers the chance to increase not just service delivery efficiency but also the effectiveness of the policing in Nigeria. Yet, with the “improvement” in such effectiveness in creating safety comes the potential for the same systems to do harm to public safety itself, civilian privacy, and civil liberties. McCarthy, renowned American computer scientist in 1956 originally defined Artificial Intelligence (AI) as the engineering and scientific process of making intelligent machines like the intelligent computer programs (Agba M. S., 2023). AI has many promises, even though it is currently determinable, the progress from decades ago are not marginal.

Rather, they have been great strides in the path of perfection. It has been shown many times over that technology can serve the interest of humankind, by improving productivity and efficiency in work. AI brings much more capabilities to the technological development discourse. There is no doubt about the capacity of AI to assist in the development of a resilient global economy, and in the creation of transformative technologies. However, AI is a double-edged technology that can bring about as much significant positive development as it can disrupt social cohesion. Public administration has been passing through a major evolution due to the intervention of AI. It has been the great driving forces of increasing efficiency, delivering better services and improving the accuracy of data. In this complex world where all countries are having to face up to very difficult problems, AI can optimize public administration, when applied in ways that promote governance, enables the automation of operations, and brings openness and clarity to the decision-making process.

The most important benefit of AI is that it can implement efficient workflow processes in public administration. By virtue of AI-supported automation, it is possible to swiftly execute repeated activities such as application processing, record keeping, and human interaction. Chatbots given that they are run by AI, can handle a lot of inquiries in a very short amount of time and provide instant answer avoiding regular workers, and thus they could deal with more difficult tasks. It is not just that it reduces the burden on thin human resource, but also the service time could be reduced making the government services which the citizens seek more available and efficient.

Without doubt, AI has the capacity to deliver in an important role for data-driven decision-making, furthermore it can serve for effective public administration. In the process of administration, Governments generate huge amounts of data, such as demographic information to economic statistics. AI algorithms can effectively analyze this data at high-level speed and accuracy, and as a result, reveal patterns and insights that could have been missed by human analysis. For instance, predictive analytics can forecast trends in public health, crime, or traffic, enabling governments to proactively address issues before they escalate. This ability to anticipate problems and allocate resources more effectively can lead to better outcomes for communities and more efficient use of public funds.

While AI promises significant improvements in government efficiency and responsiveness, it also presents significant challenges. It is crucial to use AI ethically, ensuring fairness and protecting privacy. Governments must be transparent about how AI systems work and make sure they do not unfairly target specific groups (Manyika, Silberg, & Presten, 2019). Human oversight is essential to prevent harmful outcomes (Rawashdeh, 2023). Another issue is the digital divide. AI technology must be accessible to everyone to avoid widening inequality. Investing in digital infrastructure and training is crucial to empower citizens and public servants to use AI effectively. AI can revolutionize government if handled responsibly (World Bank Group, 2021). By addressing ethical, social, and technical issues, governments can leverage AI to create a more just and efficient public sector for the future.

A Bloomberg study from June 2022 showed that several nations, including as the United States, United Kingdom, China, and Canada, are making major investments in artificial intelligence. With an estimated 1 trillion yuan (about $147.8 billion) in anticipated expenditures, China intends to become the world's leading country in artificial intelligence technology by 2030 (Agba M. S., 2023). This underscores the trajectory various legal jurisdictions across the world are moving in the developments of AI systems. It is palpable that African countries, especially Nigeria need to allocate capital in budgetary allocations to invest in Artificial Intelligence systems to enhance public administration in order to keep up with global advancements in AI systems. The value of the world AI market in 2023 was $150.2 billion USD, with an anticipated exponential annual growth rate of 36.8% by 2030 (Teremetskyi, Burylo, Stefanchuk, & Zozuliak, 2024). Unfortunately, there is still a whole lot that needs to be done by African states, when it comes to investing in technology that would benefit the advancement of society. AI has a lot to contribute in the effective management of bureaucratic affairs, especially as regards law enforcement. This is because law enforcement is a significant problem for many African countries like Nigeria.

In the context of the possible impact of AI on individual rights such as the right to privacy, there are issues that are call for concern. The proliferation of Big Data has led to an increased reliance on algorithms to guide decisions in sectors ranging from employment to finance. While artificial intelligence offers the potential for efficiency and objectivity, it also carries significant risks (Aizenberg & Hoven, 2020). These automated systems can perpetuate existing biases, leading to discriminatory outcomes in areas like hiring, lending, and criminal justice. The illusion of impartiality created by algorithms can mask human error and prejudice, making it difficult to hold institutions accountable. As a result, the widespread adoption of AI technologies has profound implications for individual rights and freedoms (Aizenberg & Hoven, 2020).

Polok *et.al* (2023) have argued that Artificial intelligence (AI) holds the promise of revolutionizing how we live and work, offering solutions to complex challenges. However, its rapid advancement also presents significant risks to human rights (Polok, el-Taj, & Rana, 2023). AI systems can inadvertently perpetuate harmful stereotypes, leading to discriminatory outcomes in areas such as employment, housing, and criminal justice.

The development of autonomous weapons raises even more profound ethical concerns, with the potential for mass casualties and the erosion of human control over the use of force. Moreover, the increasing automation of jobs due to AI threatens economic security and social stability. To fully realize the benefits of AI while mitigating its risks, it is imperative to develop robust ethical frameworks and regulations that prioritize human rights and well-being (Polok, el-Taj, & Rana, 2023). Furthermore, in the area of governance, AI presents opportunities, especially for countries that are struggling with effective bureaucracy like Nigeria. At the same time, the inherent issues with these countries can weaponize AI against human rights and further threaten freedom. Unfortunately, governments, especially authoritarian ones, acquire technology and employ everything at their disposal to silence and repress dissidence. This is why the use of AI technologies in public administration in the developing world would be subject to controversial debates.

Global Regulatory Framework of AI

The exponential increase in data infringement, security risks and privacy concerns have created a paradigm shift in the development of Artificial Intelligence. The European Union has made considerable progress in creating the first broad AI regulation framework called the Artificial Intelligence Act 2024. The primary objective of the law is to seek equilibrium between the need to promote investment and innovation in AI on the one hand, and the necessity to guarantee the security of individuals and defend their basic rights such as right to privacy on the other hand (Teremetskyi, Burylo, Stefanchuk, & Zozuliak, 2024). This legal framework is a necessary legislation to ensure public safety and responsible use of AI systems in the EU. The EU AI Act 2024 underscores the ethical consideration in the developments of AI systems. In the same vein, the Council of Europe (CoE) have initiated efforts in establishing an AI Convention and are intending to create the first universal legal framework to regulate Artificial Intelligence. This will ensure national jurisdictions and member states set forth number of domestic principles, laws and right to ensure the protection of privacy rights in the advancements of AI systems (Nwankwo, 2024).

Regulatory Gaps of AI in Nigeria

Ethical and privacy concerns in AI have been addressed by the United Nations (UN) from a variety of positions. The UN Human Rights Council said in 2021 encouraged governments to take immediate measures to protect human rights in the artificial intelligence age. The UN noted that the use of AI systems can facilitate and intensify infringement of privacy rights (Nwankwo, 2024). Conversely, there is no law regulating AI systems in Nigeria and has created increased asymmetry between innovation and privacy rights. In 2023, Nigeria just enacted a data protection law, known as the Data Protection Act and what is more is that the country is still working on a national AI strategy and not implemented any legislative instrument on AI. In the same vein, the regulatory approach for AI in Nigeria has not been extensively evaluated in consideration of privacy and data protection laws which were just enacted (Nwankwo, 2024).

Balancing Public Safety and Privacy

Nigeria has had a turbulent history with military regimes that were authoritarian and which treated dissidents with contempt, and clamped down on political opposition. Many political dissidents that had tried to engage the Nigerian government, at one time or the other had been executed. From Ken Saro Wiwa, a Nigerian journalist and activist, who had been killed during General Sani Abacha's junta to Dele Giwa, another journalist, who had been assassinated during General Babangida's regime, the Nigerian state has always reacted violently to dissident voices. It is in this clime of governance that Nigeria forged a culture of repression. This culture of repression, unfortunately makes technology like AI, which can improve policing to be at risk of unethical use when used for policing in Nigeria.

Over the decades, Nigeria has invested multi-billion dollars in surveillance technologies from other countries for public safety. However, there are sinister motives for these large investments in surveillance devices since these contracts are not in the public domain and the government's dealing with these foreign partners are not publicly debated. This has laid a bad precedent to undermine privacy rights and the legal framework to protect privacy rights is considerably weak without strong enforcement. From 2014-2023, the government spent billions of dollars to implement various security projects and to also purchase surveillance technologies (Effoduh, 2024). The right to privacy is guaranteed under the provision of section 37 of the Constitution of the Federal Republic of Nigeria. The issue with this provision which is limited in scope as argued by scholars is that section 37 included no explicit definition or limitations on privacy. It is thus anticipated that subsequent legislative enactments would bridge this gap, defining the extents of privacy rights and potential exceptions permissible under the law. (Nwankwo, 2024). Over the years, it is palpable to state that foot-dragging process to enact a specific legislative instrument to balance public safety and privacy in the development of AI systems has created unintended consequence in the lives of people by undermining privacy rights which has led to atrocious breaches. In some cases, where dispute arise as to infringement of privacy rights, the Court have taken the position to determine the perimeters of privacy rights and the extent of infringements. However, the Court cannot make laws on privacy rights (Incorporated Trustees of Digital Rights Lawyers Initiative v National Identity Management, 2020).

AI-powered monitoring can result in a "watching you all the time" society and its clear negative effects on privacy and civil rights. These systems masquerade as helpful public safety tools. Their purported benefits must be taken into account. And these systems must also be seen for what they can really do: and that's to watch, and to analyze, and to assess everyone and everything they encounter in real time and in seeming high definition, but actually all too often in bad faith.

LAW ENFORCEMENT AS PUBLIC ADMINISTRATION

In examining how AI-based systems can aid policing, it is necessary to examine how law enforcement fits into the public administration discourse. Clark (1935) considered that the control of crime is essentially a public administration problem. It is, for him, as complex as running other government agencies, like those that handle administrative laws or constitutional issues. To effectively address crime, we need to study how government agencies handle crime-related matters (Clark, 1935). This view of law enforcement is an enduring view which has led to the conception that the police or any other organization that is vested with the duty to prevent crime or secure state interests, is one with a public administrative duty. Therefore, the focus of this chapter would be the police force in Nigeria and their secret counterpart, the Department of State Services.

Law enforcement is a form of public service, one unique in itself (Schroter, Quick, Ongaro, & Hartley, 2023). There are many ways that law enforcement serves the public interest, one of such ways is the protection of the rights of the individual, which the state is responsible for, and which it does through law enforcement. It is without doubt that for the state to be successfully governed, law enforcement must be effective and in its best shape. The police must be able to contain identified threats. The law enforcement in Nigeria as a public administration is fraught with the challenges that befall any bureaucratic agency in Nigeria with a shortage of personnel, poor equipment and high-level corruption that has prevented efficiency, thereby leading to poor results in public safety. As if the challenges are not enough to prevent Nigerians from having faith in the security apparatus, human rights violations and extrajudicial killings mar any redemptive opportunity for policing in Nigeria. Technology presents policing in Nigeria with the opportunity of efficiency and precision in the investigation processes. Unfortunately, the greatest concerns with the adoption of technologies that can make law enforcement in Nigeria easier, is that they could interfere with the rights of citizens to privacy and expose people to unprecedented danger.

GLOBAL APPROACHES TO SURVEILLANCE

United States

In the United States, the Foreign Intelligence and Surveillance Act (FISA) is a legislative enactment by the US Congress to safeguard the information infrastructure of the United States against adversaries or allies who are not completely transparent (Robarge, 2024). The FISA is a highly controversial piece of legislation because the law approves intelligence gathering of foreigners but there are also areas of concerns especially the collection and retention of data of US citizens. This privacy concerns have echoed reactions from civil liberty societies and have advocated balancing public safety and privacy. The legality of section 702 of the FISA with regard to U.S citizens is highly contentious. Communication involves information across various people and entities. The communication process is not limited to foreigners alone and in the gathering of intelligence by US regulatory agencies, the communication or data of US citizens would also be accessed and examined which undermines the right to privacy (Friedman, 2024).

It is difficult for a consensus to be reached when it comes to transnational surveillance because several legal jurisdictions including allies and adversaries have deficits in transparency. In addition, the revelation by Edward Snowden in 2013, a former employee of the US National Security Agency, now a Russian citizen, on some of the spying activities conducted by the United States across online communications further undermines the confidence needed for global collaboration. (BBC, 2014). On the contrary, the practice that is universal in the various legal jurisdictions across the world is to allow surveillance practices on peoples' privacy in cases where their respective national laws permit.

European Union

All national constitutions in Europe do not explicitly outlaw mass surveillance, despite the European tradition of data protection and privacy rights, which emerged as a response to the crimes carried out by authoritarian regimes in Western and Eastern Europe prior to and during World War II (Celeste, 2024).

As far back as 1984 before the advent of Artificial Intelligence as witnessed in this digital era, the European Court of Human Rights' Justice Pettiti stated in the case *of Malone v United Kingdom* that legal jurisdictions across the world were in danger of serious violation of peoples' privacy rights because of the activities of government agencies (Malone v United Kingdom, 1984). Decades later, there are various instances were peoples' privacy rights have not only been seriously violated but governments across the world are utilizing Artificial Intelligent systems to perpetrate these violations as evidenced in their surveillance practices.

In the case of *Wieder and Guarnieri v the United Kingdom*, the European Court of Human Rights' (ECtHR) on the 12th September, 2023, held that the applicants' rights under Article 8 of the European Convention on Human Rights had been violated by the United Kingdom (UK) as a result of its surveillance practices (Shany, 2024). The Court arrived at the decision based on the principle that when a country intercept and examine private communications of individuals regardless of their territorial base, such acts amounts to an infringement of privacy rights (Shany, 2024). The judgment seeks to create a limitation on the surveillance powers of countries in conducting transnational surveillance.

Conversely, in some other legal jurisdictions like the United States, the extent in which transnational surveillance is limited is controversial, especially when the argument is based on national security. This is also the case in Nigeria. What is also clear is that the European Union established regulatory responses to the concerns connected with surveillance practices through the enactment of Data Protection laws. There can be more comprehensive provisions that regulative surveillance activities in order to provide the needed balance between public safety and privacy.

AI-DRIVEN PUBLIC ADMINISTRATION IN NIGERIA

Public administration in Nigeria at the moment is burdened by needless processes and the management of data is unwieldy. However, there have been many calls for the digitization of bureaucratic processes in Nigeria to achieve efficiency. The journey towards digitizing bureaucratic processes have been quite slow, but there are assurances that in a not-to-distant future, public administration in Nigeria would be AI-driven. This assurance is rooted in the realities of the global workplace which is increasingly reliant on digitized processes, with a large part resolved by algorithmic interventions. The investment in AI has been massive globally with these investments at about 12.4 billion US Dollars (Agba, Agba, & Obeten, 2023). And with the significant capabilities of AI, that has perpetually shown that the future will be greatly impacted by AI technologies, governments all over the world will have to rely more on the technology in public administration. With the vast population of Nigeria that continues to grow, there would be greater need for accurate processes that will also be faster, and this will spur the inclusion of AI in governance, especially in policing.

Human Rights, Policing and AI-Driven Public Administration in Nigeria

Policing at the moment in Nigeria, is quite herculean, with a burgeoning population and increased social issues, such as terrorism, kidnapping and armed robbery. Policing, like many public administrative duties in Nigeria, has failed to go through reforms and have been almost impossible with swathes of unpoliced spaces in the country, yielding to many criminal elements and activities. This has earned Nigeria a place amongst failed states on indexes ranking worst governed states. With an increasing population, the challenges that have confronted policing in Nigeria will only proliferate, thereby inclining the state to seek solution in technology. Europol (2024) has stated that artificial intelligence has the potential to change the paradigm in policing, and its outcomes (Europol, 2022). What this means for policing even in the Global South, is that there would be more demand for AI technologies in policing soon. One agency in Nigeria that would likely adopt AI-driven processes for every of its bureaucratic processes quite soon, would be the Department of State Services (DSS). The DSS is regarded as an elite security agency which came from the creation of the establishment of the "E" Department (Special Branch) at the time, and this was resident in the Office of the Inspector General of the Nigeria Police Force (Department of State Services, n.d.).

The DSS through Decree No. 16 of 1976 and Decree 19 of 1986, are empowered to prevent and apprehend any criminal activities that threaten the internal security of Nigeria, The agency is tasked with the protection of intelligence and non-classified yet very vital information to Nigeria's stability. They include the responsibilities of counter and investigations of nuisances to security of the country in areas like spying, subversion, terrorism and organized crime. Also, it offers security to the state offices, important installations and structures, top leaders, and guests from other countries. For proper governance, it provides advice to the government on any issues concerning national security business at the right time (Department of State Services, n.d.). The DSS in its policing strategies have however been high-handed in its management of apprehended persons. And they have used technology to enhance the violence that they often wreak on their victims.

In 2020, Aljazeera showed how a report by the University of Toronto's Citizen Lab exposed how Nigeria's military intelligence agency has procured technology designed to intercept and analyze Nigerians' phone calls and text messages. According to the report, a surveillance company called Circles is helping multiple government agencies across 25 countries, including Nigeria, to spy on opposition leaders, journalists, and activists using similar equipment (Aljazeera, 2020). The Pegasus spyware is an AI-based technology that has been used by governments to spy on dissidents and perceived opposition.

The powerful Pegasus spyware, created by a company called NSO Group, has blurred the lines between positive and negative uses of technology. This software has been involved in both amazing successes, like the apprehension of criminals and preventing terrorism, and terrible abuses, like spying on people and even contributing to murder. The story of NSO shows how difficult it is to control such powerful technology and make sure it is used responsibly (Kaster & Ensign, 2023). In Nigeria, the level of human rights abuses and the extreme high-handedness by the security agencies pose a concern to the effectiveness of an AI-based public administrative process like policing.

And it seems without the redefinition of what state mechanisms represent in Nigeria, technology might not yield positive results for public administration, especially for policing. There have been many anti-technology resistance in Nigeria. This is because, there is the understanding that not only can technology, especially state-of-the-art technology like AI-enabled platforms help in lessening the burden of public administrative tasks, but also ensure its efficiency. However, it is not the intention of the bureaucrats in Nigeria to want efficiency, as efficiency would only mean accountability.

THE NIGERIAN CONUNDRUM

The synopsis of global regulatory responses to surveillances practices has been discussed to lay a foundation and the lens in which the state of laws on surveillance programs in Nigeria can be analyzed. Nigeria lacks a good pedigree or reputation for the protection of personal data. The extent in which government's activities have infringed on privacy rights is incalculable. The protection of public safety has been jeopardized and privacy rights have not been upheld. It is therefore imperative to suggest that there is no balance between public safety and privacy rights when government's agencies deploy surveillance technology in public administration. Furthermore, it is a country that is notorious for human rights violations. Human rights violations in Nigeria has an ugly, brutish history.

This is because the regulatory responses to the concerns connected with the processing and retention personal data arising from surveillance practices by the government, has been relatively slow. In the same vein, the laws on surveillance is not specifically covered by the constitution, or other national laws and are sparingly entrenched across fragmented statutes despite the enormous potential of these surveillance technologies in the digital era being utilized for surveillance practices.

Historical Pedigree

Nigeria's pre-independence and brutal military regime birthed the disdain for the respect of privacy rights of its citizens. Pursuing this further, several decades after its independence which brought in democratic governance, the infringement of privacy has skyrocketed despite the constitutional right to privacy. The surveillance and the retention of data for monitoring the activities of Nigerian people has increased significantly (Oloyede, 2021). The reasons for this infringements are not far-fetched. The grundnorm, which is the Nigerian constitution contains limited provisions on privacy rights and the law that specifically protects the personal data of Nigerian citizens was only enacted in 2023 after several decades of astronomical data breaches.

Nigeria, with a population of almost 250 million, is the most populous nation in Africa. The country has seen an upsurge in incidents of violence over the last ten years that pose a danger to national harmony. The administration has used violent episodes as a justification for its surveillance activities (Oloyede, 2021). In the same vein, the Global Terrorism Index (GTI) 2023 report found that Nigeria ranks the 8th most terrorized nation in the world (Effoduh, 2024). In response, the government have increased expenditure to acquire advanced surveillance systems which include but are not limited to spyware, security cameras, databases and interception technologies (Effoduh, 2024). However, the legal issue is the asymmetry consideration of public safety and individual rights such as privacy rights.

Surveillance Technologies in Nigeria

Over the years, the federal government spent vast amount of tax payer's money to acquire surveillance technologies for national security purposes. The State Security Service (SSS), the National Intelligence Agency (NIA), the Defense Intelligence Agency (DIA), and the Office of the National Security Adviser (ONSA) collectively spent 73,736,607,928 naira to purchase surveillance technologies between 2014 and 2023. (Effoduh, 2024). Out of this total expenditure from the four security agencies in Nigeria, from 2016-2022, the Office of the National Security Adviser (ONSA) spent N58,204, 362,598; from 2014-2023, the State Security Service (SSS) spent N11, 401,833,33; from 2014-2014, the National Intelligence Agency (NIA) spent N89,300,000 and from 2020-2023, the Defense Intelligence Agency (DIA) spent N4,041,112,000 (Effoduh, 2024).

These security agencies often times decline to provide full disclosure of some of these surveillance technologies and are compelled by the court to give full disclosure of the advanced surveillance systems worth billions of naira, largely from the tax payers' money. Some of these surveillance technologies include Satellite Data and Signal Intersect, OSINT software, Data Retention System, and Digital Audio Jammer. There is limitation of data on the extent at which these surveillance systems are put into lawful use. Conversely, it is plausible that there are astronomical breaches of individual rights such as privacy rights from data retention technologies and digital audio jammer used by the federal government.

In 2013, the Nigerian government acquired surveillance technology from Elbit Systems Limited in Israel in addition to the internet and computer-based systems that collects the personal data of Nigerian citizens (Oloyede, 2021). This is a greater danger to national security because these foreign technologies are not manufactured in Nigeria and this undermines the protection of information of the Nigerian citizens. This can lead to *data flight*. The World Bank Digital Economy Diagnostic Report in 2019, states that inadequate access to digital technologies is a factor preventing cybersecurity in Nigeria. The country depends on foreign-hosted cloud services to store personal data of citizens. This is a significant threat to privacy rights. From the foregoing, there is weak protection in the cloud infrastructure as well as data protection in Nigeria (Office of the National Security Adviser, 2021).

The Nigerian government spent close to 46 billion naira (US$127.6 million) in 2017 (Budget Office of the Federation 2021) and allocated about 9 billion naira (US$22.8 million) in 2020 to acquire surveillance technology and to conduct operations connected with surveillance which did not have the complete validation of law (Oloyede, 2021). These huge amounts of spending on surveillance technology is evidenced from the security protocol of several government's organizations who demand authentication by fingerprint, facial recognition and other biometric information to again access. Closed circuit television have been configured across various places for security and surveillance purposes (Oloyede, 2021).

In July 2021, the Nigerian Senate gave the Nigerian Intelligence Agency approval to acquire the WhatsApp Interception Solution and Thuraya Interception Solution for monitoring private communications. These surveillance technologies were purchased for 4.8 billion naira (US$11 million) (Oloyede, 2021). It is palpable the Nigerian government continue to spend public resources to acquire advanced surveillance systems developed by foreign countries which undermines privacy rights. The argument is that such transactions will precipitate *personal data flight*. The government's justification to purchase these surveillance technologies to ensure national security does not in any way outweigh the atrocious data breaches associated with the utilization these surveillance technologies. Thus, it presents a counter-productive stance from the actions of the government.

What is more is that, the African Digital Network and the Institute of Development Studies revealed in September 2023 that Nigeria patronizes foreign surveillance companies more than most countries in Africa and gave more than US$2.7 billion to surveillance companies based in China, the US, Israel, Australia, the EU, and the UK to purchase surveillance technologies over a ten-year period (Effoduh, 2024). Pursuing this further, the government's intentions to increase the regulation of social media is gaining momentum. In October 2023, the Ministry of Information and National Orientation is already devising plans with law makers to amend the National Broadcasting Commission (NBC) Act 2004 to give powers to the Commission to regulate social media (Effoduh, 2024). The purported regulation of social media will be resisted by civil society groups and this will eventually be resolved by judicial intervention which is arguably compromised.

Failed Algorithms and Potential Abuses of Power

Human rights are seriously threatened by the nature of many AI algorithms, especially in places like Nigeria where power disparities and weak democratic institutions are prevalent. Artificial intelligence (AI) technologies have the potential of being used in public administration without transparency, perpetuating structural inequality and strengthening current power structures. Holding public authorities responsible for the results of an algorithm becomes difficult if the decision-making process behind it is kept secret. Under such conditions, the algorithm essentially acts as a barrier, shielding the powerful from criticism. This opacity can enable discriminatory acts, including the denial of necessary services to underprivileged populations, unfair resource allocation, and targeted monitoring. An opaque AI system can be used to uphold authoritarian leadership in a country like Nigeria, where human rights violations are common. Algorithms may be used, for example, to recognize and target political opponents, defend discriminatory laws, or quell protest. It is harder to contest or address these algorithms' negative effects if the general public is unaware of how they work.

Furthermore, power disparities already present may be made worse by AI systems' lack of transparency. The results of these systems may frequently be influenced by those who possess the technological know-how and means necessary to create and implement AI algorithms. As a result, groups who are already marginalized may become even more so since the data used to train the algorithms may not fully represent their viewpoints and interests. Democratic values and human rights are compromised by the opaqueness of AI algorithms in public administration. Making measures to guarantee accountability, openness, and public involvement in the creation and implementation of these systems is essential. Only by taking these steps will AI's possible drawbacks be reduced and its advantages made available to all societal members.

Legal Implications

The weak legal response to these atrocious breaches signal red lights in the legal framework regulating personal data of the Nigerian citizens. As pointed out earlier, developed legal jurisdictions even though are guilty of privacy infringements through their surveillance practices have responded with strong regulatory mechanisms to protects privacy rights. This appears not to be the case in Nigeria. The effectiveness of strong regulatory mechanisms underscores equally strong rule of law. This is because the rule of law in any legal jurisdiction dictates the legal and regulatory strength in the regulation and protection of rights including privacy rights. These creates incentives for both the citizens and the government to create a transparent process in the communication process which aims to balance public safety and privacy. This also underscores that the rule of law plays a significant role in the protection of privacy rights.

There are deeper issues when it comes to the legislative and regulatory framework in Nigeria. These issues undermine the efficacy of statutory enactments across the Nation and renders legislation inadequate. In assessing the rule of law in Nigeria, the nation continues to perform poorly nationally, regionally and internationally, falling to 120th out of 142th reviewed countries, with a total rating of 0.4 according to the World Justice Report in 2023 (World Justice Report, 2023). The nation also performed poorly regionally, falling to 23 out of 34 reviewed Sub-Saharan African nations in 2023. The implication of this low rating is that Nigeria has a weakened and diminished position from the assessments of government's activities and its policies. The components of rule of law include constraints of government powers, absence of corruption, open government, fundamental rights, order and security, regulatory enforcement, civil and criminal justice (World Justice Report, 2023). Nigeria has a low rating in each of these components of rule of law which guarantees privacy rights.

Nigeria is in the red zone when it comes to the protection of privacy rights due to a rating of 0.30 out of 1.0 in the 2023 WJP Rule of Law Index. The legal framework in Nigeria is designed to undermine basic privacy rights established by international law and entrenched in the Nigerian constitution. It is therefore palpable that Nigeria operates on 'rule by law' and not deserving of a 'rule of law system' which continues to undermine confidence of the citizens in the administration of justice in the protection of privacy rights.

PRIVACY RIGHTS AND REGULATION OF SURVEILLANCE ACTIVITIES IN NIGERIA

International Provisions

The National Assembly has ratified a number of international agreements that protects the right to privacy and regulates surveillance activities of the government. These legal instruments include but are not limited to:

i. African Charter on the Rights and Welfare of a Child

The right to privacy for this demography in Africa is protected in Article 10 of the Charter. The provision of this Charter is supposed to safeguard the children and regulate surveillance activities except permissible under the law (Article 10, African Charter on the Rights and Welfare of the Child). This Charter was ratified in 2001 but atrocious breaches of privacy rights of children still persists across Nigeria.

ii. Universal Declaration of Human Rights

The purpose of Article 12 in this context is to ensure that every Nigerian is entitled to their privacy and to be free from unlawful surveillance activities (Article 12, Universal Declaration of Human Rights). Conversely, this not the case as most Nigerians do not have confidence of regulatory agencies to enforce this provision.

iii. International Covenants on People and Domestic Rights

The arbitral policies and the utilization of surveillance technology to undermine privacy rights in Nigeria weakens the provision of Article 17 of the legal instrument that seeks to ensure arbitrary surveillance activities (Article 17, International Covenants on People and Domestic Rights).

iv. Economic Community of West African States Supplementary Act on Personal Data Protection

There are studies that demonstrates that Africa has a high record of personal data infringements across the world. It is palpable to state that the weak enforcement mechanism to protect privacy rights across the African states continues to undermine these international instruments on privacy rights.

National Laws

i. The Nigerian Constitution

The intention of the draftsmen is to ensure the provision of section 37 of the Constitution protect all private communications and privacy of Nigerians but in reality, there are serious violations of privacy rights (Section 37 of the Nigerian Constitution). In the same vein, section 45 of the Constitution set exceptions or limitations to section 37 which include but not limited to the interest of defense, public safety, public order, public morality, or public health. These are circumstances where privacy rights will be removed. The government does not have clear perimeters to determine the extent in which these limitations or exceptions can be applied and even if private individuals are within their protected limit to enjoy their privacy rights, the government still violate these rights.

ii. Cybercrime (Prohibition and Prevention Act) 2015

The Act was enacted in 2015 as the first law to specifically regulate cybercrimes in Nigeria. Prior to the enactment of the Cybercrime Act, there were various laws that indirectly regulated cybercrime in Nigeria. These laws created regulatory pluralism and also created conflicts in the enforcement of their provisions. Since the enactment of the Cybercrime Act about 10 years ago, the law has not been amended despite several elicited chorus from civil societies. This law in itself undermines privacy rights and it is counter-productive.

To underscore this argument, section 38(2) of the Act permit regulatory agencies or authorities to request for personal information from service providers and they are under legal obligation to comply without raising valid objections. Section 38(4) further states that the data obtained by the authorities can only be used for lawful purposes but the legal draftsmen failed to provide the perimeters that constitute lawful purposes (Section 38(4) of the Cybercrime Act, 2015). This has led to the brazen violation of privacy rights and the authorities continue to exploit this legal loopholes as a cloak to commit illegality.

iii. Mutual Assistance in Criminal Matters Act 2019

As it pertains to Nigeria, the Mutual Assistance in Criminal Matters Act 2019 is a legislation that undermines privacy rights. The reason is nor far-fetched. The purpose of the Act is to foster collaboration amongst legal jurisdictions when it comes to intelligence on suspects who have committed transnational crime. There is no guarantee that the information infrastructure and computer systems that stores these intelligence or confidential information is not being infiltrated through advanced methods such as Advanced Persistent Threat (APT). The technical analysis of the World Bank Digital Economy Diagnostic Report in 2019, that states that inadequate access to digital technologies is a factor preventing cybersecurity in Nigeria and Nigeria depends on foreign-hosted cloud services to store personal data of citizens provides a justification for this argument (National Cybersecurity Policy, 2021). This undermines the integrity of the cloud infrastructure or computer systems used in storing this personal data when they are retained across various systems that belongs to the government.

iv. Nigeria Data Protection Regulation, 2019

There have been several attempts to enact a specific legislation to protect personal data in Nigeria and these attempts have been faced with several challenges. For instance, the Nigeria Data Protection Regulation that was issued in 2013 by the National Information Technology Development Agency (NITDA) had several *lacunae* in its provisions not only but also experienced enforceability setbacks and hence, could not provide an adequate legal framework for data protection in Nigeria (Greenleaf, 2019). In the same vein, the Digital Rights and Freedom Bill also suffered setbacks as the Bill was not signed into law by the executive in March 2019 due to lack of harmonization with similar provisions in other pending bills on electronic governance which can result to statutory pluralism (Fowowe, 2019).

Even regionally, Nigeria has not ratified the African Union Data Protection Convention, otherwise known as the Malabo Convention, which was opened for signature since 2014 (Orji, 2018). After almost a decade delay without a substantial justification, the Malabo Convention finally came into effect in 2023, and the Convention has not been ratified by Nigeria, Egypt, Algeria, South Africa, Kenya, Morocco, and Ethiopia (Ifeanyi-Ajufo, 2024). The Nigeria Data Protection Regulation (NDPR) does not clearly designate a court with the authority to preserve data protection rights. The NDPR states the Federal High Court and the High Court of a State possess concurrent jurisdiction to hear and determine cases pertaining to the provisions of the regulation (Babalola, 2022). There should be a clear position on jurisdiction as specified under the Nigeria's Data Protection Act 2023. Another issue is the legislators did not expressly state whether the Data Protection Act 2023 repealed the Data Protection Regulation 2019 or both legal instruments should be harmonized which arguably can create conflicts in applicability.

v. Nigeria Data Protection Act, 2023

The Data Protection Act is divided into 13 parts with sixty-six sections (Data Protection Act, 2023). The major aim of the Act is to produce an appropriate enforcement system for the regulation of personal data, in handling how personal data is processed, and to also protect the privacy rights that are provided by the Constitution. The interpretation of section 2 of the Act does not apply to the protection of personal data of Nigerian citizens who are in another jurisdiction since the Act is limited to the processing of personal data belonging to those who reside in Nigeria (Anderson, 2023). This limitation in geographical scope undermines the transnational nature of data breaches across the globe.

Part II of the Act makes provisions for the creation, structure, authority, and the roles of the Data Protection Commission and its governing council. The primary role of the Commission is to ensure data controllers and data processors follow the data protection principles as specified by the provisions of the Act. The provisions of section 5 of the Act charged the Commission with the enforcement of the provisions of the Act. Part III of the Act makes provisions for the appointment of the Data Protection Commissioner and other employees of the Commission. The tenure of 10 years of the commissioner subject to re-election is quite monumental and the term duration under section 14 (4)(a) must be reviewed to a shorter term 4 years, subject to re-election. It is recommended that all term-limits in the Act should be further reduced.

Part V of the Act makes provisions for essential precepts and the 'legitimate interest' for the processing of personal data. The purpose for which personal data is processed must be precise, unambiguous, and lawful. The issue here is that ‘legitimate interest’ to process personal data from the government is not balanced with privacy rights and also undermines other fundamental rights. There should be clear parameters and definition of ‘legitimate interest’ under the Act which is currently not the case.

In the same vein, section 26 of the Act should be amended. For instance, when the collection of personal data is initiated by a request, the data controller must demonstrate that the data subject has expressed acceptance to the processing of his personal data. The consent must be voluntarily articulated through a communication, either expressly, orally or by affirmative action. Section 26 further states that inaction or silence is not considered consent. The mode of approval should be reviewed to ensure a clearer understanding and interpretation of approval to avoid needless ambiguity. Oral consent can be misinterpreted.

Part VI of the Act made comprehensive provisions on the rights of data subjects. Sections 34 to 38 of the Act makes provisions for these rights which include but are not limited to right to be informed on infringements of personal information, rights to access information on data processing, and right to delete personal data processed illegitimately. Section 35 states that the data subject has the right to withdraw his consent at any time. The issue is that the protection of these rights are not guaranteed.

Part VII makes provisions for the Data Security. The data controller and processor shall take all appropriate measures to ensure the safety, confidentiality and integrity of personal data collected from the data subject, in accordance to section 39 of the Act. The procedures to be taken by the data processor in the event that there is breach of personal data is provided in section 40 of the Act. The Data Protection Act did not make reference to the already existing Nigeria Data Protection Regulation 2019 (NDPR). This should be reviewed so as to enable a clear interpretation and the position of the NDPR.

Section 44 of the Data Protection Act creates an obligation for the data controllers and processors in Nigeria to register with the Commission or before the 30th June, 2024. Conversely, from the legal opinion provided to these data controllers on the need to comply with the directives of the Commission, the feedback is that these institutions are unaware of this directive to register with the Commission. There should be proper awareness and persistent communication of directives issued by the Commission to the general public.

Certainly, data protection system is failing in Nigeria due to the absence of holistic data protection law, which elicits questions about homeland safety due to the collection of personal data of Nigerians by various multilateral institutions. Given the technological developments and innovation, data protection should be a top priority for the National Assembly. The brazen violation of personal data is widespread in Nigeria as citizens frequently receive unsolicited communications. For instance, many individuals received communications from cold callers requesting support for the All Progressive Congress (APC) in the general elections of 2019. Reports found that the contact information of citizens had been collected from the Independent National Electoral Commission (INEC), from the documentation it had accumulated during the registration exercise (Ajaegbu, 2020). This is a serious violation of privacy rights.

Human Rights at Risk

The potential integration of Artificial Intelligence (AI) into public administration in Nigeria, while promising increased efficiency, poses significant threats to human rights. A primary concern is the potential for algorithmic bias. AI systems are trained on vast datasets, which often reflect societal biases. When deployed in public administration, these biases can lead to discriminatory outcomes in areas such as criminal justice, social welfare, and access to public services. Furthermore, the use of AI in surveillance and data collection raises serious privacy concerns. Without robust data protection laws and regulations, citizens risk undue intrusion into their personal lives. Mass surveillance enabled by AI can stifle dissent, hinder freedom of expression, and create a climate of fear. Another critical issue is accountability. AI systems can operate as black boxes, making it difficult to understand the decision-making process. This opacity can hinder efforts to hold government accountable for human rights violations. Moreover, the potential for job displacement due to AI automation can exacerbate economic inequality and social unrest. While AI offers potential benefits, its deployment in public administration must be approached with caution and accompanied by robust human rights safeguards. Failure to address these concerns could lead to a significant erosion of human rights in Nigeria.

Judicial Intervention

Judicial Activism undermines legal systems around the world. However, lawmakers often give too much liberty for Judges to interpret laws and as a result, these Judges can pronounce various interpretations to a legal provision and thus, creating conflicts in Judicial precedents. There are limited judicial pronouncements on privacy rights in Nigeria because the law itself undermines the protection of these rights. However, there are cases that have significant impact on privacy rights and surveillance. *In Emerging Markets Telecommunication Services Ltd v Godfrey Eneye,* the Court of Appeal upheld the right to privacy.

Conversely, the Court have been inconsistent which could be due to pressure from the government. For instance, Elbit systems received US$40 million from the Nigerian government in 2013 to procure surveillance equipment (Oloyede, 2021). Civil society groups made unsuccessful demands when these groups requested that the Nigerian government should be transparent with the procurement by providing specific information on the purchase of the surveillance equipment. In the same vein, the Court has also denied the application of these groups for the government to provide additional details on the procurements of surveillance equipment which has been utilized to undermine privacy rights (Oloyede, 2021). The Court failed to balance public safety and individual rights.

On the balance, in 2017, the Court granted the application of Paradigm initiative, a civil society group in Nigeria, and ordered the Ministry of Science and Technology to provide specific information on the intended launch of two satellites by the National Space Development and Research Agency (Oloyede, 2021). The federal government have a bad precedent of rejecting multiple requests from civil groups concerning its surveillance activities. This is disproportionate in the balance of public safety and privacy rights and underscores repressive regime of the government in the governance and enforcement of privacy rights.

CONCLUSION AND RECOMMENDATIONS

Amendment of Data Protection Act 2023

From the interpretation of section 3(2)(c) of the Data Protection Act 2023, security organization including NIA, SSS, and ONSA are exempted from obtaining the consent of data subjects before processing activities when these agencies utilize these surveillance technologies. Section 3(2)(c) excludes data controllers and processors from Part V of the Act's obligations if the processing of personal data is carried out by a competent authority and is required for national security. The agencies always justify intrusive surveillance activities under the cloak of national security concerns which continues to undermine individual rights. It is therefore imperative for an amendment of section 3(2)(c) of the Data Protection Act 2023 to include express consents of data protection and to provide a stronger justification for national security without undermining privacy rights.

Regulatory Transparency

The Nigerian government is not an open government. The lack of transparency from the government's surveillance activities undermines privacy rights. Openness in government is measured by how much a government communicates relevant information on its policies, which gives citizens the means to hold such government accountable, to encourage citizen engagement with the affairs of the country. According to the WJP Rule of Law Index 2023, Nigeria ranked 104 out of 142 countries globally in open government index score (World Justice Report, 2023). There is a decline in open government in Nigeria because the lowest rank the government recorded was in 2023. The underscore the lack of transparency in government's policies and activities which undermines confidence of the Nigerian people. It is therefore imperative for the government to be transparent in its activities by engaging citizens to participate in formulating its policies to ensure stronger enforcements of laws.

REFERENCES

Agba, M. S. (2023). Agba, Michael Sunday, GracArtificial Intelligence and Public Management and Governance in Developed and Developing Market Economies . *Journal of Public Administration, Policy and Governance Research* .

Agba, M. S., Agba, G. E., & Obeten, A. W. (2023). Artificial Intelligence and Public Management and Governance in Developed and. *Journal of Public Administration. Policy and Governance Research*, 1(2), 1–14.

Aizenberg, E., & Hoven, J. (2020). Designing for human rights in AI. *Big Data & Society*, 7(2), 2053951720949566. DOI: 10.1177/2053951720949566

Ajaegbu, C. S. (2020). The Problems of the Deficiency of Data Protection Law in Nigeria. *Chinaza Shalom Ajaegbu, 'The Problems of the Deficiency of DInternational Journal of Comparative Law and Legal Philosophy* .

Aljazeera. (2020, December 8). *Nigerian intelligence bought tool to spy on citizens: Report.* Retrieved from Aljazeera News: https://www.businesstoday.in/technology/news/story/pegasus-spyware-is-the-nso-groups-technology-good-or-evil-301878-2021-07-20

Article 10, African Charter on the Rights and Welfare of the Child . (n.d.).

Article 12, Universal Declaration of Human Rights. (n.d.).

Article 17, International Covenants on People and Domestic Rights. (n.d.).

Babalola, O. (2022). Nigeria's Data Protection Legal and Institutional Model: An Overview. *International Data Privacy Law*, 44-52.

BBC. (2014, January 17). *Edward Snowden: Leaks that exposed US spy programme.* Retrieved from BBC News.

Berryhill, J., Heang, K. K., Clogher, R., & McBride, K. (2019, November 21). Hello, World: Artificial intelligence and its use in the public sector. *OECD Working Papers on Public Governance.*

Bignami, F. (2022). Artificial Intelligence Accountability of Public Administration. *The American Journal of Comparative Law*, 2022(Supplement_1), i312–i346. DOI: 10.1093/ajcl/avac012

Celeste, E. a. (2024). Constitutionalizing Mass Surveillance in the EU: Civil Society Demands, Judicial Activism, and Legislative Inertia. *German Law Journal*, 1-20.

Clark, C. (1935). Law Enforcement and Public Administration. *Ilinois Law Review*, 30, 273.

Data Protection Act, 2023. (n.d.).

Department of State Services. (n.d.). *History of DSS*. Retrieved from Department of State Services: https://www.dss.gov.ng/dss_about

Effoduh, J. O. (2024). *Towards the Implementation of Data Protection Measures to Safeguard*. Accountability Lab Nigeria.

Europol. (2022). AI and policing: The benefits and challenges of artificial intelligence for law enforcement. European Union Agency for Law Enforcement Cooperation.

Feldstein, S. (2019, September). The Global Expansion of AI Surveillance. *Carnegie Endowment for International Peace Working Paper*.

Fowowe, S. (2019, March 20). *Buhari Declines Assent to Digital Rights and Freedom Bill and Four Others*. Retrieved from The Guardian: https://guardian.ng/news/buhari-declines-assent-to-digital-rights-and-freedom-bill-four-others/

Friedman, B. a. (2024). (Forthcoming). Indiscriminate Data Surveillance. [*Virginia Public Law and Legal Theory Research Paper.*]. *Virginia Law Review*.

Greenleaf, G. (2019). Nigeria Regulates Data Privacy: African and Global Significance. *UNSW Law Research Paper*.

Ifeanyi-Ajufo, N. (2024, February 23). *The AU took Important Action on Cybersecurity at its 2024 Summit – But More is needed*. Retrieved from Chatham House: https://www.chathamhouse.org/2024/02/au-took-important-action-cybersecurity-its-2024-summit-more-needed

Incorporated Trustees of Digital Rights Lawyers Initiative v National Identity Management, CA/IB/291/2020. (Court of Appeal 2020).

Kaster, S. D., & Ensign, P. C. (2023). Privatized espionage: NSO Group Technologies and its Pegasus spyware. *Thunderbird International Business Review*, 65(3), 355–364. DOI: 10.1002/tie.22321

Malone v United Kingdom, App. No. 8691/79 (European Court of Human Rights August 2, 1984).

Manyika, J., Silberg, J., & Presten, B. (2019, October 25). *What Do We Do About the Biases in AI?* Retrieved from Harvard Business Review: https://hbr.org/2019/10/what-do-we-do-about-the-biases-in-ai#:~:text=AI%20systems%20learn%20to%20make,or%20social%20inequities%2C%20even%20if

National Cybersecurity Policy, 2021. (n.d.).

Nwankwo, E. S. (2024). Regulating the Privacy Aspects of Artificial Intelligence Systems in Nigeria. *African Journal on Privacy and Data Protection*, 1, 220–247.

Office of the National Security Adviser. (2021). *National Cybersecurity Policy and Strategy 2021*. Office of the National Security Adviser.

Oloyede, R. (2021). *Surveillance Law in Africa: A Review of Six Countries: Nigeria Country Report.*ids.ac.uk

Orji, U. J. (2018). The African Union Convention on National Security: A Regional Response towards Cyber Security. *MUJLT*, 110.

Polok, B., el-Taj, H., & Rana, A. A. (2023). Balancing Potential and Peril: The Ethical Implications of Artificial. *Multicultural Education*, 9(6).

Rawashdeh, S. (2023, March 6). *AI's mysterious 'black box' problem, explained.* Retrieved from University of Michigan-Dearborn News: https://umdearborn.edu/news/ais-mysterious-black-box-problem-explained#:~:text=If%2C%20for%20example%2C%20an%20autonomous,we%20can't%20trace%20the

World Justice Report. (2023). *WJP Rule of Law Index 2023.* World Justice Report.

Robarge, D. (2024, June). Evolution of Surveillance Policy: US Intelligence, Domestic Surveillance and the Time of Troubles. Washington DC, United States of America.

Schroter, E., Quick, K., Ongaro, E., & Hartley, J. (2023). Insights into public management form policing: Introduction to the special issue of Public Management Review. *Public Management Review*, 25(9), 1633–1639. DOI: 10.1080/14719037.2023.2264892

Section 37 of the Nigerian Constitution. (n.d.).

Section 38(4) of the Cybercrime Act, 2015. (n.d.).

Shany, Y. (2024). Catching Up: The European Court of Human Rights Approximates its Approach to Extraterritorial Jurisdiction Over Digital Surveillance to That of the Human Rights Committee. *European Convention on Human Rights Law Review.* Vol. 5. *No. 2.*, 182-189. DOI: 10.1163/26663236-bja10089

Teremetskyi, V., Burylo, Y., Stefanchuk, M., & Zozuliak, O. (2024). Prospective Regulation of Artificial Intelligence in the European Union and its Possible Implications for Ukraine. *International Journal of Applied Engineering & Technology*, 6(1).

World Bank Group. (2021). Artificial Intelligence in the Public Sector: Summary Note. World Bank Group, Governance. Washington DC: World Bank Group.

Xia, L., Semirumi, D., & Rezaei, R. (2023). A thorough examination of smart city applications: Exploring challenges and solutions throughout the life cycle with emphasis on safeguarding citizen privacy. *Sustainable Cities and Society*, 93, 104771. DOI: 10.1016/j.scs.2023.104771

Chapter 4

AI-Driven Tools for Sustainable Public Administration:

Identification of Potential Barriers to AI Adoption in Public Administration Including Technological

Sheron Ndlovu
https://orcid.org/0000-0003-4601-9789
University of Forthare, South Africa

ABSTRACT

This chapter examines the technological, economical and societal obstacles that may prevent Artificial Intelligence from being widely used in public administration. In order to fully utilise AI's potential to improve public administration, obstacles must be addressed. Adoption of AI necessitates a large initial financial outlay, which is sometimes limited by financial constraints and conflicting goals in the public sector. Additional financial strains are incurred by long-term maintenance and training costs. Social resistance to AI originates from worries about data privacy, distrust of automated systems, and fears about job displacement. Furthermore, the acceptance of AI may be slowed down by public awareness of its ethical ramifications. In order to fully utilise AI's potential to improve public administration decision-making, efficiency, and transparency, it is imperative that these obstacles be addressed. This chapter gives a detailed analysis of these barriers, offering stakeholders and policymakers insights in advancing AI adoption.

DOI: 10.4018/979-8-3693-8372-8.ch004

INTRODUCTION

Artificial intelligence adoption in government might transform public service delivery, improve decision-making, and completely change the way government functions. However, we must consider a few potential obstacles to the use of AI in public administration.

Artificial intelligence (AI) adoption in the public administration sphere presents a potential for transforming the public administration holistically. AI not only improves service delivery but also increases efficiency and effectiveness. Despite the good that may be presented by AI adoption, it must be noted that AI is fraught with barriers in the public administration space, and these barriers fall under three main categories, namely financial, social, and technological. This chapter seeks to identify and examine these potential barriers in the public administration sector. Identifying AI barriers will assist in ensuring that there is a smooth adoption of strategies relevant to AI adoption and a smooth integration of AI adoption in public administration.

Most of the current knowledge about AI innovation in the public sector comes from theoretical perspectives and in-depth case studies of specific AI tools that are still in the early stages of development and implementation, showing how organisational, technical, ethical, and legal barriers obstruct the adoption of AI (van Noordt, Misuraca & Mergel, 2024).

Regarding technology, there are challenges prone to infrastructure in the process of trying to blend the old systems, which may be incompatible with AI adoption. This poses a significant threat to the adoption of AI, especially when considering the sensitive nature of government data across various public administration domains. The primary obstacle is the technological barrier. The development of AI applications for the public sector necessitates the machine-exploitable formalisation of a wide range of data, as well as the knowledge of governmental experts. Wirtz et al. (2021) denote that this procedure can be intricate and resource-intensive, particularly in the public sector, where data may be fragmented, unstructured, or segregated across various agencies. The public sector frequently lacks the infrastructure and technical know-how necessary to install and manage AI technologies, further hindering adoption. (Misuraca & Noordt, 2020).

Financial barriers are a significant obstacle. When embarking on any project, finances are key. With inadequate finances, it becomes a challenge to invest in the equipment, personnel, and systems required to adopt AI. In addition, the continuous maintenance and servicing of infrastructure necessitates financial resources. With limited finances, it becomes extremely challenging to implement and maintain the AI adoption process. Furthermore, securing funding in public administration presents a greater challenge compared to private enterprises. In public administration, there is limited flexibility to maintain existing resources and acquire cutting-edge technology. The financial obstacle is still another important one. The public sector may need to make large upfront investments in hardware, software, and training to implement AI technologies. This can be a major challenge because public resources are often limited, and financial priorities may conflict. We must also consider the long-term expenses of updating and maintaining AI systems, potential employment effects, and the need for retraining programs (Androutsopoulou, Karacapilidis, Loukis & Charalabidis, 2019).

Social challenges also offer a fair share of barriers that make it difficult to adopt AI in public administration. Public administration requires accountability and transparency, and AI adoption may present public trust issues. Additionally, public administration employees may face challenges related to job instability, as AI adoption could potentially jeopardise job stability. The need to upskill and reskill employees may arise, compounding the financial challenges. Ethical issues are one of the social challenges as AI adoption must adhere to AI ethics.

PUBLIC ADMINISTRATION

The political context encompasses public administration, which is why the term "public" exists. Public administration requires adherence to certain ethics and standards. Public administration may be direct or indirect. It is considered direct when it provides direct services and employs employees directly, while it is considered indirect when it subcontracts service providers for some of its services. Consider that public administration reflects the beliefs, norms, and culture of the society it serves. State statutes guide public administration as they represent a state (Shafritz, Russell, Borick & Hyde, 2022).

Public administration is key to modern society's sustainable development. Adopting stable principles and prioritising effective systems in public administration enables an effective public administration to transform the socio-economic status of any society. By adopting AI technology, digitisation contributes to the sustainability of public administration (Vasina, Monastyrskyi, Ivanova, Maistrenko, & Tsal-Tsalko, 2023). Emerging as a transformative technology, AI is poised to transform public administration through its ability to identify trends, predict, and analyse vast amounts of data, thereby enhancing the effectiveness and efficiency of the public administration's processes and procedures.

SUSTAINABILITY

Sustainable development refers to a socially and economically balanced environment that synchronises process functioning with rational resource usage while maintaining environmental safety.

Artificial Intelligence(AI)

AI, a system within a computer or machine, mimics human behaviour by carrying out tasks such as decision-making and problem-solving, and it thinks similarly to humans during operations. Despite AI's ability to execute and streamline tasks, it struggles to independently tackle certain issues, and some perspectives suggest that AI will soon surpass human intelligence (Kaplan and Haenlein 2019).

AI Applications in Public Administration

The public administration sphere is pursuing the adoption of AI for its tasks, with some countries such as the United Kingdom (UK) and the United States of America (USA) recognised as early adopters of AI in public administration. Different roles within public administration can adopt AI, including automation processes, threat and fraud detection, and knowledge management. AI can also function as a conversational assistant, providing expert or professional task support (Wirtz, Weyerer, and Geyer 2019). Ulnicane et al. (2021) have issued policy documents for the adoption of AI technology in certain instances.

Industrial processes and equipment assisted by AI systems considerably improve humans' abilities to provide digital assistance and decision-making in critical and overly complicated circumstances. As a result, it is imperative that the public sector take full advantage of AI's potential benefits. Nevertheless, AI also poses several risks to public administration. Artificial intelligence must not be viewed as a new technological advancement, as it is already in use and will likely be in the future. The first government agencies to use AI claim that the technology's enhanced productivity benefits the economy. The use of AI by public officials could be advantageous for numerous organisations in the public sector. Drone navigation, medical treatment prioritisation, bail hearings, citizen enquiries, public facility design, fraud detection, immigrant selection, and benefit distribution are a few examples. Gaining a deeper understanding of the opportunities, dangers, barriers, and rewards associated with the use of AI in the public sector is imperative (Alhosani & Alhashmi, 2024).

The efficiency, efficacy, and responsiveness of government agencies could be greatly improved by the use of artificial intelligence in the field of public administration. For example, municipal governments are starting to use AI-powered predictive analytics and decision support technology to improve service delivery and expedite workflows (Yolvi et al.,2021).

AI has the potential to improve public sector efficiency, bolster supervision and law enforcement, and assist strategic planning by enabling faster data processing and more accurate analysis. Hamirul et al., (2023) stated that AI can also be used to automate tedious jobs, giving government workers more time to concentrate on improving citizen interactions.

THREATS TO AI ADOPTION IN PUBLIC ADMINISTRATION

Public Administration Sphere's Nature

The adoption of AI in public administration faces numerous barriers, the first of which is the low adoption rate of AI within the public administration sector. When compared with private enterprises, the public administration sphere adoption of AI is still at a low level (Mikalef et al. 2021). Leaders in the public administration sector must embrace AI adoption, demonstrating a willingness to embrace the technology. Barriers to AI adoption may stem from the nature and characteristics that are prevalent in the public administration sphere. These potential barriers to AI adoption entail ethical aspects, transparency, dilemmas, which are moral, privacy, and security issues; the potential of errors, limited to no technical staff; and financial dilemmas, amongst many other potential barriers (Margetts and Dorobantu, 2019).

Late Adoption

Despite the immense potential of artificial intelligence, numerous public administration organisations continue to encounter obstacles in implementing this technology. Furthermore, there is a dearth of research that sheds light on the reasons behind the limited early adoption of AI in the public administration sector. A study also found that adoption will differ according to the stage of adoption that the organisation is in, and the factors related to the environment were considered to have minimal effects (Neumann, Guirguis & Steiner, 2022). The Diffusion of Innovation Theory further explains the adoption aspect, showing that there are different stages of adoption for every innovation, ranging from early adopters to late adopters (Dearing & Cox, 2018). In this scenario, most of the public administrators fall under the category of late adopters, hence the potential barrier.

Bureaucratic Processes

While AI appears to alleviate administrative burdens, there is a risk that it reinforces bureaucracy and bureaucratic processes in public administration (Newman, Mintrom, and O'Neill, 2022). Public administration must adhere to ethical and legislative processes when adopting and implementing AI. When public administrators implement AI, they must also adapt to the society they serve, which could potentially lead to social challenges for the citizens under their jurisdiction. In certain administrative areas, public administrators are required to consult citizens for their views prior to implementation, a process that can be lengthy. The requirement for stakeholders to express their views could potentially create a social barrier, as it necessitates citizens' initial education on the concept. This requirement can have significant implications for the public administration overall.

Security and Infrastructure

Artificial intelligence (AI) plays a crucial role in establishing the most effective communication systems in public administration, and it enhances management mechanisms (Lewallen, 2023). Electronic information systems ensure real-time communication. However, the implementation of such systems poses a security threat, and it negatively impacts the socioeconomic processes. Employees may face a security threat as electronic systems replace their manual jobs. The threat may also arise in situations where the public administration needs to purchase expensive software, leading to financial constraints and infrastructure limitations. The process necessitates advanced technology, but the public administration might not have the sophisticated information technology infrastructure to back it, leading to technological hurdles.

Acceptance

Acceptance is one of the obstacles to implementing AI in public administration. There is a need to gain the trust of the public in AI adoption. Some public administration service users may feel discriminated against due to the high degree of human touch loss associated with AI adoption. This could potentially lead to resistance from the community, including employees, who may feel hesitant to adopt the AI technology due to the potential disruption to their work routines. This presents a social challenge.

Expertise

Relevant technological training equips employees with the necessary skills to be technologically compliant. Insufficient training may prevent employees from using the technical equipment, leading to resource waste. Public administration often has shortages of the relevant technical skills and an understanding of effectively managing AI technologies. There is bound to be a shortage of personnel with sufficient technical capacity to manage the AI systems; therefore, extensive technological training may be required to impart the technical skills.

Financial Constraints

While AI projects are often considered high cost, the public administration sector is grappling with budget cuts and limited resources for its operations, making the necessity to validate new technology expenditures a perceived luxury. With constraints in the public administration budget, sufficient funds to purchase AI technology equipment is a financial barrier.

Legislative Framework and Ethics

Existing laws might not be sufficient when AI gains traction. This necessitates the creation of new AI-related policies and regulations, which could potentially impede AI adoption. Ethical dilemmas also result. We must avoid bias when making decisions. We must effectively manage accountability and transparency issues to comply with ethics and the legislative framework for AI adoption. The aforementioned factors may be a hindrance to AI technology adoption.

Technological Challenges

The use of chatbots in government defines a new area of study that presents several difficulties for the use of AI skills and their role in the provision of public services. For example, extracting and representing the expertise required to build an AI application's knowledge base is a well-known difficulty. In the public sector, this challenge intensifies due to the need to codify a multitude of data (legislative and operational) into a machine-exploitable format, alongside the expertise of governmental experts. Furthermore, to ensure data quality, we must effectively administer, organise, and aggregate heterogeneous data (Androutsopoulou, Karacapilidis, Loukis & Charalabidis, 2019).

Digital Divide

A digital divide is a disparity in access to digital infrastructure, usage, and services between people living in different geographical areas. A variety of factors, including disparities in education (learnt and unlearnt), racial segregation, age, illiteracy, language, lack of employment, policies, gender issues, and even access to digital infrastructure, contribute to the challenges of the digital divide. Issues with power may also contribute to the digital divide (Afzal, Khan, Daud, Ahmad & Butt, 2023).

A single donor will not accomplish the task of bridging the digital divide, but several community members working together will make it easier. Collaboration, even amongst different departments in the public administration sector, will be extremely helpful to solve the digital divide issue. These partnerships could involve policy formation, accountability from members of society, advocacy, and facilitators—possibly the government. A collaborative effort will also ensure that various important stakeholders are striving to close the digital gap (Ingram, 2021).

The digital divide is a major technological obstacle in public administration because it restricts equal access to digital tools and services that are essential for efficient governance. This gap frequently makes inequality worse by denying marginalised people access to digital communication platforms, e-governance opportunities, and online public services. Public servants may find it difficult to obtain the required technology or expertise, particularly in rural or underdeveloped areas. This could lead to inefficiencies and a reduction in the number of services provided.

LIMITATIONS WITH DATA

Data is the lifeblood of AI algorithms. Data from the public sector is frequently fragmented, inconsistent, incomplete, or of poor quality. Furthermore, privacy and security concerns may restrict data availability and sharing, reducing AI solutions' efficacy. One major problem is integrating and standardising data across many government entities.

Data availability and quality are two essential obstacles to the successful application of AI in the public sector. Large, high-quality datasets are necessary for AI, especially machine learning, to train and perform as intended. Several factors contribute to this problem. Data silos are another major technological impediment to AI deployment in public administration. Multiple departments and agencies disperse government data, creating data silos. This fragmentation, due to data silos and opposition to data sharing, makes it challenging to access and integrate the data required for AI adoption (Campion et al., 2022).

Inconsistent and Incomplete and Inconsistent Data

Incomplete data are among the other obstacles. The public sector's data may lack important details, be insufficient, or have inconsistent formats and structures amongst sources. This hinders the training of accurate and trustworthy AI models, a problem that the industry generally acknowledges. Another important factor is data security and privacy. Legal requirements and moral considerations related to data security and privacy may restrict data sharing and access. It is vital to strike a balance between privacy and the necessity for data. Privacy and security issues hinder data sharing in public-sector AI projects, as noted by Campion et al. (2022). The statement further supports this, highlighting data quality issues as another technological obstacle. Errors, inconsistencies, and outdated information in public sector data may impact the reliability of AI systems. Although necessary, data validation and cleaning cost money. These difficulties include data processing, privacy, and security concerns pertaining to administrative data in the public sector, which may influence the quality of the data (Abbas et al., 2023).

Integrating and analysing data from many sources is challenging in government organisations since there is a lack of common data formats and ontologies. Common data standards are essential for AI use. According to Noordt & Misuraca (2020), organisational and environmental factors, which may include data standardisation, are crucial for the effective adoption of AI in government. They also highlight the significance of elements other than data and algorithms.

The use of artificial intelligence and other cutting-edge information technology by public sector organisations leads to an increase in digital administrative data sources. This digitisation highlights the numerous processing, storage, and privacy concerns of the host departments and the nation's national statistics institutions (NSIs) (Zhang et al., 2022). Large dataset management also needs infrastructure, software, and trained personnel. Many public organisations struggle with a shortage of these resources, a problem that the larger body of research on AI in the public sector regularly highlights.

Public organisations have not yet fully integrated artificial intelligence (AI) into their operations, despite widespread optimism that it can enhance public governance. The rapid development of large language models, computer vision, generative AI, robotics, and public organisations, as demonstrated by their limited ability to develop and deploy AI and the generally slow adoption of AI in the public sector, aim to use these technologies to enhance the equity, efficiency, and effectiveness of public governance. However, they struggle to keep pace with the rapid advancements in AI (Kempeneer & Heylen, 2023). Public organisations, as demonstrated by their limited ability to develop and deploy AI and the generally slow adoption of AI in the public sector, aim to use these technologies to enhance the equity, efficiency, and effectiveness of public governance. However, they struggle to keep pace with the rapid advancements in AI (Kempeneer & Heylen, 2023). Public organisations, as demonstrated by their limited ability to develop and deploy AI and the generally slow adoption of AI in the public sector, aim to use these technologies to enhance the equity, efficiency, and effectiveness of public governance. However, they struggle to keep pace with the rapid advancements in AI (Kempeneer & Heylen, 2023). Generative AI, robotics, and other AI technologies are enabling AI to handle increasingly complex tasks (Madan & Ashok, 2023). Public organisations, despite their limited ability to develop and deploy AI and the generally slow adoption of AI in the public sector, aim to use these technologies to improve the equity, efficiency, and effectiveness of public governance. However, they find it challenging to keep up with the rapid advances in AI (Kempeneer & Heylen, 2023).

Outdated IT Systems and a Lack of AI-Compatible Infrastructure

Antiquated IT infrastructure and a lack of AI-ready technologies severely hinder the public sector's adoption of AI. These technical constraints may impede development and prevent businesses from fully utilising AI. Many public administration organisations struggle with integration with legacy systems due to their reliance on outdated IT systems that often clash with the latest AI innovations. These antiquated systems can be difficult, expensive, and time-consuming to integrate AI into. Androutsopoulou et al. (2018) mention the challenge of integrating AI technologies into current public sector systems.

A possible technological risk is the lack of processing power and storage capacity. AI, especially machine learning, requires significant processing power and storage space to process and analyse large datasets. It's possible that antiquated infrastructure lacks the resources needed to adequately support AI applications. (Abbas et al., 2023) highlight the necessity for suitable infrastructure while discussing the difficulties associated with processing, storing, and protecting the privacy of huge datasets in the public sector. Restricted connectivity and network bandwidth are threats. Large data transfers are a common feature of AI applications, necessitating high-bandwidth network connectivity. The performance of AI systems may suffer due to bottlenecks caused by outdated infrastructure with low bandwidth.

Online safety Weaknesses pose a danger When deploying AI solutions, outdated systems are frequently more susceptible to cybersecurity risks, creating worries about data security and privacy. Abbas et al. (2023) identify data security and privacy as a barrier to the public sector's adoption of modern IT, including AI. Lack of interoperability is another potential threat. It may be difficult to exchange data and seamlessly integrate AI applications with outdated systems that are incompatible with other systems, both inside and outside of government organisations. Campion et al., 2022, discuss the challenges of fostering interorganisational cooperation for the adoption of AI. A lack of interoperability may exacerbate these difficulties.

One obstacle is resistance to technological change. Employees used to the current processes and technology may be resistant to the changeover from outdated systems to contemporary, AI-compatible infrastructure. This opposition may hinder the adoption process. Modernising IT systems, updating hardware and software, and creating a strong network infrastructure are all necessary to address these infrastructure concerns. Setting interoperability and cybersecurity as top priorities is essential to guaranteeing the safe and effective application of AI in public administration (Caleb, 2024).

Financial Threats

There has been a growing interest in the application of artificial intelligence in the public sector. Scholars have emphasised the possible advantages of artificial intelligence (AI)-driven solutions in domains like decision-making, public service provision, and citizen-government relations, Hamirul et al. (2023). However, before we can widely use AI in public administration, we must overcome several obstacles. One such obstacle is financial (Valle-Cruz et al., 2019).

THE COST OF CREATING AI-BASED SOLUTIONS IS SIGNIFICANT

The substantial expense of creating and implementing AI-based solutions is one of the main financial obstacles to AI adoption in the public sector. (Margetts, 2022) Extracting and representing the knowledge of government experts, as well as encoding a large volume of data in a machine-readable manner, can be a complex and resource-intensive task. Furthermore, major hardware, software, and training expenditures may be required for the integration of AI systems into the existing public administration infrastructure (Misuraca & Noordt, 2020).

Human Capital Loss

The possible loss of human capital because of AI task automation presents another financial obstacle. Although AI-based solutions may increase the efficacy and efficiency of public services, governments and the public may be reluctant to accept new technologies due to concerns about job loss (Pizzinelli et al., 2023). Moreover, public organisations may incur financial costs for the management, updates, and continuing upkeep of AI systems (Mulyana, 2023).

Integration Challenges

Mismatches between machine learning components and operational settings can diminish efficacy and raise costs in the integration of AI systems (Lewis et al., 2019). The public sector owns and uses many noticeably big data collections for a variety of purposes. Based on the examination of this data, machine learning and artificial intelligence (ML/AI) components have a tremendous deal of potential to improve various public sector needs and functions. However, the fragility of ML/AI components and their algorithms significantly limits their fielding into public sector applications. When it comes to systems used by the government and public sector, some ML/AI system considerations, such as privacy, security, and ethics, are more pressing than in the commercial sector.

Resolving component mismatches and integrating all the components is one of the obstacles to implementing complex systems. These mismatches may have different causes and consequences for systems that use ML/AI components than for conventional software integration initiatives. Training the model on data not representative of the operating environment will significantly decrease the machine learning component's field performance. Expertise from outside software engineering is often required to field an ML/AI component within a system, regardless of software engineering considerations. Practitioners from many fields, even those in the public administration sector, may use descriptive language and assumptions to increase the difficulty of integrating machine learning and artificial intelligence components into larger systems (Lewis, Bellomo, & Galyardt, 2019).

Training and Hiring of Digitally Literate Employees

Employees that are not digitally literate may find it difficult to use AI technologies effectively, which could mean spending more on training (Medaglia & Tangi, 2022). The ability to oversee and carry out these projects is a crucial component of the emergence of data and AI-related technologies in the public sector. The public sector should have adequate people with up-to-date knowledge and practical abilities on how to use AI for public services while taking ethical and moral concerns into account, given the growing popularity of AI in all sectors, including the government. Developing these professionals' capacities and training them is one method to guarantee that governments can hire these people (Labanava et al., 2022).

Retaining Highly Qualified Employees

Lack of skilled labour and related expenses, such as attracting and keeping skilled AI professionals, including data scientists and AI engineers, necessitates offering competitive pay and benefits, which raises personnel costs. Androutsopoulou et al., (2019) alluded to the necessity for qualified workers while addressing the difficulty of extracting and representing expertise for AI development in the public sector.

A significant obstacle to the effective integration of technology in the public sector is the difficulty in retaining a staff with the necessary skills to deploy and manage these novel systems, Alqarni, (2020). When it comes to luring and retaining outstanding people, the public sector faces different obstacles than the private sector. Government organisations struggle to compete for the best and most experienced workers due to factors like lower compensation, a negative perception of their agency, and cumbersome hiring procedures. Decades have passed since the "human capital crisis" began, making it harder and harder for public organisations to retain a skilled and competent personnel. (Ciancarini et al., 2024; Arianni et al., 2023). Effective staff turnover planning and management is essential for the commercialisation of new technologies.

High Initial Investment Costs

Adoption of AI comes with a hefty upfront cost. AI system development or acquisition necessitates a substantial initial expenditure for hardware, software, and infrastructure. Nerima & Ralyte (2021) suggest that investment is necessary to achieve a state where AI adoption is viable, referencing government organisations' digital maturity phases. Berglind, Fadia, & Isherwood (2022) talk about the possible benefits of AI but skip over the precise expenses that governments could have to pay.

Budget Constraints and Little or No Return on Investment

Because of financial shortages and budgetary constraints, it is difficult to obtain sufficient funding for AI efforts in public sector organizations. These organisations frequently have limited resources and conflicting agendas. Yfantis et al. (2020) highlight the challenge of allocating public funding to AI efforts, especially when other industries may take precedence. Furthermore, Yfantis et al. (2020) highlight the uncertainty surrounding return on investment. This shows a distinct and quantifiable return on investment for AI research, which might be difficult to justify when requesting financing.

According to Valle-Cruz et al. (2019), return on investment assessments can be challenging because the outcomes of using AI in the public sector are frequently uncertain and unexpected. It will take careful planning, strategic prioritisation, and creative funding methods to get past these financial obstacles. Considering joint ventures with commercial businesses or applying for funding for AI projects can help reduce some of these difficulties.

Operational Costs

artificial intelligence (AI) systems necessitate constant upkeep, upgrades, and professional assistance, which results in high recurrent costs. This covers the price of processing, storing, and safeguarding data. It can be difficult and expensive to integrate AI into the current, frequently antiquated IT infrastructure, as well as legacy systems. According to Androutsopoulou et al. (2018), incorporating AI technologies into current public sector systems can be difficult. The price of gathering and preparing data, such as data collection, cleansing, and preparation for AI applications, can be a time-consuming and expensive procedure. Andrésopoulou et al. (2018) mention the difficulty of encoding expert knowledge and data into a machine-exploitable format, suggesting related expenses.

Significant financial barriers impede the use of AI in public administration. Limited funding, poor project management, and the need for specialised knowledge primarily cause these obstacles. Resolving these issues is imperative for successful implementation. Public sector organisations frequently set aside large sums of money for ICT; yet, poor financial planning and resource allocation are major causes of project failure (Schmidt,2023).Wilson (2021) has cited additional economic concerns such as strategic planning, budgeting, and the expenses associated with hiring outside consultants, which could lead to unnecessary spending.

Public administrations can address these obstacles by implementing a digital governance framework that prioritises personnel skill development and strategic AI investment (Misuraca & Viscusi, 2020). Involving the public in the creation of AI services can also increase the relevance and effectiveness of these projects (Medaglia & Tangi, 2022). Despite significant financial challenges, a strategic approach to budgeting and integration can facilitate the use of AI in public administration, thereby enhancing service delivery and governance.

Social Perspective

As governments increasingly integrate AI technologies into their operations, the implications for service delivery, governance, and social equity become paramount. AI has the potential to enhance public services by improving efficiency, reducing costs, and optimising resource allocation. For instance, AI applications in healthcare have demonstrated transformative capabilities, such as mining medical records and assisting in treatment planning, which can lead to better health outcomes and more efficient service delivery (Sun & Medaglia, 2019). Furthermore, research suggests that artificial intelligence (AI) can support automated decision-making procedures, which can streamline administrative duties and improve the general efficacy of public sector operations (Gualdi & Cordella, 2021; Henman, 2020). However, the successful implementation of AI in public administration necessitates the establishment of robust governance frameworks to ensure accountability and transparency, and the careful consideration of ethical considerations (Hinton, 2023; Wirtz, Weyerer, & Geyer, 2019). Even with the potential advantages, integrating AI into public administration is not without its difficulties, especially when it comes to ethical and public trust issues. Research indicates that citizens are often apprehensive about the extent to which AI can be trusted to make decisions that affect their lives, highlighting the necessity for transparency and community engagement in the AI adoption process (Schmager, Grøder, Parmiggiani, Pappas, & Vassilakopoulou, 2023). Moreover, issues of bias and discrimination in AI algorithms pose significant risks, potentially exacerbating existing inequalities within public services (Ulaşan, 2023). This necessitates a proactive approach to governance that prioritises ethical standards and safeguards against discriminatory practices (Chilunjika, Intauno, & Chilunjika, 2022). AI adoption in public administration also presents significant social opportunities. AI can be used to address urgent social challenges and support social good activities that are in line with the Sustainable Development Goals (SDGs) of the UN (Tomašev, Cornebise, Hutter, Mohamed, Picciariello, Connelly, Belgrave, Ezer, van der Haert, & Mugisha, 2020). For instance, AI technologies can facilitate data-driven policymaking, enabling governments to respond more effectively to societal needs and challenges (Loukis, Maragoudakis, & Kyriakou, 2020). Furthermore, involving the public in the co-development of AI systems can increase citizens' sense of trust and ownership, which will ultimately strengthen the legitimacy of AI-driven projects (Leikas, Johri, Latvanen, Wessberg, & Hahto, 2022).

Social Barriers

All spheres of society, including public administration, have applied Automated Decision-making (ADM) systems in an era characterised by rapid technological improvement. While these AI- and machine learning-powered systems have the potential to enhance procedures, boost productivity, and enhance service delivery, they also pose ethical concerns, especially when they affect citizens. Raising awareness of the problem is critical, given the rapid growth of these technologies, their widespread use in many spheres of society, and the blind spots in their implementation. While technologies like artificial intelligence (AI) and artificial decision-making (ADMs) have the potential to be extremely helpful and convenient for humans, improper use or programming at the wrong time can result in serious harm. Therefore, specific legislation must properly guide, control, and audit their introduction to ensure it aligns with the ethical values of good governance. These fields, like public governance and, more broadly, the public sectors, have a tangible and inevitable impact on people's lives (Toniolo, 2023).

Expertise

A major obstacle is the extraction and representation of the knowledge required to create a knowledge base that AI systems can use efficiently (Medaglia et al., 2021). This problem is especially severe in the public sector, according to Zuiderwijk et al. (2021), because of the intricate nature of governmental operations. Subject matter experts from various departments and agencies must meticulously collect a vast amount of data and translate their specialised knowledge into a format that AI-powered applications can easily integrate and use (Androutsopoulou et al., 2018).

Officials' Resistance to Adapting

Government officials may be resistant to the development and application of AI-based solutions in the public sector because they are concerned about the potential advantages or disruptions that these technologies may bring to current job roles and workflows (Noordt & Misuraca, 2020). According to Yfantis et al. (2020), there is reason to be concerned about the possibility of job displacement because of automation. To mitigate this anxiety, proactive workforce planning and the thoughtful application of AI to complement human labour rather than replace it are necessary.

Acceptance

Gaining public acceptance and trust is essential for the effective deployment of AI systems. Public resistance and scepticism might result from worries about algorithmic bias, accountability, transparency, and transparency. (Henman, 2020) talks about the issues of accountability and transparency in public administration as they apply to AI. Valle-Cruz et al. (2019) mention "algorithmic bias" as a potential drawback of AI in governmental decision-making. A lot of people might be wary or mistrustful of AI systems because they worry about potential biases, privacy invasions, or opaque decision-making.

Ethical Considerations

AI systems have the power to reinforce and magnify existing societal prejudices, resulting in biased outcomes. It is crucial to guarantee equity and fairness in AI applications. Valle-Cruz et al. (2019) explicitly mention algorithmic bias as a risk. Henman (2020) also underscores the challenge of prejudice and discrimination. The application of AI in delicate public domains such as healthcare and law enforcement raises moral questions about computers' autonomy and its effects on human rights.

Displacement of Workforce

There are worries regarding job displacement in the public sector due to AI's potential for automation. Mitigating this impact requires managing personnel migrations and providing opportunities for reskilling. (Yfantis et al., 2020) raises concerns about the potential loss of jobs to AI-driven automation, as well as the possibility of dehumanisation in public organisations (Valle-Cruz et al., 2019) and AI rejection (Wirtz et al., 2019).

Transparency and Accountability

Government organisations must place a high priority on accountability and consider how AI initiatives may affect national and public safety, as these factors may pose social barriers to the widespread deployment of AI. The field of public administration needs to concentrate on creating reliable AI. Policy changes are necessary to ensure accountability and responsibility of AI systems, particularly when they perform potentially fatal activities. Transparency is essential because it makes AI systems understandable and transparent, enabling people to comprehend how they work. Additionally, it is critical to be truthful and objective in decision-making to lessen implicit and explicit biases in AI systems that could support discrimination based on racial and gender stereotypes (Zuiderwijk, Chen & Salem, 2021).

Comprehending the decision-making process of AI systems is crucial for transparency and public confidence. Concerns of potential bias and transparency can arise with black box AI models. Henman (2020) highlights the significance of explainability and openness in AI systems utilised in public administration.

Public Service Delivery is Changing Nature

AI has the power to completely modify public service delivery, which could have an impact on citizen involvement and service accessibility. To ensure the quality of services and citizen satisfaction, competent management of these changes is required. A multifaceted strategy, including ongoing monitoring and evaluation of AI systems, workforce development programs, ethical rules, and public participation, is necessary to effectively address these societal issues (Kulal et al., 2024).

Bureaucratic Processes

One of the main obstacles to AI adoption in public administration is the opposition arising from long-standing bureaucratic procedures and standards. Employee path dependency, or the tendency to rely too much on established procedures and standards that may impede the adoption of cutting-edge technologies such as artificial intelligence, is a problem that public organisations frequently encounter. Information silos and a dearth of collaborative culture, which are common in bureaucratic contexts, exacerbate this resistance (Mikhaylov et al., 2018). Similarly, Bodemer (2023) addresses how additional obstacles may arise from the historical background and legal frameworks around AI in governance, especially in fields like healthcare where openness and trust are crucial.

Lack of infrastructure and resources complicates the integration of AI into public administration, necessitating a change in organisational culture (Moreno, 2023). Furthermore, public administration's bureaucratic structure frequently results in delayed decision-making procedures, which can inhibit innovation. The term "Algorithmic Bureaucracy," coined by Vogl et al. (2019), refers to the study of how AI can both simplify and complicate bureaucratic procedures. They contend that although artificial intelligence (AI) has the potential to simplify processes, it also brings with it additional complications that may make bureaucratic inefficiencies already present worse (Vogl et al., 2019). Understanding this paradox is critical to comprehending the challenges public administrations face when implementing AI technologies.

Regulatory frameworks are also crucial in determining how AI adoption plays out. Wang and Cai (2022) highlight the risks involved with embedding AI in government governance, stressing that the procedures and processes already in place may not adequately meet the specific problems offered by AI technology. Taeihagh (2021) concurs, emphasizing the need to reevaluate governance frameworks considering AI's rapid advancement to mitigate risks and ensure ethical deployment.

Uncertainty brought forth by unclear regulations may deter public administrations from undertaking AI efforts. Although artificial intelligence (AI) has great potential to improve public administration, bureaucratic procedures provide considerable obstacles to its adoption. We must carefully negotiate the interaction between deeply ingrained organisational cultures, regulatory frameworks, and the intricacies of current bureaucratic systems to enable a successful integration of AI technology. We must make a concentrated effort to promote an innovative culture, expedite the decision-making process, and create strong regulatory frameworks to overcome these obstacles and enable the public administration to adopt AI.

Cultural Barriers

Since traditional bureaucratic cultures frequently value human judgement and discretion over automated processes, they may be averse to technological breakthroughs like artificial intelligence (AI). While the public sector has hailed artificial intelligence (AI) for its potential benefits, such as increased efficiency and better service delivery, its practical implementation has faced numerous obstacles, preventing its widespread adoption (Valle-Cruz et al., 2019; Hamirul et al., 2023). The substantial organisational and cultural hurdles that exist in public institutions are one of the main challenges (Androutsopoulou et al., 2019; Yfantis et al., 2020). Public sector organisations often exhibit inflexible hierarchies, compartmentalised processes, and resistance to change. This strongly ingrained culture may seriously hinder the effective integration of AI (Valle-Cruz et al., 2019).

The possibility of AI-driven automation may cause government workers anxiety because they see it as a threat to their job security as well as a reduction in their professional status and decision-making power within the company (Valle-Cruz et al., 2019; Noordt & Misuraca, 2020). Furthermore, public officials may not have the technological literacy to fully understand the implications of AI due to the inherent opacity and complexity of AI systems, which can obscure decision-making processes and render them incomprehensible to non-technical personnel (Yfantis et al., 2020). This further exacerbates these concerns.

Apart from these cultural barriers, the public sector encounters substantial operational and technical challenges when using AI. A recurring issue in many government organisations has been the lack of access to high-quality, structured data, which is essential for the creation of reliable AI models (Valle-Cruz et al., 2019) (Androutsopoulou et al., 2018).

Summary for Social Challenges

The adoption of artificial intelligence (AI) in public administration faces a multitude of barriers, particularly social challenges that stem from ethical, regulatory, and operational concerns (Madan & Ashok, 2023). The successful integration of AI technology inside governmental frameworks may be severely hampered by these obstacles (Madan & Ashok, 2023; Mikalef, Lemmer, Schaefer, Ylinen, Fjørtoft, Torvatn, Gupta, & Niehaves, 2022). Lack of thorough knowledge and readiness among government agencies is one of the main barriers to AI implementation in public administration. Wirtz et al. highlight that many governments have not sufficiently addressed the range of uses of AI and have frequently overlooked related difficulties in their reports, despite the potential benefits of AI (Wirtz et al., 2019). This lack of preparedness is compounded by skill shortages within the public sector, as evidenced by Iuga's findings that indicate a noticeable gap in AI governance knowledge among public employees (Iuga & Socol, 2024). Such deficiencies impede public administration's ability to effectively leverage AI, resulting in a reluctance to adopt these technologies.

Furthermore, ethical considerations significantly influence the adoption of AI. Asilyan notes that the development of AI presents important legal and moral questions, especially about state coercion and the possibility of unrestricted digital discretion by authorities (Asilyan & Necrasova, 2023). Gupta expresses a similar concern, identifying data security and information ethics as the primary barriers that could hinder the use of AI in governance (Gupta, 2019). The people of the public and their trust in AI systems is also critical; Jobin and Ienca argue that while fostering trust is essential for ethical governance, there is a risk that such trust might diminish scrutiny of AI systems, potentially leading to ethical oversights (Jobin, Ienca, & Vayena, 2019). This paradox presents a significant barrier in public administration to the adoption of AI technologies. Social challenges also manifest in the form of public perception and acceptance of AI. Morkhat et al. emphasise that despite advancements in AI, there remains a significant gap in public understanding and acceptance of these technologies, which can lead to resistance against their implementation in public services (Morkhat, Ponkin, Markhgeym, Botnev, & Turganbayev, 2019). Zhang and Dafoe (2020) found that public trust in institutions significantly influences attitudes toward AI governance, supporting this sentiment. The challenge of building this trust is further complicated by concerns over bias and exclusion, as highlighted by Misra et al., who stress the need for clear regulatory frameworks to mitigate adverse impacts associated with AI technologies (Misra,

Das, Gupta, & Sharma, 2020). Finally, we cannot overlook the operational challenges of integrating AI into public administration. Madan and Ashok's systematic review indicates that there is a scarcity of research on the practical implementation of AI within governments, which complicates the understanding of how to create public value through AI applications (Madan & Ashok, 2023). Additionally, the procurement processes for AI technologies can be fraught with difficulties, as identified by Mcbride et al., who discuss the unique challenges faced during the public procurement of AI solutions (McBride, van Noordt, Misuraca, & Hammerschmid, 2021). These operational hurdles can slow down the adoption process and create further barriers to effective AI integration.

The barriers to AI adoption in public administration are multifaceted, encompassing a range of social challenges that include ethical concerns, public perception, skill shortages, and operational difficulties. Addressing these barriers requires a concerted effort from policymakers to develop comprehensive strategies that foster trust, enhance skills, and create robust regulatory frameworks.

AI Adoption Case Studies and Potential Barriers in Public Administration

The public administration (PA) in Italy struggled with inefficiencies and tardiness. In 2021, as part of an ambitious recovery strategy, the Italian government invested a staggering 200 billion euros to digitize PA to revitalize the nation. In a web poll that was completed by 3,000 residents in the country between the ages of 18 and 64 in March and April of 2022. More than 75% of respondents, according to the data displayed, utilised a public service online at least once. However, very few people were aware of the reform plan, and over one-third of respondents thought that the digitisation of public services would worsen the situation for the populace. The study employs regression analysis to confirm that education significantly influences the use of digital public services, surpassing the influence of other spatial and social variables. Furthermore, the study revealed a stronger trust in PA among digital public service users, which was associated with both education and work position. Thus, the poll emphasises how important it is to use education and culture as a tool to close the digital divide and advance the rights of digital citizens. It became evident that the implementation of facilitation and accompaniment procedures was necessary to avoid penalizing or excluding individuals with less digital expertise and experience under the new system, and to curb their growing mistrust of public administration and state (Mesa, 2023).

According to the perceived usefulness of a public service such as a chatbot, Williems et al. (2022) investigated the behaviour of Austrian residents regarding the privacy dilemma associated with providing their personal data and their privacy worries. The results show that although privacy concerns reduce the willingness to use AI applications, perceived value is the main factor driving their utilization. Interestingly, the trade-off between perceived utility and privacy concerns is independent of the amount of personal information necessary. These worrying findings about the discrepancy between perceptions and behaviour force public actors to think of strategies for safeguarding the public.

Another case study explores the impact of AI on organisations, highlighting the challenges associated with its implementation through a comparison of two AI applications that resulted in scandals. The Toeslagen agency's childcare allowance system in the Netherlands and the Michigan State Employment Agency's Michigan Integrated Data Automated System were the sites of these scandals. In both cases, years of persistently making the same grave mistakes resulted in significant losses and sparked public and political controversy. Even worse, many suffered terrible consequences, with some even witnessing their lives being destroyed. Organizationally, the Michigan agency's complete automation of its fraud screening procedure resulted in the layoff of one-third of its personnel (Giest and Klievink, 2024).

CONCLUSION

To address these challenges, there is a need to devise comprehensive strategies for the public administration sector. Some of these strategies entail training, adaptation by the public administration community, and adequate budget allocation for AI projects. We need to raise awareness about the advantages of adopting AI technology. Stakeholder meetings that will build trust may be introduced in the public administration sector with possible examples of institutions where the best practice of AI adoption was implemented. With careful planning, AI adoption may best be implemented, and the AI project may be piloted according to departments rather than a project for the whole organisation.

Reaching the potential of AI in public administration requires overcoming these data obstacles. Data governance frameworks with explicit norms and processes for data management, access, and sharing are just one of many strategies for improvement. Initiatives for data integration and interoperability are required to dismantle data silos and encourage agency-to-agency data sharing. Additionally, investing in data infrastructure and expertise helps to establish strong data science capabilities and data management systems. The implementation of procedures for data cleaning, validation, and standardisation will be aided by certain data quality assurance programs. The effective deployment of AI can be facilitated by public sector organisations placing a high priority on the availability and quality of data.

REFERENCES

Abbas, S. W., Hamid, M., Alkanhel, R., & Abdallah, H. A. (2023). Official Statistics and Big Data Processing with Artificial Intelligence: Capacity Indicators for Public Sector Organizations. *Systems*, 11(8), 424. DOI: 10.3390/systems11080424

Afzal, A., Khan, S., Daud, S., Ahmad, Z., & Butt, A. (2023). Addressing the Digital

Aiello, G., & Pavesi, G. (2022). Artificial intelligence in public administration: A systematic review. *Government Information Quarterly*, 40, e102751.

Alhosani, K., & Alhashmi, S. M. (2024). Opportunities, challenges, and benefits of AI innovation in government services: A review. *Discover Artificial Intelligence*, 4(1), 18. DOI: 10.1007/s44163-024-00111-w

Androutsopoulou, A., Karacapilidis, N., Loukis, E., & Charalabidis, Y. (2019). Transforming the communication between citizens and government through AI-guided chatbots. *Government Information Quarterly*, 36(2), 358–367. DOI: 10.1016/j.giq.2018.10.001

Ariyani, N., Wibowo, I., & Guswandi, G. (2023). The Influence of Leadership Style and Organizational Culture on the Performance of Functional Employees Through Motivation Within the General Secretariat Regional Representative Council of the Republic of Indonesia. *Journal of Social Research*, 2(7), 2491–2506. DOI: 10.55324/josr.v2i7.1218

Asilyan, L., & Necrasova, I. (2023). The essence of state coercion is in the mechanism of legal regulation. SHS Web of Conferences, Berglind, N., Fadia, A., & Isherwood, T. (2022). The potential value of AI—and how governments could look to capture it. *McKinsey. URL:*https://www.mckinsey.com/industries/public-and-social-sector/our-insights/the-potential-value-of-AI*, and. how governments could look to capture it.*

Bodemer, O. (2023). Artificial Intelligence in Governance: A Comprehensive Analysis of AI Integration and Policy Development in the German Government. *Authorea Preprints.*

Campion, A., Gasco-Hernandez, M., Jankin Mikhaylov, S., & Esteve, M. (2022). Overcoming the challenges of collaboratively adopting artificial intelligence in the public sector. *Social Science Computer Review*, 40(2), 462–477. DOI: 10.1177/0894439320979953

Campion, A., Gasco-Hernandez, M., Jankin Mikhaylov, S., & Esteve, M. (2022). Overcoming the challenges of collaboratively adopting artificial intelligence in the public sector. *Social Science Computer Review*, 40(2), 462–477. DOI: 10.1177/0894439320979953

Chilunjika, A., Intauno, K., & Chilunjika, S. R. (2022). Artificial intelligence and public sector human resource management in South Africa: Opportunities, challenges, and prospects. *SA Journal of Human Resource Management*, 20, 12. DOI: 10.4102/sajhrm.v20i0.1972

Ciancarini, P., Giancarlo, R., & Grimaudo, G. (2024). Digital transformation in the public administrations: A guided tour for computer scientists. *IEEE Access : Practical Innovations, Open Solutions*, 12, 22841–22865. DOI: 10.1109/ACCESS.2024.3363075

Dearing, J. W., & Cox, J. G. (2018). Diffusion of innovations theory, principles, and practice. *Health Affairs*, 37(2), 183–190. DOI: 10.1377/hlthaff.2017.1104 PMID: 29401011

Divide: Access and Use of Technology in Education. Journal of Social Sciences Review, 3(2), 883-895.DOI: 10.54183/jssr.v3i2.326

Elsyra, N. (2023). The Role of Artificial Intelligence in Government Services: A Systematic Literature Review. *Open Access Indonesia Journal of Social Sciences*, 6(3), 998–1003. DOI: 10.37275/oaijss.v6i3.163

Erkkila, T. (2020). Transparency in public administration. In *Oxford research encyclopaedia of politics*. DOI: 10.1093/acrefore/9780190228637.013.1404

Giest, S. N., & Klievink, B. (2024). More than a digital system: How AI is changing the role of bureaucrats in different organisational contexts. *Public Management Review*, 26(2), 379–398. DOI: 10.1080/14719037.2022.2095001

Gualdi, F., & Cordella, A. (2021). Artificial intelligence and decision-making: The question of accountability.

Gupta, K. (2019). Artificial intelligence for governance in India: Prioritising the challenges using the analytic hierarchy process (AHP). *Int. J. Recent Technol. Eng*, 8(2), 3756–3762. DOI: 10.35940/ijrte.B3392.078219

Hamirul, D., & Elsyra, N. (2023). The Role of Artificial Intelligence in Government Services: A Systematic Literature Review. *Open Access Indonesia Journal of Social Sciences*, 6(3), 998–1003. DOI: 10.37275/oaijss.v6i3.163

Henman, P. (2020). Improving public services using artificial intelligence: Possibilities, pitfalls, governance. *Asia Pacific Journal of Public Administration*, 42(4), 209–221. DOI: 10.1080/23276665.2020.1816188

Henman, P. (2020). Improving public services using artificial intelligence: Possibilities, pitfalls, governance. *Asia Pacific Journal of Public Administration*, 42(4), 209–221. DOI: 10.1080/23276665.2020.1816188

Hinton, C. (2023). The State of Ethical AI in Practice: A Multiple Case Study of Estonian Public Service Organizations. [IJT]. *International Journal of Technoethics*, 14(1), 1–15. DOI: 10.4018/IJT.322017

Ingram, G. (2021). Bridging the global digital divide: A platform to advance digital development in low- and middle-income countries. http://hdl.handle.net/11540/13773

Iuga, I. C., & Socol, A. (2024). Government artificial intelligence readiness and brain drain influencing factors and spatial effects in the European Union member states. *Journal of Business Economics and Management, 25*(2), 268–296-268–296.

Jobin, A., Ienca, M., & Vayena, E. (2019). The global landscape of AI ethics guidelines. *Nature Machine Intelligence*, 1(9), 389–399. DOI: 10.1038/s42256-019-0088-2

Kaplan, A., & Haenlein, M. (2019). Siri, Siri, in my hand: Who's the fairest in the land? On the interpretations, illustrations, and implications of artificial intelligence. *Business Horizons*, 62(1), 15–25. DOI: 10.1016/j.bushor.2018.08.004

Kulal, A., Rahiman, H. U., Suvarna, H., Abhishek, N., & Dinesh, S. (2024). Enhancing public service delivery efficiency: Exploring the impact of AI. *Journal of Open Innovation*, 10(3), 100329. DOI: 10.1016/j.joitmc.2024.100329

Labanava, A., Dreyling, R. M., III, Mortati, M., Liiv, I., & Pappel, I. (2022, November). Capacity Building in Government: Towards Developing a Standard for a Functional Specialist in AI for Public Services. In *International Conference on Future Data and Security Engineering* (pp. 503-516). Singapore: Springer Nature Singapore. DOI: 10.1007/978-981-19-8069-5_34

Leikas, J., Johri, A., Latvanen, M., Wessberg, N., & Hahto, A. (2022). Governing ethical AI transformation: A case study of AuroraAI. *Frontiers in Artificial Intelligence*, 5, 836557. DOI: 10.3389/frai.2022.836557 PMID: 35224480

Lewallen, J. (2023). Expertise for emerging technology: Information, prestige, and the Office of Technology Assessment. *The Review of Policy Research*.

Lewis, G. A., Bellomo, S., & Galyardt, A. (2019). Component mismatches are a critical bottleneck to fielding AI-enabled systems in the public sector. *arXiv preprint arXiv:1910.06136*.

Loukis, E. N., Maragoudakis, M., & Kyriakou, N. (2020). Artificial intelligence-based public sector data analytics for economic crisis policymaking. *Transforming Government*, 14(4), 639–662. DOI: 10.1108/TG-11-2019-0113

Madan, R., & Ashok, M. (2023). AI adoption and diffusion in public administration: A systematic literature review and future research agenda. *Government Information Quarterly*, 40(1), 101774. DOI: 10.1016/j.giq.2022.101774

Margetts, H. (2022). Rethinking AI for good governance. *Daedalus*, 151(2), 360–371. DOI: 10.1162/daed_a_01922

Margetts, H., & Dorobantu, C. (2019). Rethink government with AI. *Nature*, 568(7751), 163–165. DOI: 10.1038/d41586-019-01099-5 PMID: 30967667

McBride, K., van Noordt, C., Misuraca, G., & Hammerschmid, G. (2021). Toward a systematic understanding of the challenges of procuring artificial intelligence in the public sector.

Medaglia, R., & Tangi, L. (2022, October). The adoption of artificial intelligence in the public sector in Europe: drivers, features, and impacts. In *Proceedings of the 15th International Conference on Theory and Practice of Electronic Governance*, 10-18. DOI: 10.1145/3560107.3560110

Mesa, D. (2023). Digital divide, e-government, and trust in public service: The key role of education. *Frontiers in Sociology*, 8, 1140416. DOI: 10.3389/fsoc.2023.1140416 PMID: 36895333

Mikalef, P., & Gupta, M. (2021). Artificial intelligence capability: Conceptualisation, measurement calibration, and empirical study on its impact on organisational creativity and firm performance. *Information & Management*, 58(3), 103434. DOI: 10.1016/j.im.2021.103434

Mikalef, P., Lemmer, K., Schaefer, C., Ylinen, M., Fjørtoft, S. O., Torvatn, H. Y., Gupta, M., & Niehaves, B. (2022). Enabling AI capabilities in government agencies: A study of determinants for European municipalities. *Government Information Quarterly*, 39(4), 101596. DOI: 10.1016/j.giq.2021.101596

Misra, S. K., Das, S., Gupta, S., & Sharma, S. K. (2020). Public policy and regulatory challenges of artificial intelligence (AI). Re-imagining Diffusion and Adoption of Information Technology and Systems: A Continuing Conversation: IFIP WG 8.6 International Conference on Transfer and Diffusion of IT, TDIT 2020, Tiruchirappalli, India, December 18–19, 2020, Proceedings, Part I, Inuwa-Dutse, I., Toniolo, A., Weller, A., & Bhatt, U. (2023). Algorithmic loafing and mitigation strategies in Human-AI teams. Computers in Human Behavior: Artificial Humans, 1(2), 100024.

Misuraca, G., & Van Noordt, C. (2020). AI Watch—Artificial Intelligence in Public Services: Overview of the Use and Impact of AI in Public Services in the EU. JRC Research Reports (JRC120399).

Misuraca, G., van Noordt, C., & Boukli, A. (2020, September). The use of AI in public services results from a preliminary mapping across the EU. In *Proceedings of the 13th international conference on theory and practice of electronic governance* (pp. 90-99). DOI: 10.1145/3428502.3428513

Misuraca, G., & Viscusi, G. (2020, August). AI-enabled innovation in the public sector: A framework for digital governance and resilience. In *International Conference on Electronic Government* (pp. 110-120). Cham: Springer International Publishing. DOI: 10.1007/978-3-030-57599-1_9

Moreno, F. (2023). Ai readiness of Philippine public administration: a review of literature. DOI: 10.31219/osf.io/kpzt6

Morkhat, P. M., Ponkin, I. V., Markhgeym, M. V., Botnev, V. K., & Turganbayev, A. O. (2019). Artificial intelligence versus public administration: limitations of application.

Nerima, M., & Ralyte, J. (2021). Towards a digital maturity balance model for public organizations. In *International Conference on Research Challenges in Information Science* (pp. 295-310). Cham: Springer International Publishing. DOI: 10.1007/978-3-030-75018-3_20

Neumann, O., Guirguis, K., & Steiner, R. (2022). Exploring artificial intelligence adoption in public organisations: A comparative case study. *Public Management Review*, 26(1), 114–141. DOI: 10.1080/14719037.2022.2048685

Newman, J., Mintrom, M., & O'Neill, D. (2022). Digital technologies, artificial intelligence, and bureaucratic transformation. *Futures*, 136, 102886. DOI: 10.1016/j.futures.2021.102886

Pizzinelli, C., Panton, A. J., Tavares, M. M. M., Cazzaniga, M., & Li, L. (2023). *Labour market exposure to AI: cross-country differences and distributional implications*. International Monetary Fund.

Schmager, S., Grøder, C. H., Parmiggiani, E., Pappas, I., & Vassilakopoulou, P. (2023). What do citizens think of AI adoption in public services? Exploratory research on citizen attitudes through a social contract lens.

Schmidt, J. (2023). Mitigating risk of failure in information technology projects causes and mechanisms. *Project Leadership and Society*, 4, 100097. DOI: 10.1016/j.plas.2023.100097

Shafritz, J. M., Russell, E. W., Borick, C. P., & Hyde, A. C. (2022). *Introducing Public Administration* (10th ed.). Routledge. DOI: 10.4324/9781003191322

Sun, T. Q., & Medaglia, R. (2019). Mapping the challenges of artificial intelligence in the public sector: Evidence from public healthcare. *Government Information Quarterly*, 36(2), 368–383. DOI: 10.1016/j.giq.2018.09.008

Taeihagh, A. (2021). Governance of artificial intelligence. *Policy and Society*, 40(2), 137–157. DOI: 10.1080/14494035.2021.1928377

Tangi, L., van Noordt, C., & Rodriguez Müller, A. P. (2023, July). The challenges of AI implementation in the public sector. An in-depth case studies analysis. In Proceedings of the 24th annual international conference on digital government research (pp. 414-422). DOI: 10.1145/3598469.3598516

Tomašev, N., Cornebise, J., Hutter, F., Mohamed, S., Picciariello, A., Connelly, B., Belgrave, D., Ezer, D., van der Haert, F., & Mugisha, F. (2020). AI for social good: Unlocking the opportunity for positive impact. [In.]. *Nature Communications*, 11(1), 2468. DOI: 10.1038/s41467-020-15871-z PMID: 32424119

Toniolo, F. (2023). Artificial Intelligence and Public Administration: Ethical Implications of the Use of Automatic Decision-making Systems. https://hdl.handle.net/20.500.12880/8079

Ulaşan, F. (2023). The Dark Side of Artificial Intelligence on the basis of public administration. *Toplum Ekonomi ve Yönetim Dergisi, 4*(Özel), 301-323.

Ulnicane, I., Knight, W., Leach, T., Stahl, B. C., & Wanjiku, W. G. (2021). Framing governance for a contested emerging technology: Insights from AI policy. *Policy and Society*, 40(2), 158–177. DOI: 10.1080/14494035.2020.1855800

Valle-Cruz, D., Alejandro Ruvalcaba-Gomez, E., Sandoval-Almazan, R., & Ignacio Criado, J. (2019, June). A review of artificial intelligence in government and its potential from a public policy perspective. In *Proceedings of the 20th annual international conference on digital government research* (pp. 91-99). DOI: 10.1145/3325112.3325242

van Noordt, C., & Misuraca, G. (2022). Exploratory Insights on Artificial Intelligence for Government in Europe. *Social Science Computer Review*, 40(2), 426–444. DOI: 10.1177/0894439320980449

van Noordt, C., Misuraca, G., & Mergel, I. (2024). Analysis of driving public values of AI initiatives in government in Europe. In *Research Handbook on Public Management and Artificial Intelligence* (pp. 226–244). Edward Elgar Publishing. DOI: 10.4337/9781802207347.00024

Vasina, A., Monastyrskyi, G., Ivanova, V., Maistrenko, K., & Tsal-Tsalko, Y. (2023). Concepts of sustainable public administration: Perspectives and challenges. *Amazonia Investiga*, 12(71), 252–262. DOI: 10.34069/AI/2023.71.11.22

Vogl, T., Seidelin, C., Ganesh, B., & Bright, J. (2019, June). Algorithmic bureaucracy. In *Proceedings of the 20th Annual International Conference on Digital Government Research*, 148-153. DOI: 10.1145/3325112.3325240

Wang, W., & Cai, Y. (2022, December). The Risk of Artificial Intelligence Embedded in Government Governance: Mechanism, Process, Prevention, and Control. In 2022, 2nd International Conference on Public Management and Intelligent Society (PMIS 2022) (pp. 609-616). Atlantis Press.

Willems, J., Schmid, M. J., Vanderelst, D., Vogel, D., & Ebinger, F. (2023). AI-driven public services and the privacy paradox: Do citizens really care about their privacy? *Public Management Review*, 25(11), 2116–2134. DOI: 10.1080/14719037.2022.2063934

Wilson, T. (2021). Analysing the Budget and Strategic Plan Relationship: A Case Study Approach." Dissertation, Georgia State University, 2021. DOI: 10.57709/22629159

Wirtz, B. W., Langer, P. F., & Fenner, C. (2021). Artificial intelligence in the public sector—A research agenda. *International Journal of Public Administration*, 44(13), 1103–1128. DOI: 10.1080/01900692.2021.1947319

Wirtz, B. W., Weyerer, J. C., & Geyer, C. (2019). Artificial intelligence and the public sector—Applications and challenges. *International Journal of Public Administration*, 42(7), 596–615. DOI: 10.1080/01900692.2018.1498103

Wirtz, B. W., Weyerer, J. C., & Sturm, B. J. (2020). The Dark Sides of Artificial Intelligence: An Integrated AI Governance Framework for Public Administration. *International Journal of Public Administration*, 43(9), 818–829. DOI: 10.1080/01900692.2020.1749851

Yolvi, O. F., Alex, V. F. L., Angel, V. F. M., & Alberto, R. L. R. (2022). Artificial intelligence (AI) applied to public management. *Metaverse*, 3(2), 8. DOI: 10.54517/m.v3i2.1795

Zhang, B., & Dafoe, A. (2020, February). US public opinion on the governance of artificial intelligence. In *Proceedings of the AAAI/ACM Conference on AI, Ethics, and Society* (pp. 187-193). DOI: 10.1145/3375627.3375827

Zuiderwijk, A., Chen, Y. C., & Salem, F. (2021). Implications of the use of artificial intelligence in public governance: A systematic literature review and a research agenda. *Government Information Quarterly*, 38(3), 101577. DOI: 10.1016/j.giq.2021.101577

KEY TERMS AND DEFINITION

Artificial Intelligence: Artificial intelligence is the operation of a digital system that mimics human behaviour. By making tasks simpler, artificial intelligence (AI) is intended to increase productivity and effectiveness.

Public Administration: This is a government body which services the needs of the community it serves and these services must be offered in line with the government prescripts.

Potential Barriers: These are anticipated threats or challenges which may hinder processes or functions from occurring.

AI Driven Tools: These are applications utilised when adopting and utilising Artificial Intelligence.

Technological Barriers: These are challenges oriented to the use of Information Communication Technology and related infrastructure.

Financial Barriers: These are challenges which emanate from the limited or non-availability of funding.

Sustainability: It is a balance of the Socio-Economic factors which support functioning and processes with a minimal use of resources.

Chapter 5
AI in Public Services:
Analysing AI-Driven Tools in Healthcare, Education,Transportation, and Safety

Saroja V. B. N. H. Achanta
https://orcid.org/0000-0002-3043-0517
Zorvy Digital Private Limited, India

ABSTRACT

Artificial Intelligence (AI) is transforming public services across sectors. In healthcare, AI-driven tools enhance diagnostics, predictive analytics, and personalized treatments. Machine learning algorithms predict disease outbreaks and optimize patient care. Education benefits from AI through adaptive learning platforms, which tailor content to individual students, boosting engagement and academic performance. In transportation, AI streamlines traffic management optimizes routes, and enables autonomous vehicles, reducing congestion and accidents. Public safety uses AI in crime prevention, surveillance, and emergency response systems, improving response times and accuracy in detecting threats. While AI enhances efficiency and innovation, ethical concerns arise, such as data privacy, algorithmic bias, and accessibility. Ensuring equitable access and transparency in AI implementation is vital to its sustainable integration into public services.

DOI: 10.4018/979-8-3693-8372-8.ch005

1. INTRODUCTION

Artificial Intelligence (AI) has emerged as a transformative force across numerous sectors, and its impact on public services is particularly profound. Public services, including healthcare, education, transportation, and public safety, are integral to societal well-being and economic stability. As these services face increasing demands and complexities, AI technologies offer innovative solutions that promise to enhance their efficiency, accuracy, and accessibility. This introduction explores the significance of AI in public services and sets the stage for a deeper examination of its applications across these critical areas.

AI encompasses a range of technologies, including machine learning, natural language processing, and robotics, which can analyze vast amounts of data, recognize patterns, and make predictions. These capabilities are highly valuable in public services, where decision-making often relies on the analysis of complex and voluminous data. By leveraging AI, public services can achieve more precise and informed decisions, streamline operations, and ultimately provide better services to citizens.

In healthcare, for instance, AI is revolutionizing diagnostic practices and patient care. Advanced algorithms can analyze medical images with high accuracy, assisting radiologists in detecting conditions such as cancers or fractures at earlier stages. AI-driven tools also enable personalized treatment plans by analyzing patient data and predicting responses to various therapies, thus enhancing treatment efficacy and patient outcomes. The integration of AI in healthcare promises not only improved diagnostic precision but also greater accessibility to medical expertise, especially in underserved areas (Bajwa et al., 2021) .

Education is another domain experiencing significant transformation through AI. Traditional educational models often struggle to address the diverse needs of individual learners. AI-powered educational tools, such as adaptive learning platforms and intelligent tutoring systems, offer personalized learning experiences by tailoring content and feedback to each student's unique needs. This personalized approach helps bridge learning gaps, supports differentiated instruction, and makes educational resources more accessible to a broader audience.

In the realm of transportation, AI is optimizing systems to enhance efficiency and safety. Traffic management systems powered by AI can predict and mitigate congestion, improving the flow of vehicles and reducing travel times. Autonomous vehicles, a growing field within transportation, promise to revolutionize personal and public transport by reducing accidents and improving mobility. Predictive maintenance powered by AI also ensures that transportation infrastructure and vehicles are serviced proactively, minimizing disruptions and enhancing reliability (Ahangar et al., 2021) .

Public safety is another critical area where AI is making substantial contributions. AI-driven tools are improving crime prediction and prevention by analyzing data to identify patterns and potential threats. Surveillance systems equipped with AI capabilities enhance monitoring and response times, while emergency management systems leverage real-time data to optimize resource allocation and crisis management. These advancements contribute to safer communities and more effective public safety responses.

Despite these promising advancements, the integration of AI in public services is not without challenges. Issues such as data privacy, algorithmic bias, and the need for transparent decision-making processes must be addressed to ensure that AI technologies are deployed responsibly and ethically. As we delve deeper into the applications of AI across healthcare, education, transportation, and public safety, it is crucial to understand both the transformative potential and the complexities associated with these technologies.

In summary, AI holds the potential to significantly enhance the quality and efficiency of public services. The subsequent sections will provide a comprehensive analysis of AI applications in these sectors, exploring their benefits, challenges, and future prospects. By examining these aspects, this chapter aims to offer valuable insights into how AI can be harnessed to improve public services and contribute to a better quality of life for citizens.

2. AI IN HEALTHCARE

Artificial Intelligence (AI) has emerged as a transformative force in healthcare, fundamentally reshaping how medical conditions are diagnosed, treated, and managed. This section explores various dimensions of AI's impact on healthcare, focusing on diagnostic accuracy and efficiency, personalized treatment plans, remote patient monitoring and telehealth, and administrative efficiency. Each subsection highlights how AI algorithms, particularly those leveraging machine learning (ML), contribute to improving patient outcomes and operational efficiency in healthcare settings (Huang et al., 2022).

2.1 Diagnostic Accuracy and Efficiency

AI's application in medical diagnostics, particularly through ML algorithms, is revolutionizing the accuracy and efficiency of disease detection. Machine learning models, particularly deep learning, are adept at analyzing large volumes of medical imaging data, uncovering patterns and correlations that might be missed by human practitioners.

Cancer Detection

One of the most impactful areas of AI in diagnostics is cancer detection. AI-powered imaging tools, such as those developed for mammography and radiology, utilize deep learning algorithms to analyze images for signs of cancer. For example, Google's DeepMind has developed an AI system that analyzes retinal scans for diabetic retinopathy and age-related macular degeneration with remarkable accuracy. In mammography, AI systems like those from PathAI and Zebra Medical Vision have demonstrated the ability to detect breast cancer at an early stage, often with higher accuracy than radiologists. These systems are trained on vast datasets of annotated mammograms, learning to recognize subtle features and anomalies indicative of cancer.

Figure 1. AI detection in cancer detection

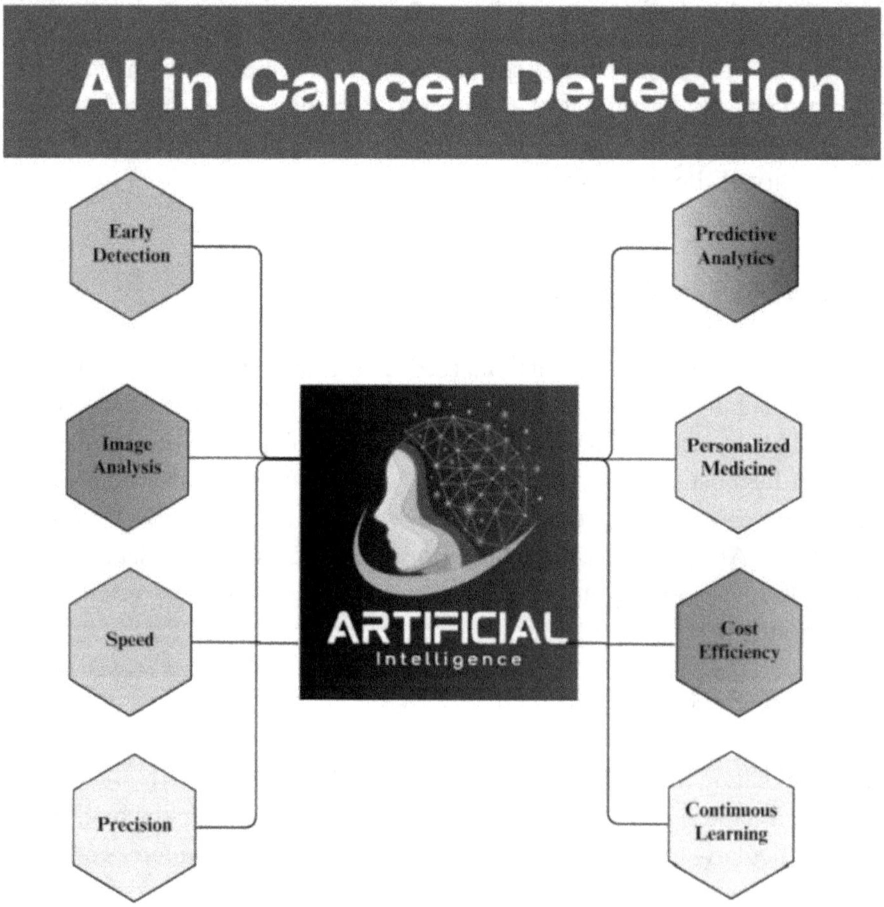

AI algorithms enhance diagnostic efficiency by automating the analysis of medical images. For instance, in the context of chest X-rays, AI tools like those developed by Aidoc analyze images to detect conditions such as pneumothorax and pulmonary embolism. These tools provide real-time alerts to radiologists, helping prioritize cases and reduce diagnostic delays. The efficiency gains are significant, as AI can process and analyze thousands of images quickly, allowing healthcare providers to focus on complex cases and clinical decision-making *(John, 2022)*.

Cardiovascular Conditions

AI's role extends to cardiovascular diagnostics, where it helps detect and manage heart diseases. Algorithms that analyze echocardiograms and electrocardiograms (ECGs) can identify abnormalities like arrhythmias, valve disorders, and cardiomyopathies with high precision.

AI tools are also used in analyzing cardiac MRI scans, where they can detect early signs of conditions such as hypertrophic cardiomyopathy and ischemic heart disease. By providing detailed and accurate assessments of cardiac structure and function, AI aids in early diagnosis and personalized treatment planning.

Neurological Disorders

In neurology, AI algorithms analyze brain imaging data to detect early signs of neurological disorders like Alzheimer's disease and multiple sclerosis. For example, AI models trained on MRI scans can detect subtle changes in brain structure that are indicative of Alzheimer's disease, often before clinical symptoms become apparent. These models can identify patterns associated with neurodegenerative diseases, enabling earlier intervention and potentially slowing disease progression.

2.2 Personalized Treatment Plans

AI's ability to analyze and integrate diverse data sources—such as a patient's medical history, genetic profile, and lifestyle factors—enables the development of personalized treatment plans. This tailored approach enhances treatment efficacy and minimizes the risk of adverse reactions.

Genomic Data and Precision Medicine

One of the most significant advancements in personalized medicine is the integration of genomic data with AI algorithms. By analyzing a patient's genetic information, AI can identify genetic mutations and variations that influence disease susceptibility and treatment responses. For instance, AI models can analyze genomic data to predict how a patient will respond to specific drugs, allowing clinicians to select treatments that are most likely to be effective (Stypińska & Franke, 2023).

Companies like Tempus and Foundation Medicine use AI to analyze genomic and clinical data, providing insights into personalized treatment options for cancer patients. These AI-driven platforms help patients with targeted therapies improving treatment.

Integrating Patient Data

AI systems integrate various data sources, including electronic health records (EHRs), lab results, and patient-reported outcomes, to create comprehensive profiles of patients. These profiles enable AI algorithms to recommend personalized treatment plans based on a patient's unique medical history and current health status. Personalized treatment plans also extend to chronic disease management. AI algorithms analyze data from wearable devices, such as glucose monitors for diabetes management, to provide real-time recommendations for insulin dosing and lifestyle adjustments. By continuously monitoring patient data and adjusting treatment plans accordingly, AI enhances disease management and improves patient outcomes (Bera et al., 2019) .

2.3 Remote Patient Monitoring and Telehealth

AI is significantly advancing remote patient monitoring and telehealth, making healthcare more accessible and efficient. Wearable devices equipped with AI algorithms provide continuous monitoring of vital signs, while AI-driven telehealth platforms enable remote consultations.

Wearable Devices

Wearable devices, such as smartwatches and fitness trackers, equipped with AI algorithms can continuously monitor vital signs like heart rate, blood pressure, and blood glucose levels. For example, devices like the Apple Watch and Fitbit utilize AI to detect irregular heart rhythms and alert users to potential health issues. These wearables can analyze data in real time, identifying anomalies and providing actionable insights to both patients and healthcare providers (Wang & Preininger, 2019) .

Telehealth Platforms

AI-driven telehealth platforms facilitate remote consultations, making healthcare more accessible to individuals in rural and underserved areas. These platforms use AI to analyze patient data, provide initial diagnoses, and recommend treatment options.

The integration of AI in telehealth has proven particularly valuable during the COVID-19 pandemic, where remote consultations have become a crucial component of healthcare delivery. AI-powered telehealth platforms have enabled healthcare providers to continue delivering care while minimizing the risk of virus transmission.

2.4 Administrative Efficiency

AI's impact extends beyond clinical care to administrative functions within healthcare organizations. By automating routine tasks and streamlining workflows, AI enhances administrative efficiency and reduces the burden on healthcare providers.

Scheduling and Appointment Management

AI algorithms can optimize scheduling and appointment management by analyzing patient data, clinician availability, and historical appointment trends. For example, AI-powered scheduling systems can predict patient no-shows and cancellations, allowing for more efficient use of appointment slots.

Figure 2. AI in personalized treatment plans

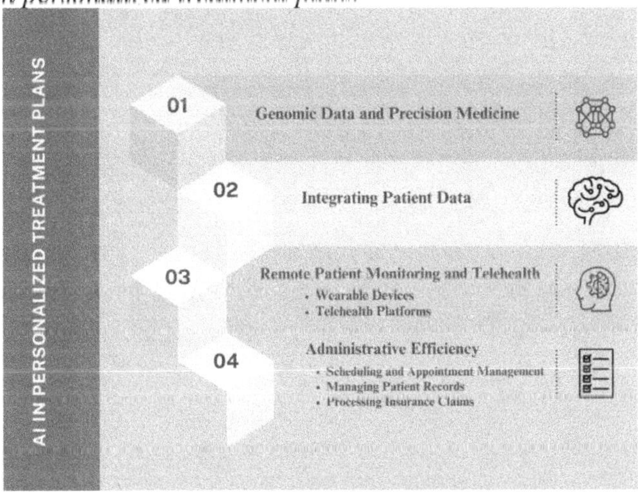

Managing Patient Records

Natural language processing (NLP) algorithms play a crucial role in managing patient records. NLP can extract relevant information from unstructured data, such as clinical notes and medical reports, and convert it into structured formats that are easily searchable and analyzable. This capability improves the accessibility of patient information, enabling healthcare providers to make more informed decisions and enhancing overall patient care.

Processing Insurance Claims

AI also streamlines the processing of insurance claims by automating the review and approval process. Machine learning models can analyze claim submissions, detect inconsistencies or errors, and flag claims for further review.

3. AI IN EDUCATION

Artificial Intelligence (AI) is significantly transforming the educational landscape by offering innovative solutions that enhance learning experiences, automate administrative tasks, and improve accessibility. This section explores how AI is reshaping education through personalized learning experiences, intelligent tutoring systems, administrative automation, and enhanced accessibility for students with disabilities (Hwang & Chen, 2023).

Figure 3. AI in education

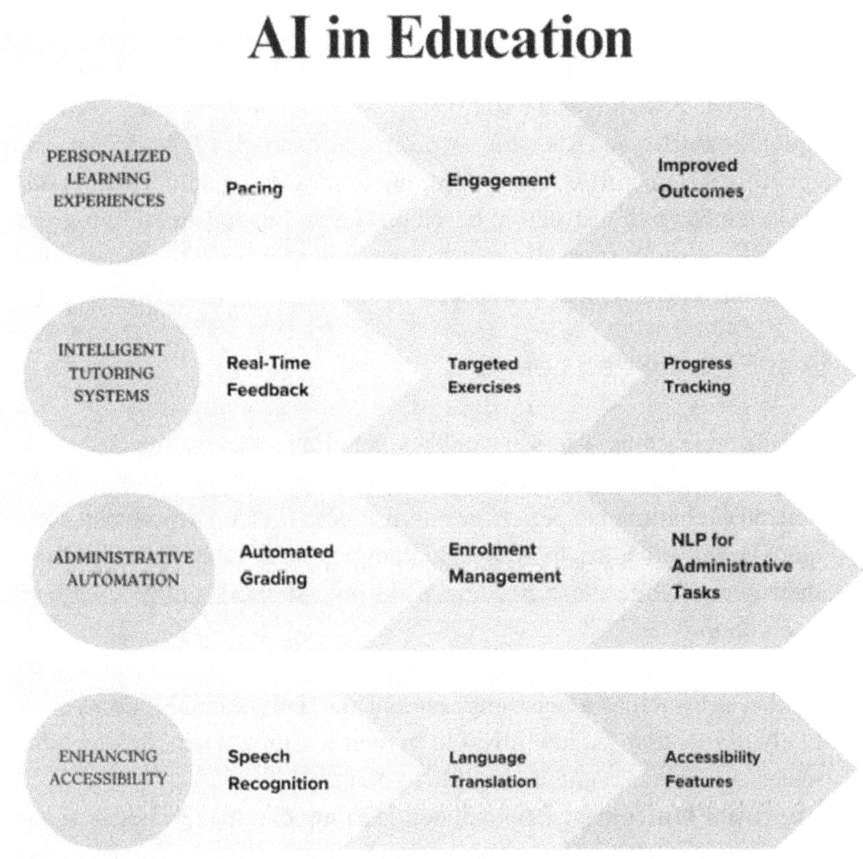

3.1 Personalized Learning Experiences

Personalized learning experiences are one of the most compelling applications of AI in education. Traditional educational models often follow a one-size-fits-all approach, which may not address the diverse needs and learning styles of individual students. AI-driven adaptive learning systems are changing this paradigm by tailoring educational content to the unique needs of each student.

Adaptive Learning Systems

Adaptive learning systems use AI algorithms to analyze data on student performance, behaviour, and learning preferences. By continuously monitoring these variables, AI systems can adjust the curriculum in real-time to meet the specific needs of each student (Srinivasan, 2022).

Example: DreamBox and Knewton are prominent examples of AI-driven adaptive learning platforms. DreamBox uses a combination of data analytics and adaptive algorithms to adjust math instruction based on student responses and progress. As students work through lessons, the system adapts in real-time, offering additional support or advanced challenges as needed.

Benefits of Personalized Learning

Personalized learning offers several key benefits:

1. **Pacing:** Students can learn at their own pace, allowing for a more individualized educational experience. For instance, students who grasp concepts quickly can advance to more challenging material without waiting for their peers, while those needing additional support can receive targeted interventions.
2. **Engagement:** By tailoring content to students' interests and learning styles, AI-driven systems increase engagement and motivation. Students are more likely to stay focused and invested in their learning when they feel that the material is relevant and accessible to them.
3. **Improved Outcomes:** Personalized learning can lead to better academic performance. Studies have shown that students who engage with adaptive learning technologies often achieve higher scores on assessments and demonstrate improved mastery of subjects.

3.2 Intelligent Tutoring Systems

Intelligent Tutoring Systems (ITS) represent another powerful application of AI in education. ITS provides real-time feedback and guidance, simulating the experience of having a personal tutor.

Functionality of ITS

ITS uses a combination of AI techniques, including natural language processing (NLP), machine learning, and knowledge representation, to interact with students and provide personalized instruction. Key features of ITS include:

Real-Time Feedback: ITS offers immediate feedback on students' work, helping them understand errors and learn from their mistakes. For example, an ITS for mathematics might provide step-by-step explanations and hints when a student struggles with a problem, guiding them toward the correct solution.
Targeted Exercises: Based on performance data, ITS can identify areas where a student needs additional practice and offer targeted exercises to address those gaps. This targeted approach ensures that students receive practice in areas where they are struggling, enhancing their understanding and retention of the material.
Progress Tracking: ITS tracks student progress over time, providing valuable insights into their learning patterns and areas of improvement. Educators can use this data to tailor their teaching strategies and provide additional support where needed.
Benefits of ITS

Intelligent Tutoring Systems offer several benefits:

1. **Enhanced Learning:** ITS provide personalized, interactive learning experiences that can lead to deeper understanding and retention of concepts. By addressing individual learning needs and offering immediate feedback, ITS help students master material more effectively.
2. **Scalability:** ITS can scale to accommodate large numbers of students, providing individualized support without requiring additional human resources. This scalability makes ITS an attractive option for educational institutions with limited staffing.
3. **Increased Engagement:** The interactive nature of ITS makes learning more engaging and enjoyable. Students benefit from a more dynamic learning experience that adapts to their needs, which can enhance motivation and interest in the subject matter.

3.3 Administrative Automation

AI is also transforming administrative functions within educational institutions by automating routine tasks and streamlining workflows. This automation reduces the administrative burden on educators and staff, allowing them to focus more on teaching and student support (Xu & Ouyang, 2022) .

Automated Grading

One of the most impactful applications of AI in administrative tasks is automated grading. AI algorithms, particularly those using NLP, can assess written assignments, essays, and even multiple-choice tests. These systems analyze student responses, evaluate correctness, and provide feedback in a fraction of the time it would take human graders.

Enrolment Management

AI-driven tools are also being used to manage student enrolments and administrative records. For instance, AI systems can automate the process of student registration, track course selections, and manage waitlists. These tools streamline administrative tasks, reducing staff workload and improving enrolment processes' efficiency.

NLP for Administrative Tasks

Natural Language Processing (NLP) algorithms play a crucial role in automating administrative tasks. NLP can extract relevant information from unstructured data, such as emails, student feedback, and course evaluations, and convert it into actionable insights.

3.4 Enhancing Accessibility

AI is playing a vital role in making education more accessible to students with disabilities. AI-powered technologies, such as speech recognition and text-to-speech systems, are helping to bridge accessibility gaps and ensure that all students have the opportunity to participate fully in educational activities (Chen et al., 2020) .

Speech Recognition and Text-to-Speech

Speech recognition and text-to-speech technologies are particularly valuable for students with visual or hearing impairments. AI-powered speech recognition systems can convert spoken language into text, enabling students with hearing impairments to access spoken content in real-time. Text-to-speech systems, on the other hand, convert written text into spoken language, assisting students with visual impairments or reading difficulties.

Language Translation

AI-driven language translation tools are breaking down language barriers, making education more inclusive for non-native speakers. Machine translation systems, powered by AI algorithms, can translate educational content into multiple languages, ensuring that students from diverse linguistic backgrounds can access and understand the material.

Accessibility Features in Educational Software

Many educational software platforms now incorporate AI-driven accessibility features to support students with disabilities. For instance, AI can be used to provide alternative formats of content, such as audio descriptions for visual content or interactive simulations for students with learning disabilities.

4. AI IN TRANSPORTATION

Artificial Intelligence (AI) is reshaping the transportation sector, offering innovations that enhance safety, efficiency, and the overall travel experience. This section delves into how AI is revolutionizing transportation through autonomous vehicles, traffic management systems, public transportation, and passenger experience enhancements. Each subsection explores the applications of AI, its benefits, and the challenges faced in integrating these technologies (Akhtar & Moridpour, 2021).

4.1 Autonomous Vehicles

Autonomous vehicles, often referred to as self-driving cars, represent one of the most exciting and transformative applications of AI in transportation. These vehicles leverage a combination of AI algorithms, sensors, and cameras to navigate roads and make real-time decisions, aiming to revolutionize how we travel.

Development and Technology

Autonomous vehicles are equipped with a range of sensors, including LIDAR (Light Detection and Ranging), radar, and cameras, which provide a comprehensive view of the vehicle's surroundings. AI algorithms process data from these sensors to understand the environment, detect objects, and make decisions about navigation and driving. Machine learning models are trained on vast amounts of driving data to recognize patterns and improve decision-making over time.

Potential Benefits

1. **Reduced Traffic Accidents:** Autonomous vehicles have the potential to significantly reduce traffic accidents. AI algorithms are designed to follow traffic laws and respond to hazards more consistently than human drivers. Studies suggest that autonomous vehicles could reduce accidents caused by human error, such as distracted or impaired driving.
2. **Improved Fuel Efficiency:** AI systems in autonomous vehicles can optimize driving patterns to enhance fuel efficiency. For instance, smooth acceleration and braking, efficient route planning, and optimized speed can reduce fuel consumption and lower emissions.
3. **Alleviated Congestion:** Autonomous vehicles can improve traffic flow by communicating with each other and adjusting their behaviour based on real-time data. This communication can help reduce traffic congestion, as vehicles can maintain optimal distances and avoid sudden stops, leading to more fluid traffic movement.
4. **Enhanced Mobility:** Autonomous vehicles can provide greater mobility for individuals who are unable to drive, such as the elderly and disabled. By offering safe and reliable transportation options, these vehicles can improve access to various services and opportunities.

Challenges and Considerations

Despite their potential, autonomous vehicles face several challenges:

- **Safety and Reliability:** Ensuring the safety and reliability of autonomous systems is crucial. AI algorithms must handle a wide range of driving scenarios and conditions, including adverse weather and complex traffic situations.
- **Regulatory and Legal Issues:** The deployment of autonomous vehicles requires regulatory approval and the establishment of legal frameworks to address liability and insurance concerns.
- **Public Acceptance:** Gaining public trust in autonomous vehicles is essential for widespread adoption. Addressing concerns about safety, privacy, and the potential loss of driving jobs is crucial for gaining acceptance.

Figure 4. AI in transportation

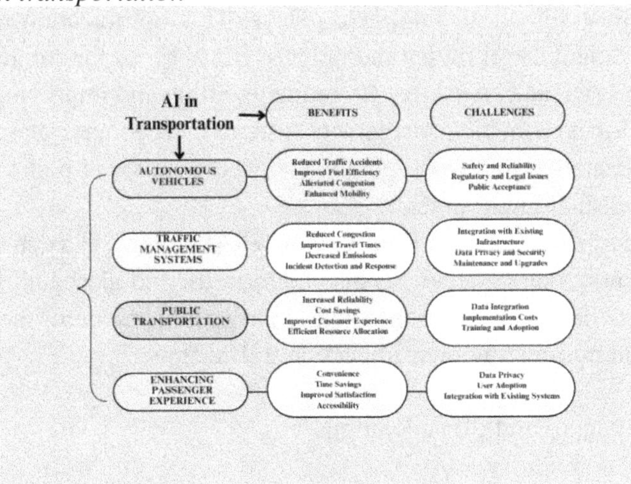

4.2 Traffic Management Systems

AI-driven traffic management systems are transforming how traffic is monitored and controlled in urban areas. These systems use data from traffic cameras, sensors, and GPS devices to optimize traffic flow and improve overall efficiency.

Functionality and Technology

Traffic management systems use AI algorithms to analyze data from various sources:

- **Traffic Cameras and Sensors:** Cameras and sensors placed at intersections and along roads collect real-time data on traffic volume, speed, and congestion. AI algorithms process this data to identify patterns and trends.
- **GPS Data:** GPS data from vehicles provides insights into traffic conditions and travel times. AI systems use this information to predict traffic patterns and make real-time adjustments.

Benefits of AI-Driven Traffic Management

1. **Reduced Congestion:** AI systems optimize traffic signal timings and adjust traffic flow based on real-time data, reducing congestion and improving travel times. By minimizing stop-and-go traffic, these systems help alleviate bottlenecks and smooth traffic flow.

2. **Improved Travel Times:** AI algorithms predict traffic patterns and adjust signals to minimize delays. This optimization leads to more efficient travel routes and reduced travel times for commuters.
3. **Decreased Emissions:** By reducing idling and improving traffic flow, AI-driven traffic management systems can decrease vehicle emissions. Efficient traffic management contributes to lower pollution levels and a cleaner environment.
4. **Incident Detection and Response:** AI systems can detect traffic incidents, such as accidents or road hazards, and alert authorities in real-time. This rapid response helps in managing incidents more effectively and minimizing their impact on traffic flow.

Challenges and Considerations

Implementing AI-driven traffic management systems involves challenges such as:

- **Integration with Existing Infrastructure:** Integrating AI systems with existing traffic infrastructure and control mechanisms can be complex and costly.
- **Data Privacy and Security:** Ensuring the privacy and security of data collected from traffic cameras and sensors is crucial. Measures must be in place to protect sensitive information and prevent misuse.
- **Maintenance and Upgrades:** Ongoing maintenance and updates are necessary to ensure the effectiveness and accuracy of AI-driven systems.

4.3 Public Transportation

AI is enhancing the efficiency and reliability of public transportation systems through predictive maintenance and optimized scheduling. These improvements lead to more dependable and effective public transit services.

Predictive Maintenance

AI-powered predictive maintenance algorithms analyze data from sensors on buses, trains, and other vehicles to anticipate and prevent mechanical failures. By identifying potential issues before they occur, these algorithms help in scheduling timely maintenance and reducing unplanned downtime.

Optimized Scheduling

AI-driven scheduling systems optimize public transportation routes and schedules based on real-time demand and historical data. These systems use machine learning algorithms to predict passenger demand, adjust schedules, and optimize routes to ensure timely and efficient service.

Benefits of AI in Public Transportation

1. **Increased Reliability:** Predictive maintenance and optimized scheduling enhance the reliability of public transportation services. Timely maintenance and efficient scheduling reduce delays and service disruptions.
2. **Cost Savings:** AI-driven predictive maintenance helps reduce maintenance costs by preventing costly repairs and extending the lifespan of vehicles. Optimized scheduling also improves operational efficiency and reduces fuel and labor costs.
3. **Improved Customer Experience:** Enhanced reliability and efficient scheduling lead to a better overall experience for passengers. Reduced wait times, fewer delays, and more consistent service contribute to higher satisfaction levels.
4. **Efficient Resource Allocation:** AI systems help allocate resources more effectively by analyzing data on passenger demand and vehicle availability. This efficient allocation improves service coverage and minimizes operational inefficiencies.

Challenges and Considerations

Challenges in integrating AI into public transportation include:

- **Data Integration:** Combining data from various sources, such as sensors, ticketing systems, and GPS, can be challenging. Ensuring data accuracy and consistency is crucial for effective AI analysis.
- **Implementation Costs:** The initial investment in AI technologies and infrastructure can be significant. Public transportation agencies must balance these costs with the anticipated benefits and savings.
- **Training and Adoption:** Training staff to effectively use AI systems and ensuring widespread adoption among users are important for successful implementation.

4.4 Enhancing Passenger Experience

AI is enhancing the passenger experience in transportation by providing real-time information, personalized recommendations, and interactive assistance. These advancements aim to make travel more convenient and enjoyable.

AI-Powered Chatbots and Virtual Assistants

AI-powered chatbots and virtual assistants offer passengers real-time information and support. These tools can provide information about routes, schedules, and delays, as well as answer frequently asked questions.

Personalisation Algorithms

AI-driven personalization algorithms recommend optimal travel routes and modes of transportation based on individual preferences and past behaviour. These algorithms analyze data on travel patterns, user preferences, and real-time conditions to suggest the best travel options.

Benefits of Enhanced Passenger Experience

1. **Convenience:** Real-time information and interactive assistance enhance the convenience of travel. Passengers can easily access information, receive updates, and get personalized recommendations without the need for manual inquiries.
2. **Time Savings:** AI-powered tools help passengers make informed decisions about their travel plans, reducing wait times and improving overall travel efficiency. Personalized route recommendations lead to faster and more efficient journeys.
3. **Improved Satisfaction:** A seamless and personalized travel experience contributes to higher passenger satisfaction. Enhanced support and convenience lead to a more positive perception of transportation services.
4. **Accessibility:** AI-driven tools provide accessible information for passengers with disabilities or special needs. For example, voice-activated assistants and text-to-speech features improve accessibility for visually impaired passengers.

Challenges and Considerations

Challenges in enhancing the passenger experience with AI include:

- **Data Privacy:** Ensuring the privacy and security of passenger data is crucial. AI systems must handle personal information responsibly and comply with data protection regulations.

- **User Adoption:** Encouraging passengers to use AI-powered tools and services requires effective communication and user-friendly interfaces.

5. AI IN PUBLIC SAFETY

Artificial Intelligence (AI) is increasingly becoming a critical tool in enhancing public safety through various applications, including crime prevention, emergency response, disaster management, and cybersecurity.

5.1 Crime Prevention and Predictive Policing

AI-driven predictive policing and crime prevention tools leverage advanced algorithms to analyze historical crime data and identify patterns that can inform law enforcement strategies. These technologies aim to prevent crime before it occurs by predicting high-risk areas and deploying resources effectively.

Predictive Policing

Predictive policing involves using AI algorithms to analyze data from past criminal activities to forecast where future crimes are likely to occur. By identifying patterns and trends in crime data, law enforcement agencies can allocate resources more efficiently and implement proactive measures to prevent crimes.

Benefits of Predictive Policing:

1. **Resource Allocation:** By predicting crime hotspots, law enforcement agencies can strategically allocate patrols and resources, enhancing their ability to prevent crimes and improve community safety.
2. **Reduced Crime Rates:** Predictive policing has the potential to reduce crime rates by allowing police to intervene before crimes occur. Early interventions can disrupt criminal patterns and deter potential offenders.
3. **Improved Efficiency:** AI-driven tools streamline the process of identifying high-risk areas, reducing the time and effort required for manual analysis and enabling more data-driven decision-making.

Challenges and Considerations:

- **Bias and Fairness:** There is concern about potential biases in predictive policing algorithms, which could lead to disproportionate targeting of certain communities. Ensuring fairness and mitigating bias in AI models is crucial for maintaining public trust and avoiding discriminatory practices.

- **Privacy Concerns:** The use of predictive policing raises privacy issues, as it involves analyzing vast amounts of personal and location data. Balancing crime prevention with individual privacy rights is essential.

Figure 5. AI in public safety

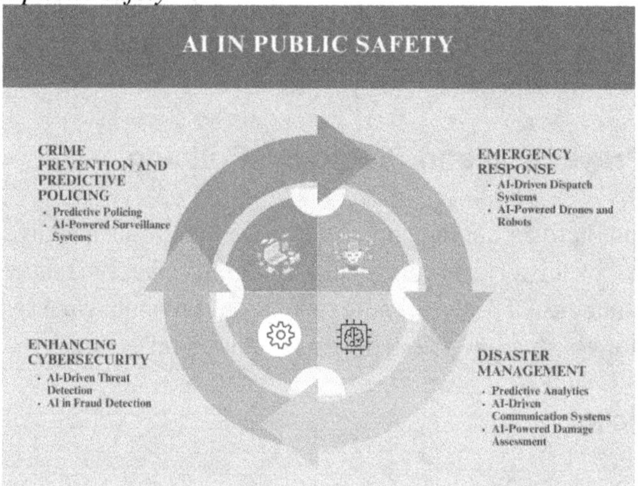

AI-Powered Surveillance Systems

AI-powered surveillance systems enhance crime prevention by analyzing video footage in real time to detect suspicious behaviour and alert authorities (Fontes & Lütge, 2022).

Benefits of AI-Powered Surveillance:

1. **Real-Time Detection:** AI systems can process video footage in real-time, enabling faster detection of suspicious activities and quicker response by law enforcement.
2. **Enhanced Accuracy:** AI algorithms can identify specific behaviours or objects of interest in video feeds, improving the accuracy of surveillance and reducing false alarms.
3. **Deterrence:** The presence of advanced surveillance systems can act as a deterrent to potential criminals, knowing that their actions are being monitored and analyzed.

Challenges and Considerations:

- **Ethical Concerns:** Continuous surveillance raises ethical issues related to privacy and civil liberties. Ensuring that surveillance practices are transparent and respect individual rights is crucial.
- **Data Security:** Securing the data collected by surveillance systems is essential to prevent unauthorized access and misuse.

5.2 Emergency Response

AI plays a significant role in improving the efficiency and effectiveness of emergency response efforts. By analyzing data from various sources, AI systems can prioritize and allocate resources more effectively, ultimately saving lives and mitigating the impact of emergencies.

AI-Driven Dispatch Systems

AI-driven dispatch systems analyze data from emergency calls to prioritize incidents and allocate resources based on urgency and severity. These systems use algorithms to evaluate factors such as the nature of the emergency, location, and available resources.

Benefits of AI-Driven Dispatch Systems:

1. **Faster Response Times:** AI systems can quickly analyze emergency data and dispatch the appropriate resources, reducing response times and improving outcomes.
2. **Improved Resource Allocation:** By evaluating the urgency and context of emergencies, AI systems ensure that resources are allocated where they are needed most, optimizing response efforts.
3. **Enhanced Coordination:** AI-driven dispatch systems facilitate better coordination among emergency services, such as police, fire, and medical teams, leading to more effective responses.

Challenges and Considerations:

- **Accuracy of Data:** The effectiveness of AI-driven dispatch systems relies on the accuracy and completeness of the data. Inaccurate or incomplete information can impact the efficiency of response efforts.
- **Integration with Existing Systems:** Integrating AI dispatch systems with existing emergency response infrastructure requires careful planning and coordination.

AI-Powered Drones and Robots

AI-powered drones and robots assist in search and rescue operations, particularly in hazardous or inaccessible environments. These technologies provide valuable support by surveying areas, locating victims, and delivering supplies.

Figure 6. Drone model

Benefits of AI-Powered Drones and Robots:

1. **Enhanced Search Capabilities:** Drones and robots equipped with AI can cover large areas quickly and gather critical information, improving search and rescue efforts.
2. **Safety for Responders:** AI-powered drones and robots can operate in hazardous environments, reducing the risk to human responders and improving overall safety.
3. **Real-Time Data Collection:** These technologies provide real-time data and imagery, aiding decision-making and coordinating rescue operations more effectively.

Challenges and Considerations:

- **Regulations and Privacy:** The use of drones and robots in emergency response must adhere to regulations and privacy considerations. Ensuring compliance with legal requirements is essential.
- **Technical Limitations:** AI-powered drones and robots have technical limitations, such as battery life and environmental constraints, which must be addressed to maximize their effectiveness.

5.3 Disaster Management

AI enhances disaster management by improving preparedness, response, and recovery efforts. Predictive analytics, communication systems, and damage assessment tools contribute to more effective disaster management strategies.

Predictive Analytics for Disaster Forecasting

Predictive analytics algorithms use AI to forecast natural disasters, such as hurricanes, earthquakes, and floods. By analyzing historical data, weather patterns, and other variables, AI models can provide early warnings and help authorities take proactive measures (Guan et al., 2020).

Benefits of Predictive Analytics:

1. **Early Warnings:** Predictive analytics provide early warnings of potential disasters, allowing authorities and communities to prepare and evacuate if necessary.
2. **Proactive Measures:** By forecasting disasters, AI enables proactive measures to minimize damage and ensure a more effective response.
3. **Improved Coordination:** Early warnings and predictive insights facilitate better coordination among emergency services, government agencies, and communities.

Challenges and Considerations:

- **Accuracy of Predictions:** The accuracy of AI predictions depends on the quality and completeness of the data used. Ensuring accurate forecasts is critical for effective disaster management.
- **Communication:** Effective communication of predictive insights to the public and authorities is essential for timely action and preparedness.

AI-Driven Communication Systems

During disasters, AI-driven communication systems provide real-time updates and coordinate rescue efforts. These systems analyze data from various sources, such as social media and emergency reports, to facilitate communication and resource allocation.

Example: The "Social Media Analytics for Crisis Response" system uses AI to monitor social media platforms and analyze posts, images, and geolocation data to provide situational awareness and coordinate response efforts.

Benefits of AI-Driven Communication Systems:

1. **Real-Time Updates:** AI systems provide real-time updates on disaster conditions, helping authorities and the public stay informed and make timely decisions.
2. **Efficient Coordination:** AI-driven communication systems facilitate coordination among emergency services, government agencies, and relief organizations, improving response effectiveness.
3. **Public Engagement:** By analyzing social media and other data sources, AI systems engage with the public and gather valuable information about disaster impacts and needs.

Challenges and Considerations:

- **Data Overload:** Managing and interpreting large volumes of data from various sources can be challenging. Ensuring relevant information is prioritized and acted upon is crucial.
- **Privacy and Security:** Handling personal data from social media and other sources must be done with consideration for privacy and security.

AI-Powered Damage Assessment

AI-powered damage assessment tools analyze satellite imagery and other data to assess the extent of damage caused by disasters. These tools help prioritize recovery efforts and allocate resources effectively.

Benefits of AI-Powered Damage Assessment:

1. **Rapid Assessment:** AI tools provide rapid damage assessments, enabling quick prioritization of recovery efforts and resource allocation.
2. **Detailed Analysis:** AI algorithms analyze high-resolution satellite imagery to assess damage with great detail, providing valuable insights for recovery planning.
3. **Resource Optimization:** Accurate damage assessments help optimize the allocation of resources and aid in effective recovery and rebuilding efforts.

Challenges and Considerations:

- **Image Quality:** The accuracy of damage assessments depends on the quality of satellite imagery and other data sources. Ensuring high-quality data is essential for accurate analysis.
- **Integration with Recovery Efforts:** Integrating AI-powered damage assessments with recovery and relief efforts requires effective coordination among various stakeholders.

5.4 Enhancing Cybersecurity

AI enhances cybersecurity within public safety by analyzing network traffic and user behaviour to identify anomalies and potential security breaches. These systems automate threat detection and response, strengthening defences against cyberattacks.

AI-Driven Threat Detection

AI-driven security systems analyze network traffic, user behaviour, and other data to detect anomalies and potential security threats. Machine learning algorithms are trained to recognize patterns indicative of cyberattacks and alert security teams to take action.

Benefits of AI-Driven Threat Detection:

1. **Early Detection:** AI systems can detect potential threats at an early stage, allowing for faster response and mitigation of cyberattacks.
2. **Reduced False Positives:** AI algorithms are designed to minimize false positives by accurately identifying genuine threats, reducing the workload on security teams.
3. **Automated Response:** AI-driven systems can automate responses to detected threats, such as blocking malicious traffic or isolating compromised systems, improving overall security.

Challenges and Considerations:

- **Evolving Threats:** Cyber threats are constantly evolving, and AI systems must be continuously updated to recognize new and emerging threats.
- **Data Privacy:** Analyzing network traffic and user behaviour raises privacy concerns. Ensuring that AI systems handle data responsibly and in compliance with privacy regulations is crucial.

AI in Fraud Detection

AI is also used to detect and prevent fraud in various public safety applications, such as financial transactions and identity verification. Machine learning algorithms analyze transaction patterns and user behaviour to identify suspicious activities and potential fraud.

Benefits of AI in Fraud Detection:

1. **Enhanced Accuracy:** AI algorithms improve the accuracy of fraud detection by analyzing complex patterns and behaviours that may be missed by traditional methods.
2. **Real-Time Monitoring:** AI systems enable real-time monitoring of transactions and activities, allowing for prompt detection and prevention of fraudulent actions.
3. **Adaptive Learning:** AI systems can adapt to new fraud techniques and patterns, improving their ability to detect evolving threats.

Challenges and Considerations:

- **False Positives:** Balancing the sensitivity of fraud detection algorithms is important to minimize false positives and avoid disrupting legitimate transactions.
- **Integration with Existing Systems:** Integrating AI-driven fraud detection with existing security and financial systems requires careful planning and coordination.

6. ETHICAL CONSIDERATIONS AND CHALLENGES IN AI INTEGRATION IN PUBLIC SERVICES

The integration of Artificial Intelligence (AI) into public services presents transformative opportunities but also significant ethical challenges (Lim & Cruz, 2024). As AI continues to evolve and be implemented across various sectors, it is imperative to address these ethical concerns to ensure that AI applications contribute positively to society.

6.1 Data Privacy and Security

The deployment of AI in public services often involves the processing of vast amounts of personal and sensitive data. This brings the issue of data privacy and security to the forefront, as the potential for data breaches, unauthorized access, and misuse of information can have far-reaching consequences.

(i)Importance of Compliance with Data Protection Regulations: AI systems that handle personal data must comply with data protection regulations such as the General Data Protection Regulation (GDPR) in the European Union or the California Consumer Privacy Act (CCPA) in the United States. Compliance is not only a legal obligation but also a fundamental ethical responsibility. Non-compliance can lead to significant penalties, legal repercussions, and loss of public trust.

(ii) **Robust Security Measures:** Implementing robust security measures is essential to protect AI systems from cyber-attacks, data breaches, and other security threats. This includes the use of encryption, secure data storage solutions, and continuous monitoring for vulnerabilities. Given that AI systems are increasingly being used to make critical decisions in areas like healthcare, law enforcement, and welfare distribution, the security of these systems cannot be overemphasized. A single breach could expose sensitive personal data, leading to identity theft, financial loss, or other forms of harm.

(iii)Challenges in Anonymization and Data De-identification: Even with anonymization and data de-identification techniques, re-identification remains a risk. Advanced algorithms can sometimes reverse anonymization, especially when combined with other data sources. Public services must therefore carefully evaluate the effectiveness of their data anonymization techniques and continuously improve them to keep pace with evolving AI capabilities.

(iv)Balancing Innovation with Privacy: While data is crucial for training AI models, there is a fine line between leveraging data for innovation and respecting individual privacy. Public institutions must find a balance between using data to improve services and protecting citizens' privacy. This often requires adopting a data minimization approach—collecting only the data that is strictly necessary for a given purpose and ensuring that it is used ethically.

Figure 7. AI in public services

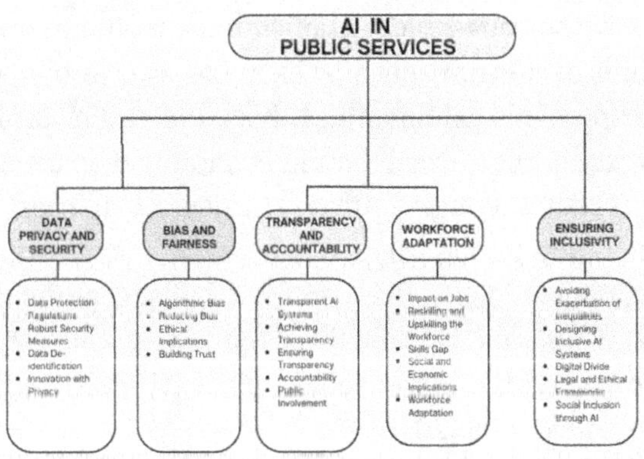

6.2 Bias and Fairness

AI systems, by their very nature, are prone to bias because they are trained on data that may reflect existing societal biases. Addressing bias and ensuring fairness in AI algorithms is crucial to avoid perpetuating discrimination and inequality.

(i)Understanding Algorithmic Bias: Algorithmic bias occurs when AI systems produce skewed results due to biased training data or biased algorithm designSimilarly, facial recognition systems have been shown to have higher error rates for people of colour, leading to concerns about racial bias in AI applications. Understanding and identifying these biases is the first step toward mitigating their impact (Chatterjee & Bhattacharjee, 2020).

(ii)Techniques for Reducing Bias: Several techniques can be employed to reduce bias in AI systems. These include:

- **Diverse and Representative Datasets:** Ensuring that the data used to train AI systems is diverse and representative of the population is crucial. This can help prevent the system from learning and perpetuating existing biases.
- **Bias Detection Tools:** There are tools and frameworks available that can detect and measure bias in AI systems. Regular audits of AI systems using these tools can help identify and address biases.
- **Algorithmic Fairness Approaches:** Developing and applying fairness-aware algorithms that explicitly consider fairness criteria during model training can help mitigate bias. Techniques such as re-weighting, re-sampling, or introducing fairness constraints are commonly used.

(iii)Ethical Implications of Unaddressed Bias: Failure to address bias in AI systems can have serious ethical implications, including reinforcing existing inequalities and discrimination. For example, if a public service AI system used for loan approvals exhibits racial bias, it could result in unfair denial of loans to minority groups, exacerbating economic disparities.

(iv)Building Trust through Fairness: Ensuring fairness in AI systems is essential to building public trust. When citizens perceive AI systems as fair and unbiased, they are more likely to trust and accept the decisions made by these systems. This trust is critical for the successful integration of AI into public services, where the consequences of biased decisions can directly impact individuals' lives (Smuha, 2019) .

6.3 Transparency and Accountability

Transparency and accountability are key ethical principles in AI deployment, particularly in public services where decisions made by AI systems can have significant consequences for individuals and communities.

(i)The Need for Transparent AI Systems: Transparency in AI systems involves making the decision-making processes of AI understandable to stakeholders, including the public. Transparent AI systems allow users to see the reasoning behind decisions, which is particularly important in public services where decisions can affect people's rights, access to resources, and overall well-being.
(ii)Challenges in Achieving Transparency: Achieving transparency in AI systems can be challenging, especially with complex models like deep learning, which operate as "black boxes" where the internal workings are not easily interpretable. This opacity raises concerns about accountability—if an AI system makes a mistake or produces a biased outcome, it can be difficult to pinpoint the cause or hold any party responsible.
(iii)Mechanisms for Ensuring Transparency: To enhance transparency, several mechanisms can be employed:

- **Explainable AI (XAI):** Techniques in explainable AI aim to make AI models more interpretable. This can involve simplifying models, providing visualizations of decision pathways, or using methods that allow for the inspection of model decisions.
- **Clear Documentation and Reporting:** Public service AI systems should include thorough documentation that explains how the system was developed, the data used, the decisions it makes, and the potential risks. Regular reporting and audits can also help in maintaining transparency.
- **User Interfaces for Transparency:** AI systems should include user interfaces that allow end-users to understand and, where appropriate, challenge the decisions made by the AI. This might include providing users with explanations or justifications for certain decisions.

(iv)Accountability in AI Deployment: Accountability involves ensuring that there is a clear understanding of who is responsible for the actions of an AI system. In the context of public services, this might mean identifying whether responsibility lies with the developers of the AI, the public agency deploying it, or a combination of both. Without accountability, there is a risk that errors or harms caused by AI systems will not be adequately addressed.

(v)Public Involvement and Oversight: Engaging the public in discussions about AI deployment in public services is crucial for transparency and accountability. Public consultations, open forums, and participatory design processes can help ensure that the views and concerns of citizens are considered in the development and implementation of AI systems.

6.4 Workforce Adaptation

As AI systems are integrated into public services, significant changes in the workforce are inevitable. While AI can enhance efficiency and productivity, it also raises concerns about job displacement, skills gaps, and the need for workforce adaptation.

(i)Impact on Jobs: The introduction of AI in public services is likely to lead to the automation of routine tasks, potentially displacing workers who perform these tasks. Jobs that involve data entry, routine decision-making, and administrative functions are particularly at risk. However, it's also important to recognize that AI can create new job opportunities, especially in areas related to AI development, maintenance, and oversight.

(ii)Reskilling and Upskilling the Workforce: To mitigate the impact of AI on jobs, there is a pressing need for reskilling and upskilling programs. Public sector workers must be provided with the training and education necessary to transition into new roles that complement AI technologies. For instance, workers who previously performed routine tasks might be retrained to oversee AI systems, manage data, or provide more specialized services that require human judgment and empathy.

(iii)Addressing the Skills Gap: The integration of AI in public services requires a workforce with skills in data science, AI ethics, cybersecurity, and other related fields. However, there is currently a significant skills gap, with demand for these skills far outstripping supply. Bridging this gap will require strategic workforce planning, partnerships with educational institutions, and initiatives to encourage more people to pursue careers in AI and related fields (Trotta et al., 2023) .

(iv)Social and Economic Implications: Workforce adaptation is not just an economic issue; it has significant social implications as well. If not managed properly, AI-driven changes in the workforce could exacerbate inequality, leading to job losses in certain sectors or regions, and contributing to social unrest. Policymakers need to consider these broader implications and take steps to ensure that the benefits of AI are distributed equitably across society.

(v)The Role of Leadership in Workforce Adaptation: Leadership plays a crucial role in guiding workforce adaptation to AI. Public sector leaders must be proactive in anticipating the changes brought about by AI and taking steps to prepare their organizations. This includes not only investing in technology but also prioritizing the development of human capital.

6.5 Ensuring Inclusivity

Inclusivity is a fundamental ethical consideration in the deployment of AI in public services. Ensuring that AI technologies are accessible to all individuals, regardless of their background or circumstances, is essential to achieving equitable outcomes.

(i)Avoiding Exacerbation of Inequalities: One of the major ethical concerns with AI is the potential to exacerbate existing inequalities. If AI systems are designed or deployed without considering the needs of marginalized or disadvantaged groups, they may unintentionally reinforce existing disparities. For example, if an AI system used for healthcare prioritizes patients based on data that reflects historical biases, it could lead to unequal access to care for certain populations.
(ii)Designing Inclusive AI Systems: Inclusive design is critical to ensuring that AI technologies serve the needs of all individuals. This involves considering the diverse needs of different populations in the design and implementation of AI systems.
(iii)Addressing the Digital Divide: The digital divide—the gap between those who have access to digital technologies and those who do not—presents a significant challenge to the inclusive deployment of AI in public services. Without access to the necessary technology or digital literacy, certain populations may be excluded from the benefits of AI driven public services.
(iv)Legal and Ethical Frameworks for Inclusivity: Ensuring inclusivity in AI deployment requires robust legal and ethical frameworks that mandate the consideration of inclusivity in the design and implementation of AI systems. These frameworks should include guidelines and standards for ensuring that AI systems are accessible to all, regardless of their socioeconomic status, race, gender, or disability.
(v)Promoting Social Inclusion through AI: AI has the potential to promote social inclusion by providing new opportunities for marginalized groups. For example, AI-powered assistive technologies can enhance the quality of life for people with disabilities, while AI-driven educational tools can provide personalized learning experiences for students from diverse backgrounds (Hastuti & Syafruddin. 2023).

7. FUTURE PROSPECTS AND RECOMMENDATIONS

As Artificial Intelligence (AI) continues to evolve, its integration into public services is poised to bring about profound changes. However, the future of AI in this domain depends not only on technological advancements but also on the frameworks, policies, and ethical guidelines that govern its use.

7.1 Technological Advancements

AI technology is rapidly advancing, with emerging trends and innovations that hold the potential to further enhance public services. These advancements are expected to improve efficiency, accuracy, and accessibility across various sectors, including healthcare, education, transportation, and public safety.

(i) **Advanced Machine Learning and AI Algorithms:** Future developments in machine learning (ML) and AI algorithms are likely to enhance the capabilities of AI systems. For instance, the continued evolution of deep learning models could lead to more accurate and reliable AI-driven predictions and decisions. These advancements may allow public services to become more proactive, identifying issues before they arise and responding to them in real-time.

(ii) **Integration of AI with the Internet of Things (IoT):** The convergence of AI and IoT represents a significant technological advancement with far-reaching implications for public services. IoT devices generate vast amounts of data, and AI can be used to analyze this data in real-time, leading to smarter and more responsive public services. In smart cities, for instance, AI can optimize traffic management by analyzing data from connected vehicles, traffic lights, and road sensors, reducing congestion and improving safety.

(iii) **Natural Language Processing (NLP) and Human-AI Interaction:** Advances in NLP will improve the ability of AI systems to understand and interact with humans in more natural and intuitive ways. This can have significant implications for public services that rely on citizen interaction, such as customer service, legal aid, and social services. AI-powered chatbots and virtual assistants are likely to become more sophisticated, providing personalized and accurate assistance to citizens.

(iv) **AI-Driven Automation and Robotics:** The future of AI in public services will likely see increased automation of routine tasks, allowing human workers to focus on more complex and high-value activities. Robotics, powered by AI, can be deployed in areas such as healthcare for tasks like surgery, patient care, and elderly assistance. In transportation, autonomous vehicles and drones could revolutionize logistics, public transportation, and emergency response.

(v)Enhanced Data Analytics and Decision-Making: AI's ability to process and analyze large datasets will continue to improve, leading to better decision-making in public services. Enhanced data analytics can help governments and public institutions make more informed policy decisions, optimize resource allocation, and identify trends that may not be immediately apparent through traditional methods.

(vi)Ethical AI and Trustworthy AI Systems: As AI technology advances, there will be a growing emphasis on developing ethical and trustworthy AI systems (Dabis & Csáki, 2024) . This includes the development of AI systems that are transparent, explainable, and free from bias. Emerging research in AI ethics will play a crucial role in shaping the future of AI in public services, ensuring that these systems operate in ways that align with societal values and ethical principles.

7.2 Policy and Regulation

The rapid advancement of AI technology necessitates the development of robust policy and regulatory frameworks to guide its responsible deployment in public services. These frameworks must balance innovation with the need to protect public interests, ensuring that AI technologies are used ethically and effectively.

(i)The Role of Government in AI Regulation: Governments play a critical role in establishing the policies and regulations that will govern the use of AI in public services. This involves setting standards for data privacy, security, and ethical AI development. Governments must also ensure that AI systems used in public services are transparent and accountable.

(ii)Developing AI Governance Structures: Effective AI governance structures are essential for overseeing the deployment of AI in public services. These structures should include mechanisms for monitoring AI systems, assessing their impact, and addressing any ethical or legal concerns that arise. This might involve the creation of independent oversight bodies tasked with evaluating the fairness, transparency, and accountability of AI systems.

(iii)Regulatory Approaches to Addressing AI Bias and Fairness: Given the ethical challenges associated with AI bias, policymakers must develop regulations that mandate fairness in AI systems. This could include requiring public institutions to use fairness-aware algorithms, conducting regular audits of AI systems for bias, and implementing corrective measures when biases are detected.

(iv)International Cooperation on AI Regulation: AI is a global technology, and its regulation requires international cooperation. International cooperation can also help address the challenges of cross-border data flows, cybersecurity threats, and the ethical use of AI. Organizations like the United Nations and the European Union can play a pivotal role in facilitating dialogue and collaboration on AI regulation.

(v)Encouraging Innovation While Ensuring Public Safety: While regulation is necessary to protect public interests, it is also important to encourage innovation in AI technology. Policymakers should strike a balance between regulating AI and fostering an environment that allows for experimentation and innovation.

(vi)Ensuring Public Trust Through Transparent Policy Development: For AI policies and regulations to be effective, they must be developed transparently and with public input. Governments should engage with citizens, industry stakeholders, and civil society in the policymaking process, ensuring that the voices of all affected parties are heard.

7.3 Collaboration and Stakeholder Engagement

Collaboration and stakeholder engagement are crucial for the successful development and deployment of AI technologies in public services. By fostering cooperation between governments, industry, academia, and civil society, we can address the challenges of AI and maximize its benefits.

(i)The Role of Governments in Fostering Collaboration: Governments can play a key role in promoting collaboration between different stakeholders. This can involve establishing public-private partnerships that bring together the expertise of industry and the public sector to develop AI solutions for public services. Governments can also facilitate collaboration by providing funding for AI research and development, creating innovation hubs, and supporting initiatives that promote knowledge-sharing between stakeholders.

(ii)Industry's Contribution to AI Development: The private sector, particularly tech companies, is at the forefront of AI innovation. Collaborating with industry can provide public services with access to cutting-edge AI technologies and expertise.

(iii)Academia's Role in Advancing AI Research: Academic institutions play a crucial role in advancing AI research and exploring its potential applications in public services. Collaborations between academia and the public sector can lead to the development of AI solutions that are grounded in scientific research and ethical considerations (Chaudhry & Kazim, 2021) .

(iv)Engaging Civil Society and the Public: Civil society organizations and the public must be actively engaged in the development and deployment of AI technologies. These stakeholders can provide valuable insights into the ethical implications of AI and help ensure that AI systems are designed in a way that serves the public good.
(v)Collaborative Approaches to Addressing Ethical Challenges: The ethical challenges associated with AI—such as bias, transparency, and accountability—cannot be addressed by any single stakeholder alone. Collaborative approaches are needed to develop ethical guidelines, standards, and best practices for AI deployment in public services.
(vi)Promoting Cross-Sector Innovation: Collaboration between different sectors can lead to innovative AI solutions that address complex societal challenges. For example, partnerships between healthcare providers, technology companies, and research institutions can lead to the development of AI tools that improve patient outcomes and reduce healthcare costs (Hwang et al., 2020).

7.4 Ethical Guidelines

The responsible deployment of AI in public services requires the development and adherence to ethical guidelines that address key concerns such as data privacy, bias, transparency, accountability, and inclusivity.

(i)Establishing Ethical Standards for AI Deployment: Ethical guidelines should establish clear standards for the deployment of AI in public services. These standards should cover issues such as data privacy, ensuring that AI systems are designed to protect the personal information of citizens and comply with relevant data protection regulations.
(ii)Ensuring Transparency and Explainability: Transparency is a key ethical principle in AI deployment. Ethical guidelines should require that AI systems used in public services are transparent and explainable, meaning that their decision-making processes can be understood by users and stakeholders.
(iii)Accountability in AI Systems: Accountability is crucial to ensuring that AI systems are used responsibly. Ethical guidelines should establish clear lines of accountability for the development, deployment, and operation of AI systems in public services. Public institutions should also be held accountable for ensuring that AI systems are used in a way that aligns with ethical standards and societal values.
(iv)Continuous Monitoring and Ethical Audits: Ethical guidelines should include provisions for the continuous monitoring and auditing of AI systems to ensure that they adhere to ethical standards over time. This might involve

regular ethical audits, where AI systems are evaluated for compliance with ethical guidelines, and corrective actions are taken if necessary.

(v)Global Collaboration on Ethical AI Guidelines: Given the global nature of AI, there is a need for international collaboration on ethical guidelines. This involves developing harmonized ethical standards that can be applied across different countries and regions, ensuring that AI is used responsibly worldwide.

8. CONCLUSION

The integration of Artificial Intelligence (AI) in public services marks a transformative shift in how societies operate, particularly in key sectors like healthcare, education, transportation, and safety. These areas, critical to public welfare, have seen profound changes as AI-driven tools introduce efficiencies, innovation, and new possibilities that were previously unattainable with traditional methods.

In **healthcare**, AI has made significant strides in enhancing diagnostics, treatment, and patient care. AI-driven diagnostic tools, such as imaging and pattern recognition systems, have also improved early detection rates for diseases like cancer, reducing the burden on healthcare systems and increasing survival rates. However, challenges such as data privacy, algorithmic transparency, and regulatory standards remain crucial in ensuring the ethical implementation of AI technologies in this field(Varnosfaderani & Forouzanfar, 2024) .

In **education**, AI has revolutionized learning experiences, with adaptive learning systems tailoring educational content to the unique needs of individual students Intelligent tutoring systems can provide students with instant feedback, making learning more interactive and effective.

In **transportation**, AI has streamlined traffic management, optimized routes, and accelerated the development of autonomous vehicles (Garikapati & Shetiya, 2024). These advancements contribute to reducing congestion, lowering emissions, and enhancing road safety. Public transportation systems, through AI-powered predictive algorithms, can adjust schedules in real time based on commuter data, improving efficiency and reducing delays. Moreover, AI's role in predictive maintenance helps avoid costly breakdowns and minimizes service disruptions.

Public safety is another critical sector where AI's potential is evident. AI-driven surveillance and facial recognition technologies have enhanced security operations, improving crime detection and prevention. Additionally, AI-enabled emergency response systems have enhanced the speed and accuracy of responses to natural disasters, fires, and medical emergencies.

The potential benefits include enhanced service delivery, optimized resource allocation, and improved outcomes across healthcare, education, transportation, and public safety. However, the rapid adoption of AI also calls for robust frameworks to address challenges such as ethical concerns, data privacy, transparency, and fairness (Abduljabbar et al., 2019) .

In conclusion, the successful deployment of AI requires thoughtful governance, interdisciplinary collaboration, and a commitment to ensuring that these technologies serve the broader goals of equity, accessibility, and sustainability. As AI continues to evolve, its role in public services will undoubtedly expand, presenting both exciting possibilities and critical responsibilities for governments and communities worldwide.

REFERENCES

Abduljabbar, R., Dia, H., Liyanage, S., & Bagloee, S. A. (2019). Applications of Artificial Intelligence in Transport: An Overview. *Sustainability (Basel)*, 11(1), 189. DOI: 10.3390/su11010189

Ahangar, M. N., Ahmed, Q. Z., Khan, F. A., & Hafeez, M. (2021). A survey of autonomous vehicles: Enabling communication technologies and challenges. *Sensors (Basel)*, 21(706), 706. Advance online publication. DOI: 10.3390/s21030706 PMID: 33494191

Akhtar, M., & Moridpour, S. (2021). A Review of Traffic Congestion Prediction Using Artificial Intelligence. *Journal of Advanced Transportation*, 2021, 1–18. DOI: 10.1155/2021/8878011

Bajwa, J., Munir, A. U., Nori, A., & Williams, B. (2021). Artificial intelligence in healthcare: Transforming the practice of medicine. *Future Healthcare Journal*, 8(2), e188–e194. DOI: 10.7861/fhj.2021-0095 PMID: 34286183

Bera, K., Schalper, K. A., Rimm, D. L., Velcheti, V., & Madabhushi, A. (2019). Artificial intelligence in digital pathology — New tools for diagnosis and precision oncology. *Nature Reviews. Clinical Oncology*, 16(11), 703–715. DOI: 10.1038/s41571-019-0252-y PMID: 31399699

Chatterjee, S., & Bhattacharjee, K. K. (2020). Adoption of artificial intelligence in higher education: A quantitative analysis using structural equation modelling. *Education and Information Technologies*, 25(5), 3443–3463. Advance online publication. DOI: 10.1007/s10639-020-10159-7

Chaudhry, M. A., & Kazim, E. (2022). Artificial Intelligence in Education (AIEd): A high-level academic and industry note 2021. *AI and Ethics*, 2(1), 157–165. DOI: 10.1007/s43681-021-00074-z PMID: 34790953

Chen, X., Xie, H., Zou, D., & Hwang, G. (2020). Application and theory gaps during the rise of Artificial Intelligence in Education. *Computers and Education Artificial Intelligence*, 1, 100002. DOI: 10.1016/j.caeai.2020.100002

Dabis, A., & Csáki, C. (2024). AI and ethics: Investigating the first policy responses of higher education institutions to the challenge of generative AI. *Humanities & Social Sciences Communications*, 11(1006), 1006. Advance online publication. DOI: 10.1057/s41599-024-03526-z

. Fontes, C., & Lütge, C. (2022). Surveillance and power relations: The use of facial recognition technologies and remote biometric identification in public spaces and impacts on public life. *Direito Público, 18*(100)

Garikapati, D., & Shetiya, S. S. (2024). Autonomous vehicles: Evolution of artificial intelligence and learning algorithms. *arXiv*, 2402.17690v2 [cs.LG]. https://arxiv.org/abs/2402.17690v2

Guan, C., Mou, J., & Jiang, Z. (2020). Artificial intelligence innovation in education: A twenty-year data-driven historical analysis. *International Journal of Innovation Studies*, 4(4), 134–147. DOI: 10.1016/j.ijis.2020.09.001

Hastuti, R., & Syafruddin, . (2023). Ethical considerations in the age of artificial intelligence: Balancing innovation and social values. *West Science Social and Humanities Studies*, 1(2), 76–87. DOI: 10.58812/wsshs.v1i02.191

Huang, J.-D., Wang, J., Ramsey, E., Leavey, G., Chico, T. J., & Condell, J. (2022). Applying artificial intelligence to wearable sensor data to diagnose and predict cardiovascular disease: A review. *Sensors (Basel)*, 22(20), 8002. DOI: 10.3390/s22208002 PMID: 36298352

Hwang, G., Xie, H., Wah, B. W., & Gašević, D. (2020). Vision, challenges, roles and research issues of Artificial Intelligence in Education. *Computers and Education Artificial Intelligence*, 1, 100001. DOI: 10.1016/j.caeai.2020.100001

Hwang, G.-J., & Chen, N.-S. (2023). Exploring the potential of generative artificial intelligence in education: Applications, challenges, and future research directions. *Journal of Educational Technology & Society*, 26(2), 1–12.

John, T. (2022). The ethical considerations of artificial intelligence in clinical decision support. In *Proceedings of the Wellington Faculty of Engineering Ethics and Sustainability Symposium* DOI: 10.26686/wfeess.vi.7649

Lim, J., & Cruz, A. (2024). Advancements in artificial intelligence applications and ethical considerations across industries. *International Journal of Applied Machine Learning and Computational Intelligence*, 14(3), 26–34.

Smuha, N. A. (2019). The EU Approach to Ethics Guidelines for Trustworthy Artificial Intelligence. *Computer Law Review International*, 20(4), 97–106. DOI: 10.9785/cri-2019-200402

Srinivasan, V. (2022). AI & learning: A preferred future. *Computers and Education: Artificial Intelligence*, 3, 100062. DOI: 10.1016/j.caeai.2022.100062

Stypińska, J., & Franke, A. (2023). AI revolution in healthcare and medicine and the (re-) emergence of inequalities and disadvantages for the ageing population. *Frontiers in Sociology*, 7, 1038854. DOI: 10.3389/fsoc.2022.1038854 PMID: 36755564

Trotta, A., Ziosi, M., & Lomonaco, V. (2023). The future of ethics in AI: Challenges and opportunities. *AI & Society*, 38(439–441), 439–441. Advance online publication. DOI: 10.1007/s00146-023-01644-x

Varnosfaderani, S. M., & Forouzanfar, M. (2024). The role of AI in hospitals and clinics: Transforming healthcare in the 21st century. *Bioengineering (Basel, Switzerland)*, 11(4), 337. DOI: 10.3390/bioengineering11040337 PMID: 38671759

. Wang, F., & Preininger, A. (2019). AI in Health: State of the Art, Challenges, and Future Directions. *Yearbook of Medical Informatics*, *28*(01), 016–026. https://doi.org/DOI: 10.1055/s-0039-1677908

Xu, W., & Ouyang, F. (2022). The application of AI technologies in STEM education: A systematic review from 2011 to 2021. *International Journal of STEM Education*, 9(1), 1–20. DOI: 10.1186/s40594-022-00377-5

Chapter 6

Implementing Artificial Intelligence in Public Administration:
Managing Challenges, Risks, and Opportunities in the Contemporary Context

Antoaneta Stoyanova
https://orcid.org/0000-0002-5186-1498
Univesity of Economics, Varna, Bulgaria

Marieta Stefanova
https://orcid.org/0000-0002-5847-0887
Nikola Vaptsarov Naval Academy, Bulgaria

ABSTRACT

Artificial Intelligence (AI) is rapidly emerging as a critical technology for improving efficiency and innovation in public administration. The implementation of AI is accompanied by many challenges and requires a clear definition of leadership positions and responsibilities in management decision-making. The aim of this study is to examine the main technical, organizational and legal challenges in the implementation of AI in public administration, as well as the role of the various leadership positions in the management of AI initiatives. In accordance with this aim, the study applies an approach inextricably linked to the assessment of RPN (Risk Priority Number) in the implementation of artificial intelligence. The results of the study urge the management of institutions within public administration to search for solutions related to the development and implementation of more effec-

DOI: 10.4018/979-8-3693-8372-8.ch006

tive and innovative tools to deal with the challenges of the present, according to the accepted context.

INTRODUCTION

Each country's adopted policies form the framework for implementing actions aimed at ensuring national, regional and local governance. Their implementation requires interactions between public institutions and the population of the relevant country. The creation of trust between the public and the various institutions within public administration rests on the reliability, security and accessibility of the services provided (Persson, Parker & Widmalm, 2017). Public administration focuses on the needs of society and functions on the basis of organizational structures, processes, roles, relationships, policies and programs. State governance necessitates the implementation of reforms, and the management of reforms is a fundamental element of public administration. The daily interactions between public administration institutions and the citizens of a society consist in the receipt of various services determined by an economic, administrative, social, health or educational context (Ingrams, Piotrowski & Berliner, 2020).

In its report on issues of the quality of public services in individual countries, the European Parliament found that it was directly related to the level of trust in the public administration, the conditions for carrying out business and public well-being (EC, 2016). The quality of public services is also a good indicator of the sustainable functioning of the state as a whole (Marques, Leitão, Carvalho & Pereira, 2021). Administration is defined as a barometer for the sustainability of the economy and the pace of economic development, welfare and guaranteeing people's well-being (Hallerod, Rothstein, Nandy, Daoud, 2013). In the current dynamic and unstable external environment, building and maintaining sustainability of the functions of public institutions is a priority for individual governments. Modern social, technological and economic changes give rise to new expectations in all interested parties towards the provided public services (Petrov, Vasilev, Kuyumdzhiev, Ivanov, 2022). Public administration is now required to monitor the implemented administrative processes and procedures and to receive feedback on the quality of the services provided with a view to improving the administration's activities (EP, 2017). The digitization of processes lays the foundation for digitalization of the activity as the main approach to achieving the desired economic results from the services of the public administration. The provision of digital services to citizens and the subsequent summarization of the resulting information are among the most important prerequisites for making available and providing information to various sectors, especially within business, healthcare, education and welfare.

Already in 2010, it was estimated that the direct impact of freely available data on the EU economy was worth EUR 32 billion, and was predicted to grow every year by 7% (Vickery, Graham, 2011).

The skills to use digital technology are becoming ever more relevant in every context, especially at the workplace, which means that one of the main goals of public administration is to recruit digitally competent personnel who can deal with problems arising from the growing volumes of services provided. Presently, the digitization of the administrative services being provided is directly dependent on the speed and distance of their implementation, while at the same time priority is given to solutions to issues related to the security of the generated data (Martin, 2017). The regulatory framework adopted in Bulgaria requires from the public administration to introduce security management mechanisms for the received, processed and provided information (Cybersecurity Act, 2018). This act of legislation proclaims that the information security system is part of the national security protection system and requires management and organization of the cybersecurity system, which is implemented by the Council of Ministers of the Republic of Bulgaria. The adoption of this framework law is fully harmonized with the requirements of Directive (EU) 2016/1148 and is in line with provisions in force at the EU level (Directive (EU) 2016/1148, 2016). Protection of information and personal data, privacy and confidentiality are essential for increasing trust and accepting the digital services provided by public administration institutions (Jolselt, 2019).

In light of the digital forms of governance in all spheres of the economy, the governments of individual countries have to operate in a demanding and developing digital environment. They face a number of challenges defined by the rapid pace of technological progress and the adoption of emerging technologies (for example, the introduction of artificial intelligence), which must be overcome so as to meet the ever-increasing expectations of citizens for hassle-free, fast and user-oriented services. The digital management of public administration is essential for the change towards automation of processes and services in ways that improve the reliability of the sector. The imposed requirements for digital transformation call for planning fundamental and adaptive governance mechanisms, a reliable and sustainable digital public infrastructure, as well as a forward-looking approach to governance through emerging technologies (OECD, 2024). Artificial Intelligence (AI) is rapidly establishing itself as a critical technology for improving efficiency and innovation in public administration. However, the implementation of AI is accompanied by numerous challenges and requires a clear definition of leadership positions and responsibilities in making management decisions (Sharma, Luthra, Joshi & Kumar, 2022).

The aim of this study is to examine the main technical, organizational and legal challenges in the implementation of AI in public administration, as well as the role of the various leadership positions in the management of AI initiatives. In accordance with this aim, the study applies an approach inextricably linked to the **assessment of RPN** (Risk Priority Number) **in the implementation of artificial intelligence in public administration**. The results of the study urge the management of institutions within public administration to search for solutions related to the development and implementation of more effective and innovative tools to deal with the challenges of the present, according to the accepted context. The applied methodology provides a systematic and objective approach to quantitative presentation of risks and measures taken for the management and mitigation of assessed risks. The obtained results will support the identification of opportunities for improvement and innovation according to the adopted requirements.

IMPLEMENTATION OF POLICIES FOR DIGITIZATION OF PUBLIC ADMINISTRATION

The pandemic also initiated and set the stage for sustainable change through strategic approaches to the digital management of public services. Achieving the effectiveness and efficiency of public sector service delivery requires every government to provide infrastructure and human resources with which to achieve compliance in implementing such changes in line with the digital transformation.

Sustainable and long-term digitization in the public sector requires implementation of established governance mechanisms (Sharik, Deepak Chaitanya, 2020). The introduction of uniform and appropriate approaches to governance, adapted to the rapidly changing conditions of the digital technological environment, is a prerequisite for working out a digital governance strategy (Kuyumdzhiev, 2019).

Measures to support the digitization of public services and e-government include planned resources that comprise a third of the digitization expenditure financed under the mechanism, making e-government and digital public services one of the most funded areas in the plan for recovery and development in the field of digitization, amounting to EUR 53 billion (EC, 2023).

A significant number of reform initiatives across Europe have focused on changes related to consolidation or redistribution of responsibilities in the official structures of public administrations in each member state (Bécue, Praça & Gama, 2021). Very often, changes in top personnel in public administration are determined by a change of the government or the introduction of AI, which ensures the implementation of algorithmic processes embedded in the activity. In most cases, the competence and experience of the human potential manager are overlooked. Actions taken towards changes in the functioning of processes and management in changing the administrative culture are also in such direction.

Regardless of the uniform strategies followed for transformations of public administrations in the EU member states, differences in the sustainability of governance in individual countries have been observed (Trondal, 2021). A survey conducted using sustainable governance indicators reports on the ability of each member state's government to have in place robust public administration policies in terms of performance and accountability. The results indicate that a significant number of countries are still barely implementing their formally adopted provisions for better policy making (Bertelsmann, 2017).

Challenges and Opportunities in the Management of Public Administration Activities

Management in the public administration is centralized at the executive branch level and the leadership of each of the structures of the public administration is deprived of autonomy and independence in making management decisions related to innovations and investments. Institutions very rarely plan independent measures and corrective actions to respond to inconsistencies in their own activities (Buis and Boex, 2015). In addition, they do not have the autonomy to plan their own resources for innovations or real structural reforms in their organizational structure. The provision of resources for the public administration comes from the state budget, and is mostly aimed at providing salaries for the personnel (Administration Act, 1998).

Public administration is the most essential part of the state governance aimed at achieving fulfilment of the adopted requirements. Therefore, in this context, it is necessary to take into account what are the most appropriate measures in the planning and implementation of administrative reforms (Pollitt, Christopher and Bouckaert, Geert, 2011). The application of appropriate management mechanisms in public administration can achieve improvement of the overall management system, through:

- Increasing the work capacity of internal operations by automating complex and recurring administrative processes and procedures;
- Generation, archiving and follow-up analysis of data related to improving the activity of the relevant structure within the scope of public administration;
- Assisting and easing the workload of civil servants at work, freeing up the time of qualified officials and ensuring the reliability of the continuous provision of public services;
- Defining and determining the powers and responsibilities based on planned resources at each administrative level;
- Improving system performance by improving the quality of relationships and collaboration.

The quality of work has to do with management of individual processes within the scope of activity and is directly related to the effectiveness or ineffectiveness of the management of the human resources used. Public administration staff in the EU make up the public sector, which is estimated to employ around 75 million people or around 25% of Europe's workforce (Berman, Bowman, West & Van Wart, 2021). Public expenditure amounts to almost 50% of the gross domestic product (GDP). In a study carried out in 2015, it was reported that the aging of civil servants is the biggest risk for public institutions in the EU. In some countries (Belgium, Spain, Italy) it has been noted that in the next 25 years up to 45% of civil servants will retire. This raises serious concerns about long-term capacity, institutional stability and service quality (Baltic Institute of Social Sciences, 2015). The same study takes into account that the increase in the number of AI users, which is most noticeable in activities involving processing of large data volumes, makes it imperative to introduce measures to organize the activity of the relevant administration (Baltic Institute of Social Sciences, 2015). Human capital has a key role not only in the implementation of reforms in the restructuring of activities, but also in the implementation of digital technologies, including the embedding of AI (Reis, Santo & Melão, 2019). Another study, focused on the use of AI in the manufacturing and financial sectors, shows alarming results regarding the inability of institutions to cope with the deadlines and speed of providing public services from the scope of their activities. This makes it necessary to look for solutions linked to implementation of policies determining the rules, approaches and mechanisms regulating the various requirements for legal and natural persons in the application of AI, by pre-evaluating the various types of risks arising from this (OECD, 2023).

Viewing the activity as a system may be an effective approach to solving problems and managing changes in it, because such approach is laid down as a basic principle in the standards that regulate requirements for management systems. One such well-established framework is the international standard ISO 27001, which is envisaged in the legislation as a basic tool for the building and implementation in public administration of Information Security Management Systems (BDS 27001:2023, 2023). Through its application, it is possible to make planned decisions, which in a subsequent stage can be evaluated as to the extent of their impact on processes and activities. The Information Security Management System in public administration includes many separate processes that influence and interact with each other to varying degrees. Their implementation is aimed at improving the overall performance of the public administration in accordance with the adopted goals (BDS ISO 27000, 2020). This standard stipulates that the fulfilment of the set goals is achieved more effectively when relevant resources and activities are managed as processes and when individual processes function together to craft an integrated response to all requirements by applying a systematic approach.

The management of processes within the scope of the activity of public administration requires defining challenges and opportunities, which are directly dependent on the influence of external and internal factors. These circumstances are very important in the planning of the activity and require that before resources are provided for this, an analysis of the risks arising from the changes in the environment be carried out. It can be summarized that the context of the public administration is bound to the surrounding environment in which it functions (Lapuente, & Van de Walle, 2020). This approach provides for identification of risks from the external and internal environment, especially in the part of applying innovative technological practices and implementation of AI, and therefore it could be concluded that the decisions made at the level of managing the activity of public administration are based on managed risks. A risk assessment is also required when changing processes and activities following a change in the objectives, the context determined by the impact of internal and external factors, the network and communication infrastructure determining the performance of activities by public administration (Ordinance on Network and Information Security, 2019).

According to some authors (Rendon & Rendon, 2015), the activities and processes in public administration can be seen as challenges that bring uncertainty and solutions should therefore be sought with measures to resolve them, such as:

- use an approach to risk assessment and management with adequate measures to control the risks;
- take advantage of the available opportunities to plan risk-related measures;

Risk management (Samani, Ismail & Leman, 2017) as a concept can be defined as the systematic application of policies, procedures and practices to manage activities, exchange information, consult, ascertain the circumstances, as well as the activities carried out for identification, analysis, assessment, engaging, monitoring and review of the risks. Risk is viewed in terms of established principles laid down in international standards (BDS ISO 31000, 2018). Risk management creates value that is preserved.

Risk management is considered as an integral part of the organizational processes within the administration's activity and is imbedded in the adopted regulatory requirements related to the security of information in an electronic environment. According to the provisions of Art. 7 of the Ordinance on the minimum requirements for network and information security in the Republic of Bulgaria, public administration bodies are required to carry out assessment of risks for the network and information security regularly, but not less than once a year, with the aim of reducing losses from incidents by reducing response time. This regulation defines the management of risks for the security of information and communication systems as part of the network and information security management policy.

It can be concluded that risk management is in essence a set of processes for identifying potential threats to information media and assets involved in the provision of electronic services, as well as for analysing and assessing the risks posed by these threats. Based on the risk analysis and assessment, the public administration plans and implements measures and activities to mitigate unacceptable risks by stipulating deadlines, responsible persons and necessary resources for the implementation of such measures.

METHODOLOGY FOR EVALUATING RPN IN THE IMPLEMENTATION OF ARTIFICIAL INTELLIGENCE IN PUBLIC ADMINISTRATION

The application of a standardized and regulator-imposed approach to risk assessment provides for revising the current concepts related to the management of information security activities in the public administration, so as to take into account the advent of Artificial Intelligence (AI). The methodology applied in the present study for assessing RPN (Risk Priority Number) in the implementation of AI in public administration consists of several basic steps adapted to contemporary challenges and opportunities.

1.1. **The first step** includes the identification of possible failures (Failure Modes) in all components and processes related to AI projects. Such analysis covers the entire range of activities and resources required to implement the projects, taking into account both technical and organizational aspects.
1.2. **The second step** is the consequence score (Severity - S) for each identified failure mode. A scale of 1 to 10 is used, where higher values indicate higher severity. This assessment helps determine how critical any potential failure is to the functioning of the public administration.
1.3. **The third step** is estimating the probability (Occurrence - O) of occurrence of each failure mode, also on a scale of 1 to 10. This gives an idea of the frequency of occurrence of such failures and allows to predict the most likely risks.
1.4. **The fourth step** is the evaluation of the possibility to detect (Detection – D) the failure before it occurs, again on a scale of 1 to 10. This score indicates how easy or difficult it is to detect a potential problem before it leads to severe consequences.

1.5. **The final step** is the calculation of the RPN as the product of the three indicators (S, O, D). High RPN values indicate a higher intervention priority. Risks are classified by RPN into four categories:

- very high risk (RPN above 800);
- high risk (RPN 340 to 799);
- moderate risk (RPN 65 to 339);
- low risk (RPN 0 to 64).

This classification allows priority treatment of the most serious and likely risks, while maintaining effective control over less critical aspects. The methodology provides a systematic and objective approach to managing risks arising from the implementation of AI in public administration, while supporting the identification of opportunities for improvement and innovation.

RESEARCH FINDINGS: RISKS AND OPPORTUNITIES FROM THE IMPLEMENTATION OF AI IN PUBLIC ADMINISTRATION

Along with the implementation of measures related to the digitization of processes in public administration, the need to assess the risks related to the management of large data sets is constantly increasing. By applying the methodology, the processes and activities that are seen as challenges or opportunities facing the public administration can be prioritized.

The challenges can be indicatively classified as follows:

- **Technical challenges concerning** the integration of AI with existing systems, thus ensuring cybersecurity and data protection through reliability and accuracy of algorithms.
- **Organizational challenges arise** from the resistance to change among employees, lack of sufficiently qualified personnel to work with AI, as well as the management of generated data and their privacy.
- **Regulatory challenges have to do** with compliance with laws and regulations on data protection, ensuring adherence to ethical aspects in the use of AI, as well as transparency and accountability in decision-making using AI.

The examined and assessed risks comprise most often:

- **Compliance risks** - New climate change compliance obligations may impact information security management systems (ISMS).
- **Risks related to leadership positions and responsibilities** are most often linked to a lack of clearly defined responsibilities, which results in

inconsistencies in the management of AI initiatives, where **insufficient support from senior management** may delay or compromise the implementation of AI. This is a consequence of the inability to adapt to rapid technological changes.

- **Risks associated with maintaining an implemented management system according to the requirements of the ISO 27001 standard** and meeting the requirements related to climate change, which are aimed at ensuring protection from weather events leading to damage to infrastructure and the resulting data loss.

The opportunities may be in turn identified as:

- **Opportunities arising from the implementation of AI aimed at improving the efficiency** and accuracy of administrative processes, reducing the number of employees in sectors dealings with complex tasks, as well as **increasing transparency and accountability** through improved service, with a view to strengthening the ties and trust between public administration and citizens;
- **Opportunities for management through the implementation of a system meeting the requirements of the ISO 27001 standard,** leading to sustainable AI by using innovations that enable the decision-making and task assignment to occur remotely;
- **The efficient execution of each individual operation fused into a single process** is associated with sustainability in the quality of the services provided in the direction of mitigating environmental impact and addressing climate change.

The data in Table 1 show which of the above challenges, opportunities and risks that have been identified, analysed and assessed should take priority. Based on the assessment of the RPN, the types of measures that will be applied to minimize them to an acceptable level are indicated. Depending on the RPN values obtained, it is prioritised and determined which types of risks require the fastest measures to ensure the execution of the processes in line with the adopted requirements. The application of this methodology helps to assess and quantify the severity of the identified risks levels, which is the basis for planning and providing all types of resources (material, financial and human) necessary for implementation of measures to mitigate the risks.

Table 1. Risk assessment and analysis of challenges and opportunities in the activity of public administration

Risk / Aspect	Consequences	Initial RPN					Actions to manage risks and opportunities	Residual RPN				Result of applied measures
		No.	Severity	Occurrence	Detection	Initial RPN		Severity	Occurrence	Detection	Residual RPN	
Technical challenges Integration of AI with existing systems.	– **Failed integration** may cause disruption to ongoing operations. – **Potential data loss** due to incompatibility. – **Increase in costs** to maintain and update the systems. – **Decrease in efficiency** and performance of existing systems. – **Possible issues with security** and privacy of data. – **Negative impact** on the trust of employees and interested parties	1	8	7	6	336	– **Planning and research.** Careful planning and thorough research of existing systems and potential integration points. – **Test stages.** Conduct test stages before the final implementation of AI. – **Staff training.** Train employees to operate with new AI systems and technologies. – **Backup systems.** Provide backup systems and data to prevent data loss. – **Monitoring and evaluation.** Continuous monitoring and evaluation of the integration process for timely detection and solution of problems. – **Cooperation with Experts.** Engage external consultants and experts to ensure a smooth transition	5	4	3	60	After implementing the risk mitigation measures, the residual RPN is significantly reduced, indicating that the risk of technical challenges in integrating AI with existing systems is better managed and controlled.

continued on following page

Table 1. Continued

Risk / Aspect	Consequences	Initial RPN					Actions to manage risks and opportunities	Residual RPN				
		No.	Severity	Occurrence	Detection	Initial RPN		Severity	Occurrence	Detection	Residual RPN	Result of applied measures
Technical challenges Ensuring cybersecurity and data protection.	– Security breaches can lead to **leakage of sensitive information**. – **Loss of trust** by citizens and interested parties. – **Financial losses** from compensations and fines paid. – **Potential legal issues and lawsuits.** – Noncompliance with statutory requirements **and data protection regulations**. – Damage to the reputation of the public administration.	2	9	6	7	378	– **Planning and research.** Conduct in-depth analyses of existing security systems and identifying potential weaknesses. – **Technological solutions.** Implement advanced cybersecurity systems such as firewalls, anti-virus software and data encryption. – **Staff training.** Conduct regular employee training on cybersecurity best practices. – **Monitoring and control.** Continuous monitoring of systems to detect anomalies and suspicious activity. – **Recovery plans.** Develop and implement disaster recovery plans, including backups and breach response strategies. – **Collaboration with experts.** Engage external consultants and experts to conduct security audits and assessments.	6	4	4	96	After implementing the risk mitigation measures, the residual RPN is significantly reduced, indicating that the risk of cyber security and data protection breaches is better managed and controlled.

continued on following page

Table 1. Continued

Risk / Aspect	Consequences	Initial RPN					Actions to manage risks and opportunities	Residual RPN				
		No.	Severity	Occurrence	Detection	Initial RPN		Severity	Occurrence	Detection	Residual RPN	Result of applied measures
Organizational challenges Resistance to change among employees.	– **Reduced productivity and efficiency** due to reluctance to adapt to new technologies. – **Increased turnover** of staff, resulting in a loss of experience and knowledge. – **Aggravation of conflicts** and deterioration of the working atmosphere. – **Extended time** to implement new systems and technologies. – **Decreased motivation** and involvement among employees. – **Potential financial losses** due to reduced efficiency and increased training and change management costs.	4	7	8	7	392	– **Communication and training.** Conduct regular communication campaigns to inform employees about the benefits of the changes and their impact. – **Organize trainings and seminars** to improve qualifications and introduce new technologies. – **Employee involvement.** Involve employees in the decision-making and change planning process. – **Create working groups and committees**, to actively participate in the change process. – **Support and encouragement.** Ensure support and encouragement from senior management. – **Recognition and awards** for employees who actively contribute to the successful implementation of changes. – **Monitoring and feedback.** Constant monitoring of moods and reactions among employees. – **Collect feedback** and suggestions for improvements. – **Phased implementation.** Implement the changes in stages to reduce stress and resistance. – **Pilot projects for testing** of new technologies and processes before their full implementation.	5	5	4	100	After the implementing the risk management measures, the residual RPN is significantly reduced, indicating that the risk of resistance to change among employees is better managed and controlled.

continued on following page

Table 1. Continued

Risk / Aspect	Consequences	Initial RPN					Actions to manage risks and opportunities	Residual RPN				
		No.	Severity	Occurrence	Detection	Initial RPN		Severity	Occurrence	Detection	Residual RPN	Result of applied measures
Lack of enough skilled personnel to operate with AI.	– **Delay in the implementation** and the development of AI projects. – **Inefficient use of AI** technologies, leading to low return on investment. – **Increased costs** for external consultants and services. – **Reduced** competitiveness of public administration. – **Increased risk of errors** and incorrect decisions due to lack of experience and knowledge. – **Potential staff turnover** due to stress and frustration at not being able to cope with tasks.	**5**	**8**	**7**	**6**	**336**	– **Training and development.** Invest in training and development of existing staff through courses, seminars and certification programs. – **Recruiting talent.** Active search for and recruitment of qualified specialists through competitions, partnerships with universities and specialized recruitment agencies. – **Partnerships and collaborations.** Establish partnerships with academic and research institutes to develop knowledge and skills in the field of AI. – **Mentoring and tutorship.** Implement mentoring programs where experienced professionals train and mentor new staff. – **Motivating and retaining staff.** Create talent retention incentives and programs through career development opportunities, competitive salaries and fringe benefits. – **External consultants.** Hire external consultants to cover critical knowledge and skills gaps pending internal capacity building.	**6**	**5**	**4**	**120**	After implementing the risk mitigation measures, the residual RPN is significantly reduced, indicating that the risk of not having enough skilled personnel to work with AI is better managed and controlled.

continued on following page

Table 1. Continued

Risk / Aspect	Consequences	Initial RPN					Actions to manage risks and opportunities	Residual RPN				
		No.	Severity	Occurrence	Detection	Initial RPN		Severity	Occurrence	Detection	Residual RPN	Result of applied measures
Data management and data privacy.	– **Leakage of sensitive information,** which could lead to serious legal and regulatory consequences. – **Loss of public trust and reputation.** – **Financial losses due to fines and compensation.** – **Noncompliance with regulatory requirements and data protection standards.** – **Possible lawsuits and legal issues.** – **Deterioration of internal processes due to ineffective data management.**	6	9	7	6	378	**Implementation of data management policies and procedures:** – Develop and implement strict **policies and procedures** for managing data and data privacy. – **Staff training.** Conduct regular employee training on the importance of data protection and compliance with regulatory requirements. – **Technological solutions.** Implement advanced data protection technologies such as encryption, multi-layer protection and breach detection systems. – **Monitoring and evaluation.** Continuous monitoring and evaluation of data management processes for early detection of weaknesses and vulnerabilities. – **Access and control.** Restrict access to sensitive data to authorized persons only and implement access tracking systems. – **Recovery plans.** Develop data recovery and business continuity plans in the event of incidents.	6	5	4	120	After implementing the risk mitigation measures, the residual RPN is significantly reduced, indicating that the risk of data management and data privacy issues is better managed and controlled.

continued on following page

Table 1. Continued

Risk / Aspect	Consequences	Initial RPN					Actions to manage risks and opportunities	Residual RPN				
		No.	Severity	Occurrence	Detection	Initial RPN		Severity	Occurrence	Detection	Residual RPN	Result of applied measures
Legal challenges Compliance with data protection laws and regulations.	– Failure to comply with regulations can result in severe **legal and financial penalties.** – **Loss of trust** by citizens and interested parties. – **Potential lawsuits** and other legal issues. – **Damage to the reputation** and the good name of the public administration. – **Additional costs** to adapt to regulatory requirements. – **Deterioration of internal processes** and reduced efficiency due to the need for urgent adjustments.	7	9	6	7	378	– **Knowledge of regulations.** Ensure thorough knowledge of existing data protection laws and regulations through consultation with legal experts and staff training. – **Conducting audits.** Conduct regular internal and external regulatory compliance audits and compliance assessment. – **Policy development.** Develop and implement data management policies and procedures in accordance with regulatory requirements. – **Staff training.** Regular employee training on new legal requirements and data protection best practices. – **Technological solutions.** Implement modern data protection technologies that meet regulatory requirements, such as encryption and access control systems. – **Monitoring and evaluation.** Continuous monitoring and assessment of data management processes for timely detection of potential breaches.	6	4	4	96	After implementing the risk mitigation measures, the residual RPN is significantly reduced, indicating that the risk of noncompliance with data protection laws and regulations is better managed and controlled.

continued on following page

Table 1. Continued

Risk / Aspect	Consequences	Initial RPN					Actions to manage risks and opportunities	Residual RPN				
		No.	Severity	Occurrence	Detection	Initial RPN		Severity	Occurrence	Detection	Residual RPN	Result of applied measures
Legal challenges Ethical issues related to the use of AI.	**– Potential violations of citizens' rights and discrimination.** **– Loss of reputation and public trust.** **– Legal sanctions and lawsuits related to ethical violations.** **– Violation of regulatory and ethical standards that may result in regulatory action.** **– Reduced acceptance of AI systems among employees and citizens.** **– Increased costs of dealing with the consequences of ethical violations and restoring trust.**	**8**	**8**	**6**	**7**	**336**	**– Development of ethical guidelines.** Develop and implement ethical guidelines and codes for the use of AI to ensure respect for citizens' rights and non-discrimination. **– Staff training.** Conduct regular training for employees on ethical issues and responsibilities related to the use of AI. **– Monitoring and evaluation.** Continuous monitoring and evaluation of AI systems to detect ethical issues and take corrective measures in a timely manner. **– Establishment of ethics committees.** Establish ethics committees to monitor and evaluate the ethical aspects of AI projects and provide recommendations. **– Transparency and accountability.** Ensure transparency in the use of AI and regularly publish reports on ethical practices and impact. **– Collaboration with experts.** Engage external experts and ethical consultants to evaluate AI projects and ensure compliance with ethical standards.	**5**	**4**	**4**	**80**	After implementing the risk mitigation measures, the residual RPN is significantly reduced, indicating that the risk of ethical issues related to the use of AI is better managed and controlled.

continued on following page

Table 1. Continued

Risk / Aspect	Consequences	Initial RPN					Actions to manage risks and opportunities	Residual RPN				
		No.	Severity	Occurrence	Detection	Initial RPN		Severity	Occurrence	Detection	Residual RPN	Result of applied measures
Risks related to leadership - Inability to adapt to rapid technological changes	– **Lagging in technological development and loss of competitiveness.** – **Inefficient use of resources** and low return on investment in new technologies. – **Loss of trust** by employees and interested parties. – **Increased risk of errors** and incorrect decisions due to outdated technological knowledge and skills. – **Decreased motivation and commitment** among employees due to lack of innovation and modern technology. – **Potential legal and regulatory issues** related to the use of outdated technologies.	12	8	8	7	448	– **Continuous training and development.** Invest in ongoing employee training and development to keep up with the latest technology trends and practices. – **Flexible strategies.** Develop flexible strategies for rapid adaptation to new technologies and market changes. – **Technology partnerships.** Create partnerships with technology companies and experts to have access to the latest innovations and solutions. – **Investments in research and development.** Invest in research and development to drive innovation and improve the organization's technological capabilities. – **Research trends.** Conduct regular research and analysis of technology trends and the market to enable informed decision-making. – **Creation of innovation teams.** Create dedicated innovation teams to focus on implementing new technologies and practices.	5	4	4	80	After implementing the risk mitigation measures, the residual RPN is significantly reduced, indicating that the risk of inability to adapt to rapid technological change is better managed and controlled.

continued on following page

Table 1. Continued

Risk / Aspect	Consequences	Initial RPN					Actions to manage risks and opportunities	Residual RPN				
		No.	Severity	Occurrence	Detection	Initial RPN		Severity	Occurrence	Detection	Residual RPN	Result of applied measures
Risks related to ISO 27001 and climate change: Damage to infrastructure.	**– Damage to data centres and network infrastructure.** **– Loss of access to critical systems and data.** **– Financial losses due to repair and restoration costs.** **– Disruption of normal operational processes.** **– Potential data Loss and service interruption.** **– Violation of information security regulations and standards.**	13	9	7	6	976	– **Risk assessment.** Regular assessment of climate change risks and their impact on infrastructure. – **Recovery plans.** Draw up and implement data recovery and business continuity plans. – **Insurance.** Take out infrastructure insurance against natural disasters and climate events. – **Strengthening the infrastructure.** Invest in strengthening and protecting the physical infrastructure, including data centres and network facilities. – **Alternative locations.** Provide alternative locations and backup data centres to minimize impact in case of damage – **Monitoring and detection.** Implement systems for monitoring and early detection of potential damage and climate risks.	6	4	4	96	After implementing the risk mitigation measures, the residual RPN is significantly reduced, indicating that the risk of damage to infrastructure in the context of ISO 27001 and climate change is better managed and controlled.

continued on following page

Table 1. Continued

Risk / Aspect	Consequences	Initial RPN					Actions to manage risks and opportunities	Residual RPN				
		No.	Severity	Occurrence	Detection	Initial RPN		Severity	Occurrence	Detection	Residual RPN	Result of applied measures
isks related to ISO 27001 Supply chain issues Unavailability of hardware and services.	**– Delay in delivery of critical components and services.** **– Inefficient functioning of information systems due to lack of necessary hardware.** **– Increased costs of finding alternative suppliers and components.** **– Disruption of planned projects and operations.** **– Increased risk of using unsafe or poor quality components.** **– Loss of trust by customers and interested parties.**	14	8	7	6	336	**– Diversification of suppliers.** Establish a network of reliable suppliers to reduce dependence on a single source. **– Maintaining stockpile.** Maintain strategic stockpile of critical components and hardware to reduce the impact of delays. **– Supply chain analysis.** Regular supply chain risk analysis and assessment, including identification of potential weaknesses and threats. **– Contractual agreements.** Enter into contracts with suppliers that include continuity of supply and compensation for delays clauses. **– Investments in local suppliers:** Invest in and collaborate with local suppliers to reduce the risk of global disruptions. **– Supply monitoring.** Continuous monitoring of supplies and maintaining close relationships with suppliers to promptly identify problems.	5	4	4	80	After implementing the risk mitigation measures, the residual RPN is significantly reduced, indicating that the risk of supply chain issues and unavailability of hardware and services in the context of ISO 27001 is better managed and controlled.

continued on following page

Table 1. Continued

Risk / Aspect	Consequences	Initial RPN					Actions to manage risks and opportunities	Residual RPN				
		No.	Severity	Occurrence	Detection	Initial RPN		Severity	Occurrence	Detection	Residual RPN	Result of applied measures
Risks related to ISO 27001 - Overheat protection costs.	– **Increased operating costs** to maintain the required temperature in data centres. – **Inefficiency of the cooling systems**, leading to potential hardware damage. – **Reduced performance** and service interruptions due to equipment overheating. – **Financial losses** due to increased costs for electricity and maintenance of cooling systems. – **Potential legal and regulatory issues,** if safety requirements are not met. – **Reduced hardware longevity due to consistently high temperatures.**	**15**	**8**	**6**	**7**	**336**	– **Investing in efficient cooling systems.** Invest in modern, energy-efficient cooling systems that minimize costs and maximize efficiency. – **Temperature monitoring.** Implement continuous temperature monitoring systems in data centres for early detection of potential problems. – **Energy efficiency.** Optimise the energy efficiency of the infrastructure by using green technologies and practices to reduce energy consumption. – **Regular maintenance.** Conduct regular maintenance and inspections of cooling systems to ensure they are operating optimally. – **Backup cooling systems.** Provide backup cooling systems to prevent overheating in case of main system failure.	**5**	**5**	**4**	**80**	After implementing the risk mitigation measures, the residual RPN is significantly reduced, indicating that the risk of incurring overheat protection costs in the context of ISO 27001 is better managed and controlled.

continued on following page

Table 1. Continued

Risk / Aspect	Consequences	Initial RPN					Actions to manage risks and opportunities	Residual RPN				
		No.	Severity	Occurrence	Detection	Initial RPN		Severity	Occurrence	Detection	Residual RPN	Result of applied measures
Risks related to ISO 27001 Power failure that threatens data integrity and availability.	**– Loss of access to critical systems and data.** **– Hardware and software damage due to unexpected interruptions.** **– Disruption of normal operational processes.** **– Potential data loss and breach of data integrity.** **– Financial losses due to interruption of services and need for recovery.** **– Reduced trust by customers and interested parties.**	16	9	7	6	378	**– Uninterruptible Power Supply (UPS).** Install uninterruptible power supplies (UPS) for critical systems to provide temporary power supply during outages. **– Backup power generators.** Provide backup generators to be activated automatically in the event of main power failure. **– Regular maintenance and testing.** Conduct regular maintenance and testing of UPS systems and generators to ensure their reliability. **– Data duplication.** Duplicate data in different locations to ensure its availability in case of interruption. **– Power supply monitoring.** Install power supply monitoring systems to warn of potential problems before they lead to outages. **– Disaster recovery plans.** Develop and implement disaster recovery plans that include power outage scenarios and rapid recovery steps.	6	4	4	96	After implementing the risk mitigation measures, the residual RPN is significantly reduced, indicating that the risk of power failure threatening the integrity and availability of data, in the context of ISO 27001, is better managed and controlled.

continued on following page

Table 1. Continued

Risk / Aspect	Consequences	Initial RPN					Actions to manage risks and opportunities	Residual RPN				Result of applied measures
		No.	Severity	Occurrence	Detection	Initial RPN		Severity	Occurrence	Detection	Residual RPN	
AI deployment opportunities: Freeing up human resources to perform more complex tasks	– **Increased productivity** and efficiency of the organization. – **Increased employee motivation** and satisfaction through relief from routine tasks. – **Improved quality of services provided by focusing** on more strategic and creative tasks. – **Improved innovation and strategic planning.** – **Better use of human capital and development of new skills.** – **Reduced operating costs** and increased return on investment.	18	8	8	7	448	– **Task analysis.** Identify routine and repetitive tasks that can be automated using AI. – **Implementation of AI solutions.** Implement AI solutions to automate the identified routine tasks. – **Training and retraining.** Train and retrain employees to perform more complex and strategic tasks. – **Reallocation of resources.** Reallocate human resources to areas where higher skills and strategic thinking are needed. – **Monitoring and evaluation.** Continuous monitoring and evaluation of the effectiveness of AI solutions and their impact on productivity and efficiency. – **Innovative projects.** Encourage employees to participate in innovative projects and initiatives that require creativity and strategic thinking.	4	4	3	48	After implementing the measures to utilize the opportunities, the residual RPN is significantly reduced, indicating that the opportunity to free up human resources to perform more complex tasks through the implementation of AI is better managed and realized.

continued on following page

Table 1. Continued

Risk / Aspect	Consequences	Initial RPN					Actions to manage risks and opportunities	Residual RPN				
		No.	Severity	Occurrence	Detection	Initial RPN		Severity	Occurrence	Detection	Residual RPN	Result of applied measures
AI deployment opportunities: Creating new jobs and developing new competencies among employees	– **Improving the qualification** and the professional development of employees. – **Creation of new jobs** related to the development, management and maintenance of AI systems. – **Increased employee motivation and commitment** by providing training and career development opportunities. – **Improving the innovation capacity** of the organization by implementing new technologies and approaches. – **Strengthening organizational culture** and attracting talent. Expanding the scope of services provided by the organization through the use of AI.	20	7	8	7	392	– **Training and development of employees.** Organise courses and training for employees aimed at acquiring new skills in the field of AI and digital technologies. – **Creation of new jobs.** Define and create new job positions related to the development, implementation and management of AI systems. – **Partnerships with academic institutions.** Cooperation with universities and training centres to develop specialized AI programs and courses. – **Stimulating innovation.** Encourage employees to participate in innovation projects and initiatives that include AI technologies. – **Career development.** Develop career paths that include opportunities for career growth in AI and related technologies. – **Monitoring and evaluation.** Continuous monitoring and evaluation of the effectiveness of training programs and their impact on the development of employee competencies.	4	4	3	48	After implementing the measures to utilize the opportunities, the residual RPN is significantly reduced, indicating that the opportunity to create new jobs and develop new competencies among employees through the implementation of AI is better managed and realized.

continued on following page

Table 1. Continued

Risk / Aspect	Consequences	Initial RPN No.	Severity	Occurrence	Detection	Initial RPN	Actions to manage risks and opportunities	Residual RPN Severity	Occurrence	Detection	Residual RPN	Result of applied measures
AI deployment opportunities: Strengthening ties and trust between public administration and citizens through improved service	– **Increased trust of citizens** in public administration. – **Increased satisfaction** of citizens through faster and more accurate service. – **Improved interaction** between the administration and the citizens. – **Reducing bureaucracy** and facilitating access to public services. – **Increased transparency** and accountability in the work of the administration. – **Strengthening public support** and the legitimacy of public administration.	**21**	**8**	**8**	**7**	**448**	– **Implementing AI in service.** Implement AI technologies to automate routine administrative tasks and provide faster and more accurate services to citizens. – **Development of interactive platforms.** Create interactive platforms and chatbots to respond to citizens' queries in real time. – **Staff training.** Train employees in the use of AI technologies to improve service and communication with citizens. – **Feedback monitoring.** Systematic collection and analysis of citizen feedback on services provided and identification of areas for improvement. – **Increasing transparency.** Publish information about processes and procedures in the administration, as well as the results of AI analyses to increase transparency. – **Improving access to services.** Develop mobile applications and online portals to facilitate citizens' access to administrative services.	**4**	**4**	**3**	**48**	After implementing the measures to utilize the opportunities, the residual RPN is significantly reduced, indicating that the opportunity to strengthen the ties and trust between the public administration and citizens through improved AI-supported service is better managed and realized.

continued on following page

Table 1. Continued

Risk / Aspect	Consequences	Initial RPN					Actions to manage risks and opportunities	Residual RPN				
		No.	Severity	Occurrence	Detection	Initial RPN		Severity	Occurrence	Detection	Residual RPN	Result of applied measures
ISO 27001 opportunities Sustainable AI Increased need for energy-efficient IT services focused on sustainability	– **Reduction of operating costs** through increased energy efficiency. – **Improving environmental sustainability** and reducing the carbon footprint. – **Increasing competitiveness** by implementing modern and sustainable technologies. – **Improving the image** of the organization as environmentally responsible and sustainable. – **Attracting more customers and partners,** who value sustainability. – **Creating new opportunities for innovation** in the field of energy efficiency and sustainable IT solutions.	**22**	**8**	**8**	**7**	**448**	– **Implementation of energy-efficient technologies.** Implement modern, energy-efficient IT solutions and infrastructure. – **Energy monitoring and management.** Use energy consumption monitoring and management systems to optimize energy efficiency. – **Adoption of sustainability policies.** Adopt and implement policies and procedures aimed at increasing sustainability and energy efficiency. – **Training and development.** Educate employees on the importance of energy efficiency and sustainability and promote good practices. – **Cooperation with external partners** and suppliers to implement sustainable technologies and solutions. – **Invest in research and innovation** for the development of new, sustainable IT services and solutions.	**4**	**4**	**3**	**48**	After implementing the measures to utilize the opportunities, the residual RPN is significantly reduced, indicating that the opportunity for sustainable AI and the increased need for energy-efficient IT services focused on sustainability is better managed and realized.

continued on following page

Table 1. Continued

Risk / Aspect	Consequences	Initial RPN					Actions to manage risks and opportunities	Residual RPN				Result of applied measures
		No.	Severity	Occurrence	Detection	Initial RPN		Severity	Occurrence	Detection	Residual RPN	
ISO 27001 opportunities Remote decision-making Transition to remote work offers opportunities to ensure remote decision-making	**– Increasing the flexibility and adaptability of the organization.** **– Increasing efficiency through faster and better-informed decision-making.** **– Reduction of costs** for physical infrastructure and travel. **– Increasing employee satisfaction** through the possibility of remote work. **– Ensuring continuity** of business in emergency situations. **– Increasing competitiveness** by reacting more quickly to market changes.	24	7	8	7	392	**– Implementation of remote work technologies.** Implement secure and reliable remote work and video conferencing platforms. **– Staff training.** Train employees to effectively use remote work and decision-making technologies. **– Security and compliance.** Ensure high levels of cybersecurity and ISO 27001 compliance when working remotely. **– Business continuity plans.** Develop and test business continuity plans that include remote decision making. **– Monitoring and evaluation.** Continuous monitoring and evaluation of the effectiveness of remote processes and decision-making. **– Investing in IT infrastructure.** Invest in modern IT infrastructure to support effective remote decision-making.	4	4	3	48	After implementing the measures to utilize the opportunities, the residual RPN is significantly reduced, indicating that the remote decision-making capability in the context of ISO 27001 is better managed and realized.

continued on following page

Table 1. Continued

Risk / Aspect	Consequences	Initial RPN					Actions to manage risks and opportunities	Residual RPN				
		No.	Severity	Occurrence	Detection	Initial RPN		Severity	Occurrence	Detection	Residual RPN	Result of applied measures
ISO 27001 opportunities Sustainability in the quality of the services provided. Addressing climate change increases brand value and customer loyalty.	– **Increasing quality** by demonstrating a commitment to sustainability and environmental responsibility. – **Strengthening the loyalty of customers** who value sustainable practices and environmental responsibility -**Strengthening the reputation** of the organization as a leader in sustainable IT services. – **Attracting new customers** and partners looking for environmentally responsible solutions. – **Increasing competitiveness** in the market through innovation and sustainable practices. Improving internal processes and efficiency by implementing sustainable technologies.	**26**	**8**	**7**	**7**	**392**	– **Implementation of sustainable practices.** Implement sustainable practices in all aspects of IT service delivery, including energy efficiency and carbon footprint reduction. – **Training and development.** Train employees on the importance of sustainability and environmental responsibility and promote good practices. – **Communication and marketing.** Actively communicate the organization's commitment to sustainability through marketing campaigns and communication strategies. – **Monitoring and evaluation.** Continuous monitoring and assessment of the sustainability of the services provided and their impact on the environment. – **Collaboration with partners.** Collaborate with partners and customers to develop sustainable IT solutions and services. – **Investing in research and innovation.** Invest in research and innovation to develop new sustainable technologies and improve the quality of services provided.	**4**	**4**	**3**	**48**	After implementing the measures to utilize the opportunities, the residual RPN is significantly reduced, indicating that the opportunity for sustainability in the quality of services provided and for increasing brand value and customer loyalty by addressing climate change in the context of ISO 27001 is better managed and realized.

The main challenges assessed as moderate risk are overcoming the *Technical challenges* of the integration of AI with existing systems, ensuring cybersecurity and data protection to achieve reliability and accuracy of algorithms. The reliability and security of information is directly related to the trust of users and interested parties and depends on the fulfilment of the legal requirements and regulations regarding cybersecurity and data protection.

Data loss is most often the result of hardware defects or failures of various types (for example: from overheating and lack of cooling, periodic failures caused by lack of maintenance and renovation, failure of the electrical supply and lack of backup power equipment).

Control over the effective implementation of these measures is aimed at minimizing the risk. The effect achieved after applying the planned measures is carefully monitored. The quantification of the effect of such actions is done by re-estimating the residual risk (residual RPN). If residual risk values are in the range that requires monitoring, follow up mechanisms need to be implemented to monitor this residual risk. This means that residual risk is managed and actions are implemented effectively. The measures taken to minimize the initial RPN related to the technical challenges are aimed at planning and researching existing systems, testing before implementation of AI, monitoring and evaluation of the integration process with the provided reliable infrastructure.

Continuous monitoring, implementation of technological solutions in accordance with the concrete practice in the digital infrastructure and constant monitoring of the data archiving process require staff training and the purchase of data archiving equipment, and are considered a necessary condition for the residual value of RPN for technical challenges (from 336 to 378) to decrease to a minimal risk level (up to 60-80).

The loss of data can also be due to insufficient capabilities for archiving the generated information, which in most cases is due to a lack of financial resources to purchase facilities or cloud space for storing data generated from the processes. Regardless of the components used in the digital infrastructure and the forms of archiving, in case of incorrect planning and organization of the data archiving activities and processes, critical inconsistencies related to the documented information and its management in general may occur. If these challenges are not taken into account, such management will, instead of reducing the values of RPN in the direction of controlling and minimizing the risk, lead to increased risk.

The organizational challenges also comprise moderate risk with RPN values of 336 to 392 and are caused by employee resistance to the digital changes in operations that are being implemented to ensure speed in the provision of each individual service. The resistance is dictated by the lack of digital skills on the part of employees, high staff turnover and lack of qualified staff to maintain and update new digitized technological solutions for the performance of the activity. The adequate identification and assessment of all specific risks for the activity of the public administration is adversely affected by the shortage or complete absence of qualified and experienced personnel capable of implementing digital technologies for the performance of the activity.

Risk management actions often include additional trainings, bringing in external experts, collaborating on software development and implementation or hiring external digital infrastructure support services. The use of AI in the digitization of public administration activities necessitates improvement of workforce skills, and therefore staff training is one of the best options for public administrations to cope with these challenges and in particular with the management of digital infrastructure.

Among the significant challenges, also posing a moderate risk, are the challenges related to solving the *ethical issues* that arise with the implementation of AI, in terms of compliance with accepted ethical standards and regulatory norms. If the measures to minimize the risk fail to mitigate the consequences, it can be concluded that the lack of adopted ethical codes for the use of AI can be considered as a violation of the rights of citizens and the cause of the resulting legal and financial sanctions to the public administration body.

Many of the assessed risks (see Table 1) constitute high risk (with RPN values from 336 to 446) and are defined as risks from the organization's activities, i.e. they can be identified as *organizational and management risks*, which are most often associated with leadership and managerial decision-making on AI initiatives. The consequences from this risk may lead to a lack of transparency and accountability due to unclearly defined responsibilities and powers for the performance of the activity, as well as to inconsistencies in the fulfilment of the requirements related to the activity. The lack of a management strategy can lead to an inability to adapt to rapid technological changes and delay the implementation of AI.

The opportunities from implementing AI are considered and evaluated as aspects with high-level of the values of the initial RPN (from 392 to 448) and are related to improving the efficiency and accuracy of administrative processes, as well as to strengthening ties and trust between public administration and citizens. The actions consist in implementation of AI technologies in order to automate routine administrative tasks and provide faster and more accurate services to citizens through real-time interactive platforms and chatbots. The application of such measures makes it possible to systematically collect and analyse data from citizen feedback on the services provided by the public administration and to identify specific areas for improvement. In this way, improved service and continuity of the provided digital services are ensured due to better data storage and improvement of the necessary infrastructure. When applying these measures, it is taken into account that the value of the residual RPN is 48. Based on the assessed risks, the possibility of sustainable AI and an increased need for energy-efficient IT services, measures are taken with focus on sustainability.

One of the important aspects of risk assessment is the *opportunities from implementing AI* with a view to improving the *efficiency and accuracy of administrative processes*. Improving the accountability and traceability of the obtained results is directly dependent on the appropriate management of the administration's activity by applying a systematic approach per the requirements of the ISO 27001 standard. The use of standardized approaches to managing the digitization of processes in the activity of the public administration is one of the main opportunities to carry out an activity that is planned, organized and controlled according to the regulatory requirements and the challenges of the environment in which it is carried out. This is how transparency and obtaining of objective, evidence-based results is achieved (the residual RPN may drop from 392 to 48).

The development and implementation of controls to prevent, detect or remove (mitigate) the risk, which are aimed at eliminating the causes of the risk, requires most often ongoing training of personnel, implementing systems for monitoring and managing climate risks that affect IT infrastructure, energy consumption monitoring and management systems to optimize energy efficiency, as well as working out and testing disaster recovery plans that include innovative approaches and technologies.

Climate change often causes extreme weather events and fires, which are extremely risky for the operation of digital infrastructure and can result in failures and the ensuing data loss.

In the case of public administrations where an information security management system has been implemented according to the requirements of the 27001 standard, measures and programs are applied, containing emergency response plans and emergency response readiness tests.

The assessment of the challenges, opportunities and risks inherent to the management of the activity allows for a constant monitoring and subsequent reassessment of the effectiveness of the applied measures and how the available opportunities are utilized. This process is the basis of the planning, organization and control of the activity of each institution within public administration.

CONCLUSION

The application of approaches laid down in established international standards creates conditions for the development of a modern information security management system at the organizational and operational level. By assessing the challenges, the opportunities can be identified and the RPN values for the relevant risk that may affect the activity of the public administration can be quantified.

The requirements of the national legislation regarding the security of information and generated data make it necessary to identify, assess and manage all manifested risks directly affecting public trust in the activities of public administration.

The measures identified in the study are aimed at mitigating or controlling the assessed risks and are directed toward minimizing the residual RPN values. Quantitative results have been obtained from how the application of new technological practices or new technological equipment, along with deployment of AI in the activity of public administration, will achieve adaptability to modern dynamic technological challenges.

The importance of information security management systems for managing the activity in the public administration sectors is one of the essential tools for dealing with the challenges of digitization of the management of various sectors of the economic, social and public development of each country.

A comprehensive situational assessment process is needed to cover not only the technological issues but also to align them with the management activities of each sector within the scope of public administration.

By determining the scope and impact of the applied risk assessment approaches when implementing artificial intelligence in public administration, the specific features of the individual challenges and opportunities are defined, which can be explored to ensure both the security of the generated information and the trust of all interested parties.

The transition to strategically planned public administration activities through the use of innovative technologies and AI reveals many challenges, but at the same time many opportunities. Technologies have the very important task of digitization and e-governance of various sectors of a country, and it is the assessment of such challenges and opportunities that drives our interest in this issue. The implementation of digital technologies is related to continuous change, which is initiated by the citizens' increasing need for accessible, fast and easily obtained administrative services. Managing activities and maintaining the trust of service users present public administrations with challenges that require quick and urgent measures.

REFERENCES

. Administration Act. Prom. SG No. 130 of 5 November 1998, add. SG No. 88 of 20 October 2023, add. SG No. 33 of 12 April 2024, Counsil of Ministers.

BDS EN ISO/IEC 27000:2020 Information technology. Security techniques. Information security management systems. Overview and vocabulary. BIS. Sofia

BDS EN ISO/IEC 27001:2023 Information security, cybersecurity and privacy protection. Information security management systems. Requirements. BIS. 2023

BDS ISO 31000:2018. Risk Management - a Practical Guide. BIS, Sofia, 2018

Bécue, A., Praça, I., & Gama, J. (2021). Artificial intelligence, cyber-threats and Industry 4.0: Challenges and opportunities. *Artificial Intelligence Review*, 54(5), 3849–3886. DOI: 10.1007/s10462-020-09942-2

Berman, E. M., Bowman, J. S., West, J. P., & Van Wart, M. R. (2021). *Human resource management in public service: Paradoxes, processes, and problems*. Cq Press.

Buis, H., & Boex, J. (2015). *Improving local government performance by strengthening their 5 core capabilities*. VNG International.

Calvino, Fl., Samek, L., Squicciarini, M., & Morris, C. (2020). Identifying and characterising AI adopters: A novel approach based on big data. ECD Science, Technology and Industry Working Papers 2022/06.

Halleröd, B., Rothstein, B., Daoud, A., & Nandy, S. (2013). Bad governance and poor children: A comparative analysis of government efficiency and severe child deprivation in 68 low-and middle-income countries. *World Development*, 48, 19–31.

Ingrams, A., Piotrowski, S., & Berliner, D. (2020). Learning from our mistakes: Public management reform and the hope of open government. *Perspectives on Public Management and Governance*, 3(4), 257–272. DOI: 10.1093/ppmgov/gvaa001

Jolselt, J. (2019). Information society: Its meanings and implications. Journal of Library. *Science Education and Learning Technology*, 1(1), 181–190.

Kuyumdzhiev, I. (2019). Metodologicheski i tehnologichni aspekti pri arhiviraneto na bazi danni. Varna: Nauka i ikonomika. p. 178. (Library Prof. Tsani Kalyandzhiev; Book 55).

Lapuente, V., & Van de Walle, S. (2020). The effects of new public management on the quality of public services. *Governance: An International Journal of Policy, Administration and Institutions*, 33(3), 461–475. DOI: 10.1111/gove.12502

Marques, I., Leitão, J., Carvalho, A., & Pereira, D. (2021). Public administration and values oriented to sustainability: A systematic approach to the literature. *Sustainability (Basel)*, 13(5), 2566. DOI: 10.3390/su13052566

Martin, W. (2017). *The global information society*. Taylor & Francis. DOI: 10.4324/9781315239385

OECD. (2023). *"Common guideposts to promote interoperability in AI risk management", OECD Artificial Intelligence Papers, No. 5*. OECD Publishing., DOI: 10.1787/ba602d18-

OECD. (2024). *"2023 OECD Digital Government Index: Results and key findings", OECD Public Governance Policy Papers, No. 44*. OECD Publishing., DOI: 10.1787/1a89ed5e-

Persson, T., Parker, C. F., & Widmalm, S. (2017). Social trust, impartial administration and public confidence in EU crisis management institutions. *Public Administration*, 95(1), 97–114. DOI: 10.1111/padm.12295

Petrov, P., Vasilev, Yu., Kuyumdzhiev, I., & Ivanov, S. Digitalizacia na procesite na upravlenie na obrazovatelnite uslugi v universitetska sreda. Varna: University Press Science and Economics, 2022, p. 134., ISBN (print) 978-954-21-1132-0 /

Pollitt, C., & Bouckaert, G. (2011), Public Management Reform: A Comparative Analysis. Oxford University Press, 2011.

Reis, J., Santo, P. E., & Melão, N. (2019). Impacts of artificial intelligence on public administration: A systematic literature review. In *2019 14th Iberian conference on information systems and technologies (CISTI)* (pp. 1-7). IEEE. DOI: 10.23919/CISTI.2019.8760893

Rendon, R. G., & Rendon, J. M. (2015). Auditability in public procurement: An analysis of internal controls and fraud vulnerability. *International Journal of Procurement Management*, 8(6), 710–730. DOI: 10.1504/IJPM.2015.072388

Samani, M. A., Ismail, N., & Leman, Z. (2017). Development of a conceptual model for risk-based quality management system. *Total Quality Management & Business Excellence*, 14(4), 1–16.

Sharik, N., & Deepak Chaitanya, M. (2020). Design and Fabrication of Fuel Level Monitoring & Alert System using IoT / N. Sharik, M. Deepak Chaitanya [IJERT]. *International Journal of Engineering Research & Technology (Ahmedabad)*, 9(10), 442–444.

Sharma, M., Luthra, S., Joshi, S., & Kumar, A. (2022). Implementing challenges of artificial intelligence: Evidence from public manufacturing sector of an emerging economy. *Government Information Quarterly*, 39(4), 101624. DOI: 10.1016/j.giq.2021.101624

The Study on the Future Role and Development of the Public Administration. (2015). *Baltic Institute of Social Sciences*. RIGA.

Trondal, J. (2021). Public administration sustainability and its organizational basis. *International Review of Administrative Sciences*, 87(2), 399–415. DOI: 10.1177/0020852319869430

Vickery, G. (2011). *Review of recent studies on PSI re-use and related market developments*. Information Economics.

KEY TERMS AND DEFINITIONS

Context of the Organization: The combination of internal and external circumstances that may influence the organization's approach to developing and achieving its goals.

Interested Parties: A person or organization that may influence, be influenced by, or be perceived as affected by a decision or activity.

Risk: Effect of uncertainty.

Digitization: A process of continuous change brought about by the increasing use of digital technologies.

Management System: A set of purposeful and coordinated actions and processes, through which the achievement of the administration's goals and the improvement of the efficiency and effectiveness its functions are ensured by using appropriate analytical tools in view of the specifics of the activity and the needs of the interested parties.

Public Administration: An organization, regardless of the legal form of incorporation, providing public services.

Chapter 7
Innovative Intelligence AI Tools Transforming Public Service Excellence

Tarun Sai Raavi
Vishwa Vishwani Institute of Systems and Management, India

Ramanchi Radhika
GITAM University, India

C. Shree Charan
GITAM University, India

ABSTRACT

This chapter provides a comprehensive framework for the implementation of Artificial Intelligence (AI) in public administration. It highlights the growing importance of AI technologies in improving public services, while emphasizing the need for a systematic approach to their deployment, also examines the literature on AI frameworks, outlines the basic benefits and risks of AI in public administration, and suggests guidelines for responsible implementation. It also seeks to provide a comprehensive understanding of the effective integration of AI tools in public management to enhance public value while upholding ethical standards.

1. INTRODUCTION

The rapid advancement of Artificial Intelligence (AI) technology has profoundly impacted many fields, including public administration. Governments face increasing demands for efficient service delivery, transparency and accountability, making AI

DOI: 10.4018/979-8-3693-8372-8.ch007

a promising tool for improving public management processes. AI can analyze vast datasets, identify trends, and generate insights to guide policymaking, improve resource allocation, and assess service needs, thereby increasing citizen participation and decision-making. Implementing AI in public administration poses ethical and regulatory hurdles such as data privacy issues, algorithmic bias and accountability.

1.1. Focus of the Study

This study presents an integrated AI architecture tailored to the unique challenges of public administration in AI implementation. The framework strives to optimize service delivery and operational efficiency while addressing ethical considerations and promoting public value generation. It emphasizes the importance of collaboration between scholars, practitioners and policy makers in disciplines such as economics, political science and administrative sciences. The research underscores the need for ethical guidelines to manage regulatory issues linked to AI technologies. Additionally, accountability is an important focus, addressing issues related to decision-making processes, data use, and algorithmic bias. The suggested framework includes criteria and monitoring and review mechanisms to ensure transparency in decision-making. Ultimately, this study aims to provide a blueprint for government agencies to effectively integrate AI while maintaining ethical governance and enhancing outcomes for citizens.

Research highlights various benefits of AI, including improved efficiency, better decision-making and improved service delivery. However, it also brings potential problems such as ethical considerations, data privacy difficulties and the need for government regulation. The evaluation concludes with the establishment of guidelines for the safe and appropriate use of AI in public services. These principles emphasize the need for openness, accountability and stakeholder engagement in the use of AI technologies. The many research gaps in this area of analysis call for more in-depth research and experimentation, which demonstrates great interest in better understanding the implications of using AI for the public sector, as it is argued that it can be greatly enhanced. Policy formulation, improving public service delivery and strengthening internal management, we elaborate in the following sections based on an extensive review of literature and cases.

1.2 Objectives of the Study

1. To explore the value of each component of an integrated AI framework in the context of public administration, highlighting the importance of monitoring and control systems.

2. To examine the economic implications of AI adoption in public management, including analyzing cost-effectiveness and improving resource allocation.
3. To establish an integrated AI framework that synthesizes the many AI applications and their implications for public administration will serve as a basic model for enhancing public services.
4. To analyze the standards and design concepts that guide the technological development and deployment of AI systems, ensuring that they are reliable, efficient and user-friendly.

2. ADVANTAGES AND DISADVANTAGES OF AI IMPLEMENTATION

The adoption of AI in public administration offers many benefits, but it also introduces risks that need to be carefully managed:

2.1 Benefits

Increased Efficiency

AI can automate routine tasks, improve service delivery and save both time and resources. By automating repetitive processes, lowering administrative costs, and freeing up staff members to concentrate on high-impact duties, artificial intelligence (AI) simplifies internal operations in public administration.

- AI has the ability to improve the efficacy and efficiency of public policy, as evidenced by its use in economic crisis policymaking
- AI applications in agriculture, especially in vertical farming, promote sustainability, efficiency, and productivity.
- AI in public accounting safe integration of AI in construction, which benefits project monitoring, quality control, and design optimization while addressing risk management issues including data privacy and quality, green AI may be used to plan cities sustainably
- AI supports automation in public agencies and reduces human error and improves decision-making. In citizen and employee interactions, conversational AI and augmented communication optimize approaches, leading to higher customer satisfaction
- AI's ability to detect anomalies such as threat detection and fraud protection with 24/7 monitoring increases security and reduces risks by enabling proactive measures.

- AI for Social Protection: digital technologies are used in welfare services, focusing on issues like accountability, equity, and efficiency AI improves regulatory measures and public safety by preventing fraud in bureaucratic processes and improving decision-making.

Better Decision-Making

AI systems can rapidly evaluate enormous datasets, generating insights that benefit decision-making processes. AI advances applications in energy efficiency, public health, social welfare, and transportation, which benefits society. It raises the standard of living by promoting sustainability, optimizing resources, and improving service quality. AI in agriculture emphasizes its role in advancing social welfare by supporting sustainability and food security. AI can help decision-making by empowering insight-driven actions, predictive analytics and public servants, resulting in more informed decisions, better strategic planning and better problem-solving.

Better Service Quality

AI applications can personalize services and provide more responsive solutions to citizens' needs. By streamlining processes, cutting expenses, and improving service accessibility, AI enhances government services. Its role in early identification, resource management, and improved support services is demonstrated by applications in criminal justice, healthcare, and education. AI solves resource constraints and boosts delivery efficiency while fortifying democratic legitimacy, accountability, and policymaking.

AI increases citizen participation which increases citizen happiness and involvement by fostering efficiency, transparency, trust, and adaptability. Self-service technologies and virtual assistants are examples of AI-based solutions that provide social value, quick task completion, and tailored experiences.

Cost Savings

By automating many procedures and optimizing the use of resources, AI can lead to significant cost reductions in government operations. Through cost reductions, automation, and increased efficiency across a range of industries, AI generates financial gains. It contributes to economic growth by increasing productivity in e-government, smart cities, and agriculture. AI also benefits the financial and auditing industries, freeing up specialists to concentrate on activities that generate value.

2.2 Risks

Data Privacy Issues

Processing sensitive personal data, such as medical records, financial data, and behavioral patterns, is frequently necessary when using AI. Because breaches or misuse of such data could result in identity theft, financial fraud, or even harm to one's reputation, this presents serious privacy and security issues. Furthermore, people are reluctant to share their information with AI systems due to ambiguous data governance policies and weak encryption standards, which worsen risks. Strict data protection regulations, like the GDPR, are designed to allay these worries, but different firms' compliance levels result in different protections.

Displacement of Jobs

AI's ability to automate laborious and repetitive processes could result in a large loss of jobs, especially in sectors like manufacturing, retail, and administrative services. In order to assist displaced workers in acquiring new skills appropriate for developing roles in a technology-driven economy, this change calls for workforce retraining. However, there are educational, financial, and logistical obstacles to putting large-scale retraining initiatives into action. Transitions are made more difficult by psychological effects including job uncertainty and unwillingness to change, in addition to economic displacement. In order to develop inclusive strategies that strike a balance between workforce well-being and technological growth, policymakers and organizations must work together.

Absence of Openness

Artificial intelligence systems frequently include intricate structures, such deep learning networks that function as "black boxes" and make it challenging to understand how they make decisions. Users may become distrustful of this lack of openness, particularly in high-stakes industries where accountability is essential, such as healthcare, law enforcement, and financial services. Users and stakeholders lose faith in an AI system's fairness and dependability when they are unable to comprehend how it makes its decisions. To allay these worries and guarantee ethical use, explainable AI (XAI) technologies must be developed and explicit algorithmic accountability requirements must be put in place.

Discrimination and Bias

AI systems rely heavily on the caliber of the data they use for training. The resulting algorithms may reinforce and even magnify historical biases or societal injustices reflected in the training data. Biased employment algorithms, for example, may disadvantage some groups while favoring others, resulting in discriminatory behaviors. In a similar vein, race and gender differences in accuracy have been observed in facial recognition technologies. It is crucial to create fairness criteria, audit datasets for bias, and include a range of viewpoints in the design of AI systems in order to overcome these problems. Minimizing unintentional discrimination and promoting equal outcomes require proactive steps like continuous monitoring and inclusive policymaking.

Opposition to Culture

Organizational and societal opposition to AI adoption is a problem. There is widespread public ignorance, irrational expectations, and fear of losing one's work. Workers frequently oppose AI because they fear losing their jobs, and socioeconomic and cultural disparities make it more difficult to enact policies. Fears of social inequity brought on by hurdles to digital access and bad experiences with previous technologies serve as further fuels for resistance.

Limitations of Technology

Implementing AI is hampered by technical issues such inadequate infrastructure, scarce data, and faulty algorithms. Unfair results may arise from bias in AI systems, and system maintenance and monitoring are hampered by a shortage of qualified personnel. Significant obstacles also arise from the intricacies of integrating AI with current infrastructures and guaranteeing dependable performance.

Budgetary Restrictions

AI adoption is hampered by high infrastructure, technology, and training expenses. Insufficient funding impacts citizen-led projects and impedes testing, experimentation, and innovation. Financial obstacles are especially noticeable in the healthcare industry, as exorbitant expenses affect patient care and access.

Insufficient Trust

Adoption is hampered by a lack of trust in AI systems as well as worries about accountability and transparency. Particularly in delicate domains like clinical decision-making, care planning, and parenting, citizens frequently doubt the intelligence and compassion of AI technologies like chatbots. For AI to be accepted in industries like healthcare and agriculture, trust must be established.

To address fragmentation in public administration, there is a growing consensus on the need for integrated AI techniques. An integrated framework provides a holistic view of AI applications, highlighting causal interconnections and connections between systems to align projects with strategic goals. This model facilitates collaboration between stakeholders—policymakers, engineers, and researchers—allowing insights and best practices to be shared, ultimately enhancing AI applications.

3. A REVIEW OF CURRENT LITERATURE ON AI FRAMEWORKS IN PUBLIC MANAGEMENT

The literature on AI frameworks in public administration addresses several basic themes. Fragmentation of AI applications is a common issue, as existing frameworks often focus on specialized technology or use cases without considering larger implications for public administration. This fragmentation leads to a lack of coherence in understanding how different AI systems interact and the overall impact they have on service delivery and governance.

To address this problem, academics have called for integrated approaches that combine multiple AI methods into coherent frameworks. Such integrated frameworks provide a more comprehensive understanding of the role of AI in public management, allowing the identification of causal links and interdependencies between different applications. For example, some frameworks emphasize the need to integrate AI activities with strategic goals, while others focus on the ethical implications of AI deployment.

Several criteria can be used in classifying existing frameworks, including their focus on specific AI technologies (e.g., machine learning, natural language processing), their applicability to different areas of public management (e.g., healthcare, transportation, social services). Characterizing these frameworks, researchers can find gaps in the literature and areas for additional inquiry, ultimately helping to build a more robust integrated AI framework for public management.

Job displacement from AI in the public sector underscores the need for social support as technology reshapes the workforce. In addition, the rapid development of AI raises regulatory issues that authorities must address while supporting innovation.

Successful application of AI in public administration requires interdisciplinary collaboration. Diverse perspectives from policy makers, technologists, researchers and practitioners promote integrated solutions. Collaboration supports shared goals, creativity and best practices while ensuring ethical considerations are embedded in AI systems. Capacity building through information sharing will strengthen the skills of public sector employees to successfully use AI technologies in their job.

The literature study provides a thorough examination of existing research on AI frameworks in public administration. It emphasizes how concentration on particular AI applications leads to fragmented knowledge of the subject. This fragmentation makes it challenging to find broad success criteria and interdependencies between different AI systems.

The integration of AI into public services has gained momentum in many disciplines, raising debates on its potential, problems and consequences. AI is being deployed to increase efficiency, decision-making and service delivery, but its adoption comes with significant challenges around ethics, transparency and stakeholder engagement. This review combines literature analyzing the impact of AI in areas such as performance management, health care governance, library services, and municipal government.

3.1. AI and Performance Management in Public Service

Numerous researches addressing a wide range of topics center on the potential of AI in decision-making and value creation. These include providing high-quality public services, improving citizen engagement in politics, regulating AI by the government, boosting citizen satisfaction and trust in AI, and broad applications. These studies discuss common tools like chatbots and virtual assistants, including how they improve communication between citizens and governments, build trust, improve administrative and customer service processes, and benefit citizens who interact with virtual assistants . Additionally, the ethical use of AI in local public services and robotic process automation (RPA) as a means of generating public value in municipal government are investigated.

Table 1. AI applications and their impacts on public engagement in the public sector

Public Sector Setting	AI Application	Impacts on Public Engagement
Parks	Managing Crowd Levels	Elimination of crowds can be exhausting for park staff, freeing up time for other park activities and public engagement programs.
Government, daily Services	Job Search and Matching	Reduced mismatches and missed matches for both local job seekers and potential employers lead to better job searches and greater career opportunities.
Smart Estates, Efficient and Seamless Municipal Services	Mass Transit Urban Rail System Management with a Customer-Centric Monitoring Approach	Faster and better ways to respond to service issues across the entire rail network, increasing customer satisfaction.
Smart Estates, Efficient and Seamless Municipal Services	Municipal Services Office and the One Service Chatbot	An easy and simple interface for citizens to report issues and get comments, leading to a more responsive and intelligent back-end system.
Education, K-12	Adaptive Learning and Assessment for Personalized Public-School Education	Teachers can select and target student time in subject areas that are more specialized and suit specific student needs.
Border Security	Contactless (Breeze Through) Immigration Clearance at Border Control Checkpoints	Reduced waiting period, less physical contact between travelers and checkpoint officials, more convenient and quicker border crossings

Source: Miller (2023)

The table lists the many kinds of AI and how they are used in government. It demonstrates how several AI technologies increase the effectiveness of the public sector through better communication, automation, and predictive insights. For example, rule-based systems aid in the simplification of typical government work, while predictive analytics and natural language processing provide methods for anticipating and comprehending citizen requirements. Speech recognition facilitates communication and service delivery, while robotics and computer vision enhance services like surveillance and healthcare. All things considered, AI helps governments to offer the public more efficient, timely, and customized services.

The implementation of AI in public services brings both potential and limitations. Efe (2023) analyzes how performance management in the Turkish public sector can benefit from AI tools, highlighting the importance of good forecasting and management systems. The report identifies several approaches to address inefficiencies in public service delivery, such as multidimensional stakeholder management and AI-supported automation. He suggests a novel application of AI in performance management in the public sector, showing its potential to eliminate inefficiencies in traditional approaches such as nepotism and subjectivity. His study underscores the need for AI-supported automation to promote accountability and transparency while coordinating with multidimensional approaches such as the balanced scorecard and stakeholder management. The study also suggests that AI, as a solution to existing problems in public performance systems, offers development prospects leading to better service delivery. Similarly, Calliontzi and Delinavelli (2024) outline the steps municipalities should take to integrate AI into policy-making processes, emphasizing the need to understand local contexts, stakeholder involvement, and technological readiness. They propose that transparency and public trust in government decisions can be enhanced by developing user-centric AI tools. Furthermore, Arnaout and Virani (2024) studied the responsible implementation of AI tools in health care in British Columbia. Their study underscores the importance of clinical governance to protect patient and provider safety, cultural safety, and equity in the AI adoption process. They suggest developing systematic evaluation tools and ethical review systems to reduce risks. Similarly, Li and Segumpan (2024) discusses the challenges of AI adoption in China's public sector, highlighting that while AI can enhance service efficiency, barriers such as job losses and lack of data integrity significantly impact its effectiveness. Their study aims to examine existing AI frameworks in public management by identifying their strengths and weaknesses through a comprehensive literature review. Rahmani (2023) analyzes the integration of AI into public library services, describing the benefits and barriers to its implementation. Background analysis suggests that while AI increases operational efficiency and service delivery, issues such as technical barriers, staff training demands, and financial constraints must be addressed for successful deployment. The findings underscore the need for strategic planning and ethical considerations in AI implementation. In home ownership and public service coproduction, as noted by Zhang (2024), the importance of household ownership in public service coproduction has been under-researched. This study suggests that household ownership drives individuals to engage in public service coproduction by protecting their economic interests and enhancing their understanding of government processes. Examination of survey data from individuals in Beijing indicates that homeowners are more inclined to report public service concerns, showing that financial stakes influence civic engagement. These observations have significance for promoting public service coproduction, as policy makers can use home ownership as a factor in improving community involvement. Sawhn, P., and Torres, R. (2023), ML and a regulatory sandbox for public sector services powered by AI. The authors of this study investigate how Machine Learning Operations (MLOps) and the regulatory sandbox can help with the integration of AI technologies in public sector services. They assert that these frameworks offer a secure setting for testing AI applications while guaranteeing adherence to regulatory requirements. These strategies improve the efficiency and quality of services provided by public institutions by fostering greater cooperation among stakeholders. Toivonen, M., and Heilala, S. (2023), sentiment analysis techniques based on AI for extensive data areas of public and security concern. The application of AI-based sentiment analysis in the public and security domains is examined in this research. It assesses the capacity of machine learning models to examine enormous volumes of textual data and offer insights into public sentiment. Through an awareness of community needs, the study highlights how these technologies can improve public service performance and boost communication approaches. Ismail, R., and Zakaria, Z. (2017), techniques used by blue ocean leadership (BOL) to improve public service employee engagement. Blue ocean leadership is proposed in this study as a way to increase public sector staff engagement. The authors contend that disengagement results from traditional leadership practices' frequent disregard for employee feedback. Leaders in the public sector can improve service delivery and organizational effectiveness by using BOL practices and fostering an inclusive atmosphere that encourages engagement. The article "I Hub: Idea to Innovative Service - AI Service Hub for Bangladesh Citizens to Accelerate Implementation of Smart Bangladesh" by Majumdar Hussain (2024) explores how artificial intelligence (AI) might help Bangladesh get closer to being a Smart Bangladesh. An AI repository, capacity building, and a collaboration platform are the three primary parts of the AI Service Hub's integrated ecosystem concept. While capacity building initiatives concentrate on reskilling and skilling residents, the AI repository centralizes AI models, algorithms, and applications to address regional issues. The platform for collaboration accelerates AI activities across sectors and encourages interdisciplinary innovation. Strong technical infrastructure, extensive stakeholder involvement, and government policy backing are necessary for the Hub's successful deployment. By democratizing access to AI, the Hub hopes to enhance governance, promote socioeconomic progress, and advance the goal of Smart Bangladesh 2041. The potential of the AI Hub to revolutionize civic services, encourage innovation, and advance economic growth is examined in this article Artificial Intelligence (AI) in public services is transforming a number of industries, most notably hospitality and education. The UTAUT2 model is extended by Kavitha and Joshit (2024) to investigate the factors impacting Gen Z's propensity to use AI tools in Indian higher education institutions. According to their findings, 34.2% of the explanatory power for Gen Z's adoption of AI may be attributed to hedonic motivation, perceived task perfection, conducive conditions, and performance expectations. In their study of cognitive training techniques in Taiwanese food and beverage service training programs, Chande and Verma (2023) emphasize the impact of mentor-apprentice relationships on learning satisfaction. Their quasi-experimental study provides insights into effective occupational training by demonstrating that cognitive training considerably improves learning results when compared to traditional techniques. Leading the National Association of Schools of Public Affairs and Administration (NASPAA) is the main emphasis of Rubaii (2012), who highlights the importance of cooperation in defining public affairs education. The difficulties AI poses for public service journalism are discussed by Jones and Luger (2022), especially the disconnect between journalists' knowledge of these technologies and their use in news production, which compromises accountability. They suggest actions to advance AI literacy in communities, businesses, and individuals. According to Thinthong and Suttavet's (2022) research on local hospital success in Thailand, respect, community involvement, and sound policymaking are important components of operational performance. In their analysis of the obstacles to AI deployment in China's public sector, Li and Segumpan (2024) identify issues with personnel preparedness, data, and algorithmic knowledge. To tackle these challenges, their research recommends astute partnerships, sensible legislation, and investments in AI infrastructure. With an emphasis on patient safety, equity, and trust, Arnout and Virani (2024) investigate clinical governance in British Columbia for the proper application of AI in healthcare.

In their investigation of the function of professional moderators in controlling offensive remarks on online forums, Stockinger and Lecheler (2023) point out the shortcomings of automatic moderation methods and argue for the necessity for more complex legislation. Adawiya and Hera (2021) investigate the use of AI in Banyuwangi, Indonesia, emphasizing how it might improve public services for individuals with disabilities. In his discussion of the changing role of the state in an AI-driven society, Mokanu (2022) emphasizes the necessity of legal frameworks that can keep up with technical advancements while also ensuring moral governance. A focus on productivity led to more stress and less employee autonomy, according to Mattos and Schlindwein's (2015) investigation of the effects of a new management tool in a public agency in the Amazon region. They stress the necessity of well-rounded management techniques that put workers' welfare first. In their study of AI deployment in the public sector, Kawakami and Zhu (2024) demonstrate how power dynamics impact choices about AI design and use, arguing in favor of a participatory approach to overcome power and knowledge disparities. Ismail & Wang (2023) look exploring integrating blockchain technology into a dental service system with the goal of improving data security and appointment scheduling while fostering privacy and trust. In their study of public discourse on generative AI, Braun & Flaherty (2023) analyze the technology's changing social standing and effects, with a focus on creativity and sector application. Milan-Vargas & Valle-Cruz (2024) investigate the obstacles to AI adoption in the State of Mexico's public sector, highlighting the necessity of overcoming these issues in order to enhance public services. They cite costs, technical capabilities, and connection as the main obstacles. Marup & Rokhman (2024): titled "Use of Artificial Intelligence (AI) Chatbots in Improving Public Services: A Meta-Analysis Study", This meta-analysis analyzes the performance of AI chatbots in public service delivery under multiple conditions. Analyzing 30 studies, the authors found that AI chatbots can significantly improve efficiency, reduce response time, and increase customer happiness. The results reveal that contexts such as service type and task complexity determine the success of chatbots, providing key information for policymakers on integrating AI into public services.

Public Service Motivation (PSM) is typically investigated in Western contexts, but current research highlights the need for deeper knowledge about PSM in non-Western settings. Wall and Mussagulova (2023) provide a comprehensive evaluation of PSM scholarship outside the Western world that emphasizes the importance of cultural values and social attitudes. Their findings suggest that different motivators shape PSM in different cultural contexts, bringing new insights into the link between PSM and public service ethics. The study recommends collaboration among scholars in non-Western institutions to further explore regional specificities and deepen understanding of PSM.

3.2 Ethical Considerations in AI Deployment

As AI technologies become increasingly popular, ethical questions about their use in public services become increasingly important. Baronchelli (2023) highlights the urgent need for new rules in the deployment of AI, focusing on the problems of developing these rules amid rapid technological progress. The study underscores the importance of an open and inclusive public discourse in defining societal responses to the expanding impact of AI. Dobson and Whittaker (2024) raised this issue by investigating patient perceptions of the use of their health data for AI development. The study found that while patients are generally fine with data use, they emphasize the importance of governance, privacy and transparency, suggesting that ethical considerations must be in place for the application of AI in healthcare.

3.3 AI Governance in Healthcare

Arnaout and Virani (2024) contribute to the discourse by exploring the responsible deployment of AI technologies in healthcare systems, focusing on the British Columbia Provincial Health Services Authority (PHSA). Their work underscores the importance of creating rigorous clinical governance for the use of AI in healthcare. The authors suggest a comprehensive approach to evaluating AI tools, including ethics reviews, risk assessments, and provider training. They propose that a transparent, comprehensive governance system is critical to maintaining trust and providing equitable access to AI technologies in healthcare settings.

3.4 AI in Library Services

Rahmani (2023) points to public libraries where AI integration can help streamline operations and increase user engagement. This study demonstrates that while AI has enhanced service delivery through technologies such as chatbots and automated systems, barriers related to technical barriers, staff training and financial constraints still hinder full adoption. Rahmani proposes strategic planning and ethical AI methods to enable successful integration. The study emphasizesincreasing operational efficiency and accessibility. Calliontji and Delinavelli (2024) provide insights into the integration of AI into municipal policy making, particularly under the AI4PublicPolicy Horizon 2020 project. Their research underscores the need to understand local ecosystems and build internal capabilities for AI adoption. They have also pushed for transparency by creating explainable AI (XAI) services to increase public trust. The study addresses issues of data availability, ethical compliance, and stakeholder engagement, while underscoring the promise of AI in shaping citizen-centric government policies. Studies such as Khorunissa and Suhender (2024) on service quality in Bandung Public Service Mall highlight the direct impact of service quality on public satisfaction. Although the focus is not entirely on AI, research shows that AI-based service improvements can increase citizens' perceptions and trust. These findings demonstrate a growing understanding of how AI can optimize service processes and create positive public interaction.

4. KEY THEMES IN PUBLIC SERVICE AI APPLICATIONS

Artificial Intelligence (AI) research in public management has shown some fundamental themes that are critical to understanding its consequences and guiding its implementation. These themes include the fragmentation of AI applications, the need for integrated approaches, and the driving forces and risks associated with AI technologies.

Optimizing human resource allocation: AI increases the efficiency of staff, ensuring better deployment of people based on real-time demands and talent.
Improving Fraud and Corruption Detection: AI tools enable more accurate detection, monitoring and accountability of fraudulent activities or corruption.
Improving maintenance operations: AI-based predictive maintenance helps optimize infrastructure management, reducing downtime costs.
Strengthening financial management: AI can promote more effective budgeting, financial planning and resource allocation in public institutions.

Strengthens organizational cyber security: AI systems enable advanced threat detection and protection, protecting public sector organizations from cyberattacks.
Streamlining Public Procurement: AI will simplify procurement processes, increase transparency and efficiency in procuring products and services.
Improving Recruiting Services: AI improves hiring by automating applicant selection and matching, leading to more successful hiring processes.

The proposed Integrated AI Framework for Public Administration serves as a basic model to guide the responsible application of AI technology. Its primary purpose is to connect various AI applications and provide a better understanding of their impact on public administration while emphasizing ethical considerations and public value gene

5. IDENTIFICATION AND CLASSIFICATION OF EXISTING FRAMEWORKS

Identification and classification of existing AI frameworks in public administration is an important step in understanding how these technologies can be effectively integrated into public services. A comprehensive assessment of the current literature indicates a wide variety of frameworks that have been developed to guide the adoption of AI in various public administration scenarios. These frameworks vary in their focus, scope, and underlying concepts, reflecting the complexity of AI applications and the specific problems facing public organizations.

5.1 Components of a Framework for AI in Public Management

Integrating Artificial Intelligence (AI) into public administration calls for a systematic framework that spans multiple components to ensure effective implementation and monitoring. This model is designed to maximize their potential benefits in solving the challenges of AI technology. The core components of this framework include monitoring and regulation, economic efficiency and technical design. Each of these components plays an important role in guiding the responsible use of AI in public services.

Oversight and control: Establishing oversight measures to ensure that AI systems operate as planned and in accordance with ethical principles, thus maintaining public trust.

Economic efficiency: Evaluating the cost-effectiveness of AI initiatives to inform resource allocation and prioritize projects that provide maximum value to citizens.

Technical Design: Focusing on hard technical features to deliver successful data collection, processing and analysis, maximizing the performance and scalability of AI solutions.

Ethical Considerations: Integrate ethical standards and regulatory oversight to limit risks of bias, discrimination and privacy violations, foster accountability and transparency.

Interdisciplinary Collaboration: Promoting communication between various stakeholders to leverage expertise and identify best practices for AI application in public administration.

5.2 AI Technology Infrastructure Layer

The AI technology infrastructure layer serves as the foundational backbone for AI systems, how data is acquired, processed and incorporated into higher-level applications. This layer includes the hardware and software components required for data collection, including sensors, databases, and processing units. It allows capturing primary data through direct inputs from devices and retrieving secondary data from existing databases such as machine logs and cloud storage. By providing the appropriate technical infrastructure, this layer facilitates the efficient deployment of AI applications and services, ensuring that data is accurately captured, stored, and available for analysis and decision making. Ultimately, the AI technology infrastructure layer is critical to support the overall performance and scalability of AI-based solutions across multiple domains, including public service.

5.3. AI Functional Layer

The AI functional layer consists of architectures and mechanisms that allow the internal interconnection and collaboration of the hardware and software components of an AI system. It starts with gadgets that sense their environment and collect data, which is then analyzed and stored in databases. This layer covers several functions such as data collection, processing and integration, enabling the system to understand and act on information. By integrating machine learning algorithms and inference engines, the AI functional layer enables intelligent decision-making and automation, ultimately increasing the efficiency and effectiveness of applications in public service and other sectors.

5.4. AI Applications and Services Layer

The AI applications and services layer is the top tier of AI frameworks, focusing on the integration and interaction of various AI techniques and applications to effectively deliver services. This layer includes a range of AI-based tools and solutions aimed at improving user experience and operational efficiency in public service and other areas. It includes functionalities such as customer assistance systems, automated service delivery and data-driven decision-making tools that enable the connection between individuals and government agencies. By using AI technology, this layer will speed up processes, improve service accessibility and promote communication between multiple government agencies, ultimately contributing to a more responsive efficient governance model.

5.5 An Integrated AI Framework for Public Management

The Integrated AI Framework for Public Management provides a structured strategy for the adoption of AI technologies in public institutions. It describes real-time scenarios in which AI can improve government operations, improve service delivery, enhance decision-making efficiency, and stimulate increased civic engagement, revolutionizing how public services are delivered to communities.

Table 2. Types of AI and their applications in government

AI Type	Description	Government Applications
Predictive Analytics	Predicting future events using machine learning	Forecasting resource needs, predicting crime rates, identifying potential fraud
Natural Language Processing (NLP)	Understanding and processing human language	Chatbots for citizen services, analyzing public sentiment, translating documents
Rule-Based Systems	Implementing predefined rules for decision-making	Automating routine tasks, enforcing compliance, managing workflows
Robotics	Physical tasks performed by machines	Healthcare, disaster response, logistics, surveillance
Computer Vision	Interpreting and understanding visual information	Analyzing images and videos for surveillance, license plate recognition, document scanning
Speech Recognition	Recognizing and understanding spoken language	Voice-activated services, transcription, call centers

Source: Created by the authors

This table lists several AI applications in diverse public sector contexts along with their beneficial effects on public participation. AI is revolutionizing the way public services are provided, increasing efficiency and raising citizen satisfaction in everything from controlling park crowd levels to better matching people with jobs.

An Integrated AI Framework for Public Management covers several real-time applications that highlight the role of AI in enhancing public services.

AI technology is revolutionizing public services through many new applications.

6 REAL-TIME CASES OF AI IN PUBLIC SERVICE

Artificial intelligence (AI) is gradually being integrated into government service sectors, changing how governments operate and provide services to residents. Here are several real-time scenarios that highlight AI's role in strengthening public sector capacity, improving decision-making and promoting citizen participation.

6.1. Predictive Policing

One of the most important applications of AI in public service is predictive policing. Police departments in places like Los Angeles and Chicago have adopted AI algorithms to analyze crime data and predict where crimes will occur. By assessing previous crime trends, socio-economic characteristics and environmental data, these systems can help law enforcement agencies allocate resources more effectively. For example, the Los Angeles Police Department uses a system called PredPol, which generates daily predictions of where crimes are likely to occur, allowing police to proactively monitor high-risk areas. This method has led to a decrease in crime rates in some neighborhoods, highlighting the potential of AI to increase public safety.

6.2. Smart Traffic Management

AI can also be applied to improve traffic management in urban areas. Cities like Barcelona and Singapore have installed AI-based traffic management systems that evaluate real-time traffic data from cameras and sensors. These systems can dynamically change traffic signals to optimize traffic flow, eliminate congestion and reduce travel times. For example, Singapore's Intelligent Transport System uses AI algorithms to predict traffic conditions and control traffic signals appropriately, resulting in smoother traffic and reduced emissions. This application not only increases the efficiency of transport systems but also contributes to environmental sustainability.

6.3. Chatbots for Citizen Engagement

Governments are increasingly using AI-powered chatbots to encourage citizen engagement and improve service delivery. For example, the city of Los Angeles has implemented a chatbot called "LA 311" that allows users to report problems such as potholes, graffiti and streetlight outages through a conversational interface. The chatbot uses natural language processing to understand public requests and provide immediate responses, speeding up the reporting process. It not only improves the efficiency of service requests but also increases citizen happiness by providing instant assistance.

6.4. Health Care Services

AI is making tremendous progress in public health services, especially in disease prediction and management. The National Health Service (NHS) in the United Kingdom has implemented AI algorithms to analyze patient data and predict the spread of diseases such as the flu. By using historical health data and real-time information, AI systems can predict trends and future outbreaks, enabling healthcare professionals to effectively allocate resources and adopt preventative measures. This proactive approach improves public health response skills and improves overall community health outcomes.

6.5. Disaster Response and Management

AI technology is also applied in disaster response and management. For example, during natural disasters such as hurricanes or wildfires, AI systems can scan satellite photos and social media data to assess damage and identify areas in need of immediate assistance. The Federal Emergency Management Agency (FEMA) in the United States has applied AI to improve its disaster response practices by predicting the impact of disasters and optimizing resource allocation. This application of AI enhances the performance of emergency services and ensures that relief reaches those in need more quickly.

6.6. Fraud Detection in Social Services

AI is playing a key role in detecting fraud in social welfare programs. Governments are using machine learning algorithms to evaluate patterns in data linked to welfare claims, tax filings and other public assistance programs. For example, the US Department of Agriculture uses AI to find irregularities in food stamp applications, which helps prevent fraudulent claims. By automating the identification process,

AI not only saves taxpayers money but also ensures that resources are provided to people who actually need help.

7. AI TOOLS FOR PUBLIC SERVICE

AI Tools for Public Service refers to a number of artificial intelligence technologies and applications aimed at improving the efficiency, effectiveness and accessibility of government services. These solutions use data analysis, machine learning and automation to improve decision making, speed up procedures and deliver better services to citizens. Here are some key aspects of AI tools in public service:

Table 3. Research studies on AI applications, methodologies, and impacts in public sector services

Reference	Algorithm/ Methodology	Key Features	Evaluation Criteria	Performance Summary
Abane&Phinaitrup (2022)	Multiple regression techniques	Public service motivation, performance management practices in local government	Regression analysis predicting variance in the dependent variable	A positive link was found between public service motivation and performance management. Together, the public service motivation subscales strongly predict changes in performance management practices.
Naik (2023)	Cloud computing &big data	Data-driven decision-making, healthcare resource management, public policy management	Data security, responsiveness, efficiency	Significant productivity gains have been demonstrated using cloud computing and big data analytics, particularly in healthcare and public service delivery.
Syam&Moenta (2021)	Empirical research with conceptual approach	Transparency, participation, public service, governance principles	Transparency and participation optimization	It is concluded that the principles of transparency and participation in public services are not fully optimized. More SOP communication and complaint handling through multiple channels is recommended for better governance.

continued on following page

Table 3. Continued

Reference	Algorithm/ Methodology	Key Features	Evaluation Criteria	Performance Summary
Jumanne&Njoroge (2018)	Multiple linear regression using Microsoft Excel Analysis ToolPak	Structural change management, employee performance in Public sector organizations	Cronbach's alpha reliability, regression analysis	Structural change management has had a significant positive Impact on employee performance in the Kenya Parliamentary Service Commission. Additional study in different fields is recommended.
Sala-Garrido&Maziotis (2023)	Cross-efficiency techniques	Benchmarking performance of productive units	Empirical approach	Applied cross-efficiency Applying Cross-Efficiency Benchmarking to Water Corporations to Increase Efficiency in Service Management and Resource Utilization
David &Makhamara (2022)	Survey research design, regression analysis	Benchmarking (external, internal, functional, process), service delivery in Kenya's National Police Service	Content validity, Cronbach's alpha reliability, regression analysis	It has been established that benchmarking procedures have favorably improved service delivery. Recommended continuous performance review and idea-sharing strategies to close performance gaps in police service delivery.

continued on following page

Table 3. Continued

Reference	Algorithm/ Methodology	Key Features	Evaluation Criteria	Performance Summary
Umar &Misnawati (2019)	Qualitative approach, case study design	One-Stop Service policy, bureaucratic reform, public service in Indonesia	Data reduction, presentation, conclusion & verification	It identified several challenges in implementing a one-stop service, including lack of human resources and poor socialization patterns. Improvements in human resource management and better organizational collaboration are recommended.
Fountain (2001)	Theoretical analysis	Customer service paradoxes in government	Political inequality, customer service as public management objective	It highlighted the paradoxes that customer service policies improve service quality but increase political inequality. It suggested that customer satisfaction measures should be re-examined for public sector changes.
Chatzoglou&Diamantidis (2013)	SERVQUAL instrument	Public service quality, Citizen's Service Centers (CSCs) in Greece, citizen participation	Modified SERVQUAL, random sampling, questionnaire analysis	Measured the service quality of CSCs in Greece, highlighting the relevance of public involvement in service development and provision. Service quality is rated above average, but recommendations are given for additional improvements in citizen participation.

continued on following page

Table 3. Continued

Reference	Algorithm/ Methodology	Key Features	Evaluation Criteria	Performance Summary
Lefebvre & Flora (1988)	Social marketing, behavior change strategies	Public health intervention, social marketing for community-based health education	Consumer orientation, exchange theory, marketing mix	Proposed the use of social marketing strategies to improve public health treatments. Highlighted the importance of audience segmentation, channel analysis and monitoring mechanisms for more successful, scalable health education programs.
Arifin&Afriansyah (2024)	Credit score assessment, data analytics, ML	E-governance, personnel management, credit score optimization for supervision in e-government	Data-driven decision-making, resource allocation, risk assessment	Demonstrated how data analytics and machine learning can optimize credit score evaluations, enhance monitoring and administrative control in e-governance. Highlighted efficiency improvements in personnel management decisions.
Firdaus&Yuningsih (2023)	Case study method	Digital service transformation, public relations, bureaucratic reform in West Java	Observation, interviews, literature study	Examined the digital evolution of the ministry's website during the pandemic, identifying important steps and strategies. In the context of bureaucratic reforms, digital communication approaches have been found to be helpful in increasing ease of service and public relations.

continued on following page

Table 3. Continued

Reference	Algorithm/ Methodology	Key Features	Evaluation Criteria	Performance Summary
Fadhilah&Alhadi (2024)	Qualitative approach, descriptive methods	Flood disaster management in Solok City	Data reduction, data presentation, drawing conclusions	Identifies driving and constraining factors in flood management. It was decided to proceed with the implementation due to issues such as insufficient stakeholder cooperation. Recommendations for better collaboration are provided.
Naidoo & Fields (2019)	Factor analysis, structural equation modeling (SEM)	Lean methodology initiation in public hospitals, critical success factors	Statistical factor analysis, SEM	Highlighted critical success factors for Lean approach in hospitals. They found that successful initiation depends on staff participation, proper training and management support. Further research on long-term Lean implementation is suggested.
Khairati& Putra (2022)	Backpropagation Neural Network (BPNN)	Drug usage prediction in health services, Artificial Neural Network (ANN)	Prediction accuracy, MAPE	An ANN model (12-12-1 architecture) was developed with 97.87% accuracy to predict drug consumption, particularly paracetamol. Recommends model for health care service planning.

continued on following page

Table 3. Continued

Reference	Algorithm/ Methodology	Key Features	Evaluation Criteria	Performance Summary
Gomide& Oliveira (2023)	Descriptive analysis, situational analysis	Hepatitis C virus transmission control in chronic kidney care units	Active search, transmission routes, management protocol	The effectiveness of focused treatments and prevention strategies in controlling hepatitis C transmission has been demonstrated. No new cases were found after the intervention, confirming the success of the interdisciplinary efforts.
Aljahdali& Xu (2013)	Resource allocation techniques, security design in IaaS	Cloud computing, multi-tenancy security, Infrastructure as a Service (IaaS)	Resource allocation, security by design	proposed a security-based resource allocation technique for enhancing multi-tenant security in cloud systems. Advances in data privacy and cloud computing security have been discovered with this approach.
Fazila&Husna (2022)	Qualitative research	Stunting reduction strategies in Nagan Raya Districts	Data reduction, data management, conclusion drawing	Analyzed methods of stunting reduction and identified specific difficulties related to use of money and stakeholder alignment. Suggest changes in government knowledge and money allocation for better implementation of lagging interventions.

continued on following page

Table 3. Continued

Reference	Algorithm/ Methodology	Key Features	Evaluation Criteria	Performance Summary
Serikandi&Ghivary (2022)	None specified	Role of product manager, 12 tools for development	Service efficiency, feature integration	Product managers will start the effective development of the Si Cantik application for public service, combining tools for better service results
Nazaruddin&Yani (2022)	None specified	Electronic Resident Card (KTP-el)	Tangibility, reliability, assurance, empathy	Service quality is strong in terms of awareness and reliability, but lacks assurance and empathy, indicating areas for improvement
Mieniyailova (2020)	None specified	Innovative investment development in public catering	IT integration, resource-saving technologies	Positive state debt schemes stimulate innovation in public catering, but credit conditions require improvement
Considine& Painter (1997)	None specified	Public sector reforms in Australia	Performance indicators, corporate management	Public sector reforms have enhanced performance management, but have raised concerns about compromising public service ethics
Rai (2013)	Case-Based Reasoning (CBR)	Temporal abstractions, intelligent data analysis	Risk evaluation, control of metabolic situation	AI-based risk assessment algorithms improve type 1 diabetes care, leading to cost-effective, tight metabolic control

continued on following page

Table 3. Continued

Reference	Algorithm/ Methodology	Key Features	Evaluation Criteria	Performance Summary
Charoensiriwatana&Waiyasilp (2003)	ELISA, IRMA, Guthrie's Test, Fluorometry	Congenital hypothyroidism, phenylketonuria screening	Coverage, follow-up rates, incidence rates	Newborn screening programs are well established in Thailand, leading to better detection and higher quality of life for newborns
Madya&Pasaribu (2022)	None specified	AI capabilities in public service	Resource-based theory, AI investment	Organizations must invest in complementary resources to gain performance improvements from AI adoption

Source: Created by Authors

This table lists several AI applications in diverse public sector contexts along with their beneficial effects on public participation. AI is revolutionizing the way public services are provided, increasing efficiency and raising citizen satisfaction in everything from controlling park crowd levels to better matching people with jobs.

8. MONITORING AND CONTROL

8.1 Mechanisms for Monitoring and Evaluation of AI Systems

Monitoring and regulation are critical to ensure that AI systems operate within ethical and regulatory constraints. This component includes architecture systems for monitoring that can analyze the performance and effectiveness of AI applications in real time.

- Performance metrics: Developing accurate performance metrics is critical to evaluating the success of AI systems. These measures should have several characteristics such as accuracy, efficiency, user satisfaction and compliance with ethical standards. Systematic reviews against these measures can help identify areas for improvement and ensure AI systems are achieving their intended goals.
- Transparency and Accountability: Transparency in AI decision-making processes is vital to building public trust. Mechanisms must be in place to explain how AI systems reach their judgments, especially in high-stakes do-

mains such as law enforcement or social services. This includes the use of interpretable AI (XAI) tools that provide insights into the performance of algorithms. In addition, accountability mechanisms should be created to hold stakeholders accountable for the consequences of AI applications.

- Regulatory compliance: AI systems must comply with existing rules and regulations, including data protection and privacy laws. Continuous monitoring helps ensure AI systems meet these regulatory standards, reducing risks associated with data theft or ethical violations.
- Stakeholder engagement: Engaging stakeholders, including citizens, policymakers, and technologists, in the monitoring process strengthens accountability of AI systems. Feedback channels should be built for stakeholders to voice concerns and contribute to the evaluation of AI applications.

8.2 Economic Impact Assessment of AI Projects

Economic efficiency is a core component of the AI framework, focusing on the cost-effectiveness and economic implications of AI implementations in public management. This requires examining both the direct and indirect economic implications of AI projects.

- Cost-Benefit Analysis: It is important to conduct a thorough cost-benefit analysis before adopting AI projects. This analysis should examine the initial investment, operational costs and future savings provided by AI applications. By measuring economic benefits, government agencies can make educated judgments about resource allocation and prioritize projects that provide the highest return on investment.
- Resource optimization: AI has the potential to optimize resource allocation in public services. By automating routine jobs and improving decision-making processes, AI can lead to massive cost reductions. For example, AI-based predictive analytics can help agencies allocate resources more effectively, ensuring that services are delivered where they are most needed.
- Long-term economic impact: Beyond immediate cost savings, the long-term economic impact of AI projects should be considered. This includes examining how AI can increase productivity, create new job opportunities and spur economic growth. Policymakers should address the broader economic ramifications of AI adoption, including its ability to spur innovation and improve public service delivery.
- Sustainability considerations: Economic efficiency should also include sustainability. AI projects should be scrutinized for their environmental impact, ensuring they contribute to sustainable development goals. For example,

AI applications in energy management can optimize resource use and reduce carbon footprints, combining financial efficiency with environmental responsibility.

8.3. Technical Design

Technical specifications and design principles for AI systems

The technical design component of the framework focuses on standards and principles that guide the development and implementation of AI systems in public administration. This ensures that AI applications are developed on a strong technological base.

- Robust architecture: AI systems should be created with a robust architecture that can handle massive data and complex algorithms. This includes choosing the right machine learning models, data storage options, and processing capabilities. A well-structured architecture helps the reliability and scalability of AI applications.
- Interoperability: Ensuring interoperability between multiple AI systems and existing public service infrastructure is critical. AI applications should be built to easily connect with various technologies and platforms used in public administration. It promotes data sharing and collaboration across departments, increasing overall service performance.
- Security and Privacy: Technology design must prioritize security and privacy considerations. AI systems must have strong security mechanisms to protect sensitive data from breaches and illegal access. In addition, privacy-preserving policies such as differential privacy should be applied to protect personal data while still allowing for relevant analysis.
- User-centered design: The design of AI systems should prioritize user experience. Public agencies must consider the needs and preferences of end users, including citizens and public servants, when designing AI applications. User-centered design concepts maximize usability, ensuring that AI technologies are accessible and successful in satisfying user goals.

10. FUTURE RESEARCH DIRECTIONS

To ensure the continued use and relevance of AI in public management, various avenues for further study should be explored:

Exploration of specific case studies: Conducting in-depth case studies of successful AI implementations in public services can provide useful insights into best practices, obstacles and lessons learned. These case studies can serve as models for other agencies trying to implement AI technologies.

Consideration of long-term consequences: Research should focus on the long-term consequences of AI on public administration, including its impact on service delivery, citizen participation and workforce dynamics. Understanding these implications can help politicians make informed judgments about future AI programs.

Development of criteria for evaluating the effectiveness of AI: It is important to establish unambiguous criteria for evaluating the effectiveness of AI applications in public services. These metrics should examine not only executive efficiency, but also quality of service delivery and citizen satisfaction. Ongoing review allows agencies to adapt their AI initiatives to meet changing public needs.

Interdisciplinary Research Initiatives: Encourage interdisciplinary research initiatives that bring together experts from multiple domains to investigate the implications of AI in public management. Collaborative research can lead to new solutions and gain deeper knowledge about the ethical, social and economic components of AI integration.

11. CONCLUSION

In summary, the integration of AI in public administration offers enormous opportunities to improve service delivery and create public value. However, it also presents issues that must be addressed through responsible and successful implementation strategies. By implementing the practical rules given above, involving diverse stakeholders and exploring future research areas, policy makers and practitioners can harness the revolutionary potential of AI while ensuring ethical concerns and responsibilities.

The proposed integrated AI framework serves as a basic model for the adoption of AI technology in public services. It emphasizes the need for continuous review, interdisciplinary collaboration and stakeholder involvement in developing a public administration that is responsive to residents' demands. Ultimately, the successful integration of AI into public management depends on responsible use, openness, and a focus on delivering public value for all.

The chapter concludes by underlining the potential of AI to transform public management, but also underlines the issues that need to be addressed to harness its full benefits. The integrated AI framework proposed by the chapter serves as a foundational model for future research and practical applications in the public sector with the aim of promoting responsible and effective use of AI technologies. The chapter concludes with a detailed description of an integrated AI framework for public management, which includes three primary components: monitoring and control, economic efficiency, and technical design. The framework seeks to provide a structured approach to implementing AI technology in public administration and emphasizes ethical considerations and public value generation.

REFERENCES

Abane, D., & Phinaitrup, B. (2022). *Performance management practices and motivation in developing countries: A further validation of the public service motivation construct in Ghana*. Management and Economics Research Journal.

Adawiyah, R., & Haerah, M. (2021). Implementation of artificial intelligence: The use of technology on diffable public service in Banyuwangi. *IOP Conference Series: Earth and Environment, 1019*, 012016. https://doi.org/DOI: 10.1088/1755-1315/717/1/012046

Aljahdali, S., & Xu, C. (2013). Resource allocation techniques and security design in Infrastructure as a Service (IaaS): Enhancing multi-tenancy security in cloud computing. *Journal of Cloud Computing Advances, Security, and Applications*, 10(2), 55–67.

Arifin, A., & Afriansyah, M. (2024). Optimizing credit score assessment for supervision and administrative control of e-government-based personnel analysts. *Proceedings of the 4th International Conference on Social Science, Humanity and Public Health (ICoSHIP 2023)*. DOI: 10.4108/eai.18-11-2023.2342550

Arnaout, T., & Virani, R. (2024). Shaping the future of healthcare in British Columbia: Establishing provincial clinical governance for responsible deployment of AI tools. *Healthcare Management Forum*. https://doi.org/DOI: 10.1177/08404704231154085

Chande, A., & Verma, R. (2023). Cognitive learning & data mining optimization strategies in sustainable training for restaurant food and beverage service excellence. *2023 International Conference on Communication, Security and Artificial Intelligence (ICCSAI)*. DOI: 10.1109/ICCSAI59793.2023.10420934

Charoensiriwatana, W., & Waiyasilp, P. (2003). Neonatal screening program in Thailand. *The Southeast Asian Journal of Tropical Medicine and Public Health*. PMID: 15906708

Chatzoglou, P. D., & Diamantidis, A. D. (2013). Service quality in the public sector: The case of the Citizen's Service Centers (CSCs) of Greece. *International Journal of Public Sector Management*.

Considine, M., & Painter, M. (1997). Managerialism: The great debate. *Public Administration Review*.

David, K., & Makhamara, A. (2022). Benchmarking practices and service delivery in the national police service in Mombasa County, Kenya. *International Journal of Business and Management*.

Dobson, R., & Whittaker, J. (2024). What do health service users think about the use of their data for AI development? *Medinfo*. Advance online publication. DOI: 10.3233/SHTI231146 PMID: 38269996

Efe, S. (2023). A discussion on problems and solutions of innovative performance management in the public service and government. *Uluslararası Akademik Yönetim Bilimleri Dergisi*, 8(1), 45–62. DOI: 10.51947/yonbil.1247897

Firdaus, I., & Yuningsih, M. (2023). Digital service transformation and public relations reform in West Java. *Journal of Digital Governance*.

Fountain, J. E. (2001). Customer service paradoxes in government: Balancing political inequality and public management objectives. *Public Administration Review*.

Gomide, F., & Oliveira, S. (2023). Measures to contain the transmission of Hepatitis C in a chronic kidney care hospital unit in the Triângulo Mineiro in Brazil: A case study. *International Journal of Public Health*, 68, 1605914. DOI: 10.3389/ijph.2023.1605914 PMID: 37325177

Heilala, S., & Toivonen, M. (2023). *AI-based sentiment analysis approaches for large-scale data domains of public and security interests*. AHFE International. DOI: 10.54941/ahfe1003738

Ismail, N., & Wong, C. (2023). Dental service system into blockchain environment. *International Journal of Innovative Computing*. Advance online publication. DOI: 10.11113/ijic.v13n1.394

Jones, T., & Luger, J. (2022). AI 'everywhere and nowhere': Addressing the AI intelligibility problem in public service journalism. *Digital Journalism (Abingdon, England)*, 10(10), 1731–1755. DOI: 10.1080/21670811.2022.2145328

Jumanne, A., & Njoroge, M. (2018). Structural change management and employee performance in public sector organizations in Kenya: Case of the Parliamentary Service Commission. *Journal of Strategic Management*.

Kalliontzi, E., & Delinavelli, M. (2024). Data-driven policy development of municipalities: Preparation steps for integrating AI tools in the policymaking process. *The International Archives of the Photogrammetry, Remote Sensing and Spatial Information Sciences*, XLVIII-4/W10-2024, 85–91. DOI: 10.5194/isprs-archives-XLVIII-4-W10-2024-85-2024

Kavitha, S., & Joshith, R. (2024). Factors shaping the adoption of AI tools among Gen Z: An extended UTAUT2 model investigation using CB-SEM. *Bulletin of Science, Technology & Society*, 44(1-2), 12–32. DOI: 10.1177/02704676241283362

Kawakami, Y., & Zhu, M. (2024). Studying up public sector AI: How networks of power relations shape agency decisions around AI design and use. *arXiv.org*.

Khairati, N., & Putra, A. (2022). Drug usage prediction in health services using Backpropagation Neural Network (BPNN): A case study on paracetamol consumption. *Journal of Health Informatics and Artificial Intelligence*, 14(3), 45–58.

Khairati, N., & Putra, R. (2022). Drug usage prediction using backpropagation neural networks. *Health Informatics Journal*.

Lefebvre, R. C., & Flora, J. A. (1988). Social marketing strategies for community-based health education. *American Journal of Public Health*.

Li, Y., & Segumpan, T. (2024). Challenges of AI adoption in China public service and its impact on efficiency and performance. *International Journal of Academic Research in Business & Social Sciences*.

Ma'rup, R., & Rokhman, I. (2024). *Utilization of artificial intelligence (AI) chatbots in improving public services: A meta-analysis study*. Open Access Indonesia Journal of Social Sciences.

Madya, F., & Pasaribu, H. (2022). AI capabilities in public service: A resource-based theory perspective. *Journal of Organizational Innovation*.

Malíčková, J. (2024). Extracting retrospective information through the public sharing of female golfers' contributions in a digital environment: An analytical perspective of their impact on shaping golf communities. *Proceedings of the International Conference on Business Excellence*.

Mattos, P., & Schlindwein, S. (2015). Excellence and productivity: New management imperatives in public service. *Revista de Administração Pública*.

Mazumder, S., & Hossain, M. (2024). AI Hub: Idea to innovative service - An AI Service Hub for the citizens of Bangladesh to accelerate the implementation of Smart Bangladesh. *International Journal of Scientific Research and Management*.

Mieniyailova, Y. (2020). Innovative investment development in public catering through IT integration. *Economic Development Review (Schiller Park, Ill.)*.

Mieniyailova, Y. (2020). Innovative investment development in public catering through IT integration. *Economic Development Review (Schiller Park, Ill.)*.

Millan-Vargas, M., & Valle-Cruz, J. (2024). *Impact and barriers to AI in the public sector: The case of the State of Mexico*. Digital Government Research.

Miller, S. (2023). Singapore's AI applications in the public sector: Six examples. *Management and Business Review, 3*(1–2). https://ssrn.com/abstract=4599495

Mocanu, I. (2022). What is the state's role in a world driven by AI tools? *Central and Eastern European eDem and eGov Days, 40–50.* https://doi.org/DOI: 10.24984/ceeed.2022.40

Naidoo, P., & Fields, D. (2019). Critical success factors for the successful initiation of Lean in public hospitals in KwaZulu-Natal: A factor analysis and structural equation modelling study. *Human Resources for Health*, 17(1), 69. DOI: 10.1186/s12960-019-0405-1 PMID: 31443719

Naik, P. (2023). A methodological study on big data and cloud computing for public policy management. *International Journal for Research in Applied Science and Engineering Technology*, 11(10), 992–999. DOI: 10.22214/ijraset.2023.56118

Nazaruddin, R., & Yani, E. (2022). Electronic resident card-making services (KTP-el). *International Journal of Public Administration Studies.*

Rahmani, H. (2023). *Exploring the integration of AI in public library services.* AI and Tech in Behavioral and Social Sciences. DOI: 10.61838/kman.aitech.1.4.6

Rai, A. (2013). Application of artificial intelligence for virtually assisted prognosis of diabetes: A NODDS project.

Rubaii, N. (2012). Leading by example: Modeling global public service excellence. *Public Administration Review*, 72(1), 1–5.

Sala-Garrido, R., & Maziotis, A. (2023). Benchmarking the performance of productive units using cross-efficiency techniques: An empirical approach for water companies. *Water Resources Management*, 37(14), 5459–5476. DOI: 10.1007/s11269-023-03614-w

Sartori, A., & Bocca, B. (2022). Minding the gap(s): Public perceptions of AI and socio-technical imaginaries. *AI & Society.*

Serikandi, T., & Ghivary, P. (2022). The role of product managers in public service application development. *Journal of Public Sector Innovation.*

Stockinger, D., & Lecheler, S. (2023). Navigating the gray areas of content moderation: Professional moderators' perspectives on uncivil user comments and the role of (AI-based) technological tools. *New Media & Society*, 25(4), 837–855. DOI: 10.1177/14614448231190901

Syam, D., & Moenta, H. (2021). *Implementing transparency and participation: An overview in public service.* International Journal Paper Public Review.

Thienthong, K., & Suttawet, C. (2022). Developing local hospitals for public health excellence. *Journal of Public Health and Development.*

Tran, N., Luu, T. T., Trinh, N. K., & Nguyen, X. N. (2023). How do normative public values promote service innovative behavior in public organizations: The roles of felt responsibility for change and responsible leadership. *Public Performance & Management Review*, 46(5), 1207–1236. DOI: 10.1080/15309576.2023.2241453

Umar, A., & Misnawati. (2019). One-stop service policy as a bureaucratic reform in Indonesia. *Public Policy Review.*

Wal, Z., & Mussagulova, M. (2023). Developing public service motivation in the non-Western world. *Asia Pacific Journal of Public Administration.*

Yefremova, I. (2024). Using the AI service RunwayML for data visualization. *Dnipro Academy of Continuing Education Herald. Series: Philosophy. Pedagogy.*

Zhang, L. (2024). How does homeownership shape public service coproduction? Evidence from a public complaint system in Beijing, China.

Chapter 8
Metropolitan Managers' Perspectives on Artificial Intelligence (AI) Technologies

Mustafa Demirkol
https://orcid.org/0000-0002-9860-8836
Tekirdağ Namık Kemal University, Turkey

ABSTRACT

This qualitative study examines the perspectives of 60 public authorities from six metropolitan areas: Copenhagen, Helsinki, Bucharest, Milan, Prague, and Berlin, regarding the use of AI technologies in public service provision. The research explores both the potential benefits and challenges associated with AI implementation. Many respondents expressed positive attitudes towards AI as a tool to improve public service delivery, while others voiced concerns about AI's developmental stage. A portion of the participants indicated that their lack of familiarity and technological literacy regarding AI was a barrier to its effective adoption. This highlights the need for training programs to equip local authorities with the skills to utilize AI in enhancing public services. The study also analyzes the data using MAXQDA software to categorize themes and provide structured insights. The findings emphasize the importance of preparing metropolitan managers for AI integration and offer strategic proposals for its successful implementation in public administration.

DOI: 10.4018/979-8-3693-8372-8.ch008

INTRODUCTION

The use of artificial intelligence (AI) in local services is growing in popularity every day. Undoubtedly, in this case, there is an opportunity for AI to improve all phases of the services provided to citizens, both for the practitioner and the beneficiary. It can help relevant processes run more smoothly, so to speak, and decisions can be made better (Mulyana, 2023). Globally, local/metropolitan governments are exploring how AI can help make public works and operations more effective and efficient and improve services (Algosaibi et al. 2020; Sousa et al. 2019).

AI usage in the local services has been increasingly utilized to streamline workflows (Yolvi et al., 2021). Particularly adept, at managing repetitive tasks like organizing documents and handling citizen queries AI technology allows public servants to dedicate their time to projects and strategic initiatives. This enhanced efficiency is not onlyboosts productivity but also ensures quicker responses and improved service quality for citizens as per the study (Levesque et al., 2023).

Public agencies benefit greatly from utilizing AI driven analytics and decision support tools alongside automation. These tools provide insights that enable agencies to make decisions based on data and strategy. They are adept, at recognizing patterns and predicting requirements while enhancing the allocation of resources, for improved policies and increased citizen satisfaction (Alenezi 2022; Hamirul et al., 2023; OECD 2020).

AI is also essential, in improving safety and security by detecting threats to maintaining order, in society early on through advanced AI systems—like unusual behavior or irregular data patterns—thus enhancing law enforcement actions and ensuring the safety of the public (Shams et al., 2018; Ardabili et al., 2023).

While there are benefits, to using AI in services there are also various obstacles to overcome. Issues such as safeguardin data privacy upholding standards in AI applications and building public confidence, in these new technologies are major concerns. To maximize the advantages of AI while minimizing risks, governments must implement thought out policies and establish strong regulatory frameworks (Schiff et al., 2024; Ben Ishai et al., 2024; Hamirul et al., 2023; Madhavan et al., 2020).

In the end AI technologies hold promise, for transforming administration. There is a shift towards using these technologies not to boost the efficiency of public services and manage resources better but also to improve transparency in governance. However the crucial factor in fully harnesslng the potential of AI is the integration and utilization of these technologies, by governments. This, in depth research project delves into the perceptions of AI in public service delivery by conducting interviews with 60 authorities across six metropolitan regions (including Copenhagen, Helsinki, Bucharest, Milan, Prague and Berlin). It explores the challenges encountered during the implementation of AI. Provides insights into its role in public administration and local services offering a detailed evaluation of the current status of AI adoption, among local authorities.

RELATIONSHIP BETWEEN ARTIFICIAL INTELLIGENCE TECHNOLOGIES AND LOCAL SERVICE DELIVERY

In the era of technology known as the age or information era there has been a notable transition, towards utilizing data driven systems. The growth in data availability and the capacity to gather information have driven the advancement of AI technologies. AI is seen as a tool in enhancing services. Both national and local governments are required to incorporate these advancements resulting in modifications, to their policies and service offerings. AI brings advantages in the realms of economy and society by leveraging technologies to revolutionize the way services are provided (Saygılı, 2020).

AI technology has a range of uses, in government services. Plays a significant role, in how local services are provided to the public today.After the integration of information and communication technologies (ICT) local governments have had to adjust to the era. This change has transformed how citizens interact with their local authorities by encouraging participation. As local governments modernize their services digitally, citizens now have the convenience of completing transactions without visiting offices saving their valuable time and energy. The AI intervenes to adapt to changing citizen demands by improving services to cater effectively to their requirements (Önder & Saygılı, 2018).

Technology advancements, like AI are transforming sectors such as healthcare and transportation while also impacting education and agriculture fields significantly. AIs incorporation in administrations involves utilizing machine learning techniques alongside technologies like blockchain, reality, Internet of Things (IoT) and big data analysis. These advancements have an influence on life interpersonal connections and work practices. Urban centers such as Helsinki and Amsterdam are leading the way, in implementing AI in services to boost accessibility and effectiveness by employing AI for chatbot assistance traffic management and community engagement (Floridi, (2020).

AI technology is influencing the development of cities well; it's important for local authorities to guarantee that AI tools are clear cut and trustworthy, in addition to being ethical. A case in point is Molenlanden in the Netherlands which has gone digital by delivering services (Bletz, 2016). Implementations of AI in services can help address issues, like waste disposal and traffic management while also aiding social care professionals with interventions (LGC 2022).

There are important obstacles, to implementing AI in public service provision. However the worry about job losses among workers is a serious concern even though AI is intended to ease workloads rather, than displace jobs as mentioned by Ribeiro (2016). Governments are actively exploring AI driven solutions like creating chatbots and leveraging sensors to enhance service delivery and efficiency These initiatives streamline tasks and also enhance real time data collection and decision making processes (Damar et al., 2024).

The benefits of AI, in revolutionizing government are clear as it streamlines tasks and allows employees to concentrate on more intricate matters.In the context of city initiatives AI aids in handling amounts of data resultinging in smarter decision making and better public services (Yiğitcanlar et al., 2020). In the long run AI holds great promise for cost reduction,elevated productivity and heightened citizen contentment.It is crucial for governments to continue backing AI exploration and advancement to ensure its application, in addressing issues.

PURPOSE AND IMPORTANCE OF THE RESEARCH

The primary focus of the research is the assessment of the metropolitan city managerrs' comprehension and attitudes towards artificial intelligence technologies, obtaining their opinion on the application of these technologies in public services, and recognizing the barriers in the process of the AI adoption. The justification for selecting metropolitan managers as the sample in this research is the fact that most human beings reside in metropolitan areas nowadays. Thus, the right of the metropolitan management personnel is critical for the implementation of such technologies that can affect vast numbers of people. Metropolitans are the areas where most of the people live today, hence adding to the growing importance of the role of metropolitan managers in the use of such technologies that can affect a large number of population. In this regard, public administration's effective use of AI tech is very important since the AI can provide benefits in the areas of efficiency, transparency, and sustainability.

METHODOLGY

This research was a qualitative study using a semi-structured interview method that involved 60 local authorities from six metropolitan regions. The aim of the interviews was to find out what the participants knew about AI technologies and how they perceived them, as well as their views on the possible use of these technologies in the public service domain. The interview data was then analyzed thematically using MAXQDA software to conclude that AI technology adoption challenges and opportunities. The findings revealed the challenges and opportunities in the adoption of AI technologies.

FINDINGS

In general, the views of the interviewers can be classified in three different group. The mightiness of AI technologies in other areas like public services delivery is what the interviewees generally have. The majority of the respondents were confident that AI has the potential to assist in their job tasks. Nevertheless, a small segment showed a prejudiced disposition towards AI, while another group claimed that AI is not yet matured and that these technologies may eventually be of use when they mature. In the analysis, the major part of the interviewees showed that they have not yet experienced any AI technology and do not have sufficient knowledge and technological literacy in this field.

Such a situation contains the evidence of the necessity of training and informing local authorities in order to properly use AI technologies in public services. The research brings out the ignorance of local authorities who are not familiar with AI technologies and they do not know how they can facilitate the lives of their people with AI technologies and the steps that need to be taken to overcome these deficiencies. Besides, this research was done with the help of MAXQDA software. It promotes the idea of training managers for efficient use of AI technology in public administration and puts forward strategic recommendations for ensuring the adoption of AI technology in public services.

The MAXQDA coding outcomes show some significant results that this study thoroughly explores the understanding levels and perspectives of local authorities (city councillors) concerning the incorporation of AI technologies in public services as well as their current use and challenges faced in implementing them effectively and training requirements associated with AI utilization in public services. Additionally considers ethical and social considerations related to AI future prospects are assessed alongside recommendations stemming from the study results. The findings are such:

1. General Knowledge and Perceptions of AI Technologies

A significant majority of the 60 local government officials involved in the study indicated that they possess limited knowledge of AI technologies. Particularly among older participants, there was a noticeable disinterest in technological innovations and a resistance to adopting new technologies. This phenomenon is identified as a critical factor that could slow down technological transformation processes in local governments. This is because the sample of this study consists of representatives of one of the most important mechanisms of local government units, namely council members. Considering the importance of municipal councils in both decision-making, implementation and supervision, the importance of the issue can be understood much better. In contrast, relatively younger respondents showed a much more interested and open attitude towards AI technology, and even those without any technical knowledge of AI developed thoughts about the potential advantages and disadvantages of this new technology.

2. Advantages and Disadvantages of AI Technologies

In this part of the research we delve into the perspectives shared by the participants regarding the pros and cons of implementing AI in services.The insights gathered from the responses of those interviewed can be outlined as follows:

Advantages:

- **Increased Efficiency:** Most people interviewed mentioned that AI has the capability to automate step, by step and repetitive tasks so that human workers can concentrate on strategic responsibilities.This shift is viewed by those interviewed as having the potential to greatly enhance the effectiveness of services. In areas, like big dataset analysis and streamlining processes.
- **Faster Decision-Making:** Many people believed that the ability of AI to analyze datasets could help city administrators make more efficient decisions.
- **Cost Savings:** Most interviewers believe that AI could help cut down on employee expenses and handle tasks with little need, for human involvement.
- **Improved Service Quality:** Interviewees believe that AI has the potential to offer services consistently. This would allow citizens benefiting from services to access faster and more efficient assistance.
- **Data Analysis and Prediction:** During the interviews conducted with individuals mentioned how AI technology has the potential to forecast trends and contribute to the creation of public policies.

Disadvantages:

- **Ethical Concerns:** Most of the people interviewed expressed concerns, about how AI could struggle with ensuring fairness and transparency, in decision making processes and being held accountable for its Many agreed that biased algorithms could harm marginalized communities.

- **Job Losses:** Outsourcing tasks to AI automation might result in public sector employees facing potential job loss, which stands out as a significant drawback.
- **Security and Privacy Risks:** Interviewees have expressed worries regarding the security and privacy of data handled by AI systems.
- **Lack of Familiarity with Technology:** To fully leverage AIs benefits, in their work processes and decision making strategies public administrators must enhance their understanding and expertise in AI technologies. According to those interviewed the absence of training, in this area hinders the application of AI solutions.
- **Responsibility Ambiguities:** Participants raised numerous concerns that the use of AI in decision-making could create uncertainties in terms of responsibility and accountability.

3. Current Applications and Potential Benefits

Several participants mentioned that they were using AI technologies in their municipalities for some tasks, like planning in transportation and implementing chatbots, for various applications as well as for data analysis purposes. However most interviewees admitted they did not have sufficient understanding of AI technologies or the extent to which these tools were being used in ongoing municipal activities.

Potential Benefits:

- **Increased Efficiency and Decision-Making:** Participants emphasized that AI has the potential to significantly contribute to efficiency improvements and faster decision-making processes.
- **Personalized Services:** AI can offer customized solutions tailored to the needs of citizens in public services.
- **Improved Data Management:** AI's capacity for data management and analysis can enhance the effectiveness of public services.

4. Integration Challenges and Barriers

The incorporation of AI, in services encounters numerous obstacles such as limited funding resources and staff shortages, alongside data handling difficulties and ethical dilemmas according to respondents who noted that the effective integration of AI would entail a combination of technical and social initiatives.

Key Challenges:

- **Resource and Budget Constraints:** The integration of AI technologies requires significant financial investments, and municipal budget limitations pose a barrier to such investments.
- **Personnel Shortages and Training Needs:** The lack of education necessary to understand and utilize AI technologies is seen as a major obstacle.
- **Data Management and Privacy:** AI's dependence on large volumes of data raises significant challenges, particularly regarding personal data management and privacy.

5. Education and Knowledge Needs

Attendees emphasized the necessity of initiatives covering AI concepts and practices, in data handling and ethics as well as proficient project supervision to maximize the benefits of AI tools in operations.They also underscored the significance of being well versed in planning, for the extended usage of AI endeavors.

6. Ethical and Social Concerns

The primary ethical considerations surrounding the implementation of AI, in public services center on matters, like safeguardin data integrity and privacy of individuals sensitizing transparency and accountability. Importantly it was emphasized by participants that human involvement should not be completely eliminated from decision making processes guided by AI.

7. Future Expectations

Participants believe that AI will be more widely used in public services in the future. In particular, AI is expected to play a key role in areas such as data management, personalised services and smart city applications. However, participants also emphasised the need for adequate infrastructure and training in public administration to ensure the successful implementation of these technologies.

Analysis

The findings of this study reveal that while AI presents significant opportunities in public services, there are substantial challenges to its widespread adoption. A majority of participants reported a lack of knowledge and awareness regarding AI technologies, which hinders the full realization of AI's potential advantages. According to the result of the analysis, there are two main factor:

Technological Integration and Training Needs: Successful AI integration requires the development of both technical infrastructure and personnel competence within local governments. The lack of education is a primary factor limiting the feasibility of AI projects, underscoring the need for comprehensive and continuous training programs.

Ethical and Social Dimensions: The ethical dimensions of AI, particularly concerning transparency, accountability, and social equity, raise serious concerns. Participants voiced worries that AI-driven decisions could disproportionately affect disadvantaged groups.

Discussion and Suggestions

This study reveals discoveries, about the knowledge levels of governmental officials and managers when it comes to utilizing AI technologies in public administration effectively and the necessary training they require for it to be successful in delivering public services efficiently. To ensure the use of AI technologies in services by administrators through proper training and awareness is crucial for their successful integration into public administration practices at large as outlined in our research findings. Furthermore the study aims to facilitate the adoption of AI technologies, in administration by offering actionable recommendations and strategic guidance. Additionally, MAXQDA software was utilized to assess our research outcomes effectively.

This proposal, for a chapter delves into an in depth study aimed at understanding how AI technologies are perceived in administration and the challenges encountered during their integration process.The findings from our research indicate that offering training and information to managers plays an important role in the effective incorporation of AI technologies, within public services. Some recommendations were put forth to address knowledge deficiencies in this domain.

The results indicate that local governments face difficulties in the process of adopting AI technologies which are mostly lack of knowledge, lack of technological literacy, and mistrust of these technologies. This situation makes it imperative for the managers to be trained extensively to make the most out of AI technologies. Just as general comprehensive trainings such as "training of educators" were organized in educational institutions for a period, similarly, it would be appropriate to organize theoretical and practical trainings on artificial intelligence in all institutions providing public services with a theme such as "training of managers". Continuous training programs, awareness campaigns on AI technologies, and sharing best practices should be the suggested strategies to improve the AI knowledge level of metropolitan governments and managers.

Besides, the sociocultural and moral consequences of AI deployment in the public sector must be taken into consideration. Artificial Intelligence (AI) technology adoption in public organizations is likely to encounter challenges such as data privacy, security, and transparency. Thus, while making the regulations and policies about the use of AI technologies in the public administration, the ethical and social aspects of these technologies should be paid attention too.

This research shows that AI technology has the potential to improve efficiency and lower costs while enhancing service quality, in public services sector.. Local governments encounter challenges such as lack of knowledge ethical dilemmas and technological limitations when implementing these innovations. The main discoveries of the study point to a pressing requirement, for training programs and awareness initiatives to empower government officers to utilize AI technologies proficiently. To address social hurdles successfully necessitates prioritizing transparency, in operations and data safety while centering decision making processes around values and concerns. Implementing AI in services has the capability to enhance the effectiveness of local governments by cutting costs and enhancing services, for citizens. It's essential to establish legal structures and training programs for staff to ensure successful deployment.

CONCLUSION

This research thoroughly explores how city managers view the integration of AI technology, in delivering services within urban areas. The results emphasize AIs potential to enhance the effectiveness and quality of services while also reducing costs in settings. Many interview participants see AI as a game changing tool that can simplify processes and improve decision making to offer tailored services to local residents. The study also reveals obstacles, to effectively incorporating AI technologies into local governance initiatives.

One of the challenges that stands out is the level of technological knowledge, among local/metropolitan government officials in various cities and towns who are not familiar with AI technology. This lack of understanding hinders them from utilizing the benefits of AI. As a result of this issue highlighted in the research report it is stressed that there is a need for robust training initiatives to prepare administrators adequately for implementing and overseeing AI systems. Without training the true impact of AI, on revolutionizing governance may not be fully achieved.

In addition, to that are issues related to the use of AI in services such as worries about data privacy and fairness in algorithms which are important areas that require focus and discussion. As AI becomes more integrated, into the operations of services provided by local/metropolitan governments guidelines and regulations must be put in place to ensure transparency protect peoples privacy and maintain trust in these advancing technologies.

In conclusion of the conversation while artificial intelligence offers advantages for managing cities its effective use relies on overcoming challenges related to knowledge gaps and infrastructure issues well as ethical concerns. By providing training, for local/metropolitan government officials and setting standards local authorities can optimize AI for improving services and ultimately boosting the quality of life for city dwellers. The practical recommendations outlined in this study serve as a roadmap, for bridging knowledge gaps. Incorporating AI into the workings of metropolitan governments is essential, for maximizing the benefits of AI technology.

ACKNOWLEDGEMENTS

This work was supported by the 2219 TÜBİTAK Postdoctoral Research Program and was conducted as a Visiting Researcher under the coordination of Dr. Lina Olsson at the Department of Urban Studies, Malmö University, Sweden. I would like to express my deepest gratitude to TÜBİTAK, Dr. Lina Olsson, and Malmö University for their invaluable support.

REFERENCES

Alenezi, M. (2022). Understanding Digital Government Transformation. Cornell University. https://doi.org//arXiv.2202.01797DOI: 10.48550

AlGosaibi, A. A., Abdul, R. W. S., AlOthman, A. F., & AlHamed, S. (2020). Developing an Intelligent Framework for Improving the Quality of Service in the Government Organizations in the Kingdom of Saudi Arabia [IJACSA]. *International Journal of Advanced Computer Science and Applications*, 11(12). Advance online publication. DOI: 10.14569/IJACSA.2020.0111233

Ardabili, B. R., Pazho, A. D., Noghre, G. A., Neff, C., Bhaskararayuni, S. D., Ravindran, A., Reid, S., & Tabkhi, H. (2023). Understanding Policy and Technical Aspects of AI-enabled Smart Video Surveillance to Address Public Safety. *Computational Urban Science*, 3(1), 21. DOI: 10.1007/s43762-023-00097-8

Ben-Ishai, G., Dean, J., Manyika, J., Porat, R., Varian, H., & Walker, K. (2024). AI and the Opportunity for Shared Prosperity: Lessons from the History of Technology and the Economy. *arXiv preprint arXiv:2401.09718* or https://synthical.com/article/f8f3e908-a6ff-4e36-8fd2-74e92786bd03

Bletz, J. (2016). Molenwaard: The world's first digital municipality. Retrieved from https://joinup.ec.europa.eu/collection/egovernment/document/molenwaard-worlds-first-digital-municipality (Accessed: October 2, 2024).

Damar, M., Özen, A., Çakmak, Ü. E., Özoğuz, E., & Erenay, F. S. (2024). Super AI, generative AI, narrow AI and chatbots: An assessment of artificial intelligence technologies for the public sector and public administration. *Journal of AI*, 8(1), 83–106. DOI: 10.61969/jai.1512906

Floridi, L. (2020). Artificial intelligence as a public service: Learning from Amsterdam and Helsinki. *SSRN*. https://ssrn.com/abstract=3827084 or http://dx.doi.org/DOI: 10.2139/ssrn.3827084

Hamirul, D., & Elsyra, N. (2023). The Role of Artificial Intelligence in Government Services: A Systematic Literature Review. *Open Access Indonesia Journal of Social Sciences*, 6(3), 998–1003. DOI: 10.37275/oaijss.v6i3.163

Levesque, V. R., Bell, K. P., & Johnson, E. S. (2023). The role of municipal digital services in advancing rural resilience. *Government Information Quarterly*, 41(1), 101883–101883. DOI: 10.1016/j.giq.2023.101883

LGC. (2022). What does AI mean for councils? We asked an AI system to tell us. *Local Government Chronicle*. Retrieved from https://www.lgcplus.com/politics/lgcbriefing/what-does-ai-mean-for-councils-we-asked-an-ai-system-to-tell-us-14-12-2022/ (Accessed: October 20, 2023).

Madhavan, R., Kerr, J. A., Corcos, A. R., & Isaacoff, B. P. (2020). Toward Trustworthy and Responsible Artificial Intelligence Policy Development. *IEEE Intelligent Systems*, 35(5), 103–108. DOI: 10.1109/MIS.2020.3019679

Mulyana, Y. (2023). The Impact of Using Artificial Intelligence on Public Services in Indonesia. *The International Journal of Science in Society*, 5(3), 356–365. DOI: 10.54783/ijsoc.v5i3.745

OECD. (2020). *"Open, Useful and Re-usable data (OURdata) Index: 2019", OECD Public Governance Policy Papers, No. 01*. OECD Publishing., DOI: 10.1787/45f6de2d-

Önder, M., & Saygılı, H. (2018). Yapay zeka ve kamu yönetimine yansımaları. *Türk İdare Dergisi*, 90(487), 629–668.

Ribeiro, R. (2016). Are chatbots in state IT's future? *StateTech Magazine*. Retrieved from https://statetechmagazine.com/article/2016/11/are-chatbots-state-its-future (Accessed: August 9, 2024).

Saygılı, H. (2020). *Public policies on artificial intelligence: Comparison of the USA and China's AI public policies* (Unpublished master's thesis). Ankara Yıldırım Beyazıt University, Institute of Social Sciences, Department of Political Science and Public Administration, Ankara.

Schiff, D., Borenstein, J., Biddle, J., & Laas, K. (2021). AI Ethics in the Public, Private, and NGO Sectors: A Review of a Global Document Collection. *IEEE Transactions on Technology and Society*, 2(1), 31–42. DOI: 10.1109/TTS.2021.3052127

Shams, S., Goswami, S., Lee, K., Yang, S., & Park, S.-J. (2018). Towards Distributed Cyberinfrastructure for Smart Cities Using Big Data and Deep Learning Technologies, *IEEE 38th International Conference on Distributed Computing Systems (ICDCS)*, Vienna, Austria, pp. 1276-1283, DOI: 10.1109/ICDCS.2018.00127

Sousa, W. G. D., Melo, E. R. P. D., Bermejo, P. H. D. S., Farias, R A S., & Gomes, A. D. O. (2019, July 25). How and where is artificial intelligence in the public sector going? A literature review and research agenda. *Government Information Quarterly*, 36(4), 101392–101392. DOI: 10.1016/j.giq.2019.07.004

Yiğitcanlar, T., Desouza, K. C., Butler, L., & Rashidi, F. (2020). Contributions and risks of artificial intelligence (AI) in building smarter cities: Insights from a systematic review of the literature. *Energies*, 13(6), 1473. Retrieved November 25, 2022, from. DOI: 10.3390/en13061473

Yolvi, O. F., Luis Alex, V. F., Miguel Angel, V. F., & Raúl Alberto, R.-L. (2022). Artificial intelligence (AI) applied to public management. *Metaverse*, 3(2), 8–8. DOI: 10.54517/m.v3i2.1795

APPENDIX I

Study Questions

The questions used in the interviews conducted in the field within the scope of the study are as follows:

General Information and Perceptions about Artificial Intelligence Technologies:
How do you assess your general level of knowledge about artificial intelligence technologies?
What advantages and disadvantages do you think the use of AI technologies in public services can bring?

Existing Usage Areas and Potential Benefits:

Are you currently using AI technologies in your administration? If so, in which areas and how?
What do you think are the biggest potential benefits of AI technologies in public service delivery?

On Challenges and Obstacles:

What are the biggest challenges you face in integrating AI technologies into public services?
What are the factors that hinder the adoption of AI technologies? What are your recommendations to overcome these barriers?

On Training and Information Needs:

What training or information do you need in order to use AI technologies more effectively?

What kind of training programs would be useful for local authorities to better understand and use AI technologies?

On Ethical and Social Dimensions:

Do you have ethical or social concerns about the use of AI technologies in public services? If so, what are they?
What policies or regulations are needed to address these concerns?

Future Prospects and Recommendations:

What do you think about the future of AI technologies in public services?
What are your suggestions for a more widespread and effective use of AI technologies?
Do you have any other comments or suggestions you would like to add within the scope of this research or on AI and public services in general?

Chapter 9
Natural Language Processing (NLP) for Sustainable Public Administration

Hilal Saygili Balci
https://orcid.org/0000-0002-2668-838X
Ankara Yıldırım Beyazıt University, Turkey

İlyas Balci
https://orcid.org/0000-0003-2221-6219
Ankara Yıldırım Beyazıt University, Turkey

ABSTRACT

Technology with Artificial intelligence (AI) continues to evolve daily and transform public administrations. This study focuses on natural language processing (NLP), one of the effective AI technologies. Sustainability will be addressed within the context of sustainable public administration which is the long-term impact and sustainability of public services. This study suggests that NLP is a vital tool for reform and enhancement in public administration, proposing assumptions on its potential to improve the efficiency, transparency, and inclusiveness of public administration. It explains the usage areas of NLP in public administration with application examples. Thus, three main sustainability issues are examined: environmental, economic and social. In addition, critical challenges of NLP such as language diversity, data privacy and ethical issues are addressed, and solutions are sought. This study aims to present the significant potential of NLP in promoting sustainability in public administration. It creates an important roadmap for researchers, policy makers and practitioners.

DOI: 10.4018/979-8-3693-8372-8.ch009

1. INTRODUCTION

The rapid development of technology has transformative effects in the field of public administration, as in every field. Public administration needs speed, innovations and infrastructure in terms of both providing public services and making the right decisions for the public good. Actually, the most important technological development that can meet these needs today is artificial intelligence (AI). The transformative effect of AI on public administration is incontrovertible, especially in terms of sustainability, which is one of the main points of this study. Natural Language Processing (NLP), one of the AI technologies, is a technology that can contribute to the sustainability of public administration as a transformative technology capable of understanding, interpreting and producing human language. These features of NLP are cut out for sustainable public administration.

Sustainable public administration refers to the understanding of considering the long-term effects of public services and policies. This means providing public services and public benefits in a short span of time, with the most effective solutions and in a renewable way. In this context, three main areas of sustainability in public administration stand out: environmental sustainability, economic sustainability and social sustainability. The application of sustainability in public administration requires the formulation, implementation and monitoring of relevant policies. NLP gains significance during this phase since it can help relatively much thanks to its advanced data processing ability.

NLP is composed of the unification of computer science, AI, and linguistics. NLP is aimed to provide computers with the ability to understand and respond to human language. Thus, computers are enabled to process text or audio input in a meaningful and useful way. NLP is composed of three main technologies which are morphological analysis, syntactic analysis and semantic analysis.

Morphological analysis examines the structure of words and their formation rules. Syntactic analysis analyzes sequences of symbols in natural language according to grammatical rules. Semantic analysis examines the meaning of words and how they come together to compose meaningful sentences. In public administration, NLP has quite different application areas. For example, in environmental management, NLP can supervise pollution levels, forecast environmental disasters, and optimize resource usage by analyzing large data sets thanks to the sensors and social media. In economic sustainability, it accelerates administrative processes, diminishes costs, and develops services. On the other hand, it increases governance inclusiveness by dissolving language problems, increasing transparency, and encouraging public participation in social fields.

NLP technology has a significant space in public administration. In the public administration literature, there are a number of studies regarding the usage of NLP in public administration. AI technologies have a distinctive ability of learning different data sets in real time. Algorithmic bureaucracies are the most preferred fields in which AI systems are used in public administration. In general, such preferences comprise the NLP to deploy conversational agents or chatbots to provide public services to the citizens at 24 hours without the requirement of human presence (Cortés-Cediel et al., 2023, p. 1). The AI algorithms in question provides the analysis of wide data sets and provides the policy makers critical data on the newly developing trends, demands, which enables them to take the relevant precautions (Vogl et al., 2020, p. 946). With this regard, AI can foresee the trends in public health and provide and the necessary knowledge to the policy makers and executers to take necessary precautions in policy making and distribution of resources. Such assistance of AI in public administration can be enlarged since it can be benefited in areas like public education, transportation, security etc. in which it is vital to detect and analyze the recent trends and foresee the most possible future threats or developments.

Another study in the literature underlines the benefits of the usage of AI and NLP in public administration. It emphasizes the reduction of costs achieved thanks to the usage of NLP technology in the automation of repetitive duties (Androutsopoulou et al., 2019, pp. 358–359). The reduction of costs in the relevant jobs provides the public administration with the ability to deploy the relevant public personnel in other critical positions and hard duties.

The usage of AI and NLP in public administration increases the righteousness and coherence of public services. The application of these technologies augments the reliability of public services, reinforces relations with shareholders and creates an environment of trust thanks to the decrease in human error and standardized responses (Miner et al., 2020, p. 1). NLP provides reliable analysis of grand data to the public administrators easily, which creates more safe relations between citizens and government. AI and NLP also increase the transparency, openness, accountability and citizen participation in public administration since they can make public data accessible more (Kalampokis et al., 2023, p. 4).

The usage of AI technologies in public administration has some difficulties. For example, necessity of change in organizational structure and the increase in the skills of public personnel. Furthermore, the increase in openness, accountability and transparency in public administration requires public personnel to be more careful about their duties (Madan & Ashok, 2023, p. 2). Language diversity, data privacy and ethical issues are other potential difficulties in AI and NLP usage in public administration. Since NLP must understand and process many languages existing in the world correctly, it may create some errors or lead to dissemination of classified information. Therefore, usage of AI and NLP in public administration requires enhanced security protocols and precautions.

Although NLP poses such challenges in its application in public administration, the challenges in question can be easily overcome since NLP becomes the center of the PA services thanks to the supplementary precautions. Such precautions and efforts become quite meaningful when the advantages and benefits NLP provides are taken into consideration together with its costs and disadvantages. Furthermore, NLP can enhance the sustainability, decision-making process, citizen participation in public administration when the NLP is combined with other AI technologies such as big data analytics and the Internet of Things (IoT). It will also provide huge amounts of data and working area to the researchers, policy makers and practitioners.

The 21st century brings many difficulties with it for public sector and NLP plays crucial role in the addressing of those difficulties. For the sustainability of government operations, NLP usage is indispensable since it decreases costs of public services and increases openness, citizen participation and accountability in public administration. With this regard, this study aims to provide a comprehensive overview of the impact and possibilities of NLP on sustainable public administration and to provide key strategies for researchers and policy makers achieving sustainability in public administration.

2. CONCEPTUAL FRAMEWORK

The conceptual framework of this study mainly consists of natural language processing and sustainability. With this regard, the regarding concepts will be analyzed.

2.1. Definition and Key Concepts of Natural Language Processing (NLP)

NLP has a rich history dating back to the 1940s when Roberto Busa, an Italian Jesuit priest, pioneered computational linguistics by analyzing the complete works of St. Thomas Aquinas. In 1949, Busa induced IBM founder Thomas J. Watson to support his project, the Index Thomisticus, which ultimately eclectics Aquinas' works into a computer-readable format over 30 years, using more than 11 million punch cards (Eggers et al., 2019). NLP acquired widespread recognition in the 1950s, sitting at the crossroads of AI and linguistics (Nadkarni et al., 2011, p. 544). In fact, NLP emerged as a branch of AI and Linguistics intended to enable computers to understand expressions or words written in human languages (Figure 1). It was developed to make easier users' tasks and to fulfill the desire to communicate with computers in natural language (Khurana et al., 2023, p. 3714). Fueled by advancements in machine learning, NLP has become a well-established domain within AI, linguistics, computer science, and information technology (Egger & Gokce, 2022, p. 308). Recent advances in NLP are driven by deep learning and neural networks, which mimic brain neuron functions for better performance. On the contrary traditional algorithms, deep learning NLP can learn from examples autonomously.

NLP is a branch of computer science and AI that strengthens machine learning to help machines understand and interact using human language. NLP enables computers and digital devices to recognize, comprehend, and produce text and speech by integrating rule-based modeling of human language with statistical modeling, machine learning, and deep learning techniques (IBM, 2024). NLP involves a variety of computational methods, driven by theoretical principles, aimed at analyzing and representing naturally occurring texts across multiple levels of linguistic analysis. The aim is to reach human-like language processing for various tasks and applications (Liddy, 2021, p. 3).

NLP comprises several key technologies that make easier the understanding and processing of human language. Morphological analysis focuses on the structure of words, delivering the identification of roots, affixes, and word formations, which is essential for understanding various linguistic patterns (Manning & Schutze, 1999, p. 81). Syntactic analysis examines sentence structure and the relationships between words, employing grammar rules to analyze sentences and ensure grammaticl correctness. Semantic analysis searches into the meanings of words and phrases, determining how context influences meaning, which is crucial for accurately interpreting language. Additionally, sentiment analysis identifies and categorizes emotions expressed in text, providing valuable insights into public opinion and customer feedback (Pang & Lee, 2008, p. 25). Relation inference focuses on identifying relationships between entities within a text, which aids in information retrieval and knowledge graph construction. Finally, automatic summarization generates brief summaries of lengthy texts, enhancing information accessibility and comprehension. Together, these technologies form the backbone of NLP, enabling machines to effectively interact with human language.

The aim of NLP is to achieve language processing that looks like human capabilities. The term 'processing' is deliberately chosen and should not be substituted with 'understanding.' Although the early days of AI referred to this field as Natural Language Understanding (NLU), it is widely recognized today that, while the ultimate objective of NLP is real NLU, this goal has not yet been fully realized (Liddy, 2021, p. 4).

Figure 1. The evaluation of NLP underlying algorithms

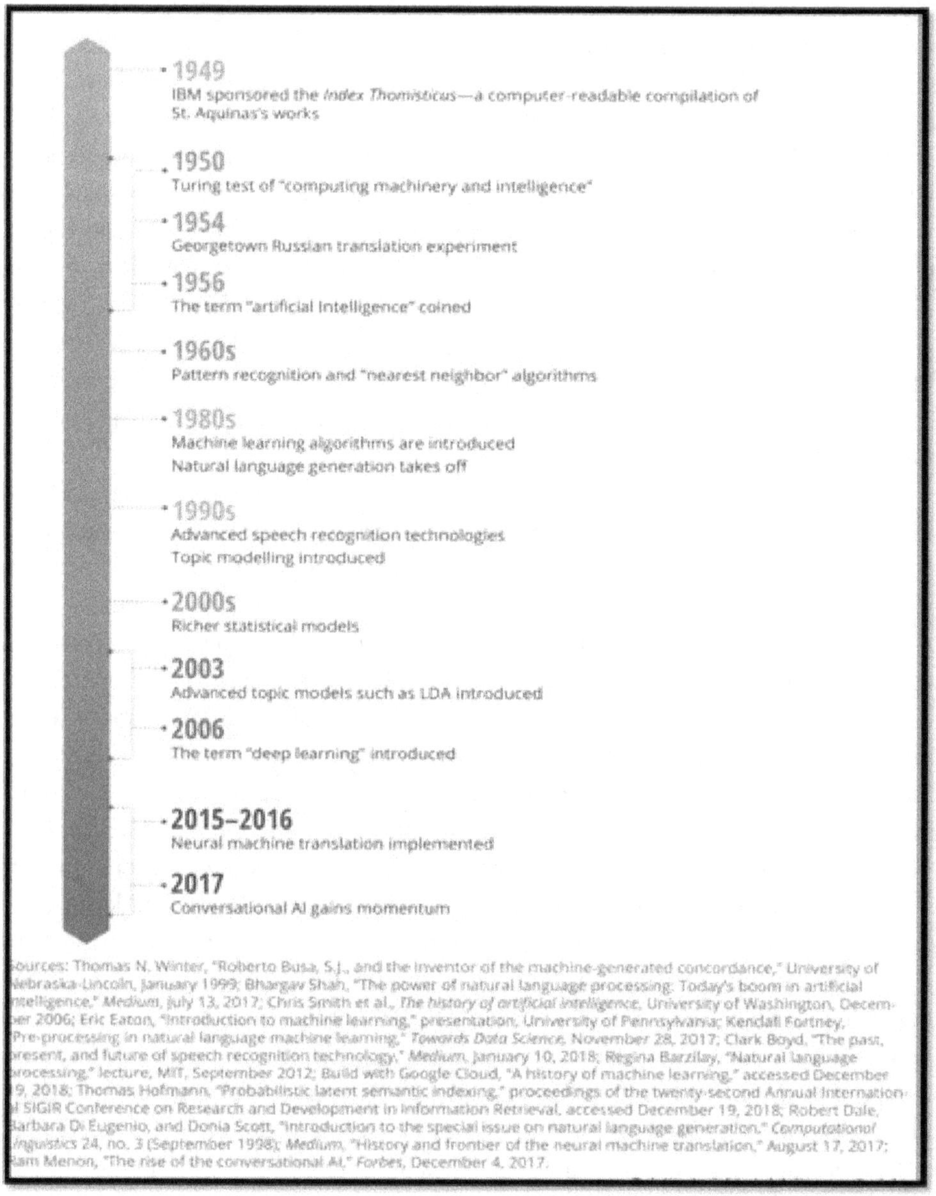

2.2. The Significance of Sustainability in Public Administration

The evaluation of the concept of sustainability in the context of public administration began with the adoption of an approach that comprises not only environmental and development issues but also social justice and economic balance. In this context, sustainable public administration means that states and public institutions develop policies and practices that use resources efficiently and effectively while considering the needs of future generations. As the Prime Minister of Norway, Brundtland chaired the UN World Commission on Environment and Development and popularized the concept of sustainable development. The Brundtland Report underlies the foundation for integrating the concept of sustainability into public policies. The report emphasized that sustainable public administration provides a framework that reunites environmental protection, economic development, and social equity (UN, 1987). This is considered one of the cornerstones of sustainability in public administration literature.

The UN Conference on Environment and Development, held in 1992, discussed how sustainable development in public administration could be implemented through applicable policies. The "Agenda 21" document emphasized that sustainable development should be applied at the local government level. The UN conference in question and its documents composed a guide for the adoption and implementation of sustainable development strategies in public sector (UN, 1992).

In their work, Bryson and George (2024, pp. 3–4) underlines some serious and global challenges encountered by public and nonprofit sector leaders and managers such as rapid technological advancements, demographic changes, climate change, and economic instability. Such global changes create complex environments and difficulties for leaders and require strategic planning for effective action and solution. Thus, sustainable administration involves strategic planning in dealing with such challenges.

Bryson and George (2024, pp. 5–6) put forth that that strategic planning has critical importance for public and nonprofit sector in the solution of problems led by such developments. According to Bryson and George, strategic planning plays a huge role in organizations' adaptation of changes, creation of public value, and maintenance of sustainable development goals. This process involves comprehension the interconnected issues like influencing organizations, including technological changes, migration, aging populations, climate change, inequality, violence, economic management, and declining trust in public institutions. Furthermore, strategic planning supports ability of organizations, to develop comprehensive approaches that consolidate environmental, economic, and social considerations, necessary for sustainability. Therefore, sustainable public administration requires effective leadership. Because of the desire to adopt and implement the relevant strategic plan addressing the emerging and changing global developments.

Public and non-profit sectors must adapt themselves in accordance with the changes in technological developments especially in AI, robotics, and virtual workspaces. Strategic planning is the key point for these sectors to embrace such developments in cost efficient and sustainable ways. Sustainability in public administration emphasizes the need for long-term planning comprising environmental, social, and economic aspects. To ensure that resources can be available for future generations as well. Sustainable public administration, thus, aims to reduce waste and conserve resources by promoting resource efficiency. Furthermore, sustainability comprises addressing social equity and justice issues. Sustainable public administration aims to create policies that benefit all segments of society by ensuring that vulnerable populations have access to essential services and opportunities. Sustainable public administration supports and leads to more effective and responsive governance by promoting citizens' active participation in decision-making processes.

Sustainability prepares public organizations for environmental and social changes, such as climate change and demographic shifts by increasing robustness through strategic plans and relevant sustainable practices, precautions and regulations. Furthermore, sustainable public administration supports economic growth and employment through its encouragements of innovations in green technologies.

Sustainable public administration also prevents the potential legal and financial penalties due to the violation of the sustainability regulations which are always being upgraded since sustainable public administrations already adapt themselves to the changing rules. Furthermore, sustainable practices increase the public's life quality and health through the clean air and water, green environment and preserved nature.

Additionally, sustainability promotes the development of metrics and indicators for the assessment of social, environmental and economic performance of policies. It leads to permanent development and accountability in the relevant fields. Public administrators, on the other hand, can deal with changing global problems by promoting sustainable practices which enhances the quality of life and health of public.

2.3. The Relationship Between NLP and the Three Pillars of Sustainability: Environmental, Economic, and Social

Government agencies and public services manage and analyze a large amount of text-based data. This data includes public records, legal documents, and comments from the public. This information helps in decision-making and improving services. Even so it would be impossible to manually examine all this data. This is where NLP comes in. By automating the analysis of this data, NLP can reveal insights that are difficult to find manually. This helps the government make better decisions and improve public services and sectors (Cogent, 2024).

3. APPLICATIONS OF NLP IN SUSTAINABLE PUBLIC ADMINISTRATION

There are so many application areas of NLP in sustainable public administration in the world. In this section, the most prominent NLP applications in the world will be discussed. These applications will be presented through selected country examples. It has been determined that NLP applications for sustainable public administration are more common, especially in countries that have adopted AI technologies relatively more (such as the US, UK, and European countries). The figure titled "Natural Language Processing Applications in Public Administration" highlights various areas where NLP technologies can be applied within the realm of public administration. These applications include analyzing citizen feedback, automating document processing, providing policy recommendations, detecting fraud, deploying virtual assistants, monitoring public opinion, ensuring regulatory compliance, offering translation services, managing emergency responses, and enhancing transparency and accountability (Figure 2). The mentioned application areas will be examined in the following section of the study in the context of environmental, economic, and social sustainability.

Figure 2. Natural language processing applications in public administration

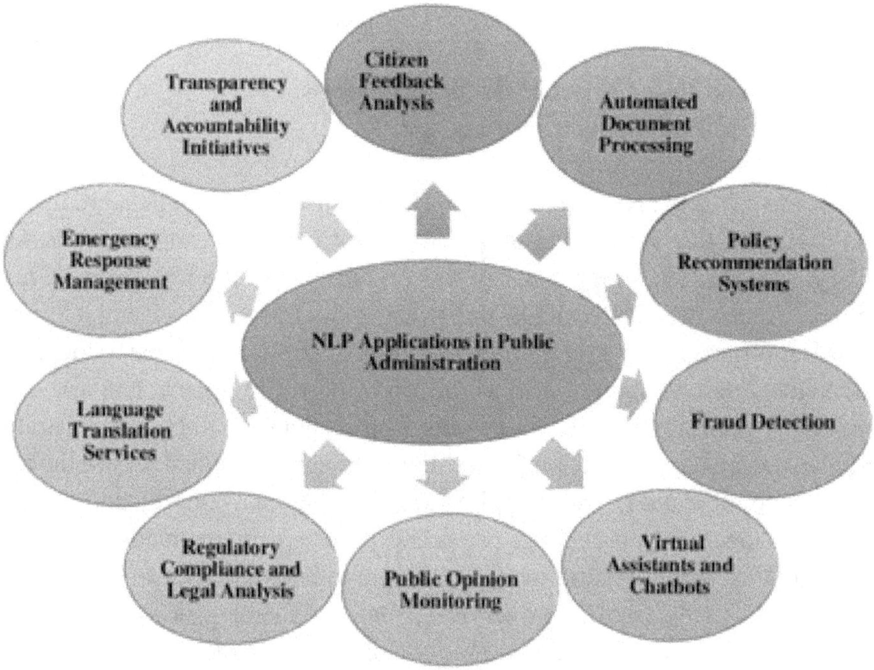

The integration of NLP technologies in public administration has sweeping effects for sustainability. By developing environmental, economic and social sustainability, NLP applications help create a more efficient, coherent, and inclusive government. NLP in public administration both increases the quality of public services but composes an easy way for public sector to deal with the challenges in sustainable way. The ongoing research would create new opportunities for the public sector' NLP usage in creating sustainable social, economic and environmental space.

Government agencies try to analyze large amounts of data in policy analysis and decision-making processes. NLP makes the work of these agencies easier by doing such analyses. In the U.S. Department of Defense (DoD), analysts Tom is a notable example of this since it processes data from a various of sources, including weather reports, traffic information, military movements, and social media. Much of this data consists of unstructured text. Making it difficult to identify patterns and draw actionable conclusions (Eggers et al., 2019). Defense Advanced Research Projects Agency (DARPA) serving under The DoD developed the Deep Text Exploration and Filtering (DEFT) program to address these challenges. NLP provides the program with the relevant data automatically from unstructured sources. Thus, it contributes analysts in identifying important trends and knowledge. This approach develops the decision-making and service delivery across a variety of government sectors varying from defense, and transportation to public safety and healthcare (OECD, 2024, p. 10).

NLP-based software continues to develop and is utilized in the public sector increasingly. NPL based chatbots and virtual assistants increase public participation by answering questions correctly, providing information in public services, and helping in paperwork through natural language understanding. NLP based software are benefited by the policy makers as well since they can assess the public reactions and adjust their policies accordingly thanks to the NLP based analysis of news articles and social media sources. For example, sentiment analysis can assess public opinions on issues like immigration and border control. Sentiment analysis, thus, leads to the emergence of more popular and fact-based policies. NLP also plays a significant role in fraud detection by analyzing large amounts of text data to identify activities such as money laundering and tax evasion. In this context, federal revenue agencies use NLP to determine potential fraud in tax returns, and it can detect corruption in public procurement data. In traffic management, NLP analyzes data from traffic sensors and social media to identify density and traffic patterns. Major cities use NLP to foresee traffic conditions, aiding in informed decision-making regarding road design and signal timings, thus decreasing congestion and improving efficiency. NLP can also evaluate the impact of major events on traffic by analyzing social media, enabling real-time adjustments like road closures and traffic light changes (Cogent, 2024).

3.1. Environmental Sustainability

In his work "The Concept of Environmental Sustainability," Robert Goodland defines "environmental sustainability" as the preservation of natural capital. He presents this concept as distinct from, yet interconnected with, social and economic sustainability (Goodland, 1995, p. 2). Environmental sustainability could be defined as a condition of balance, resilience, and interconnectedness that allows human society to satisfy its needs while neither exceeding the capacity of its supporting ecosystems to continue to regenerate the services necessary to meet those needs nor by our actions diminishing biological diversity (Morelli, 2013, p. 5). environmental sustainability as fulfilling the resource and service needs of both current and future generations without jeopardizing the health of the ecosystems that provide those resources. More specifically, it is characterized as a state of balance, resilience, and interconnectedness that enables human society to meet its needs while not surpassing the capacity of supporting ecosystems to regenerate the essential services needed or diminishing biological diversity through our actions.

NLP applications in public administration significantly contribute to environmental sustainability. For instance, by analyzing large volumes of citizen feedback and public opinion, governments can better understand public sentiment towards environmental policies and initiatives. This enables the creation of more effective and widely accepted environmental regulations. Additionally, automated document processing and policy recommendation systems help streamline administrative processes, reducing paper usage and promoting digital workflows, which contribute to lower carbon footprints. Emergency response management through NLP can also increase the efficiency of disaster response, mitigating the impact on the environment.

AI has become a vital tool in addressing key environmental sustainability challenges such as biodiversity, energy, transportation, and water management. In biodiversity research, machine learning and NLP are used to estimate ecosystem services. These technologies also have a significant potential in struggling with climate change. For example, AI-supported buses can decrease emissions by 50 percent by 2050 by optimizing routes for maximum efficiency. AI applications in agriculture have increased productivity as indicated in the example of India (Yadav & Singh, 2023, p. 216).

NLP has become an important thing in the struggle with misinformation related to climate change. A study conducted in the US indicates that NLP helps identify misleading information. Thus, the use of NLP is becoming widespread. Application of NLP is not only important for developing strategies to prevent the dissemination of misinformation, but also vital for promoting environmental sustainability efforts since it ensures that public and private sector initiatives are based on true information (Farrell, 2019, p. 7).

The US has adopted NLP based systems considerably much to augment its policymaking and implementation efforts for environmental sustainability. The US' public agencies like the Environmental Protection Agency (EPA) is able to analyze huge amounts of environmental monitoring reports, social media data, and public feedback thanks to the NLP based softwares (Table 1). This data-driven approach increases comprehension and awareness of environmental issues and public sentiment. Furthermore, it promotes the development of more effective and responsive environmental policies (Application of Artificial Intelligence in EPA Homeland Security, 2022).

As NLP is utilized in almost every aspect of life in advanced economies, agriculture is a crucial part that NLP takes. The Netherlands as one of the perfect users of NLP applies NLP technologies to develop agricultural productivity and support sustainable practices. The Netherlands is analyzing detailed and huge data from agricultural research reports, farmer feedback, and environmental monitoring sources with NLP (as shown in Table 1 below). It enables the Dutch government, and agricultural organizations comprehend the key trends and insights that shape decision making. This approach allows for optimized farming practices, such as precision in agriculture, which augments crop yield while decreasing resource consumption and costs. For instance, the Netherlands benefits from NLP to evaluate reports on soil health, crop performance, and climate patterns. It integrates the findings to inform the relevant parties about the potential threats and opportunities for sustainable land use and resource management. This way includes reducing the need for chemical inputs and monitoring crop health to prevent potential waste and environmental impact. Moreover, information gathered from farmer feedback through NLP-based sentiment analysis helps policymakers understand local challenges and supports better alignment of agricultural policy with the realities of sustainable farming needs. Thus, the needs, threats and opportunities of farmers and other parties of agriculture are best detected and assessed by the state and relevant steps or decisions can be taken for obtaining sustainable agriculture.

Another significant field that NLP plays important role environmental policies executed in the United Kingdom. The UK government benefits from NLP technologies to assess environmental data and develops environmental policies accordingly. Such policies are mainly generated on air quality monitoring, energy efficiency, and biodiversity (as shown in Table 1 below). The NLP technology in question enhances accuracy, precision and quality environmental decision-making processes. The UK government's air quality policies focus on reducing harmful substances due to their adverse health effects. As part of the UK Clean Air Strategy, the government has set a sustainable policy target by 2030, with the goal of protecting public health and the environment. In order to acquire its targets, the UK is using a bunch of technologies, including NLP, to make an automatic analysis of large amounts of data collected from air quality sensors located in varying points of the country. The UK obtains the pollution hotspots and measures the effectiveness level of its environmental policies thanks to the analysis made by the NLP. The UK's environmental plan in which NLP plays critical role promotes the local governments to use their regulatory powers more effectively to reach defined national air quality targets (Department for Environment, Food & Rural Affairs, 2023).

Climate change has been a challenging and threatening issue for our lives. NLP with its wide range of usage can be a robust solution to address such a huge threat. In this context, Australia becomes a prominent country case which uses NLP in its struggle with climate change. It uses NLP to analyze environmental reports and data on climate change (as indicated in Table 1 below). Australia deployed NLP to identify automatically the relationships between climate actions and the United Nations Sustainable Development Goals (SDGs). Australia's initiative enables its policymakers to comprehend the synergies worldwide and adopt policies against climate change along with the world (Zhou et al., 2022, p. 3). Furthermore, Australian public agencies uses NLP techniques to analyze climate-related literature, which enables it to be familiar with the regional effects of climate change (Mallick & Murphy, 2024). Although Australia records a good development in struggling with climate change, there is a lot for it to do for obtaining policies based on the analysis of wide variety of knowledge sources. Australia can achieve it by establishing large datasets and creating models that can summarize findings. Such an initiative can boosts Australia's ability to combat climate change and its challenges.

Japan, on the other hand, gives considerably high attention to the biodiversity since its first National Biodiversity Strategy published in 1993. It is using NLP technologies to enhance its biodiversity efforts as part of its new "National Biodiversity Strategy and Action Plan for 2023-2030" (Table 1). Japan aims to achieve a "nature-positive" society by 2030, with important strategies focusing on ecosystem integrity, nature-based solutions, and recognizing biodiversity's value in everyday life (Japan's National Biodiversity Strategy and Action Plan 2023-2030, 2023). One of the significant initiatives in Japan is the "30by30 Alliance for Biodiversity". It aims to conserve at least 30% of the nation's continental and naval areas by the year 2030. This initiative supports collaboration among various sectors, including public, private enterprises, and academic institutions, to develop biodiversity monitoring and reporting. The use of NLP is particularly advantageous for processing existing datasets of biodiversity assessments and surveys. Thanks to it, public authorities obtained the ability of recognition of important trends and assisting in relevant policy formulation (Kutty & Tochibayashi, 2022). NLP is beneficial in analyzing large datasets from biodiversity reports and surveys. It also helps to catch the trends and shape policy decisions.

Energy is the main source of the contemporary world's functioning. However, the emergence and usage of such energy should harm the environment. Furthermore, energy should be utilized efficiently so that further generations can benefit from it. With this regard green projects and smart technologies supporting sustainable energy management are vital. Germany appears as the prominent case in integrating NLP technologies into its energy efficiency and renewable energy policies (showed in Table 1). With this regard, Germany deploys NLP to analyze environmental reports, governmental reports, public consultations and feedback, and scientific literature, ultimately informing policy decisions and fostering a more sustainable energy landscape. This analysis significantly enhances the accuracy of its policies on sustainable energy management by extracting key themes from stakeholder feedback, ensuring that energy policies are evidence-based and aligned with public needs. NLP technologies facilitate the renewable energy initiatives in the country that automate data extraction from monitoring reports, helping to track progress toward national energy goals. (IRENA, 2015).

Green building initiatives are popular around the world. Singapore is the most prominent of them since it uses NLP and other technologies effectively in this field. In Singapore, NLP technology is widely used to evaluate public sentiment regarding green building initiatives, particularly through the "Building and Construction Authority (BCA)" and its "Green Building Masterplan" (Table 1). This plan comprises public engagement efforts, where surveys and consultations are conducted to gather insights from citizens. For example, over 5,000 individuals discussed about their perspectives on green buildings, and the results were unified into policy recommendations (Green Building Masterplans, 2024). NLP plays a crucial role in analyzing the feedback collected during these public consultations. By processing textual data, NLP helps identify common themes, concerns, and levels of support related to green building projects. This data-driven approach allows policymakers to designate their strategies to better align with public expectations and needs. Also, through ongoing assessments of public sentiment, Singapore aims to develop community involvement and promote greater acceptance of sustainable building practices, ensuring that 80% of its buildings are green by 2030.

Table 1. Harnessing NLP for environmental sustainability: Sectoral insights

Sector	Country	NLP Application	Purpose
Environmental Monitoring	United States	Analyzing environmental reports and social media data	To develop effective environmental policies by understanding public sentiment and environmental conditions.
Agriculture	Netherlands	Analyzing agricultural research data	To enhance agricultural sustainability and policy development through insights from farmer feedback and studies.
Air Quality Management	United Kingdom	Evaluating air quality reports and public opinions	To improve air quality policies by assessing community concerns and data analytics.
Climate Change	Australia	Analyzing climate change impact reports	To develop strategies addressing climate change effects based on analyzed environmental data.
Biodiversity	Japan	Monitoring public feedback on biodiversity conservation	To support conservation policies by utilizing public input and environmental reports for biodiversity efforts.
Energy Sector	Germany	Analyzing reports on renewable energy usage	To optimize energy policies and improve the transition to renewable sources through detailed data analysis.
Urban Planning	Singapore	Evaluating public sentiment on green building initiatives	To enhance urban sustainability practices and support the development of eco-friendly infrastructure.

Source: Authors

The application of NLP across various countries plays a crucial role for increasing environmental sustainability through developed public engagement, data analysis, and informed policymaking. Nations like US, Netherlands UK, Australia, Japan, Germany and the Singapore set good examples how NLP can facilitate better understanding and response to environmental concerns, thereby supporting sustainable practices.

3.2. Economic Sustainability

The concept of sustainability has become widely recognized and accepted in international development and environmental policy communities. Organizations like the World Resources Institute, World Bank, World watch Institute, and the International Union for the Conservation of Nature and Natural Resources have all identified sustainability as a crucial policy objective (Foy, 1990, p. 771). Economic sustainability refers to the ability of an economy to support a defined level of economic production indefinitely. This includes maintaining the necessary financial, social, and environmental resources to ensure ongoing productivity and economic growth without depleting the natural resources and environmental assets that future generations will need to thrive (Foy, 1990, p. 776).

According to the World Bank, the public sector is crucial for a country's development and economic growth, as it provides the essential technical and technological infrastructure needed to drive progress. Economic development would not be possible without the efforts of the public sector, as governments make direct investments in various economic sectors, including industry, agriculture, and commerce, to stimulate growth (Bolívar, 2017, p. 3). The high levels of debt and deficits have weakened public service delivery due to reduced revenues and expenditure cuts. Decentralization has led to significant territorial disparities and duplicated services, challenging public administrations' ability to maintain service quality and quantity. This situation has increased the demand for better financial transparency and sustainability to ensure effective public administration.

Economic sustainability is supported by NLP applications through improved efficiency and cost savings in public administration. For example, fraud detection systems which are supported by NLP can identify and prevent fraudulent transactions, ensuring significant public fund savings. Virtual assistants and chatbots decrease the need for extensive human resources by handling routine citizen demands, allowing governments to allocate resources more effectively. Policy recommendation systems based on NLP can provide data-driven insights. Leading to better decision-making and optimized allocation of financial resources. These applications not only reduce operational costs but also provide that public funds are utilized in the most effective manner, supporting long-term economic stability.

Effective economic management is important for sustainability, especially in the face of financial crises and economic recessions (Bryson & George, 2024, p. 7). In the context of public administration, leveraging NLP plays a critical role in achieving economic sustainability. By utilizing NLP, government bodies can analyze large volumes of text data to gain insights into resource management, policy impacts, and public sentiment. This can cause more informed decision-making processes that balance economic growth with the preservation of environmental assets.

The US uses NLP technologies to develop sustainability in the energy sector (Table 2). The Department of Energy (DOE) benefits from NLP applications to analyze energy usage data and environmental reports, thereby optimizing energy policies (DOE Announces New Actions to Enhance America's Global Leadership in Artificial Intelligence, 2024). This makes it possible to enhance energy efficiency and support the use of renewable energy sources. The U.S. Department of Energy's "Oak Ridge National Laboratory" is benefiting NLP to assemble and analyze data related to components of the energy ecosystem. This initiative aims to rank the leading clean energy innovation ecosystems across the US. The laboratory describes how it analyzes large amounts of textual and numerical data related to clean energy innovation with NLP techniques and transforms this data into measurable indicators. The laboratory can map developments in energy innovation geographically thanks to which investors and policy makers can see which regions are intensively populated with energy innovation. (Eggers et al., 2019, p. 12). This case promotes energy efficiency policies and renewable energy sources. The Consumer Financial Protection Bureau (CFPB) uses NLP technologies to analyze consumers' financial data and develops consumer protection policies, which augments economic sustainability.

The Netherlands is an important country using NLP in different ways to control agricultural reports and trends. Without any doubt, it has a significant impact on its status as one of the largest agricultural exporters worldwide (Table 2). Dutch agricultural authorities, such as the Ministry of Agriculture, Nature and Food Quality (LNV), use NLP to analyze vast amounts of data from agricultural reports, literature, and economic indicators. Such analysis allows Netherlands for the monitoring of structural developments, economic significance, and international trade within the agricultural sector (Rintoul, 2023). NLP technologies are used in the Netherlands to evaluate the environmental performance of agricultural practices by monitoring sustainability initiatives, greenhouse gas emissions, and compliance with regulations. These technologies analyze research papers and policy documents to assess the sector's contributions to sustainability goals.

In the UK, on the other hand, NLP plays a crucial role in analyzing feedback to raise economic sustainability in healthcare (Table 2). NLP helps identify common concerns and sentiments, which enables healthcare providers to enable processes and assign resources more effectively because of the data collected from large volumes of patient feedback (Fairie et al., 2021, p. 1). The focus on efficiency is crucial for decreasing waste and maintaining budgetary constraints for the UK. NLP thus encourages cost-saving opportunities by analyzing feedback to highlight gaps in the system thorugh patient experiences (HDR UK, 2021). This reduces the need for expensive measures and their costs while it creates an environment for improvements to be made.

In Australia, NLP is used to understand community concerns about environmental policies for economic sustainability concerns (Table 2). This approach allows policymakers to analyze public feedback from various sources (like social media and surveys) to describe key community sentiments and priorities related to environmental initiatives. NLP enables authorities to categorize and quantify public sentiments related to environmental issues, ensuring policies align with community expectations and fostering public support. Technology assesses perceptions of the economic implications of environmental policies, such as job creation in green sectors or costs associated with climate adaptation. NLP enables to evaluate the effectiveness of existing policies, which also gives clues on the public expectations(Climate Change Authority, 2019).

In Finland, NLP is used to evaluate public feedback on educational services, particularly in the context of economic sustainability (Table 2). NLP technologies are used to analyze feedback from surveys, social media, and public forums. It identifies the main concerns, preferences, and recommendations of society regarding the quality of education and access to education. This analysis plays a crucial role in informing policymakers about public sentiment and priorities. Furthermore, it also informs policymakers on whether educational reforms collaborate with economic sustainability goals. For example, understanding the demand for skills that adjust the job market enables and promotes educational institutions to adapt curricula, which promotes a workforce that supports economic growth while maintaining social equity (Ministry of Education and Culture, 2024).

In Singapore, NLP is used to optimize transportation systems to attain economic sustainability (Table 2). NLP applications analyze data from various sources and inform authorities to make precise decisions about public transport and private vehicle usage. For instance, Singapore's Land Transport Authority (LTA) uses NLP to utilize public sentiment regarding transport policies, identify areas for improvement, and assess the effectiveness of existing services. This feedback cycle enables the continuous development of transportation strategies to align with economic sustainability goals (Md Nur, 2022).

Table 2. Harnessing NLP for economic sustainability: Sectoral insights

Sector	Country	NLP Application	Purpose
Energy Sector	United States	Analyzing energy consumption data	To optimize energy policies and practices based on insights from energy usage reports.
Consumer Finance	United States	Analyzing consumer feedback and complaints	To aid in developing consumer protection policies by understanding public sentiment regarding financial services.
Agriculture	Netherlands	Monitoring agricultural reports and trends	To improve agricultural policies and sustainability initiatives through data analysis from farmers and research.
Public Health	United Kingdom	Analyzing health-related public feedback	To guide equitable health policies by assessing public needs and opinions in health services.
Environmental Protection	Australia	Understanding community concerns on environmental policies	To enhance environmental regulations and promote sustainability initiatives by analyzing social media and feedback.
Education	Finland	Evaluating public feedback on educational services	To improve education access and economic opportunities through processed feedback on educational policies.
Transport	Singapore	Optimizing transportation systems	To create more efficient transportation policies by analyzing traffic and public transport data using NLP.

Source: Authors

The use of NLP in various countries serves as an important mechanism for providing economic sustainability through improved public sector engagement and data-driven policymaking. Countries like the US, the UK, Finland, Singapore, Australia, and the Netherlands illustrate how NLP can transform the way governments interact with citizens, make more reliable and precise decisions while it enables a more responsive and adaptive approach in addressing social needs.

3.3. Social Sustainability

Social sustainability is improved by NLP applications that promote transparency, inclusiveness, and accessibility in public administration. Government data becomes more accessible and understandable through NLP technologies. This situation enhances trust between citizens and the government. For example, NLP technologies such as language translation services facilitate access to essential public services for individuals with different native languages, which promotes inclusiveness and equality. NLP applications are used in various ways to support social sustainability comprises social equality, justice, community health, and cultural richness in different countries in the world.

In the US, the Consumer Financial Protection Bureau (CFPB) utilized NLP to analyze public opinions and complaints related to financial services, which augments social sustainability (Deloitte, 2013). This analysis enables policymakers to understand consumer complaints better and improve financial products and services to solve the problems in question (Table 3). NLP technologies classify and organize complaints by various categories, such as debt collection and mortgage issues (Craven, 2021).

The UK government used NLP to analyze public sentiments and opinions, particularly in the health and education spheres (Table 3). For example, the Health Foundation conducts surveys to evaluate public perceptions of the National Health Service (NHS) and social care (Buzelli et al., 2022, p. 25). Their findings indicate that a significant portion of the public believes the quality of care has declined due to the waiting times and staff. The UK government utilizes NLP to analyze feedback from various sources, including social media and public consultations (Dray, 2019).

The Indian government utilizes NLP to analyze public feedback on social assistance programs, which significantly contributes to social sustainability (Table 3). The government can process and interpret large volumes of public opinions collected from different sources, including social media, surveys, and feedback forms, which enables them to gain information into the effectiveness and impact of programs designed to decrease poverty, improve healthcare, and enhance educational opportunities. This data-driven approach allows policymakers to adapt programs based on the actual needs and concerns of the community (Mehra, 2021).

The Canadian government benefits from NLP to analyze feedback from indigenous communities, which is essential for protecting their rights and shaping socially sustainable policies (Table 3). This involves integration of indigenous knowledge through approaches like "Two-Eyed AI" which combines Indigenous and Western methodologies to develop that technology serves Indigenous interests rather than consolidating historical biases. The public authorities can evaluate community sentiments and identify systemic issues in existing policies thanks to the NLP analysis from different sources (Dubay, 2021).

In Australia, the government uses NLP to analyze public data concerning women's rights, focusing on enhancing economic opportunities for women as part of broader social sustainability efforts (Table 3). This involves utilizing NLP technologies to evaluate sentiments and opinions expressed in various forums, including social media, public consultations, and surveys. The information gathered through NLP, help policymakers identify barriers that women face in accessing economic opportunities and develop targeted initiatives to address these challenges. For instance, Australia's "10-Year Plan to Unleash the Full Capacity and Contribution of Women to the Australian Economy" emphasizes the importance of removing systemic barriers and promoting women's economic equality. Moreover, by monitoring public feedback, the government can adapt its strategies to align more closely with community needs and expectations, fostering an environment that supports women's participation in the workforce and economic activities. Australia aims to create a more overarching economy that recognizes and utilizes the full potential of its female population thanks to the more alignment with NLP (Australian Government, 2021).

In South Korea, NLP is adopted to analyze social media and public data to understand the needs of the elderly (Table 3). The government recognizes the necessity for innovative strategies to address the evolving demands of this demographic change since the estimations indicates that over 20% of South Koreans will be aged 65 and older by 2025. With this regard, a key initiative is the Korean Longitudinal Healthy Aging Study which began in 2021 to search the needs of the new generations of elderly people (Han et al., 2023). Through these efforts, South Korea aims to create more inclusive and sustainable policies that augment the quality of life for its aging population.

In Finland, the government employs NLP to analyze public feedback related to educational services with the aim of developing equitable educational policies (Table 3). This analysis is crucial in identifying the various needs and experiences of students, teachers, and parents, particularly in enhancing the inclusiveness of the education system. Finnish authorities can efficiently process large amounts data obtained from the feedback from various sources, including social media, surveys, and educational forums with this technology. The government addresses the problems arising from differences in educational access and outcomes through this information by promoting an environment where all learners can thrive regardless of their backgrounds (Finceed, 2024).

Table 3. Harnessing NLP for social sustainability: Sectoral insights

Sector	Country	NLP Application	Purpose
Consumer Protection	United States	The Consumer Financial Protection Bureau (CFPB) uses NLP to analyze public opinions and consumer complaints related to financial services.	Aids in developing consumer protection policies and promotes economic equality.
Social Policy Development	United Kingdom	The UK government uses NLP to understand public opinions in developing social policies, especially in health and education.	Improves social equity and addresses community health needs.
Poverty Alleviation	India	The Indian government utilizes NLP to analyze public feedback on social assistance programs.	Helps identify effective strategies to combat poverty.

continued on following page

Table 3. Continued

Sector	Country	NLP Application	Purpose
Indigenous Rights	Canada	Canada employs NLP to analyze feedback from Indigenous communities to protect their rights and develop social policies.	Aims to preserve cultural values and improve living conditions.
Gender Equality	Australia	The Australian government uses NLP to analyze public data related to women's rights to enhance economic opportunities for women.	Supports the development of gender equality policies.
Elderly Services	South Korea	The South Korean government analyzes social media and public data to identify the needs of the elderly population.	Improves social support services and enhances the quality of life for seniors.
Education	Finland	The Finnish government analyzes public feedback related to education using NLP to develop equitable educational policies.	Ensures equal opportunities in education and improves student outcomes.

Source: Authors

NLP has become an important tool for providing social sustainability across various nations since it promotes more informed and responsive governance. Governments can understand better the needs of citizens and can create policies that promote inclusiveness and equity thanks to the NLP technologies. For instance, countries like the US and the UK utilize NLP to improve financial services and healthcare policies, while India focuses on social assistance programs to ensure support reaches marginalized communities. Similarly, nations such as Canada and Australia benefit from NLP to hear Indigenous communities' voices and promote gender equality. It demonstrates the adaptability of NLP applications in addressing complex social issues. Overall, the integration of NLP in public policies not only facilitates the identification of trends and gaps but also strengthens the relationship between governments and their citizens while it promotes more equitable and sustainable future.

4. CHALLENGES AND ETHICAL CONSIDERATIONS

AI is seen as a huge potential for the world as well as it is seen a monster for some of them. Since the emergence of AI with Turing in 1950s, the viewpoint of AI has changed. Stephan Hawking and Bill Gates claimed that it is a great threat for the world. In fact, doubts about AI were neither limited to them nor did they reach a conclusion. Challenges about the use of NLP for sustainable public administration include challenges about AI. The primary challenge of NLP is the ability of interpretation. NLP technology is not able to completely interpret natural language (Abro et al., 2023, p. 1532). There are also claims that NLP algorithms can be biased like humans (Cogent, 2024). There are some challenges and ethical consideration like these, are examined in this section.

4.1. Language Diversity and Accessibility Issues

There are so many languages and dialects on the world. So, this is a challenge to the use of NLP in public administrations (Shelf, 2024). Because public administrations serve linguistically diverse populations. NLP technologies often present service widely spoken languages, while minority and indigenous languages receive less attention. The diversity of languages and dialects found worldwide is one of the primary challenges to the use of NLP technologies in public administration (Shelf, 2024). The biggest drawback of traditional language models is that they operate in only one direction, which limits the variety of pre-training architectures that can be used (Abro et al., 2023, p. 1533).

Many NLP models are built primarily on widely spoken languages, often neglecting smaller languages and dialects. As De-Dios-Flores and Campos (2023, p. 8) note that in multilingual contexts like Spain, NLP systems should be expert at handling multiple languages to provide fair and effective public service. Public administration aims to address and serve the needs of all citizens equitably; thus, handling diverse linguistic needs becomes important. For public administration, this creates a challenge in collecting representative data and providing inclusivity in decision-making. Addressing these issues requires reconciled NLP models that account for local language variations and dialects.

Each language has its own linguistic and cultural nuances. Cai (2021, p. 1218) emphasizes that multilingual NLP should not only translate but also contextualize language use in urban governance to make public administration accessible and relevant to diverse communities. Adopting this approach in public administration is vital to increasing citizens' compliance with government policies and developing more sustainable governance frameworks that respect cultural identities.

Accessibility is also a central subject in the sustainable application of NLP in public administration. In this context, accessibility means that NLP systems must be designed to address a wide range of users, including those with varying levels of digital literacy, socioeconomic backgrounds, and physical abilities. However, significant challenges exist there. NLP systems often suppose a standard level of language proficiency and technical understanding, which can alienate users who do not meet these expectations. Esfahani (2024, p. 97) argues that NLP applications in education must account for users with different reading and comprehension abilities to ensure that public services are inclusive.

4.2. Data Privacy and Security Challenges

Public authorities acquire and store huge amounts of data some of which are sensitive and private. The private and sensitive data in question should be stored by the public authorities securely. Furthermore, NLP based technologies analyze large amounts of data obtained during measurement of public sentiment, policy impacts, or environmental feedback. The data in question should be kept highly secure and classified in order to prevent misuse (Xu & He, 2023). The data obtained by the NLP applications is often stored in centralized or cloud-based systems which are mostly vulnerable to cyber-attacks (Jim et al., 2024, p. 23). Unauthorized access can reveal sensitive data, violate personal privacy and abuse sensitive or private information. In order to prevent such unintended cases, the data in question should be obtained and stored under multi-layered security protocols. Data encryption is one of the most secure ways which should be used by any public authority deploying NLP. Multiple control measures for storage and access would augment the security of the data stored.

The number of participants in the analysis is significant for the security of the research and result data of NLP since some of the members of small groups can be identifiable through their distinctive features. NLP unintentionally reveal or hide such sort of information belonging to the members of small populations since it may not understand the identifiability of some certain members with distinctive characteristics (Jim et al., 2024, p. 25).

The risk in question raises during the NLP analysis of sensitive small groups since it can disseminate the identities of some members. In order both to avoid such situations and ensure the maintenance of NLP analysis, advanced anonymization methods are indispensable in the public services conducted on NLP.

Jim et al (2024, p. 25) underlines that legal constraints may occur when the NLP based tools are used to analyze social media comments of citizens since it can reveal personal information of users. With this regard, ethical data usage policies should be in conjunction with NLP if the data in question is collected without specific consent. Therefore, transparent data collection practices and policies are the best solutions that can address such ethical issues.

Another obstacle is that NLP may contain biases of the data producers since it is a data-driven technology. It can sometimes reinforce those biases, and it may thus bear the risks for biased decision-making. If NLP is not steered and monitored carefully, its algorithms can distort results and increase social inequalities in contrary to the principle of equal access and fair treatment in public services. However, impartiality in public services can be maximized when the data is precisely collected, processed and analyzed by NLP based tools.

When the NLP based tools are being established by the institutions, the data privacy laws and frameworks should be kept under consideration for the data collection, storage, use, and disposal. Hence, the design of technology should be composed in accordance with such rules.

4.3. Solutions for Addressing These Challenges

Up to this point of study, some challenges of NLP applications in the context of sustainable public administration have been mentioned. Alternative solutions to these challenges will be compiled in this part of the study. These are about enhancing transparency and explainability, reducing bias and ensuring fairness, strengthening privacy and data security, establishing accountability in automated decision-making and ethical data collection and informed consent.

Enhancing Transparency and Explainability

It is important to develop NLP models that will make decision-making processes transparent. Because these are among the most important criteria for sustainable public administration. That can be achieved with algorithms (Magnini et al., 2000, p. 5). This involves adopting interpretable algorithms, such as decision trees or rule-based models. These make it easier for users to understand how decisions are reached. Public administrations should establish guidelines for regularly reporting model decisions. Especially, in high-impact areas like policy evaluation. These transparency reports can develop public understanding of how NLP influences policies and public services.

Reducing Bias and Ensuring Fairness

Fair and objective application of NLP technologies is of vital significance for sustainable public administration to obtain accurate information. NLP models should be trained on diverse and representative data sets and regularly inspected to prevent any discriminatory behavior in their outputs. According to research, the techniques deployed to decrease bias include prioritizing the training data or using fairness-oriented algorithms (Cerrillo Martinez, 2019, p. 53). In order to reduce bias in automated analyses via NLP, such techniques can be utilized and they can contribute to more equitable results. Furthermore, outside oversight and support would increase the detection of unseen errors in the processes. With this regard, research collaborations with universities and independent institutions can help improve bias detection and correction processes. Such collaborations can enable continuous improvement in NLP algorithms and ensure the preservation of justice

(Behera et al., 2023, p. 26). Preventing bias contributes to providing fairer and more reliable services to citizens in public administration, which increases public trust.

Strengthening Privacy and Data Security

In the contemporary world, data is the biggest power, and its privacy thus gains huge significance. Protecting sensitive information of persons or institutions requires strong anonymization and encryption methods. Implementing differential privacy mechanisms reduces the risk of re-identifying individuals in datasets. Moreover, federated learning can train models on decentralized data, which preserves privacy by avoiding data transfer. In addition, clear communication of data processing methods can augment transparency and user confidence, which are necessary for sustainable public administration.

Establishing Accountability in Automated Decision-Making

NLP based tools for sustainable public administration are both necessary and vital. However, its sole establishment cannot be sufficient without establishing clear and comprehensive accountability mechanisms. In this context, accountability frameworks should clarify the roles of NLP practitioners, developers, and policymakers to ensure responsible NLP implementation. Moreover, assigning oversight roles and creating audit trails in decision-making processes enable public authorities to trace errors and to obtain responsible use of AI tools. In addition, regulatory bodies should oversee NLP applications in public administration, especially in high-stakes cases, potentially enforcing model validation and certification standards to ensure ethical compliance. Thus, vital public administration principles of accountability, reliability and transparency in public services are ensured during NLP based technologies compose the continuity of the sustainable public administration.

Ethical Data Collection and Informed Consent

Ethical considerations are of vital significance in the contemporary world. Ethical data collection is a concept that requires informed consent of the people whose information is to be used. With this regard, the people in question should be informed about where and how their information is going to be utilized. In this context, public policies should offer transparent, accessible explanations and should provide the ability of withdrawal options if possible.

Public administrations can obtain responsible data sharing practices by augmenting public awareness through initiatives that explain the benefits and risks of NLP in governance. In order to ensure this, collaborative action among public administrators, policymakers, technical experts, and the general public is vital since they can address the ethical and technical challenges of NLP in public administration. Such initiative contributes much to sustainable, fair, and effective governance practices that build citizen trust and promote long-term sustainability goals.

5. CONCLUSION

AI has transformed into indispensable, useful and functional technology that facilitates human life. Although it has disadvantages like job displacement, over-reliance in human life; its advantages are countless and has revolutionary effect worldwide. NLP, which is an AI technology examined in this study, continues to develop its influence progressively. NLP enables human-computer interaction and is crucial for sustainable public administration. NLP changes the relation between human and technology since NLP makes technology more accessible. It has the potential to revolutionize human interaction with technology by making it simpler and more convenient. As long as NLP maintains its progress, it will play a vital role in advancing user experiences in a different applications area such as citizen participation, public service delivery, monitoring public health, environment, commerce, agriculture etc. which are essential for sustainable public administration.

Like customer orientation in business administration, citizen-centered services in public administration become attainable with the NLP based technologies since it provides a healthy and reliable relation-communication-interaction between public authorities and citizens with numerous tools and contexts. Virtual assistants and chatbots are the most prominent examples of such NLP-based tools which are used by almost any public institution worldwide today. Human language and machine comprehension becomes no longer a problem thanks to the NLP based tools. Furthermore, it creates new opportunities for data analysis and generation while enabling public authorities to respond more efficiently to citizens' needs and concerns.

This study has indicated that numerous public institutions around the world have been using NLP to implement a citizen-centered approach in public administration in different context and services. The citizens in such countries are met faster, effective and reliable public services with the NLP-based systems which understand and communicate human language. Furthermore, public service delivery became simpler and easier; data analysis became more reliable and precise in such cases. Thanks to the precise analysis of citizen feedback and sentiment through NLP tools, more inclusive citizen participation and data-based decision-making process can be realized.

Although NLP is of vital importance for the sustainable public administration, it also brings some unclear and unpredictable challenges which can yield adverse results arising from the ambiguity and nuance inherent in natural language due to the abundance of language in the world. The abundance in question makes the language learning process complex. However, it is not impossible to overcome which makes NLP a fascinating area of research that is constantly pushing the boundaries of what machines can achieve in the field of public administration. NLP not only serves practical purposes in improving communication within public services, it also raises important questions about the implications of machines understanding human emotions and intentions in the public sector.

REFERENCES

Abro, A. A., Talpur, M. S. H., & Jumani, A. K. (2023). Natural Language Processing Challenges and Issues: A Literature Review. *Gazi University Journal of Science*, 36(4), 4. Advance online publication. DOI: 10.35378/gujs.1032517

Androutsopoulou, A., Karacapilidis, N., Loukis, E., & Charalabidis, Y. (2019). Transforming the communication between citizens and government through AI-guided chatbots. *Government Information Quarterly*, 36(2), 358–367. DOI: 10.1016/j.giq.2018.10.001

Application of Artificial Intelligence in EPA Homeland Security. (2022). https://cfpub.epa.gov/si/si_public_record_report.cfm?Lab=CESER&dirEntryId=357842

Australian Government. (2021). *Second Australian National Action Plan on Women, Peace and Security 2021–2031 | Australian Government Department of Foreign Affairs and Trade*. Australian Government. https://www.dfat.gov.au/publications/second-australian-national-action-plan-on-women-peace-and-security-2021-2031, https://www.dfat.gov.au/publications/second-australian-national-action-plan-on-women-peace-and-security-2021-2031

Behera, R. K., Bala, P. K., & Rana, N. P. (2023). Responsible Natural Language Processing: A

Bryson, J., & George, B. (2024). *Strategic Planning for Public and Nonprofit Organizations: A Guide to Strengthening and Sustaining Organizational Achievement* (6th ed.).

Buzelli, L., Cameron, G., Duxbury, K., Gardner, T., Rutherford, S., Williamson, S., & Alderwick, H. (2022). *Public perceptions of health and social care: What the new government should know - The Health Foundation*. The Health Foundation. https://www.health.org.uk/publications/reports/public-perceptions-of-health-and-social-care-what-government-should-know

Cerrillo i Martinez, A. (2019). How Can We Open the Black Box of Public Administration? Transparency and Accountability in the Use of Algorithms. Revista Catalana de Dret Públic, Cai, M. (2021). Natural language processing for urban research: A systematic review. *Heliyon*, 7(12), 1218.

Climate Change Authority. (2019). *Australia's climate change policies at the Australian and state and territory government levels: A stocktake* (Australia). Commonwealth of Australia 2019. https://apo.org.au/node/224211

Cogent. (2024). *NLP in the Public Sector*. NLP in the Public Sector. https://www.cogentinfo.com/resources/nlp-examples-in-the-public-sector

Cortés-Cediel, M. E., Segura-Tinoco, A., Cantador, I., & Rodríguez Bolívar, M. P. (2023). Trends and challenges of e-government chatbots: Advances in exploring open government data and citizen participation content. *Government Information Quarterly*, 40(4), 101877. DOI: 10.1016/j.giq.2023.101877

Craven, L. S. (2021). CFPB Releases Report Analyzing Consumer Complaint Data By Demographics | Insights & Resources | Goodwin. *Goodwin*. https://www.goodwinlaw.com/en/insights/blogs/2021/10/cfpb-releases-report-analyzing-consumer-complaint

De-Dios-Flores, I., & Pichel Campos, J. R. (2023). Language technologies for a multilingual public administration in Spain. Journal of Language & Law, 8.

Deloitte. (2013). *CFPB's consumer complaint database Analysis reveals valuable insights*. Deloitte.

Department for Environment. Food & Rural Affairs. (2023). *The air quality strategy for England*. https://www.gov.uk/government/publications/the-air-quality-strategy-for-england

DOE Announces New Actions to Enhance America's Global Leadership in Artificial Intelligence. (2024). Energy.Gov. https://www.energy.gov/articles/doe-announces-new-actions-enhance-americas-global-leadership-artificial-intelligence

Dray, M. (2019). Natural Language Processing in government – Data in government. *Natural Language Processing in Government*. https://dataingovernment.blog.gov.uk/2019/06/14/natural-language-processing-in-government/

Dubay, L. (2021). Creating an equitable AI policy for Indigenous communities. *First Policy Response*. https://policyresponse.ca/creating-an-equitable-ai-policy-for-indigenous-communities/

Egger, R., & Gokce, E. (2022). Natural Language Processing (NLP): An Introduction. In Egger, R. (Ed.), *Applied Data Science in Tourism: Interdisciplinary Approaches, Methodologies, and Applications* (pp. 307–334). Springer International Publishing., DOI: 10.1007/978-3-030-88389-8_15

Eggers, W. D., Malik, N., & Gracie, M. (2019). Using AI to unleash the power of unstructured government data. *Deloitte Insights*. https://www2.deloitte.com/us/en/insights/focus/cognitive-technologies/natural-language-processing-examples-in-government-data.html

Esfahani, M. N. (2024). Content analysis of textbooks via natural language processing. *American Journal of Education and Learning*, 9(2), 97.

Fairie, P., Zhang, Z., D'Souza, A. G., Walsh, T., Quan, H., & Santana, M. J. (2021). Categorising patient concerns using natural language processing techniques. *BMJ Health & Care Informatics*, 28(1), e100274. Advance online publication. DOI: 10.1136/bmjhci-2020-100274 PMID: 34193519

Farrell, J. (2019). The growth of climate change misinformation in US philanthropy: Evidence from natural language processing. *Environmental Research Letters*, 14(3), 1–10. DOI: 10.1088/1748-9326/aaf939

Finceed. (2024). *Exploring Finnish Digital Education | Finnish National Agency for Education*. https://www.oph.fi/en/exploring-finnish-digital-education

Foy, G. (1990). Economic sustainability and the preservation of environmental assets. *Environmental Management*, 14(6), 771–778. DOI: 10.1007/BF02394171

GDPR. (2018). *General Data Protection Regulation (GDPR) – Legal Text*. General Data Protection Regulation (GDPR). https://gdpr-info.eu/

Goodland, R. (1995). The Concept of Environmental Sustainability. *Annual Review of Ecology and Systematics*, 26(1), 1–24. DOI: 10.1146/annurev.es.26.110195.000245

Green Building Masterplans. (2024). BCA Corp. https://www1.bca.gov.sg/buildsg/sustainability/green-building-masterplans

Han, E.-J., Han, Z. A., Kim, H., & Jung, T. R. (2023). Monitoring healthy ageing for the next decade: South Korea's perspective. *Age and Ageing*, 52(Supplement_4), iv10–iv12. DOI: 10.1093/ageing/afad102 PMID: 37902513

HDR UK. (2021). *The National Text Analytics Project*. HDR UK. https://www.hdruk.ac.uk/case-studies/the-national-text-analytics-project/

IBM. (2024). *What Is NLP (Natural Language Processing)? | IBM*. https://www.ibm.com/topics/natural-language-processing

IRENA. (2015). *RENEWABLE ENERGY PROSPECTS: GERMANY*. The International Renewable Energy Agency (IRENA).

Japan's National Biodiversity Strategy and Action Plan 2023-2030. (2023). UNEP Law and Environment Assistance Platform. https://leap.unep.org/en/countries/jp/national-legislation/japans-national-biodiversity-strategy-and-action-plan-2023-2030

Jim, J. R., Talukder, M. A. R., Malakar, P., Kabir, M. M., Nur, K., & Mridha, M. F. (2024). Recent advancements and challenges of NLP-based sentiment analysis: A state-of-the-art review. *Natural Language Processing Journal*, 6, 100059. DOI: 10.1016/j.nlp.2024.100059

Kalampokis, E., Karacapilidis, N., Tsakalidis, D., & Tarabanis, K. (2023). Understanding the Use of Emerging Technologies in the Public Sector: A Review of Horizon 2020 Projects. *Digit. Gov.: Res. Pract.*, 4(1), 4–28. DOI: 10.1145/3580603

Khurana, D., Koli, A., Khatter, K., & Singh, S. (2023). Natural language processing: State of the art, current trends and challenges. *Multimedia Tools and Applications*, 82(3), 3713–3744. DOI: 10.1007/s11042-022-13428-4 PMID: 35855771

Kutty, N., & Tochibayashi, N. (2022). *Will new initiatives succeed in protecting Japan's biodiversity?* World Economic Forum. https://www.weforum.org/agenda/2022/12/japan-biodiversity/

Liddy, E. (2021). *Natural Language Processing Natural Language Processing*. https://surface.syr.edu/cgi/viewcontent.cgi?article=1043&context=istpub

Madan, R., & Ashok, M. (2023). AI adoption and diffusion in public administration: A systematic literature review and future research agenda. *Government Information Quarterly*, 40(1), 101774. DOI: 10.1016/j.giq.2022.101774

Mallick, T., & Murphy, J. (2024). Analyzing Regional Impacts of Climate Change using Natural Language Processing Techniques. *ArXiv*. https://ar5iv.labs.arxiv.org/html/2401.06817

Manning, C., & Schutze, H. (1999). *Foundations of Statistical Natural Language Processing*. MIT Press.

Md Nur, N. (2022, August 4). *Driving into a smart mobility future*. The Edge Singapore. https://www.theedgesingapore.com/digitaledge/digital-economy/driving-smart-mobility-future

Mehra, S. (2021). *Leveraging language technology for national good: Initiatives by the Indian govt*. INDIAai. https://indiaai.gov.in/article/leveraging-language-technology-for-national-good-initiatives-by-the-indian-govt

Miner, A. S., Laranjo, L., & Kocaballi, A. B. (2020). Chatbots in the fight against the COVID-19 pandemic. *NPJ Digital Medicine*, 3(1), 1–4. DOI: 10.1038/s41746-020-0280-0 PMID: 32377576

Ministry of Education and Culture. (2024). *Ministry of Education and Culture cooperation in UN and UNESCO - OKM - Ministry of Education and Culture, Finland*. Ministry of Education and Culture Cooperation in UN and UNESCO - OKM - Ministry of Education and Culture, Finland. https://okm.fi/en/un-and-unesco

Morelli, J. (2013). Environmental Sustainability: A Definition for Environmental Professionals. *Journal of Environmental Sustainability*, 1(1), 1–10. Advance online publication. DOI: 10.14448/jes.01.0002

Nadkarni, P. M., Ohno-Machado, L., & Chapman, W. W. (2011). Natural language processing: An introduction. *Journal of the American Medical Informatics Association : JAMIA*, 18(5), 544–551. DOI: 10.1136/amiajnl-2011-000464 PMID: 21846786

Nee, J., Smith, G. M., & Rustagi, I. (2022). Linguistic justice as a framework for designing, developing, and managing NLP tools. Big Data & Society, OECD. (2024). *Governing with Artificial Intelligence*. OECD. https://www.oecd.org/en/publications/governing-with-artificial-intelligence_26324bc2-en.html

Pang, B., & Lee, L. (2008). Opinion Mining and Sentiment Analysis. *Foundations and Trends® in Information Retrieval, 2*(1–2), 1–135. DOI: 10.1561/1500000011

Principlist Framework for Social Benefits. Technological Forecasting and Social Change, Elsevier, Bolívar, M. P. R. (2017). *Financial Sustainability in Public Administration: Exploring the Concept of Financial Health*. Palgrave Macmillan. https://proxy.hacibayram.edu.tr:2708/ehost/ebookviewer/ebook/bmxlYmtfXzE1NzM2OTRfX0FO0?sid=c64b32ab-098c-4a02-aa34-1101f9b635d7@redis&vid=2&format=EB&rid=2

Rintoul, J. (2023). *Farming for the future: Why the Netherlands is one of the largest food exporters in the world | DutchReview*. Https://Dutchreview.Com/. https://dutchreview.com/culture/innovation/second-largest-agriculture-exporter/

Shelf. (2024). *Challenges and Considerations in Natural Language Processing*. Shelf. https://shelf.io/blog/challenges-and-considerations-in-nlp/

UN. (1987). *Our Common Future*. World Commission on Environment and Development. https://www.are.admin.ch/are/en/home/medien-und-publikationen/publikationen/nachhaltige-entwicklung/brundtland-report.html

UN. (1992). *Agenda 21* (United Nations Conference on Environment & Development). United Nations. https://sustainabledevelopment.un.org/outcomedocuments/agenda21

Vogl, T. M., Seidelin, C., Ganesh, B., & Bright, J. (2020). Smart Technology and the Emergence of Algorithmic Bureaucracy: Artificial Intelligence in UK Local Authorities. *Public Administration Review*, 80(6), 946–961. DOI: 10.1111/puar.13286

Xu, Q., & He, X. (2023). *Security Challenges in Natural Language Processing Models.* https://emnlp2023-nlp-security.github.io/

Yadav, M., & Singh, G. (2023). ENVIRONMENTAL SUSTAINABILITY WITH ARTIFICIAL INTELLIGENCE. [IJMR]. *EPRA International Journal of Multidisciplinary Research*, 213–217, 213–217. Advance online publication. DOI: 10.36713/epra13325

Zhou, X., Jain, K., Moinuddin, M., & McSharry, P. (2022). Using Natural Language Processing for Automating the Identification of Climate Action Interlinkages within the Sustainable Development Goals.

Chapter 10
Algorithmic Governance and Its Transformative Role in Decision-Making

Elif Davutoğlu
https://orcid.org/0009-0001-6381-7857
TED University, Turkey

ABSTRACT

This chapter explores how algorithmic governance, also known as "algocracy," has become a key force in decision-making today. It examines how algorithms have evolved from simple tools of convenience to essential parts of how both public and private sectors operate. Tracing their historical roots, the chapter highlights algorithms' role in shaping regulatory frameworks and discusses their societal implications, particularly around transparency, accountability, and potential biases. By analyzing concepts such as "algorithmic governmentality" and "algorithmic regulation," the chapter unpacks both the benefits and ethical challenges these systems bring, highlighting their transformative impact on governance structures.

INTRODUCTION

The emergence of algorithms as key instruments in governance has redefined decision-making processes in contemporary societies. With advancements in computing and big data, the role of algorithms extends beyond computational tools; they have become crucial in governing and regulating both individual and societal behaviors. This chapter explores the concept of algorithmic governance—often referred to as "algocracy"—and delves into its historical origins, its role in regulatory frameworks, and the profound social implications it has introduced. As algorithms

DOI: 10.4018/979-8-3693-8372-8.ch010

continue to permeate public and private sectors, understanding their impact on governance and society is essential for addressing the ethical, political, and practical challenges they pose.

With the rise of technological developments specifically in computing and dataism, algorithms have been an indispensable part of governance both in the process of designing, operating, and evaluating policies and analysing the system. As a natural result of this coalescence, the rise of algorithms in governance has been accompanied by a proliferation of terms that describe this phenomenon, including "algorithmic governmentality" (Rouvroy et al., 2013), "algorithmic regulation" (Yeung, 2018), and "algorithmic governance" (Gritsenko & Wood, 2020). While these terms are not identical, they share a common theme: algorithms are not just tools of convenience but have become central to the operation and evolution of governance systems.

This chapter begins by discussing the rise of algorithmic governance and its historical roots, with an emphasis on the evolution of algorithms from simple mathematical procedures to complex systems that now underpin major social and political decisions. This is followed by a discussion on the regulatory frameworks shaped by algorithmic governance, highlighting the benefits and challenges of such systems. Finally, the chapter will address the societal impacts of algorithms, with particular attention to issues of transparency, accountability, bias, and discrimination in the context of public and political life.

THE RISE OF ALGOCRACY

The term "algocracy" was first introduced by Aneesh (2002) to describe the increasing reliance on algorithms for governance. Even though there have been many claiming algocracy is the software version of bureaucracy, Aneesh (2009) stated that "there is no common meta-language shared by bureaucratic (legal code) and algocracy (binary code) systems of governance" (p. 355). In his view, algocracy represents a fundamental shift from traditional forms of bureaucratic governance, which relied on legal and hierarchical systems, to a new form of governance based on the execution of binary code. Unlike bureaucracy, which is characterized by structured legal codes and procedures, algocracy operates through algorithms that are capable of processing large amounts of data to produce decisions and outcomes. Therefore, he argues that this shift is transformative because algorithms do not operate within the same normative frameworks that govern human decision-makers.

Instead, they are built upon binary code, making decisions through processes that are neither fully visible nor interpretable to the public.

Several scholars have built upon Aneesh's concept of algocracy, introducing variations that capture different facets of algorithmic governance. Rouvroy (2013) coined the term "algorithmic governmentality" to describe the broader paradigm shift in knowledge production and modes of power resulting from the rise of algorithms. She expressed skepticism about the implications of this shift, particularly regarding the production of "knowledge without truth"—a reference to the idea that algorithmic decision-making often bypasses traditional forms of human reasoning and judgment. Yeung (2018) introduced the term "algorithmic regulation," which she defined as decision-making systems that manage risk and alter behavior through the continuous computational generation of knowledge. Unlike earlier forms of regulation, which relied on fixed legal frameworks, algorithmic regulation adapts in real-time based on data inputs, making it highly dynamic and responsive to changing conditions.

Gritsenko and Wood (2020) further expanded the discussion with the term "algorithmic governance," which they described as design-based governance modes that rely on algorithmic systems. According to Gritsenko and Wood, algorithmic governance is characterized by its reliance on algorithms to create "design-based" solutions that work in conjunction with hierarchical, self-governance, and co-governance modes. The defining feature of these governance modes is their ability to adapt and refine their operations automatically, without the need for direct human intervention. This aspect of algorithmic governance is particularly appealing to policymakers and regulators, as it promises greater efficiency and accuracy in decision-making.

Despite these varied terminologies, the underlying theme remains consistent: algorithms are fundamentally reshaping how governance is conducted. As societies become more reliant on data-driven systems, algocracy is increasingly seen as an inevitable progression in governance models. However, the rise of algocracy also raises critical questions about transparency, accountability, and the role of human judgment in decision-making processes. While algorithms offer significant advantages in terms of efficiency and precision, their opacity and complexity often leave little room for human oversight, raising concerns about the legitimacy of algorithmic decisions.

Historical Perspective on Algorithms

The concept of the algorithm may sound ultramodern since it has been associated basically with computers and supremely with artificial intelligence, but its origins date back to ancient times. Early examples of algorithms can be found in the mathematical practices of Babylonian and Egyptian civilizations, which used division algorithms to solve arithmetic problems (Barbin et al., 1999). Also, Greek mathematicians developed their own algorithms, such as the sieve of Eratosthenes for identifying prime numbers and the Euclidean algorithm for calculating the greatest common divisor (Cooke, 2005).

The term "algorithm" itself is derived from the name of the 9th-century Persian mathematician Mu ammad ibn Musa al-Khwarizmi, whose work on the Hindu-Arabic numeral system laid the groundwork for later mathematical innovations (Miyazaki, 2012). Al-Khwarizmi's works were translated into Latin, where his name became "Algorizmi" (Brezina, 2006), from which the term "algorithm" eventually emerged. In the centuries that followed, algorithms evolved into general problem-solving procedures, though it wasn't until the 19th century that they began to be associated with mechanical computation. Ada Lovelace's work on Charles Babbage's Analytical Engine, which produced the first algorithm intended for mechanical execution, marked the beginning of modern computational algorithms (Barbin et al., 1999).

The evolution of algorithms from ancient mathematical procedures to their modern form took a significant leap in the 19th century, when Ada Lovelace designed the first algorithm intended to be run on a mechanical computer (Barbin et al., 1999). Lovelace's work marked the beginning of the modern use of algorithms as tools for automating calculations. However, it was not until the 1930s that algorithms started to be used in electronic computers, thanks to the pioneering work of Alan Turing.

Turing's 1937 paper, "On Computable Numbers," introduced the concept of the Turing Machine, a theoretical device capable of performing any computation that could be described by a set of instructions. Turing's work laid the foundation for modern algorithmic theory by demonstrating that any computational problem could be solved through a series of logical steps (Turing, 1937). The Turing Machine became the standard model for understanding algorithms, and its influence extended far beyond the realm of mathematics. In many ways, Turing's work anticipated the rise of algorithmic governance, as it demonstrated the potential for machines to perform tasks traditionally reserved for human decision-makers.

Over the following decades, algorithms evolved from simple computational tools into complex systems that underpin decision-making processes. This evolution was accelerated by the development of general-purpose computers and the growth of artificial intelligence (AI), which allowed algorithms to process increasingly complex data. Today, algorithms operate in nearly every aspect of modern life, from healthcare and finance to social media and national security. The role of algorithms has expanded to the extent that they now influence major social, political, and economic decisions, raising questions about their impact on human autonomy, justice, and fairness.

ALGORITHMIC REGULATION AND GOVERNANCE

As algorithms have become more sophisticated, they have also become central to governance systems. The concept of algorithmic regulation, as defined by Yeung (2018), refers to decision-making systems that regulate activities by continuously collecting and analyzing data in real-time. These systems are designed to manage risks and modify behavior by refining their operations based on data inputs. In this sense, algorithmic regulation represents a departure from traditional forms of governance, which relied on fixed legal frameworks and human judgment to make decisions.

One of the key advantages of algorithmic regulation is its ability to adapt quickly to changing conditions. Unlike traditional regulatory systems, which often require lengthy legislative processes to implement changes, algorithmic systems can modify their operations automatically based on new data. This makes them particularly effective in managing dynamic and complex environments, where real-time data processing is essential for effective decision-making.

Algorithmic regulation is already being applied in a number of domains, including law enforcement, immigration, and finance. In the United States, for example, law enforcement agencies use predictive policing algorithms to forecast where crimes are most likely to occur. Tools such as PredPol and ShotSpotter analyze historical crime data and identify areas where police presence may be needed to prevent or respond to criminal activity. These tools are designed to allocate resources more efficiently, allowing police departments to focus their efforts on areas with the highest crime risk.

In China, algorithmic regulation plays an even more significant role in governance. The Chinese government has implemented a number of algorithmic systems to monitor and control its population. The Integrated Joint Operations Platform (IJOP), for instance, collects vast amounts of data on citizens' activities and uses algorithms to identify individuals who may pose a threat to social stability. This system is part of China's broader "social credit" initiative, which uses data to assign scores to individuals based on their behavior and compliance with government regulations. Those with low scores may face restrictions on travel, access to financial services, and other aspects of daily life.

In the realm of immigration, algorithms are increasingly being used to assess and prioritize individuals for entry or deportation. The algorithms with the support of data may offer a rather detailed inquiry for those who are prioritised as potential illegal immigrants (European Migration Network, 2022). The system uses facial recognition and other biometric data to assess the likelihood that a traveler is attempting to cross the border illegally. While these systems promise to enhance the efficiency of immigration procedures, they also raise concerns about privacy, transparency, and accountability. In the European Union, the iBorderCtrl system (the name of the programme changed to iCROSS later) was developed to screen travelers at border checkpoints, but it has been suspended after a time as a result of a court decision by the Court of Justice of the EU because of emerging controversies.

Despite the potential benefits of algorithmic regulation, its use in governance is not without controversy. One of the primary concerns is the opacity of these systems. Because algorithms often operate as "black boxes" (Pasquale, 2013), it can be difficult for individuals to understand how decisions are being made or to challenge those decisions when they believe they are unjust. This lack of transparency raises significant ethical and legal questions about the fairness and legitimacy of algorithmic governance.

Another concern is the potential for algorithmic systems to reinforce existing biases and inequalities. Machine learning algorithms, which are commonly used in algorithmic regulation, rely on large datasets to make predictions. If the data used to train these algorithms contains biases—such as racial or gender disparities—the algorithms may reproduce or even amplify these biases in their decision-making processes. This has been observed in predictive policing, where algorithms have been found to disproportionately target minority communities.

The Social Impacts of Algorithmic Governance

The increasing reliance on algorithmic systems in governance brings significant social consequences that extend beyond their technical functionalities. As algorithms shape decision-making processes, they transform the relationship between individuals and institutions, often raising concerns about the impact on autonomy, social justice, and human agency.

One of the most significant social impacts of algorithmic governance lies in its capacity to influence decisions with little to no human oversight, often operating as opaque systems. Danaher (2016) argues that as algorithms become central to decision-making, they may pose legitimacy problems because they reduce human participation in such processes. This creates a barrier between citizens and the decisions that affect their lives, as algorithms—unlike human decision-makers—do not offer easily understandable reasoning for their outcomes. This challenge is exacerbated by what Rouvroy (2013) describes as the paradigm shift toward "knowledge without truth," where decisions are made based on correlations in data rather than interpretative, human-centric knowledge.

The social impacts of algorithmic governance are evident in various domains, particularly in areas where algorithms influence individual behavior. Gillespie (2014) describes "public relevance algorithms" as systems that shape information ecosystems by prioritizing, classifying, and filtering content. Gillespie outlines six dimensions of public relevance algorithms—patterns of inclusion, cycles of anticipation, the evaluation of relevance, the promise of objectivity, entanglement with practice, and the production of calculated publics—all of which demonstrate the ways in which algorithms influence societal structures and shape public perception. The dimensions identified by Gillespie (2014) highlight the extent to which algorithms dictate what information is visible to the public and how people understand their social reality. For example, algorithms that prioritize certain types of content or filter information based on user profiles can reinforce particular viewpoints, potentially creating echo chambers and limiting exposure to diverse perspectives.

The use of predictive policing algorithms, such as PredPol in the United States or the Integrated Joint Operations Platform (IJOP) in China, exemplifies how algorithmic governance can impact social structures by directing law enforcement resources to specific areas based on historical crime data. However, these predictive models are often trained on biased data, leading to the over-policing of certain communities and perpetuating existing social inequalities (European Migration Network, 2022). This reliance on algorithmic predictions can undermine trust between communities and law enforcement, as the impartiality of these systems comes into question.

In addition to affecting public perception and social structures, algorithmic governance can significantly impact individual autonomy. Danaher (2016) suggests that algorithms, by operating autonomously and without human review, remove an individual's ability to understand or control the decisions that govern their lives. This detachment from the decision-making process can leave individuals feeling powerless, as they are unable to engage with or challenge decisions that affect their daily experiences. The erosion of individual agency in decision-making raises ethical concerns, especially when algorithms are used in sensitive areas such as immigration, healthcare, or social services.

Transparency and Accountability in Algorithmic Governance

The opacity of algorithmic systems poses a serious challenge to transparency and accountability, key pillars of democratic governance. In traditional governance systems, decision-makers are held accountable through established legal and political mechanisms. However, when decisions are made by algorithms, these mechanisms are often insufficient because the processes behind the decisions are concealed within complex, technical operations.

As Danaher (2016) points out, the reliance on algorithms in decision-making can threaten the legitimacy of governance because it becomes difficult for individuals to understand or challenge the decisions that affect them.This opacity stems from several factors. First, the technical complexity of algorithms means that even the individuals responsible for deploying them may not fully understand how they arrive at their conclusions, especially in the case of machine learning systems that evolve over time based on the data they process. Second, algorithms often operate under secrecy laws, or their intellectual property is protected, making it even harder for outsiders to scrutinize them.

The Association for Computing Machinery (2017) reveals that algorithmic systems can be opaque due to three main reasons "including technical (the algorithm may not lend itself to easy explanation), economic (the cost of providing transparency may be excessive, including the compromise of trade secrets), and social (revealing input may violate privacy expectations)" (p.1), which leads scholars to think over the taxonomy of algorithmic opacity (Burrell, 2016; Creel, 2020; Facchini & Termine, 2021). Therefore, algorithmic transparency is not a binary phenomenon because it can be possible to investigate the algorithms backwards for its developers, but the process or even input can be hidden from society because of other causes. In other words, the design of the system can be transparent whereas the implementation may not, or vice versa. Hence, algorithmic transparency is a matter of degree rather than a dichotomy because full-transparency may harm privacy as a result of disclosure of personal data whereas complete opacity may cause discrimination, manipulation, and inequalities.

Efforts to address these transparency challenges have included proposals for "human review of algorithms" (Danaher, 2016). However, as Danaher acknowledges, implementing human oversight is difficult in practice due to the complexity of algorithmic systems and the scale at which they operate. The solution might lie in a combination of approaches, such as integrating sousveillance technologies that allow citizens to monitor algorithmic decisions and form partnerships with algorithms to ensure greater accountability (Mann, 2013).

Furthermore, Kitchin (2017) suggests that studying algorithms through discursive analysis, ethnographies of coding teams, and reverse engineering may help demystify the processes behind algorithmic systems and offer pathways for greater transparency. However, he also warns that these approaches have limitations, particularly when it comes to understanding the broader social and political implications of algorithmic decisions. For instance, reverse engineering focuses on uncovering the functionality of an algorithm but does not explain the motivations or socio-political context behind its design.

Despite these proposals, accountability in algorithmic governance remains an unresolved issue. As Neyland and Möllers (2017) explain, the power of algorithms often lies in their associations and the data they process. Algorithms interpret and prioritize certain data points based on their programming, which can lead to biases that are difficult to detect or rectify. Creating robust accountability mechanisms will require not only technical solutions but also regulatory frameworks that provide individuals with the means to contest algorithmic decisions and ensure that these systems operate fairly.

BIAS AND DISCRIMINATION IN ALGORITHMIC SYSTEMS

The potential for bias and discrimination in algorithmic systems is one of the most pressing challenges in algorithmic governance. Algorithms are often perceived as objective tools that operate free from human prejudice; however, they are fundamentally shaped by the data they process and the design choices made by developers. As a result, algorithms may inadvertently encode and perpetuate societal biases, leading to discriminatory outcomes in areas such as criminal justice, finance, and employment.

Machine learning algorithms, which form the backbone of many governance systems, are trained on large datasets that reflect historical inequalities. If the data used to train these algorithms contain biases—such as racial, gender, or socioeconomic inequalities—these biases are likely to be embedded in the algorithm's predictions and decisions. As a result, these algorithms may reproduce and even amplify biases that exist in society. As Neyland and Möllers (2017) note, "power derives from algorithmic association" (p.46), meaning that the patterns algorithms detect in data can reinforce existing power dynamics. This is particularly evident in areas such as predictive policing, where algorithms like PredPol rely on historical crime data that may disproportionately target minority communities (European Migration Network, 2022). Consequently, these algorithms may reinforce discriminatory policing practices rather than providing impartial assessments.

This issue extends to other domains where algorithms are used to make consequential decisions. In hiring practices, for example, algorithms that screen candidates may favor applicants from certain demographic backgrounds if trained on biased data. Similarly, algorithms used to assess creditworthiness may disadvantage individuals from lower-income backgrounds, perpetuating economic disparities. Also, algorithms used in healthcare may provide biased recommendations if they are trained on datasets that do not adequately represent diverse populations.

Addressing bias in algorithmic systems requires more than just improving the quality of data. It also involves questioning the assumptions and goals that guide the development of these systems. As Katzenbach and Ulbricht (2019) argue, algorithms are not neutral; they are shaped by the epistemic practices of their designers and the institutions that deploy them. This means that efforts to mitigate bias must take into account the broader social and political contexts in which algorithms are created and used.

One potential solution to mitigating bias in algorithmic systems is to implement fairness constraints. Fairness constraints are designed to ensure that algorithms do not produce outcomes that disproportionately affect specific groups. However, as Danaher (2016) notes, defining fairness in the context of algorithms is challenging, as different stakeholders may have competing definitions of what constitutes a fair outcome. Additionally, fairness constraints may not address the underlying structural inequalities that give rise to bias in the first place, limiting their effectiveness.

Another approach to addressing bias is to adopt a reflexive approach to algorithm design, as advocated by Kitchin (2017) and Neyland (2016). This approach involves critically examining the assumptions and values embedded in algorithms and considering their broader social impacts. By designing algorithms that are sensitive to these concerns, developers may be able to reduce the risk of bias and create systems that are more equitable. However, achieving true fairness in algorithmic systems remains an ongoing challenge, and further research is needed to develop effective strategies for mitigating bias.

THE FUTURE OF ALGORITHMIC GOVERNANCE

As algorithmic systems become increasingly embedded in governance structures, their future impact is a subject of intense debate. While these systems offer significant benefits in terms of efficiency and precision, their growing role in decision-making raises ethical, political, and social concerns. The future of algorithmic governance will likely revolve around addressing these challenges while leveraging the potential of algorithms to enhance decision-making across various domains.

A major issue facing the future of algorithmic governance is the tension between the autonomy of algorithmic systems and the need for human oversight. As Danaher (2016) notes, algorithms can undermine the legitimacy of governance by diminishing human participation in decision-making processes. This reduction of human oversight creates a gap in accountability, especially when algorithms operate as opaque systems, where it is unclear how decisions are made or how outcomes can be challenged. The potential for machine learning algorithms to evolve and adapt autonomously compounds these concerns, as their decision-making processes become increasingly difficult for humans to interpret or control (Danaher, 2016).

Rouvroy's (2013) notion of "algorithmic governmentality" reflects the broader paradigm shift in governance, where decision-making is increasingly driven by correlations in data rather than interpretive, human-driven processes. This shift, Rouvroy argues, leads to "knowledge without truth," as algorithms prioritize efficiency and data processing over deeper forms of understanding that are central to traditional governance. This tension between human judgment and algorithmic logic will continue to shape the future of governance, as societies grapple with the role of algorithms in shaping knowledge, power, and societal order.

Looking forward, addressing issues of transparency and accountability will be critical for ensuring the legitimacy of algorithmic governance. Yeung's (2018) work on algorithmic regulation highlights the importance of balancing the technical efficiency of algorithms with broader social and ethical considerations. One of the main concerns is that algorithms, especially those involved in real-time decision-making, often operate without sufficient human oversight or transparency. As Kitchin (2017) suggests, efforts to enhance the transparency of algorithmic systems will need to go beyond technical fixes like explainable AI and require the development of legal and institutional frameworks that ensure accountability.

In the realm of accountability, Danaher (2013) proposes several strategies for addressing the opacity of algorithmic systems. These include the implementation of human oversight, sousveillance technologies, and epistemic enhancement of human beings to ensure that individuals can engage with and understand algorithmic decisions. However, the practical implementation of these strategies remains challenging, particularly given the complexity of many algorithmic systems and the scale at which they operate.

As algorithmic governance continues to evolve, it is essential to address the risks of bias and discrimination, which remain central concerns for the future. As Neyland and Möllers (2017) argue, algorithmic power is derived from the associations that algorithms make, which are often shaped by biased data and existing power structures. Therefore, the future of algorithmic governance will likely involve efforts to develop more equitable and just systems that minimize the risk of perpetuating societal inequalities. These efforts will require not only technical solutions, such as fairness optimization in algorithmic design but also a more reflexive approach to the development of algorithms that takes into account their broader social and political implications (Kitchin, 2017).

In addition to technical and ethical challenges, the future of algorithmic governance will involve determining how these systems can be integrated into existing governance frameworks. Gritsenko and Wood (2020) describe algorithmic governance as design-based modes of governance that operate alongside hierarchical and co-governance systems. As algorithmic systems become more widespread, they will need to be integrated with traditional forms of governance to ensure that they complement, rather than replace, human decision-making processes. This integration will require ongoing collaboration between technologists, policymakers, and civil society to develop systems that are both technically robust and aligned with democratic values.

Finally, the future of algorithmic governance will depend on how societies address the ethical implications of these systems. As Yeung (2018) points out, algorithmic regulation should not solely focus on optimizing efficiency and managing risks but must also consider the broader social and ethical goals of governance. This requires a shift in the design and implementation of algorithmic systems to ensure that they reflect human values such as fairness, justice, and equality.

All in all, while algorithmic governance presents many opportunities for improving decision-making processes, its future will depend on how societies navigate the ethical, political, and social challenges it presents. Ensuring transparency, accountability, and fairness in algorithmic systems will be critical for maintaining public trust and ensuring that these systems serve the broader public interest.

CONCLUSION

Algorithmic governance represents a fundamental shift in how societies are organized and regulated. As algorithms become more deeply embedded in decision-making processes, they offer both significant opportunities and profound challenges. While algorithms have the potential to enhance the efficiency, accuracy, and fairness of governance systems, they also raise important ethical questions about transparency, accountability, bias, and discrimination.

In order to navigate these challenges, it is essential that societies develop robust mechanisms for overseeing and regulating algorithmic systems. This will require a combination of technical solutions, such as explainable AI and fairness constraints, as well as regulatory frameworks that promote transparency, accountability, and ethical decision-making. By addressing the limitations of algorithmic governance and ensuring that these systems are designed with human values in mind, it is possible to harness the potential of algorithms to create more just and equitable societies.

REFERENCES

Aneesh, A. (2002). Technologically coded authority: The post-industrial decline in bureaucratic hierarchies.

Aneesh, A. (2009). Global labor: Algocratic modes of organization. *Sociological Theory*, 27(4), 347–370. DOI: 10.1111/j.1467-9558.2009.01352.x

Association for Computing Machinery US Public Policy Council. (2017). Principles for algorithmic transparency and accountability https://www.acm.org/binaries/content/assets/publicpolicy/2017_usacm_statement_algorithms.pdf

Barbin, E., Borowczyk, J., Chabert, J.-L., Guillemot, M., Michel-Pajus, A., & Bernard, L. C. (1999). *A history of algorithms: From the pebble to the microchip* (Chabert, J.-L., Ed.). Springer.

Brezina, C. (2006). *Al-Khwarizmi: The inventor of algebra*. The Rosen Publishing Group.

Burrell, J. (2016). How the machine 'thinks': Understanding opacity in machine learning algorithms. *Big Data & Society*, 3(1), 2053951715622512. Advance online publication. DOI: 10.1177/2053951715622512

Cooke, R. L. (2005). *The history of mathematics: A brief course*. John Wiley & Sons. DOI: 10.1002/9781118033098

Creel, K. A. (2020). Transparency in complex computational systems. *Philosophy of Science*, 87(4), 568–589. DOI: 10.1086/709729

Danaher, J. (2016). The threat of algocracy: Reality, resistance and accommodation. *Philosophy & Technology*, 29(3), 245–268. DOI: 10.1007/s13347-015-0211-1

European Migration Network. (2022). *The use of digitalisation and artificial intelligence in migration management*. https://emn.ie/publications/accurate-timely-interoperable-data-manage-

Facchini, A., & Termine, A. (2021). Towards a taxonomy for the opacity of AI systems. In Müller, V. C. (Ed.), *Philosophy and Theory of Artificial Intelligence 2021* (pp. 73–89). Springer., DOI: 10.1007/978-3-031-09153-7_7

Gillipsc, T. (2014). The relevance of algorithms. In Gillespie, T., Boczkowski, P. J., & Foot, K. A. (Eds.), *Media technologies: Essays on communication, materiality, and society*. The MIT Press., DOI: 10.7551/mitpress/9780262525374.003.0009

Gritsenko, D., & Wood, M. (2020). Algorithmic governance: A modes of governance approach. *Regulation & Governance*. Advance online publication. DOI: 10.1111/rego.12367

Katzenbach, C., & Ulbricht, L. (2019). Algorithmic governance. *Internet Policy Review*, 8(4). Advance online publication. DOI: 10.14763/2019.4.1424

Kitchin, R. (2017). Thinking critically about and researching algorithms. *Information Communication and Society*, 20(1), 14–29. DOI: 10.1080/1369118X.2016.1154087

Mann, S. (2013). Veilance and reciprocal transparency: Surveillance versus sousveillance, AR glass, lifeglogging, and wearable computing. *2013 IEEE International Symposium on Technology and Society (ISTAS): Social Implications of Wearable Computing and Augmediated Reality in Everyday Life*, 1-12. https://doi.org/DOI: 10.1109/ISTAS.2013.6613094

Miyazaki, S. (2012). Algorhythmics: Understanding micro-temporality in computational cultures. *Computational Culture*, 1–22. http://computationalculture.net/article/algorhythmics-understanding-micro-temporality-in-computational-cultures

Neyland, D. (2016). Bearing account-able witness to the ethical algorithmic system. *Science, Technology & Human Values*, 41(1), 50–76. DOI: 10.1177/0162243915598056

Neyland, D., & Möllers, N. (2017). Algorithmic IF … THEN rules and the conditions and consequences of power. *Information Communication and Society*, 20(1), 45–62. DOI: 10.1080/1369118X.2016.1156141

Pasquale, F. (2013). The emperor's new codes: reputation and search algorithms in the finance sector. *Governing Algorithms*, 1–86.

Rouvroy, A., Berns, T., & Carey-Libbrecht, L. (2013). Algorithmic governmentality and prospects of emancipation: Disparateness as a precondition for individuation through relationships? *Reseaux (London)*, 177(1), 163–196. DOI: 10.3917/res.177.0163

Turing, A. M. (1937). On computable numbers, with an application to the Entscheisungsproblem. Proceedings of the London Mathematical Society, s2-42(1), 230–265. https://doi.org/DOI: 10.1112/plms/s2-43.6.544

Yeung, K. (2018). Algorithmic regulation: A critical interrogation. *Regulation & Governance*, 12(4), 505–523. DOI: 10.1111/rego.12158

Chapter 11
Cost-Effective Sustainable Energy Solutions for Turkey: AI Driven Renewables

Esin Okay
Independent Scholar, Istanbul, Turkey

ABSTRACT

Artificial intelligence (AI) is an essential high value technology that upgrades science globally increasing wealth and decreasing costs. Intersection of renewable energy and AI can lead to great achievement and progress for global eco-efficiency enhancing and widespreading alternative sources of energy all over the world. By all means, there is considerable energy investments combined with AI in the eco-efficient countries. However, AI global readiness is still not enough. Interestingly, Turkey's adaptation of AI level is even better than the renewable energy dependency rank by prolonged practices of renewables. Turkey is still far beyond the desired level of eco-efficiency and affordable energy. After all, economic disruption deepened in Turkey since pandemic, with huge corporate debts worsening financial situation and decreasing investments that unfortunately affect both AI and any type of renewable energy projects. This study emphasizes the great potential of renewables in Turkey and yet needs transformation by the help of AI driven projects.

DOI: 10.4018/979-8-3693-8372-8.ch011

INTRODUCTION

Artificial intelligence (AI) increased the potential solutions for decreasing costs and especially considering energy research and development. Tendency of sophisticated high technology and AI can eliminate the unsolved disadvantages of renewable energy so that the clean energy solutions conquer the earth hopefully. AI should be the source of elavating investments in the the long run for cost-effective sustainable and infinite energy.

As ecological technology improves every day and advanced engineering leads energy science, improvements expand opportunities for carbon reductions. Ecoefficient countries put so much effort to enhance energy investments combined with AI. Experts say smart systems, as playing a distinctive role in the future process of greening cities, will handle increasing amounts of variable renewable energy from local sources, incorporate local energy storage, and provide greater flexibility, efficiency, and transparency in the power distribution grid all by the help of new technologies mainly the AI. Nevertheless, the index- AI global readiness- shows that AI is not yet widespread in the world (Oxford Insights, 2023).

EU 2030 digital compass policy advises for emhancing AI based practices in every field. United Kingdom announced a progressive inactment for AI strategy in 2021 (EU, 2021). USA inacted National AI R&D Strategic Plan in 2023, which follows national AI R&D strategic plans issued in 2016 and 2019, reaffirming strategies and adds a ninth one to underscore a principled and coordinated approach to international collaboration in AI research (NITRD, 2023).

On the other hand, the second division of this study -energy and the future of energy - seems uncertain but can be predicted and AI is a powerful solution. The range of possible future energy solutions become greater and so does the uncertainty. As long as the technology enables favorable outcomes, the global energy policy is to bring energy use and carbon emissions to decline 70% below today's levels, in 2050 according to International Renewable Energy Agency (IRENA, 2019). Furthermore, natural sources of energy like wind, hydro, solar, geothermal, biomass, and biofuel is cheap and clean for protecting earth and acquiring sustainable clean environment. In the last decade, high energy prices and shortages grew fast as global demand increases enormously. Understanding the benefits of natural energy sources, countries are forced to work on legislature to provide incentives for and renewable energy based on new technologies.

This study finally addresses solutions for Turkey, specifically. Turkey has a considerable potential for a sustainable, creative and cheap form of future energy. But there is a sign of incompetence in policy making which challenges renewable energy utilization in Turkey. Nowadays, renewable energy is widely accepted with the crucial benefits of environmental protection and reduction of carbon emissions.

There is still an expectation Turkey sufficiently fulfilling the strategic purposes of energy plan sustaining and distributing energy to ensure the future energy demand. As Turkey having a huge potential for renewable energy solutions especially like solar energy, the adoption of strategic plan is crucially important to meet the predicted demand of future energy.

The chapter is a hypothetical study on the future of AI based energy investments and the status of Turkey regarding the topic. This study is to gain insights for future of AI based energy from the infrastructural problems in energy sector and financial services showing the inadequate status in Turkey. The study has three main objectives. The first objective is to emphasize the importance of AI and AI solutions. In this context, global AI strategy and action plans are presented in the background of the paper. The second objective is to extend the renewables and AI driven energy solutions showing the huge potential for a cost-effective sustainable energy. The last objective is all about Turkey that contributes to the energy outlook, potential in renewables and economic review. The study concludes with the recommendations for a transition to modernize energy market by the help of AI driven solutions in Turkey.

BACKGROUND

Artificial Intelligence

AI has become a hot topic that attracts a lot of public attention both in economy and science. EU 2030 digital compass policy advises for emhancing AI based practices in every field. United Kingdom announced a progressive inactment for AI strategy in 2021 (EU, 2021). AI needs further regulations as AI global readiness shows that it is not yet widespread in the global energy system, too (Oxford Insights, 2023) .

Goldman Sachs predicts that the business world is making strategies to deal with AI as an opportunity and challenge. At the same time, there are even legal and political regulations and policies proposed to deal with AI (Wang 2019). However, as the definitions clearly show AI is a favorable mechanism. It may be stated that AI has the ability to copy human intelligence as a science and engineering of solving, especially making the best intelligent machines in order to achieve goals in the world (McCarthy, 2004).

More than half of businesses are so far implementing some form of new wave of AI technologies in 2020. These developments are important because AI provides inestimable possibilities for enhancing people's lives in a variety of areas, including their homes, safety, transportation healthcare, education, and employment. Simply, AI and AI systems can be considered as valuable automatic helpers (Berente et al, 2021). AI can support three important business needs: automating business processes, gaining insight through data analysis, and engaging with customers and employees (Davenport, Ronanki, 2018).

Figure 1. Sentiment towards AI tools in development among professional developers, 2023 (Maslej, N. et al., 2024)

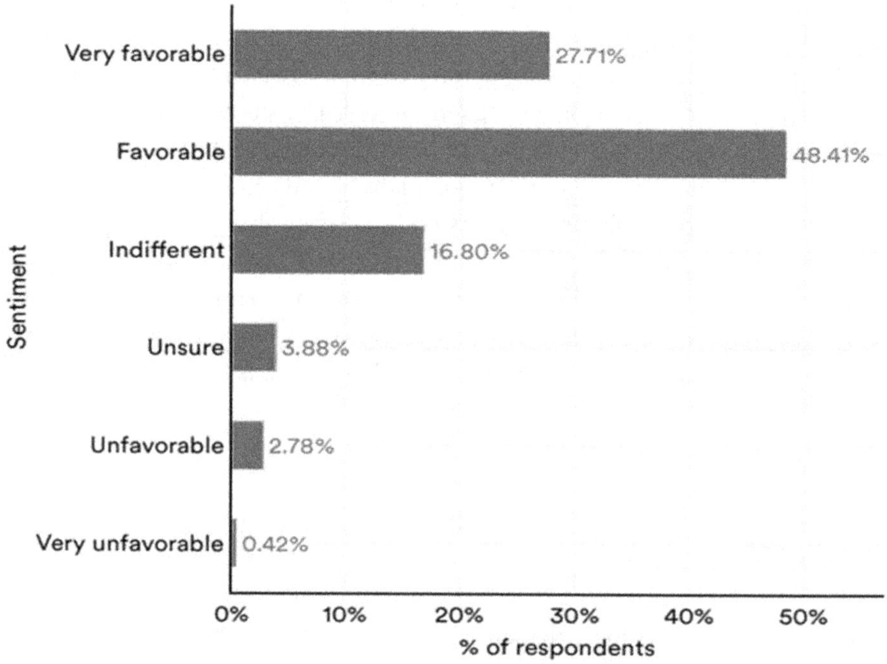

One of the most important part of AI is supervised learning that has led to automatic zip code recognition, speech recognition, self-driving cars, and a continually improving understanding of the human intellegince. AI is based on learning algorithms that automatically learn features from unlabeled data (Ng, 2011).

AI solutions basically can be divided into two groups. One of them is virtual AI solutions that use algorithms, data analysis, and computational power to automate processes, make predictions, and learn from data. AI-based systems are mainly software-based, acting in the virtual world. And the other one can be described as physical AI for the sake of automation. Robotics can be defined as 'AI in action in the physical world' (European Commission, 2018).

Figure 2. AI Adoption and AI investments by sector (Chui J., J. Manyika, M. Miremadi, 2018)

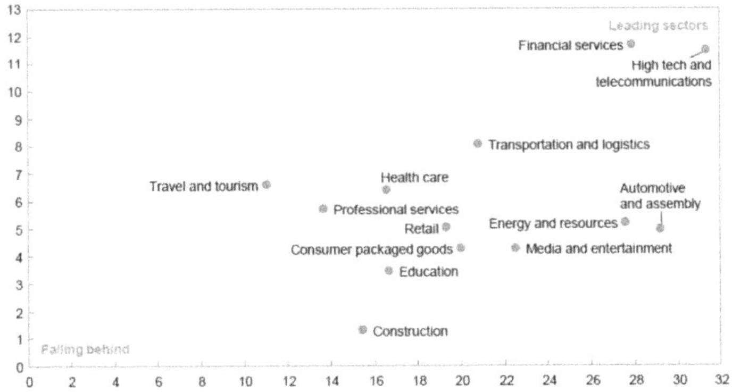

AI sector is experiencing an unprecedented growth. U.S. generative AI companies alone have garnered $8 billion in investments between 2020-2022, whereas the global AI economy is forecasted to reach a staggering $32 trillion by 2027 (Global AI Ecosystem, 2022). Figure 2 shows that Financial Services -using blockchain, IoT, and cloud computing for elevating accuracy and efficiency (Okay, Sencer, Taskin, 2024) - has been one of the leading sectors globally when it comes to AI adoption (National Strategy for Artificial Intelligence of India, 2018).

In 2023, the total Global AI investment dropped to $189.2 billion, a decrease of approximately 20% from 2022. Despite a slight reduction in private investment, the most significant downturn occurred in mergers and acquisitions, which fell by 31.2% from the previous year. However, over the past decade, AI related investments have increased thirteenfold (Maslej et al., 2024).

On the other hand, these rapid changes also raise profound ethical concerns. These arise from the potential AI systems have to embed biases, contribute to climate degradation, threaten human rights and more. Such risks associated with AI have already begun to compound on top of existing inequalities, resulting in further harm (European Parliament, 2023).

Figure 3. AI economy size indicators (Global AI Ecosystem, 2022)

Figure 4. Private investment in AI, 2013-23 (Maslej, N. et al., 2024)

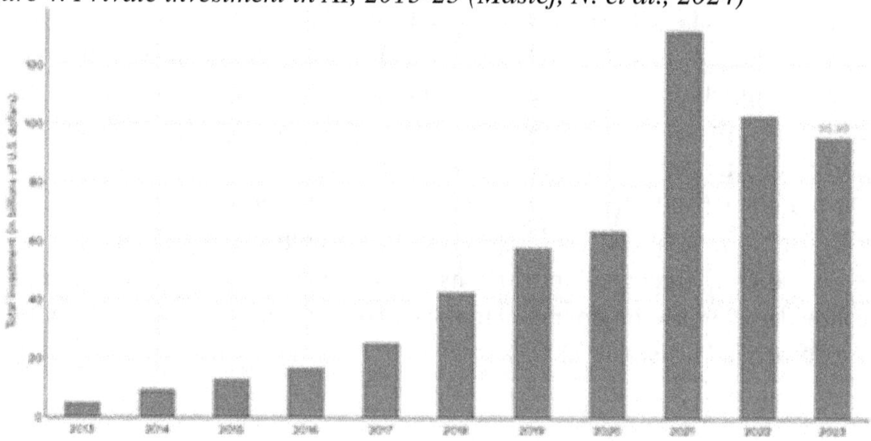

Figure 5. Private investment in AI by country, 2013-23 (Maslej, N. et al., 2024)

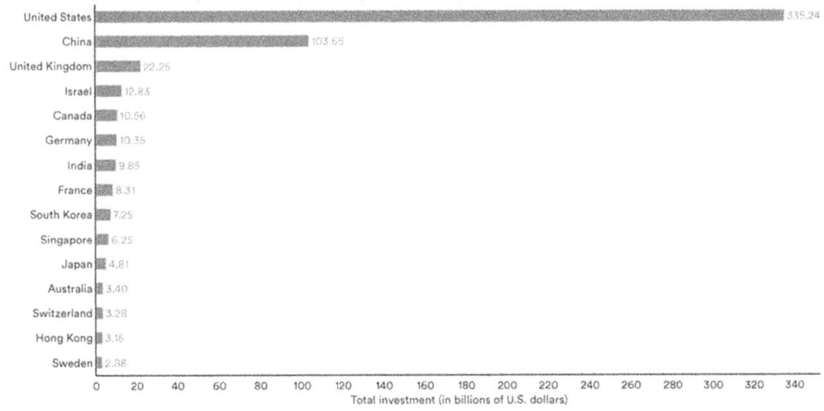

Renewable Energy

Renewable energy is still a critical issue regarding energy supply and and/or environmental action. High energy consumption with huge carbon emissions still raises the threats of global warming and climate change. Therefore, energy is a non-stop hot issue having a strong impact on both economy and environment. Global economy still needs to obtain sustainable and clean sources of energy, which is an issue of finance.

Achieving a low carbon economy involves tackling uncertainty and ambiguity about the future energy supply, energy mix, energy use and efficiency and working out how to address behavioural change and adaption. Future energy studies will be shaped primarily by increased carbon emissions, energy demand and prices, and climate change effects. Renewables integration, energy efficiency, smart grids driven by high technology energy systems will be the important areas of energy research and innovation in the future.

On the other hand, developing countries more challenged by costs and risks face problems of energy sourcing and financing. But it is widely accepted that using the natural sources of renewable energy is cheap and clean. Therefore, developing economies must develop energy strategies based on renewable energy solutions.

Global economic concerns increase as the growth rate falls down by the on going high volatility in asset prices, uncertainty level and risks. Global growth is expected to flow around 3.1% in 2024, the same as the 3.1% in 2023, followed by a slight pick-up to 3.2% in 2025. Significant uncertainty remains. Inflation may stay higher for longer, resulting in slower-than-expected reductions in policy interest rates and leading to further financial vulnerabilities (OECD, 2024a).

According to the report of World Economic Situation and Prospects as of mid-2024, the world economy is now projected to grow by 2.7% in 2024 (+0.3% from the January forecast) and 2.8% in 2025. Developing economies face persistent challenges despite global disinflationary trend. It is stated that international cooperation will remain crucial to facilitate technology transfers and financing to developing countries, combat illicit financial flows and ensure the supply of the critical minerals (UN Critical Energy Transition Minerals Action Plan enhancing renewables) needed for the green transition (UN, 2024).

Renewable capacity accounted for 3.9 TW or 43.0% out of the 9.0 TW of global total capacity including nonrenewables. It indicates an unprecedented 14.0% increase from 2022. Such growth established a recent trend of 10.0% compound annual growth rate from 2017 to 2023 (IRENA, 2024a). Renewable investment reached almost $500 billion globally in 2022, amounting to 83% of new electric capacity that year. Renewables accounted for 28% of electric generation in 2021, consisting of hydro (55%), wind (23%), biomass (13%), solar (7%) and geothermal (1%) (Statista, 2024a).

Figure 6. Global energy capacity shares 2023 (IRENA, 2024a)

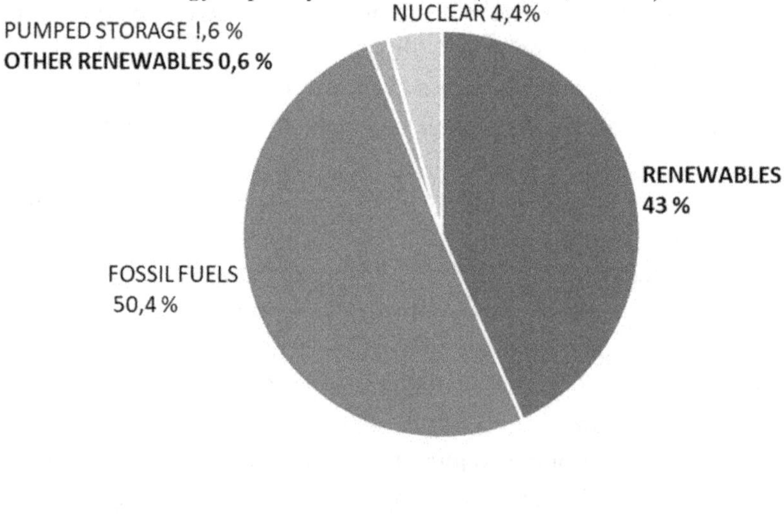

After the economic downturn regarding pandemic, global energy investment is set to exceed USD 3 trillion for the first time in 2024, with USD 2 trillion going to clean energy technologies and infrastructure. The goal of doubling the pace of energy efficiency improvement requires an even greater additional effort by tripling the renewable capacity by 2030. Yet much more needs to be done. In most cases, this growth comes from a very low base and many of the least-developed economies are being left behind as several face acute problems servicing high levels of debt (IEA, 2024).

Of course, there is a significant impact between income levels and energy investment, As developing economies struggle with economical distress and financial fragility energy investments decline. Most countries face problems of energy sourcing due to costs and risks such as Turkey (Okay, 2020). After all, risk is the greatest obstacle to investment in markets. Economic units exposed to energy are increasingly challenged by high prices, competitive economies, volatile markets, and costly complex regulations and obligations. Rapid changes regarding the energy market require additional emphasis on risk strategy, analytics, reporting, systems, and governance mainly called as energy risk management.

Risk can come from many sources. In many markets, there is limited awareness of what mechanisms or methodologies can be used to measure and verify savings after project implementation. This lack of standardization may contribute to the view held by many potential investors that energy efficiency is a risky investment. In the future, energy world needs new financial products and appraisal tools in order to raise funds and borrowing capacity. Financial institutions and customers need more incentives. Policy makers should coordinate a better standardization and good energy system for all.

According to Sustainable Development Scenario of IEA, almost 35% of the cumulative CO2 emissions reductions seen in the Sustainable Development Scenario by 2070 compared with the current trajectory come from technologies that are currently at the prototype or demonstration phase and that will not become available at scale without further R&D (including commercial demonstrators) and technical improvements. A further 40% of the cumulative emissions reductions rely on *high technologies like**AI*** that have not yet been commercially deployed in mass-market applications. (IEA, 2020).

AI-Driven Renewables in the World

More regulatory agencies turn their attention toward AI. The number of US. regulatory agencies issuing AI regulations increased to 21 in 2023 from 17 in 2022, indicating a growing concern over AI regulation. One of them is the US Department of Energy which enacted AI related regulations for the first time in 2023 (Maslej et al., 2024).

USA points to an urgent need to design resource-aware AI algorithms, systems, and applications that consider broader notions of sustainability beyond simply energy consumption. Sustainable AI also depends on research in environmental sustainability within and across all layers of the computing stack and the data management and use lifecycle. This requires a shift in research toward embracing design for sustainability that treats sustainability impacts as first-order metrics and on equal standing with performance, reliability, usability, and operational energy efficiency (NITRD, 2023).

Despite the rapid rise in AI that has created many opportunities globally providing efficiencies through automated tasks, there are ethical concerns (UNESCO, 2023). Therefore, EU deals on comprehensive rules for trustworthy AI, restricting and upgrading the use of AI especially on the behalf of sectors like energy industry (European Parliament, 2023). US officials predict that the real-world performance and energy efficiency of AI models remain poorly quantified. Development and adoption of standards, including the documentation of hardware and training details, may allow better management of the nuances of the environmental performance of AI (NITRD, 2023). Therefore, AI and AI in energy solutions needs further preparedness in the world. As stated before, we know AI global readiness is not adequate enough that it is not widespread in the global energy system, too. (Oxford Insights, 2023).

The potential usage of AI systems in the energy sector include energy system modelling and forecasting to decrease unpredictability and increase efficiency in power balancing and usage. In renewable energy systems, AI can enable storage of energy through intelligent grids enabled by smart meters, provide incremental value through improved routing and energy management, to act of sowing seeds helping decisions and also improve productivity, the reliability and affordability of photovoltaic energy. AI may also be deployed for predictive maintenance of grid infrastructure (National Strategy for Artificial Intelligence, 2018). Efforts enhancing AI to provide sustainability may represent a promising tool for achieving energy reductions, algorithms and computational processes. Calculating energy consumption in AI systems, carbon footprint is important as well as the development and implementation of regulation and the promotion of AI practices (Canedo et al., 2024).

Figure 7. AI in energy sector (Instellas, 2024)

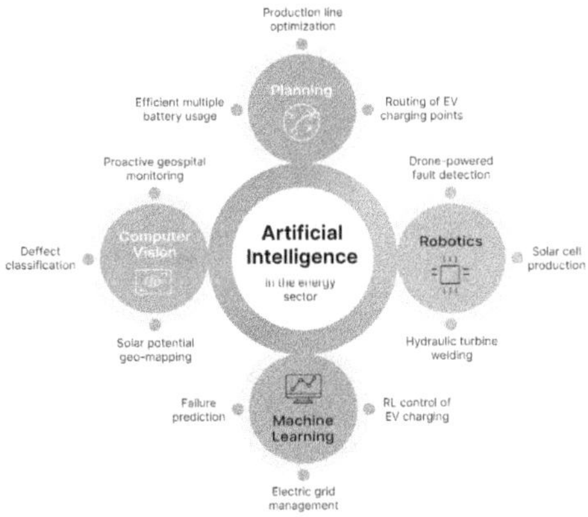

AI is uniquely tested to support the simultaneous growth of smart grids and the massive quantities of data they generate. Smart meters produce and send several thousand times more data points to utilities than their analogue predecessors. New devices for monitoring grid power flows funnel more than an order of magnitude more data to operators than the technologies they are replacing. And the global fleet of wind turbines is estimated to produce more than 400 billion data points per year. This is a key reason energy firms see AI as an increasingly critical resource. A recent estimate suggests that AI already serves more than 50 different uses in the energy system, and that the market for the technology in the sector could be worth up to USD 13 billion (IEA, 2023) Based on present and future trends, the market size is estimated to double in the period from 2019 to 2031 (Cognitive Market Research, 2024).

Figure 8. AI in global energy market share (%) 2019-2031 (Cognitive Market Research, 2024)

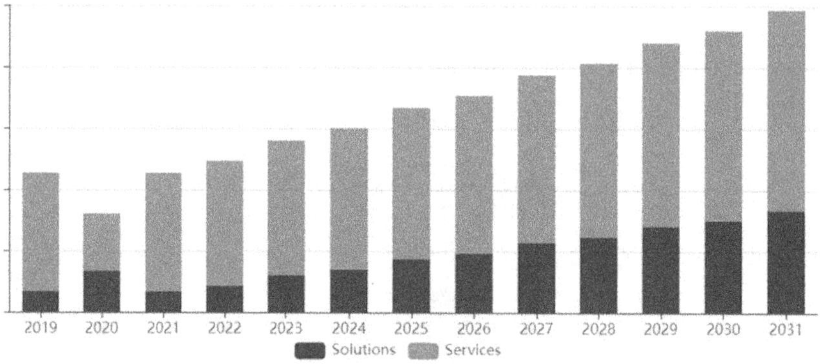

The world's five economies — the US, China, Japan, India and Germany — are each building AI ecosystems. (World Economic Forum, 2024). Ecosytem is a combination of benefits that people obtain. Eco- efficiency is the word that provides building ecosystem in countries. Clean energy and renewables, climate regulation, water purification, flood control are some of the ecosystem services (UNDP, 2024)

Smart city act (EU Directorate General for Internal Policies, 2014), too combines diverse technologies to reduce environmental impact and offer modern urban health and renewal. Smart city concept is related with eco-city and sustainable city, too. Nowadays there are 20 smart cities (Statista, 2024b) that have been upgraded by AI Technologies. The top leading first 5 are, Zuric, Oslo, Canberra, Copenhagen and Lausanne (We World Forum, 2024). Smart energy including renewables based on Information and Communications Technology- Environment enabled energy grids, metering, pollution control and monitoring, renovation of buildings and amenities, green buildings, green urban planning, as well as resource use efficiency, re-use and resource substitution which serves the above goals. Urban services such as street lighting, waste management, drainage systems, and water resource systems that are monitored to evaluate the system, reduce pollution and improve water quality are also good examples (Okay, 2016)

Figure 9. Ecosystem proposal by green AI (Canedo V.B. et al., 2024)

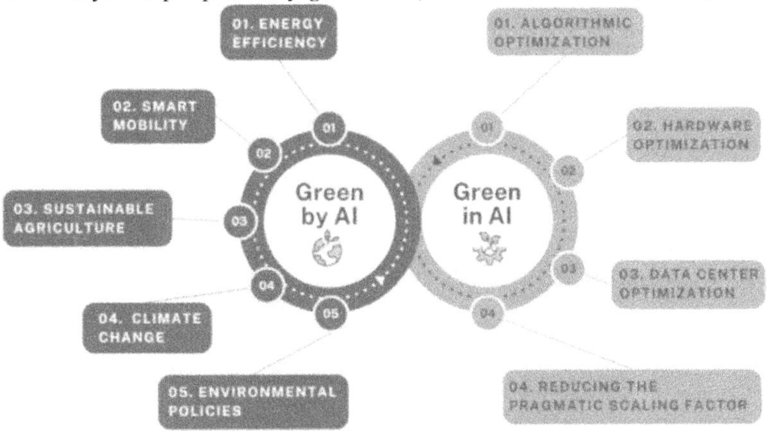

AI can play a pivotal role in reducing GHG emissions and enhancing efficiency across sectors encompassing energy production and consumption, agriculture, land use, biodiversity management, communications, transportation, and smart mobility (Canedo et al., 2024).

Figure 10. Benefits of AI tools for professional developers, 2023 (Maslej, N. et al., 2024)

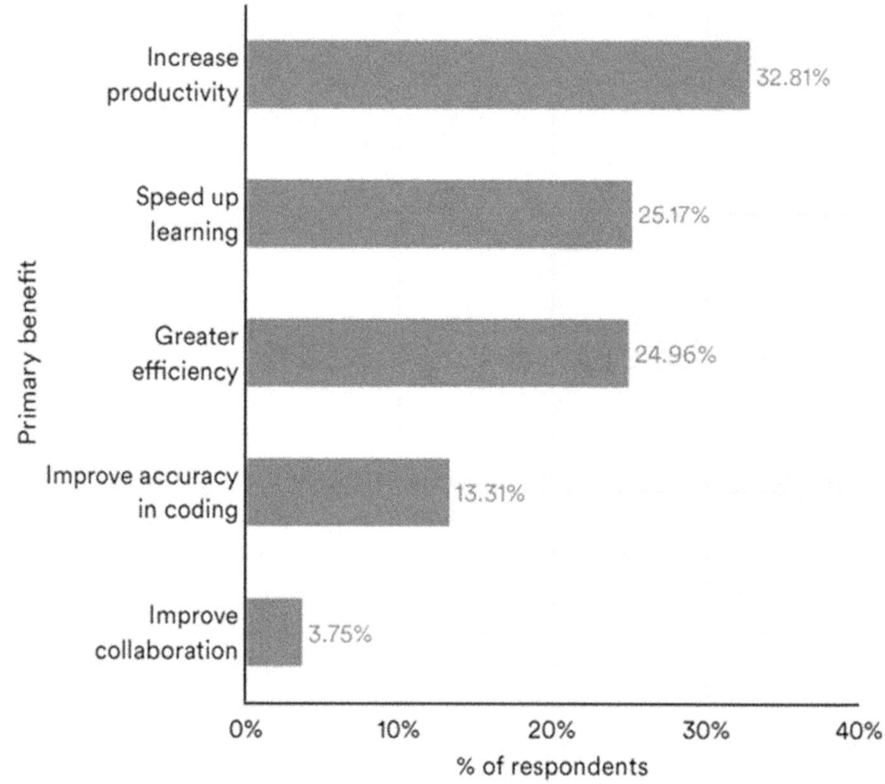

One of the branches of AI ecosystems is advanced clean energy technologies, including small modular reactors (SMRs), fusion, high-temperature geothermal energy, and advanced energy storage can complement more mature renewable technologies in a future net-zero energy system. The implementation of AI energy provides 24/7 power that is a friendly financial solution too, reducing costs (World Economic Forum). It is no surprise that managing the grids of the future will require more powerful analytical tools, with a critical role for AI (IEA,2023).

AI can contribute positively to environmental sustainability (UNDP, 2024). AI applications include enhancing thermal energy system management, improving pest control strategies, and boosting urban air quality. For instance, AI has a friendly aid for energy efficiency by optimizing the energy usage associated with air-conditioning (Luo et al., 2022). At the same time, AI can help anticipating thermal energy needs and managing thermal energy storage systems (Olabi et al., 2023). Another contribution of AI is to improve waste mangement saving time and costs in waste-to-energy conversion, waste sorting, and waste monitoring (Fang et al., 2023). AI can provide urban air quality forecasting and predicting the air quality (Shams et al., 2021). AI can also prevent grid failures, increasing reliability and security (IEA,2023).

Figure 11. Comparision of global private investments in AI by focus area, 2017–23 [Total investment (in billions of U.S. dollars)] (Maslej, N. et al., 2024)

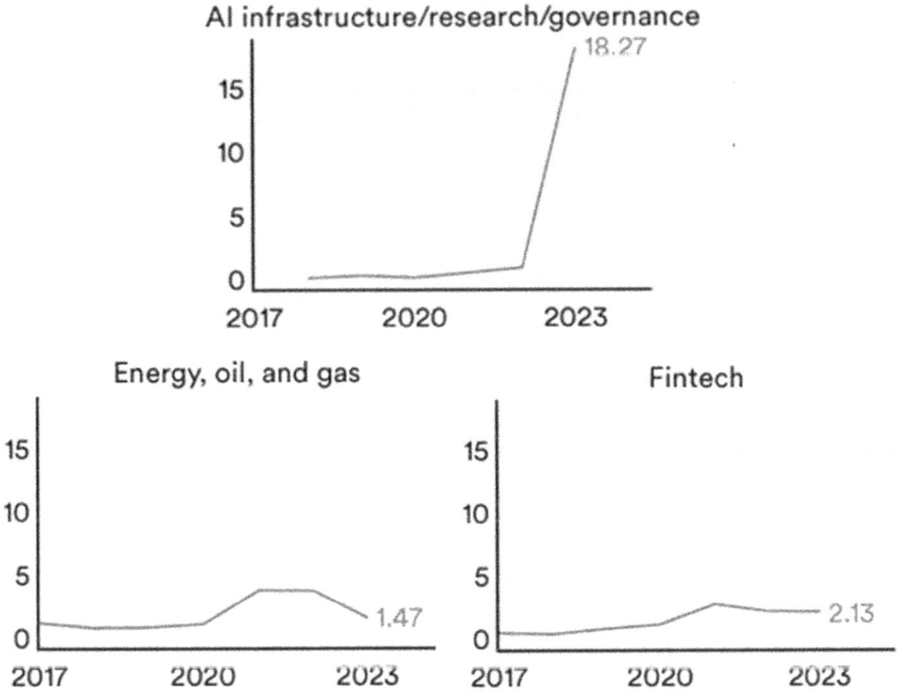

Figure 11 shows the comparison of investments of AI by sector. The highest trend percentage of AI investments by sector is in infrastructure/research/governance and data management, processing. Unfortunately, the data shows that the energy sector needs more concern for improving investments in AI, having a similar level of trend for financial services.

This is because the sectors face different types of obstacles regarding AI investments. For instance, AI driven energy technologies remain in different stages of development and large scale deployment of advanced energy solutions face a range of challenges, including technical, economic, regulator and supply chain issues (World Economic Forum). Energy sector will struggle by AI driven applications because of outdated infrastructure, lack of theoretical knowledge, lack of practical expertise and financial pressure. Especially, outdated infrastructures are the biggest obstacle to the use of AI in the energy sector (InsightTurkey, 2022).

TURKEY

Renewable Energy in Turkey

Renewable energy production and dependency is very low in Turkey as well as conventional energy. Although Turkey implemented policies to improve renewables and energy efficiency in line with EU requirements, there are inadequacies regarding both capital and legislative issues in the energy market. Turkey does not have enough conventional energy but very large potential of renewable energy resources. (Okay 2020). But still, Turkey is ranked by IEA for the year 2020 as the 70th of country list in share of modern renewables in final energy consumption global ranking (IEA, 2021). The floowing year, Turkey is ranked by IRENA for the year 2021, as the 90th of country list with a %35,4 of renewables in electricity production from renewables with 16.7% hydro, 9.4% wind, 4.2% solar, 1.8% biomass, 3.2% geomagnetic (IRENA, 2024b). Lastly, according to Energy Transition Index, Turkey is ranked as the 65th of country list regarding renewables (World Economic Forum, 2023).

By the end of August 2024, the installed capacity of Turkey has reached 113,932 MW. As of the end of August 2024, the distribution of installed capacity by resources is as follows: 28.3% hydraulic, 21.7% natural gas, 19.2% coal, 10.8% wind, 16.2% solar, 1.5% geothermal and 2.4% other sources (Ministery of Energy and Natural Resources of Turkey, 2024)

Figure 12. Turkey's renewable energy capacity shares 2024 (Ministery of Energy and Natural Resources of Turkey, 2024)

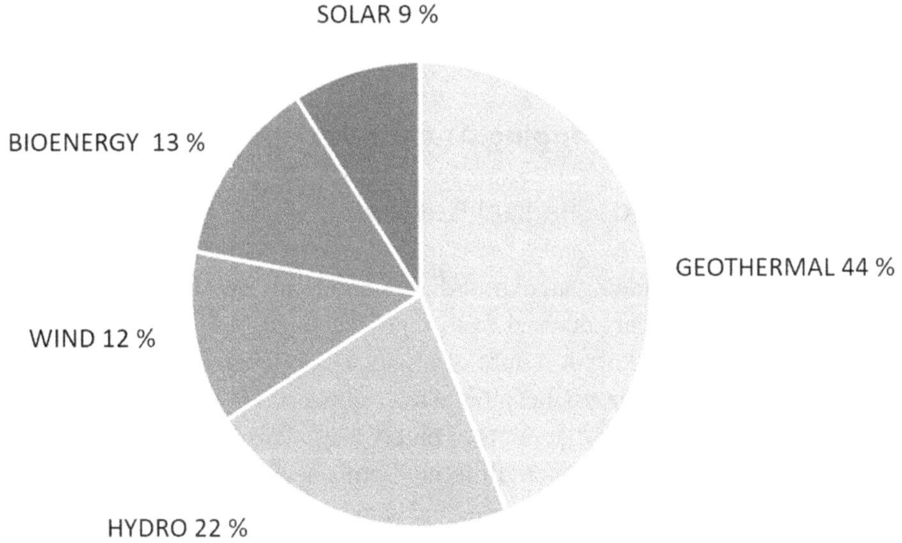

The economical concerns and the risks of financing huge energy projects still preserve caution that Turkey needs to depend on investing in the cheapest forms of creative energy solutions. The latest enactment, 2nd National Energy Efficiency Action Plan 2014 covering the period between 2024 and 2030, aims to reduce energy intensity by 15% compared to its 2023 level. According to National Energy Efficiency 2030 Strategy, Turkey aims to reduce energy consumption by %16 and contribute to 100 million tons of emission reduction and to invest $20 billion in energy efficiency schemes in the public and private sectors by 2030 (Ministery of Energy and Natural Resources of Turkey, 2024).

Turkey's reliance on natural gas use has grown along with rising oil and gas imports, leaving the Turkish economy increasingly exposed to the volatility in oil and gas prices. Turkey aims to promote sustainable economic growth whereas the IEA urges the government to set a longer term energy policy agenda for 2030. (IEA, 2016). Furthermore, Turkey needs more solar, wind, and geothermal energy projects. There is no doubt that Turkey has to promote this energy with an easy and affordable energy plan. Government in Turkey plays a crucial role in determining and establishing frameworks for a better energy sector to provide cheap and clean future energy with creative solutions of renewables. The enactment of raising awareness for green policies and reducing costs of energy efficiency should be the first priority of government.

Carbon reductions in Turkey are possible when government acts for incentives regarding industry players to provide *modern technological solutions like**AI.*** Government in Turkey has to convince and help the public and energy sector that the best way to provide energy security is to promote clean and affordable energy technologies.

What Lies Behind Challenging Any Action Plan in Turkey?

Turkey's Economic and Financial Review

Nowadays, Turkey is facing an extraordinary economic and financial situation different than previous years derived from high exchange rates and inflation but primarily provoked by persistent failure of monetary policies over and over again never seen before. The other risks can be listed as uncertainty affecting economy, business environment, huge dollar debts of enterprises alarming debt turnover rate and growing concerns; weak lira; credit rating firm's negative reports and ratings; rising government debts, investment status and banking sector and incredible delays in structural reform implementation.

Turkey's economy started to slow down since 2020 pandemic period. Although governing party continuously has the parliament majority, political environment is still incompetent under high inflation for an economic stability and recovery. Nevertheless, continous erosion of institutions has already cost Turkey its investment status and business environment causing uncertainty. The economic slow-down worsened by 2023-2024 mainly because of unfortunate monetary policies by the government. Unfortunately, fiscal spending continued to rise and exports were subject to exchange rate fluctuations. At the same time, currency risk exposure flew high in 2023-2024. The suppress on economy and finance still continues stressing the paybacks of enterprises that threatens the Turkish banks, ever.

Economy has deteriorated dramatically by the persistent inflationary affect in the last years where it is headed into contraction. The Turkish lira crashed many times in the last 5 years, losing more that 80% of its value against the dollar, increasing import and foreign debt costs and dramatically weakening the purchasing power of Turkish economic units (CNBCE, 2024).

Despite tighter financial conditions, inflation still remains stubbornly high in 2024. Further monetary policy tightening may be required most probably, if inflation expectations remain unanchored. The projections assume the policy rate will remain at 50% until well into 2025. The government announced fiscal policy tightening as part of a multi-pronged effort to put Turkey's economy back on a sustainable path (OECD, 2024b).

Credit ratings and expectations have not recovered back since 2020 where started falling apart immensely. Rating institutions respectively announced negative reports about uncertainty and risks, downgraded ratings and revised the outlook of Turkey to negative. Then, the extreme weakening of Turkish lira repeatedly influenced the 3 rating institutions respectively to announce reports. After consecutive negative reports and ratings -as government initiated tight monetary policies- Standard and Poor's, Moody's, and Fitch upgraded Turkey.

Firstly, Standard and Poor's upgraded Turkey to B+ level with positive outlook in 2024. The agency does not anticipate the inflation rate in Turkey dropping to single digits until 2028. Turkey needs immediate structural reform implementations and the agency expects authorities will take steps during 2024 to better coordinate fiscal, monetary, and incomes policies, including cuts to current nonwage expenditure. (S&P, 2024).

Respectively, Moody's upgraded Turkey to B1 level with positive outlook in 2024. (Moody's, 2024). The rating was upgraded two notches to B1, from B3, with a positive outlook because Turkey has efforts of reducing major macroeconomic imbalances. Turkey still remains four notches below investment grade. Moody's sees inflation slowing to around 30% in 2025 expecting the current account deficit to be 2.4% of GDP this year and below 2% of GDP in 2025 (Bloomberg, 2024).

Lastly, Fitch upgraded Turkey to BB- level with stable outlook in 2024. Despite the risk of policy reversals remain present in Turkey, the agency improved the tight monetary policies to lower inflation, fiscal policy and better external buffers (Fitch Ratings, 2024). Fitch said that stricter monetary policies, planned budget cuts, and wage adjustments will lead to lower inflation and current account deficits, ultimately helping to maintain better foreign currency reserves. (Reuters, 2024).

Despite the upgraded ratings, Turkey still remains below investment grade considered to be speculative. It means that Turkey is vulnerable to financial and economic conditions but currently has the capacity to meet financial commitments. So, the rank points to a risky investment environment that lower investment capacity.

SOLUTIONS AND RECOMMENDATIONS

AI-Driven Renewable Energy Investments and Solutions for Turkey

Turkey implemented policies in line with EU requirements to improve renewables and energy efficiency approved by EU (European Commision, 2012). In a decade of change, Turkish industry and municipal sectors aimed to catalyze walking out of traditional and inadequate models in energy sector. First of all Turkey focused on transition to low carbon economy and efficiency, sustainable agriculture and access to food, sustainable industry for eco- efficiency and social inclusion. Then, Turkey invested in value added energy projects regrading high technologies targeting AI solutions. *But there is no regulation or a guidance like AI driven energy action plan in Turkey.*

It is forecasted that renewable energy sources are accounted for 66% of the total electricity generation capacity in Turkey by 2035, compared with 55% in 2023, according to GlobalData's power capacity and generation database (Euro Monitor, 2024). GlobalData mainly reports about major 10 projects regarding power plants, thermal power plants and hydro power plants (GlobalData, 2024).

As said before, the records show that interestingly Turkey's adaptation of AI - country rank is 47th according to AI Global Index- is even better than the renewable energy dependency country rank which is 69th according to by prolonged practices of renewables (Oxford Insights, 2023). Although the AI index is levelling up, the AI driven renewable projects are not enough and the transition to a high tech based energy act is new (Unsal et.al, 2024). Turkey is still far beyond the desired level of eco-efficiency and affordable energy. What's more, Turkey's financial and economical situation can no longer allow a continuous demand for conventional energy. After all, economic disruption deepened in Turkey since pandemic, with huge corporate debts worsening financial situation and decreasing investments that unfortunately affect both AI and any type of renewable energy projects. Research and development projects are new in AI based energy field and that unfortunately, *there is insıfficient evidence and few studies in Turkey.*

The market size in Turkey's AI market is projected to reach US$1.62bn in 2024. The market size is expected to show an annual growth rate (CAGR 2024-2030) of 28.72%, resulting in a market volume of US$7.37bn by 2030. In global comparison, the largest market size will be in the United States (US$50.16bn in 2024) (Statista, 2024c).

Turkey needs a change of pace, like modernization by AI driven energy management. Such an AI energy plan should include managing and controlling grids, using an array of data from sensors, smart meters and other internet-of-things devices to observe and control the flow of power in the network, particularly at the distribution level. A system that AI facilitating demand response, using a range of processes such as forecasting electricity prices, scheduling and controlling response loads, and setting dynamic pricing. Turkey could provide improved energy services by using AI (InsightTurkey, 2022).

In fact, Turkey is growing on AI by industrial robotics (IFR,2023) and national defense sector (National Artificial Intelligence Strategy of Turkey, 2021) based on machine learning which are the highest market sizes in robotics of the country

(Statista, 2024c) But Turkey needs a focus of change and attention to some other strategic areas like energy sector related to economical concerns.

AI must be implemented to renewable energy sector in Turkey. Afterall, despite the challenging economical frustrations Turkey must be willing to allocate an impressive budget and accept the risks of changing the outdated systems in the country. Turkish universities should upgrade both technology related engineering fields by establishing new or developing the existing computer science and energy related institutes, departments, degree-granting programs, and EEL related official certificate programs. They must hold organizations like conferences and workshops regarding AI.

According to Artificial Intelligence Index Report 2024, the comparison records of European countries show that Turkey has huge growth in new informatics, CS, CE, and IT education compared to a decade ago. Turkey has seen the greatest growth in new CS, CE, and information PhD graduates, in the last decade which is the highest change in Europe. In other education levels, Turkey (197%) achieved one of the greatest percentage growth in new informatics, CS, CE, and IT master's graduates, whereas, with a lower but still one of the promising percentage growth (118%) in new informatics, CS, CE, and IT bachelor's graduates (Maslej et al., 2024).

Moreover, Turkey needs an AI university. Afterall, the records show that AI educational trend results of Turkey are valuable and promising for future AI related investments and labour. Therefore, AI university can help achieving more growth rate, AI investments, patents and revenues. Beyond that, universities can collaborate with policy makers and authorities for developing effective methods of risk identification and evaluation in order to help sound and vast opportunities for future energy market.

CONCLUSION

Although Turkey has a considerable potential for renewable energy sources and adopted sustainable energy action plans there is still a sign of incompetence both in practice and policy making which challenges renewable energy utilisation and adopting the eco-energy standards. At the same time, Turkey has severe economic burdens nowadays and inability to provide investments, projects, transitional measures or action plans for energy and sustainability. Turkey is facing a severe economic difficulty ongoing in the last years that affects the energy companies. Companies have debts that need restructuring. As this financial situation and payment difficulties continue the credibility of energy market decrease detoriating the investment environment.

Despite the efforts in both AI and energy sector seperately, AI driven energy attempts and transition is new and needs further attention. The major target should be to fix the economic downturn and reverse it with sound monetary and fiscal policies and structural reforms supporting renewables and AI implementations. For a change of pace, AI could be a source to renovate energy action plan in Turkey, modernizing renewable energy management. Moreover, a mixed regulation could cover a new transition towards both renewables and AI related solutions decreasing energy burden and improving a better and healthier environment in Turkey.

Universities could play a major role as AI educational trend results are promising. This is crossing with Turkey's level in AI Global index. Turkey should take the necessary steps in order to provide a robust system pertaining AI driven cost-effective sustainable energy action plan for future energy solutions by maintaining a stable economic and investment environment both for the energy market and financial services.

REFERENCES

Bloomberg. (2024). Turkey Wins Rating Upgrade From Moody's After Over a Decade. Retrieved from https://www.bnnbloomberg.ca/investing/2024/07/19/turkey-wins-rating-upgrade-from-moodys-after-over-a-decade/

Brunette, E. S., Flemmer, R. C., & Flemmer, C. L. "A review of artificial intelligence," 2009 4th International Conference on Autonomous Robots and Agents, Wellington, New Zealand, 2009, pp. 385-392. Retrieved from https://www.researchgate.net/publication/220774315

Canedo, V. B., Fernández, L. M., Cancela, B., & Betanzos, A. A. (2024), A review of green artificial intelligence: Towards a more sustainable future, Neurocomputing, Volume 599, 128096, ISSN 0925-2312, Retrieved from https://doi.org/DOI: 10.1016/j.neucom.2024.128096

Chui, J. J., & Miremadi, M. (2018). AI adoption and use survey. McKinsey Global Institute. Retrieved from https://www.mckinsey.com/capabilities/quantumblack/our-insights/what-ai-can-and-cant-do-yet-for-your-business?cid=other-soc-fce-mip-mck-oth-1801&kui=JM_dauoGBH5BzmJfYriUSw

CNBCE. (2024). Turkish lira hits fresh record low against the U.S. dollar. Retrieved from https://www.cnbc.com/2024/01/11/turkish-lira-hits-fresh-record-low-against-the-dollar.html

Cognitive Market Research. (2024). Artificial Intelligence in Energy Market Report 2024 (Global Edition). Retrieved from https://www.cognitivemarketresearch.com/artificial-intelligence-in-energy-market-report?

Davenport, T. H., & Ronanki, R. (2018). Artificial intelligence for the real world. Harvard Business Review, January-February, Retrieved from https://blockqai.com/wp-content/uploads/2021/01/analytics-hbr-ai-for-the-real-world.pdf

EU. (2021). EU Digital Strategy. Retrieved from https://eufordigital.eu/discover-eu/eu-digital-strategy/

EuroMonitor. (2024). Energy transition in Turkey. Retrieved from https://www.energymonitor.ai/data-insights/energy-transition-in-turkey/?cf-view

European Commision. (2012). Turkey's Energy Strategy, Retrieved from https://ec.europa.eu/enlargement/pdf/european_energy_policy/turkeys_energy_strategy_en.pdf

European Parliament. (2023). European Union Artificial Intelligence (AI) Act. Retrieved from https://www.europarl.europa.eu/topics/en/article/20230601STO93804/eu-ai-act-first-regulation-on-artificial-intelligence

Fang, B., Yu, J., Chen, Z., Osman, A. I., Farghali, M., Ihara, I., Hamza, E. H., Rooney, D. W., & Yap, P.-S. (2023). Artificial intelligence for waste management in smart cities: A review. *Environmental Chemistry Letters*, 21(4), 1959–1989. Advance online publication. DOI: 10.1007/s10311-023-01604-3 PMID: 37362015

Fitch Ratings. (2024). Fitch Upgrades Turkiye to 'BB-; Outlook Stable Retrieved from. https://www.fitchratings.com/research/sovereigns/fitch-upgrades-turkiye-to-bb-outlook-stable-06-09-2024

Global, A. I. Ecosystem, (2022). https://www.ai-ecosystem.org/

GlobalData. (2024). Turkey Power Market Outlook 2024. Retrieved from https://6obp2b8hjd9m4pjtra8i2gct80-GDPE2346ICR_SP.pdf

IEA. (2016). Turkey Review. Retrieved from_https://www.iea.org/publications/freepublications/publication/EnergyPoliciesofIEACountriesTurkey.pdf

IEA. (2020). Energy Technology Perspectives. Retrieved from https://www.iea.org/reports/energy-technology-perspectives-2020

IEA. (2021), Turkey, Renewables. Retrieved from https://www.iea.org/countries/turkiye/renewables

IEA. (2023), Why AI and energy are the new power couple, IEA, Paris Retrieved from https://www.iea.org/commentaries/why-ai-and-energy-are-the-new-power-couple

IEA. (2024). World Energy Investment 2024. Retrieved from https://iea.blob.core.windows.net/assets/60fcd1dd-d112-469b-87de-20d39227df3d/World EnergyInvestment2024.pdf

Insight Turkey. (2022). Energy Supply Security and Artificial Intelligence Applications. Retrieved from https://www.insightturkey.com/articles/energy-supply-security-and-artificial-intelligence-applications

Instellas, (2024). Artificial Intelligence in the Energy Sector: Benefits and Use Cases. Retrieved from https://intellias.com/ai-in-energy-sector-benefits/

IRENA. (2019). Global Energy Transformation. Retrieved from https://www.irena.org/apps/DigitalArticles/-/media/652AE07BBAAC407ABD1D45F6BBA8494B.ashx

IRENA. (2024a). Renewable energy highlights. Retrieved from https://www.irena.org/-/media/Files/IRENA/Agency/Publication/2024/Jul/Renewable_energy_highlights_FINAL_July_2024.pdf

IRENA. (2024b), Turkey Profile. Retrieved from https://www.irena.org/-/media/Files/IRENA/Agency/Statistics/Statistical_Profiles/Eurasia/Turkiye_Eurasia_RE_SP.pdf

Luo, J., Paduraru, C., Voicu, O., Chervonyi, Y., & Munns, S. (2022). Controlling Commercial Cooling Systems Using Reinforcement Learning. 10.48550/arXiv.2211.07357

Maslej, N., ... (2024). Artificial Intelligence Index Report 2024. Standford University & US Human-Centered Artifical Intelligence, Retrieved from https://aiindex.stanford.edu/report/

McCarthy. (2004). What is Artificial Intelligence? Retrieved from https://www-formal.stanford.edu/jmc/whatisai.pdf

Ministery of Energy and Natural Resources of Turkey. (2024). Info Bank: Energy. Retrieved from https://enerji.gov.tr/infobank-energy-electricity

Moody's. (2024). B1posistive: Update following to B1, Outlook remains positive. Retrieved from https://www.moodys.com/reports?region=Turkiye

National Artificial Intelligence Strategy of Turkey. (2021). Retrieved from https://cbddo.gov.tr/SharedFolderServer/Genel/File/TRNationalAIStrategy2021-2025.pdf

National Strategy for Artificial Intelligence of India. (2018). Retrieved from https://www.niti.gov.in/sites/default/files/2023-03/National-Strategy-for-Artificial-Intelligence.pdf

Ng, A. (2011). Sparse Autoencoder. CS294A Lecture Notes, 72, 1-19. Retrieved from https://web.stanford.edu/class/archive/cs/cs294a/cs294a.1104/sparseAutoencoder.pdf

NITRD. (2023). National AI R&D Strategic Plan 2023. Retrieved from https://www.nitrd.gov/pubs/National-Artificial-Intelligence-Research-and-Development-Strategic-Plan-2023-Update.pdf

OECD. (2024a). Economic outlook: Steady global growth expected for 2024 and 2025. Retrieved from https://www.oecd.org/en/about/news/press-releases/2024/05/economic-outlook-steady-global-growth-expected-for-2024-and-2025.html

OECD. (2024b).. . *Economic Outlook*, 2024(1), •••. https://www.oecd-ilibrary.org/docserver/2b72fc41-en.pdf?expires=1727124085&id=id&accname=guest&checksum=5EE3CF374CFD1BD4F79D9443A5B8E755

Okay, C. N., Sencer, A., & Taskin, N. (2024). Quantitative indicators for environmental and social sustainability performance assessment of the supply chain. *Environment, Development and Sustainability*. Advance online publication. DOI: 10.1007/s10668-024-05210-3

Okay, E. (2016). Towards Smart Cities in Turkey? Transitioning from Waste to Creative, Clean and Cheap Eco- Energy. In *Handbook of Research on Waste Management Techniques for Sustainability (SCOPUS), Hersey*. IGI Global. DOI: 10.4018/978-1-4666-9723-2.ch015

Okay, E. (2017). Investment on Heat Pumps: Geothermal Green Solutions for Turkey Lowering Energy Costs. In *Handbook of Research on Supply Chain Management for Sustainable Development (SCOPUS), (194-217). Hersey*. IGI Global.

Okay E. (2018). A New Barrier for the Future of Energy Market in Turkey: Internal Capital Adequacy Assessment Process (ICAAP). *in Ethics and Sustainability in Global Supply Chain Management* (SCOPUS),, (178-196). Hersey: IGI Global.

Okay, E. (2020). *More Obstacles to the Growth of ESCOs in Turkey: Stumble In the Midst of a Financial Distress in Handbook of Research on Creating Sustainable Value in the Global Economy, Hersey*. IGI Global. DOI: 10.4018/978-1-7998-1196-1.ch008

Olabi, A. G., Abdelghafar, A. A., Maghrabie, H. M., Sayed, E. T., Rezk, H., Radi, M. A., Obaideen, K., & Abdelkareem, M. A. (2023). Application of Artificial Intelligence for Prediction, Optimization, and Control of Thermal Energy Storage Systems. *Thermal Science and Engineering Progress*, 39, 101730. DOI: 10.1016/j.tsep.2023.101730

Oxford Insights. (2023). Government AI Readiness Index 2023. Retrieved from https://oxfordinsights.com/wp-content/uploads/2023/12/2023-Government-AI-Readiness-Index-2.pdf

Reuters, (2024). Fitch upgrades Turkey's rating to "BB-" on improved fiscal policy. Retrieved from https://www.reuters.com/world/middle-east/fitch-upgrades-turkeys-rating-bb-improved-fiscal-policy-2024-09-06/

Shams, S. R., Jahani, A., Kalantary, S., Moeinaddini, M., & Khorasani, N. (2021). Artificial intelligence accuracy assessment in NO2 concentration forecasting of metropolises air. *Scientific Reports*, 11(1), 1805. DOI: 10.1038/s41598-021-81455-6 PMID: 33469146

Standard and Poor's. (2024). Turkiye Upgraded To 'B+' On Economic Rebalancing; Outlook Positive. Retrieved from https://disclosure.spglobal.com/ratings/en/regulatory/article/-/view/type/HTML/id/3165137

Statista, (2024a). Renewable energy investments worldwide - statistics & facts. Retrieved from https://www.statista.com/topics/10992/global-renewable-energy-investments/#topicOverview

Statista, (2024b). Ranking of leading 20 smart cities globally in 2023, by human development index (HDI) score. Retrieved from https://www.statista.com/statistics/1410416/hdi-smart-city-index-worldwide/

Statista, (2024c). Market Insights: Artificial Intelligence -Turkey. Retrieved from https://www.statista.com/outlook/tmo/artificial-intelligence/turkey

UN. (2024). World Economic Situation and Prospects as of mid-2024. Retrieved from_https://desapublications.un.org/publications/world-economic-situation-and-prospects-mid-2024?_ga=2.152444025.1736376011.1727109015-126811107.1727108980

UNESCO. (2023). Ethics of Artificial Intelligence. Retrieved from https://unesdoc.unesco.org/ark:/48223/pf0000385082.page=4

Unsal, D. B., Aksoz, A., Oyucu, S., Guerrero, J. M., & Guler, M. (2024). A Comparative Study of AI Methods on Renewable Energy Prediction for Smart Grids: Case of Turkey. MDPI. Volume 16, Issue 7, . Retrieved from https://www.mdpi.com/2071-1050/16/7/2894DOI: 10.3390/su16072894

Wang, P. (2019). On Defining Artificial Intelligence. *Journal of Artificial General Intelligence*, 10(2), 1–37. https://sciendo.com/article/10.2478/jagi-2019-0002. DOI: 10.2478/jagi-2019-0002

World Economic Forum. (2023) Fostering Effective Energy Transition 2023, Retrieved from https://www3.weforum.org/docs/WEF_Fostering_Effective_Energy_Transition_2023.pdf

World Economic Forum. (2024). These 5 cities are making innovative use of generative AI. Retrieved from https://www.weforum.org/agenda/2024/07/generative-ai-smart-cities/

ADDITIONAL READING

Abisoye, O., Sun, Y., & Zenghui, W. A. (2024). Survey of artificial intelligence methods for renewable energy forecasting: Methodologies and insights. Energy Focus, 48. https://www.sciencedirect.com/science/article/pii/S1755008423001254

Akkucuk, U. (2016). *Handbook of Research on Waste Management Techniques for Sustainability, SCOR Model and the Green Supply Chain, Hersey*. IGI Global.

Andretta, A. (2014). Key enablers for the future of Smart Cities. Philips Lighting. Retrieved from_https://www.theclimategroup.org/sites/default/files/archive/files/Dubai-Philips---Business-Case-1.pdf

Baars, B. J. (1988). *A cognitive theory of consciouness*. Cambridge University Press.

Bostrom, N. (2014). *Superintelligence: Paths, Dangers, Strategies* (1st ed.). Oxford University Press.

Brachman, R. J. (2006). (AA)AI — More than the sum of its parts, 2005 AAAI Presidential Address. *AI Magazine*, 27(4), 19–34. https://ojs.aaai.org/aimagazine/index.php/aimagazine/article/view/1907

Chandler, J. (2009). Trendy solutions: Why do states adopt sustainable energy portfolio standards. *Energy Policy*, 37(8), 3274–3281. https://www.sciencedirect.com/science/article/abs/pii/S0301421509002870. DOI: 10.1016/j.enpol.2009.04.032

Cohen, P. R. (2005). If Not Turing's Test, then what? *AI Magazine*, 26, 61–67. https://ojs.aaai.org/aimagazine/index.php/aimagazine/article/view/1849

Davis, R. (1998). What are intelligence? and why? 1996 AAAI Presidential Address. *AI Magazine*, 19(1), 91–111. https://dl.acm.org/doi/abs/10.1609/aimag.v19i1.1356

Dennett, D. C. (1984). Cognitive wheels: the frame problem of AI. In *Mind, Machines, and Evolution*. Cambridge University Press.

Dorian, J. P., Herman, T. F., & Dale, R. S. (2006). Global challenges in energy. Energy Policy, 34(15), 1984–1991. Retrieved fromhttps://www.sciencedirect.com/science/article/abs/pii/S0301421505000972

Gamble, C., & Gao, J. Safety-first ai for autonomous data centre cooling and industrial control. Retrieved from https://www.deepmind.com/blog/safety-first-ai-for-autonomous-datacentre-cooling-and-industrial-control

Huang, C. J., & Kuo, P. H. Multiple-Input Deep Convolutional Neural Network Model for Short-Term Photovoltaic Power Forecasting. IEEE Access 2019, 7, 74822–74834. Retrieved from https://ieeexplore.ieee.org/abstract/document/8732333

International Network for Sustainable Energy. (2010). Europe, Sustainable Energy Vision 2050: A Global Vision for 2050. Retrieved from http://www.inforse.org/europe/VisionWorld.htm

Jensen, J.O., S. B. Nielsen, J.R. (2013). Greening public buildings: ESCO Contracting in Danish municipalitics. Energies, 6, 2407–2427. 64

Kleindorfer, R. P. (2011). Risk management for energy efficiency projects in developing countries. United Nations. Working paper 6/ 2011. Retrieved from https://www.unido.org/api/opentext/documents/download/9925425/unido-file-9925425

Kostka, G., & Shin, K. (2013). Energy conservation through energy service companies: Empirical analysis from China. *Energy Policy*, 52, 748–759. DOI: 10.1016/j.enpol.2012.10.034

KPMG. (2016). Commodity & Energy Risk Management. Retrieved from https://assets.kpmg/content/dam/kpmg/pdf/2016/04/Commodity-and-Energy-Risk-Management.pdf

Langlois, P., & Hansen, S. (2013). *World ESCO Outlook*. The Fairmont Press.

Liehr, G. (2010). Energy Services: Potentials and Future Applications. *European Association of Energy Service Companies European Energy Service Day* 9.13.2010. Retrieved from https://www.euesco.org/cms/upload/downloads/presentations/LiehreuESCO100910_.pdf

Okay, E. (2014). The Risks of Financing Energy in Turkey: Heading for Rocky Road. *Open Journal of Energy Efficiency*, 3(1), 1–13. DOI: 10.4236/ojee.2014.31001

Okay, E. (2015). Creative Energy Alternatives: Cheap and Future Energy for Turkey. in *Handbook of Research on Developing Sustainable Value in Economics, Finance, and Marketing*. (157-178). Hersey: IGI Global.

Okay E., N. Okay, U. Akman (2008). Views on Trukey's impending ESCO market: Is it promising? Energy Policy 2008, 36, 1821–1825. 67.

Okay, E., Okay, N., & Akman, U. (2012). Turkey chapter. In *World ESCO Outlook* (pp. 396–403). The Fairmont Press.

Okay, E., Okay, N., & Akman, U. (2013). Current Snapshot of the Turkish ESCO Market (SSCI). *Energy Policy*, 60, 106–115. DOI: 10.1016/j.enpol.2013.04.080

Turkish Ministry of Energy and Natural Resources. (2018). National Energy Efficiency Action Plan (2017-2023). Ankara. Retrieved from https://www.yegm.gov.tr/document/20180102M1_2018_eng.pdf

Zhang, Z., Chong, A., Pan, Y., Zhang, C., & Lam, K. P. (2019). Whole building energy model for hvac optimal control: A practical framework based on deep reinforcement learning. *Energy and Building*, 199, 472–490. https://www.sciencedirect.com/science/article/abs/pii/S0378778818330858. DOI: 10.1016/j.enbuild.2019.07.029

KEY TERMS AND DEFINITIONS

AI: The science and engineering of making intelligent machines, especially intelligent computer programs

AI-Based Energy Solutions: Optimising solutions based on AI for the storage and distribution of energy from energy sources (renewables)

AI-Driven Cost-Effective Sustainable Energy: Sustainable and cheap solutions based on AI for the storage and distribution of energy from energy sources

Cost-Effective Energy: Energy solutions reducing costs, cost of supplying, producing and creating energy

Eco-Efficiency: Goods and services to meet human needs and improve quality of life while progressively reducing environmental side effects

Energy Efficiency: Low cost and effective energy solutions and reductions of carbon ensuring a safe, reliable, affordable and sustainable energy system

Renewable Energy: Natural sources of energy derived from wind, sun, and biomass.

Sustainable Energy: Ability to maintain or support energy over time

Turkey: Turkey is a developing country located between Europe and Asia

Chapter 12
Intentions and Premises: An Analysis of Sustainability in U.S. Security Institutions' AI Strategies

Alp Cenk Arslan
https://orcid.org/0000-0002-5526-2089
Turkish National Police Academy, Turkey

ABSTRACT

This chapter evaluates the sustainability premises of the strategy documents on AI for U.S. security institutions regarding intent, and foundational assumptions. While doing so, the paper covers a discussion of the position of AI in public administration and how sustainability is captured within these strategies in the security sector. These results indicate that U.S. security institutions work toward enhancing effectiveness in operations using AI, but also address the long-term, critical challenges on energy efficiency, social equity, and economic responsibility. The concept of sustainability is based on assumptions, such as the fact that AI should serve today's needs while protecting those of future generations. This can also be interpreted to mean a far stronger integration of secure-by-design principles and a much wider focus on minimizing negative societal impacts of AI. It therefore helps provide an insight into how AI governance evolves through a complex adaptive system in framing strategic foresight of sustainability in developing balanced and ethical AI applications.

DOI: 10.4018/979-8-3693-8372-8.ch012

INTRODUCTION

The rapid development of AI technologies in recent years has significantly transformed public administration and security. The U.S. security institutions primarily, have determined the operational effectiveness of these technologies and the need to evaluate their long-term societal, environmental, and economic effects while designing their AI strategies. In this context, sustainability has become a theme that has gained significance in AI strategies.

The sustainability premises within the AI strategy documents of the U.S. security institutions have a critical role in the design and adoption of AI technologies. These premises aim to reach short-term strategic objectives and long-term sustainability goals. In this context, sustainability aims to sustain AI's impacts on the security sector to be balanced and persistent by assuming the environmental, societal, and economic dimensions. How AI could be sustainable in the long term has become a vital subject regarding social benefits and the protection of global stability.

The integration of AI technologies into public administration processes is a significant development that enhances the operational capacities of states and gives them an opportunity to present more effective services to their people. These technologies provide considerable benefits to public administration in processing data rapidly and effectively, solving complex problems, and automating processes. However, the use of technology in a more sustainable way has become a crucial point, in addition to AI's advantages above.

Sustainability is an approach that considers the long-term social, environmental, and economic impacts of using AI, especially in public administration. Public administration has broad responsibilities, such as protecting the well-being of societies, ensuring financial stability, and supporting the sustainable use of natural resources. In this context, AI applications should meet current needs and consider future generations' demands. The sustainable application of AI ensures that these technologies contribute to long-term social benefits by supporting social justice, environmental balance, and economic prosperity.

When evaluating the significance of sustainability in the context of public administration, it is primarily required to approach the environmental effects of these technologies. Since AI systems require considerable amounts of data for processing, they consume extreme energy. Thus, ecological sustainability brings the subjects of energy efficiency and reduction of carbon footprint. If these technologies are not appropriately governed, there is a risk of extinction of energy resources and climate change. Accordingly, strategies of ecological sustainability create a necessity for AI to be governed with solutions that increase energy efficiency.

Societal sustainability is related to the impacts of AI technologies on society. The extensive use of AI in public administration affects social issues such as data privacy, ethical responsibilities, and the transformation of the workforce. Safeguarding social justice in AI-based decision processes builds fundamental elements of equity, respect for human rights, and sustainable governing of these technologies (Kulkov et al., 2023; Szalkowski & Johansen, 2023). For instance, making erroneous decisions or excluding several social groups while using AI in public services could deepen social inequalities. The principles of social inclusion and equality should be at the forefront of AI applications in public administration to prevent this negative effect.

Economic sustainability includes the responsible and efficient use of resources and contributing to economic growth by this method. The extensive use or problematic design and planning of these technologies could bring liabilities to public finance in the long term. Economic sustainability requires the careful governing of public resources and the long-term benefits of AI investments (Nishant et al., 2020). In an ideal system, public administration focuses on the long-term economic benefits rather than the short-term costs. Also, AI technologies form a significant effect on the workforce in this term. The use of AI in automation processes could affect the workforce negatively. To prevent this kind of social risk, it is necessary to focus on building education and skill-sharing programs for the workforce to adapt to these new technologies.

Sustainability is related to not only short-term benefits and technological effectiveness but also long-term societal, environmental, and economic dimensions. It is a multidimensional approach. Adopting AI technologies in public administration in a sustainable way allows these technologies to contribute to society, the environment, and the economy while guaranteeing the minimizing of potential negative impacts. In this regard, the principles of sustainability need to be central to the AI strategy documents.

This study will evaluate the intentions, foundations, and related possibilities in the AI strategy documents of U.S. security institutions. The main research question is, "What are the underlying intentions, premises, and possibilities on the sustainability premises of the AI strategy documents of U.S. security institutions?"

This research question reveals several significant elements. Firstly, the concept of intentions points to the goals the security institutions try to reach while designing their AI strategy documents. The long-term strategic goals that are set by security institutions with regard to sustainability in the use of AI technologies are prior to understanding the intentions behind the documents. It is noteworthy to ask whether AI technological systems are being employed only to enhance operational effectiveness or whether a broader vision is being pursued, such as promoting social, environmental, and economic sustainability. This initial part of the research will comprehensively analyze the goals behind the sustainability propositions of the U.S.

security institutions. Secondly, the concept of premises refers to the assumptions on which strategy documents are based. A strategy document is based on essential premises about why a particular approach should be implemented in order to reach a strategic goal. The U.S. security institutions' societal assumptions should be taken into account for the sustainable use of AI. Finally, the term of possibilities is the insights into how the sustainability premises contained in the strategy documents of the institutions will be shaped in the future. How these technologies could be governed sustainably in the security sector and what kind of possibilities will appear are valuable questions to be responded. The applicability of the sustainability propositions in the strategy documents of the U.S. security institutions has the potential to reveal what possibilities that these documents contain in the context of social, environmental, and economic sustainability.

The three main dimensions of the research seek to understand not only how premises of sustainability are present in the AI strategy documents but also how these premises would evolve in the future. Sustainability in the U.S. security institutions' AI strategy documents both meet current needs and make predictions about what methods would be decided in the future in terms of security and social sustainability.

Accordingly, the research question aims to conduct a comprehensive analysis of how the premises of sustainability are designed in the documents. The questions of what are the intentions behind these premises, what their foundations are, and what the future implications of these premises are deserve to be answered in the analysis. Assessing the sustainability premises in the documents from a broader perspective would provide significant insights.

The main objective of this chapter is to examine the strategic AI frameworks of key United States (U.S.) security institutions, including the Department of State (DoS), the Department of Defense (DoD), the Department of Homeland Security (DHS), Cybersecurity and Infrastructure Security Agency (CISA), and the Directorate of National Intelligence (DNI). The chapter will also examine the sustainability intentions and premises of these institutions' strategy documents. By subjecting these AI strategy documents to a meticulous review, this chapter will elucidate the strategic intentions, premises, and prospective possibilities inherent in the adoption of AI into national security frameworks.

This chapter has a structure that is both theoretical and practical. The structure and methodology used in the analysis are designed to provide a comprehensive understanding of the topic. First, it will demonstrate the place of security institutions and strategies in the paradigm of AI-driven public administration. Then, it will analyze the practical documents. The chapter is structured in four main pillars to analyze the subject: an examination of security institutions as complex adaptive systems, AI strategies in the context of AI-driven public administration paradigm, an analysis of the AI strategy documents of the U.S. security institutions, and a conclusion.

The first section of the chapter posits security institutions as complex adaptive systems. Complex adaptive systems theory is employed to comprehend systems in which different components interact with each other dynamically and continuously. This understanding is suitable for large and multi layered organizations such as security agencies. The reason for this is that these organizations operate in a constantly changing environment with a variety of actors, processes, and technologies. The use of AI in security institutions transforms the nature of the complex structures of the institutions. The chapter will explain how security institutions are considered complex systems. The chapter will also explain how these institutions adapt to changing threat environments and technological innovations. It will focus on how flexible or resilient the structures of these institutions are in achieving their sustainability goals.

The following section analyzes the role of AI in public administration. It also examines the strategies developed in this context. In a rapidly digitizing planet, public administration employs advanced technologies such as AI to provide more effective and efficient services. The AI strategies of the U.S. security institutions will be discussed in the context of digital transformation in public services in this section. What role does sustainability play in the use of AI in public administration, do AI-driven public policies focus only on short-term operational gains or long-term sustainability goals are the questions to be responded to. The chapter will examine AI strategies in the literature and raise a discussion how public administration transforms from a sustainability perspective. The impact of the strategies in the security sector and how these strategies are positioned will be examined.

The third section is the central part of the research. It presents a detailed analysis of the AI strategy documents of the U.S. security institutions. The sustainability premises in the strategy documents will be analyzed using qualitative analysis methods in this section. The sustainability themes that are prominent in the strategy documents will be analyzed in depth. The research methodology will be thematic analysis. The thematic analysis allows for an in-depth analysis of the main themes emerging in the documents. This method is also suitable to understand the underlying dimensions of sustainability.

The final section will summarize the analyses that were conducted in the previous chapters. It will draw conclusions from the analyses. It will discuss how effective sustainability premises are in the AI strategies of U.S. security institutions and how these premises shape long-term security policies. This section will also discuss the main findings of the study. It will also provide recommendations for future research. It will discuss how the sustainability approach of the U.S. security institutions could serve as a model for other countries or international security organizations. Finally, an overview of the potential of AI technologies in achieving sustainability goals and their capacity to generate more inclusive security governance will be provided.

SECURITY INSTITUTIONS AS COMPLEX ADAPTIVE SYSTEMS IN AI-DRIVEN PUBLIC ADMINISTRATION

Security institutions can be conceptualized as complex adaptive systems (CAS) in the context of AI-driven public administration. This perspective is fundamental for understanding the field in which these institutions operate and evolve in an increasingly interconnected and dynamic environment. CAS are characterized by their capacity to adapt and respond to changes in their environment. This process operates with the interaction of their components, which are mostly and frequently autonomous. The autonomous character of the components are interdependent at the same time. Security institutions, including law enforcement bodies, intelligence services, and military units, contain these characteristics in several important ways.

CASs are characterized by a complex structure arising from the interactions of different components. These components are actors, processes, and technologies. One of their main determining features is the absence of central authority. This decentralization is because of the system's behavior emerging from the interactions of individual components. Due to this characteristic, CASs become different from hierarchical and centralized systems (Vieira, 1992; Gell-Mann, 1999).

The fundamental characteristics of CAS could be listed as follows (Holland, 2006; Levin, 2002; Holden, 2005):

1. A multi-component structure is a defining characteristic of CASs. It contains a multitude of independent components that interact with each other. The components interact in harmony with a set of defined rules. The interactions among them collectively form the overall dynamics of the system.
2. CASs are capable of self-organization as a result of interactions between components in the absence of central control. This decentralization enables the system to rapidly adapt to change in the environment.
3. CASs are capable of going through structural or functional transitions in response to environmental change. This adaptation capacity is vital to persist in complex and uncertain situations.
4. In CASs, the interactions of components with each other are subject to constant review. It is not valid only for the interactions among components but also for the results of these interactions. By constantly reviewing the interactions and their results, the system behavior is continuously updated.

Security institutions are constructed of a multitude of interacting elements. These elements include human agents, technological systems, organizational structures, policies, and strategies. These elements are in constant interaction with each other and external factors. The external factors include political directives, social changes, and technological innovations (Burns et al. 2017). The interactions within these systems become more complex because of the introduction of new variables and capabilities that are inherent to AI technologies, in a public administration environment where AI is a dominant factor. If we give an example, AI could facilitate predictive policing activities by detecting and identifying potential threats by the analysis of large datasets which influences decision-making processes within law enforcement bodies. This situation forms a feedback loop in which the organization needs to continuously adapt its strategies and operations based on AI-providing insights.

Another aspect of the CAS-type understanding of security institutions is because of their inherent decentralized nature. "Security institutions as CAS" are decentralized, with decision-making dispatched across various levels and units. This process of decentralization is fundamental for the system's flexibility and adaptability. This situation enables the institution to respond rapidly to emerging threats and challenges. Nevertheless, it presents challenges in terms of coordination and consistency (Pianini et al., 2019). These challenges are valid, particularly in the adoption of AI technologies. AI systems frequently operate autonomously. They make decisions or recommendations based on data analysis without human control. It can lead to tensions within the institution. Primarily, it leads to tensions with various sectors adopting AI tools at different speeds or interpreting AI-generated insights differently. This dispatched decision process could result in fragmented responses to security threats (Shnitko, 2003).

A final aspect is that the capacity of security institutions to adapt is contingent on their capability to learn. In CASs, learning happens by the accumulation of experiences and continuous adaptation to highly changing circumstances (Allen, 2001). In the aspect of security institutions, it marks the capacity to learn from AI-generated data. It also modifies policies and strategies in harmony with learning and adopts new technologies in several methods that enhance their effectiveness and efficiency. The adoption of AI into security administration requires a more open-minded organizational culture. This type of culture will re-examine established practices in light of new insights and capabilities.

Similarly, "security institutions as CAS" are subject to the influence of the environment where they operate. It confines both technological space and legal, ethical, and social contexts. The adoption and integration of AI in security give rise to important questions regarding the protection of privacy, the assurance of accountability, and the biases in decision-making processes. It is critical for security institutions to address these challenges. It is also crucial for them to maintain public trust while ensuring that the adoption of AI is compatible with democratic values and human rights standards (Mukhin et al., 2016).

The recognition that security institutions function as CAS has essential implications for sustainability. The concept of sustainability forms not only environmental considerations but also the need for organizational and operational balance and resilience. It is significant that security institutions embrace sustainable strategies to achieve long-term goals (Pereira & Ruysenaar, 2012). In this context, accepting "security institutions as CAS" allows them to maintain flexibility and resilience.

Their function in the context of sustainability is to secure the effective and efficient management of resources. It is vital for them where they operate within limited resources (Crampton, 2013). AI provides optimization in resource management and functions as an essential tool for sustainable operations.

Risk management is another aspect. Security institutions conduct operations in an environment full of uncertainties (Goralski & Tan, 2020). CASs facilitate the management of these uncertainties. It enables organizations to mitigate long-term risks. AI-supported analysis and modeling could increase and enhance the efficiency and effectiveness of risk management. Sustainability requires both the mitigation of current vulnerabilities and the preparation for future threats. With the help of CAS characteristics, security institutions could quickly adapt to changing conditions. They also could better cope with unexpected situations thanks to their flexible structures.

Evaluating "security institutions as CAS," or this kind of thinking, has positive implications, such as contribution to AI strategies in these institutions. Security institutions are large and multi-layered organizations (Lorenzoli et al., 2007). They need to respond to a wide range of threats, changing technological developments, and uncertainties at the international level. They are not static and predictable. However, they are somewhat dynamic, self-organizing and renewing, and adaptive systems. The approach of CAS provides a robust framework for comprehending the operation of these institutions and designing their strategies. CAS is an understanding employed to describe systems that constantly evolve and adapt by the interactions of different, independent actors. CAS understanding enables security institutions to design their AI strategies. It guarantees these strategies are sustainable and flexible (Al-Guesbi, 2020).

CASs are built of decentralized and constantly interacting components. The institutions also have a structure with different units, technologies, and individuals. These units, technologies, and individuals who are members of security institutions constantly interact. Centralized control in these systems could be restricted due to the system's success, which depends on how all of the components operate together and adapt (Ioannou, 1986). Adoption of new technologies, such as AI, into these systems, increases the complexity of strategies and introduces new dynamics. Thus, designing and developing of AI strategies become a process in which CAS understanding could help create solutions. These solutions allow security institutions to respond to changing circumstances flexibly.

The contribution of CAS understanding to AI strategies in security institutions could be evaluated in seven points. These are 1) decentralized control and autonomous systems, 2) internal communication and feedback loops, 3) adaptability and ability to learn, 4) coordination of multiple actors and systems, 5) ability to cope with uncertainty, 6) sustainability and resilience, and 7) inclusive strategy development.

CAS thinking emphasizes a decentralized control structure. This decentralization in security institutions empowers the ability of various units and levels to act independently. Designing and developing AI strategies facilitate institutions to build more autonomous systems and units without positing them under centralized control. AI-based security systems could enhance operational flexibility by adapting to local circumstances. They also increase flexibility by making rapid and timely decisions that are independent of a centralized structure (Arcaini et al., 2017). This situation is necessary in security threats and crises due to the requirement for fast response. CAS understanding enhances the ability of AI systems to learn and adapt in the autonomous system constantly. It helps security institutions respond to changing threat environments more rapidly and effectively.

Another key contribution of CASs is that they operate on continuous feedback loops. Security institutions are large-scale organizations, and they have various units that have a continuous exchange of information and feedback among each other (Ryan et al., 2007). This mechanism increases the overall effectiveness of the system. In terms of CAS understanding, we need to focus on how to make the feedback mechanism more effective in the design of AI strategies. AI technologies collect large amounts of data. They analyze it and provide constant feedback to security institutions. These mechanisms enable dynamic evaluation, continuous renewal, and updates of strategies (Ma et al., 2012). Evaluating feedback processes more effectively facilitates the creation of AI systems that evolve and adapt. Security institutions' threat detection and analysis systems could reach more accurate predictions by constantly learning from the data collected and building strategic decisions consistent with the threats.

A significant contribution of CASs is their adaptability and ability to learn. This ability continuously adapts the organizations to changing circumstances. The system enhances its ability to learn in the process. AI strategies of security institutions need constant adaptation and learning because they work in a complex threat and operational environment. AI systems could constantly optimize the operations of these institutions. They could develop more effective strategies against threats due to their features, such as data analysis. CAS understanding allows security institutions to renew their strategy dynamically. Adopting AI could help to avoid developing static solutions and employ new data and experience for better strategy development (Nadimpalli et al., 2023). While the institutions design and develop AI strategies with a CAS understanding, they could make their learning processes stronger and more effective. Analyzing the results of decisions built in past crises could help make more accurate decisions for similar future situations. Adaptation and learning capability contribute to the processes of institutions being more flexible and resilient.

CAS thinking also contributes to the coordination of multiple actors and systems. These systems often operate with an interaction of many independent actors. Security institutions possess a similar organizational structure. Continuous coordination is a necessity among different units, departments, and partners. The development and adoption of AI strategies in this complexity should be evaluated carefully. CAS understanding presents a roadmap for multiple actors working in harmony. Security systems supported by AI technologies have an opportunity to share information rapidly for different levels of units and actors (Ma et al., 2022). These systems could enhance coordination among multiple actors with the help of data analysis and decision-support mechanisms. They also facilitate security operations to conduct them effectively. As different bodies of security institutions are required to operate in coordination, AI technologies could promote cooperation with rapid and accurate information sharing. CAS understanding has noteworthy implications for AI operating in these multi-layered systems. AI could contribute to the operational objectives of each body. This situation creates more effective security management (Raimundo & Rosário, 2021).

Uncertainty is a significant characteristic of today's world. Security institutions need to cope with uncertainty in every level and environment. CAS understanding addresses how institutions could survive and provide resilient solutions in uncertain and chaotic situations. These institutions face a changing threat environment and uncertainties. Designing and development of AI strategies should include management of uncertainty. AI systems could reduce uncertainties by big data analysis. They also could employ prediction algorithms and provide more valuable predictions to security institutions (Weiser & Krogh, 2023). Accepting security institutions as CAS enables understanding AI systems' adaptation to uncertain situations and developing flexible strategies. CAS understanding contributes to security organizations to develop AI strategies in a more flexible, adaptive and sustainable manner (Li, 2007).

Aforementioned characteristics of CAS understanding that are decentralized control, feedback mechanism, adaptability, coordination of multiple and diverse actors, and coping with uncertainty provide an enhancement of the effectiveness of AI strategies. The strategies allow for an easier base for security institutions to adapt to rapidly changing environments, threats, and technological advancements. AI's capacity to respond to evolving dynamics enhances the strategic flexibility and resilience of the institutions. This is vital to reaching the success and sustainability of the security paradigm.

There are two concluding points regarding CAS understanding's contribution to sustainability and AI strategies. These are CAS understanding's implications for resilience and inclusive strategy development. Adaptation and resilience are the core principles of CAS understanding. They are directly related to sustainability goals. Long-term sustainability goals require not only responding to current threats but also being prepared for potential future threats. This is relevant not only for threats but also for opportunities. Future opportunities should also be taken into account for security institutions. AI strategies provide the required flexibility and resilience to adapt to changing situations. CAS understanding facilitates security institutions to design and develop strategies adaptable to uncertainties while reaching their long-term sustainability goals (Maldonado et al., 2020). AI systems enable sustainable strategic goals by employing big data analytics and using optimization for operational processes. CAS understanding's promotion of flexible structure could manage AI in harmony with sustainability criteria. By these opportunities, security institutions could achieve more sustainable outcomes both strategically and operationally.

CAS understanding also promotes inclusiveness in the design and development phases of strategies. Various actors, variables, and dynamics in CASs require an inclusive strategy development. Different dynamics and actors should be taken into account when designing and developing AI strategies. CAS understanding facilitates the integration of diverse disciplines, technologies, and agencies in the development process of strategies. The integration could make strategies more inclusive and robust in the way of sustainability. Thus, CAS understanding could make AI strategies more inclusive and open to collaboration for sustainability. AI strategies of security institutions should focus on social peace and environmental balance as well as addressing security threats. Accordingly, the results of security operations could benefit society at large and support sustainability. When we think of the nature of the new security paradigm which is not only related to military or security operations but also related to societal and environmental factors, inclusiveness becomes at the forefront.

As a result, multi-layered and dynamic structure suggested by CAS understanding facilitates the creation of AI strategies in a more innovative, flexible and sustainable way. By embracing this kind of understanding, security institutions could cope with various and complex threats while at the same time achieving long-term sustainability goals. Consequently, considering "security institutions as CAS" offers a significant framework for seizing the sustainability premises of these institutions' AI strategies. The augmentation of these systems' functionality allows for the effectiveness of security policies. This perspective highlights the requirement for these institutions to be flexible, decentralized, and capable of learning in order to effectively integrate AI systems. This perspective also responds to the evolving security terrain. By embracing the principles of CASs, security institutions could improve their resilience and adaptability, thereby becoming better equipped to face the imminent challenges.

AI SECURITY STRATEGIES IN THE WAKE OF AI-DRIVEN PUBLIC ADMINISTRATION

Deployment of AI technologies in public administration and the design and development of security strategies in this context have been increasingly crucial in academic discussions in recent years. Potential of AI in data analysis, decision-making processes, and service delivery create a more effective, transparent, and rapid operation process for public institutions. However, this situation requires the redesigning of security strategies (Borges et al., 2020). One of the most common uses of AI in public administration is big data analysis. AI creates an environment for public institutions that allows for processing immense data sets. It, then, facilitates drawing meaningful conclusions. Data analysis of AI has a significant role in security strategies. AI-supported data analysis could analyze immense amounts of data required to identify security threats, assess risks, and sustain public safety.

Chun and Warner (2010) examine the role of AI in data analysis. They suggest that these systems have a potential in creating proactive strategies before security threats. AI enables security institutions to incorporate data from diverse sources to reach insights. It also could identify vulnerabilities by data analysis. AI could identify cyber attack patterns and develop strategies to prevent them by analyzing big data against changing threat environments. This ability of AI technologies could enhance themselves by machine learning and deep learning. These methods allow for readiness in a dynamic environment with data analysis and risk management.

Likewise, Meijer and Bolívar (2016) emphasize that the rapid and accurate outcomes of AI data analysis have contributions to decision-making processes. Preventive security strategies in public administration are created by data analysis. AI systems could identify frauds and security threats in advance and guide strategic decisions of security institutions. AI-supported data analysis also creates opportunities for integration among diverse data sources. It enables comprehensive assessment of security threats.

An additional use of AI in public administration and security strategies is the enhancement in decision-making processes. AI's contribution to decision-making processes have been discussed in terms of its role in the development of security strategies. AI allows for more accurate and informed decisions by analyzing large amounts of data and modeling diverse scenarios. This opportunity offers an important advantage for security institutions.

Booyse and Scheepers (2023) have conducted significant studies on the adoption of AI technologies in decision-making mechanisms. It reveals that AI-supported decision support systems could offer clearer and faster recommendations to human decision-makers. It is valid also in the design of security strategies. AI systems could provide vital information to decision-makers by drawing analysis in terms of geographical and other types of priorities. AI also provides help for the distribution of scarce resources. AI reduces the risk of human error and gives optimal strategies.

Schemmer (2022) examined the effects of AI on the speed and accuracy of decision-making processes. AI-supported decision systems are more effective in the identification and management of security threats. In cases where threats are required to be detected quickly in public administration, AI technologies offer rapid data analysis and outcomes. It allows decision-makers to drive timely strategic actions.

Nevertheless, there are also significant concerns about the employment of AI in decision-making processes. Zerilli et al. (2018) discusses the lack of transparency in the AI-supported decision-making processes. Although AI supports decision-making processes, the issue of the consequences of the decisions raised by these systems and who is responsible for these decisions is still contentious. It is emphasized that AI-supported decision-making processes should be organized within an ethical framework and structured in harmony with the principles of transparency.

AI also has a substantial role in delivering public services more efficiently. AI-supported systems facilitate more rapid reaction to citizens' demands and more personalized delivery of public services. The contributions of AI to providing security in service delivery and efficient use of public resources have been frequently discussed. Margetts and Dunleavy (2023) examine the effects of AI systems on digitizing public services and raising security standards. They demonstrate that AI enhances the efficiency of public administration by enabling it to respond effectively to citizens' needs. AI-based chatbots could automatically respond to citizens' applications to public institutions and provide the necessary documents. As such applications reduce the workload of public administration, they also present significant advantages in terms of security. AI could detect possible fraud attempts in service delivery, provide a more reliable service to citizens and close the security gaps of public institutions in the process.

Also, Fan et al. (2023) highlight the role of AI technologies in sustainability and efficient use of resources in public services. AI allows public services to be delivered to a wider audience using fewer resources. AI-supported systems create more personalized delivery of healthcare services by analyzing patient data. This both improves public health and reduces security risks in the healthcare sector.

Despite aforementioned positive effects of AI in service delivery, there are discussions on diverse challenges in the enactment of these technologies. Sousa el al. (2019) emphasize that a strong technological infrastructure is needed for the effective use of AI systems in public services. This infrastructure is lacking in some public institutions. In addition, concerns are also valid that these systems could have negative consequences in relations with citizens by completely eliminating the human factor.

AI security strategies offer great potential in public administration in areas such as data analysis, decision-making processes and service delivery. AI enhances security in public administration, enabling more efficient and reliable services to citizens, accelerating decision-making processes and helping to develop proactive security strategies through data analysis. However, there are also some challenges and restrictions related to the application of AI-supported security strategies.

The main challenges faced in the adoption of AI in security strategies are stated as inadequate technological infrastructure, data privacy, lack of transparency of algorithms, and the risks of undermining the human factor. Sousa (2019) and Osborne and Brown (2016) demonstrate that new technologies could only be employed effectively with robust technological infrastructure and qualified personnel. Training and reskilling processes should be implemented in order for public institutions to adapt to AI technologies.

Additionally, the adoption of AI in security strategies carries important privacy and ethical issues related to the collection and processing of personal data. Hagendorff (2019) and Kim (2023) highlight that the ethical structure of AI-supported decision systems, responsibility for the decisions reached by these systems, and the transparency of algorithms should be examined in depth.

There are also opportunities for AI in security strategies. Some such contributions of AI in public administration include but are not limited to the development of more effective, efficient, and reliable security solutions, increasing personalization and comprehensiveness in public service delivery, and starting to provide more data-driven solutions in decision-making processes. Essien and Petrounias (2022) argue that AI systems can be used to underpin key decisions in public safety and crisis management while proactively assisting public organizations in closing more gaps in security.

The general trend, in relation to these, seemed to emerge from the literature contributions on AI security strategies, underlining that, along with great advantages offered, technologies must be approached with a view to serious issues: ethical responsibility, data security, the human factor, and infrastructural needs.

All these varied aspects of literature have ranged from data analysis and decision-making to service delivery in public administration using AI security strategies. While AI can be utilized in enhancing public safety and ensuring better operational efficiency of public organizations, much is yet to be questioned regarding the ethical, legal, and operational dimensions of the technology. Such an integration of the AI-based security strategy into the public administration has to be done with these issues in focus, in due implementation within a sustainable, transparent, accountable framework.

It is evident that this, on the one hand, increases the efficiency of working in various sectors of the industry, on the other hand, urges a review and elaboration of strategies for security in this field. Among AI's competencies come such issues as maintenance of social order and public safety, effective serving of citizens, and raising the efficiency of state structures and institutions. Such processes could be accelerated by integrating AI into public administration in order to establish an effective, transparent, and efficient management system (Larsson & Heintz, 2020). On the other hand, such integration shows several opportunities and challenges with respect to its security implications. Discussing the effect of AI security strategies on public administration, is bound to cover detailed opportunities and challenges upon the strategies.

AI provides a variety of powerful tools that enforce security, speed up the process of threat detection, and optimize resource utilization. Big data analytics combined with machine learning techniques will further speed up the pace of crucial decision-making processes within that part of public administration where early detection and rapid response against the threat will be highly required, particularly through AI-driven security systems (Flügge et al., 2021). While most decision-making processes take long periods to finalize in traditional forms of public administration due to the presence of several bureaucratic obstacles and coordination issues, AI can analyze vast amounts of data with speed to show vulnerabilities and advise appropriate strategies for the enhancement of efficiency. It helps in the identification of terrorist threats and cyber-attacks in the incubation stage with the use of AI, thus making respective institutions take fast action (Kaloudi & Li, 2020).

Publicly, AI can be used proactively in managing public safety. The normal existing methods of security have usually been reactive; that is, they respond after an incident has occurred. However, an AI system, aided by predictive models and forecasting algorithms, can easily identify and plan against impending security threats. It will, therefore, be possible, in the case of public administration, to plan strategies much in advance that lower the rate of crime, damage caused by natural calamities, and disturbance to public peace. In relation to considering crime history trends, for instance, the crime forecasting system can identify which areas within a region are bound to commit crime, and precautionary measures should be put in place to give more resources to such areas (Li et al., 2023).

AI security strategies are also significant for the better use of resources within public administration. Public institutions are normally characterized by resource limitations. Therefore, it is important to consider effective ways of managing those sets of resources to deliver quality services. While optimizing the resources of the security units and public administration, AI systems are enabling getting more work done with few resources. Thanks to AI, it would be possible to avoid the dispersal of resources at the emergency management and crisis response processes by providing intervention in the most important areas (Zuiderwijk et al., 2021).

Moreover, AI will be making efficiencies in public service through quick responses to its citizens' needs and improving service delivery. AI security strategies give way to developing data-driven policies in public administration, particularly critical in public safety and the building of citizen trust. The massive amount of data-articulated AI systems enables much more precise decision-making to be made. To that end, it helps in the carrying out of one more transparent, liable, and proper public administration. Information gained through city cameras and surveillance could be used as a catalyst for anti-crime policy implementation (Corbett et al., 2023). In turn, it will enhance the level of confidence among citizens in state institutions as this kind of technology could allow the delivery of public services more effectively.

In this regard, besides all the gains that are possible through AI security strategies, several challenges exist in the integration of these technologies into public administration. These must be faced on levels of both technology and ethics. Hence, AI systems gather lots and process much information. However, the gathered information stands in danger and will continue to be a huge threat to the privacy of entities. It also means that AI applied in public administration is necessary to collect and process high volumes of personal data of citizens (Wirtz & Müller, 2018). This may amount to an acute risk to the privacy of a person. In situations where AI is employed in the security sector, misutilization of personal data threatens to perpetuate a surveillance society. Public administration should strengthen its mechanism with respect to the protection of data privacy in tune with its ethical commitments in that regard (Perina et al., 2022). Breaches of data or data misuse would lead to exposure of public security and the loss of public confidence in the state's institutions.

The biases in the data sets infect algorithms used for the creation of AI systems. It has serious implications both for public safety and the proper administration of justice. The algorithms of crime prediction take, for instance, a certain risk in discriminating against communities on account of biased historical data. AI systems reproduce biases intrinsic in datasets and result in unjust security policies (Srinivasan & Chander, 2021). Public administration, while deploying the use of AI, has to be aware of such bias and ensure the working of algorithms in a manner that is fair, impartial, and ethical. Otherwise, AI systems will continue to perpetuate inequity.

Effective application of AI systems depends on good technological infrastructure in public administration. Still, a number of public institutions will find difficulty in implementing AI into their working process due to the presence of legacy systems and inferior technological infrastructure (Fortuna et al., 2023). These organizations require big investments in technology, as making their security strategy AI-supported actually means renaming them. However, AI systems also face a greater challenge in alignment with the traditional bureaucratic and operational system (Presuel & Sierra, 2023). Above all, the AI-based system needs to be upgraded regularly and also protected from a certain kind of security vulnerability. Inadequate technological infrastructure might slacken the implementation of the AI system and raise possible threats to citizens' safety.

It's the integration of AI technologies within the framework of public administration that, however, presupposes proper competencies and equipment in personnel by the use of those systems. However, an important barrier is the shortage of capabilities for the effective use of AI technologies in state institutions. The right method of implementation involves qualified personnel in its management and evaluation. Similarly, the personnel already present in the public administration must be trained in AI technologies. AI-based security strategies could simply not work without human resources. That also means that the security strategies are not enacted, nor are the benefits of AI developed in public administration. Inadequate expertise will lead to mismanagement of the AI systems or not integrating them well enough. Such will lead to the failure of appropriate analysis of security threats or failure to identify an important weakness in the system (Gehlhaus, 2021).

The other major limiting factor in AI security strategy implementation is the inadequacy of legal and regulatory frameworks. Not every country has fully developed legal frameworks regulating the use of AI systems. This further creates a lot of uncertainties during the implementation of AI security strategies. Strong regulations in the use of AI in public administration are required, thus, for the protection of the security and rights of the citizenry (Cuéllar & Huq, 2022). However, the rapid development of AI technologies turned an existing legal system lethargic. In this respect, public administration, while carrying out the strategy of AI, has to consider gaps in law and contribute to the creation of mechanisms of regulation (Dignam, 2020).

The regulatory frameworks should also touch base on security and ethics in the usage of AI systems. Misuse of AI-based systems creates social unrest and security vulnerability. As governments develop their AI security strategy, so too should the legal regulations that will determine the limits and responsibilities of these technologies (Rakha, 2023).

This will, in turn, enable a number of significant alterations in the future concerning public administration in case more AI security strategies are implemented in the sphere of public administration. Finally, AI is able to improve public administration due to its effectiveness, reliability, and efficiency. However, their creation presumes sophisticated and unpredictable security risks (Rahman et al., 2023). Through their rapid development, the technologies of AI mean that the public administration has to deal with new challenges and change its security strategy in correspondence with them.

In the future, AI applications within the framework of public administration will be so much better integrated that public administration will, because of this, have much more operational capacity and reactive potential against security threats. If the AI security policies are to succeed completely, the public administration should make updates on those systems, constantly closing the security gaps. It is also very important that the public administration develops mechanisms that ensure that the AI systems are used in an ethical and transparent way.

Lastly, despite the major benefits that are availed to public administration, through the AI security strategy, varied challenges presented by such implementation are cardinal to be addressed. Using AI technologies, public administration can develop a more proactive, effective, and secure structure, but each and every ethical, legal, and technical aspect related to these technologies should be carefully evaluated. All the security strategies regarding AI will operate if only public institutions develop appropriate policies and implement continuous adaptation procedures that create the preconditions for overcoming all those challenges.

AI STRATEGY DOCUMENTS OF U.S. SECURITY INSTITUTIONS: AN ANALYSIS

The U.S leads in the integration of AI into national security and defense. A series of key documents on AI strategy has been published in the last few years through various US security agencies, hence setting the increased centrality of AI in national security, military capability, and new threats. This section discusses a few of the goals, guiding principles, and effects of those strategy documents on the wider security environment.

In this part of the study, the intentions and premises of sustainability and resilience are thematically analyzed in the current AI strategy documents of U.S. security institutions. The documents under analysis are as follows: The Department of State's "Enterprise AI Strategy" (2023), The Department of Defense's "Data, Analytics, and Artificial Intelligence Adoption Strategy" (2023), The Department of Homeland Security's "Artificial Intelligence (AI) Roadmap" (2024), The Directorate of National Intelligence's "The Intelligence Community (IC) Data Strategy" (2023), and The Cybersecurity and Infrastructure Security Agency's "The CISA Roadmap for Artificial Intelligence" (2023).

The "Enterprise AI Strategy" of the U.S. Department of State addresses basic guiding principles in focusing on sustainability and resilience when looking into ways to harness AI responsibly in support of its goals of diplomacy and statecraft. The first strong theme mentioned within the document is "sustainability with secure and responsible AI use". It emphasizes "responsible and secure use of AI" as one aspect of insuring sustainability at both levels of its core diplomacy and support functions. It is conceptualized that, even as AI continues to revolutionize Government functions, the Department must make sure that applications of AI are informed by sustainable infrastructures in support of security, data privacy, and ethics. Basic intentions within this theme are: 1) ensure AI technologies are implemented in a way that is safe, ethical, and responsible to protect data, people, and the integrity of the Department; and 2) enable AI in a way that allows sustainable gains in productivity with a reduction in employee operational burden by automating tasks that are repetitive. The basic premises are 1) AI technology should be incorporated into an infrastructure that allows it to be secure for long-term, scaled uses. Sustainability herein ensures that AI adoption in no way compromises data security and privacy, which would damage the very diplomatic effort. 2) There is recognition that without due governance, AI deployment could risk biased outcomes, unethical usage, or violation of privacy. This view is basic to the goal of assuring long-term viability and trust in AI solutions.

The second theme is "resilience through AI innovation and risk mitigation". In fact, there is resilience across this whole document as a key theme, particularly with respect to a Department's response to these emerging diplomatic and security challenges. Capacity for "anticipation, management, and recovery from potential disruptions" through the insights and innovations of AI is emphasized. The intentions involve: 1) creating "resilient diplomatic capabilities" through the utilization of AI in the form of: rapid collection of information, analysis of foreign policy, and crisis management with reduced vulnerabilities in operations; and 2) deployment of AI-powered solutions that will enable real-time insight and proactive security toward creating a resiliency posture in U.S. diplomatic missions. First premises would be something like the following: 1) AI is a "risk management" tool that guarantees continuity in these times when everything seems uncertain-from geopolitical tension to cybersecurity. This is through ramping up AI technologies that are adaptable much more quickly to the changes in circumstances and threats; 2) through emphasizing "responsible experimentation" and "scaling AI successes," it tries to make sure that the Department will be innovative yet resilient to technological change and associated risks. AI resiliency is encouraged through governance structures and controls that seek to reduce the risks of algorithms and make certain of accuracy in trusted output.

The third important theme is "alignment to wider government sustainability goals". The strategy is further in tune with other initiatives across the government, such as the National Security Strategy (NSS) and the Joint Strategic Plan (JSP), in highlighting the turn towards modernization of national security capabilities with sustainable AI technologies. That would mean, within the existing policy and legal framework, amplification of AI capability for the sustainable use of technology in service of the foreign policy and national security objectives of the U.S. My assumption is that the department is aware that the development of AI has to be congruent with the sustainable goals of the nation by making the instruments transformational and able to meet up with the challenges of changing times. This will be done through the infusing of global AI ecosystems with sustainable AI practices, ensuring "interagency collaboration" for strategic partnerships that can amplify these ends.

The components of sustainability and resiliency describe the vision of "responsible AI integration" in the context of ethics in usage, data privacy, risk management, and finally, long-term viability. In so doing, by securing AI deployment in an increasingly complex technological and geopolitically complex environment in a safe, ethical, and sustainable manner, the Department is assured of cementing diplomatic effectiveness and leadership in the world.

The Department of Defense (DoD) "Data, Analytics, and Artificial Intelligence Adoption Strategy" underpins sustainability and resilience in functions of military and organization concerned with advanced data, analytics, and AI technologies. Therein lies an ability, while trying to draw broad themes from the document, to understand key intentions and premises of sustainability and resilience across all layers of this strategy-from data management up to AI integration and governance.

As the first theme, there is "sustainability through data as a foundational resource". Included among the key premises of the strategy are the ideas that the Department shall treat data as a sustainable resource, in order to support the operational and strategic objectives of the DoD. The intentions here range from "maintain and improve the quality of data, governance, and accessibility for long-term use across the organization." This thematic pillar is very important for the successful decision-making process and further development of AI and analytics capability.

The strategy treats "data as a product" that is cared for, curated, and maintained with the purpose of enabling military operations and informing decisions. Furthering the sustainable life of the data could be achieved if it were "visible", "accessible", "trustworthy", and "secure" throughout its life. This approach emphasizes continuous investment in quality to ensure "sustainability of operations" whereby the data is always ready for use in analytics and AI development.

Another critical premise of "sustainability" in the implementation of "open standard architectures" includes extensive collaboration with industry, academia, and allies. Since the strategy targets interoperable and federated systems, it ensures "longevity" in the infrastructure for managing data, scaling up the adoption of new technologies as those evolve. In so doing, it positions the DoD to meet whatever challenge may arise in the future and "sustainable growth" engendered into the core of its discipline for managing data.

The second fundamental theme is "resilience through AI-enabled decision advantage". This is recurrently emphasized through the rapid, scalable deployment of data, analytics, and AI capabilities so as to retain "decision advantage" across all military and operational contexts. It is how DoD is going to be more agile and responsive to the need of providing the leadership with superior, faster, and best-informed decisions resilient in the dynamic environment.

The strategy emphasizes "agile," user-centered AI and data systems able to dynamically adapt in a global threat environment in constant flux. Resilience shall be baked into the design and deployment of AI-enabled systems, establishing infrastructures ready to stand firm against an array of internal and external stresses. As a matter of fact, the "agile approach" in developing technologies involves rapid iteration and learning in order to make the systems relevant, "resilient against disruptions," and continuously improving.

It realizes that scalable infrastructure underlies good data and AI technologies. The DoD declares it will continue investment in "federated, flexible, and secure infrastructures" to allow an environment that bolsters innovation and rapid adoption to evolving military problems. This federated infrastructure will allow for "AI experimentation" with the needed assurance over "resilient deployment environments" for the scale and complexity of military operations.

A third theme centers around "sustainable and resilient talent and workforce development." This approach greatly emphasizes how "building a more sustainable and resilient workforce" can first of all implement such advanced AI, data, and analytics, and then secondly, manage them. This is critical for the sustainability of DoD development of the human capital so that whatever is achieved is maintained-and also its resilience against a host of emerging challenges.

The prominent intention shows up at this point. Entrusted with building a "digital workforce" proficient in AI, analytics, and data science, it underlines the road map for up-skilling and reskilling both service members and civilians to such critical needs inside the workforce, thus making the latter durable in nature. Establishing a culture of lifelong learning and innovation, it was entrusted with "sustaining the long-term viability" of its workforce while making it resilient in response to new technological challenges.

Another underline of the strategy is the further development of "flexible service structures" to preserve talented people and make possible nonstandard tours of duties in technological areas. Workforce resilience, in that respect, will contribute to conditions whereby the DoD can "adapt to the workforce demand" without facing a shortage of talent which may seriously impede its capabilities to realize new technologies.

The fourth theme is "sustainability through responsible AI governance". This may be the key thematic premise underlying the need for "responsible AI" governance and "ethical deployment", which directly enhances both the theme of "sustainability" and that of "resilience". The strategy requires "strong governance structures able to ensure AI systems will be secure, trustworthy, and ethical" through the whole life of the system, lowering any potential risk of algorithmic bias or other unintended consequences.

What that means here, as an intention, is that AI systems shall be "developed responsibly", fielding consistent with ethical principles consonant with the DoD values, and the "sustainability" of AI initiatives assured through "transparent governance frameworks" that sustain public and institutional trust in AI technologies at minimal risks to national security. This responsible governance will engender resilience by which the ability of AI systems to evolve effects without the introduction of new vulnerabilities.

While the strategy puts forth "mitigating bias" as the necessary guiding principle for making the decision-making processes resilient-through paying close attention to "transparent testing, evaluation, and validation" of the models-DoD is trying not to let biases in that would drastically worsen the effectiveness and equity of AI applications and thus hurt the "long-term resilience" of the DoD's AI infrastructure.

Another major theme tackled along in this strategic framework is "resilience in operational capabilities and decision-making". The document has zoomed enough on "resilience in operational capabilities" that was achieved through various data and AI technologies with respect to enhancement in "decision-making". Wherewithal has been endeavored to provide to the leadership at DoD, commanders, and personnel to conduct countering of a threat with "precision, speed, and adaptability".

Common threads of resilience include attaining and maintaining a "decision advantage" through enhanced "battlespace awareness", "adaptive force planning", and "resilient sustainment". Another way of saying this, the approach presumes that the integration of AI and analytics will enable the DoD to "adapt quickly" against emergent adversaries, hence "build operational resilience", whereby DoD will be able to outrun its enemies.

The strategy mentioned "experimentation" in order to scale up and develop AI use cases. It's all about an iterative approach that will make the process resilient and help the DoD "rapidly learn from actual applications" for continuous refinement of their systems to make them capable of dealing with newer challenges.

The intentions and premises of sustainability and resilience put force into the "Data, Analytics, and AI Adoption Strategy" of the DoD: sustainably managing data, talent, and AI systems with resiliency through fast experimentation, agile development, and responsible governance. It is this way that the basics can be laid for the operation of the Department to move at speed relevant to the leading edges of military operations and decisions, both today and in the future, against a dynamically shifting global security environment.

The Department of Homeland Security (DHS) "Artificial Intelligence (AI) Roadmap 2024" articulates a path to integrating AI technologies throughout the DHS mission to standards set by sustainability and resilience. There are strong themes of the key intents and premises on sustainability and resilience within the debates on responsible use, building infrastructure, safety, and collaboration.

The first point is "sustainability in AI use and governance." It sets out key intentions on the responsible use of AI. Indeed, one of the key themes within this document in its entirety speaks to "the responsible use" of AI-not to harm people or society. It provides guidelines on how to avoid "bias, privacy violations, and civil liberties infringement", underscoring that AI shall be transparent and explainable. Sustainability is part and parcel with "ethical governance" of AI technologies as a premise. The department outlines policies in concert with the AI Bill of Rights and the National Institute of Standards and Technology's (NIST) AI Risk Management Framework to make certain that the application of AI within DHS is sustainable, or it maintains legal and ethical thresholds. The resultant vision is to plant a mechanism of sound and durable governance that will continue with changes in technology to serve the public interest without furthering inequity.

One of the biggest themes in sustainability deals with the intention of protecting individual privacy and civil liberties. The policies were instituted to ensure that the design and deployment of AI systems protect these rights. By embedding these kinds of principles at the outset of AI use, DHS is making sure that the long-term sustainability of AI deployment will be guaranteed. That would be through underlining civil liberties, making AI models more open, thus fostering public confidence, which acts as an ingredient that is needed in the continued and scalable use of AI in government operations.

The second point is "resilience through technological integration and security powered by AI". Therein lies the pretty explicit purpose-showing the "resilience" aspect in integrating AI into national security, especially in "cyber-defense". AI is known both in the role of a tool that hardens defenses and as a threat vector upon which adversaries may lean-that premise holds good in this document, too. The way to improve resilience through the use of AI "to detect and mitigate cybersecurity risks" is brought in by the roadmap.

It understands that even the AI systems can become the target of various malicious attacks, hence it proposes "robust testing, validation, and security measures" to be taken for their protection. CISA's collaboration with international partners for AI security guidance is based on a premise of resilience in which DHS pre-acts to create those systems which resist sophisticated attacks and allow the continuity of critical infrastructural service provision.

The DHS roadmap is overtly obvious in envisioning strong, scalable infrastructure that enables each sustainable and resilient AI ecosystem by creating secure environments in data management and machine learning (ML) operations, including constant monitoring in AI systems.

It is in the light of this "premise of sustainability" that this roadmap places a core focus on infrastructure in building towards long-term AI adoption. DHS acknowledges how desirable a federated infrastructure would be-for instance, the USCG's SURVEYOR Integrated Data Environment-which extends scalability and adaptability of AI solutions through diverse operational contexts. Hence, investment in such infrastructures allows for the resiliency of the AI capability in response to changing operational demands and technological changes.

The third point is "sustainability by way of cross-sector and international collaboration". One of the key themes of sustainability to emerge explicitly in the document is that of partnership. DHS recognizes that "private industry, academia, other government agencies, and international bodies" have a role to play in the resilience and security of the whole life cycle of AI systems.

Its premise of sustainability is pegged on "shared knowledge and global standards" that promise to be even more effective than the isolated efforts in securing the AI technologies. In this light, some of the collaboration works include but are not limited to the AI Safety and Security Board (AISSB) and the joint work that DHS does with the National Cyber Security Centre in the UK in furthering the creation of a sustainable AI ecosystem. It allows DHS to develop "future-proof," scalable, and secure AI technologies across many different sectors and regions through building relations and sharing best practices.

Another important thematic area of sustainability is "promoting AI safety standards". This is, among other reasons, because there is a need for international standards in securing and making AI responsible. This was evidenced by how the roadmap was in line with the Executive Order 14110 by President Biden.

The premise underlines that, therefore, the belief that "global cooperation" is needed in ensuring that AI technologies usage will be long-term. In furthering these standards, DHS will make certain that AI systems are effective, secure from adversary use, and resilient, with reduced long-term risk.

DHS's intention is to "leverage AI to strengthen core homeland security missions" such as border security, cybersecurity, and management of disasters. Several real-time applications of AI have already been tried; a few of them include the "detection of fentanyl" by Customs and Border Protection (CBP), damage assessment in disasters conducted by FEMA, and the identification of threats within the cyber systems.

It's the continued development that the AI systems further develop the premise for resilience in accomplishing those mission-critical tasks. An "agile approach" follows suite, where rapid adaptation with iteration through AI tools can take place, hence resiliency is maintained through new threats and challenges. Continuous capability for improvement in itself is a "resilience strategy" looking ahead at responsiveness with adaptiveness against variably changing threat landscapes.

It regards AI as a means to further enhance "emergency preparedness" and "response capabilities" of the general nature of natural disasters and national emergencies. Looking at the application of AI within the DHS's FEMA with respect to disaster response and risk mitigation planning, this really reflects the high echelon of "resilience premise" where AI is baked into the infrastructure of emergency management. By developing and using AI for underserved communities-while making processes faster-DHS enhances its "capacity to respond effectively" in crisis situations, ensuring a resilient immediate and long-term response within their emergency management systems.

Various intentions and premises set in "DHS AI Roadmap 2024" are deeply related to the notions of sustainability and resilience. These are indicative of AI governance steered by ethics in nature, construction of privacy, civil liberties, infrastructure building toward scalable AI, increased cybersecurity, partnership, continuous innovation, and implementation of AI in critical homeland security missions. Together, these themes underscore the DHS's commitment to using AI responsibly while ensuring long-term effectiveness and adaptability in the face of evolving challenges.

The Directorate of National Intelligence's (DNI) "The Intelligence Community Data Strategy 2023-2025" had a primary focus on data management, interoperability, and innovation-all future imperatives if the US is to maintain an intelligence advantage. Guided by thematic analysis, major intentions and premises of sustainability and resilience could be grasped from the strategic vision in the use of data across the Intelligence Community.

The first point is "sustainability in data management and utilization" in the document. One of the key themes of this document is the strategic focus on "end-to-end data management." It is thus hoped that the IC will be able to create data management plans across the total data life cycle, from collection/acquisition to exploitation, dissemination, and to eventual disposal. This is a strategy with the aim of making certain that data is well-governed, ethically utilized, and secure throughout its life.

The approach to sustainability is, therefore, pretty clear in the way the IC has admitted that information is, in fact, several decades-old asset to start with and mindful management thereof is required in order to create mission value. Sustainable data management includes standardization of processes such as data tagging, handling, and labeling for proper use that remains permissive under ethics and laws related to data privacy and civil liberties. This would place sustainability into the core data processes as the IC seeks to establish data as a long-term strategic asset in support of current and future missions.

It looks to data as more than a near-term facilitator of current intelligence but as a "strategic asset" in granting long-term intelligence and decision-making advantage. This approach explicitly calls for a plan to integrate data into plans, not as an ancillary function but at the heart of the core operation.

It means that, in simple words, sustainability refers to "long-term usability and relevance of data." Contrarily, through deliberate design, IC focuses on the intentional exploitation of data derived from insights. It would, therefore, assure that the collected data will be reused in several missions and varied domains to bring better value without redundancy or obsolesce.

As a second point, there is "resilience in data systems and cybersecurity". In each entity in the IC, the strategy insists there be "data interoperability". The focus is on following a data-centric model where the data is found, analyzed, and given out in a timely and safe way. It is not only important for immediate needs of intelligence, but rather it is very important for the long-term function and operational capability.

In such a context, the "premise of resilience" would be an IC able to absorb operational challenges and threats through an agile and interoperable data system. This will be warranted by the data-centric architecture: adaptability of the intelligence systems to the missions and threats in evolution, keeping the highest standards concerning privacy and security. Agility and flexibility stress a "resilient infrastructure" able to operate in crisis situations and allowing continuity of operation.

It intends to employ "advanced data analytics and AI." AI, as used by the IC, would accelerate data discovery, increase the time of processing, and enhance quality about information leading to action. Resilience comes in with the commitment of the IC to embracing AI-driven automation for quickened data processing and decision-making. It gives credence to the focus on AI-enabled analytics, underpinning the recognition that the IC makes use of technology in trying to outpace the adversary through real-time, resilient intelligence operations. A shortening cycle between data collection and mission insight further enables the IC to function within an increasingly complex security environment.

The third point is "sustainability through collaboration and partnerships". The strategic focus that comes out is to deepen and widen partnerships with the private sector, academia, and foreign partners for continued innovation in the data and digital landscape. In such a perspective, the way the IC approaches collaboration embeds by itself sustainability: resources and expertise of external partners will be leveraged to enable continued innovation within the IC-second to none in data technologies. There, the implication is that partnerships expand the "long-term sustainability" of the IC's data systems and better allow the IC to adopt new technological advances and apply new solutions to intelligence problems.

The other related thrust is the improvement in the sharing of data within the intelligence community and outside it. The strategy, therefore, lays emphasis on achieving free sharing through the development of interoperable systems. Resilience underlines the very intention of creating a data-sharing infrastructure that is resilient against organizational silos and operational barriers-so that the IC is able to provide one unified and agile response toward emerging threats, hence resilient in case of disruptions or operational changes.

And thc fourth point is "building a resilient workforce". In that context, huge emphasis has been placed on "training and transforming the workforce" to be data-savvy as it tries to fight complexities in intelligence operations through data. This indeed requires operational, tactical, and leadership levels of data acumen. The resilience herein would mean preparation of the workforce for the rapid changes ushered in by technology. The development of a cadre proficient in data handling, analysis, and decision-making will provide the IC with the ability to build human capital-people-into long-term sustainable enhancement of its intelligence capabilities. It will be a human-centered approach to resilience-an assurance that the IC rests not on technologies alone but on expertise to see it through.

The fifth point is "sustainability and resilience in ethical and legal governance". It defines the need to fix "privacy and civil liberties protections" at the core of every data management and operational process, compliance with U.S. laws and ethical standards, and a principle of sustainability understood as long-term attention to "ethical data governance". The integration of legal protections, including privacy into information practices by the IC fosters the sustainable operation of activities that reflect U.S. values. In this way, the IC will better protect the rights of persons, which improves the legitimacy, and, when necessary, the trustworthiness of the intelligence activities, hence making them sustainable.

By explicitly identifying "AI and advanced data technologies" within the strategy, there is an ethical commitment toward the deployment commitment to ways in which not to violate civil liberties and create other harms unintended. Resilience has also been related to the ability of the IC capability to retain a high level of ethical standards by deploying the most advanced technologies. In putting a premium on ethics and legality, an IC is thereby setting up an environment of confidence and responsibility wherein it can consider future technologies while never jeopardizing its values or integrity of operation.

The "IC Data Strategy 2023-2025" indicates how embedding of sustainability and resilience will be reflected within the IC data practices by means of long-term data management, ethical governance, and partnership for continuity toward further innovation. It will be resilient-interoperable, agile, secure data systems which would scale with the dynamic intelligence environment. Emphasizing data as an asset, continuing to use a data-informed workforce, embedding advanced technology including AI-positions the IC to hold the edge in the information age while safeguarding its values relating to privacy and civil liberties.

The roadmap entitled "CISA Roadmap for Artificial Intelligence (2023-2024)" articulates a clear strategic vision on AI issues within the cybersecurity and protection of critical infrastructure context. The thematic analysis demonstrates major intentions that form the base with sustainability and resilience premises.

The first point is "sustainability in AI governance and ethical use". In support, CISA upholds a commitment to "responsible, ethical, and safe" use of AI in all its operations, befitting the Constitution and the rule of law. It will involve the creation of oversight processes, embedding privacy and civil rights, and assurance of AI governance through programmatic structures.

The premise of sustainability is based on the certainty that AI technologies are deployed not only to meet current needs but also to handle long-term ethical management. Enveloping such thoughts within the AI adoption itself, CISA envisions a future where AI systems will be sustained over time, minimizing harm while achieving maximum utility. Governance and ethics are the driving ethos that will make the developed AI system trusted and hold in high regard the values that have been set in society for generations.

CISA is committed to "limiting bias" in the AI systems for the maintenance of fairness in AI output. In the roadmap, biases are to be identified at the development, testing, and implementation of AI technologies. The sustainability of the AI seems tied with fairness and equity in its deployment because a focus on the mitigation of bias and ensuring fairness entails that CISA is assured no AI system will disproportionately impact or discriminate against a certain group. The approach presented hence will contribute to the sustainable development of AI systems that will be trustworthy and acceptable for a wide array of stakeholders, including the general public and institutional level.

The second point relates to "resilience in AI security and risk mitigation." CISA's roadmap does bring out needs around "assuring AI systems" through cyber threat-hardening, needing "secure by design," and the need to develop best practices for secure AI deployment. That will entail implementation of the NIST AI Risk Management Framework, other guidance around security with the implementation of robust vulnerability management practices.

Whereas, "premise of resilience" shall concern the ability of AI systems with operational survivability and recoverability pertaining to cyber threats and vulnerabilities. In fact, CISA is wanting to create such strong security protocols and resilience frameworks that keep the important infrastructures and government networks safe from all types of AI-related risks. This secure-by-design approach enables AI systems to maintain the evolving nature of security challenges and ensures continuity of operation.

CISA intends to formulize "red teaming" and adversarial machine learning the centerpieces of its AI security strategy. Red Teaming, for the purposes described below, is a means of stress-testing AI systems for vulnerabilities, while Adversarial Machine Learning represents ways to attack AI models.

It is in all these efforts that the different dimensions reside-the very pivot of resilience wherein even CISA itself invests in trying to foresee how such threats emanating from AI can be tried out and mitigated well before they could realistically occur. Through red teaming and adversarial machine learning, CISA develops systems that work well under ideal conditions and are resistant to intentional adversarial attacks. This allows continuity of operation and delivery of value from AI systems in hostile conditions.

The third point is "sustainability through collaboration and partnership". CISA's strategy will heavily depend on "collaboration" with interagency, international partners, and the general public to develop a whole-of-government AI security policy and framework. Contribute to whole-of-DHS approaches to AI, including international partner engagement on global AI security best practices.

The premise of sustainability is baked into the very recognition herein that AI security is a matter of global collaboration. Working across agencies, sectors, and borders, CISA said it wants to craft AI policies and standards that adapt and last in a range of contexts. This, in turn, will involve ensuring that AI systems and their policies can scale and are sustainable, evolving with rapid changes in technologies and global security challenges.

CISA is also at the leading edge of "driving innovation in AI", working extensively with the private sector, other government agencies, and even academic research institutions to identify security challenges, share threats, and develop AI tools through its application in all aspects of critical infrastructure.

Sustainability also emanates from emphasizing constant innovation and partnership. In this regard, CISA calls for cooperation with various parties in the continuous updating and adaptability of AI instruments and technologies to new challenges. This would constitute a means of supporting long-term sustainability in the sense that it results in an ecosystem where AI technologies remain relevant, effective, and secure within a constantly changing landscape of technologies.

The last point is "building a resilient workforce for AI". Building a "data-savvy workforce" that can exploit all kinds of AI technologies underlying the effective development of CISA's roadmap involves hiring more experts in this field; this also includes training the current workforce on how to use AI, including technical aspects and the ethics involved in AI.

Here, the premise of resilience is connected to human capital, which manages and deploys AI systems. In this respect, investment in training and recruitment by CISA will contribute to building a workforce that can take on present and future challenges thrown up by AI. The resilient workforce may mean agile with regard to the adoption of new technologies and threats, hence it will help in maintaining business efficiency and security irrespective of changes in the technological landscape.

Apart from the technical training, the organization would engage the workforce in understanding the "legal, ethical, and policy" implications of using AI. It would, in that respect, effectively deploy AI but responsibly. Sustainability means the responsible and ethical use of AI. By embedding legal and ethical considerations in workforce training, CISA gave cause to implementable use of AI technologies in a sustainable manner that respects privacy, civil rights, and civil liberties, makes sure AI use is conformed to the long-term values of society and is legally framed.

The "CISA Roadmap for Artificial Intelligence 2023-2024" is fully engaged in the effort to root sustainability and resilience in its AI strategy. It is sustainable in that it puts great concern into ethical governance, reduction of bias, and long-term collaboration with its partners. That is resilient, too, because it talks about AI security, adversarial testing, and building a workforce that would adapt to the shifting landscapes of AI. Focusing these themes, CISA has kept a watch to ensure that AI systems continue to advance cybersecurity and defense of critical infrastructure-that is, adaptive, secure, in conjunction with greater societal values-for years to come.

CONCLUSION

This chapter has revisited the open-access U.S. security institution strategy documents related to AI with respect to intent and premise in light of possible pathways toward sustainability. Analysis of the continuing organizations indicates that the root patterns for integrating AI technologies are comprehensive, combining immediate operational needs with long-term sustainability goals, all within the social, environmental, and economic dimensions.

The AI strategy documents underpin a number of items, in particular ethical governance and responsible use of AI technologies. What that means is, in the research field of AI, deployment shall be compatible with societal values, respect for the rule of law, and respect for human rights and dignity; it would include privacy of data, protection of civil rights, and transparency regarding the AI application. These documents also note the importance of vigorous oversight mechanisms against the possible detriments of bias, theft of privacy, and potential prejudicial impact unintended on some social groups.

Another buttressing reason is the fact that sustainability in AI governance impresses fairness and inclusiveness in every decision-making aspect made by AI. This ensures the AI technologies will not perpetuate societal inequalities but contribute toward the course of social justice and equity. The strategies note that AI holds a bidirectional possibility-to enhance or harm the well-being of societies; thus, responsible and sustainable governance is core to long-term success.

The strategies acknowledge the negative impact of AI on the environment, mostly in terms of energy consumption and carbon emission owing to data processing. Many AI systems are very computationally intensive, hence highly energy-consuming. In relation to this, the rationale for environmental sustainability has been the reduction in the carbon footprint resulting from technological use of AI and the assurance of energy efficiency. The documents also indicate a shift toward creating and deploying AI in an ecologically non-destructive manner: optimization of energy use in data centers, or using more efficient algorithms.

Ecological sustainability forms the core of any possible future use of AI in public administrative and security domains. Neglecting the environmental cost of AI will surely lead to further acceleration of climate change and exhaustion of natural resources, which may well undermine, in their turn, the very same security objectives its use is supposed to underpin.

While AI technologies could contribute to economic growth, the successful integration of those technologies requires careful resource management and long-term planning. The documents make one thing quite clear: economic sustainability is reached within the optimal use of public resources, together with an adequate return on the investments developed in AI in the long, not the short, term. Therefore, an AI strategy has to make some cost balances in comparison, for instance, to the increase in economic benefits like higher productivity, better decision-making, and automation of routine tasks.

A key takeout is the realization of impending economic hazards in the event of non-prudent AI systems. In this context, the reason for strained public finances or workforce disruption might be due to overdependence on AI. Thus, the concept of economic viability is well-linked with that of responsibility and prudent use of means: AI investments must be able to guarantee long-term economic benefits.

Some of the major social challenges wrought by AI involve job changes. Automation and AI-driven processes may, in fact, displace jobs, and governments need to invest in education and reskilling programs for such workers. This strategy places a lot of emphasis on making a data-savvy workforce able to manage and work with AI technologies. It is not just technical training; it's also legally, ethically, and societally educated about AI.

Social sustainability as a premise in this context would have AI for service to each member in society, including the employed. Security institutions, in focusing on re-skilling and upskilling, will prevent AI from increasing the gap that divides the skilled and unskilled labors. Their strategies proliferate this vision: AI enhances human capacity, not taking its place, to make society more socially fair and sustainable.

It embeds in AI strategies the resilience of adapting to technological disruptions or cyber threats. Throughout the documents, articulation reiterates in developing secure-by-design AI systems that are resistant to the attack, hence operational under adversarial conditions. This may also involve implementing cybersecurity measures such as red teaming and adversarial testing in scrutinizing weaknesses in the AI systems.

That premise of resilience extends to the general infrastructure that has something to do with supporting the AI technologies. Strategies call to action that there must be scalable, federated, and flexible infrastructures that will enable a rapid development in AI capabilities. To such an extent, it makes AI systems being deployed today relevant and effective during times when new challenges and threats are arising, one after another.

Another keen observation has been that of collaboration between the government agencies, the private sector inclusive of academia, and their international partners. For example, all the strategy documents on AI have proposed a whole-of-government approach in AI governance where best practices are shared and efforts are aligned to national and international standards. This kind of collaboration will be essential in the quest for sustainability and resilience since it allows various institutions to pool their resources and share knowledge toward the development of interoperable systems that can resist global challenges.

The assumption that underpins collaboration in the premise of sustainability, therefore, plays off the assumption wherein no institution is fully endowed to deal with the complexity in AI governance. Building in partnerships allows US security institutions to conceptualize the development and utilization of a global ecosystem in AI technologies responsibly, through long-term sustainability and resilience.

Overall, the AI strategies devised by U.S. security institutions would seem to reflect comprehensive and extensive mappings in the integration of AI technologies in socially, environmentally, and economically sustainable ways. An emphasis on ethical governance, energy efficiency, and labor adaptation underlines the fact that AI technologies will serve immediate mission needs while working in the interest of long-term societal benefits.

It also emphasizes resilience through the deployment of secure, flexible, and adaptive AI systems that would be resistant to technological and security challenges. In sum, the proposed measures will help in maintaining the integrity and effectiveness of AI systems against evolving threats across the globe.

Further research has to be conducted to find out where these assumptions of sustainability and resilience are actually realized. Where are these strategies continuing their obvious benefits socially, environmentally, and economically? Researchers must also investigate how transferable the approaches to achieve sustainability are for application in other sectors or countries. That would mean U.S. security institutions serve as a role model for the global regime of AI governance-responsible development and deployment of AI underpin increasingly more inclusive, secure, and sustainable governance arrangements.

The AI strategies so far presented by U.S. security institutions provide a way toward responsible and sustainable integration. Putting sustainability and resilience at the forefront of AI governance, they afford a vision as to how AI can be used in order to meet present and future security challenges while fostering broader societal goals.

REFERENCES

Al-Guesbi, H. (2020). A new concept of adaptive complexity. [PEN]. *Periodicals of Engineering and Natural Sciences*, 8, 1687–1700. DOI: 10.21533/PEN.V8I3.1580.G655

Allen, P. (2001). A COMPLEX SYSTEMS APPROACH TO LEARNING IN ADAPTIVE NETWORKS. *International Journal of Innovation Management*, 05(2), 149–180. DOI: 10.1142/S136391960100035X

Arcaini, P., Riccobene, E., & Scandurra, P. (2017). Formal Design and Verification of Self-Adaptive Systems with Decentralized Control. [TAAS]. *ACM Transactions on Autonomous and Adaptive Systems*, 11(4), 1–35. DOI: 10.1145/3019598

Booyse, D., & Scheepers, C. (2023). Barriers to adopting automated organisational decision-making through the use of artificial intelligence. *Management Research Review*. Advance online publication. DOI: 10.1108/MRR-09-2021-0701

Borges, A., Laurindo, F., Spínola, M., Gonçalves, R., & Mattos, C. (2020). The strategic use of artificial intelligence in the digital era: Systematic literature review and future research directions. *International Journal of Information Management*, 57, 102225. DOI: 10.1016/j.ijinfomgt.2020.102225

Burns, A., Posey, C., Courtney, J., Roberts, T., & Nanayakkara, P. (2017). Organizational information security as a complex adaptive system: Insights from three agent-based models. *Information Systems Frontiers*, 19(3), 509–524. DOI: 10.1007/s10796-015-9608-8

Chun, S. A., & Warner, J. (2010). Government 2.0: Making connections between citizens, data and government. *Information Polity*, 15(1-2), 1–9. DOI: 10.3233/IP-2010-0205

Corbett, E., Denton, E., & Erete, S. (2023). Power and Public Participation in AI. *Proceedings of the 3rd ACM Conference on Equity and Access in Algorithms, Mechanisms, and Optimization*. https://doi.org/DOI: 10.1145/3617694.3623228

Crampton, J. (2013). Is Security Sustainable? *Environment and Planning. D, Society & Space*, 31(4), 571–577. DOI: 10.1068/d3104com

Cuéllar, M., & Huq, A. (2022). Artificially Intelligent Regulation. *Daedalus*, 151(2), 335–347. DOI: 10.1162/daed_a_01920

Cybersecurity and Infrastructure Security Agency. (2023), CISA Roadmap for Artificial Intelligence, https://www.cisa.gov/sites/default/files/2023-11/2023-2024_CISA-Roadmap-for-AI_508c.pdf

Department of Defense. (2023), *Data, Analytics, and Artificial Intelligence Adoption Strategy: Accelerating Decision Advantage*, https://media.defense.gov/2023/Nov/02/2003333300/-1/-1/1/DOD_DATA_ANALYTICS_AI_ADOPTION_STRATEGY.PDF#page=5.06

Department of Homeland Security. (2024), *Artificial Intelligence Roadmap 2024*, https://www.dhs.gov/sites/default/files/2024-03/24_0315_ocio_roadmap_artificialintelligence-ciov3-signed-508.pdf

Department of State. (2023), *Enterprise Artificial Intelligence Strategy FY2024-FY2025: Empowering Diplomacy Through Responsible AI*, https://www.state.gov/wp-content/uploads/2023/11/Department-of-State-Enterprise-Artificial-Intelligence-Strategy.pdf

Dignam, A. (2020). Artificial intelligence, tech corporate governance and the public interest regulatory response. *Cambridge Journal of Regions, Economy and Society*, 13(1), 37–54. DOI: 10.1093/cjres/rsaa002

Dunleavy, P., & Margetts, H. (2023). Data science, artificial intelligence and the third wave of digital era governance. *Public Policy and Administration*, •••, 09520767231198737. DOI: 10.1177/09520767231198737

Essien, A., & Petrounias, I. (2022). An Artificial Intelligence (AI)-Based Decision-Making Framework for Crisis Management. *Advances in Electronic Government, Digital Divide, and Regional Development*, 84–98. Advance online publication. DOI: 10.4018/978-1-7998-9815-3.ch007

Fan, Z., Yan, Z., & Wen, S. (2023). Deep Learning and Artificial Intelligence in Sustainability: A Review of SDGs, Renewable Energy, and Environmental Health. *Sustainability (Basel)*, 15(18), 13493. Advance online publication. DOI: 10.3390/su151813493

Flügge, A., Hildebrandt, T., & Møller, N. (2021). Street-Level Algorithms and AI in Bureaucratic Decision-Making. *Proceedings of the ACM on Human-Computer Interaction*, 5(CSCW1), 1–23. DOI: 10.1145/3449114

Fortuna, C., Yetgin, H., & Mohorčič, M. (2023). Smart Infrastructures: Artificial Intelligence-Enabled Lifecycle Automation. *IEEE Industrial Electronics Magazine*, 17(2), 37–47. DOI: 10.1109/MIE.2022.3165673

Gehlhaus, D., Koslosky, L., Goode, K., & Perkins, C. (2021). U.S. AI Workforce: Policy Recommendations. . https://doi.org/. –DOI: 10.51593/20200087

Gell-Mann, M. (1999). Complex adaptive systems. *Complexity*, •••, 17–45.

Goralski, M., & Tan, T. (2020). Artificial intelligence and sustainable development. *International Journal of Management Education*, 18(1), 100330. Advance online publication. DOI: 10.1016/j.ijme.2019.100330

Hagendorff, T. (2019). The Ethics of AI Ethics: An Evaluation of Guidelines. *Minds and Machines*, 30(1), 99–120. DOI: 10.1007/s11023-020-09517-8

Holden, L. (2005). Complex adaptive systems: Concept analysis. *Journal of Advanced Nursing*, 52(6), 651–657. DOI: 10.1111/j.1365-2648.2005.03638.x PMID: 16313378

Holland, J. (2006). Studying Complex Adaptive Systems. *Journal of Systems Science and Complexity*, 19(1), 1–8. DOI: 10.1007/s11424-006-0001-z

Ioannou, P. (1986). Decentralized adaptive control of interconnected systems. *IEEE Transactions on Automatic Control*, 31(4), 291–298. DOI: 10.1109/TAC.1986.1104282

Kaloudi, N., & Li, J. (2020). The AI-Based Cyber Threat Landscape. *ACM Computing Surveys*, 53(1), 1–34. DOI: 10.1145/3372823

Kim, H. (2023). *Suggestions for Ethical Decision-Making Model through Collaboration between Human and AI.* J-INSTITUTE., DOI: 10.22471/ai.2023.8.12

Kulkov, I., Kulkova, J., Rohrbeck, R., Menvielle, L., Kaartemo, V., & Makkonen, H. (2023). Artificial intelligence - driven sustainable development: Examining organizational, technical, and processing approaches to achieving global goals. *Sustainable Development.* Advance online publication. DOI: 10.1002/sd.2773

Larsson, S., & Heintz, F. (2020). Transparency in artificial intelligence. *Internet Policy Review*, 9(2). Advance online publication. DOI: 10.14763/2020.2.1469

Levin, S. (2002). Complex adaptive systems: Exploring the known, the unknown and the unknowable. *Bulletin of the American Mathematical Society*, 40(1), 3–19. DOI: 10.1090/S0273-0979-02-00965-5

Li, D., & Du, Y. (2007). Artificial Intelligence with Uncertainty. *Artificial Intelligence with Uncertainty.*, 2. Advance online publication. DOI: 10.1201/9781584889991

Li, G., Wang, J., & Wang, X. (2023). Construction and Path of Urban Public Safety Governance and Crisis Management Optimization Model Integrating Artificial Intelligence Technology. *Sustainability (Basel)*, 15(9), 7487. Advance online publication. DOI: 10.3390/su15097487

Lorenzoli, D., Tosi, D., Venticinque, S., & Micillo, R. (2007). Designing multi-layers self-adaptive complex applications., 70-77. https://doi.org/.DOI: 10.1145/1295074.1295088

Ma, C., Li, J., Wei, K., Liu, B., Ding, M., Yuan, L., Han, Z., & Poor, H. (2022). Trusted AI in Multiagent Systems: An Overview of Privacy and Security for Distributed Learning. *Proceedings of the IEEE*, 111(9), 1097–1132. DOI: 10.1109/JPROC.2023.3306773

Ma, Y., Jiang, W., Sang, N., & Zhang, X. (2012). ARCSM: A Distributed Feedback Control Mechanism for Security-critical Real-time System. *2012 IEEE 10th International Symposium on Parallel and Distributed Processing with Applications*, 379-386. https://doi.org/DOI: 10.1109/ISPA.2012.56

Maldonado, A., Morales, M., Aguilera, P., & Salmerón, A. (2020). Analyzing Uncertainty in Complex Socio-Ecological Networks. *Entropy (Basel, Switzerland)*, 22(1), 123. Advance online publication. DOI: 10.3390/e22010123 PMID: 33285898

Meijer, A. J., & Bolívar, M. P. R. (2016). Governing the smart city: A review of the literature on smart urban governance. *International Review of Administrative Sciences*, 82(2), 392–408. DOI: 10.1177/0020852314564308

Mukhin, V., Kornaga, Y., Steshyn, V., & Mostovoy, Y. (2016). Adaptive security system based on intelligent agents for distributed computer systems. *2016 International Conference on Development and Application Systems (DAS)*, 320-325. https://doi.org/DOI: 10.1109/DAAS.2016.7492595

Nadimpalli, V., Hauser, F., Bittner, D., Grabinger, L., Staufer, S., & Mottok, J. (2023). Systematic Literature Review for the Use of AI Based Techniques in Adaptive Learning Management Systems. *Proceedings of the 5th European Conference on Software Engineering Education.* https://doi.org/DOI: 10.1145/3593663.3593681

Nishant, R., Kennedy, M., & Corbett, J. (2020). Artificial intelligence for sustainability: Challenges, opportunities, and a research agenda. *International Journal of Information Management*, 53, 102104. DOI: 10.1016/j.ijinfomgt.2020.102104

Office of the Directorate of National Intelligence. (2023), *The IC Data Strategy 2023-2025: The IC Data-Driven Future Unlocking Mission Value and Insight*, https://www.dni.gov/files/ODNI/documents/IC-Data-Strategy-2023-2025.pdf

Osborne, S. P., & Brown, L. (2013). *Handbook of innovation in public services.* Edward Elgar Publishing., DOI: 10.4337/9781849809757

Pereira, L., & Ruysenaar, S. (2012). Moving from traditional government to new adaptive governance: The changing face of food security responses in South Africa. *Food Security*, 4(1), 41–58. DOI: 10.1007/s12571-012-0164-5

Perino, D., Katevas, K., Lutu, A., Marin, E., & Kourtellis, N. (2022). Privacy-preserving AI for future networks. *Communications of the ACM*, 65(4), 52–53. DOI: 10.1145/3512343

Pianini, D., Casadei, R., & Viroli, M. (2019). Security in Collective Adaptive Systems: A Roadmap. *2019 IEEE 4th International Workshops on Foundations and Applications of Self* Systems (FAS*W)*, 86-91. https://doi.org/.DOI: 10.1109/FAS-W.2019.00034

Presuel, R., & Sierra, J. (2023). The Adoption of Artificial Intelligence in Bureaucratic Decision-making: A Weberian Perspective.. *Digital Government: Research and Practice*. https://doi.org/.DOI: 10.1145/3609861

Rahman, M., Arshi, A., Hasan, M., Mishu, S., Shahriar, H., & Wu, F. (2023). Security Risk and Attacks in AI: A Survey of Security and Privacy. *2023 IEEE 47th Annual Computers, Software, and Applications Conference (COMPSAC)*, 1834-1839. https://doi.org/DOI: 10.1109/COMPSAC57700.2023.00284

Raimundo, R., & Rosário, A. (2021). The Impact of Artificial Intelligence on Data System Security: A Literature Review. *Sensors (Basel)*, 21(21), 7029. Advance online publication. DOI: 10.3390/s21217029 PMID: 34770336

Rakha, N. (2023). The impacts of Artificial Intelligence (AI) on business and its regulatory challenges. *International Journal of Law and Policy*. https://doi.org/.DOI: 10.59022/ijlp.23

Ryan, J., Ludwig, J., & Mcalpine, C. (2007). Complex adaptive landscapes (CAL): A conceptual framework of multi-functional, non-linear ecohydrological feedback systems. *Ecological Complexity*, 4(3), 113–127. DOI: 10.1016/j.ecocom.2007.03.004

Schemmer, M., Hemmer, P., Nitsche, M., Kuhl, N., & Vossing, M. (2022). A Meta-Analysis of the Utility of Explainable Artificial Intelligence in Human-AI Decision-Making. *Proceedings of the 2022 AAAI/ACM Conference on AI, Ethics, and Society*. https://doi.org/DOI: 10.1145/3514094.3534128

Shnitko, A. (2003). Adaptive security in complex information systems. *7th Korea-Russia International Symposium on Science and Technology, Proceedings KORUS 2003. (IEEE Cat. No.03EX737)*, 2, 206-210 vol.2.

Shrestha, Y. R., & Yang, Y. (2019). Organizational adoption of artificial intelligence in public administration: Literature review and research agenda. *Government Information Quarterly*, 36(4), 101391. DOI: 10.1016/j.giq.2019.07.001

Sousa, W., Melo, E., Bermejo, P., Farias, R., & Gomes, A. (2019). How and where is artificial intelligence in the public sector going? A literature review and research agenda. *Government Information Quarterly*, 36(4), 101392. Advance online publication. DOI: 10.1016/j.giq.2019.07.004

Srinivasan, R., & Chander, A. (2021). Biases in AI Systems. *ACM Queue; Tomorrow's Computing Today*, 19(2), 45–64. DOI: 10.1145/3466132.3466134

Szalkowski, G., & Johansen, C. (2023). Defining and measuring the effects of digital technologies on social sustainability: A systematic literature review. *Sustainable Development*. Advance online publication. DOI: 10.1002/sd.2741

Vieira, R. (1992). Complex Adaptive Systems. *Daedalus*, 121(1), 17–30. DOI: 10.1007/978-3-319-71059-4_11-1

Weiser, A., & Krogh, G. (2023). Artificial intelligence and radical uncertainty. *European Management Review*, 20(4), 711–717. Advance online publication. DOI: 10.1111/emre.12630

Wirtz, B., & Müller, W. (2018). An integrated artificial intelligence framework for public management. *Public Management Review*, 21(7), 1076–1100. DOI: 10.1080/14719037.2018.1549268

Zerilli, J., Knott, A., MacLaurin, J., & Gavaghan, C. (2018). Transparency in Al gorithmic and Human Decision-Making: Is There a Double Standard? *Philosophy & Technology*, •••, 1–23. DOI: 10.1007/s13347-018-0330-6

Zuiderwijk, A., Chen, Y., & Salem, F. (2021). Implications of the use of artificial intelligence in public governance: A systematic literature review and a research agenda. *Government Information Quarterly*, 38(3), 101577. DOI: 10.1016/j.giq.2021.101577

Chapter 13

Mitigating Financial Anomalies Dimensions Vulnerability and Stratagem in Service Organizations:

Policy and Ethical Considerations in Public Administration

Arjun J. Nair
https://orcid.org/0000-0002-2287-3174
Chitkara University, Canada

Satish Rao A. B.
https://orcid.org/0009-0003-5379-9688
Manipal University, India

ABSTRACT

The chapter examines the intricate landscape of financial fraud within public administration, emphasising the vulnerabilities that service organisations face in an increasingly complex environment. It delineates the concepts of vulnerability and stratagem, elucidating how determinants such as opportunity, pressure, and rationalisation contribute to fraud susceptibility. The chapter offers a comprehensive exploration of effective fraud detection and prevention strategies, highlighting the importance of robust policy frameworks and ethical standards. By integrating vulnerability assessments into operational practices and developing strategic responses, public administrators fortify their organisations against fraudulent activities.

DOI: 10.4018/979-8-3693-8372-8.ch013

Through illustrative case studies and practical applications, the chapter underscores the critical need for transparency and accountability and advocates for continuous improvement and collaboration among stakeholders.

1. INTRODUCTION

The nexus between public administration and the financial architecture of service organisations is becoming increasingly intricate in an era defined by heightened scrutiny, globalisation, and the incessant proliferation of digital finance mechanisms. Within this sphere, policy and ethical considerations play an indispensable role in safeguarding the integrity of financial transactions, mitigating anomalies, and shielding the most vulnerable strata of society from economic exploitation (Riefa & Saintier, 2020; Radanliev et al., 2024). Public administration, traditionally viewed through the lens of bureaucratic efficiency and regulatory oversight, now assumes a more dynamic and multi-dimensional role as a custodian of ethical governance and a bulwark against financial improprieties. The manifold complexities of this role are particularly pronounced within service organisations, where the fluidity of transactions and the intangibility of services render them uniquely susceptible to a panoply of financial irregularities. In the wake of financial crises and emerging vulnerabilities exacerbated by rapid digitalisation, service organisations have become focal points for financial anomalies ranging from fraud and embezzlement to more nuanced transgressions such as financial misreporting and unethical fiscal practices (Markowitz et al., 2021; Hilal et al., 2022). The chapter seeks to explore these dimensions, offering a comprehensive discourse on how policy frameworks and ethical considerations in public administration can be harnessed to both identify and mitigate the vulnerabilities inherent in financial systems within service organisations. The discourse will unfold through an examination of the operational and strategic intricacies that characterise modern financial systems, delving into the nuances of vulnerability that exist at the confluence of public oversight and organisational financial practices. At the heart of this analysis lies an investigation into the multidimensional nature of financial anomalies, which, far from being singular events, often arise from systemic weaknesses embedded within the organisational structure. These weaknesses are not merely technical or operational but are deeply intertwined with ethical lapses, policy ambiguities, and strategic oversights. As service organisations are increasingly compelled to balance profitability with accountability, the susceptibility to financial anomalies intensifies, calling for a more robust policy apparatus and an ethical recalibration within the domain of public administration.

Furthermore, the digital transformation of financial systems has introduced novel vulnerabilities that transcend traditional fraud paradigms (Kamuangu, 2024).

Cybersecurity risks, digital fraud, and algorithmic malfeasance have emerged as significant concerns, necessitating the evolution of public policy and administrative ethics to keep pace with technological advancements. In this context, the role of public administration extends beyond its conventional regulatory functions, encompassing the development of ethical standards that can guide service organisations in navigating the complex interplay between innovation and financial integrity. The digital age, while offering unprecedented opportunities for financial growth and efficiency, simultaneously presents an environment ripe for exploitation, where traditional ethical frameworks falter under the weight of technological complexity (Kamuangu, 2024; George, 2024). The vulnerability of financial systems within service organisations is not a monolithic construct rather, it manifests in various dimensions, each presenting unique challenges for mitigation. These dimensions include, but are not limited to, governance structures, internal control mechanisms, regulatory compliance, and the organisational culture that underpins financial decision making (Rahman & Marjerison, 2020; Manginte, 2024). Each of these elements needs to be critically examined through the lens of policy and ethics, as they collectively shape the organisational landscape within which financial anomalies are either prevented or perpetuated. For instance, weak governance structures allow unethical financial practices to proliferate unchecked, while ineffective internal controls create opportunities for embezzlement or fraud (Okoye et al., 2021). Similarly, regulatory non-compliance, often stemming from a lack of clarity or coherence in policy frameworks, exacerbates the vulnerability of service organisations to financial anomalies (Engvall, 2024; Rajesh et al., 2024). Ethical considerations are paramount in this discourse, as they provide the moral compass by which public administration navigates the treacherous waters of financial oversight (Heng, 2024). In the absence of a strong ethical foundation, policy frameworks, no matter how well-intentioned or meticulously crafted, are likely to be rendered ineffective in the face of sophisticated financial malfeasance. The ethical dimension of public administration is thus not a peripheral concern but is central to the efficacy of any strategy aimed at mitigating financial anomalies in service organisations. The chapter will explore how ethical principles can be operationalised within the public administration framework to strengthen the resilience of financial systems and reduce susceptibility to anomalies.

The stratagem for mitigating financial anomalies in service organisations needs to be multi-faceted, encompassing both preventive and corrective measures. Preventive strategies include the establishment of robust governance frameworks, the enhancement of internal control systems, and the promotion of a culture of transparency and accountability (Nair, Manohar, et al., 2023b; Manginte, 2024). On the other hand, corrective strategies focus on the detection and rectification of anomalies once they have occurred through mechanisms such as audits, investigations, and the imposition of sanctions (Hao et al., 2023). Both sets of strategies are contingent upon a strong policy infrastructure that is informed by ethical considerations, and that can adapt to the evolving nature of financial vulnerabilities. Public administration plays a pivotal role in the development and enforcement of such strategies, serving as both a regulator and a facilitator of ethical financial practices within service organisations (Sigfrids et al., 2022; Adaga et al., 2024). However, the effectiveness of public administration in this regard is often contingent upon its ability to navigate the complexities of power, politics, and influence that permeate the financial landscape. Service organisations, particularly those that operate on a global scale, often wield considerable economic and political clout, which can complicate efforts to impose stringent regulatory measures or to hold them accountable for financial transgressions. As such, public administrators need to possess not only technical expertise but also political acumen to effectively mitigate financial anomalies while maintaining the delicate balance between regulatory oversight and organisational autonomy (Madan & Ashok, 2023; J. Nair et al., 2024). Moreover, the globalisation of financial systems has further complicated the task of mitigating financial anomalies in service organisations. Cross-border transactions, multinational operations, and the increasingly international nature of financial markets have created a regulatory environment that is both fragmented and inconsistent (Challapalli, 2023). In such an environment, public administration needs to contend with the challenge of harmonising disparate regulatory frameworks while ensuring that ethical standards are upheld across jurisdictions. This necessitates a more collaborative and integrated approach to public administration, where national and international bodies work in concert to address the vulnerabilities that arise from the globalisation of financial systems. Therefore, the chapter will argue that the mitigation of financial anomalies in service organisations requires a holistic approach that integrates policy, ethics, and strategic oversight. Public administration, as the guardian of ethical governance, needs to rise to the challenge of navigating the complexities of modern financial systems, where vulnerability is an ever-present concern. By fostering a culture of accountability, transparency, and ethical responsibility, public administration can play a crucial role in safeguarding the financial integrity of service organisations, thereby ensuring that they continue to fulfil their societal obligations while operating within the bounds of legality and morality. Through a detailed exploration of the policy and ethical dimensions of financial anomaly mitigation, the chapter seeks to contribute to the ongoing discourse on the role of public administration in fostering a more just and equitable financial system in the service sector.

2. STRATAGEM: STRATEGIES FOR DETECTION AND PREVENTION IN FINANCIAL FRAUD

In the realm of financial fraud, particularly within the context of public administration, the deployment of a robust and well-crafted stratagem is essential for safeguarding the integrity of service organisations. A stratagem can be succinctly defined as a carefully devised set of strategies or schemes designed to detect, prevent, and respond to fraudulent activities, specifically targeting vulnerabilities inherent in financial operations (Sarkar & Shukla, 2023; Ozkan-Ozay et al., 2024; Amiri et al., 2024). The art of developing and implementing such stratagems lies not merely in identifying fraudulent acts but in building a systemic and sustained resistance to the ever-evolving tactics employed by fraudsters. At its core, a stratagem in the context of fraud prevention refers to the formulation and execution of a sophisticated array of methods designed to detect and deter fraudulent activities (Hilal et al., 2022; Ezeji, 2024; Nair & Manohar, 2024). Unlike ad hoc or reactive measures, a stratagem is pre-emptive, systematic, and embedded within the organisation's governance framework. It operates as a continuous mechanism for safeguarding financial resources, ensuring compliance with regulatory standards, and maintaining public trust. Public administrators entrusted with vast financial assets and services need to employ stratagems that not only address current fraud risks but also anticipate future vulnerabilities. The success of any stratagem hinges upon its adaptability and resilience, given that fraudulent techniques often evolve in response to new technologies and regulatory frameworks (Manohar et al., 2023; Obi et al., 2024). The intricacies of stratagem extend beyond mere policy enforcement, they encompass the integration of technological, managerial, and ethical frameworks aimed at bolstering the organisation's defensive capabilities (Papagiannidis, 2024). A successful stratagem needs to weave together various strands of organisational processes, internal controls, human resource management, and technology deployment to create an impervious system resistant to fraud.

The first pillar of a robust fraud prevention strategy is the development and implementation of detection methods. Detection, as a proactive measure, involves identifying fraudulent activities either in their nascent stages or before they can cause significant damage (Khalid et al., 2023). In service organisations, where the scale of financial transactions and data handling is vast, detection methods need to be dynamic, scalable, and precise. Detection methods typically fall into two categories, manual and automated. Manual detection involves human oversight, such as the review of financial statements, auditing processes, and cross-checking documentation for inconsistencies (Chowdhury, 2021; Nair et al., 2024). While manual detection can be effective, it is inherently limited by the capacity and expertise of the personnel involved. Moreover, human error and oversight can create gaps in the detection process, allowing sophisticated fraud schemes to slip through unnoticed. To augment manual detection, many public service organisations have increasingly turned to automated detection systems, which leverage the power of technology to identify fraudulent activities in real time. Automated detection utilises advanced technologies, such as artificial intelligence (AI), machine learning, and data analytics (Jarrett & Choo, 2021). AI algorithms can analyse vast amounts of transactional data, identifying patterns and anomalies that indicate fraudulent behaviour. For instance, an AI system might detect unusual spending patterns or discrepancies in document submissions that suggest fraud. These systems not only increase the speed and accuracy of fraud detection but also allow organisations to operate with greater efficiency. The implementation of detection methods requires a careful balance between innovation and practicality. Public administrators need to ensure that new technologies are compatible with existing systems and are accessible to personnel responsible for monitoring and managing fraud detection. Moreover, detection methods need to be continuously updated and refined to keep pace with the ever-evolving tactics employed by fraudsters. While detection is essential, prevention remains the ultimate goal of any fraud stratagem. Prevention techniques are proactive measures designed to minimise the opportunities for fraud, reducing the likelihood that fraudulent activities will occur in the first place (Taherdoost, 2021; Nair, Manohar, et al., 2023a). In the context of public administration, prevention needs to be embedded in every layer of the organisation, from its governance structures to its operational processes.

One of the most effective prevention techniques is the implementation of internal controls. Internal controls refer to policies, procedures, and systems designed to ensure the integrity of financial operations (Al-Mashhadi, 2021; Nair, Manohar, Mittal, et al., 2023). These controls include the segregation of duties, ensuring that no single individual has control over all aspects of a financial transaction. By dividing responsibilities among multiple individuals, the opportunity for fraud is significantly reduced. Additionally, regular audits and compliance checks can serve as preventative measures, as they discourage individuals from engaging in fraud due to the heightened likelihood of detection (Kassem, 2022). Technological solutions also play a critical role in fraud prevention. For example, encryption technologies can protect sensitive financial data, making it more difficult for fraudsters to gain access to critical information. Similarly, multi-factor authentication systems ensure that only authorised individuals can approve financial transactions or access sensitive documents (Mohammed et al., 2023). Blockchain technology, with its decentralised and immutable ledger, is another promising tool for preventing fraud, as it makes tampering with financial records virtually impossible (Javaid et al., 2022). However, the success of prevention techniques depends not only on their technical sophistication but also on their application within the organisation. Prevention techniques need to be tailored to the specific needs and vulnerabilities of the organisation. Public administrators are recommended to conduct regular risk assessments to identify areas where fraud is most likely to occur and implement targeted prevention measures accordingly (Gotelaere & Paoli, 2022). Furthermore, the organisation's culture needs to promote ethical behaviour and integrity, as a culture that tolerates or ignores minor infractions can create an environment conducive to large-scale fraud (Hilend et al., 2023). While detection and prevention are critical components of a fraud stratagem, an organisation also needs to be prepared to respond effectively when fraud is detected. Response strategies involve the actions taken by public administrators and service organisations to address fraudulent activities, mitigate their impact, and prevent their recurrence (Mugellini et al., 2021; Gotelaere & Paoli, 2022). The first step in any response strategy is the immediate containment of the fraudulent activity. Once fraud is detected, it is crucial to halt any further financial losses or damage to the organisation. This involves freezing accounts, suspending transactions, or temporarily shutting down compromised systems. The next step is to conduct a thorough investigation into the nature and scope of the fraud. This investigation is recommended to be carried out by internal or external auditors, forensic accountants, or fraud investigators who can trace the origins of the fraudulent activity and identify the individuals responsible (Isaac & Uhunmwenma, 2021). Following the investigation, the organisation needs to take steps to rectify the situation. This involves recovering lost funds, reinstating compromised systems, and implementing stronger controls to prevent future fraud. In cases where employees or contractors are found to have engaged in fraudulent activities, disciplinary action is necessary, ranging from termination of employment to legal prosecution. Finally, the organisation needs to engage in a process of learning and improvement. Each instance of fraud provides valuable insights into the organisation's vulnerabilities, and public administrators are recommended to use these insights to strengthen their fraud prevention stratagem. By analysing the circumstances surrounding the fraud and addressing any weaknesses in internal controls, service organisations can build a more resilient system.

Numerous real-world examples illustrate the successful implementation of fraud prevention stratagems in service organisations. One such example comes from a municipal government, where the integration of AI-driven fraud detection systems led to a significant reduction in fraudulent welfare claims (Yigitcanlar et al., 2021; Tariq, 2024). By analysing patterns in claim submissions, the system was able to identify and flag anomalies that would have otherwise gone unnoticed. The system's success not only resulted in substantial financial savings but also restored public confidence in the government's ability to manage welfare programs. Another example is found in a national healthcare system, where blockchain technology was employed to secure patient data and prevent fraudulent billing practices (Attaran, 2022). The decentralised nature of blockchain ensured that all financial transactions and patient records were immutable and transparent, reducing the opportunities for fraudsters to manipulate data for financial gain. The implementation of this stratagem significantly reduced instances of fraudulent claims, saving the healthcare system millions of pounds annually. Therefore, the development and implementation of a sophisticated stratagem are vital for the detection, prevention, and response to financial fraud in public administration. Stratagems need to be adaptable, employing a combination of manual oversight, technological innovations, and ethical governance to combat the ever-evolving tactics of fraudsters. By integrating detection methods, prevention techniques, and effective response strategies, service organisations can build a resilient system capable of safeguarding public resources and maintaining the trust of the public. Through the examination of real-world case studies, it is evident that well-executed stratagems not only reduce the occurrence of fraud but also enhance the overall integrity and efficiency of public administration.

3. POLICY AND ETHICAL CONSIDERATIONS IN FRAUD PREVENTION IN PUBLIC ADMINISTRATION

In the intricate landscape of public administration, the governance of financial resources is bound by a complex web of ethical standards and policy frameworks, particularly in the realm of fraud prevention. Given the high stakes involved both in terms of financial integrity and public trust, public administrators are charged with the dual responsibility of enforcing robust fraud prevention measures while maintaining the ethical principles that underpin their service to society (Redmond, 2020). Ethical standards in public administration are the bedrock upon which all governance activities are founded. They serve not only as moral guidelines but also as the principles that ensure the legitimacy and credibility of public institutions. In the context of fraud prevention, ethical standards are paramount, as they dictate the way public administrators are recommended to approach their responsibilities, prioritising the public interest above all else. At the heart of these ethical standards is the principle of integrity. Public administrators are custodians of public resources, and it is their ethical duty to protect these resources from misuse, including fraudulent activities (Kassem, 2022). Integrity demands a steadfast commitment to honesty and fairness in all dealings, ensuring that fraud prevention strategies are implemented without prejudice or bias. In practical terms, this means creating an environment where financial transparency is not just a procedural requirement but a moral obligation. Public administrators need to exhibit ethical leadership, setting an example for their staff and fostering a culture of accountability within their organisations. Another crucial ethical standard in public administration is justice.

Fraud prevention measures need to be designed and enforced in a manner that is equitable and just (Rashid et al., 2022). This requires administrators to ensure that their policies do not disproportionately target or discriminate against any particular group. For instance, while stringent measures are necessary to prevent fraud, these measures are recommended not to infringe upon the rights of individuals or marginalised groups. Justice in fraud prevention also extends to ensuring that the consequences of fraud are met with appropriate and fair responses, where culpable individuals are held accountable in a manner that reflects the severity of their actions (Gotelaere & Paoli, 2022). Lastly, the principle of public service needs to guide all ethical considerations in fraud prevention. Public administrators are expected to act in the best interests of the citizens they serve, prioritising the collective good over individual or organisational gain (Olney, 2020). This means designing policies that not only protect public resources but also serve to enhance public confidence in governmental institutions.

Effective fraud prevention requires a robust and comprehensive policy framework that integrates both ethical standards and practical measures. Such a framework needs to be dynamic and able to respond to the evolving tactics of fraudsters while upholding the ethical principles of public service (Figure 1). In public administration, fraud prevention policies need to be carefully crafted to address the specific vulnerabilities within an organisation's financial processes while ensuring that these policies do not inadvertently create new risks or ethical dilemmas. A sound policy framework for fraud detection and prevention typically begins with the establishment of clear guidelines for identifying and responding to fraudulent activities. These guidelines are recommended to delineate the responsibilities of public administrators, outlining the specific steps to be taken when fraud is detected and ensuring that there are no ambiguities in the enforcement of fraud prevention measures. Such policies need to be communicated clearly to all members of the organisation, fostering a culture of vigilance and responsibility at every level. The integration of technological solutions into fraud prevention policies has become increasingly important in recent years. Advances in artificial intelligence, data analytics, and machine learning have enabled public administrators to develop sophisticated detection systems capable of identifying fraudulent activities in real time (Bello et al., 2023). However, the deployment of these technologies needs to be carefully governed by policy frameworks that account for ethical concerns, such as the potential for misuse of personal data or the inadvertent targeting of innocent individuals. A comprehensive policy framework is recommended to also include procedural safeguards to prevent the misuse of fraud detection and prevention mechanisms. For example, the use of automated fraud detection systems needs to be accompanied by stringent oversight protocols to ensure that false positives do not result in unjust consequences for individuals or organisations. Similarly, policies are recommended to mandate regular audits and evaluations of fraud prevention systems to ensure their continued efficacy and ethical alignment. Transparency and accountability are indispensable to the maintenance of public trust in public administration, particularly in the area of fraud prevention. The public's confidence in governmental institutions hinges on the perception that these institutions operate with openness and integrity and that they are accountable for their actions. Transparency in fraud prevention refers to the openness with which public administrators communicate their policies, procedures, and actions. This includes providing the public with clear information about the measures being taken to detect and prevent fraud, as well as the outcomes of these measures. Transparency helps to reassure the public that their resources are being managed responsibly and that the government is actively working to prevent fraudulent activities. However, transparency needs to be balanced with the need for confidentiality in certain aspects of fraud prevention. For instance, while public administrators are recommended to strive to be open about their fraud prevention efforts, they also need to protect sensitive information that could compromise the effectiveness of these efforts if made public. A delicate balance needs to be struck between providing the public with enough information to maintain trust while safeguarding the integrity of fraud detection systems.

Figure 1. Financial fraud in public administration diagram

Accountability is closely tied to transparency and refers to the obligation of public administrators to answer for their actions, particularly in the event of failures in fraud prevention (Samaratunge & Alam, 2021). Public administrators need to be willing to take responsibility for lapses in fraud detection or prevention, and there needs to be mechanisms in place to ensure that those responsible for such failures are held to account. This is critical for maintaining public trust, as citizens need to be assured that the government is committed to rectifying any shortcomings in its fraud prevention efforts. Accountability also extends to the enforcement of ethical standards within public administration. Public administrators need to not only be accountable for their actions but also for ensuring that their staff adhere to the same ethical principles. This requires the establishment of clear accountability structures within the organisation, ensuring that every individual understands their role in preventing fraud and the consequences of failing to do so. One of the most challenging aspects of fraud prevention in public administration is the need to balance security with the maintenance of public trust (Yamamoto & Schührer, 2023). Fraud prevention measures are inherently restrictive, as they involve the implementation of stringent security protocols aimed at safeguarding public resources. However, these measures need to be implemented in a manner that does not erode public trust or create the perception that the government is overly intrusive or authoritarian. Public administrators need to ensure that their fraud prevention strategies are proportionate to the risks involved. Overzealous security measures, such as excessive surveillance or the blanket use of automated fraud detection systems, can undermine public confidence in the fairness and transparency of governmental institutions (Jameaba, 2024). To avoid this, administrators need to adopt a risk-based approach to fraud prevention, tailoring security measures to the specific vulnerabilities of the organisation while avoiding unnecessary intrusions into the privacy or rights of individuals. Engagement with the public is crucial in maintaining trust while implementing security measures. Public administrators are recommended to strive to involve citizens in the development and evaluation of fraud prevention policies, ensuring that these policies reflect the concerns and expectations of the public. By fostering a dialogue with citizens, public administrators can build a sense of shared responsibility for the prevention of fraud, helping to maintain public confidence in the government's efforts. Ultimately, the success of any fraud prevention strategy depends on its ability to balance the need for security with the ethical imperative to maintain public trust. This requires public administrators to act with transparency, accountability, and integrity, ensuring that their actions are guided by the highest standards of public service ethics. Hence, the integration of ethical standards and policy frameworks into fraud detection and prevention is essential for the effective governance of public administration. Public administrators need to navigate the complex interplay between security and public trust, ensuring that their fraud prevention measures are both effective and ethically sound. By upholding the principles of transparency, accountability, and integrity, public administrators can build a robust defence against financial fraud while maintaining the confidence and trust of the citizens they serve. Through the careful crafting of policy frameworks and the judicious application of ethical considerations, public administration can successfully navigate the challenges of fraud prevention in the modern era.

4. INTEGRATING VULNERABILITY AND STRATAGEM IN PRACTICE: A STRATEGIC APPROACH TO FRAUD PREVENTION

In the ongoing battle against financial anomalies and fraud in public administration, the effective integration of vulnerability assessment and strategic countermeasures or stratagems is crucial. Fraud prevention cannot be a mere theoretical exercise it needs to manifest in daily operations and evolve continuously to meet the ever-changing tactics of fraudsters. To mitigate the risk of financial fraud, service organisations need to embed vulnerability assessments into their everyday processes. This requires not only periodic evaluations but also a systematised approach where vulnerabilities are consistently monitored. The key to this integration is the development of an organisational culture that prioritises the identification and management of potential fraud risks, thereby reducing opportunities for fraudulent activity to take root (Alazzabi et al., 2023). Operational integration begins with the acknowledgement that vulnerability to fraud is a dynamic variable influenced by internal and external pressures (Knisley & Lin, 2022). Public administrators need to conduct regular assessments that analyse the interplay of opportunity, pressure, and rationalisation within their organisations. Vulnerability assessments are recommended to examine every facet of the operational framework, including procurement processes, financial reporting, and document submissions, as well as interpersonal interactions that could present fraud risks. For this to be practical, administrators need to establish internal protocols that institutionalise these assessments. For instance, assigning specific teams or departments the responsibility for regular vulnerability audits ensures that fraud detection becomes an inherent part of the organisation's fabric. Additionally, fostering an environment where employees are encouraged to report suspicious activities without fear of reprisal can serve as an early warning system, helping to prevent minor vulnerabilities from escalating into significant threats. Moreover, the use of technology-driven solutions plays a pivotal role in this operationalisation. Modern fraud prevention software, coupled with data analytics, enables public administrators to detect unusual patterns that signal fraud (Tang & Karim, 2019). These tools, when integrated into daily operational systems, ensure that vulnerability assessments are not limited to sporadic reviews but are part of a continuous, automated process.

Once vulnerabilities are identified, the next step is to develop stratagems tailored to address these specific risks. The concept of stratagem refers to the deliberate and strategic formulation of methods to detect and prevent fraud (Trompeter et al., 2013). The effectiveness of any fraud prevention strategy is contingent upon the precision with which it addresses the unique vulnerabilities of an organisation. Designing effective stratagems begins with a thorough analysis of the vulnerability assessment outcomes. Public administrators need to categorise these vulnerabilities, differentiating between those that require immediate action and those that can be monitored over time. High-risk vulnerabilities, such as gaps in financial oversight or inadequate vetting processes for document submission, demand the swift implementation of targeted measures. A critical component of stratagem design is the balance between proactive and reactive measures. Proactive measures, such as establishing strict verification protocols for document submission or employing forensic accounting techniques, help to pre-empt fraud by making it difficult for fraudsters to exploit organisational weaknesses. Conversely, reactive measures involve the development of response strategies for when fraud is detected, ensuring that administrators can act swiftly to minimise damage and recover losses. Additionally, employee training and awareness need to be an integral part of the stratagem. Employees are often the first line of defence against fraud, and their awareness of potential vulnerabilities can significantly enhance the organisation's overall fraud prevention efforts (Murphy & Dacin, 2011). Regular training sessions that educate staff on the latest fraud detection techniques, as well as updates on evolving fraud schemes, are vital in maintaining a vigilant workforce.

Case Studies and Practical Applications

The successful implementation of vulnerability assessments and stratagems can be best understood through the examination of real-world case studies. Consider, for example, the case of a public healthcare organisation that experienced substantial losses due to fraudulent billing practices (Barnes). Through a vulnerability assessment, it was discovered that the organisation's billing department lacked adequate oversight, providing an opportunity for fraudulent claims to be processed without scrutiny. In response, the organisation developed a stratagem that involved the installation of automated billing verification systems and the establishment of a dedicated fraud detection unit. This proactive approach not only reduced fraud but also increased overall efficiency in the billing process. In another instance, a government department responsible for infrastructure projects uncovered vulnerabilities in its procurement process, where collusion between contractors and employees resulted in inflated project costs (Pattanayak & Verdugo-Yepes, 2020). The vulnerability assessment revealed insufficient segregation of duties in the procurement chain, allowing employees to manipulate tendering procedures. By implementing a stratagem that introduced greater transparency, including third-party auditing and the mandatory rotation of procurement officers, the department was able to significantly reduce its fraud risk. These cases underscore the importance of customising fraud prevention strategies based on the specific vulnerabilities of an organisation. A one-size-fits-all approach is rarely effective in the nuanced field of fraud prevention. Instead, each organisation needs to analyse its unique risk profile and craft stratagems that address these risks with precision.

While the initial implementation of vulnerability assessments and stratagems is essential, their efficacy is only as good as their capacity to evolve. Fraudsters are constantly refining their techniques, and as such, public administrators need to remain vigilant, ensuring that their fraud prevention measures are continuously evaluated and enhanced (Sarkar & Shukla, 2023). Evaluations are recommended to occur at both the operational and strategic levels. At the operational level, public administrators are recommended to regularly review the outcomes of their vulnerability assessments, updating their fraud detection systems as new risks emerge. This includes recalibrating automated fraud detection systems to account for emerging fraud patterns, as well as revising employee training programs to reflect the latest developments in fraud tactics. At the strategic level, administrators are recommended to conduct periodic audits of their fraud prevention policies to ensure that they remain aligned with both legal requirements and ethical standards. These audits are recommended to assess not only the effectiveness of existing stratagems but also their potential impact on the organisation's overall operational efficiency and public reputation. In some cases, fraud prevention measures can become so restrictive that they impede normal operations, leading to inefficiencies that ultimately harm the organisation (Kaur et al., 2023). Continuous improvement, therefore, involves striking a balance between vigilance and practicality. Moreover, the feedback loop created by regular evaluation ensures that lessons learned from both successful and failed fraud prevention efforts are integrated into future strategies. Public administrators are recommended to encourage a culture of learning within their organisations, where the findings of vulnerability assessments and the outcomes of stratagem implementation are shared and discussed openly. This fosters an environment where continuous improvement becomes a collective responsibility rather than a task relegated to a select few. The integration of vulnerability assessment and stratagem design into the daily operations of service organisations is not merely a procedural necessity but a strategic imperative. By embedding vulnerability assessments into everyday activities, public administrators can ensure that fraud detection remains a dynamic and continuous process. Stratagems, carefully crafted in response to identified vulnerabilities, provide a robust framework for both preventing and responding to fraud. However, the true efficacy of these measures lies in their constant evaluation and refinement. Public administration, by its very nature, is an evolving field, and fraud prevention strategies need to evolve alongside it. Through diligent application of vulnerability assessments and the thoughtful design of stratagems, public administrators can build a resilient defence against fraud, safeguarding public resources and maintaining the trust of the citizens they serve.

5. CHALLENGES AND FUTURE DIRECTIONS IN POLICY AND ETHICAL CONSIDERATIONS FOR FINANCIAL FRAUD PREVENTION

In the domain of public administration, the imperative to safeguard service organisations from the scourge of financial fraud remains ever-present. Despite the advancements in fraud detection technologies and the implementation of robust policy frameworks, significant challenges continue to arise, not least in the realms of policy and ethics. Furthermore, it provides insights into future directions for research and practice alongside concrete recommendations for policymakers tasked with pre-empting the evolving nature of fraud. One of the foremost challenges in the realm of public administration is the delicate balance between stringent security measures and the preservation of ethical standards, particularly those pertaining to transparency and accountability (Graf & Bitencourt, 2024). Policymakers are confronted with the task of developing robust anti-fraud protocols while ensuring that these measures do not encroach upon civil liberties or erode public trust (Alfian et al., 2023). Striking this balance is inherently difficult, as the implementation of invasive security mechanisms such as comprehensive data surveillance or stringent document verification processes is perceived as infringing upon individual rights or overstepping the bounds of reasonable governance. Additionally, the ethical dimension of fraud prevention extends beyond the mere protection of public resources. Public administrators need to also contend with the moral implications of their anti-fraud strategies, ensuring that these measures do not disproportionately target vulnerable or marginalised groups within society. For example, overly restrictive fraud detection mechanisms could inadvertently discriminate against individuals who, due to socio-economic disadvantages, struggle to provide the necessary documentation for service access (Ruiu & Ragnedda). Policymakers need to be acutely aware of the potential for unintended consequences, ensuring that anti-fraud measures are both equitable and ethically defensible. The challenge of globalisation further complicates the policy landscape, as financial fraud schemes often transcend national borders. This requires public administrators to collaborate with international bodies and other jurisdictions to implement effective cross-border fraud prevention strategies. However, such cooperation is fraught with complexities, ranging from legal jurisdiction issues to variances in ethical standards across different regions. The harmonisation of policies across borders, while desirable, remains an elusive goal, exacerbating the challenges faced by public administrators in curbing global financial fraud.

The landscape of financial fraud is continuously evolving, with fraudsters employing increasingly sophisticated tactics that exploit technological advancements and regulatory gaps. One of the most prominent emerging trends is the rise of cyber-enabled fraud, wherein malicious actors leverage digital platforms to perpetrate fraud at a scale previously unimagined (Yu et al., 2024). These include schemes such as phishing, identity theft, and ransomware attacks, which are becoming increasingly prevalent within public administration sectors, particularly those that handle vast quantities of sensitive personal data. Furthermore, the proliferation of cryptocurrencies and other forms of decentralised finance presents new avenues for fraud (Hossain, 2023). These technologies, while offering legitimate benefits in terms of financial innovation and accessibility, have also enabled criminals to bypass traditional regulatory frameworks, facilitating money laundering, tax evasion, and other forms of financial crime. Public administrators are thus faced with the dual challenge of regulating these new technologies without stifling innovation whilst also developing strategies to mitigate the potential for their misuse in fraudulent schemes. Another emerging trend in financial fraud is the use of AI and machine learning to perpetrate more targeted and deceptive attacks (Nicholls et al., 2021). Fraudsters are increasingly using AI to analyse large datasets and identify weaknesses within public administration systems, enabling them to execute highly personalised fraud schemes that are difficult to detect. The sophistication of these attacks, combined with the speed at which they can be deployed, underscores the need for public administrators to stay ahead of technological developments and ensure that their anti-fraud strategies are equally advanced.

Given the dynamic and evolving nature of financial fraud, there is a pressing need for continuous research and innovation in fraud prevention strategies. Future research needs to focus on the development of next-generation fraud detection technologies, particularly those that leverage AI, big data analytics, and blockchain technology. These tools have the potential to revolutionise fraud prevention by enabling real-time detection of suspicious activities and providing immutable records of financial transactions that can be audited for signs of fraud. In terms of policy development, future efforts are recommended to be directed towards the creation of more flexible and adaptive regulatory frameworks. Current regulatory models are often static and slow to adapt to the rapid changes in the fraud landscape, leaving public administrators ill-equipped to respond to emerging threats. A more agile approach to regulation, wherein policies can be quickly adjusted in response to new fraud schemes, would significantly enhance the resilience of public administration systems. Moreover, fostering collaboration between governments, the private sector, and academia will be critical to the development of innovative fraud prevention solutions. On the ethical front, future research is recommended to explore the implications of emerging technologies such as AI and blockchain on privacy and civil liberties. As public administrators increasingly rely on these technologies to detect and prevent fraud, there is a growing need to ensure that they are deployed in a manner that upholds ethical principles and respects individual rights. Research into ethical AI frameworks and the responsible use of data analytics will be paramount in ensuring that future anti-fraud strategies do not compromise public trust or violate ethical standards. In light of the challenges and trends discussed above, several recommendations can be made to assist public administrators in their ongoing efforts to combat financial fraud. First and foremost, public administrators need to adopt a proactive and anticipatory approach to fraud prevention. Rather than simply reacting to fraud after it has occurred, administrators are recommended to invest in predictive analytics and other tools that can identify potential fraud risks before they materialise. This shift towards a preventative mindset is essential in an era where fraud schemes are becoming increasingly complex and difficult to detect. Secondly, public administrators need to prioritise the development of cross-jurisdictional partnerships and information-sharing mechanisms. As financial fraud becomes more globalised, it is no longer sufficient for public administrators to operate in isolation. Collaborative efforts between governments, law enforcement agencies, and international organisations are necessary to combat fraud on a global scale. Establishing data-sharing agreements and harmonising regulatory standards across borders will greatly enhance the ability of public administrators to detect and prevent transnational fraud schemes.

Moreover, public administrators are recommended to focus on fostering a culture of ethical integrity within their organisations. This entails not only ensuring that anti-fraud policies are ethically sound but also instilling a sense of responsibility and accountability in employees at all levels of the organisation. Training programs that emphasise the ethical dimensions of fraud prevention, combined with transparent reporting mechanisms that allow employees to report suspicious activities without fear of retaliation, are key components of an ethical organisational culture. Lastly, public administrators need to remain committed to continuous learning and adaptation. The fraud landscape is constantly evolving, and the strategies that are effective today become obsolete tomorrow. Public administrators are recommended to engage in ongoing professional development, staying abreast of the latest research and innovations in fraud prevention. Additionally, they are recommended to establish feedback loops within their organisations, regularly evaluating the effectiveness of their fraud prevention strategies and making adjustments as needed to ensure their continued relevance. The challenges of financial fraud in public administration are manifold, particularly in the context of policy and ethical considerations. Emerging trends, such as cyber-enabled fraud and the rise of cryptocurrencies, present new and formidable obstacles that require innovative solutions. Future research and practice need to focus on the development of advanced fraud detection technologies and adaptive regulatory frameworks while also addressing the ethical implications of these measures. Public administrators need to adopt a proactive, collaborative, and ethically grounded approach to fraud prevention, ensuring that they are well-equipped to navigate the evolving fraud landscape and maintain public trust. Through continuous evaluation and improvement, public administrators can build a resilient defence against the ever-present threat of financial fraud.

6. CONCLUSION: SAFEGUARDING PUBLIC ADMINISTRATION FROM FINANCIAL FRAUD

As the chapter draws this discourse to a close, it becomes imperative to encapsulate the myriads of considerations and strategies discussed throughout the chapter, reinforcing the overarching narrative regarding the necessity of addressing financial fraud within public administration. The ramifications of financial anomalies are profound, affecting not only the economic fabric of society but also the very trust and integrity that underpin public institutions. Thus, it is with a sense of urgency that summarised key points reflect upon their significance and extend a clarion call to action for public administrators and policymakers alike. Throughout our exploration, the chapter has delineated the multifaceted nature of financial fraud as it pertains to public administration, emphasising the critical need to understand both vulnerability and stratagem in this context. The definition of vulnerability in financial fraud illuminates the various factors, namely, opportunity, pressure, and rationalisation, that predispose service organisations to fraudulent activities. By employing illustrative case studies, the chapter has elucidated how these vulnerabilities manifest in real-world scenarios, emphasising the necessity for rigorous vulnerability assessments as a foundational element of any anti-fraud strategy. Furthermore, the discussion surrounding stratagem has underscored the imperative of developing effective detection and prevention methods. The chapter examined various techniques, such as advanced data analytics and behavioural monitoring, which can be deployed to pre-empt fraudulent activities. The integration of these stratagems with ethical considerations and policy frameworks is paramount. Effective fraud prevention cannot exist in a vacuum devoid of ethical integrity and public trust. The dynamic landscape of financial fraud necessitates continuous research and adaptation, particularly in the face of emerging threats such as cyber-enabled fraud and the exploitation of digital currencies. In this light, the role of collaborative partnerships and the establishment of transparent frameworks for fraud detection and prevention cannot be overstated.

The significance of addressing financial fraud within public administration extends beyond mere financial implications. It is a matter of upholding the principles of accountability, transparency, and ethical governance. Financial fraud undermines public trust, erodes the legitimacy of institutions, and diverts essential resources away from critical public services. As it can be seen, the repercussions of fraud are not confined to the immediate victims they reverberate throughout society, perpetuating a cycle of distrust that ultimately hampers effective governance and service delivery. Public administrators are tasked with the noble responsibility of safeguarding public resources while promoting the common good. In fulfilling this mandate, they need to be vigilant against the insidious nature of fraud, which can manifest in myriad forms, often eluding detection until significant damage has been inflicted. The cultivation of a robust anti-fraud culture within public organisations is thus not only prudent but essential. This involves fostering an environment where ethical behaviour is championed, and individuals are encouraged to report suspicious activities without fear of reprisal. Moreover, the commitment to continuous improvement in fraud prevention strategies cannot be overstated. As financial fraud evolves, so too do our responses. Public administrators need to embrace innovation, leveraging advancements in technology and data analytics to stay ahead of fraudsters. By cultivating a proactive approach characterised by ongoing assessment and adaptation, public administrators can fortify their organisations against emerging threats. In light of the comprehensive analysis presented herein, it is imperative that public administrators and policymakers heed this call to action. The time for complacency has long since passed stakeholders need to mobilise to implement the strategies and considerations outlined throughout this chapter. First and foremost, public administrators need to prioritise the integration of vulnerability assessments into their daily operations. This entails the development of systematic processes for identifying and evaluating vulnerabilities within their organisations, coupled with the implementation of tailored stratagems designed to mitigate these risks. The engagement of all levels of staff in this endeavour is crucial, as a collective commitment to fraud prevention fosters a culture of accountability and vigilance.

Policymakers, for their part, need to champion the establishment of comprehensive policy frameworks that facilitate collaboration among various stakeholders, including law enforcement, regulatory bodies, and civil society. Such frameworks are recommended to be designed to promote the sharing of information and best practices, ensuring that public administrators are equipped with the tools and knowledge necessary to respond effectively to emerging fraud threats. Furthermore, the integration of ethical considerations into the policy-making process is vital. Policymakers need to recognise that effective fraud prevention strategies cannot sacrifice ethical standards or public trust. Instead, they are recommended to strive to create policies that not only protect public resources but also uphold the principles of transparency and accountability. The implementation of training programs focused on ethical governance, and fraud awareness is a necessary component of this endeavour. Lastly, it is imperative that public administrators engage in continuous learning and professional development. The landscape of financial fraud is dynamic, and ongoing education in fraud detection techniques, emerging trends, and ethical considerations is essential for effective governance. By fostering a culture of lifelong learning, public administrators can remain at the forefront of fraud prevention efforts, adapting to new challenges as they arise.

The imperative to address financial fraud in public administration cannot be overstated. Explored throughout the chapter, the interplay of vulnerability and stratagem is fundamental to developing effective fraud prevention strategies. The challenges posed by the evolving nature of fraud demand concerted action from public administrators and policymakers alike. By prioritising ethical considerations, fostering collaboration, and committing to continuous improvement, stakeholders can safeguard service organisations from the pervasive threat of financial fraud.

REFERENCES

Adaga, E. M., Egieya, Z. E., Ewuga, S. K., Abdul, A. A., & Abrahams, T. O. (2024). A comprehensive review of ethical practices in banking and finance. *Finance & Accounting Research Journal*, 6(1), 1–20. DOI: 10.51594/farj.v6i1.705

Al-Mashhadi, A. S. J. (2021). Review on development of the internal control system. *technology, 31*, 35.

Alazzabi, W. Y. E., Mustafa, H., & Karage, A. I. (2023). Risk management, top management support, internal audit activities and fraud mitigation. *Journal of Financial Crime*, 30(2), 569–582. DOI: 10.1108/JFC-11-2019-0147

Alfian, A., Ritchi, H., & Adrianto, Z. (2023). Fraud analytics practices in public-sector transactions: A systematic review. *Journal of Public Budgeting, Accounting & Financial Management*, 35(5), 685–710. DOI: 10.1108/JPBAFM-11-2022-0175

Amiri, Z., Heidari, A., Jafari, N., & Hosseinzadeh, M. (2024). Deep study on autonomous learning techniques for complex pattern recognition in interconnected information systems. *Computer Science Review*, 54, 100666. DOI: 10.1016/j.cosrev.2024.100666

Attaran, M. (2022). Blockchain technology in healthcare: Challenges and opportunities. *International Journal of Healthcare Management*, 15(1), 70–83. DOI: 10.1080/20479700.2020.1843887

Barnes, N. *Financial controls of a healthcare fund to mitigate fraud risk in the expenses cycle* University of Johannesburg].

Bello, O. A., Ogundipe, A., Mohammed, D., Adebola, F., & Alonge, O. A. (2023). AI-Driven Approaches for Real-Time Fraud Detection in US Financial Transac tions: Challenges and Opportunities. *European Journal of Computer Science and Information Technology*, 11(6), 84–102.

Challapalli, S. (2023). Benefits and Constraints Associated with the Harmonization of Financial Regulations: An Overview. *Asian Journal of Economics. Business and Accounting*, 23(15), 49–56.

Chowdhury, E. K. (2021). Prospects and challenges of using artificial intelligence in the audit process. *The Essentials of Machine Learning in Finance and Accounting*, 139-156.

Engvall, N. (2024). The Influence of Institutional Factors on AI adoption in EU banking cybersecurity:: A narrative literature review.

Ezeji, C. L. (2024). Artificial Intelligence for detecting and preventing procurement fraud. *International Journal of Business Ecosystem & Strategy (2687-2293), 6*(1), 63-73.

George, A. S. (2024). Emerging Trends in AI-Driven Cybersecurity: An In-Depth Analysis. *Partners Universal Innovative Research Publication*, 2(4), 15–28.

Gotelaere, S., & Paoli, L. (2022). Prevention and control of financial fraud: A scoping review. *European Journal on Criminal Policy and Research*, •••, 1–21. DOI: 10.1007/s10610-022-09532-8

Graf, J. O., & Bitencourt, C. M. (2024). Digital government and the handling of sensitive data in the execution of public policies: challenges and possibilities. *Araucaria: Revista Iberoamericana de Filosofía, Política. Humanidades y Relaciones Internacionales*, 26(56), 139–153.

Hao, Y., Vand, B., Delgado, B. M., & Baldi, S. (2023). Market manipulation in stock and power markets: A study of indicator-based monitoring and regulatory challenges. *Energies*, 16(4), 1894. DOI: 10.3390/en16041894

Heng, L. J. (2024). Strategic Overview of Applying Artificial Intelligence on the Future Battlefield.

Hilal, W., Gadsden, S. A., & Yawney, J. (2022). Financial fraud: A review of anomaly detection techniques and recent advances. *Expert Systems with Applications*, 193, 116429. DOI: 10.1016/j.eswa.2021.116429

Hilend, R., Bell, J. E., Griffis, S. E., & Macdonald, J. R. (2023). Illicit activity and scarce natural resources in the supply chain: A literature review, framework, and research agenda. *Journal of Business Logistics*, 44(2), 198–227. DOI: 10.1111/jbl.12331

Hossain, M. Z. (2023). Emerging Trends in Forensic Accounting: Data Analytics, Cyber Forensic Accounting, Cryptocurrencies, and Blockchain Technology for Fraud Investigation and Prevention. *Cyber Forensic Accounting, Cryptocurrencies, and Blockchain Technology for Fraud Investigation and Prevention (May 16, 2023).*

Isaac, U., & Uhunmwenma, A. J. (2021). Forensic accounting and financial malpractices: A conceptual review. *SAARJ Journal on Banking & Insurance Research*, 10(4), 1–8. DOI: 10.5958/2319-1422.2021.00026.6

Jameaba, M.-S. (2024). Digitalization, emerging technologies, and financial stability: challenges and opportunities for the Indonesian banking sector and beyond. *Emerging Technologies, and Financial Stability: Challenges and Opportunities for the Indonesian Banking Sector and Beyond (April 26, 2024).*

Jarrett, A., & Choo, K. K. R. (2021). The impact of automation and artificial intelligence on digital forensics. *WIREs Forensic Science*, 3(6), e1418. DOI: 10.1002/wfs2.1418

Javaid, M., Haleem, A., Singh, R. P., Suman, R., & Khan, S. (2022). A review of Blockchain Technology applications for financial services. *BenchCouncil Transactions on Benchmarks. Standards and Evaluations*, 2(3), 100073.

Kamuangu, P. (2024). A Review on Cybersecurity in Fintech: Threats, Solutions, and Future Trends. *Journal of Economics. Finance and Accounting Studies*, 6(1), 47–53.

Kassem, R. (2022). Elucidating corporate governance's impact and role in countering fraud. *Corporate Governance (Bradford)*, 22(7), 1523–1546. DOI: 10.1108/CG-08-2021-0279

Kaur, B., Sood, K., & Grima, S. (2023). A systematic review on forensic accounting and its contribution towards fraud detection and prevention. *Journal of Financial Regulation and Compliance*, 31(1), 60–95. DOI: 10.1108/JFRC-02-2022-0015

Khalid, M. N. A., Al-Kadhimi, A. A., & Singh, M. M. (2023). Recent developments in game-theory approaches for the detection and defense against advanced persistent threats (APTs): A systematic review. *Mathematics*, 11(6), 1353. DOI: 10.3390/math11061353

Knisley, R. J., & Lin, H. (2022). A review of literature and experimental evidence on fraud motivation: Differentiating incentive and pressure. *Journal of Financial Accounting Research*, 7(1), 184–209. DOI: 10.2308/JFAR-2020-024

Madan, R., & Ashok, M. (2023). AI adoption and diffusion in public administration: A systematic literature review and future research agenda. *Government Information Quarterly*, 40(1), 101774. DOI: 10.1016/j.giq.2022.101774

Manginte, S. Y. (2024). Fortifying Transparency: Enhancing Corporate Governance through Robust Internal Control Mechanisms. *Advances in Management & Financial Reporting*, 2(2), 72–84. DOI: 10.60079/amfr.v2i2.173

Manohar, S., Nag, I., Mittal, A., & Nair, A. J. (2023, August 18-19). 2023). Omni Channeling Healthcare: Chaining Details, Information and Predictions for Extemporize Service Delivery. 2023 7th International Conference On Computing, Communication, Control And Automation (ICCUBEA), Markowitz, H., Guerard, J., Xu, G., & Beheshti, B. (2021). Financial anomalies in portfolio construction and management. *Journal of Portfolio Management*, 47(6), 51–64.

Mohammed, A. H. Y., Dziyauddin, R. A., & Latiff, L. A. (2023). Current multi-factor of authentication: Approaches, requirements, attacks and challenges. *International Journal of Advanced Computer Science and Applications*, 14(1). Advance online publication. DOI: 10.14569/IJACSA.2023.0140119

Mugellini, G., Della Bella, S., Colagrossi, M., Isenring, G. L., & Killias, M. (2021). Public sector reforms and their impact on the level of corruption: A systematic review. *Campbell Systematic Reviews*, 17(2), e1173. DOI: 10.1002/cl2.1173 PMID: 37131927

Murphy, P. R., & Dacin, M. T. (2011). Psychological pathways to fraud: Understanding and preventing fraud in organizations. *Journal of Business Ethics*, 101(4), 601–618. DOI: 10.1007/s10551-011-0741-0

Nair, A. J., & Manohar, S. (2024). Green Service Consumption: Unlocking Customer Expectations on Technological Transformations Enhancing Purchase Experience in Retail Store. *International Journal of Information Management Data Insights*, 4(2), 100277. https://doi.org/https://doi.org/10.1016/j.jjimei.2024.100277. DOI: 10.1016/j.jjimei.2024.100277

Nair, A. J., Manohar, S., & Chaudhry, R. (2024). Role of Knowledge Management in Enhancing the Effectiveness of the Gig Economy. In Ordóñez de Pablos, P., Almunawar, M. N., & Anshari, M. (Eds.), *Strengthening Sustainable Digitalization of Asian Economy and Society* (pp. 161–175). IGI Global., DOI: 10.4018/979-8-3693-1942-0.ch009

Nair, A. J., Manohar, S., & Mittal, A. (2023a, August 18-19). 2023). Enhancing Customer Experience with Teleportation Technology: The Future of Travel and Tourism Industry. *2023 Second International Conference On Smart Technologies For Smart Nation (SmartTechCon)*

Nair, A. J., Manohar, S., & Mittal, A. (2023b, 14-16 Dec. 2023). Robotic Vision with Micro Expression Analysis: Revolutionizing Customer Experiences in the Tourism and Hospitality Industry. 2023 IEEE Technology & Engineering Management Conference - Asia Pacific (TEMSCON-ASPAC),

Nair, A. J., Manohar, S., & Mittal, A. (2024). AI-enabled FinTech for innovative sustainability: promoting organizational sustainability practices in digital accounting and finance. International Journal of Accounting & Information Management, ahead-of-print(ahead-of-print). doi:DOI: 10.1108/IJAIM-05-2024-0172

Nair, A. J., Manohar, S., Mittal, A., & Khanna, V. (2023, 14-16 Sept. 2023). Revolutionizing Tourism and Hospitality Services: Integrating AI in the Metaverse. 2023 6th International Conference on Contemporary Computing and Informatics (IC3I)

Nicholls, J., Kuppa, A., & Le-Khac, N.-A. (2021). Financial cybercrime: A comprehensive survey of deep learning approaches to tackle the evolving financial crime landscape. *IEEE Access : Practical Innovations, Open Solutions*, 9, 163965–163986.

Obi, O. C., Akagha, O. V., Dawodu, S. O., Anyanwu, A. C., Onwusinkwue, S., & Ahmad, I. A. I. (2024). Comprehensive review on cybersecurity: Modern threats and advanced defense strategies. *Computer Science & IT Research Journal*, 5(2), 293–310. DOI: 10.51594/csitrj.v5i2.758

Okoye, N. J., Okonkwo, V. I. P., & Okaro, C. P. (2021). FRAUD AND CORRUPTION'S EFFECTS ON NIGERIA'S CAPITAL MARKET PERFORMANCE: CONCEPTUAL REVIEW. *Journal of Global Accounting Department of Accountancy*, 7(1).

Olney, S. (2020). Serving the Public, But Not Public Servants? *The Palgrave Handbook of the Public Servant*, 1-19.

Ozkan-Ozay, M., Akin, E., Aslan, Ö., Kosunalp, S., Iliev, T., Stoyanov, I., & Beloev, I. (2024). A Comprehensive Survey: Evaluating the Efficiency of Artificial Intelligence and Machine Learning Techniques on Cyber Security Solutions. *IEEE Access : Practical Innovations, Open Solutions*, 12, 12229–12256. DOI: 10.1109/ACCESS.2024.3355547

Papagiannidis, E. (2024). Responsible AI governance in practice: The strategic impact of responsible AI governance on business value and competitiveness.

Pattanayak, S., & Verdugo-Yepes, C. (2020). Protecting public infrastructure from vulnerabilities to corruption: a risk-based approach. *Well Spent: How Strong Infrastructure Governance Can End Waste in Public Investment. Pg*, 175-200.

Radanliev, P., Santos, O., & Brandon-Jones, A. (2024). Capability hardware enhanced instructions and artificial intelligence bill of materials in trustworthy artificial intelligence systems: analyzing cybersecurity threats, exploits, and vulnerabilities in new software bills of materials with artificial intelligence. *The Journal of Defense Modeling and Simulation*, 15485129241267919.

Rahman, J. M., & Marjerison, R. K. (2020). *Sustaining competitive advantage through good governance and fiscal controls: Risk determinants in internal controls.* Corporate Ownership & Control.

Rajesh, Y., Kumar, V. K., & Poojari, A. (2024). A Unified Approach Toward Security Audit and Compliance in Cloud Computing. *Journal of The Institution of Engineers (India): Series B, 105*(3), 733-750.

Rashid, M. A., Al-Mamun, A., Roudaki, H., & Yasser, Q. R. (2022). An overview of corporate fraud and its prevention approach. *Australasian Accounting. Business and Finance Journal*, 16(1), 101–118.

Redmond, T. (2020). Independent review into the oversight of local audit and the transparency of local authority financial reporting. *London, available at:https://assets. publishing. service. gov. uk/government/uploads/system/uploads/attachment_data/file/916217/Redmond_Review. pdf.*

Riefa, C., & Saintier, S. (2020). *Vulnerable consumers and the law: consumer protection and access to justice*. Routledge. Ruiu, M. L., & Ragnedda, M. Digital-Environmental Poverty.

Samaratunge, R., & Alam, Q. (2021). Accountability and transparency in emerging countries: Governance, democratic currents and change. *Public Administration and Development*, 41(4), 147–156. DOI: 10.1002/pad.1963

Sarkar, G., & Shukla, S. K. (2023). Behavioral analysis of cybercrime: Paving the way for effective policing strategies. *Journal of Economic Criminology*, 100034.

Sigfrids, A., Nieminen, M., Leikas, J., & Pikkuaho, P. (2022). How should public administrations foster the ethical development and use of artificial intelligence? A review of proposals for developing governance of AI. *Frontiers in Human Dynamics*, 4, 858108. DOI: 10.3389/fhumd.2022.858108

Taherdoost, H. (2021). A review on risk management in information systems: Risk policy, control and fraud detection. *Electronics (Basel)*, 10(24), 3065. DOI: 10.3390/electronics10243065

Tang, J., & Karim, K. E. (2019). Financial fraud detection and big data analytics–implications on auditors' use of fraud brainstorming session. *Managerial Auditing Journal*, 34(3), 324–337. DOI: 10.1108/MAJ-01-2018-1767

Tariq, M. U. (2024). The Role of Emerging Technologies in Shaping the Global Digital Government Landscape. *Emerging Developments and Technologies in Digital Government*, 160-180.

Trompeter, G. M., Carpenter, T. D., Desai, N., Jones, K. L., & Riley, R. A.Jr. (2013). A synthesis of fraud-related research. *Auditing*, 32(Supplement 1), 287–321. DOI: 10.2308/ajpt-50360

Yamamoto, K., & Schührer, S. (2023). Finance and accounting: recent developments and challenges building efficiency and public accountability. *Handbook of Public Administration Reform*, 90-110.

Yigitcanlar, T., Corchado, J. M., Mehmood, R., Li, R. Y. M., Mossberger, K., & Desouza, K. (2021). Responsible urban innovation with local government artificial intelligence (AI): A conceptual framework and research agenda. *Journal of Open Innovation*, 7(1), 71. DOI: 10.3390/joitmc7010071

Yu, J., Yu, Y., Wang, X., Lin, Y., Yang, M., Qiao, Y., & Wang, F.-Y. (2024). The Shadow of Fraud: The Emerging Danger of AI-powered Social Engineering and its Possible Cure. *arXiv preprint arXiv:2407.15912*.

Chapter 14
The Use of Artificial Intelligence in the Turkish Judiciary

Fatih Ulaşan
https://orcid.org/0000-0003-3301-4823
Adalet Bakanlığı, Turkey

ABSTRACT

The Turkish judicial system is very fragmented and each unit has its own rules, it is more accurate to focus on the benefits of AI to the Turkish judicial system in general rather than examining the units in the Turkish judicial system one by one. In addition, preliminary preparations are vital for governmental duties, education and legal strategies in order to use AI more efficiently. The proposed ways for the application of AI-based tools for the utilization of the AI-based technology in Turkish courts will be analyzed. The problem of acceptability and serviceability of AI in the Turkish judiciary will be analyzed by the help of previous studies, legal reasonings, current examples and existing theories. Firstly, examples around the world regarding the usage of AI systems in law will be discussed. Secondly, examples from Türkiye regarding the usage of AI in law will be discussed. Finally, whether the decision-making mechanism in Turkish law is compatible with the AI systems will be discussed and recommendations will be made to increase the use of the AI systems.

INTRODUCTION

Artificial intelligence (AI) technology is a system that can perform certain tasks by imitating human intelligence so as to fulfill orders and improve itself by repeating the information it collects. The progress of the AI-based technology led to an

DOI: 10.4018/979-8-3693-8372-8.ch014

upsurge in the features of computers and the ability to store millions of information efficiently and the use of the data effectively. AI started to perform numerous connections and tasks and became useful in various fields. Also, AI made a great progress and increased significantly in value since it was first put forward in 1956 at the Dartmouth conference (Moor, 2006, p. 86). Today, the speed of technology in AI is at an unprecedented level. Thanks to technological advances like deep learning, machine learning and big data, AI affects humans' lives positively by providing work productivity, cost reduction and resource optimization (Ulaşan, 2023, p. 303). Intelligent robots with natural language processing, image analysis and computer vision have been produced (Zhang and Lu, 2021). AI-based systems develop and are transformed into higher systems thanks to their interactions with people. AI transforms data into a self-reinforcing cycle, making it easier for people to do their jobs financially, scientifically, and socially. AI systems make great contributions to humanity by simplifying many situations that are difficult for people. AI systems that determine the most appropriate route to use to find any address, applications that find the most suitable products by creating a personal recommendation list for shopping, autonomous cars that minimize the risk of accidents, systems that perform risk analysis, systems that analyze people's preferences and make personal recommendations to them, chatbots and many other AI products provide people with huge advantages in terms of time, labor, cost and workforce (Coşkun & Gülleroğlu, 2021, p. 954). Due to this, today, AI has become popular and widely used in almost every area of life. AI studies in a lot of fields such as law, public finance, public administration and national defense give opportunities which make humans' lives easier.

Especially, one of areas where the usage of the AI technology is widespread is public administration. Public administration is related to a wide area that deals with structures and functioning of countries in theoretical and practical terms. Public administration, defined as the organization established for the purpose of producing and providing public services, represents the face of the country reflected to citizens. Public administration, which aims to meet the needs of the public, has been shaped by different understandings in different periods of history. The New Public Administration approach emerged after the 1970s and was an administrative approach that interpreted and directed the changes in the activities and structure of the administrative and economic system as an alternative to traditional management thought (Çamur & Aydın, 2022, p. 149). This understanding is basically defined as an approach that tries to give place to a market or semi-market understanding in services by going to a structure where decentralization and corporatization will be dominant in public services (Demirel, 2015, p. 140). This trend has many dimensions. First of all, a new management focused on public services has been adopted instead of the old-style public management and the need for contracts and performance-oriented incentives of employees have increased the possibility of implementing them for greater efficiency in public services (Lapsley, 1999, p. 201). In addition, new public management contributes to the growth of information technology and automation in the distribution and production of public services. New public management has developed a more global agenda focusing on general subjects about policy strategy, decision types and intergovernmental collaboration (Hood, 1991, p. 3). With the impact of globalization, AI has reached a level where it can guide government policies, public demands, and world trade, allowing public administration to be viewed from a global perspective (Uzun, Yildiz, & Onder, 2022, p. 433). The highest effect of AI on public administration can be seen in public services. Many public institutions are integrating AI applications into their bodies so as to adapt to the changing world by meeting the demands and expectations of citizens. First of all, many states such as the USA and China, South Korea, France, India, and the UK have created strategies to utilize AI in various areas such as the healthcare sector. AI has been utilized efficiently by countries in the health sector and public administration against COVID-19 (Ulaşan, 2023b, pp. 639-640). South Korea and China have tracked citizens through credit cards, CCTV cameras and phones and have called citizens they have identified as at risk for testing (Ulaşan, 2023a, p. 118). Also, AI systems used in education can provide excellence in certain routine tasks in the classroom and help teachers spend more time with their students. AI systems help increase student success by adapting the level of education to the capacity of each student (Ulaşan, 2023d). In particular, AI supports policy makers by helping to define problems in public administration, set the agenda, analyze problems in the public opinion, and define problems. AI can analyze citizens' problems by helping to collect and analyze data through various sensors. With AI, social media platforms can become information sources and citizens' tendencies can be understood. AI systems check common trends in the public opinion and suggest policies that can be implemented (Ulaşan, 2023e, p. 523). Thanks to AI applications in public administration, making the right decisions with reliable data becomes more effort less. With AI, governments can easily identify the least risky and most beneficial situation on specific issues and make policies for each situation, and also control the effectiveness of these policies by understanding the data better (Önder & Saygılı, 2018, pp. 651-652).

There are discussions on the usage of AI for legal industry. The idea of finding solutions to legal problems with AI systems is a bold step, but it also carries certain risks. The basic contribution of AI to legal systems may be to perform more tasks in a shorter time and automate routine processes (Turan, Kemaloğlu, & Küçüksille, 2020). But with recent developments, AI started to be complicated and flourish. Especially in judicial systems, AI is thought to be very helpful in terms of speed, accuracy, support, quality, etc. For example, AI systems are also used as a prediction technology in current judicial systems. In fact, what is expected from AI is that the decision-making mechanism of a human judge can be imitated. The use of the AI prediction technologies in criminal proceedings is widespread. Basically, it is possible to address the area of use of AI in the judiciary under three headings; Information Organization/Management Related Systems, Advising/Supporting Systems and Prediction Systems (Sümer, 2021, p. 1559). These systems are different from humans in many ways. For example, they do not make mistakes due to fatigue, lack of knowledge and experience and personal problems. In addition, the AI system makes decisions without emotions such as fear, favoritism, hesitation. They can work at any time and in the medium and long term the systems become much cheaper, while the infrastructures of the systems are expensive. The decisions of AI are consistent. People can understand what the judge may decide on their case based on previous decisions. AI is possible to be utilized especially in fields where the legal system is prone to automation. Since the Turkish judicial system is very fragmented and each unit has its own rules, it is more accurate to focus on the benefits of AI to the Turkish judicial system in general rather than examining the units in the Turkish judicial system one by one. In addition, preliminary preparations are vital for governmental duties, education and legal strategies in order to use AI more efficiently. The proposed ways for the application of AI-based tools for the utilization of the AI-based technology in Turkish courts will be analyzed. The problem of acceptability and serviceability of AI in the Turkish judiciary will be analyzed by the help of previous studies, legal reasonings, current examples and existing theories. Firstly, examples around the world regarding the usage of AI systems in law will be discussed. Secondly, examples from Türkiye regarding the usage of AI in law will be discussed. Finally, whether the decision-making mechanism in Turkish law is compatible with the AI systems will be discussed and recommendations will be made to increase the use of the AI systems.

Scope of the Study

The aims of the study are to observe Türkiye's current AI capacity, analyze the Turkish judiciary's need for AI systems, and decide which AI-based legal analysis tools should be utilized in the Turkish judiciary. To achieve this, it is necessary to investigate the possibility of automating steps of decision-making processes in the Turkish judiciary and to analyze whether AI tools fit into the Turkish legal basis. The study may help especially lawyers, administrators, engineers and politicians to understand which preparations should be made in order to utilize AI tools in the Turkish judiciary. The purpose of the study is to understand the possibility of AI tools in the Turkish judiciary and to analyze what preparations need to be made to make the Turkish judiciary ready for AI-based legal analysis systems. Creating applications/services with AI and algorithms is not the subject of the study.

Objective of the Study

The study analyzes the effects of AI on the basis of the Turkish judiciary and measures the usability of AI-based systems in terms of legal analysis. Examples of the use of AI in courts will be given from states like the United States and China, and the ways in which AI is used will be analyzed. Then, the possibility of using AI in its current form in the Turkish judiciary will be emphasized and examples of AI-based systems used in the Turkish judiciary from Türkiye will be emphasized. Even if AI decision-making tools start operating in the Turkish legal system in the future, AI tools need to be consistent with the Turkish law. This study searches possible legal categories and rules for the usage of AI tools and concentrates on how existing rules can be applied to AI tools. In general, Machine Learning, Deep Learning, natural networks and other feedback loops are utilized to create AI tools. All these systems allow AI to decide through an evolutionary and adaptive course rather than an engineering design course. The core issue of the study is to analyze the possibility of the usage of AI techniques in the Turkish legal system. Researches on the application of AI in the Turkish legal system requires a comprehensive approach that includes a systemic analysis. Since each case has its own specific characteristics, AI tools should be made to contribute to the success of the aim of consistency and speed in trials by avoiding incomplete and improper procedural procedures and malicious behaviors that try to prolong the duration of the case. Designers have to take into account that AI tools get a system which permits human intervention at appropriate and necessary times.

LITERATURE REVIEW

In recent years, AI applications in legal systems have been developed rapidly and have been increasingly used. The usage of AI tools in legal systems offers efficiency, especially in processes such as file classification, contract review, case prediction and legal research, and saves time and costs. AI applications can contribute to the rule of law with the acceleration of legal processes and more accurate decisions. Text classification models using various neural networks for judicial verdict prediction was created and it analyzed the content of the cases, defenses and articles of law and reached results. In this way, fast and accurate results are obtained in the analysis of complex legal texts (Turan, Kemaloğlu, & Küçüksille, 2020, pp. 147,148-152). In addition, AI systems' ability to make predictions in litigation processes supports lawyers and judges in their decision-making processes with their ability to predict the outcome of cases. In this sense, AI provides a great advantage in applications such as contract review, judicial case prediction and electronic discovery. Situation determination and previously given decisions can be analyzed by AI and the outcome of the case can be predicted. In addition, data can be collected from the decision history of the judge who make decisions and an evaluation can be made about the current case. Software templates can be created with the help of document automation based on data entry (Efe, 2022, p. 102). Research on AI and law at Tulane University has helped judges make decisions on more than 50,000 convictions in Virginia. The AI system scores each offender's risk of reoffending and makes recommendations to judges on sentencing options (prison only or alternative sentences). As a result, AI systems can help correct gender and racial prejudice which may play an important role in judges' discretionary decisions (Brunette, 2024).

In contrast, there may be many difficulties in the integration of AI into legal systems. The most important one is that AI is prone to make biased predictions. There are risks of bias and error in the data sets on which AI algorithms are trained, which can lead to wrong decisions. In order to ensure a fair trial process, AI systems must be impartial. However, if the data obtained by existing algorithms produces biased information, the results obtained by AI will also be biased. Skewed datasets, biased algorithmic design and subjective preferences of developers can drive discrimination and lead to unfair outcomes. AI tools trained on historically prejudiced data might favor one over another in custody cases in family law without clear and robust justification (Zafar, 2024). There is a serious lack of infrastructure for AI-based law practices in Türkiye. Digitizing existing data and creating high-quality data sets are necessary for the proper operation of AI-based legal systems. However, the data formats (such as PDF, JPG) used in legal databases such as UYAP in Türkiye make it difficult for AI algorithms to work efficiently. Organizing the data sets is important for AI to be integrated into legal processes more effectively (Kandır, 2023).

In Türkiye, significant studies have been conducted on the use of AI in law. With the contributions of the Union of Turkish Bar Associations, the Istanbul, Ankara and Izmir Bar Associations have organized various workshops and published reports on the relationship between AI and law. These studies have evaluated how legal technologies, especially AI, can be used more effectively in the field of law. The report emphasizes the importance of digital transformation in law schools and states that more experts should be trained on AI and digitalization (İstanbul, Ankara ve İzmir Baroları Çalıştay Raporu, 2019). However, the utilization of AI tools in legal processes in Türkiye is still limited. Although there are some AI applications in existing systems such as case law search engines, these systems are largely keyword search based and are not yet fully AI-assisted in estimating or analyzing case law. In Türkiye, AI-based legal assistant and case analysis systems need to be developed (Kandır, 2023).

In conclusion and in terms of future fields of study, the current literature on the utilization of AI tools in legal world shows that it is quite beneficial in terms of efficiency, speed and accuracy. However, difficulties such as data quality, ethical issues and bias in algorithms should also be taken into consideration. More research and a stronger infrastructure are needed to integrate AI-based systems into legal processes. For this purpose, it is recommended to increase both national and international collaborations and to develop various educational programs for the adaptation of law schools to technology.

THE USE OF ARTIFICIAL INTELLIGENCE IN COURTS IN THE WORLD

The use of robot judges around the world is being implemented in a few countries, either in a trial phase or as pilot projects, with the aim of increasing automation and providing faster results, especially in judicial systems. Some of the prominent countries are China, Estonia and Canada. These countries aim to speed up justice services and reduce costs by integrating AI-supported systems into courts with different methods. However, these initiatives have ethical and legal limitations as well as benefits. If AI robots are employed in courts without complying with ethical and legal limitations, AI robots can do more harm than good to the justice system, so it is necessary to be very careful about the utilization of AI tools in courts.

China is considered one of the most advanced countries in the utilization of AI tools in the judiciary. China's internet courts began in 2017 and are now largely conducted in a virtual environment. Internet courts help users quickly resolve their online cases through AI-powered "robot judges." These systems have been used particularly in matters such as online commercial disputes, intellectual property and digital rights violations, paving the way for individuals and institutions to file lawsuits without having to physically go to court. While an average case in China takes 40 days in online courts, a hearing is completed in about 37 minutes. These systems have been observed to increase efficiency in terms of cost and time. However, concerns have also been expressed about whether AI-based decisions are fair and how citizens can exercise their rights to appeal (Vasdani T., 2020). For instance, Xiaofa is an AI robot used by China in the Beijing No. 1 Intermediate People's Court, which advises on legal issues and teaches people about legal terminology. It is possible to answer more than 40,000 case questions and handle 30,000 legal problems. In particular, Chinese courts utilize AI tools to analyze comments and messages on social media platforms as evidence (Harris, 2018). In 2019, a court in Hangzhou began using AI systems in its cases. The assistant judge, called Xiao Zhi 3.0 or "Little Wisdom," was first used to try a case involving ten people who could not repay their bank loans. Although 10 separate cases have to be filed in advance to solve this problem, Xiao Zhi 3.0 allows all cases to be resolved by a single judge in a single hearing, with a verdict given in 30 minutes. Initially, Xiao Zhi 3.0 performed repetitive tasks such as announcing court procedures in hearings. It was later utilized to record testimony with voice recognition, evaluate case materials, and confirm information from a database in real time. It is primarily utilized in cases about basic financial problems. However, the similar technology has been applied by a court in Suzhou to disputes involving traffic accidents. The Xiao Baogong Intelligent Sentence Prediction System can be called as a legal AI platform utilized by judges and public prosecutors in criminal law. The tool recommends punishments based on data analysis of case information and previous convictions from similar cases (Deutsche Welle, 2023).

Estonia, like China, is among the countries that have adopted AI-powered judicial systems. Studies are carried out in Estonia on AI-based decision-making systems in the judicial process. This system, developed for small-scale cases, is being used in courts as a pilot application. These Estonian projects aim to reduce the workload of the courts and speed up the judicial process. AI judges are limited to making decisions only in certain types of cases, and final decisions are not made without the approval of human judges. In Canada and the UK, AI is particularly preferred in mediation and conciliation processes. Online dispute resolution platforms such as "Smartsettle ONE" used in Canada help resolve disputes through mediation by analyzing the parties' demands through AI. These systems provide a mechanism that allows offers and counter-offers to be made privately between parties to resolve disputes. In countries such as the UK and Canada, the use of robot mediators is particularly advantageous in terms of low cost and accessibility, and offers effective solutions to small-scale commercial disputes. These methods are considered useful in reducing the burden on the justice system and ensuring that citizens obtain quick solutions (Vasdani T., 2019).

The use of AI judge and mediator systems enables justice processes to be completed faster and at lower costs. In the examples of China and Estonia, it is seen that processes are shorter and costs are reduced. However, the implementation of these systems requires a significant infrastructure investment and the initial costs are high. However, in the long term, especially with the continuous development of AI, it is expected that these investments will reduce the cost of the justice system. Although the use of AI-supported judges and robot mediators has the potential to provide faster and more efficient justice processes, it is still controversial in terms of issues such as ethics, privacy and human rights. It is seen that these systems, which can replace human judges, increase concerns about the provision of justice. As in Estonia, methods such as not allowing AI to be completely independent in the decision-making process and keeping it under human control are presented as a response to ethical concerns. When the different approaches of China and Estonia are considered, it is understood that it is important to carefully implement such projects in accordance with the national legal infrastructure. In general, within the scope of the measures that should be taken for AI to become functional in judicial activities, measures should be taken to eliminate the possible risks which might arise with the utilization of AI tools in ethical problems like personal privacy, data security, transparency, etc. and reliable international regulations should be made regarding the application of AI in public service and judicial activities and national legislation should be harmonized with these regulations. In addition, the ethical and legal dimensions of AI should be evaluated by taking international examples into account and models and guides should be published. In-service training should be provided to judicial personnel on the impact of AI technologies on the legal and criminal liability regime and on the transformed intellectual property rights. Pilot AI applications should be carried out and the level of awareness among all partners regarding the regulation and implementation of legislation in terms of the safety of personal data and data governance in the area of AI should be increased (Bilgin, 2022, p. 417).

The Use of Artificial Intelligence in Turkish Courts

The use of AI-supported systems in courts has already been common especially in administrative tasks such as data processing and file management. The use of similar systems is increasing in Türkiye, and it is thought that justice services will become faster and more effective thanks to these technologies. In addition, judges and public prosecutors can be supported in the decision-making process by AI-based decision support systems in order to reach more accurate decisions with stability (Töngel, 2024). When evaluating developments in the field of AI in Türkiye, it is necessary to take into account the "Artificial Intelligence Strategy 2021 2025", which was published and started being effective in 2021 by the help of the Presidency of Digital Transformation Office and the Ministry of Industry and Technology. According to the strategy text, activities will be carried out to evaluate ethical and legal dimensions of AI tools, international studies will be followed, and various initiatives are mentioned to identify and solve new legal and ethical problems that arise with the spread of AI technologies. The strategic goals determined within the scope of the National AI Strategy produce governance mechanisms that facilitate algorithmic accountability with the operation of an agile and comprehensive legal harmonization method for the testing of ethical and legal situations and the auditing of impartiality, data privacy and ethical values (TRAI, 2024, p. 23).

There have been no advanced AI applications such as robot judges in courts in Türkiye yet. However, studies have been conducted on some AI-based software with more limited functions to support judicial processes. These include consultant robots to increase efficiency in the work processes of law firms or software that can perform automatic document classification and analysis. For example, in the workshops organized by the Turkish Artificial Intelligence Initiative (TRAI), topics such as how AI can contribute to an independent and fair judiciary and how it can be made compatible with existing legal frameworks were discussed. There are academic and sectoral discussions on how AI can be used in the digital transformation of the judiciary. Some steps have been taken in the Turkish judicial system in terms of digitalization and data management. These developments may enable the integration of AI-based solutions into the Turkish legal system in the future. For example, National Judiciary Informatics System (UYAP in Turkish), Türkiye's central judicial management system, with high-resolution data and converting the data into formats that can be processed by AI algorithms may pave the way for the use of smarter systems in courts in the future. As the use of digital data in the judicial system increases, it will become more possible to quickly analyze similar cases and provide support in decision-making processes (TRAI, 2024). Within the scope of the Project to Strengthen the Institutional Capacity of the Court of Cassation in Türkiye, it has been announced that there is a study in which summaries of precedent decisions will be made available quickly using the AI system. An AI-supported Jurisprudence Center has been established in order to popularize the Court of Cassation precedents. Thanks to this software, lawyers and applicants can evaluate precedent decisions and evaluate in advance whether their cases have a chance of success. This AI tool can be an example of the predictive AI for the Court of Cassation in Türkiye (Yargıtay, 2023). AI will be used in processes such as writing reasoned decisions and preparing reports, distributing the workload fairly, distributing files, conducting preliminary investigations, and measuring the performance of employees (Hürriyet, 2023).Minister of Justice of the Republic of Türkiye stated that there are some issues that are decided just in light of data expect for human element and that AI will be used in a certain part of the judiciary in relation to these issues (Çakır, Karaduman, & Zobar, 2024).

Numerous samples can be given like decision search engines, UYAP, Celse, e-Tahsilat and etc. These systems are primarily designed for lawyers. For example, the Lawyer Identity Card (Barokart) is one of the technological products traditionally used in the legal profession. Lawyers can load money onto this and this card is specially designed card to shop for clothing, fuel, food and etc. and benefit from special services. In addition, file debts and case expenses can be collected via credit card from the E-Collection System, which works integrated with Barokart. The mobile lawyer communication system called (mAV-İ), which is compatible with UYAP and developed by the Ankara Bar Association, provides lawyers with information about the cases they represent and helps to view the status of the cases on the court list and predict when the hearing may start (Buluz, 2019, p. 38). In recent years, especially, the new interface and new features of the UYAP mediator portal have been put into effect. Within the scope of the UYAP version III study, the mediator portal interface has been renewed and improvements have been made to the existing screens by fixing the detected errors. The "Big Data and Artificial Intelligence Applications Branch Directorate" has been established under the General Directorate of Information Processing within the Ministry of Justice (T.C. Adalet Bakanlığı, 2023). The Ministry of Justice is trying to make the justice system smarter and more efficient by using big data and AI applications at the institutional level (Yalçın, 2024, p. 205). In addition, lawyers can log in to the system via the UYAP Lawyer Portal and obtain data about cases, make payments and add documents to case files by using electronic signatures. Citizens can log in to the system via the UYAP Citizen Portal and understand the subjects, parties, date and stage of their cases. UYAP integrates with other computers in the public sector and provides the necessary information and document flow. For example, it enables courts to automatically obtain criminal records from the Criminal Record Information System, population records from MERNIS and address records from the Address Registration System, driver's license records from POLNET, exchange rates from the Central Bank, and land registry and cadastral records from TAKBIS (Akçakaya, 2017, p. 23). However, there are also software such as Turklex that finds court decisions and presents them systematically. This software analyzes case results and helps create a case file automatically (Buluz, 2019, p. 38).

The "Enforcement Document Classification" AI project was developed under the main title of AI in Enforcement in UYAP and uploaded to UYAP in January 2022. Thanks to this project, the scanning, classification, image and text classification of the enforcement offices' documents were carried out and 94 million documents were digitized. In addition, the issues that the Court of Appeals chambers handle were determined according to the division of labor. If the Court of Appeals concludes that it is not authorized according to this division of labor during the preliminary examination phase, it sends the file to the chamber it deems authorized. When an appeal is filed, the decision on this issue due to being sent to the wrong chamber causes the trial process to be prolonged. So as to overcome the problem in UYAP, an AI model was developed on 50 issues based on the issues that were most frequently decided in civil courts. Thanks to these AI models, an 88% accuracy rate was achieved in sending the file to the correct chamber according to the division of labor. In order to prevent human errors and incomplete data entry in prosecution files and to increase the accuracy of judicial statistics data and reports requested by auditing institutions, AI models were developed and uploaded to UYAP to match terrorist organization information with terrorist organization information registered in the system by estimating the information about terrorist organizations through AI (Birtane, 2024, pp. 254-255). Supported by the TUBITAK Individual Young Entrepreneurs Support Program, the ARYA AI system based on natural language processing is a system that brings Supreme Court decisions containing the answers to the questions lawyers look for and predicts with a 90% accuracy rate which divorce case decisions will fall into three categories: 'approval', 'revelsal and 'approval with correction'. This software in question is still in development phase. The AI-based Legal Assistant Adalet Hanım is a system with legal analysis, legal text editing and virtual office management capabilities (Buluz, 2019, p. 39).

Evaluation Of the Use of Artificial Intelligence in The Turkish Judiciary

AI can make positive and negative contributions to judicial and legal processes. In addition, AI systems attract attention in terms of effectiveness, efficiency and economy. Especially due to the disruptions in traditional public administration that emerged in the COVID-19 period, the way for the utilization of AI-based systems in public administration has been opened. Given the impact of COVID-19 on the delivery of justice, the judiciary's approach to non-intrusive AI involvement should also be positive. Considering the success of courts in facilitating virtual hearings through UYAP and the introduction of e-filing during the pandemic, the contributions of AI to the courts can be invaluable. Although AI has great advantages, it can become vulnerable to interventions such as hacking, cyber-attacks, etc. In addition, if the decisions made by an AI software are used, the decisions made by humans may come to a point where they are not considered important, and the quality of the decisions made by humans may decrease over time. The contributions that AI will make to the justice system should be well considered. AI can be useful if it increases the quality of human decisions and prevents unnecessary loss of time and cost. It is possible to think that AI systems can have a positive impact on judicial processes, especially when evaluated in terms of "procedural economy", which envisages the resolution of a case in the shortest possible time, with less bureaucratic procedures and in a fair manner. The postponement of the case is a situation that must be overcome in terms of justice. By using predictive analytics for reconciliation and visualization, AI can reduce the time in which cases wait in courts and help courts to force the parties to an out-of-court settlement. An AI system that reads, understands and summarizes the content of documents can make the court's job easier. Human errors can be based on many external and internal factors, and even if an error is noticed, it is very difficult to notice the reason. However, as long as AI systems have an algorithm trained with accurate data, the chance of making a mistake is very low, and even if they make a mistake, it is easier to understand the reason compared to humans. AI will be very efficient if used with patience and caution in the judiciary. It is very important to teach the inferences and logic of decisions to the machine during the algorithm design and construction phase. Electronic management information systems (e-MIS) tools derived from AI algorithms can accelerate case flow management, prevent processes that slow down justice, and facilitate administrative aspects. It seems more appropriate to establish a structure where AI assists human decision making processes (Efe, 2022, pp. 112-113).

The utilization of digitalization and AI-based applications in courts is increasing day by day. The duty of the judiciary is to ensure that justice is served in every case. Public prosecutors and judges try to conduct a fair trial by processing the information given to them or obtained. The right to a fair trial aims to guarantee that each individual is treated fairly and equally in trials. It allows people to actively join cases, give evidence, demand witnesses and defend themselves (Ulaşan, 2024, p. 158). Judges use techniques of interpreting laws and rules of logic in decision making processes. For example, the principle of legality in crime and punishment appears as a guarantee for the safety of individuals' rights and freedom. With this principle, the boundaries of the freedom to impose punishment are drawn by determining the crimes and the sanctions to be applied to these crimes in advance. This means that since the crime is defined in the article of the law and the type and amount of the sanction are determined, the judge's discretionary power is limited (Şenyüz, 2022, p. 11). The criteria sought for the principle of legality to be accepted as valid can be listed as; "principle of certainty", "prohibition of analogy", "prohibition of retroactivity", "prohibition of punishment based on customary law" and "prohibition of stipulating criminal and criminal law sanctions with regulatory acts of the administration" (Karaca, 2022). These situations make the job of AI easier in the decision-making process. In addition, AI systems can have a positive impact on judicial processes, especially when viewed from the perspective of "procedural economy", which envisages a quick completion of the case, less bureaucratic procedures and a fair resolution. The quick and definitive resolution of disputes between individuals is important in terms of procedural economy as well as protecting the parties to the case against grievances that may arise due to the prolongation of the case (Yılmaz, 2019, p. 274). The result is reached by applying these rules to the concrete case systematically. The verdict is reached by applying legal rules to the concrete case. Therefore, it can be said that the information processing processes in law should be compatible with working methods of AI-based systems. Law is based on practical reasoning, which involves applying a set of logical steps resulting from applying law to real situations to reach a decision. The decision making requires knowledge for reasonable conclusions. Judgmental reasoning is considered a type of knowledge generated by the process of reasoning. The way AI adapts to judgmental reasoning occurs in 2 main methods. Rule-based reasoning (RBR) and case-based reasoning (CBR) occurred as 2 significant and complementary reasoning methodologies in AI-based systems (Duttai & Bonissone, 1993, p. 163).

Mainly RBR utilizes inductive rules to decide whether problems should be inspected, while CBR uses similarity-based matching to discover the most similar cases to the new problem on a case-by-case basis (Lee, 2008). When codes are used to decide on a case, an RBR inference engine can produce a solution by adapting the legal definitions and penalties given by laws, constitutions and regulations to the events. Rules are determined by laws, constitutions, regulations, etc. In Türkiye, the administrative jurisdiction is primarily written with numerous legal procedures. RBR seems appropriate for the Turkish administrative jurisdiction. But it is unavoidable that some values which can be created by administrative courts to meet the evolving needs arising from the lack of codification of administrative law will be taken into account in the judicial process. Decisions regarding the unification of conflicting decisions are compulsory. Provided that a rule is not totally understandable, AI CBR can be seen as the database by finding cases similar to previous cases with case law. Also, hybrid systems can be utilized effectively in Türkiye (Ulaşan, 2023c, pp. 287-288). For instance, the applicability of AI in the Turkish criminal law seems difficult, especially when considering basic principles such as the right to a fair trial, transparency, responsibility, data security and impartiality in criminal proceedings. However, thanks to certain application areas and support mechanisms, AI can be used to assist the Turkish criminal law. AI systems can be used in areas such as decision support systems, analysis and prediction processes or data management in the Turkish criminal law. AI can be used as a decision support system to help judges and public prosecutors make decisions. Such systems can analyze certain judicial decisions according to the types of crimes and provide sample decisions to judges and public prosecutors. It is possible to use AI systems as a supporting tool, especially in crime analysis, judicial case analysis and event prediction processes. When making a decision, judges shape their decisions by looking at court precedents and doctrine, which are considered as secondary sources, in addition to the primary source, such as the law, constitution, etc. The practice of utilization of court precedents allows the judge to save both time and effort. This method serves similar practices regarding similar events, equal justice, and unity and harmony in court decisions. In Türkiye, precedents are not the main source, but auxiliary sources. Therefore, the decision given by the court is not binding for the other court as a rule; however, in practice, judges give importance to precedents. It is almost as important as the primary source for both lawyers and the Supreme Court. However, the decisions of the Supreme Court of Appeals to combine precedents are binding and judges are obliged to comply with them (Gedik & Koç, 2009, pp. 157-158). In these matters, AI can perform legal researches in a much shorter time due to its data processing capacity. For example, AI can find the relevant section in the entire case law in a very short time. In addition, AI can show the basic elements of the case, such as the provisions to be applied in the case according to the claims of the parties. AI can also be used for secondary tasks. Examples of this situation are the direct transcription of verbal statements in trials from voice to text and the ability to hold hearings remotely. In addition, the identities of the parties can be verified with facial recognition technology in remote hearings. In terms of our country, since the remote hearing application has started in our courts due to the special conditions of the COVID-19, this system has contributed to the judiciary. Apart from this, it is possible for AI judges to decide on some disputes that are not very complex. The first step on the path to AI judges may be internet-based and technically-oriented issues or some consumer disputes (Yılmaz O. G., 2021, pp. 403-407). AI can contribute to criminal law in functions such as analyzing crime rates, mapping and predicting crimes on a local and national basis. Such analysis can allow police and other law enforcement agencies to better manage their resources. However, this requires a data processing process that is unbiased and in accordance with ethical values. The fact that AI makes predictions based on biases in past data can create problems in terms of the principle of fair trial (Kılıç, 2024).

In order for AI to be generally implemented in the Turkish law, an ethical and legal framework needs to be established in Türkiye. This framework should include principles such as fair treatment of the offender, confidentiality, impartiality, data security and transparency. In particular, since erroneous results or biased data analysis during the process of determining guilt can have serious effects on the freedom of the individual, it is essential that these systems operate with full transparency and are under human control. In addition, since AI is not expected to operate with full autonomy in legal processes, it is necessary to use it within certain limits and under human control (Yılmaz O. G., 2021).

Under the General Directorate of Information Processing within the Ministry of Justice, the "Big Data and Artificial Intelligence Applications Branch Directorate" is one of the institutional structures in the field of AI within the national framework. In the studies to be carried out by the Big Data and Artificial Intelligence branch for the transfer of archive files to UYAP, "Enforcement Document Classification" under the title of "Artificial Intelligence in Enforcement" is provided to minimize human workload and automatically detect the relevant document type, "Important Slang and Object Detection from Image", which detects slang and offensive words in the texts in the image in order to eliminate the confusion and problems experienced while uploading visuals of movable and immovable properties related to the tender to the E-Sales Portal, and AI-supported chatbot applications are provided via the E-Sales

Portal, Lawyer Portal, Institution Portal and Citizen Portal. In the referral of the files appealed in the civil courts to the regional courts of justice, training data was collected according to the selected division of labor information, and in the light of the collected data, an information message was given to the judge during the division of labor selection, thus enabling an AI-supported selection opportunity. The judge will be able to refer the file to the appeal with the division of labor suggested by AI or with the division of labor he/she chooses. With the implementation of this project, the workload in regional courts of justice will be reduced by ensuring that the file is sent to the competent department and therefore the trial periods can be shortened. In criminal courts, the failure to correctly identify and enter the different types of files opened depending on the documents added to the files of different types of work causes significant loss of rights. For example, if the petition for objection to arrest is recorded as other and the objection is accepted, no release document will be created, and this will cause data inconsistency between the prison and the court. Again, since the decisions for the removal of arrest, judicial control and judicial control decisions are actions to be carried out immediately, it is of great importance to open the files in the correct type in such actions. With this project, the correct workflow will be ensured by preventing the user from selecting the incoming request incorrectly or the sending unit from selecting the wrong document. In addition, the disruptions experienced during the investigation phase and the workload received as a request for correction will be prevented. It is an AI service developed to prevent errors and complications in organization information name entries to the UYAP Information System. This project aims to prevent human errors in the files of the Chief Public Prosecutor's Office, to prevent incomplete data entries, to increase the accuracy of statistical data and to ensure the reliability of reports requested by auditing institutions (Adalet Bakanlığı Bilgi İşlem Genel Müdürlüğü, 2024).

CONCLUSION

Today, technological advances happen at a dizzying pace. This process, which started with the industrial revolution, has accelerated with computers and the internet and has reached a dizzying point with the emergence of tools that learn and think like people and this process has caused the role of people in law to begin to alter. The AI technology is a system that can perform certain tasks by imitating human intelligence so as to fulfill orders and improve itself by repeating the information it collects. In recent years, the developments of the AI technology have led to a growth in features and the ability of computers to store millions of data efficiently and the use of the information effectively. These developments have economic, cultural, social and even artistic effects, and their echoes are felt in almost every area of human life. A society should accept AI applications in the legal system only if there is a possibility of providing better social welfare than the current one. AI always contains this possibility. Law is one of the areas where this possibility emerges. AI has the potential to process data and countless variables that are too large for a human to reason about very quickly, and can contribute to the prevention of crime and serve to conduct trials with fewer resources and more efficiently. Due to the workload of the courts, structural difficulties in the judicial organization and insufficiencies of judges, there are disruptions in the justice system. It is seen that AI systems have exhibited noteworthy advances about judgment.

AI should be designed to be prepared for risks that may arise suddenly and should contribute to the enhancement of processes in courts. Since every case obtains its own characteristics, the AI-based tools should be planned in a way that prevents procedural procedures from being faulty, prevents pointless actions, and prevents malevolent behaviors that try to prolong the duration of cases, thus contributing to the achievement of consistency and speed goals in the trial. AI needs human intervention at appropriate times. The arrival of AI systems will not reduce the need for judges and public prosecutors. On the contrary, AI will emphasize the quality of judges and public prosecutors and their importance in the justice system. For example, before the widespread use of cameras, the fact that painters could convey what they saw in the same way was an indication of the success of painters. However, the profession of painting did not disappear after cameras became widespread. On the contrary, while painters who depicted exactly what they saw lost their importance, creative painters gained more value than before. Painting began to transform into a field where those who added their own perspective to their paintings were valued. The utilization of AI-based tools in the legal system will have the same effect. AI will develop and take away the repetitive and uncreative work of judges and public prosecutors, creating the opportunity for them to think creatively and improve themselves. With the utilization of AI-based tools in the legal system, there might be a decrease in the number of judges and public prosecutors. However, there will be an increase in the quality of judges and public prosecutors.

Legal technology is rapidly developing in the world and the research on the ethical and legal aspects of new technologies is increasing. Many states are looking for ways to improve their justice mechanisms with AI. Some of these states are the United States and China. China, in particular, has started to actively use AI systems in courts. Adaption and advantages of new technologies are very important for the development of states and the welfare of the people. Only societies and states that can adapt to the times can live their lives in prosperity. It is very important to raise awareness in every segment of society by conducting studies on future technologies and their social and political effects, to provide an education that will broaden the horizons of the new generation of students so that they can create new jobs of the future, to pave the way for growth by providing the necessary support to companies, and to save money by using new technologies and to increase the efficiency of the public.

In the world, AI-supported systems help justice services become faster and more effective, especially in administrative tasks such as data processing and file management. The use of similar systems has increased in Türkiye. It is aimed to provide effective and fast public services by integrating AI systems into systems such as UYAP. In addition, AI systems can support judges and public prosecutors in the decision-making process in order to reach more stable and accurate decisions. AI systems should initially be designed to support judges and public prosecutors rather than making completely independent decisions. Smart court applications used in countries such as China facilitate the work of judges and speed up the decision-making process. In Türkiye, such systems can first be useful for classifying cases or analyzing previous decisions made in similar cases. This can reduce the workload of judges and provide a fairer trial process. The combination of AI systems with the Turkish legal system can increase the speed and consistency of the judicial process. It can facilitate the work of judges, especially those with intensive workloads, and reduce errors by providing standard decision suggestions in similar cases. In addition, automatic data analysis performed by AI systems can reduce long-lasting trial processes. However, the cost of integrating AI into the justice mechanism is high. In addition, high budgets may be required for issues such as software development, data security, and infrastructure compatibility in the justice system of AI. In addition, in the process of making these systems compatible with Turkish law, attention should be paid to sensitive issues such as the safety of personal data and human rights. AI-based tools cannot currently be considered as independent decision-makers such as judges and public prosecutors in Turkish law. For now, AI can provide objective data analysis and legal support without interfering with elements based on the conscientious opinion of judges and public prosecutors. If AI technologies are adopted in the field of legal education, a new generation of lawyers will emerge. In Türkiye, AI systems may function as decision support systems rather than independent decision-makers in the short term. When the necessary legal regulations are made for the integration of this technology, the efficiency and consistency of the justice system will increase.

In summary, the combination of AI-based systems with the Turkish legal system includes both potential benefits and significant challenges. The inclusion of technology in judicial and legal processes can provide significant contributions in terms of speed, efficiency and accuracy. The use of AI, especially in areas such as decision support systems, big data analytics and arbitration/mediation, has the potential to alleviate the current workload and provide faster solutions to the parties. However, attention should be paid to ethical and legal frameworks for the combination of AI-based systems into the legal system. Transparency, justice and impartiality should be valid for AI systems. Resolving issues such as data privacy, algorithmic biases and legal liability should be a prerequisite for the use of AI. The Turkish National Artificial Intelligence Strategy supports the use of AI-based applications in various sectors, as well as preparing the ground for possible applications in law. Provided that ethical standards, data security and human control issues are overcome, the way can be opened for the application of AI in the legal world. However, the ability of AI-based systems to make autonomous decisions should be considered as a long-term goal. In the Turkish law, the application of AI technologies must be under human control, within certain limits and in accordance with legal principles. If this technology is used correctly, the benefits of AI systems can be maximized while fundamental human rights and fair trial principles can be secured.

REFERENCES

Adalet Bakanlığı, T. C. (2023, December 12). *Uzlaştırmacı Uyap*. Retrieved October 31, 2024, from https://uzlastirmaci.uyap.gov.tr

Adalet Bakanlığı Bilgi İşlem Genel Müdürlüğü. (2024). *UYAP Yapay Zeka Uygulamaları İle Güçleniyor.* Ankara: T.C. Adalet Bakanlığı. Retrieved November 23, 2024, from https://portal.uyap.gov.tr/duyuru-detay/

Akçakaya, D. (2017). E-Devlet Anlayışı Ve Türk Kamu Yönetiminde Edevlet Uygulamaları. *Yüzüncü Yıl Üniversitesi İktisadi ve İdari Bilimler Fakültesi Dergisi*, (3), 8–31.

Bilgin, H. (2022). Yapay Zekânın Mahkeme Kararlarında Kullanımına Uluslararası Bir Bakış Ve Robot Hâkimler Hakkında Düşünceler. *İnönü Üniversitesi Hukuk Fakültesi Dergisi, 13*(2), 405-419.

Birtane, Ş. (2024). Hakime Yardımcı Yapay Zekâ. *Türkiye Adalet Akademisi Dergisi*, (59), 233–272. DOI: 10.54049/taad.1515051

Brunette, A. (2024, October 25). *Humanizing Justice: The transformational impact of AI in courts, from filing to sentencing*. Retrieved October 30, 2019, from Thomsonreuters: https://www.thomsonreuters.com/en-us/posts/ai-in-courts/humanizing-justice/

Buluz, B. (2019). Türkiye'de Avukatlık ve Teknoloji. In Çetin, S. (Ed.), *Yapay zekâ Çağında Hukuk.* Ankara ve İzmir Baroları Çalıştay Raporu.

Çakır, F., Karaduman, M., & Zobar, G. (2024, September 06). *Adalet Bakanı Tunç: Yargı hizmetlerinin hızlandırılması anlamında da yapay zekanın kullanılması lazım.* Retrieved October 31, 2024, from Anadolu Ajansı: https://www.aa.com.tr/tr/gundem/adalet-bakani-tunc-yargi-hizmetlerinin-hizlandirilmasi-anlaminda-da-yapay-zekanin-kullanilmasi-lazim/3323172

Çamur, Ö., & Aydın, A. (2022). Yeni Kamu Yönetimi Anlayışının Etik Temelleri ve Kamu Yönetiminde Etik Yönetimin Gelişmesi Üzerindeki Etkisi. *Denetişim*, 25, 148–159.

Coşkun, F., & Gülleroğlu, H. D. (2021). Yapay Zekanın Tarih İçindeki Gelişimi ve Eğitimde Kullanılması. [JFES]. *Ankara University Journal of Faculty of Educational Sciences*, 54(3), 947–966.

Demirel, D. (2015). Üçüncü yol politikalarında yeni kamu yönetiminin izleri. *Atatürk Üniversitesi İktisadi ve İdari Bilimler Dergisi*, 29(1), 137–153.

Deutsche Welle. (2023, January 20). *How China's AI is automating the legal system.* Retrieved from https://www.taiwannews.com.tw/news/4787354

Duttai, S., & Bonissone, P. P. (1993). Integrating case- and rule-based reasoning. *International Journal of Approximate Reasoning*, 8(3), 163–203. DOI: 10.1016/0888-613X(93)90001-T

Efe, A. (2022). Yargısal ve Hukuki Süreçlerde Yapay Zekâ Kullanan Araçlar Üzerine Bir Araştırma. *Bilgi Yönetimi*, 5(1), 92–117. DOI: 10.33721/by.971873

Gedik, F., & Koç, E. (2009). Hüküm Kurma ve İçtihat. *Ankara Barosu Dergisi*, (2), 157–163.

Harris, B. (2018, July 11). *Could an AI Ever Replace a Judge in Court.* Retrieved from World Government Summit: https://www.worldgovernmentsummit.org/observer/articles/2017/detail/could-an-ai-ever-replace-a-judge-in-court

Hood, C. (1991). A public management for all seasons? *Public Administration Review*, (69), 3–19.

Hürriyet. (2023, September 03). *Yargıtay Başkanı Mehmet Akarca: 'Yapay zekâ' karar yazacak.* Retrieved October 31, 2024, from https://www.hurriyet.com.tr/gundem/yargitay-baskani-mehmet-akarca-yapay-zeka-karar-yazacak-42324616

İstanbul. (2019). *Ankara ve İzmir Baroları Çalıştay Raporu.* Yapay Zekâ Çağında Hukuk.

Kandır, M. O. (2023, August 13). *Türk Hukukunda Yapay Zeka Kullanımı.* Retrieved from Hukukvebilisim: https://hukukvebilisim.org/turk-hukukunda-yapay-zeka-kullanimi/

Karaca, E. (2022, Nisan 25). *Kanunilik İlkesi Bağlamında Belirlilik ve Kıyas Yasağı.* Retrieved November 02, 2024, from https://blog.lexpera.com.tr/kanunilik-ilkesi-baglaminda-belirlilik-ve-kiyas-yasagi/

Kılıç, B. (2024, August 06). *Türkiye'nin 2024 Yılı Ulusal Yapay Zekâ Stratejisi: Geleceğe Dönük Bir Projeksiyon.* Retrieved November 03, 2024, from https://hukukvebilisim.org/turkiyenin-2024-yili-ulusal-yapay-zeka-stratejisi-gelecege-donuk-bir-projeksiyon/

Lapsley, I. (1999). Accounting and the New Public Management: Instruments of Substantive Effiency or a Rationalising Modernity? *Financial Accountability & Management*, 15(3-4), 201–207. DOI: 10.1111/1468-0408.00081

Lee, G. H. (2008). Rule-based and case-based reasoning approach for internal audit of bank. *Knowledge-Based Systems*, 21(2), 140–147. DOI: 10.1016/j.knosys.2007.04.001

Moor, J. (2006). The Dartmouth College Artificial Intelligence Conference: The Next Fifty Years. *AI Magazine*, 27(4), 87–91.

Önder, M., & Saygılı, H. (2018). Yapay Zekâ ve Kamu Yönetimine Yansımaları. *Türk İdare Dergisi*, 2(487), 629–670.

Şenyüz, D. (2022). *Vergi Ceza Hukuku* (12. ed.). Bursa: Ekin Yayınevi.

Sümer, S. Y. (2021). Ceza Yargılamasının Geleceği: Robot Hakim. *Dokuz Eylül Üniversitesi Hukuk Fakültesi Dergisi*, 23(2), 1543–1591.

Töngel, B. (2024, July 11). *Hukukta Yapay Zeka Kullanımı: Genel Bakış*. Retrieved from Blog.kalem.ai: https://blog.kalem.ai/hukukta-yapay-zeka-kullanimi/

TRAI. (2024). *Türkiye Yapay Zeka İnisiyatif 2024 Çalıştayı Raporu.* Türkye Yapay Zeka İnisiyatifi (TRAI). Retrieved October 31, 2024, from https://turkiye.ai/wp-content/uploads/2024/07/TRAI-2024-Calistay-Raporu.pdf

TRAI. (2024). *Yapay Zekâ Etik İlkeleri Ve Hukuki Düzenlemeler Raporu.* Türkiye Yapay Zekâ İnisiyatifi. Retrieved October 31, 2024, from https://turkiye.ai/wp-content/uploads/2024/06/TRAI-Yapay-Zeka-Etik-Ilkeleri-ve-Hukuki-Duzenlemeler-Raporu-Mayis-2024-5.pdf

Turan, T., Kemaloğlu, N., & Küçüksille, E. C. (2020). Hukuk'ta Yapay Zeka: Çalışmalar ve Gelecek Öngörüleri. *Mehmet Akif Ersoy Üniversitesi Fen Bilimleri Enstitüsü Dergisi*, 11(2), 246–255. DOI: 10.29048/makufebed.748843

Ulaşan, F. (2023). The Dark Side Of Artificial Intelligence On The Basis Of Public Administration. . *Toplum Ekonomi Ve Yönetim Dergisi, 4*(Özel), 301-323.

Ulaşan, F. (2023a). Koronavirüsle Mücadelede Yapay Zekânın Yerinin Kamu Yönetimi Temelinde Değerlendirilmesi. *3.International Mediterranean Congress* (pp. 109-123). Mersin: Iksad Global.

Ulaşan, F. (2023b). The Impact of Korean Local Government's Public Health and Urban Planning Policies in Combating COVID-19. *Kent Akademisi*(16).

Ulaşan, F. (2023c). *The Possibility of Using Artificial Intelligence for Turkish Administrative Jurisdiction*. İksad Yayınevi.

Ulaşan, F. (2023d). The Use of Artificial Intelligence in Educational Institutions: Social Consequences of Artificial Intelligence in Education. *Korkut Ata Türkiyat Araştırmaları Dergisi*(Özel Sayı 1), 1305-1324.

Ulaşan, F. (2023e). The Use Of Artificial Intelligence In The Defense System Within The Framework Of The Policy Making Cycle: The Case Of The United States. *Uluslararası Toplumsal Bilimler Dergisi*, 7(3), 517–535.

Ulaşan, F. (2024). Contributions Of Declaration Of Ethics For Turkish Judiciary To The Right To A Fair Trial In Terms Of Effective Participation In Trials. *Adalet Dergisi*, (72), 155–177. DOI: 10.57083/adaletdergisi.1483988

Uzun, M. M., Yildiz, M., & Onder, M. (2022). Big questions of artificial intelligence (AI) in public administration and policy. *SİYASAL: Journal of Political Sciences*, 31(2), 423–442. DOI: 10.26650/siyasal.2022.31.1121900

Vasdani, T. (2019). *From Estonian AI judges to robot mediators in Canada, U.K.* Retrieved from Lexisnexis: https://www.lexisnexis.ca/en-ca/ihc/2019-06/from-estonian-ai-judges-to-robot-mediators-in-canada-uk.page

Vasdani, T. (2020, 05 February). *Robot justice: China's use of Internet courts*. Retrieved from LexisNexis: https://www.lexisnexis.ca/en-ca/ihc/2019-06/from-estonian-ai-judges-to-robot-mediators-in-canada-uk.page

Yalçın, A. (2024). Türkiye'de Kamu Kurumlarınn Toplum İçin Geliştirdiği Yapay Zekâ Uygulamaları. *İstanbul Aydın Üni versitesi Sosyal Bilimler Dergisi, 16*(2), 185-215.

Yargıtay. (2023, July 19). *Yargıtayın Kurumsal Kapasitesinin Güçlendirilmesi Projesi Kapanış Konferansı" Gerçekleştirildi*. Retrieved October 31, 2024, from Türkiye Cumhuriyeti Yargıtay Başkanlığı: https://www.yargitay.gov.tr/icerik/1727/yargitayin-kurumsal-kapasitesinin-guclendirilmesi-projesi-kapanis-konferansi-gerceklestirildi

Yılmaz, D. (2019). "Usul Ekonomisi İlkesi" Çerçevesinde Türk İdari Yargılama Usulünde Sözlülük İlkesine İlişkin Bazı Değerlendirmeler. *Ankara Hacı Bayram Veli Üniversitesi Hukuk Fakültesi Dergisi*, 23(2), 267–320. DOI: 10.34246/ahbvuhfd.585054

Yılmaz, O. G. (2021). Yargı Uygulamasinda Yapay Zekâ Kullanımı - Yapay Zekâ Hâkim Cübbesini Giyebilecek mi? *Adalet Dergisi*, (66), 379–415.

Zafar, A. (2024). Balancing the scale: navigating ethical and practical challenges of artificial intelligence (AI) integration in legal practices. *Discover Artificial Intelligence, 4*(27).

Compilation of References

Abane, D., & Phinaitrup, B. (2022). *Performance management practices and motivation in developing countries: A further validation of the public service motivation construct in Ghana*. Management and Economics Research Journal.

Abbas, S. W., Hamid, M., Alkanhel, R., & Abdallah, H. A. (2023). Official Statistics and Big Data Processing with Artificial Intelligence: Capacity Indicators for Public Sector Organizations.*Systems*, 11(8), 424. DOI: 10.3390/systems11080424

Abduljabbar, R., Dia, H., Liyanage, S., & Bagloee, S. A. (2019). Applications of Artificial Intelligence in Transport: An Overview.*Sustainability (Basel)*, 11(1), 189. DOI: 10.3390/su11010189

Abioye, S. O., Oyedele, L. O., Akanbi, L., Ajayi, A., Davila Delgado, J. M., Bilal, M., Akinade, O. O., & Ahmed, A. (2021). Artificial intelligence in the construction industry: A review of present status, opportunities and future challenges.*Journal of Building Engineering*, 44, 103299. DOI: 10.1016/j.jobe.2021.103299

Abro, A. A., Talpur, M. S. H., & Jumani, A. K. (2023). Natural Language Processing Challenges and Issues: A Literature Review.*Gazi University Journal of Science*, 36(4), 4. Advance online publication. DOI: 10.35378/gujs.1032517

Adaga, E. M., Egieya, Z. E., Ewuga, S. K., Abdul, A. A., & Abrahams, T. O. (2024). A comprehensive review of ethical practices in banking and finance.*Finance & Accounting Research Journal*, 6(1), 1–20. DOI: 10.51594/farj.v6i1.705

Adalet Bakanlığı Bilgi İşlem Genel Müdürlüğü. (2024). *UYAP Yapay Zeka Uygulamaları İle Güçleniyor.* Ankara: T.C. Adalet Bakanlığı. Retrieved November 23, 2024, from https://portal.uyap.gov.tr/duyuru-detay/

Adalet Bakanlığı, T. C. (2023, December 12). *Uzlaştırmacı Uyap*. Retrieved October 31, 2024, from https://uzlastirmaci.uyap.gov.tr

Adawiyah, R., & Haerah, M. (2021). Implementation of artificial intelligence: The use of technology on diffable public service in Banyuwangi. *IOP Conference Series: Earth and Environment, 1019*, 012016. https://doi.org/DOI: 10.1088/1755-1315/717/1/012046

Afzal, A., Khan, S., Daud, S., Ahmad, Z., & Butt, A. (2023). Addressing the Digital

Agba, M. S. (2023). Agba, Michael Sunday, GracArtificial Intelligence and Public Management and Governance in Developed and Developing Market Economies . *Journal of Public Administration, Policy and Governance Research* .

Agba, M. S., Agba, G. E., & Obeten, A. W. (2023). Artificial Intelligence and Public Management and Governance in Developed and. *Journal of Public Administration. Policy and Governance Research*, 1(2), 1–14.

Ahangar, M. N., Ahmed, Q. Z., Khan, F. A., & Hafeez, M. (2021). A survey of autonomous vehicles: Enabling communication technologies and challenges.*Sensors (Basel)*, 21(706), 706. Advance online publication. DOI: 10.3390/s21030706 PMID: 33494191

Ahn, M. J., & Chen, Y. C. (2020, June). Artificial intelligence in government: Potentials, challenges, and the future. In *Proceedings of the 21st Annual International Conference on Digital Government Research* (pp. 243–252). DOI: 10.1145/3396956.3398260

Aidonojie, P. A., Ikubanni, O. O., Okuonghae, N., & Oyedeji, A. I. (2021). The challenges and relevance of technology in administration of justice and human security in nigeria: Amidst the covid19 pandemic.*Cógito (Salvador)*, 13(3), 149–171.

Aiello, G., & Pavesi, G. (2022). Artificial intelligence in public administration: A systematic review.*Government Information Quarterly*, 40, e102751.

Aizenberg, E., & Hoven, J. (2020). Designing for human rights in AI.*Big Data & Society*, 7(2), 2053951720949566. DOI: 10.1177/2053951720949566

Ajaegbu, C. S. (2020). The Problems of the Deficiency of Data Protection Law in Nigeria. *Chinaza Shalom Ajaegbu, 'The Problems of the Deficiency of DInternational Journal of Comparative Law and Legal Philosophy* .

Akçakaya, D. (2017). E-Devlet Anlayışı Ve Türk Kamu Yönetiminde Edevlet Uygulamaları.*Yüzüncü Yıl Üniversitesi İktisadi ve İdari Bilimler Fakültesi Dergisi*, (3), 8–31.

Akhtar, M., & Moridpour, S. (2021). A Review of Traffic Congestion Prediction Using Artificial Intelligence.*Journal of Advanced Transportation*, 2021, 1–18. DOI: 10.1155/2021/8878011

Akinrinola, O., Okoye, C.C., Ofodile, O.C., & Ugochukwu, C.E. (2024). Navigating and reviewing ethical dilemmas in AI development: Strategies for transparency, fairness, and accountability. *GSC Advanced Research and Reviews, 18*(3), 050–058.

Alazzabi, W. Y. E., Mustafa, H., & Karage, A. I. (2023). Risk management, top management support, internal audit activities and fraud mitigation.*Journal of Financial Crime*, 30(2), 569–582. DOI: 10.1108/JFC-11-2019-0147

Alenezi, M. (2022). Understanding Digital Government Transformation. Cornell University. https://doi.org//arXiv.2202.01797DOI: 10.48550

Alfian, A., Ritchi, H., & Adrianto, Z. (2023). Fraud analytics practices in public-sector transactions: A systematic review.*Journal of Public Budgeting, Accounting & Financial Management*, 35(5), 685–710. DOI: 10.1108/JPBAFM-11-2022-0175

Alghamdi, M., Alsolami, R., Alghamdi, W., & Almehmadi, Y. (2020). Personalizing government services through AI: Opportunities and challenges. In *2020 4th International Conference on Computer and Communication Systems (ICCCS)* (pp. 595–599). IEEE.

AlGosaibi, A. A., Abdul, R. W. S., AlOthman, A. F., & AlHamed, S. (2020). Developing an Intelligent Framework for Improving the Quality of Service in the Government Organizations in the Kingdom of Saudi Arabia[IJACSA]. *International Journal of Advanced Computer Science and Applications*, 11(12). Advance online publication. DOI: 10.14569/IJACSA.2020.0111233

Al-Guesbi, H. (2020). A new concept of adaptive complexity.[PEN]. *Periodicals of Engineering and Natural Sciences*, 8, 1687–1700. DOI: 10.21533/PEN.V8I3.1580.G655

Alhosani, K., & Alhashmi, S. M. (2024). A review of the opportunities, challenges, and benefits of AI innovation in government services.*Discover Artificial Intelligence*, 4(1), 18. DOI: 10.1007/s44163-024-00111-w

Ali, O., Abdelbaki, W., Shrestha, A., Elbasi, E., Alryalat, M. A. A., & Dwivedi, Y. K. (2023). A systematic literature review of artificial intelligence in the healthcare sector: Benefits, challenges, methodologies, and functionalities.*Journal of Innovation & Knowledge*, 8(1), 100333. DOI: 10.1016/j.jik.2023.100333

Aljahdali, S., & Xu, C. (2013). Resource allocation techniques and security design in Infrastructure as a Service (IaaS): Enhancing multi-tenancy security in cloud computing.*Journal of Cloud Computing Advances, Security, and Applications*, 10(2), 55–67.

Aljazeera. (2020, December 8). *Nigerian intelligence bought tool to spy on citizens: Report.* Retrieved from Aljazeera News: https://www.businesstoday.in/technology/news/story/pegasus-spyware-is-the-nso-groups-technology-good-or-evil-301878-2021-07-20

Allam, Z., & Dhunny, Z. A. (2019). On big data, artificial intelligence, and smart cities.*Cities (London, England)*, 89, 80–91. DOI: 10.1016/j.cities.2019.01.032

Allam, Z., & Jones, D. (2018). Towards a circular economy: A case study of waste conversion into housing units in Cotonou, Benin.*Urban Science (Basel, Switzerland)*, 2(4), 118. DOI: 10.3390/urbansci2040118

Allam, Z., & Newman, P. (2018). Redefining the smart city: Culture, metabolism, and governance.*Smart Cities*, 1(1), 4–25. DOI: 10.3390/smartcities1010002

Allen, P. (2001). A COMPLEX SYSTEMS APPROACH TO LEARNING IN ADAPTIVE NETWORKS.*International Journal of Innovation Management*, 05(2), 149–180. DOI: 10.1142/S136391960100035X

Al-Mashhadi, A. S. J. (2021). Review on development of the internal control system. *technology, 31*, 35.

Amiri, Z., Heidari, A., Jafari, N., & Hosseinzadeh, M. (2024). Deep study on autonomous learning techniques for complex pattern recognition in interconnected information systems.*Computer Science Review*, 54, 100666. DOI: 10.1016/j.cosrev.2024.100666

Androutsopoulou, A., Karacapilidis, N., Loukis, E., & Charalabidis, Y. (2019). Transforming the communication between citizens and government through AI-guided chatbots.*Government Information Quarterly*, 36(2), 358–367. DOI: 10.1016/j.giq.2018.10.001

Aneesh, A. (2002). Technologically coded authority: The post-industrial decline in bureaucratic hierarchies.

Aneesh, A. (2009). Global labor: Algocratic modes of organization.*Sociological Theory*, 27(4), 347–370. DOI: 10.1111/j.1467-9558.2009.01352.x

Aoki, N. (2020). An experimental study of public trust in AI chatbots in the public sector.*Government Information Quarterly*, 37(4), 101490. DOI: 10.1016/j.giq.2020.101490

Application of Artificial Intelligence in EPA Homeland Security. (2022). https://cfpub.epa.gov/si/si_public_record_report.cfm?Lab=CESER&dirEntryId=357842

Arcaini, P., Riccobene, E., & Scandurra, P. (2017). Formal Design and Verification of Self-Adaptive Systems with Decentralized Control.[TAAS]. *ACM Transactions on Autonomous and Adaptive Systems*, 11(4), 1–35. DOI: 10.1145/3019598

Ardabili, B. R., Pazho, A. D., Noghre, G. A., Neff, C., Bhaskararayuni, S. D., Ravindran, A., Reid, S., & Tabkhi, H. (2023). Understanding Policy and Technical Aspects of AI-enabled Smart Video Surveillance to Address Public Safety.*Computational Urban Science*, 3(1), 21. DOI: 10.1007/s43762-023-00097-8

Arifin, A., & Afriansyah, M. (2024). Optimizing credit score assessment for supervision and administrative control of e-government-based personnel analysts. *Proceedings of the 4th International Conference on Social Science, Humanity and Public Health (ICoSHIP 2023)*. DOI: 10.4108/eai.18-11-2023.2342550

Ariyani, N., Wibowo, I., & Guswandi, G. (2023). The Influence of Leadership Style and Organizational Culture on the Performance of Functional Employees Through Motivation Within the General Secretariat Regional Representative Council of the Republic of Indonesia.*Journal of Social Research*, 2(7), 2491–2506. DOI: 10.55324/josr.v2i7.1218

Arnaout, T., & Virani, R. (2024). Shaping the future of healthcare in British Columbia: Establishing provincial clinical governance for responsible deployment of AI tools. *Healthcare Management Forum*. https://doi.org/DOI: 10.1177/08404704231154085

Article 10, African Charter on the Rights and Welfare of the Child . (n.d.).

Article 12, Universal Declaration of Human Rights. (n.d.).

Article 17, International Covenants on People and Domestic Rights. (n.d.).

Asilyan, L., & Necrasova, I. (2023). The essence of state coercion is in the mechanism of legal regulation. SHS Web of Conferences, Berglind, N., Fadia, A., & Isherwood, T. (2022). The potential value of AI—and how governments could look to capture it. *McKinsey. URL*.:https://www.mckinsey.com/industries/public-and-social-sector/our-insights/the-potential-value-of-AI, *and. how governments could look to capture it.*

Association for Computing Machinery US Public Policy Council. (2017). Principles for algorithmic transparency and accountability https://www.acm.org/binaries/content/assets/publicpolicy/2017_usacm_statement_algorithms.pdf

Attaran, M. (2022). Blockchain technology in healthcare: Challenges and opportunities.*International Journal of Healthcare Management*, 15(1), 70–83. DOI: 10.1080/20479700.2020.1843887

Australian Government. (2021). *Second Australian National Action Plan on Women, Peace and Security 2021–2031 | Australian Government Department of Foreign Affairs and Trade*. Australian Government. https://www.dfat.gov.au/publications/second-australian-national-action-plan-on-women-peace-and-security-2021-2031, https://www.dfat.gov.au/publications/second-australian-national-action-plan-on-women-peace-and-security-2021-2031

Ayling, J., & Chapman, A. (2022). Putting AI ethics to work: Are the tools fit for purpose?*AI and Ethics*, 2(3), 405–429. DOI: 10.1007/s43681-021-00084-x

Babalola, O. (2022). Nigeria's Data Protection Legal and Institutional Model: An Overview. *International Data Privacy Law*, 44-52.

Bachner, J. (2013). *Predictive policing: Preventing crime with data and analytics*. IBM Center for the Business of Government.

Bajwa, J., Munir, A. U., Nori, A., & Williams, B. (2021). Artificial intelligence in healthcare: Transforming the practice of medicine.*Future Healthcare Journal*, 8(2), e188–e194. DOI: 10.7861/fhj.2021-0095 PMID: 34286183

Barbin, E., Borowczyk, J., Chabert, J.-L., Guillemot, M., Michel-Pajus, A., & Bernard, L. C. (1999). *A history of algorithms: From the pebble to the microchip* (Chabert, J.-L., Ed.). Springer.

Barnes, N. *Financial controls of a healthcare fund to mitigate fraud risk in the expenses cycle* University of Johannesburg].

Barns, S., Cosgrave, E., Acuto, M., & McNeill, D. (2016). Digital infrastructures and urban governance.*Urban Policy and Research*, 35(1), 20–31. DOI: 10.1080/08111146.2016.1235032

BBC. (2014, January 17). *Edward Snowden: Leaks that exposed US spy programme*. Retrieved from BBC News.

BDS EN ISO/IEC 27000:2020 Information technology. Security techniques. Information security management systems. Overview and vocabulary. BIS. Sofia

BDS EN ISO/IEC 27001:2023 Information security, cybersecurity and privacy protection. Information security management systems. Requirements. BIS. 2023

BDS ISO 31000:2018. Risk Management - a Practical Guide. BIS, Sofia, 2018

Bécue, A., Praça, I., & Gama, J. (2021). Artificial intelligence, cyber-threats and Industry 4.0: Challenges and opportunities.*Artificial Intelligence Review*, 54(5), 3849–3886. DOI: 10.1007/s10462-020-09942-2

Behera, R. K., Bala, P. K., & Rana, N. P. (2023). Responsible Natural Language Processing: A

Bello, O. A., Ogundipe, A., Mohammed, D., Adebola, F., & Alonge, O. A. (2023). AI-Driven Approaches for Real-Time Fraud Detection in US Financial Transactions: Challenges and Opportunities.*European Journal of Computer Science and Information Technology*, 11(6), 84–102.

Ben-Ishai, G., Dean, J., Manyika, J., Porat, R., Varian, H., & Walker, K. (2024). AI and the Opportunity for Shared Prosperity: Lessons from the History of Technology and the Economy. *arXiv preprint arXiv:2401.09718* or https://synthical.com/article/f8f3e908-a6ff-4e36-8fd2-74e92786bd03

Bera, K., Schalper, K. A., Rimm, D. L., Velcheti, V., & Madabhushi, A. (2019). Artificial intelligence in digital pathology — New tools for diagnosis and precision oncology.*Nature Reviews. Clinical Oncology*, 16(11), 703–715. DOI: 10.1038/s41571-019-0252-y PMID: 31399699

Berawi, M. (2019). The role of Industry 4.0 in achieving sustainable development goals.*International Journal of Technology*, 10(4), 644–647. DOI: 10.14716/ijtech.v10i4.3341

Berman, E. M., Bowman, J. S., West, J. P., & Van Wart, M. R. (2021). *Human resource management in public service: Paradoxes, processes, and problems*. Cq Press.

Berryhill, J., Heang, K. K., Clogher, R., & McBride, K. (2019, November 21). Hello, World: Artificial intelligence and its use in the public sector. *OECD Working Papers on Public Governance*.

Biermann, F., Hickmann, T., & Sénit, C. A. (2022). *The political impact of the Sustainable Development Goals: Transforming governance through global goals?*-Cambridge University Press. DOI: 10.1017/9781009082945

Bignami, F. (2022). Artificial Intelligence Accountability of Public Administration. *The American Journal of Comparative Law*, 2022(Supplement_1), i312–i346. DOI: 10.1093/ajcl/avac012

Bilgin, H. (2022). Yapay Zekânın Mahkeme Kararlarında Kullanımına Uluslararası Bir Bakış Ve Robot Hâkimler Hakkında Düşünceler. *İnönü Üniversitesi Hukuk Fakültesi Dergisi, 13*(2), 405-419.

Birtane, Ş. (2024). Hakime Yardımcı Yapay Zekâ.*Türkiye Adalet Akademisi Dergisi*, (59), 233–272. DOI: 10.54049/taad.1515051

Bletz, J. (2016). Molenwaard: The world's first digital municipality. Retrieved from https://joinup.ec.europa.eu/collection/egovernment/document/molenwaard-worlds-first-digital-municipality (Accessed: October 2, 2024).

Bloomberg. (2024). Turkey Wins Rating Upgrade From Moody's After Over a Decade. Retrieved from https://www.bnnbloomberg.ca/investing/2024/07/19/turkey-wins-rating-upgrade-from-moodys-after-over-a-decade/

Bodemer, O. (2023). Artificial Intelligence in Governance: A Comprehensive Analysis of AI Integration and Policy Development in the German Government. *Authorea Preprints*.

Booyse, D., & Scheepers, C. (2023). Barriers to adopting automated organisational decision-making through the use of artificial intelligence.*Management Research Review*. Advance online publication. DOI: 10.1108/MRR-09-2021-0701

Borges, A., Laurindo, F., Spínola, M., Gonçalves, R., & Mattos, C. (2020). The strategic use of artificial intelligence in the digital era: Systematic literature review and future research directions.*International Journal of Information Management*, 57, 102225. DOI: 10.1016/j.ijinfomgt.2020.102225

Brezina, C. (2006). *Al-Khwarizmi: The inventor of algebra*. The Rosen Publishing Group.

Brunette, A. (2024, October 25). *Humanizing Justice: The transformational impact of AI in courts, from filing to sentencing*. Retrieved October 30, 2019, from Thomsonreuters: https://www.thomsonreuters.com/en-us/posts/ai-in-courts/humanizing-justice/

Brunette, E. S., Flemmer, R. C., & Flemmer, C. L. "A review of artificial intelligence," 2009 4th International Conference on Autonomous Robots and Agents, Wellington, New Zealand, 2009, pp. 385-392. Retrieved from https://www.researchgate.net/publication/220774315

Bryson, J., & George, B. (2024). *Strategic Planning for Public and Nonprofit Organizations: A Guide to Strengthening and Sustaining Organizational Achievement* (6th ed.).

Buis, H., & Boex, J. (2015). *Improving local government performance by strengthening their 5 core capabilities*. VNG International.

Buluz, B. (2019). Türkiye'de Avukatlık ve Teknoloji. In Çetin, S. (Ed.), *Yapay zekâ Çağında Hukuk*. Ankara ve İzmir Baroları Çalıştay Raporu.

Burns, A., Posey, C., Courtney, J., Roberts, T., & Nanayakkara, P. (2017). Organizational information security as a complex adaptive system: Insights from three agent-based models.*Information Systems Frontiers*, 19(3), 509–524. DOI: 10.1007/s10796-015-9608-8

Burrell, J. (2016). How the machine 'thinks': Understanding opacity in machine learning algorithms.*Big Data & Society*, 3(1), 2053951715622512. Advance online publication. DOI: 10.1177/2053951715622512

Busuioc, M. (2021). Accountable artificial intelligence: Holding algorithms to account.*Public Administration Review*, 81(5), 825–836. DOI: 10.1111/puar.13293 PMID: 34690372

Buzelli, L., Cameron, G., Duxbury, K., Gardner, T., Rutherford, S., Williamson, S., & Alderwick, H. (2022). *Public perceptions of health and social care: What the new government should know - The Health Foundation*. The Health Foundation. https://www.health.org.uk/publications/reports/public-perceptions-of-health-and-social-care-what-government-should-know

Çakır, F., Karaduman, M., & Zobar, G. (2024, September 06). *Adalet Bakanı Tunç: Yargı hizmetlerinin hızlandırılması anlamında da yapay zekanın kullanılması lazım*. Retrieved October 31, 2024, from Anadolu Ajansı: https://www.aa.com.tr/tr/gundem/adalet-bakani-tunc-yargi-hizmetlerinin-hizlandirilmasi-anlaminda-da-yapay-zekanin-kullanilmasi-lazim/3323172

Calvino, Fl., Samek, L., Squicciarini, M., & Morris, C. (2020). Identifying and characterising AI adopters: A novel approach based on big data. ECD Science, Technology and Industry Working Papers 2022/06.

Campion, A., Gasco-Hernandez, M., Jankin Mikhaylov, S., & Esteve, M. (2022). Overcoming the challenges of collaboratively adopting artificial intelligence in the public sector.*Social Science Computer Review*, 40(2), 462–477. DOI: 10.1177/0894439320979953

Çamur, O., & Aydın, A. (2022). Yeni Kamu Yönetimi Anlayışının Etik Temelleri ve Kamu Yönetiminde Etik Yönetimin Gelişmesi Üzerindeki Etkisi.*Denetişim*, 25, 148–159.

Canedo, V. B., Fernández, L. M., Cancela, B., & Betanzos, A. A. (2024), A review of green artificial intelligence: Towards a more sustainable future, Neurocomputing, Volume 599, 128096, ISSN 0925-2312, Retrieved from https://doi.org/DOI: 10.1016/j.neucom.2024.128096

Celeste, E. a. (2024). Constitutionalizing Mass Surveillance in the EU: Civil Society Demands, Judicial Activism, and Legislative Inertia. *German Law Journal*, 1-20.

Cerrillo i Martinez, A. (2019). How Can We Open the Black Box of Public Administration? Transparency and Accountability in the Use of Algorithms. Revista Catalana de Dret Públic, Cai, M. (2021). Natural language processing for urban research: A systematic review.*Heliyon*, 7(12), 1218.

Challapalli, S. (2023). Benefits and Constraints Associated with the Harmonization of Financial Regulations: An Overview. *Asian Journal of Economics. Business and Accounting*, 23(15), 49–56.

Chande, A., & Verma, R. (2023). Cognitive learning & data mining optimization strategies in sustainable training for restaurant food and beverage service excellence.*2023 International Conference on Communication, Security and Artificial Intelligence (ICCSAI)*. DOI: 10.1109/ICCSAI59793.2023.10420934

Charoensiriwatana, W., & Waiyasilp, P. (2003). Neonatal screening program in Thailand.*The Southeast Asian Journal of Tropical Medicine and Public Health.* PMID: 15906708

Chatterjee, S., & Bhattacharjee, K. K. (2020). Adoption of artificial intelligence in higher education: A quantitative analysis using structural equation modelling. *Education and Information Technologies*, 25(5), 3443–3463. Advance online publication. DOI: 10.1007/s10639-020-10159-7

Chatzoglou, P. D., & Diamantidis, A. D. (2013). Service quality in the public sector: The case of the Citizen's Service Centers (CSCs) of Greece.*International Journal of Public Sector Management.*

Chaudhry, M. A., & Kazim, E. (2022). Artificial Intelligence in Education (AIEd): A high-level academic and industry note 2021.*AI and Ethics*, 2(1), 157–165. DOI: 10.1007/s43681-021-00074-z PMID: 34790953

Chen, H.. (2023). Algorithmic fairness in municipal AI systems.*Government Information Quarterly*, 40(1), 101–115.

Chen, T., Guo, W., Gao, X., & Liang, Z. (2021). AI-based self-service technology in public service delivery: User experience and influencing factors.*Government Information Quarterly*, 38(4), 101520. DOI: 10.1016/j.giq.2020.101520

Chen, X., Xie, H., Zou, D., & Hwang, G. (2020). Application and theory gaps during the rise of Artificial Intelligence in Education.*Computers and Education Artificial Intelligence*, 1, 100002. DOI: 10.1016/j.caeai.2020.100002

Chilunjika, A., Intauno, K., & Chilunjika, S. R. (2022). Artificial intelligence and public sector human resource management in South Africa: Opportunities, challenges, and prospects.*SA Journal of Human Resource Management*, 20, 12. DOI: 10.4102/sajhrm.v20i0.1972

Chowdhury, E. K. (2021). Prospects and challenges of using artificial intelligence in the audit process. *The Essentials of Machine Learning in Finance and Accounting*, 139-156.

Chui, J. J., & Miremadi, M. (2018). AI adoption and use survey. McKinsey Global Institute. Retrieved from https://www.mckinsey.com/capabilities/quantumblack/our-insights/what-ai-can-and-cant-do-yet-for-your-business?cid=other-soc-fce-mip-mck-oth-1801&kui=JM_dauoGBH5BzmJfYriUSw

Chung, I. H., Williams, D. W., & Do, M. R. (2022). For better or worse? Revenue forecasting with machine learning approaches.*Public Performance & Management Review*, 45(5), 1133–1154. DOI: 10.1080/15309576.2022.2073551

Chun, S. A., & Warner, J. (2010). Government 2.0: Making connections between citizens, data and government.*Information Polity*, 15(1-2), 1–9. DOI: 10.3233/IP-2010-0205

Ciancarini, P., Giancarlo, R., & Grimaudo, G. (2024). Digital transformation in the public administrations: A guided tour for computer scientists.*IEEE Access : Practical Innovations, Open Solutions*, 12, 22841–22865. DOI: 10.1109/ACCESS.2024.3363075

Clark, C. (1935). Law Enforcement and Public Administration.*Ilinois Law Review*, 30, 273.

Climate Change Authority. (2019). *Australia's climate change policies at the Australian and state and territory government levels: A stocktake* (Australia). Commonwealth of Australia 2019. https://apo.org.au/node/224211

CNBCE. (2024). Turkish lira hits fresh record low against the U.S. dollar. Retrieved from https://www.cnbc.com/2024/01/11/turkish-lira-hits-fresh-record-low-against-the-dollar.html

Cogent. (2024). *NLP in the Public Sector*. NLP in the Public Sector. https://www.cogentinfo.com/resources/nlp-examples-in-the-public-sector

Cognitive Market Research. (2024). Artificial Intelligence in Energy Market Report 2024 (Global Edition). Retrieved fromhttps://www.cognitivemarketresearch.com/artificial-intelligence-in-energy-market-report?

Considine, M., & Painter, M. (1997). Managerialism: The great debate.*Public Administration Review.*

Cooke, R. L. (2005). *The history of mathematics: A brief course.* John Wiley & Sons. DOI: 10.1002/9781118033098

Corbett, E., Denton, E., & Erete, S. (2023). Power and Public Participation in AI.*Proceedings of the 3rd ACM Conference on Equity and Access in Algorithms, Mechanisms, and Optimization.* https://doi.org/DOI: 10.1145/3617694.3623228

Cortés-Cediel, M. E., Segura-Tinoco, A., Cantador, I., & Rodríguez Bolívar, M. P. (2023). Trends and challenges of e-government chatbots: Advances in exploring open government data and citizen participation content.*Government Information Quarterly*, 40(4), 101877. DOI: 10.1016/j.giq.2023.101877

Coşkun, F., & Gülleroğlu, H. D. (2021). Yapay Zekanın Tarih İçindeki Gelişimi ve Eğitimde Kullanılması.[JFES].*Ankara University Journal of Faculty of Educational Sciences*, 54(3), 947–966.

Crampton, J. (2013). Is Security Sustainable?*Environment and Planning. D, Society & Space*, 31(4), 571–577. DOI: 10.1068/d3104com

Craven, L. S. (2021). CFPB Releases Report Analyzing Consumer Complaint Data By Demographics | Insights & Resources | Goodwin. *Goodwin.* https://www.goodwinlaw.com/en/insights/blogs/2021/10/cfpb-releases-report-analyzing-consumer-complaint

Creel, K. A. (2020). Transparency in complex computational systems.*Philosophy of Science*, 87(4), 568–589. DOI: 10.1086/709729

Cuéllar, M., & Huq, A. (2022). Artificially Intelligent Regulation.*Daedalus*, 151(2), 335–347. DOI: 10.1162/daed_a_01920

Cugurullo, F. (2020). Urban artificial intelligence: From automation to autonomy in the smart city.*Frontiers in Sustainable Cities*, 2, 38. DOI: 10.3389/frsc.2020.00038

Cybersecurity and Infrastructure Security Agency. (2023), CISA Roadmap for Artificial Intelligence, https://www.cisa.gov/sites/default/files/2023-11/2023-2024_CISA-Roadmap-for-AI_508c.pdf

Dabis, A., & Csáki, C. (2024). AI and ethics: Investigating the first policy responses of higher education institutions to the challenge of generative AI.*Humanities & Social Sciences Communications*, 11(1006), 1006. Advance online publication. DOI: 10.1057/s41599-024-03526-z

Damar, M., Özen, A., Çakmak, Ü. E., Özoğuz, E., & Erenay, F. S. (2024). Super AI, generative AI, narrow AI and chatbots: An assessment of artificial intelligence technologies for the public sector and public administration.*Journal of AI*, 8(1), 83–106. DOI: 10.61969/jai.1512906

Danaher, J. (2016). The threat of algocracy: Reality, resistance and accommodation. *Philosophy & Technology*, 29(3), 245–268. DOI: 10.1007/s13347-015-0211-1

Daneshjou, R., Smith, M. P., Sun, M. D., Rotemberg, V., & Zou, J. (2021). Lack of transparency and potential bias in artificial intelligence data sets and algorithms: A scoping review.*JAMA Dermatology*, 157(11), 1362–1369. DOI: 10.1001/jamadermatol.2021.3129 PMID: 34550305

Data Protection Act, 2023. (n.d.).

Davenport, T. H., & Ronanki, R. (2018). Artificial intelligence for the real world. Harvard Business Review, January-February, Retrieved from https://blockqai.com/wp-content/uploads/2021/01/analytics-hbr-ai-for-the-real-world.pdf

David, K., & Makhamara, A. (2022). Benchmarking practices and service delivery in the national police service in Mombasa County, Kenya.*International Journal of Business and Management.*

Dearing, J. W., & Cox, J. G. (2018). Diffusion of innovations theory, principles, and practice.*Health Affairs*, 37(2), 183–190. DOI: 10.1377/hlthaff.2017.1104 PMID: 29401011

De-Dios-Flores, I., & Pichel Campos, J. R. (2023). Language technologies for a multilingual public administration in Spain. Journal of Language & Law, 8.

Deloitte. (2013). *CFPB's consumer complaint database Analysis reveals valuable insights*. Deloitte.

Demirel, D. (2015). Üçüncü yol politikalarında yeni kamu yönetiminin izleri.*Atatürk Üniversitesi İktisadi ve İdari Bilimler Dergisi*, 29(1), 137–153.

Department for Environment. Food & Rural Affairs. (2023). *The air quality strategy for England*. https://www.gov.uk/government/publications/the-air-quality-strategy-for-england

Department of Defense. (2023), *Data, Analytics, and Artificial Intelligence Adoption Strategy: Accelerating Decision Advantage*, https://media.defense.gov/2023/Nov/02/2003333300/-1/-1/1/DOD_DATA_ANALYTICS_AI_ADOPTION_STRATEGY.PDF#page=5.06

Department of Homeland Security. (2024), *Artificial Intelligence Roadmap 2024*, https://www.dhs.gov/sites/default/files/2024-03/24_0315_ocio_roadmap_artificialintelligence-ciov3-signed-508.pdf

Department of State Services. (n.d.). *History of DSS*. Retrieved from Department of State Services: https://www.dss.gov.ng/dss_about

Department of State. (2023), *Enterprise Artificial Intelligence Strategy FY2024-FY2025: Empowering Diplomacy Through Responsible AI*, https://www.state.gov/wp-content/uploads/2023/11/Department-of-State-Enterprise-Artificial-Intelligence-Strategy.pdf

Desouza, K. C., Dawson, G. S., & Chenok, D. (2020). Designing, developing, and deploying artificial intelligence systems: Lessons from and for the public sector. *Business Horizons*, 63(2), 205–213. DOI: 10.1016/j.bushor.2019.11.004

Deutsche Welle. (2023, January 20). *How China's AI is automating the legal system*. Retrieved from https://www.taiwannews.com.tw/news/4787354

Devlin, C., & Coaffee, J. (2023). Planning and technological innovation: The governance challenges English local authorities face in adopting planning technologies. *International Journal of Urban Sciences, 27*(sup1), 149–163.

Di Vaio, A., Palladino, R., Hassan, R., & Escobar, O. (2020). Artificial intelligence and business models in the sustainable development goals perspective: A systematic literature review.*Journal of Business Research*, 121, 283–314. DOI: 10.1016/j.jbusres.2020.08.019

Dignam, A. (2020). Artificial intelligence, tech corporate governance and the public interest regulatory response.*Cambridge Journal of Regions, Economy and Society*, 13(1), 37–54. DOI: 10.1093/cjres/rsaa002

Divide: Access and Use of Technology in Education. Journal of Social Sciences Review, 3(2), 883-895.DOI: 10.54183/jssr.v3i2.326

Dobson, R., & Whittaker, J. (2024). What do health service users think about the use of their data for AI development?*Medinfo*. Advance online publication. DOI: 10.3233/SHTI231146 PMID: 38269996

DOE Announces New Actions to Enhance America's Global Leadership in Artificial Intelligence. (2024). Energy.Gov. https://www.energy.gov/articles/doe-announces-new-actions-enhance-americas-global-leadership-artificial-intelligence

Dray, M. (2019). Natural Language Processing in government – Data in government. *Natural Language Processing in Government*. https://dataingovernment.blog.gov.uk/2019/06/14/natural-language-processing-in-government/

Dubay, L. (2021). Creating an equitable AI policy for Indigenous communities. *First Policy Response*. https://policyresponse.ca/creating-an-equitable-ai-policy-for-indigenous-communities/

Dunleavy, P. & Margetts, H. (2023). Data science, artificial intelligence and the third wave of digital era governance. *Public Policy and AdministrationSpecial Issue: Artificial Intelligence and Public Administration: Actors, Governance, and Policies*. 1-30.

Dunleavy, P., & Margetts, H. (2023). Data science, artificial intelligence and the third wave of digital era governance.*Public Policy and Administration*, •••, 09520767231198737. DOI: 10.1177/09520767231198737

Duttai, S., & Bonissone, P. P. (1993). Integrating case- and rule-based reasoning. *International Journal of Approximate Reasoning*, 8(3), 163–203. DOI: 10.1016/0888-613X(93)90001-T

Efe, A. (2022). Yargısal ve Hukuki Süreçlerde Yapay Zekâ Kullanan Araçlar Üzerine Bir Araştırma.*Bilgi Yönetimi*, 5(1), 92–117. DOI: 10.33721/by.971873

Efe, S. (2023). A discussion on problems and solutions of innovative performance management in the public service and government.*Uluslararası Akademik Yönetim Bilimleri Dergisi*, 8(1), 45–62. DOI: 10.51947/yonbil.1247897

Effoduh, J. O. (2024). *Towards the Implementation of Data Protection Measures to Safeguard*. Accountability Lab Nigeria.

Egger, R., & Gokce, E. (2022). Natural Language Processing (NLP): An Introduction. In Egger, R. (Ed.), *Applied Data Science in Tourism: Interdisciplinary Approaches, Methodologies, and Applications* (pp. 307–334). Springer International Publishing., DOI: 10.1007/978-3-030-88389-8_15

Eggers, W. D., Malik, N., & Gracie, M. (2019). Using AI to unleash the power of unstructured government data. *Deloitte Insights*. https://www2.deloitte.com/us/en/insights/focus/cognitive-technologies/natural-language-processing-examples-in-government-data.html

Elsyra, N. (2023). The Role of Artificial Intelligence in Government Services: A Systematic Literature Review.*Open Access Indonesia Journal of Social Sciences*, 6(3), 998–1003. DOI: 10.37275/oaijss.v6i3.163

Engvall, N. (2024). The Influence of Institutional Factors on AI adoption in EU banking cybersecurity:: A narrative literature review.

Erkkila, T. (2020). Transparency in public administration. In *Oxford research encyclopaedia of politics*. DOI: 10.1093/acrefore/9780190228637.013.1404

Esfahani, M. N. (2024). Content analysis of textbooks via natural language processing.*American Journal of Education and Learning*, 9(2), 97.

Essien, A., & Petrounias, I. (2022). An Artificial Intelligence (AI)-Based Decision-Making Framework for Crisis Management.*Advances in Electronic Government, Digital Divide, and Regional Development*, 84–98. Advance online publication. DOI: 10.4018/978-1-7998-9815-3.ch007

EU. (2021). EU Digital Strategy. Retrieved from https://eufordigital.eu/discover-eu/eu-digital-strategy/

EuroMonitor. (2024). Energy transition in Turkey. Retrieved from https://www.energymonitor.ai/data-insights/energy-transition-in-turkey/?cf-view

European Commision. (2012). Turkey's Energy Strategy, Retrieved fromhttps://ec.europa.eu/enlargement/pdf/european_energy_policy/turkeys_energy_strategy_en.pdf

European Migration Network. (2022). *The use of digitalisation and artificial intelligence in migration management.* https://emn.ie/publications/accurate-timely-interoperable-data-manage-

European Parliament. (2023). European Union Artificial Intelligence (AI) Act. Retrieved from https://www.europarl.europa.eu/topics/en/article/20230601STO93804/eu-ai-act-first-regulation-on-artificial-intelligence

Europol. (2022). AI and policing: The benefits and challenges of artificial intelligence for law enforcement. European Union Agency for Law Enforcement Cooperation.

Ezeji, C. L. (2024). Artificial Intelligence for detecting and preventing procurement fraud. *International Journal of Business Ecosystem & Strategy (2687-2293), 6*(1), 63-73.

Facchini, A., & Termine, A. (2021). Towards a taxonomy for the opacity of AI systems. In Müller, V. C. (Ed.), *Philosophy and Theory of Artificial Intelligence 2021* (pp. 73–89). Springer., DOI: 10.1007/978-3-031-09153-7_7

Fairie, P., Zhang, Z., D'Souza, A. G., Walsh, T., Quan, H., & Santana, M. J. (2021). Categorising patient concerns using natural language processing techniques.*BMJ Health & Care Informatics*, 28(1), e100274. Advance online publication. DOI: 10.1136/bmjhci-2020-100274 PMID: 34193519

Fang, B., Yu, J., Chen, Z., Osman, A. I., Farghali, M., Ihara, I., Hamza, E. H., Rooney, D. W., & Yap, P.-S. (2023). Artificial intelligence for waste management in smart cities: A review.*Environmental Chemistry Letters*, 21(4), 1959–1989. Advance online publication. DOI: 10.1007/s10311-023-01604-3 PMID: 37362015

Fan, Z., Yan, Z., & Wen, S. (2023). Deep Learning and Artificial Intelligence in Sustainability: A Review of SDGs, Renewable Energy, and Environmental Health. *Sustainability (Basel)*, 15(18), 13493. Advance online publication. DOI: 10.3390/su151813493

Farazmand, A. (2009). Building administrative capacity for an age of rapid globalization: A modest prescription for the twenty-first century.*Public Administration Review*, 69(6), 1007–1020. DOI: 10.1111/j.1540-6210.2009.02054.x

Farida, I., Ningsih, W., Lutfiani, N., Aini, Q., & Harahap, E. (2023). Responsible urban innovation working with local authorities: A framework for artificial intelligence (AI).*Scientific Journal of Informatics*, 10(2), 121–126. DOI: 10.15294/sji.v10i2.43818

Farrell, J. (2019). The growth of climate change misinformation in US philanthropy: Evidence from natural language processing.*Environmental Research Letters*, 14(3), 1–10. DOI: 10.1088/1748-9326/aaf939

Feldstein, S. (2019, September). The Global Expansion of AI Surveillance. *Carnegie Endowment for International Peace Working Paper.*

Finceed. (2024). *Exploring Finnish Digital Education | Finnish National Agency for Education.* https://www.oph.fi/en/exploring-finnish-digital-education

Firdaus, I., & Yuningsih, M. (2023). Digital service transformation and public relations reform in West Java. *Journal of Digital Governance.*

Fitch Ratings. (2024). Fitch Upgrades Turkiye to 'BB-; Outlook Stable Retrieved from. https://www.fitchratings.com/research/sovereigns/fitch-upgrades-turkiye-to-bb-outlook-stable-06-09-2024

Floridi, L. (2020). Artificial intelligence as a public service: Learning from Amsterdam and Helsinki.*SSRN*. https://ssrn.com/abstract=3827084 or http://dx.doi.org/ DOI: 10.2139/ssrn.3827084

Flügge, A., Hildebrandt, T., & Møller, N. (2021). Street-Level Algorithms and AI in Bureaucratic Decision-Making.*Proceedings of the ACM on Human-Computer Interaction*, 5(CSCW1), 1–23. DOI: 10.1145/3449114

Fortuna, C., Yetgin, H., & Mohorčič, M. (2023). Smart Infrastructures: Artificial Intelligence-Enabled Lifecycle Automation.*IEEE Industrial Electronics Magazine*, 17(2), 37–47. DOI: 10.1109/MIE.2022.3165673

Fountain, J. E. (2001). Customer service paradoxes in government: Balancing political inequality and public management objectives.*Public Administration Review*.

Fowowe, S. (2019, March 20). *Buhari Declines Assent to Digital Rights and Freedom Bill and Four Others*. Retrieved from The Guardian: https://guardian.ng/news/buhari-declines-assent-to-digital-rights-and-freedom-bill-four-others/

Foy, G. (1990). Economic sustainability and the preservation of environmental assets.*Environmental Management*, 14(6), 771–778. DOI: 10.1007/BF02394171

Friedman, B. a. (2024). (Forthcoming). Indiscriminate Data Surveillance.[*Virginia Public Law and Legal Theory Research Paper*.]. *Virginia Law Review*.

Garikapati, D., & Shetiya, S. S. (2024). Autonomous vehicles: Evolution of artificial intelligence and learning algorithms. *arXiv*, 2402.17690v2 [cs.LG]. https://arxiv.org/abs/2402.17690v2

GDPR. (2018). *General Data Protection Regulation (GDPR) – Legal Text*. General Data Protection Regulation (GDPR). https://gdpr-info.eu/

Gedik, F., & Koç, E. (2009). Hüküm Kurma ve İçtihat.*Ankara Barosu Dergisi*, (2), 157–163.

Gehlhaus, D., Koslosky, L., Goode, K., & Perkins, C. (2021). U.S. AI Workforce: Policy Recommendations. . https://doi.org/. –DOI: 10.51593/20200087

Gell-Mann, M. (1999). Complex adaptive systems.*Complexity*, •••, 17–45.

George, A. S. (2024). Emerging Trends in AI-Driven Cybersecurity: An In-Depth Analysis.*Partners Universal Innovative Research Publication*, 2(4), 15–28.

Gesk, T. S., & Leyer, M. (2022). Artificial intelligence in public services: When and why citizens accept its usage.*Government Information Quarterly*, 39(3), 101704. DOI: 10.1016/j.giq.2022.101704

Giest, S. N., & Klievink, B. (2024). More than a digital system: How AI is changing the role of bureaucrats in different organisational contexts.*Public Management Review*, 26(2), 379–398. DOI: 10.1080/14719037.2022.2095001

Gillipse, T. (2014). The relevance of algorithms. In Gillespie, T., Boczkowski, P. J., & Foot, K. A. (Eds.), *Media technologies: Essays on communication, materiality, and society*. The MIT Press., DOI: 10.7551/mitpress/9780262525374.003.0009

Glemarec, Y., & Puppim de Oliveira, J. A. (2012). The role of the visible hand of public institutions in creating a sustainable future.*Public Administration and Development*, 32(3), 200–214. DOI: 10.1002/pad.1631

Global, A. I. Ecosystem, (2022). https://www.ai-ecosystem.org/

GlobalData. (2024). Turkey Power Market Outlook 2024. Retrieved from https://6obp2b8hjd9m4pjtra8i2gct80-GDPE2346ICR_SP.pdf

Gomide, F., & Oliveira, S. (2023). Measures to contain the transmission of Hepatitis C in a chronic kidney care hospital unit in the Triângulo Mineiro in Brazil: A case study.*International Journal of Public Health*, 68, 1605914. DOI: 10.3389/ijph.2023.1605914 PMID: 37325177

Goodland, R. (1995). The Concept of Environmental Sustainability.*Annual Review of Ecology and Systematics*, 26(1), 1–24. DOI: 10.1146/annurev.es.26.110195.000245

Goralski, M., & Tan, T. (2020). Artificial intelligence and sustainable development. *International Journal of Management Education*, 18(1), 100330. Advance online publication. DOI: 10.1016/j.ijme.2019.100330

Gotelaere, S., & Paoli, L. (2022). Prevention and control of financial fraud: A scoping review.*European Journal on Criminal Policy and Research*, •••, 1–21. DOI: 10.1007/s10610-022-09532-8

Graf, J. O., & Bitencourt, C. M. (2024). Digital government and the handling of sensitive data in the execution of public policies: challenges and possibilities. *Araucaria: Revista Iberoamericana de Filosofía, Política. Humanidades y Relaciones Internacionales*, 26(56), 139–153.

Green Building Masterplans. (2024). BCA Corp. https://www1.bca.gov.sg/buildsg/sustainability/green-building-masterplans

Greenleaf, G. (2019). Nigeria Regulates Data Privacy: African and Global Significance. *UNSW Law Research Paper*.

Gritsenko, D., & Wood, M. (2020). Algorithmic governance: A modes of governance approach.*Regulation & Governance*. Advance online publication. DOI: 10.1111/rego.12367

Gualdi, F., & Cordella, A. (2021). Artificial intelligence and decision-making: The question of accountability.

Guan, C., Mou, J., & Jiang, Z. (2020). Artificial intelligence innovation in education: A twenty-year data-driven historical analysis. *International Journal of Innovation Studies*, 4(4), 134–147. DOI: 10.1016/j.ijis.2020.09.001

Guarini, E., Mori, E., & Zuffada, E. (2022). Localizing the sustainable development goals: A managerial perspective. *Journal of Public Budgeting, Accounting & Financial Management*, 34(5), 583–601. DOI: 10.1108/JPBAFM-02-2021-0031

Guerrero, L. A., Maas, G., & Hogland, W. (2013). Solid waste management challenges for cities in developing countries. *Waste Management (New York, N.Y.)*, 33(1), 220–232. DOI: 10.1016/j.wasman.2012.09.008 PMID: 23098815

Gupta, K. (2019). Artificial intelligence for governance in India: Prioritising the challenges using the analytic hierarchy process (AHP). *Int. J. Recent Technol. Eng*, 8(2), 3756–3762. DOI: 10.35940/ijrte.B3392.078219

Gwagwa, A., Kraemer-Mbula, E., Rizk, N., Rutenberg, I., & De Beer, J. (2020). Artificial intelligence (AI) deployments in Africa: Benefits, challenges, and policy dimensions. *The African Journal of Information and Communication*, 26(26), 1–28. DOI: 10.23962/10539/30361

Hagendorff, T. (2019). The Ethics of AI Ethics: An Evaluation of Guidelines. *Minds and Machines*, 30(1), 99–120. DOI: 10.1007/s11023-020-09517-8

Halleröd, B., Rothstein, B., Daoud, A., & Nandy, S. (2013). Bad governance and poor children: A comparative analysis of government efficiency and severe child deprivation in 68 low-and middle-income countries. *World Development*, 48, 19–31.

Han, E.-J., Han, Z.-A., Kim, H., & Jung, T. R. (2023). Monitoring healthy ageing for the next decade: South Korea's perspective. *Age and Ageing*, 52(Supplement_4), iv10–iv12. DOI: 10.1093/ageing/afad102 PMID: 37902513

Hao, K. (2019). Training a single AI model can emit as much carbon as five cars in their lifetimes. *MIT's Technology Review*, 75, 103.

Hao, Y., Vand, B., Delgado, B. M., & Baldi, S. (2023). Market manipulation in stock and power markets: A study of indicator-based monitoring and regulatory challenges. *Energies*, 16(4), 1894. DOI: 10.3390/en16041894

Haque, M. S., Ramesh, M., Puppim de Oliveira, J. A., & Gomide, A. A. (2021). Building administrative capacity for development: Limits and prospects. *International Review of Administrative Sciences*, 87(2), 211–219. DOI: 10.1177/00208523211002605

Harris, B. (2018, July 11). *Could an AI Ever Replace a Judge in Court.* Retrieved from World Government Summit: https://www.worldgovernmentsummit.org/observer/articles/2017/detail/could-an-ai-ever-replace-a-judge-in-court

Hastuti, R., & Syafruddin, . (2023). Ethical considerations in the age of artificial intelligence: Balancing innovation and social values.*West Science Social and Humanities Studies*, 1(2), 76–87. DOI: 10.58812/wsshs.v1i02.191

HDR UK. (2021). *The National Text Analytics Project.* HDR UK. https://www.hdruk.ac.uk/case-studies/the-national-text-analytics-project/

Heilala, S., & Toivonen, M. (2023). *AI-based sentiment analysis approaches for large-scale data domains of public and security interests.* AHFE International. DOI: 10.54941/ahfe1003738

He, M., Li, Z., Liu, C., Shi, D., & Tan, Z. (2020). Deployment of artificial intelligence in real-world practice: Opportunities and challenges.*Asia-Pacific Journal of Ophthalmology*, 9(4), 299–307. DOI: 10.1097/APO.0000000000000301 PMID: 32694344

Heng, L. J. (2024). Strategic Overview of Applying Artificial Intelligence on the Future Battlefield.

Henman, P. (2020). Improving public services using artificial intelligence: Possibilities, pitfalls, governance.*Asia Pacific Journal of Public Administration*, 42(4), 209–221. DOI: 10.1080/23276665.2020.1816188

Hilal, W., Gadsden, S. A., & Yawney, J. (2022). Financial fraud: A review of anomaly detection techniques and recent advances.*Expert Systems with Applications*, 193, 116429. DOI: 10.1016/j.eswa.2021.116429

Hilend, R., Bell, J. E., Griffis, S. E., & Macdonald, J. R. (2023). Illicit activity and scarce natural resources in the supply chain: A literature review, framework, and research agenda.*Journal of Business Logistics*, 44(2), 198–227. DOI: 10.1111/jbl.12331

Hinton, C. (2023). The State of Ethical AI in Practice: A Multiple Case Study of Estonian Public Service Organizations.[IJT]. *International Journal of Technoethics*, 14(1), 1–15. DOI: 10.4018/IJT.322017

Holden, L. (2005). Complex adaptive systems: Concept analysis.*Journal of Advanced Nursing*, 52(6), 651–657. DOI: 10.1111/j.1365-2648.2005.03638.x PMID: 16313378

Holland, J. (2006). Studying Complex Adaptive Systems.*Journal of Systems Science and Complexity*, 19(1), 1–8. DOI: 10.1007/s11424-006-0001-z

Hood, C. (1991). A public management for all seasons?*Public Administration Review*, (69), 3–19.

Hossain, M. Z. (2023). Emerging Trends in Forensic Accounting: Data Analytics, Cyber Forensic Accounting, Cryptocurrencies, and Blockchain Technology for Fraud Investigation and Prevention. *Cyber Forensic Accounting, Cryptocurrencies, and Blockchain Technology for Fraud Investigation and Prevention (May 16, 2023).*

Hossain, S. T., Yigitcanlar, T., Nguyen, K., & Xu, Y. (2024). Cybersecurity in local governments: A review and framework of key challenges.*SSRN*. DOI: 10.2139/ssrn.4631885

Huang, J.-D., Wang, J., Ramsey, E., Leavey, G., Chico, T. J., & Condell, J. (2022). Applying artificial intelligence to wearable sensor data to diagnose and predict cardiovascular disease: A review.*Sensors (Basel)*, 22(20), 8002. DOI: 10.3390/s22208002 PMID: 36298352

Hürriyet. (2023, September 03). *Yargıtay Başkanı Mehmet Akarca: 'Yapay zekâ' karar yazacak*. Retrieved October 31, 2024, from https://www.hurriyet.com.tr/gundem/yargitay-baskani-mehmet-akarca-yapay-zeka-karar-yazacak-42324616

Hwang, G.-J., & Chen, N.-S. (2023). Exploring the potential of generative artificial intelligence in education: Applications, challenges, and future research directions. *Journal of Educational Technology & Society*, 26(2), 1–12.

Hwang, G., Xie, H., Wah, B. W., & Gašević, D. (2020). Vision, challenges, roles and research issues of Artificial Intelligence in Education.*Computers and Education Artificial Intelligence*, 1, 100001. DOI: 10.1016/j.caeai.2020.100001

IBM. (2024). *What Is NLP (Natural Language Processing)? | IBM*. https://www.ibm.com/topics/natural-language-processing

IEA. (2016). Turkey Review. Retrieved fromhttps://www.iea.org/publications/freepublications/publication/EnergyPoliciesofIEACountriesTurkey.pdf

IEA. (2020). Energy Technology Perspectives. Retrieved fromhttps://www.iea.org/reports/energy-technology-perspectives-2020

IEA. (2021), Turkey, Renewables. Retrieved from https://www.iea.org/countries/turkiye/renewables

IEA. (2023), Why AI and energy are the new power couple, IEA, Paris Retrieved from https://www.iea.org/commentaries/why-ai-and-energy-are-the-new-power-couple

IEA. (2024). World Energy Investment 2024. Retrieved from https://iea.blob.core.windows.net/assets/60fcd1dd-d112-469b-87de-20d39227df3d/WorldEnergyInvestment2024.pdf

Ifeanyi-Ajufo, N. (2024, February 23). *The AU took Important Action on Cybersecurity at its 2024 Summit – But More is needed.* Retrieved from Chatham House: https://www.chathamhouse.org/2024/02/au-took-important-action-cybersecurity-its-2024-summit-more-needed

Incorporated Trustees of Digital Rights Lawyers Initiative v National Identity Management, CA/IB/291/2020. (Court of Appeal 2020).

Ingram, G. (2021). Bridging the global digital divide: A platform to advance digital development in low- and middle-income countries. http://hdl.handle.net/11540/13773

Ingrams, A., Piotrowski, S., & Berliner, D. (2020). Learning from our mistakes: Public management reform and the hope of open government.*Perspectives on Public Management and Governance*, 3(4), 257–272. DOI: 10.1093/ppmgov/gvaa001

Insight Turkey. (2022). Energy Supply Security and Artificial Intelligence Applications. Retrieved from https://www.insightturkey.com/articles/energy-supply-security-and-artificial-intelligence-applications

Instellas, (2024). Artificial Intelligence in the Energy Sector: Benefits and Use Cases. Retrieved from https://intellias.com/ai-in-energy-sector-benefits/

Ioannou, P. (1986). Decentralized adaptive control of interconnected systems. *IEEE Transactions on Automatic Control*, 31(4), 291–298. DOI: 10.1109/TAC.1986.1104282

IRENA. (2015). *RENEWABLE ENERGY PROSPECTS: GERMANY*. The International Renewable Energy Agency (IRENA).

IRENA. (2019). Global Energy Transformation. Retrieved from https://www.irena.org/apps/DigitalArticles/-/media/652AE07BBAAC407ABD1D45F6BBA8494B.ashx

IRENA. (2024a). Renewable energy highlights. Retrieved from https://www.irena.org/-/media/Files/IRENA/Agency/Publication/2024/Jul/Renewable_energy_highlights_FINAL_July_2024.pdf

IRENA. (2024b), Turkey Profile. Retrieved from https://www.irena.org/-/media/Files/IRENA/Agency/Statistics/Statistical_Profiles/Eurasia/Turkiye_Eurasia_RE_SP.pdf

Isaac, U., & Uhunmwenma, A. J. (2021). Forensic accounting and financial malpractices: A conceptual review.*SAARJ Journal on Banking & Insurance Research*, 10(4), 1–8. DOI: 10.5958/2319-1422.2021.00026.6

Ismail, N., & Wong, C. (2023). Dental service system into blockchain environment. *International Journal of Innovative Computing*. Advance online publication. DOI: 10.11113/ijic.v13n1.394

İstanbul. (2019). *Ankara ve İzmir Baroları Çalıştay Raporu*. Yapay Zekâ Çağında Hukuk.

Iuga, I. C., & Socol, A. (2024). Government artificial intelligence readiness and brain drain influencing factors and spatial effects in the European Union member states. *Journal of Business Economics and Management, 25*(2), 268–296-268–296.

Jameaba, M.-S. (2024). Digitalization, emerging technologies, and financial stability: challenges and opportunities for the Indonesian banking sector and beyond. *Emerging Technologies, and Financial Stability: Challenges and Opportunities for the Indonesian Banking Sector and Beyond (April 26, 2024).*

Janssen, M., Janowski, T., & Scholl, H. J. (2021). AI for personalized e-participation. *Government Information Quarterly*, 38(2), 101571.

Japan's National Biodiversity Strategy and Action Plan 2023-2030. (2023). UNEP Law and Environment Assistance Platform. https://leap.unep.org/en/countries/jp/national-legislation/japans-national-biodiversity-strategy-and-action-plan-2023-2030

Jarrett, A., & Choo, K. K. R. (2021). The impact of automation and artificial intelligence on digital forensics.*WIREs Forensic Science*, 3(6), e1418. DOI: 10.1002/wfs2.1418

Javaid, M., Haleem, A., Singh, R. P., Suman, R., & Khan, S. (2022). A review of Blockchain Technology applications for financial services. *BenchCouncil Transactions on Benchmarks. Standards and Evaluations*, 2(3), 100073.

Javed, A. R., Shahzad, F., Rehman, S., Zikria, Y. B., Razzak, I., Jalil, Z., & Xu, G. (2022). Future smart cities: Requirements, emerging technologies, applications, challenges, and future aspects.*Cities (London, England)*, 129, 103794. DOI: 10.1016/j.cities.2022.103794

Jha, A. K., Ghimire, A., ... (2021). A review of AI for urban planning: Towards building sustainable smart cities. In *2021 6th International Conference on Inventive Computation Technologies (ICICT)* (pp. 937-944). Coimbatore, India.

Jim, J. R., Talukder, M. A. R., Malakar, P., Kabir, M. M., Nur, K., & Mridha, M. F. (2024). Recent advancements and challenges of NLP-based sentiment analysis: A state-of-the-art review.*Natural Language Processing Journal*, 6, 100059. DOI: 10.1016/j.nlp.2024.100059

Jobin, A., Ienca, M., & Vayena, E. (2019). The global landscape of AI ethics guidelines.*Nature Machine Intelligence*, 1(9), 389–399. DOI: 10.1038/s42256-019-0088-2

John, T. (2022). The ethical considerations of artificial intelligence in clinical decision support. In *Proceedings of the Wellington Faculty of Engineering Ethics and Sustainability Symposium*DOI: 10.26686/wfeess.vi.7649

Jolselt, J. (2019). Information society: Its meanings and implications. Journal of Library.*Science Education and Learning Technology*, 1(1), 181–190.

Jones, T., & Luger, J. (2022). AI 'everywhere and nowhere': Addressing the AI intelligibility problem in public service journalism.*Digital Journalism (Abingdon, England)*, 10(10), 1731–1755. DOI: 10.1080/21670811.2022.2145328

Jumanne, A., & Njoroge, M. (2018). Structural change management and employee performance in public sector organizations in Kenya: Case of the Parliamentary Service Commission. *Journal of Strategic Management*.

Kalampokis, E., Karacapilidis, N., Tsakalidis, D., & Tarabanis, K. (2023). Understanding the Use of Emerging Technologies in the Public Sector: A Review of Horizon 2020 Projects.*Digit. Gov.: Res. Pract.*, 4(1), 4–28. DOI: 10.1145/3580603

Kalliontzi, E., & Delinavelli, M. (2024). Data-driven policy development of municipalities: Preparation steps for integrating AI tools in the policymaking process. *The International Archives of the Photogrammetry, Remote Sensing and Spatial Information Sciences*, XLVIII-4/W10-2024, 85–91. DOI: 10.5194/isprs-archives-XLVIII-4-W10-2024-85-2024

Kaloudi, N., & Li, J. (2020). The AI-Based Cyber Threat Landscape.*ACM Computing Surveys*, 53(1), 1–34. DOI: 10.1145/3372823

Kamuangu, P. (2024). A Review on Cybersecurity in Fintech: Threats, Solutions, and Future Trends. *Journal of Economics. Finance and Accounting Studies*, 6(1), 47–53.

Kandır, M. O. (2023, August 13). *Türk Hukukunda Yapay Zeka Kullanımı*. Retrieved from Hukukvebilisim: https://hukukvebilisim.org/turk-hukukunda-yapay-zeka-kullanimi/

Kaplan, A., & Haenlein, M. (2019). Siri, Siri, in my hand: Who's the fairest in the land? On the interpretations, illustrations, and implications of artificial intelligence. *Business Horizons*, 62(1), 15–25. DOI: 10.1016/j.bushor.2018.08.004

Karaca, E. (2022, Nisan 25). *Kanunilik İlkesi Bağlamında Belirlilik ve Kıyas Yasağı*. Retrieved November 02, 2024, from https://blog.lexpera.com.tr/kanunilik-ilkesi-baglaminda-belirlilik-ve-kiyas-yasagi/

Kassem, R. (2022). Elucidating corporate governance's impact and role in countering fraud.*Corporate Governance (Bradford)*, 22(7), 1523–1546. DOI: 10.1108/CG-08-2021-0279

Kaster, S. D., & Ensign, P. C. (2023). Privatized espionage: NSO Group Technologies and its Pegasus spyware.*Thunderbird International Business Review*, 65(3), 355–364. DOI: 10.1002/tie.22321

Katzenbach, C., & Ulbricht, L. (2019). Algorithmic governance.*Internet Policy Review*, 8(4). Advance online publication. DOI: 10.14763/2019.4.1424

Kaur, B., Sood, K., & Grima, S. (2023). A systematic review on forensic accounting and its contribution towards fraud detection and prevention.*Journal of Financial Regulation and Compliance*, 31(1), 60–95. DOI: 10.1108/JFRC-02-2022-0015

Kavitha, S., & Joshith, R. (2024). Factors shaping the adoption of AI tools among Gen Z: An extended UTAUT2 model investigation using CB-SEM.*Bulletin of Science, Technology & Society*, 44(1-2), 12–32. DOI: 10.1177/02704676241283362

Kawakami, Y., & Zhu, M. (2024). Studying up public sector AI: How networks of power relations shape agency decisions around AI design and use. *arXiv.org*.

Kerr, A., Barry, M., & Kelleher, J. D. (2020). Expectations of artificial intelligence and the performativity of ethics: Implications for communication governance.*Big Data & Society*, 7(1), 2053951720915939. DOI: 10.1177/2053951720915939

Khairati, N., & Putra, A. (2022). Drug usage prediction in health services using Backpropagation Neural Network (BPNN): A case study on paracetamol consumption.*Journal of Health Informatics and Artificial Intelligence*, 14(3), 45–58.

Khairati, N., & Putra, R. (2022). Drug usage prediction using backpropagation neural networks.*Health Informatics Journal*.

Khalid, M. N. A., Al-Kadhimi, A. A., & Singh, M. M. (2023). Recent developments in game-theory approaches for the detection and defense against advanced persistent threats (APTs): A systematic review.*Mathematics*, 11(6), 1353. DOI: 10.3390/math11061353

Khurana, D., Koli, A., Khatter, K., & Singh, S. (2023). Natural language processing: State of the art, current trends and challenges.*Multimedia Tools and Applications*, 82(3), 3713–3744. DOI: 10.1007/s11042-022-13428-4 PMID: 35855771

Kılıç, B. (2024, August 06). *Türkiye'nin 2024 Yılı Ulusal Yapay Zekâ Stratejisi: Geleceğe Dönük Bir Projeksiyon.* Retrieved November 03, 2024, from https://hukukvebilisim.org/turkiyenin-2024-yili-ulusal-yapay-zeka-stratejisi-gelecege-donuk-bir-projeksiyon/

Kim, B., Park, J., & Suh, J. (2020). Transparency and accountability in AI decision support: Explaining and visualizing convolutional neural networks for text information.*Decision Support Systems*, 134, 113302. DOI: 10.1016/j.dss.2020.113302

Kim, H. (2023). *Suggestions for Ethical Decision-Making Model through Collaboration between Human and AI.* J-INSTITUTE., DOI: 10.22471/ai.2023.8.12

Kim, N. J., & Kim, M. K. (2022, March). Teacher's perceptions of using an artificial intelligence-based educational tool for scientific writing.[). Frontiers Media SA.]. *Frontiers in Education*, 7, 755914. DOI: 10.3389/feduc.2022.755914

Kitchin, R. (2017). Thinking critically about and researching algorithms.*Information Communication and Society*, 20(1), 14–29. DOI: 10.1080/1369118X.2016.1154087

Knisley, R. J., & Lin, H. (2022). A review of literature and experimental evidence on fraud motivation: Differentiating incentive and pressure.*Journal of Financial Accounting Research*, 7(1), 184–209. DOI: 10.2308/JFAR-2020-024

Kommisctty, P. D. N. K. (2022). Leading the Future: Big Data Solutions, Cloud Migration, and AI-Driven Decision-Making in Modern Enterprises.*Educational Administration: Theory and Practice*, 28(03), 352–364.

Konidena, B. K., Malaiyappan, J. N. A., & Tadimarri, A. (2024). Ethical considerations in the development and deployment of AI systems.*European Journal of Technology*, 8(2), 41–53. DOI: 10.47672/ejt.1890

Kulal, A., Rahiman, H. U., Suvarna, H., Abhishek, N., & Dinesh, S. (2024). Enhancing public service delivery efficiency: Exploring the impact of AI.*Journal of Open Innovation*, 10(3), 100329. DOI: 10.1016/j.joitmc.2024.100329

Kulkov, I., Kulkova, J., Rohrbeck, R., Menvielle, L., Kaartemo, V., & Makkonen, H. (2023). Artificial intelligence - driven sustainable development: Examining organizational, technical, and processing approaches to achieving global goals.*Sustainable Development*. Advance online publication. DOI: 10.1002/sd.2773

Kutty, N., & Tochibayashi, N. (2022). *Will new initiatives succeed in protecting Japan's biodiversity?* World Economic Forum. https://www.weforum.org/agenda/2022/12/japan-biodiversity/

Kuyumdzhiev, I. (2019). Metodologicheski i tehnologichni aspekti pri arhiviraneto na bazi danni. Varna: Nauka i ikonomika. p. 178. (Library Prof. Tsani Kalyandzhiev; Book 55).

Kuziemski, M., & Misuraca, G. (2020). AI governance in the public sector: Three tales from the frontiers of automated decision-making in democratic settings.*Telecommunications Policy*, 44(6), 101976. DOI: 10.1016/j.telpol.2020.101976 PMID: 32313360

Labanava, A., Dreyling, R. M., III, Mortati, M., Liiv, I., & Pappel, I. (2022, November). Capacity Building in Government: Towards Developing a Standard for a Functional Specialist in AI for Public Services. In *International Conference on Future Data and Security Engineering* (pp. 503-516). Singapore: Springer Nature Singapore. DOI: 10.1007/978-981-19-8069-5_34

Ladislas, E. S. (2024). Personalizing government services through artificial intelligence: Opportunities and challenges. *Indian Journal of Artificial Intelligence and Neural Networking (IJAINN, 3*(5), 13-18.

Lahdili, N. (2023). Citizen participation in local government: A case study of Safi [Doctoral dissertation, Ankara Yıldırım Beyazıt University]. *ResearchGate.* https://doi.org/DOI: 10.1234/researchgate.374477797

Lahdili, N., Önder, M., & Nyadera, I. N. (2024). Artificial intelligence and citizen participation in governance: Opportunities and threats.*Amme Idaresi Dergisi*, 57(3), 202–229.

Lahdili, N., Önder, M., & Nyadera, I. N. (2024). Artificial Intelligence and Citizen Participation in Governance: Opportunities and Threats.*Amme Idaresi Dergisi*, 57(3).

Lapsley, I. (1999). Accounting and the New Public Management: Instruments of Substantive Effiency or a Rationalising Modernity?*Financial Accountability & Management*, 15(3-4), 201–207. DOI: 10.1111/1468-0408.00081

Lapuente, V., & Van de Walle, S. (2020). The effects of new public management on the quality of public services.*Governance: An International Journal of Policy, Administration and Institutions*, 33(3), 461–475. DOI: 10.1111/gove.12502

Larsson, S., & Heintz, F. (2020). Transparency in artificial intelligence.*Internet Policy Review*, 9(2). Advance online publication. DOI: 10.14763/2020.2.1469

Lee, G. H. (2008). Rule-based and case-based reasoning approach for internal audit of bank.*Knowledge-Based Systems*, 21(2), 140–147. DOI: 10.1016/j.knosys.2007.04.001

Lefebvre, R. C., & Flora, J. A. (1988). Social marketing strategies for community-based health education.*American Journal of Public Health.*

Leikas, J., Johri, A., Latvanen, M., Wessberg, N., & Hahto, A. (2022). Governing ethical AI transformation: A case study of AuroraAI.*Frontiers in Artificial Intelligence*, 5, 836557. DOI: 10.3389/frai.2022.836557 PMID: 35224480

Levesque, V. R., Bell, K. P., & Johnson, E. S. (2023). The role of municipal digital services in advancing rural resilience.*Government Information Quarterly*, 41(1), 101883–101883. DOI: 10.1016/j.giq.2023.101883

Levin, S. (2002). Complex adaptive systems: Exploring the known, the unknown and the unknowable.*Bulletin of the American Mathematical Society*, 40(1), 3–19. DOI: 10.1090/S0273-0979-02-00965-5

Lewallen, J. (2023). Expertise for emerging technology: Information, prestige, and the Office of Technology Assessment.*The Review of Policy Research.*

Lewis, G. A., Bellomo, S., & Galyardt, A. (2019). Component mismatches are a critical bottleneck to fielding AI-enabled systems in the public sector. *arXiv preprint arXiv:1910.06136.*

LGC. (2022). What does AI mean for councils? We asked an AI system to tell us. *Local Government Chronicle*. Retrieved from https://www.lgcplus.com/politics/lgcbriefing/what-does-ai-mean-for-councils-we-asked-an-ai-system-to-tell-us-14-12-2022/ (Accessed: October 20, 2023).

Li, C. (2024). Future trends and technological innovations of private AI deployment. *Science. Technology and Social Development Proceedings Series*, 1, 1–14. DOI: 10.70088/6fmynz86

Li, D., & Du, Y. (2007). Artificial Intelligence with Uncertainty.*Artificial Intelligence with Uncertainty.*, 2. Advance online publication. DOI: 10.1201/9781584889991

Liddy, E. (2021). *Natural Language Processing Natural Language Processing.* https://surface.syr.edu/cgi/viewcontent.cgi?article=1043&context=istpub

Li, G., Wang, J., & Wang, X. (2023). Construction and Path of Urban Public Safety Governance and Crisis Management Optimization Model Integrating Artificial Intelligence Technology.*Sustainability (Basel)*, 15(9), 7487. Advance online publication. DOI: 10.3390/su15097487

Lim, J., & Cruz, A. (2024). Advancements in artificial intelligence applications and ethical considerations across industries.*International Journal of Applied Machine Learning and Computational Intelligence*, 14(3), 26–34.

Liu, C., & Ke, L. (2023). Cloud assisted Internet of things intelligent transportation system and the traffic control system in the smart city.*Journal of Control and Decision*, 10(2), 174–187. DOI: 10.1080/23307706.2021.2024460

Liu, H., Shen, J., & Xu, Z. (2020). The integration of artificial intelligence and e-government: Opportunities and challenges.*International Journal of Information Management*, 50, 28–37.

Li, Y., & Segumpan, T. (2024). Challenges of AI adoption in China public service and its impact on efficiency and performance.*International Journal of Academic Research in Business & Social Sciences*.

Lorenzoli, D., Tosi, D., Venticinque, S., & Micillo, R. (2007). Designing multi-layers self-adaptive complex applications., 70-77. https://doi.org/.DOI: 10.1145/1295074.1295088

Loukis, E. N., Maragoudakis, M., & Kyriakou, N. (2020). Artificial intelligence-based public sector data analytics for economic crisis policymaking.*Transforming Government*, 14(4), 639–662. DOI: 10.1108/TG-11-2019-0113

Lu, L., Zhang, J., Xie, Y., Gao, F., Xu, S., Wu, X., & Ye, Z. (2020). Wearable health devices in health care: Narrative systematic review.*JMIR mHealth and uHealth*, 8(11), e18907. DOI: 10.2196/18907 PMID: 33164904

Luo, J., Paduraru, C., Voicu, O., Chervonyi, Y., & Munns, S. (2022). Controlling Commercial Cooling Systems Using Reinforcement Learning. 10.48550/arXiv.2211.07357

Ma, Y., Jiang, W., Sang, N., & Zhang, X. (2012). ARCSM: A Distributed Feedback Control Mechanism for Security-critical Real-time System. *2012 IEEE 10th International Symposium on Parallel and Distributed Processing with Applications*, 379-386. https://doi.org/DOI: 10.1109/ISPA.2012.56

Ma'rup, R., & Rokhman, I. (2024). *Utilization of artificial intelligence (AI) chatbots in improving public services: A meta-analysis study*. Open Access Indonesia Journal of Social Sciences.

Ma, C., Li, J., Wei, K., Liu, B., Ding, M., Yuan, L., Han, Z., & Poor, H. (2022). Trusted AI in Multiagent Systems: An Overview of Privacy and Security for Distributed Learning.*Proceedings of the IEEE*, 111(9), 1097–1132. DOI: 10.1109/JPROC.2023.3306773

Madan, R., & Ashok, M. (2023). AI adoption and diffusion in public administration: A systematic literature review and future research agenda. *Government Information Quarterly*, 40(1), 101774. DOI: 10.1016/j.giq.2022.101774

Madhavan, R., Kerr, J. A., Corcos, A. R., & Isaacoff, B. P. (2020). Toward Trustworthy and Responsible Artificial Intelligence Policy Development. *IEEE Intelligent Systems*, 35(5), 103–108. DOI: 10.1109/MIS.2020.3019679

Madya, F., & Pasaribu, H. (2022). AI capabilities in public service: A resource-based theory perspective. *Journal of Organizational Innovation*.

Mahendra, S. (2021). Artificial intelligence and urban design. *AI Plus Info*. https://www.aiplusinfo.com/blog/artificial-intelligence-and-urban-design

Maldonado, A., Morales, M., Aguilera, P., & Salmerón, A. (2020). Analyzing Uncertainty in Complex Socio-Ecological Networks. *Entropy (Basel, Switzerland)*, 22(1), 123. Advance online publication. DOI: 10.3390/e22010123 PMID: 33285898

Malíčková, J. (2024). Extracting retrospective information through the public sharing of female golfers' contributions in a digital environment: An analytical perspective of their impact on shaping golf communities. *Proceedings of the International Conference on Business Excellence*.

Mallick, T., & Murphy, J. (2024). Analyzing Regional Impacts of Climate Change using Natural Language Processing Techniques. *ArXiv*. https://ar5iv.labs.arxiv.org/html/2401.06817

Malone v United Kingdom, App. No. 8691/79 (European Court of Human Rights August 2, 1984).

Manginte, S. Y. (2024). Fortifying Transparency: Enhancing Corporate Governance through Robust Internal Control Mechanisms. *Advances in Management & Financial Reporting*, 2(2), 72–84. DOI: 10.60079/amfr.v2i2.173

Manning, C., & Schutze, H. (1999). *Foundations of Statistical Natural Language Processing*. MIT Press.

Mann, S. (2013). Veilance and reciprocal transparency: Surveillance versus sousveillance, AR glass, lifeglogging, and wearable computing. *2013 IEEE International Symposium on Technology and Society (ISTAS): Social Implications of Wearable Computing and Augmediated Reality in Everyday Life*, 1-12. https://doi.org/DOI: 10.1109/ISTAS.2013.6613094

Manohar, S., Nag, I., Mittal, A., & Nair, A. J. (2023, August18-19). 2023). Omni Channeling Healthcare: Chaining Details, Information and Predictions for Extemporize Service Delivery. 2023 7th International Conference On Computing, Communication, Control And Automation (ICCUBEA), Markowitz, H., Guerard, J., Xu, G., & Beheshti, B. (2021). Financial anomalies in portfolio construction and management.*Journal of Portfolio Management*, 47(6), 51–64.

Manyika, J., Silberg, J., & Presten, B. (2019, October 25). *What Do We Do About the Biases in AI?* Retrieved from Harvard Business Review: https://hbr.org/2019/10/what-do-we-do-about-the-biases-in-ai#:~:text=AI%20systems%20learn%20to%20make,or%20social%20inequities%2C%20even%20if

Margetts, H. (2022). Rethinking AI for good governance.*Daedalus*, 151(2), 360–371. DOI: 10.1162/daed_a_01922

Margetts, H., & Dorobantu, C. (2019). Rethink government with AI.*Nature*, 568(7751), 163–165. DOI: 10.1038/d41586-019-01099-5 PMID: 30967667

Marques, I., Leitão, J., Carvalho, A., & Pereira, D. (2021). Public administration and values oriented to sustainability: A systematic approach to the literature.*Sustainability (Basel)*, 13(5), 2566. DOI: 10.3390/su13052566

Martin, W. (2017). *The global information society*. Taylor & Francis. DOI: 10.4324/9781315239385

Maslej, N., ... (2024). Artificial Intelligence Index Report 2024. Standford University & US Human-Centered Artifical Intelligence, Retrieved from https://aiindex.stanford.edu/report/

Mattos, P., & Schlindwein, S. (2015). Excellence and productivity: New management imperatives in public service.*Revista de Administração Pública*.

Mazumder, S., & Hossain, M. (2024). AI Hub: Idea to innovative service - An AI Service Hub for the citizens of Bangladesh to accelerate the implementation of Smart Bangladesh. *International Journal of Scientific Research and Management*.

McBride, K., van Noordt, C., Misuraca, G., & Hammerschmid, G. (2021). Toward a systematic understanding of the challenges of procuring artificial intelligence in the public sector.

McCarthy. (2004). What is Artificial Intelligence? Retrieved from https://www-formal.stanford.edu/jmc/whatisai.pdf

Md Nur, N. (2022, August 4). *Driving into a smart mobility future*. The Edge Singapore. https://www.theedgesingapore.com/digitaledge/digital-economy/driving-smart-mobility-future

Medaglia, R., & Tangi, L. (2022, October). The adoption of artificial intelligence in the public sector in Europe: drivers, features, and impacts. In *Proceedings of the 15th International Conference on Theory and Practice of Electronic Governance*, 10-18. DOI: 10.1145/3560107.3560110

Mehra, S. (2021). *Leveraging language technology for national good: Initiatives by the Indian govt.* INDIAai. https://indiaai.gov.in/article/leveraging-language-technology-for-national-good-initiatives-by-the-indian-govt

Meijer, A. J., & Bolívar, M. P. R. (2016). Governing the smart city: A review of the literature on smart urban governance.*International Review of Administrative Sciences*, 82(2), 392–408. DOI: 10.1177/0020852314564308

Mesa, D. (2023). Digital divide, e-government, and trust in public service: The key role of education.*Frontiers in Sociology*, 8, 1140416. DOI: 10.3389/fsoc.2023.1140416 PMID: 36895333

Meskó, B., & Topol, E. J. (2023). The imperative for regulatory oversight of large language models (or generative AI) in healthcare.*NPJ Digital Medicine*, 6(1), 120. DOI: 10.1038/s41746-023-00873-0 PMID: 37414860

Mieniyailova, Y. (2020). Innovative investment development in public catering through IT integration.*Economic Development Review (Schiller Park, Ill.)*.

Mikalef, P., & Gupta, M. (2021). Artificial intelligence capability: Conceptualisation, measurement calibration, and empirical study on its impact on organisational creativity and firm performance.*Information & Management*, 58(3), 103434. DOI: 10.1016/j.im.2021.103434

Mikalef, P., Lemmer, K., Schaefer, C., Ylinen, M., Fjørtoft, S. O., Torvatn, H. Y., Gupta, M., & Niehaves, B. (2022). Enabling AI capabilities in government agencies: A study of determinants for European municipalities.*Government Information Quarterly*, 39(4), 101596. DOI: 10.1016/j.giq.2021.101596

Millán-Vargas, A. O., Sandoval-Almazán, R., & Valle-Cruz, D. (2024). Impact and barriers to AI in the public sector: The case of the State of Mexico.*Proceedings of the 25th Annual International Conference on Digital Government Research*, 81- 89. DOI: 10.1145/3657054.3657249

Millan-Vargas, M., & Valle-Cruz, J. (2024). *Impact and barriers to AI in the public sector: The case of the State of Mexico*. Digital Government Research.

Miller, S. (2023). Singapore's AI applications in the public sector: Six examples. *Management and Business Review, 3*(1–2).https://ssrn.com/abstract=4599495

Miner, A. S., Laranjo, L., & Kocaballi, A. B. (2020). Chatbots in the fight against the COVID-19 pandemic.*NPJ Digital Medicine*, 3(1), 1–4. DOI: 10.1038/s41746-020-0280-0 PMID: 32377576

Ministery of Energy and Natural Resources of Turkey. (2024). Info Bank: Energy. Retrieved from https://enerji.gov.tr/infobank-energy-electricity

Ministry of Education and Culture. (2024). *Ministry of Education and Culture cooperation in UN and UNESCO - OKM - Ministry of Education and Culture, Finland*. Ministry of Education and Culture Cooperation in UN and UNESCO - OKM - Ministry of Education and Culture, Finland. https://okm.fi/en/un-and-unesco

Misra, S. K., Das, S., Gupta, S., & Sharma, S. K. (2020). Public policy and regulatory challenges of artificial intelligence (AI). Re-imagining Diffusion and Adoption of Information Technology and Systems: A Continuing Conversation: IFIP WG 8.6 International Conference on Transfer and Diffusion of IT, TDIT 2020, Tiruchirappalli, India, December 18–19, 2020, Proceedings, Part I, Inuwa-Dutse, I., Toniolo, A., Weller, A., & Bhatt, U. (2023). Algorithmic loafing and mitigation strategies in Human-AI teams. Computers in Human Behavior: Artificial Humans, 1(2), 100024.

Misuraca, G., & Van Noordt, C. (2020). AI Watch—Artificial Intelligence in Public Services: Overview of the Use and Impact of AI in Public Services in the EU. JRC Research Reports (JRC120399).

Misuraca, G., van Noordt, C., & Boukli, A. (2020, September). The use of AI in public services results from a preliminary mapping across the EU. In *Proceedings of the 13th international conference on theory and practice of electronic governance* (pp. 90-99). DOI: 10.1145/3428502.3428513

Misuraca, G., & Viscusi, G. (2020, August). AI-enabled innovation in the public sector: A framework for digital governance and resilience. In *International Conference on Electronic Government* (pp. 110-120). Cham: Springer International Publishing. DOI: 10.1007/978-3-030-57599-1_9

Miyazaki, S. (2012). Algorhythmics: Understanding micro-temporality in computational cultures. *Computational Culture*, 1–22. http://computationalculture.net/article/algorhythmics-understanding-micro-temporality-in-computational-cultures

Mocanu, I. (2022). What is the state's role in a world driven by AI tools? *Central and Eastern European eDem and eGov Days, 40–50.* https://doi.org/DOI: 10.24984/ceeed.2022.40

Mohammed, A. H. Y., Dziyauddin, R. A., & Latiff, L. A. (2023). Current multi-factor of authentication: Approaches, requirements, attacks and challenges.*International Journal of Advanced Computer Science and Applications*, 14(1). Advance online publication. DOI: 10.14569/IJACSA.2023.0140119

Moody's. (2024). B1posistive: Update following to B1, Outlook remains positive. Retrieved from https://www.moodys.com/reports?region=Turkiye

Moor, J. (2006). The Dartmouth College Artificial Intelligence Conference: The Next Fifty Years.*AI Magazine*, 27(4), 87–91.

Morelli, J. (2013). Environmental Sustainability: A Definition for Environmental Professionals.*Journal of Environmental Sustainability*, 1(1), 1–10. Advance online publication. DOI: 10.14448/jes.01.0002

Moreno, F. (2023). Ai readiness of Philippine public administration: a review of literature.DOI: 10.31219/osf.io/kpzt6

Morkhat, P. M., Ponkin, I. V., Markhgeym, M. V., Botnev, V. K., & Turganbayev, A. O. (2019). Artificial intelligence versus public administration: limitations of application.

Mugellini, G., Della Bella, S., Colagrossi, M., Isenring, G. L., & Killias, M. (2021). Public sector reforms and their impact on the level of corruption: A systematic review.*Campbell Systematic Reviews*, 17(2), e1173. DOI: 10.1002/cl2.1173 PMID: 37131927

Mukhin, V., Kornaga, Y., Steshyn, V., & Mostovoy, Y. (2016). Adaptive security system based on intelligent agents for distributed computer systems.*2016 International Conference on Development and Application Systems (DAS)*, 320-325. https://doi.org/DOI: 10.1109/DAAS.2016.7492595

Mullick, M., & Patnaik, A. (2022). Pandemic management, citizens, and the Indian smart cities: Reflections from the right to the smart city and the digital divide. *City. Cultura e Scuola*, 30, 100474. DOI: 10.1016/j.ccs.2022.100474

Mulyana, Y. (2023). The Impact of Using Artificial Intelligence on Public Services in Indonesia.*The International Journal of Science in Society*, 5(3), 356–365. DOI: 10.54783/ijsoc.v5i3.745

Murphy, P. R., & Dacin, M. T. (2011). Psychological pathways to fraud: Understanding and preventing fraud in organizations.*Journal of Business Ethics*, 101(4), 601–618. DOI: 10.1007/s10551-011-0741-0

Nadimpalli, V., Hauser, F., Bittner, D., Grabinger, L., Staufer, S., & Mottok, J. (2023). Systematic Literature Review for the Use of AI Based Techniques in Adaptive Learning Management Systems.*Proceedings of the 5th European Conference on Software Engineering Education*. https://doi.org/DOI: 10.1145/3593663.3593681

Nadkarni, P. M., Ohno-Machado, L., & Chapman, W. W. (2011). Natural language processing: An introduction.*Journal of the American Medical Informatics Association : JAMIA*, 18(5), 544–551. DOI: 10.1136/amiajnl-2011-000464 PMID: 21846786

Naidoo, P., & Fields, D. (2019). Critical success factors for the successful initiation of Lean in public hospitals in KwaZulu-Natal: A factor analysis and structural equation modelling study.*Human Resources for Health*, 17(1), 69. DOI: 10.1186/s12960-019-0405-1 PMID: 31443719

Naik, P. (2023). A methodological study on big data and cloud computing for public policy management.*International Journal for Research in Applied Science and Engineering Technology*, 11(10), 992–999. DOI: 10.22214/ijraset.2023.56118

Nair, A. J., Manohar, S., & Mittal, A. (2023b, 14-16 Dec. 2023). Robotic Vision with Micro Expression Analysis: Revolutionizing Customer Experiences in the Tourism and Hospitality Industry. 2023 IEEE Technology & Engineering Management Conference - Asia Pacific (TEMSCON-ASPAC),

Nair, A. J., Manohar, S., & Mittal, A. (2024). AI-enabled FinTech for innovative sustainability: promoting organizational sustainability practices in digital accounting and finance. International Journal of Accounting & Information Management, ahead-of-print(ahead-of-print). doi:DOI: 10.1108/IJAIM-05-2024-0172

Nair, A. J., Manohar, S., Mittal, A., & Khanna, V. (2023, 14-16 Sept. 2023). Revolutionizing Tourism and Hospitality Services: Integrating AI in the Metaverse. 2023 6th International Conference on Contemporary Computing and Informatics (IC3I)

Nair, A. J., & Manohar, S. (2024). Green Service Consumption: Unlocking Customer Expectations on Technological Transformations Enhancing Purchase Experience in Retail Store.*International Journal of Information Management Data Insights*, 4(2), 100277. https://doi.org/https://doi.org/10.1016/j.jjimei.2024.100277. DOI: 10.1016/j.jjimei.2024.100277

Nair, A. J., Manohar, S., & Chaudhry, R. (2024). Role of Knowledge Management in Enhancing the Effectiveness of the Gig Economy. In Ordóñez de Pablos, P., Almunawar, M. N., & Anshari, M. (Eds.), *Strengthening Sustainable Digitalization of Asian Economy and Society* (pp. 161–175). IGI Global., DOI: 10.4018/979-8-3693-1942-0.ch009

Nair, A. J., Manohar, S., & Mittal, A. (2023a, August18-19). 2023). Enhancing Customer Experience with Teleportation Technology: The Future of Travel and Tourism Industry.*2023 Second International Conference On Smart Technologies For Smart Nation (SmartTechCon)*

Nallaperuma, D., Nawaratne, R., Bandaragoda, T., Adikari, A., Nguyen, S., Kempitiya, T., De Silva, D., Alahakoon, D., & Pothuhera, D. (2019). Online incremental machine learning platform for big data-driven smart traffic management.*IEEE Transactions on Intelligent Transportation Systems*, 20(12), 4679–4690. DOI: 10.1109/TITS.2019.2924883

Nasim, S. F., Qaiser, A., Abrar, N., & Kulsoom, U. (2023). Implementation of AI in traffic management: Need, current techniques, and challenges.*Pakistan Journal of Scientific Research*, 3(1), 20–25. DOI: 10.57041/pjosr.v3i1.942

Nassar, A., & Kamal, M. (2021). Ethical dilemmas in AI-powered decision-making: A deep divc into big data driven ethical considerations *International Journal of Responsible Artificial Intelligence*, 11(8), 1–11.

National Artificial Intelligence Strategy of Turkey. (2021). Retrieved from https://cbddo.gov.tr/SharedFolderServer/Genel/File/TRNationalAIStrategy2021-2025.pdf

National Cybersecurity Policy, 2021. (n.d.).

National Strategy for Artificial Intelligence of India. (2018). Retrieved from https://www.niti.gov.in/sites/default/files/2023-03/National-Strategy-for-Artificial-Intelligence.pdf

Nazaruddin, R., & Yani, E. (2022). Electronic resident card-making services (KTP-el). *International Journal of Public Administration Studies.*

Nee, J., Smith, G. M., & Rustagi, I. (2022). Linguistic justice as a framework for designing, developing, and managing NLP tools. Big Data & Society, OECD. (2024). *Governing with Artificial Intelligence.* OECD. https://www.oecd.org/en/publications/governing-with-artificial-intelligence_26324bc2-en.html

Nerima, M., & Ralyte, J. (2021). Towards a digital maturity balance model for public organizations. In *International Conference on Research Challenges in Information Science* (pp. 295-310). Cham: Springer International Publishing. DOI: 10.1007/978-3-030-75018-3_20

Neumann, O., Guirguis, K., & Steiner, R. (2022). Exploring artificial intelligence adoption in public organisations: A comparative case study.*Public Management Review*, 26(1), 114–141. DOI: 10.1080/14719037.2022.2048685

Newman, J., Mintrom, M., & O'Neill, D. (2022). Digital technologies, artificial intelligence, and bureaucratic transformation.*Futures*, 136, 102886. DOI: 10.1016/j.futures.2021.102886

Neyland, D. (2016). Bearing account-able witness to the ethical algorithmic system.*Science, Technology & Human Values*, 41(1), 50–76. DOI: 10.1177/0162243915598056

Neyland, D., & Möllers, N. (2017). Algorithmic IF … THEN rules and the conditions and consequences of power.*Information Communication and Society*, 20(1), 45–62. DOI: 10.1080/1369118X.2016.1156141

Ng, A. (2011). Sparse Autoencoder. CS294A Lecture Notes, 72, 1-19. Retrieved from https://web.stanford.edu/class/archive/cs/cs294a/cs294a.1104/sparseAutoencoder.pdf

Nicholls, J., Kuppa, A., & Le-Khac, N.-A. (2021). Financial cybercrime: A comprehensive survey of deep learning approaches to tackle the evolving financial crime landscape.*IEEE Access : Practical Innovations, Open Solutions*, 9, 163965–163986.

Nishant, R., Kennedy, M., & Corbett, J. (2020). Artificial intelligence for sustainability: Challenges, opportunities, and a research agenda.*International Journal of Information Management*, 53, 102104. DOI: 10.1016/j.ijinfomgt.2020.102104

NITRD. (2023). National AI R&D Strategic Plan 2023. Retrieved fromhttps://www.nitrd.gov/pubs/National-Artificial-Intelligence-Research-and-Development-Strategic-Plan-2023-Update.pdf

Nwankwo, E. S. (2024). Regulating the Privacy Aspects of Artificial Intelligence Systems in Nigeria.*African Journal on Privacy and Data Protection*, 1, 220–247.

Obi, O. C., Akagha, O. V., Dawodu, S. O., Anyanwu, A. C., Onwusinkwue, S., & Ahmad, I. A. I. (2024). Comprehensive review on cybersecurity: Modern threats and advanced defense strategies.*Computer Science & IT Research Journal*, 5(2), 293–310. DOI: 10.51594/csitrj.v5i2.758

OECD. (2020). *"Open, Useful and Re-usable data (OURdata) Index: 2019", OECD Public Governance Policy Papers, No. 01*. OECD Publishing., DOI: 10.1787/45f6de2d-

OECD. (2023). *"Common guideposts to promote interoperability in AI risk management", OECD Artificial Intelligence Papers, No. 5*. OECD Publishing., DOI: 10.1787/ba602d18-

OECD. (2024). *"2023 OECD Digital Government Index: Results and key findings", OECD Public Governance Policy Papers, No. 44*. OECD Publishing., DOI: 10.1787/1a89ed5e-

OECD. (2024a). Economic outlook: Steady global growth expected for 2024 and 2025. Retrieved from https://www.oecd.org/en/about/news/press-releases/2024/05/economic-outlook-steady-global-growth-expected-for-2024-and-2025.html

OECD. (2024b).. . *Economic Outlook*, 2024(1), •••. https://www.oecd-ilibrary.org/docserver/2b72fc41-en.pdf?expires=1727124085&id=id&accname=guest&checksum=5EE3CF374CFD1BD4F79D9443A5B8E755

Office of the Directorate of National Intelligence. (2023), *The IC Data Strategy 2023-2025: The IC Data-Driven Future Unlocking Mission Value and Insight*, https://www.dni.gov/files/ODNI/documents/IC-Data-Strategy-2023-2025.pdf

Office of the National Security Adviser. (2021). *National Cybersecurity Policy and Strategy 2021*. Office of the National Security Adviser.

Okay E. (2018). A New Barrier for the Future of Energy Market in Turkey: Internal Capital Adequacy Assessment Process (ICAAP). *in Ethics and Sustainability in Global Supply Chain Management* (SCOPUS),, (178-196). Hersey: IGI Global.

Okay, C. N., Sencer, A., & Taskin, N. (2024). Quantitative indicators for environmental and social sustainability performance assessment of the supply chain. *Environment, Development and Sustainability*. Advance online publication. DOI: 10.1007/s10668-024-05210-3

Okay, E. (2016). Towards Smart Cities in Turkey? Transitioning from Waste to Creative, Clean and Cheap Eco- Energy. In *Handbook of Research on Waste Management Techniques for Sustainability (SCOPUS), Hersey*. IGI Global. DOI: 10.4018/978-1-4666-9723-2.ch015

Okay, E. (2017). Investment on Heat Pumps: Geothermal Green Solutions for Turkey Lowering Energy Costs. In *Handbook of Research on Supply Chain Management for Sustainable Development (SCOPUS), (194-217). Hersey*. IGI Global.

Okay, E. (2020). *More Obstacles to the Growth of ESCOs in Turkey: Stumble In the Midst of a Financial Distress in Handbook of Research on Creating Sustainable Value in the Global Economy, Hersey*. IGI Global. DOI: 10.4018/978-1-7998-1196-1.ch008

Okoye, N. J., Okonkwo, V. I. P., & Okaro, C. P. (2021). FRAUD AND CORRUPTION'S EFFECTS ON NIGERIA'S CAPITAL MARKET PERFORMANCE: CONCEPTUAL REVIEW.*Journal of Global Accounting Department of Accountancy*, 7(1).

Olabi, A. G., Abdelghafar, A. A., Maghrabie, H. M., Sayed, E. T., Rezk, H., Radi, M. A., Obaideen, K., & Abdelkareem, M. A. (2023). Application of Artificial Intelligence for Prediction, Optimization, and Control of Thermal Energy Storage Systems.*Thermal Science and Engineering Progress*, 39, 101730. DOI: 10.1016/j.tsep.2023.101730

Olney, S. (2020). Serving the Public, But Not Public Servants? *The Palgrave Handbook of the Public Servant*, 1-19.

Oloyede, R. (2021). *Surveillance Law in Africa: A Review of Six Countries: Nigeria Country Report.*ids.ac.uk

Onder, M., & Saygılı, H. (2018). Yapay Zekâ ve Kamu Yönetimine Yansımaları / Artificial Intelligence and the Reflections on Public Administration. *Türk İdare Dergisi*, 90(487), 629–668.

Önder, M., & Saygılı, H. (2018). Yapay Zekâ ve Kamu Yönetimine Yansımaları. *Türk İdare Dergisi*, 2(487), 629–670.

Önder, M., & Saygılı, H. (2018). Yapay zeka ve kamu yönetimine yansımaları.*Türk İdare Dergisi*, 90(487), 629–668.

Onder, M., & Uzun, M. M. (2021). Roles of Artificial Intelligence (AI) on COVID-19 pandemic crisis management policies.[IJPADA]. *International Journal of Public Administration in the Digital Age*, 8(2), 1–13. DOI: 10.4018/IJPADA.294122

Orji, U. J. (2018). The African Union Convention on National Security: A Regional Response towards Cyber Security. *MUJLT*, 110.

Osborne, S. (2020). *Public service logic: Creating value for public service users, citizens, and society through public service delivery*. Routledge. DOI: 10.4324/9781003009153

Osborne, S. P., & Brown, L. (2013). *Handbook of innovation in public services*. Edward Elgar Publishing., DOI: 10.4337/9781849809757

Oskam, I., Bossink, B., & de Man, A. P. (2021). Valuing value in innovation ecosystems: How cross-sector actors overcome tensions in collaborative sustainable business model development.*Business & Society*, 60(5), 1059–1091. DOI: 10.1177/0007650320907145

Oxford Insights. (2023). Government AI Readiness Index 2023. Retrieved from https://oxfordinsights.com/wp-content/uploads/2023/12/2023-Government-AI-Readiness-Index-2.pdf

Ozkan-Ozay, M., Akin, E., Aslan, Ö., Kosunalp, S., Iliev, T., Stoyanov, I., & Beloev, I. (2024). A Comprehensive Survey: Evaluating the Efficiency of Artificial Intelligence and Machine Learning Techniques on Cyber Security Solutions.*IEEE Access : Practical Innovations, Open Solutions*, 12, 12229–12256. DOI: 10.1109/ACCESS.2024.3355547

Pang, B., & Lee, L. (2008). Opinion Mining and Sentiment Analysis. *Foundations and Trends® in Information Retrieval, 2*(1–2), 1–135. DOI: 10.1561/1500000011

Papagiannidis, E. (2024). Responsible AI governance in practice: The strategic impact of responsible AI governance on business value and competitiveness.

Pasquale, F. (2013). The emperor's new codes: reputation and search algorithms in the finance sector. *Governing Algorithms*, 1–86.

Pattanayak, S., & Verdugo-Yepes, C. (2020). Protecting public infrastructure from vulnerabilities to corruption: a risk-based approach. *Well Spent: How Strong Infrastructure Governance Can End Waste in Public Investment. Pg*, 175-200.

Pencheva, I., Esteve, M., & Mikhaylov, S. J. (2020). Big Data and AI–A transformational shift for government: So, what next for research?*Public Policy and Administration*, 35(1), 24–44. DOI: 10.1177/0952076718780537

Perdana, A., & Mokhtar, I. A. (2022). Seniors are adopting digital devices and virtual event platforms in Singapore during COVID-19.*Technology in Society*, 68, 101817. DOI: 10.1016/j.techsoc.2021.101817 PMID: 34785827

Pereira, L., & Ruysenaar, S. (2012). Moving from traditional government to new adaptive governance: The changing face of food security responses in South Africa. *Food Security*, 4(1), 41–58. DOI: 10.1007/s12571-012-0164-5

Perino, D., Katevas, K., Lutu, A., Marin, E., & Kourtellis, N. (2022). Privacy-preserving AI for future networks.*Communications of the ACM*, 65(4), 52–53. DOI: 10.1145/3512343

Persson, T., Parker, C. F., & Widmalm, S. (2017). Social trust, impartial administration and public confidence in EU crisis management institutions.*Public Administration*, 95(1), 97–114. DOI: 10.1111/padm.12295

Petrov, P., Vasilev, Yu., Kuyumdzhiev, I., & Ivanov, S. Digitalizacia na procesite na upravlenie na obrazovatelnite uslugi v universitetska sreda. Varna: University Press Science and Economics, 2022, p. 134., ISBN (print) 978-954-21-1132-0 /

Pianini, D., Casadei, R., & Viroli, M. (2019). Security in Collective Adaptive Systems: A Roadmap. *2019 IEEE 4th International Workshops on Foundations and Applications of Self* Systems (FAS*W)*, 86-91. https://doi.org/.DOI: 10.1109/FAS-W.2019.00034

Pizzinelli, C., Panton, A. J., Tavares, M. M. M., Cazzaniga, M., & Li, L. (2023). *Labour market exposure to AI: cross-country differences and distributional implications*. International Monetary Fund.

Pollitt, C., & Bouckaert, G. (2011), Public Management Reform: A Comparative Analysis. Oxford University Press, 2011.

Polok, B., el-Taj, H., & Rana, A. A. (2023). Balancing Potential and Peril: The Ethical Implications of Artificial.*Multicultural Education*, 9(6).

Prasad, A. (2021). *Examining bureaucratic responsiveness in India: A comparative study of municipal services* (Doctoral dissertation, The George Washington University).

Presuel, R., & Sierra, J. (2023). The Adoption of Artificial Intelligence in Bureaucratic Decision-making: A Weberian Perspective.. *Digital Government: Research and Practice*. https://doi.org/.DOI: 10.1145/3609861

Principlist Framework for Social Benefits. Technological Forecasting and Social Change, Elsevier, Bolívar, M. P. R. (2017). *Financial Sustainability in Public Administration: Exploring the Concept of Financial Health*. Palgrave Macmillan. https://proxy.hacibayram.edu.tr:2708/ehost/ebookviewer/ebook/bmxlYmtfXzE1NzM2OTRfX0FO0?sid=c64b32ab-098c-4a02-aa34-1101f9b635d7@redis&vid=2&format=EB&rid=2

Radanliev, P., Santos, O., & Brandon-Jones, A. (2024). Capability hardware enhanced instructions and artificial intelligence bill of materials in trustworthy artificial intelligence systems: analyzing cybersecurity threats, exploits, and vulnerabilities in new software bills of materials with artificial intelligence. *The Journal of Defense Modeling and Simulation*, 15485129241267919.

Rahman, M., Arshi, A., Hasan, M., Mishu, S., Shahriar, H., & Wu, F. (2023). Security Risk and Attacks in AI: A Survey of Security and Privacy. *2023 IEEE 47th Annual Computers, Software, and Applications Conference (COMPSAC)*, 1834-1839. https://doi.org/DOI: 10.1109/COMPSAC57700.2023.00284

Rahmani, H. (2023). *Exploring the integration of AI in public library services*. AI and Tech in Behavioral and Social Sciences. DOI: 10.61838/kman.aitech.1.4.6

Rahman, J. M., & Marjerison, R. K. (2020). *Sustaining competitive advantage through good governance and fiscal controls: Risk determinants in internal controls.* Corporate Ownership & Control.

Rai, A. (2013). Application of artificial intelligence for virtually assisted prognosis of diabetes: A NODDS project.

Raimundo, R., & Rosário, A. (2021). The Impact of Artificial Intelligence on Data System Security: A Literature Review. *Sensors (Basel)*, 21(21), 7029. Advance online publication. DOI: 10.3390/s21217029 PMID: 34770336

Rajesh, Y., Kumar, V. K., & Poojari, A. (2024). A Unified Approach Toward Security Audit and Compliance in Cloud Computing. *Journal of The Institution of Engineers (India): Series B, 105*(3), 733-750.

Rakha, N. (2023). The impacts of Artificial Intelligence (AI) on business and its regulatory challenges. *International Journal of Law and Policy*. https://doi.org/ .DOI: 10.59022/ijlp.23

Rashid, M. A., Al-Mamun, A., Roudaki, H., & Yasser, Q. R. (2022). An overview of corporate fraud and its prevention approach. *Australasian Accounting. Business and Finance Journal*, 16(1), 101–118.

Rawashdeh, S. (2023, March 6). *AI's mysterious 'black box' problem, explained.* Retrieved from University of Michigan-Dearborn News: https://umdearborn.edu/news/ais-mysterious-black-box-problem-explained#:~:text=If%2C%20for%20example%2C%20an%20autonomous,we%20can't%20trace%20the

Redmond, T. (2020). Independent review into the oversight of local audit and the transparency of local authority financial reporting. *London, available at: https://assets. publishing. service. gov. uk/government/uploads/system/uploads/attachment_data/file/916217/Redmond_Review. pdf.*

Regona, M., Yigitcanlar, T., Xia, B., & Li, R. Y. (2022). Opportunities and adoption challenges of AI in the construction industry: A PRISMA review. *Journal of Open Innovation*, 8(1), 45. DOI: 10.3390/joitmc8010045

Reis, J., Santo, P. E., & Melão, N. (2019). Impacts of artificial intelligence on public administration: A systematic literature review. In *2019 14th Iberian conference on information systems and technologies (CISTI)* (pp. 1-7). IEEE. DOI: 10.23919/CISTI.2019.8760893

Rendon, R. G., & Rendon, J. M. (2015). Auditability in public procurement: An analysis of internal controls and fraud vulnerability. *International Journal of Procurement Management*, 8(6), 710–730. DOI: 10.1504/IJPM.2015.072388

Reuters, (2024). Fitch upgrades Turkey's rating to “BB-” on improved fiscal policy. Retrieved from https://www.reuters.com/world/middle-east/fitch-upgrades-turkeys-rating-bb-improved-fiscal-policy-2024-09-06/

Ribeiro, R. (2016). Are chatbots in state IT’s future? *StateTech Magazine*. Retrieved from https://statetechmagazine.com/article/2016/11/are-chatbots-state-its-future (Accessed: August 9, 2024).

Riefa, C., & Saintier, S. (2020). *Vulnerable consumers and the law: consumer protection and access to justice*. Routledge. Ruiu, M. L., & Ragnedda, M. Digital-Environmental Poverty.

Rintoul, J. (2023). *Farming for the future: Why the Netherlands is one of the largest food exporters in the world | DutchReview*. Https://Dutchreview.Com/. https://dutchreview.com/culture/innovation/second-largest-agriculture-exporter/

Robarge, D. (2024, June). Evolution of Surveillance Policy: US Intelligence, Domestic Surveillance and the Time of Troubles. Washington DC, United States of America.

Robles, P., & Mallinson, D. J. (2023). Artificial intelligence technology, public trust, and effective governance.*The Review of Policy Research*, ropr.12555. DOI: 10.1111/ropr.12555

Rosenbloom, D. H., Kravchuk, R. S., & Clerkin, R. M. (2022). *Public administration: Understanding management, politics, and law in the public sector*. Routledge.

Rouvroy, A., Berns, T., & Carey-Libbrecht, L. (2013). Algorithmic governmentality and prospects of emancipation: Disparateness as a precondition for individuation through relationships?*Reseaux (London)*, 177(1), 163–196. DOI: 10.3917/res.177.0163

Rubaii, N. (2012). Leading by example: Modeling global public service excellence. *Public Administration Review*, 72(1), 1–5.

Ruggiero, A. F., Owusu, T. D., & Staley, J. J. (2022). Ransomware in local government: Risk factors, vulnerabilities, and exploitation during a global pandemic. *Issues in Information Systems*, 23(4).

Ryan, J., Ludwig, J., & Mcalpine, C. (2007). Complex adaptive landscapes (CAL): A conceptual framework of multi-functional, non-linear ecohydrological feedback systems.*Ecological Complexity*, 4(3), 113–127. DOI: 10.1016/j.ecocom.2007.03.004

Sala-Garrido, R., & Maziotis, A. (2023). Benchmarking the performance of productive units using cross-efficiency techniques: An empirical approach for water companies.*Water Resources Management*, 37(14), 5459–5476. DOI: 10.1007/s11269-023-03614-w

Samani, M. A., Ismail, N., & Leman, Z. (2017). Development of a conceptual model for risk-based quality management system.*Total Quality Management & Business Excellence*, 14(4), 1–16.

Samaratunge, R., & Alam, Q. (2021). Accountability and transparency in emerging countries: Governance, democratic currents and change.*Public Administration and Development*, 41(4), 147–156. DOI: 10.1002/pad.1963

Sanchez, T., Shumway, H., Gordner, T., & Lim, T. (2022). The prospects of artificial intelligence in urban planning. *International Journal of Urban Sciences*.

Saner, R., Saner-Yiu, N., & Gollub, L. (2017). Implementing the SDGs by subnational governments: Urgent need to strengthen administrative capacities.*Public Administration and Policy*, 20(2), 23–40.

Santoro, P. (2019). The sustainability of institutions: An unstable condition.*International Review of Administrative Sciences*, 85(4), 609–626. DOI: 10.1177/0020852317741533

Sarkar, G., & Shukla, S. K. (2023). Behavioral analysis of cybercrime: Paving the way for effective policing strategies. *Journal of Economic Criminology*, 100034.

Sartori, A., & Bocca, B. (2022). Minding the gap(s): Public perceptions of AI and socio-technical imaginaries.*AI & Society*.

Saygılı, H. (2020). *Public policies on artificial intelligence: Comparison of the USA and China's AI public policies* (Unpublished master's thesis). Ankara Yıldırım Beyazıt University, Institute of Social Sciences, Department of Political Science and Public Administration, Ankara.

Schemmer, M., Hemmer, P., Nitsche, M., Kuhl, N., & Vossing, M. (2022). A Meta-Analysis of the Utility of Explainable Artificial Intelligence in Human-AI Decision-Making.*Proceedings of the 2022 AAAI/ACM Conference on AI, Ethics, and Society*. https://doi.org/DOI: 10.1145/3514094.3534128

Schiff, D., Borenstein, J., Biddle, J., & Laas, K. (2021). AI Ethics in the Public, Private, and NGO Sectors: A Review of a Global Document Collection. *IEEE Transactions on Technology and Society*, 2(1), 31–42. DOI: 10.1109/TTS.2021.3052127

Schmager, S., Grøder, C. H., Parmiggiani, E., Pappas, I., & Vassilakopoulou, P. (2023). What do citizens think of AI adoption in public services? Exploratory research on citizen attitudes through a social contract lens.

Schmidt, J. (2023). Mitigating risk of failure in information technology projects causes and mechanisms.*Project Leadership and Society*, 4, 100097. DOI: 10.1016/j.plas.2023.100097

Schroter, E., Quick, K., Ongaro, E., & Hartley, J. (2023). Insights into public management form policing: Introduction to the special issue of Public Management Review.*Public Management Review*, 25(9), 1633–1639. DOI: 10.1080/14719037.2023.2264892

Scupola, A., & Mergel, I. (2022). Co-production in digital transformation of public administration and public value creation: The case of Denmark.*Government Information Quarterly*, 39(1), 101650. DOI: 10.1016/j.giq.2021.101650

Section 37 of the Nigerian Constitution. (n.d.).

Section 38(4) of the Cybercrime Act, 2015. (n.d.).

Şenyüz, D. (2022). *Vergi Ceza Hukuku* (12. ed.). Bursa: Ekin Yayınevi.

Serikandi, T., & Ghivary, P. (2022). The role of product managers in public service application development. *Journal of Public Sector Innovation.*

Shafritz, J. M., Russell, E. W., Borick, C. P., & Hyde, A. C. (2022). *Introducing Public Administration* (10th ed.). Routledge. DOI: 10.4324/9781003191322

Shams, S., Goswami, S., Lee, K., Yang, S., & Park, S.-J. (2018). Towards Distributed Cyberinfrastructure for Smart Cities Using Big Data and Deep Learning Technologies, *IEEE 38th International Conference on Distributed Computing Systems (ICDCS)*, Vienna, Austria, pp. 1276-1283, DOI: 10.1109/ICDCS.2018.00127

Shams, S. R., Jahani, A., Kalantary, S., Moeinaddini, M., & Khorasani, N. (2021). Artificial intelligence accuracy assessment in NO2 concentration forecasting of metropolises air.*Scientific Reports*, 11(1), 1805. DOI: 10.1038/s41598-021-81455-6 PMID: 33469146

Shany, Y. (2024). Catching Up: The European Court of Human Rights Approximates its Approach to Extraterritorial Jurisdiction Over Digital Surveillance to That of the Human Rights Committee.*European Convention on Human Rights Law Review.* Vol. 5. *No. 2.*, 182-189. DOI: 10.1163/26663236-bja10089

Shao, Z., Zhao, R., Yuan, S., Ding, M., & Wang, Y. (2022). Tracing the evolution of AI in the past decade and forecasting the emerging trends.*Expert Systems with Applications*, 209, 118221. DOI: 10.1016/j.eswa.2022.118221

Sharik, N., & Deepak Chaitanya, M. (2020). Design and Fabrication of Fuel Level Monitoring & Alert System using IoT / N. Sharik, M. Deepak Chaitanya[IJERT]. *International Journal of Engineering Research & Technology (Ahmedabad)*, 9(10), 442–444.

Sharma, M., Luthra, S., Joshi, S., & Kumar, A. (2022). Implementing challenges of artificial intelligence: Evidence from public manufacturing sector of an emerging economy.*Government Information Quarterly*, 39(4), 101624. DOI: 10.1016/j.giq.2021.101624

Shelf. (2024). *Challenges and Considerations in Natural Language Processing*. Shelf. https://shelf.io/blog/challenges-and-considerations-in-nlp/

Shnitko, A. (2003). Adaptive security in complex information systems.*7th Korea-Russia International Symposium on Science and Technology, Proceedings KORUS 2003. (IEEE Cat. No.03EX737)*, 2, 206-210vol.2.

Shrestha, Y. R., & Yang, Y. (2019). Organizational adoption of artificial intelligence in public administration: Literature review and research agenda.*Government Information Quarterly*, 36(4), 101391. DOI: 10.1016/j.giq.2019.07.001

Shvets, K., Onyshchenko, A., Kudin, V., Korchak, N., & Ivanii, O. (2024). Application of artificial intelligence in modern public administration: New opportunities and challenges. *International Journal of Informatics and Communication Technology (IJ-ICT), 13*(3), 509–518.

Sigfrids, A., Nieminen, M., Leikas, J., & Pikkuaho, P. (2022). How should public administrations foster the ethical development and use of artificial intelligence? A review of proposals for developing governance of AI.*Frontiers in Human Dynamics*, 4, 858108. DOI: 10.3389/fhumd.2022.858108

Sinha, S., & Lee, Y. M. (2024). Challenges with developing and deploying AI models and applications in industrial systems.*Discover Artificial Intelligence*, 4(1), 55. DOI: 10.1007/s44163-024-00151-2

Smuha, N. A. (2019). The EU Approach to Ethics Guidelines for Trustworthy Artificial Intelligence.*Computer Law Review International*, 20(4), 97–106. DOI: 10.9785/cri-2019-200402

Sousa, W. G. D., Melo, E. R. P. D., Bermejo, P. H. D. S., Farias, R A S., & Gomes, A. D. O. (2019, July25). How and where is artificial intelligence in the public sector going? A literature review and research agenda.*Government Information Quarterly*, 36(4), 101392–101392. DOI: 10.1016/j.giq.2019.07.004

Srinivasan, R., & Chander, A. (2021). Biases in AI Systems.*ACM Queue; Tomorrow's Computing Today*, 19(2), 45–64. DOI: 10.1145/3466132.3466134

Srinivasan, V. (2022). AI & learning: A preferred future.*Computers and Education: Artificial Intelligence*, 3, 100062. DOI: 10.1016/j.caeai.2022.100062

Standard and Poor's. (2024). Turkiye Upgraded To 'B+' On Economic Rebalancing; Outlook Positive. Retrieved fromhttps://disclosure.spglobal.com/ratings/en/regulatory/article/-/view/type/HTML/id/3165137

Statista, (2024a). Renewable energy investments worldwide - statistics & facts. Retrieved from https://www.statista.com/topics/10992/global-renewable-energy-investments/#topicOverview

Statista, (2024b). Ranking of leading 20 smart cities globally in 2023, by human development index (HDI) score. Retrieved from https://www.statista.com/statistics/1410416/hdi-smart-city-index-worldwide/

Statista, (2024c). Market Insights: Artificial Intelligence -Turkey. Retrieved from-https://www.statista.com/outlook/tmo/artificial-intelligence/turkey

Stockinger, D., & Lecheler, S. (2023). Navigating the gray areas of content moderation: Professional moderators' perspectives on uncivil user comments and the role of (AI-based) technological tools.*New Media & Society*, 25(4), 837–855. DOI: 10.1177/14614448231190901

Stylos, N., Zwiegelaar, J., & Buhalis, D. (2021). Big data empowered agility for dynamic, volatile, and time-sensitive service industries: The case of tourism sector. *International Journal of Contemporary Hospitality Management*, 33(3), 1015–1036. DOI: 10.1108/IJCHM-07-2020-0644

Stypińska, J., & Franke, A. (2023). AI revolution in healthcare and medicine and the (re-) emergence of inequalities and disadvantages for the ageing population.*Frontiers in Sociology*, 7, 1038854. DOI: 10.3389/fsoc.2022.1038854 PMID: 36755564

Sultan, S., Taimuri, U., Basnan, S. A., Ai-Orabi, W. K., Awadallah, A., Almowald, F., & Hazazi, A. (2020). Low vitamin D and its association with cognitive impairment and dementia.*Journal of Aging Research*, 2020(1), 6097820. DOI: 10.1155/2020/6097820 PMID: 32399297

Sümer, S. Y. (2021). Ceza Yargılamasının Geleceği: Robot Hakim.*Dokuz Eylül Üniversitesi Hukuk Fakültesi Dergisi*, 23(2), 1543–1591.

Sun, T. Q., & Medaglia, R. (2019). Mapping the challenges of artificial intelligence in the public sector: Evidence from public healthcare.*Government Information Quarterly*, 36(2), 368–383. DOI: 10.1016/j.giq.2018.09.008

Syam, D., & Moenta, H. (2021). *Implementing transparency and participation: An overview in public service*. International Journal Paper Public Review.

Szalkowski, G., & Johansen, C. (2023). Defining and measuring the effects of digital technologies on social sustainability: A systematic literature review.*Sustainable Development*. Advance online publication. DOI: 10.1002/sd.2741

Taeihagh, A. (2021). Governance of artificial intelligence.*Policy and Society*, 40(2), 137–157. DOI: 10.1080/14494035.2021.1928377

Taherdoost, H. (2021). A review on risk management in information systems: Risk policy, control and fraud detection.*Electronics (Basel)*, 10(24), 3065. DOI: 10.3390/electronics10243065

Tangi, L., van Noordt, C., & Rodriguez Müller, A. P. (2023, July). The challenges of AI implementation in the public sector. An in-depth case studies analysis. In Proceedings of the 24th annual international conference on digital government research (pp. 414-422). DOI: 10.1145/3598469.3598516

Tang, J., & Karim, K. E. (2019). Financial fraud detection and big data analytics–implications on auditors' use of fraud brainstorming session.*Managerial Auditing Journal*, 34(3), 324–337. DOI: 10.1108/MAJ-01-2018-1767

Tapscott, D., & Tapscott, A. (2015). *Blockchain revolution: How the technology behind Bitcoin is changing money, business, and the world*. Penguin/Portfolio.

Tariq, M. U. (2024). The Role of Emerging Technologies in Shaping the Global Digital Government Landscape. *Emerging Developments and Technologies in Digital Government*, 160-180.

Teremetskyi, V., Burylo, Y., Stefanchuk, M., & Zozuliak, O. (2024). Prospective Regulation of Artificial Intelligence in the European Union and its Possible Implications for Ukraine.*International Journal of Applied Engineering & Technology*, 6(1).

The Study on the Future Role and Development of the Public Administration. (2015). *Baltic Institute of Social Sciences*. RIGA

Thienthong, K., & Suttawet, C. (2022). Developing local hospitals for public health excellence. *Journal of Public Health and Development*.

Toll, D., Lindgren, I., Melin, U., & Madsen, C. Ø. (2020). Values, benefits, considerations, and risks of AI in government: A study of AI policies in Sweden.*JeDEM: EJournal of EDemocracy and Open Government*, 12(1), 40–60. DOI: 10.29379/jedem.v12i1.593

Tomašev, N., Cornebise, J., Hutter, F., Mohamed, S., Picciariello, A., Connelly, B., Belgrave, D., Ezer, D., van der Haert, F., & Mugisha, F. (2020). AI for social good: Unlocking the opportunity for positive impact.[In.]. *Nature Communications*, 11(1), 2468. DOI: 10.1038/s41467-020-15871-z PMID: 32424119

Töngel, B. (2024, July 11). *Hukukta Yapay Zeka Kullanımı: Genel Bakış*. Retrieved from Blog.kalem.ai: https://blog.kalem.ai/hukukta-yapay-zeka-kullanimi/

Toniolo, F. (2023). Artificial Intelligence and Public Administration: Ethical Implications of the Use of Automatic Decision-making Systems. https://hdl.handle.net/20.500.12880/8079

TRAI. (2024). *Türkiye Yapay Zeka İnisiyatif 2024 Çalıştayı Raporu.* Türkye Yapay Zeka İnisiyatifi (TRAI). Retrieved October 31, 2024, from https://turkiye.ai/wp-content/uploads/2024/07/TRAI-2024-Calistay-Raporu.pdf

TRAI. (2024). *Yapay Zekâ Etik İlkeleri Ve Hukuki Düzenlemeler Raporu.* Türkiye Yapay Zekâ İnisiyatifi. Retrieved October 31, 2024, from https://turkiye.ai/wp-content/uploads/2024/06/TRAI-Yapay-Zeka-Etik-Ilkeleri-ve-Hukuki-Duzenlemeler-Raporu-Mayis-2024-5.pdf

Tran, N., Luu, T. T., Trinh, N. K., & Nguyen, X. N. (2023). How do normative public values promote service innovative behavior in public organizations: The roles of felt responsibility for change and responsible leadership.*Public Performance & Management Review*, 46(5), 1207–1236. DOI: 10.1080/15309576.2023.2241453

Trompeter, G. M., Carpenter, T. D., Desai, N., Jones, K. L., & Riley, R. A.Jr. (2013). A synthesis of fraud-related research.*Auditing*, 32(Supplement 1), 287–321. DOI: 10.2308/ajpt-50360

Trondal, J. (2021). Public administration sustainability and its organizational basis.*International Review of Administrative Sciences*, 87(2), 399–415. DOI: 10.1177/0020852319869430

Trotta, A., Ziosi, M., & Lomonaco, V. (2023). The future of ethics in AI: Challenges and opportunities.*AI & Society*, 38(439–441), 439–441. Advance online publication. DOI: 10.1007/s00146-023-01644-x

Turan, T., Kemaloğlu, N., & Küçüksille, E. C. (2020). Hukuk'ta Yapay Zeka: Çalışmalar ve Gelecek Öngörüleri.*Mehmet Akif Ersoy Üniversitesi Fen Bilimleri Enstitüsü Dergisi*, 11(2), 246–255. DOI: 10.29048/makufebed.748843

Turing, A. M. (1937). On computable numbers, with an application to the Entscheisungsproblem. Proceedings of the London Mathematical Society, s2-42(1), 230–265. https://doi.org/DOI: 10.1112/plms/s2-43.6.544

Ulaşan, F. (2023). The Dark Side Of Artificial Intelligence On The Basis Of Public Administration. . *Toplum Ekonomi Ve Yönetim Dergisi, 4*(Özel), 301-323.

Ulaşan, F. (2023). The Dark Side of Artificial Intelligence on the basis of public administration. *Toplum Ekonomi ve Yönetim Dergisi, 4*(Özel), 301-323.

Ulaşan, F. (2023a). Koronavirüsle Mücadelede Yapay Zekânın Yerinin Kamu Yönetimi Temelinde Değerlendirilmesi. *3.International Mediterranean Congress* (pp. 109-123). Mersin: Iksad Global.

Ulaşan, F. (2023b). The Impact of Korean Local Government's Public Health and Urban Planning Policies in Combating COVID-19. *Kent Akademisi*(16).

Ulaşan, F. (2023d). The Use of Artificial Intelligence in Educational Institutions: Social Consequences of Artificial Intelligence in Education. *Korkut Ata Türkiyat Araştırmaları Dergisi*(Özel Sayı 1), 1305-1324.

Ulaşan, F. (2023c). *The Possibility of Using Artificial Intelligence for Turkish Administrative Jurisdiction*. İksad Yayınevi.

Ulaşan, F. (2023e). The Use Of Artificial Intelligence In The Defense System Within The Framework Of The Policy Making Cycle: The Case Of The United States. *Uluslararası Toplumsal Bilimler Dergisi*, 7(3), 517–535.

Ulaşan, F. (2024). Contributions Of Declaration Of Ethics For Turkish Judiciary To The Right To A Fair Trial In Terms Of Effective Participation In Trials.*Adalet Dergisi*, (72), 155–177. DOI: 10.57083/adaletdergisi.1483988

Ulnicane, I., Knight, W., Leach, T., Stahl, B. C., & Wanjiku, W. G. (2021). Framing governance for a contested emerging technology: Insights from AI policy.*Policy and Society*, 40(2), 158–177. DOI: 10.1080/14494035.2020.1855800

Umar, A., & Misnawati. (2019). One-stop service policy as a bureaucratic reform in Indonesia. *Public Policy Review*.

UN. (1987). *Our Common Future*. World Commission on Environment and Development. https://www.are.admin.ch/are/en/home/medien-und-publikationen/publikationen/nachhaltige-entwicklung/brundtland-report.html

UN. (1992). *Agenda 21* (United Nations Conference on Environment & Development). United Nations. https://sustainabledevelopment.un.org/outcomedocuments/agenda21

UN. (2024). World Economic Situation and Prospects as of mid-2024. Retrieved fromhttps://desapublications.un.org/publications/world-economic-situation-and-prospects-mid-2024?_ga=2.152444025.1736376011.1727109015-126811107.1727108980

UNESCO. (2023). Ethics of Artificial Intelligence. Retrieved from https://unesdoc.unesco.org/ark:/48223/pf0000385082.page=4

Unsal, D. B., Aksoz, A., Oyucu, S., Guerrero, J. M., & Guler, M. (2024). A Comparative Study of AI Methods on Renewable Energy Prediction for Smart Grids: Case of Turkey. MDPI. Volume 16, Issue 7, . Retrieved from https://www.mdpi.com/2071-1050/16/7/2894DOI: 10.3390/su16072894

Uzun, M. M., Yıldız, M., & Önder, M. (2022). Big Questions of AI in Public Administration and Policy.*Siyasal: Journal of Political Sciences*, 31(2), 423–442. DOI: 10.26650/siyasal.2022.31.1121900

Valle-Cruz, D., Alejandro Ruvalcaba-Gomez, E., Sandoval-Almazan, R., & Ignacio Criado, J. (2019, June). A review of artificial intelligence in government and its potential from a public policy perspective. In *Proceedings of the 20th annual international conference on digital government research* (pp. 91-99). DOI: 10.1145/3325112.3325242

Valle-Cruz, D., & García-Contreras, R. (2023). Towards AI-driven transformation and smart data management: Emerging technological change in the public sector value chain.*Public Policy and Administration*, 0(0), 09520767231188401. Advance online publication. DOI: 10.1177/09520767231188401

Van Noordt, C., & Misuraca, G. (2022). Artificial intelligence for the public sector: Results of landscaping the use of AI in government across the European Union. *Government Information Quarterly*, 39(3), 101714. DOI: 10.1016/j.giq.2022.101714

van Noordt, C., & Misuraca, G. (2022). Exploratory Insights on Artificial Intelligence for Government in Europe.*Social Science Computer Review*, 40(2), 426–444. DOI: 10.1177/0894439320980449

van Noordt, C., Misuraca, G., & Mergel, I. (2024). Analysis of driving public values of AI initiatives in government in Europe. In *Research Handbook on Public Management and Artificial Intelligence* (pp. 226–244). Edward Elgar Publishing. DOI: 10.4337/9781802207347.00024

Varnosfaderani, S. M., & Forouzanfar, M. (2024). The role of AI in hospitals and clinics: Transforming healthcare in the 21st century.*Bioengineering (Basel, Switzerland)*, 11(4), 337. DOI: 10.3390/bioengineering11040337 PMID: 38671759

Vasdani, T. (2019). *From Estonian AI judges to robot mediators in Canada, U.K.* Retrieved from Lexisnexis: https://www.lexisnexis.ca/en-ca/ihc/2019-06/from-estonian-ai-judges-to-robot-mediators-in-canada-uk.page

Vasdani, T. (2020, 05 February). *Robot justice: China's use of Internet courts*. Retrieved from LexisNexis: https://www.lexisnexis.ca/en-ca/ihc/2019-06/from-estonian-ai-judges-to-robot-mediators-in-canada-uk.page

Vasina, A., Monastyrskyi, G., Ivanova, V., Maistrenko, K., & Tsal-Tsalko, Y. (2023). Concepts of sustainable public administration: Perspectives and challenges.*Amazonia Investiga*, 12(71), 252–262. DOI: 10.34069/AI/2023.71.11.22

Vickery, G. (2011). *Review of recent studies on PSI re-use and related market developments*. Information Economics.

Vieira, R. (1992). Complex Adaptive Systems.*Daedalus*, 121(1), 17–30. DOI: 10.1007/978-3-319-71059-4_11-1

Vinuesa, R., Azizpour, H., Leite, I., Balaam, M., Dignum, V., Domisch, S., Felländer, A., Langhans, S. D., Tegmark, M., & Fuso Nerini, F. (2020). The role of artificial intelligence in achieving the sustainable development goals.*Nature Communications*, 11(1), 233. DOI: 10.1038/s41467-019-14108-y PMID: 31932590

Vogl, T. M. (2021). Artificial intelligence in local government: Enabling artificial intelligence for good governance in UK local authorities.

Vogl, T. M., Seidelin, C., Ganesh, B., & Bright, J. (2020). Smart Technology and the Emergence of Algorithmic Bureaucracy: Artificial Intelligence in UK Local Authorities.*Public Administration Review*, 80(6), 946–961. DOI: 10.1111/puar.13286

Vogl, T., Seidelin, C., Ganesh, B., & Bright, J. (2019, June). Algorithmic bureaucracy. In *Proceedings of the 20th Annual International Conference on Digital Government Research*, 148-153. DOI: 10.1145/3325112.3325240

Vrabie, C. (2023). E-Government 3.0: An AI model to use for enhanced local democracies.*Sustainability (Basel)*, 15(12), 9572. DOI: 10.3390/su15129572

Walker, R. M., & Andrews, R. (2015). Local government management and performance: A review of evidence.*Journal of Public Administration: Research and Theory*, 25(1), 101–133. DOI: 10.1093/jopart/mut038

Wal, Z., & Mussagulova, M. (2023). Developing public service motivation in the non-Western world.*Asia Pacific Journal of Public Administration*.

Wang, W., & Cai, Y. (2022, December). The Risk of Artificial Intelligence Embedded in Government Governance: Mechanism, Process, Prevention, and Control. In 2022, 2nd International Conference on Public Management and Intelligent Society (PMIS 2022) (pp. 609-616). Atlantis Press.

Wang, P. (2019). On Defining Artificial Intelligence.*Journal of Artificial General Intelligence*, 10(2), 1–37. https://sciendo.com/article/10.2478/jagi-2019-0002. DOI: 10.2478/jagi-2019-0002

Weiser, A., & Krogh, G. (2023). Artificial intelligence and radical uncertainty. *European Management Review*, 20(4), 711–717. Advance online publication. DOI: 10.1111/emre.12630

Willems, J., Schmid, M. J., Vanderelst, D., Vogel, D., & Ebinger, F. (2023). AI-driven public services and the privacy paradox: Do citizens really care about their privacy?*Public Management Review*, 25(11), 2116–2134. DOI: 10.1080/14719037.2022.2063934

Wilson, T. (2021). Analysing the Budget and Strategic Plan Relationship: A Case Study Approach." Dissertation, Georgia State University, 2021. DOI: 10.57709/22629159

Wilson, R., & Lee, J. (2023). Technical challenges in municipal AI implementation. *Digital Government: Research and Practice*, 4(2), 1–18.

Wirtz, B. W., Langer, P. F., & Fenner, C. (2021). Artificial intelligence in the public sector—A research agenda.*International Journal of Public Administration*, 44(13), 1103–1128. DOI: 10.1080/01900692.2021.1947319

Wirtz, B. W., Weyerer, J. C., & Geyer, C. (2019). Artificial intelligence and the public sector—Applications and challenges.*International Journal of Public Administration*, 42(7), 596–615. DOI: 10.1080/01900692.2018.1498103

Wirtz, B. W., Weyerer, J. C., & Sturm, B. J. (2020). The dark sides of artificial intelligence: An integrated AI governance framework for public administration.*International Journal of Public Administration*, 43(9), 818–829. DOI: 10.1080/01900692.2020.1749851

Wirtz, B., & Müller, W. (2018). An integrated artificial intelligence framework for public management.*Public Management Review*, 21(7), 1076–1100. DOI: 10.1080/14719037.2018.1549268

World Bank Group. (2021). Artificial Intelligence in the Public Sector: Summary Note. World Bank Group, Governance. Washington DC: World Bank Group.

World Economic Forum. (2023) Fostering Effective Energy Transition 2023, Retrieved from https://www3.weforum.org/docs/WEF_Fostering_Effective_Energy_Transition_2023.pdf

World Economic Forum. (2024). These 5 cities are making innovative use of generative AI. Retrieved from https://www.weforum.org/agenda/2024/07/generative-ai-smart-cities/

World Justice Report. (2023). *WJP Rule of Law Index 2023.* World Justice Report.

Xia, L., Semirumi, D., & Rezaei, R. (2023). A thorough examination of smart city applications: Exploring challenges and solutions throughout the life cycle with emphasis on safeguarding citizen privacy.*Sustainable Cities and Society*, 93, 104771. DOI: 10.1016/j.scs.2023.104771

Xu, Q., & He, X. (2023). *Security Challenges in Natural Language Processing Models*. https://emnlp2023-nlp-security.github.io/

Xu, W., & Ouyang, F. (2022). The application of AI technologies in STEM education: A systematic review from 2011 to 2021.*International Journal of STEM Education*, 9(1), 1–20. DOI: 10.1186/s40594-022-00377-5

Yadav, M., & Singh, G. (2023). ENVIRONMENTAL SUSTAINABILITY WITH ARTIFICIAL INTELLIGENCE.[IJMR]. *EPRA International Journal of Multidisciplinary Research*, 213–217, 213–217. Advance online publication. DOI: 10.36713/epra13325

Yalçın, A. (2024). Türkiye'de Kamu Kurumlarının Toplum İçin Geliştirdiği Yapay Zekâ Uygulamaları. *İstanbul Aydın Üni versitesi Sosyal Bilimler Dergisi, 16*(2), 185-215.

Yamamoto, K., & Schührer, S. (2023). Finance and accounting: recent developments and challenges building efficiency and public accountability. *Handbook of Public Administration Reform*, 90-110.

Yargıtay. (2023, July 19). *Yargıtayın Kurumsal Kapasitesinin Güçlendirilmesi Projesi Kapanış Konferansı" Gerçekleştirildi*. Retrieved October 31, 2024, from Türkiye Cumhuriyeti Yargıtay Başkanlığı: https://www.yargitay.gov.tr/icerik/1727/yargitayin-kurumsal-kapasitesinin-guclendirilmesi-projesi-kapanis-konferansi-gerceklestirildi

Yefremova, I. (2024). Using the AI service RunwayML for data visualization. *Dnipro Academy of Continuing Education Herald. Series: Philosophy. Pedagogy.*

Yen, C. P., & Hung, T. W. (2021). Achieving equity with predictive policing algorithms: A social safety net perspective.*Science and Engineering Ethics*, 27(3), 1–16. DOI: 10.1007/s11948-021-00312-x PMID: 34075448

Yeung, K. (2018). Algorithmic regulation: A critical interrogation.*Regulation & Governance*, 12(4), 505–523. DOI: 10.1111/rego.12158

Yigitcanlar, T., Corchado, J. M., Mehmood, R., Li, R. Y. M., Mossberger, K., & Desouza, K. (2021). Responsible urban innovation with local government artificial intelligence (AI): A conceptual framework and research agenda.*Journal of Open Innovation*, 7(1), 71. DOI: 10.3390/joitmc7010071

Yiğitcanlar, T., Desouza, K. C., Butler, L., & Rashidi, F. (2020). Contributions and risks of artificial intelligence (AI) in building smarter cities: Insights from a systematic review of the literature.*Energies*, 13(6), 1473. Retrieved November 25, 2022, from. DOI: 10.3390/en13061473

Yigitcanlar, T., Li, R. Y., Inkinen, T., & Paz, A. (2022). Public perceptions on application areas and adoption challenges of AI in urban services.*Emerging Science Journal*, 6(6), 1199–1236. DOI: 10.28991/ESJ-2022-06-06-01

Yılmaz, D. (2019). "Usul Ekonomisi İlkesi" Çerçevesinde Türk İdari Yargılama Usulünde Sözlülük İlkesine İlişkin Bazı Değerlendirmeler.*Ankara Hacı Bayram Veli Üniversitesi Hukuk Fakültesi Dergisi*, 23(2), 267–320. DOI: 10.34246/ahbvuhfd.585054

Yılmaz, O. G. (2021). Yargı Uygulamasinda Yapay Zekâ Kullanımı - Yapay Zekâ Hâkim Cübbesini Giyebilecek mi?*Adalet Dergisi*, (66), 379–415.

Yolvi, O. F., Alex, V. F. L., Angel, V. F. M., & Alberto, R. L. R. (2022). Artificial intelligence (AI) applied to public management.*Metaverse*, 3(2), 8. DOI: 10.54517/m.v3i2.1795

Yu, J., Yu, Y., Wang, X., Lin, Y., Yang, M., Qiao, Y., & Wang, F.-Y. (2024). The Shadow of Fraud: The Emerging Danger of AI-powered Social Engineering and its Possible Cure. *arXiv preprint arXiv:2407.15912*.

Zafar, A. (2024). Balancing the scale: navigating ethical and practical challenges of artificial intelligence (AI) integration in legal practices. *Discover Artificial Intelligence, 4*(27).

Zerilli, J., Knott, A., MacLaurin, J., & Gavaghan, C. (2018). Transparency in Algorithmic and Human Decision-Making: Is There a Double Standard?*Philosophy & Technology*, •••, 1–23. DOI: 10.1007/s13347-018-0330-6

Zhang, L. (2024). How does homeownership shape public service coproduction? Evidence from a public complaint system in Beijing, China.

Zhang, B., & Dafoe, A. (2020, February). US public opinion on the governance of artificial intelligence. In *Proceedings of the AAAI/ACM Conference on AI, Ethics, and Society* (pp. 187-193). DOI: 10.1145/3375627.3375827

Zhang, J., & Zhang, Z. M. (2023). Ethics and governance of trustworthy medical artificial intelligence.*BMC Medical Informatics and Decision Making*, 23(1), 7. DOI: 10.1186/s12911-023-02103-9 PMID: 36639799

Zhou, X., Jain, K., Moinuddin, M., & McSharry, P. (2022). Using Natural Language Processing for Automating the Identification of Climate Action Interlinkages within the Sustainable Development Goals.

Zuiderwijk, A., Chen, Y. C., & Salem, F. (2021). Implications of the use of artificial intelligence in public governance: A systematic literature review and a research agenda. *Government Information Quarterly*, 38(3), 101577. DOI: 10.1016/j.giq.2021.101577

About the Contributors

Ulas Akkucuk is an Associate Professor of Quantitative Methods at Bogazici University Department of Management, Usak, Turkey. Dr. Akkucuk has a BS in Industrial Engineering from Bilkent University (1997), an MBA from Bogazici University (2000), and a PhD in Management Science and Information Systems from Rutgers University (2004). He has taught Statistics, CRM & Data Mining, and Global Aspects of Management courses, among others, at both graduate and undergraduate levels. He is Editor in Chief for International Journal of Environmental Sustainability and Green Technologies, Associate Editor for International Journal of E-Business Research and Subject Area Editor for Journal of Global Business Insights. He has edited 11 books with IGI Global two of which have been indexed by WoS.

Murat Önder is Professor at Bogaziçi University, Turkiye. Ph.D. in Public Administration and Policy from Florida State University. Research interests are in the topics of comparative public administration, methodology, strategic management, performance, quality, NGOs, public policy analysis, governance, and artificial intelligence.

***

Saroja Achanta, a seasoned Senior Financial Management Professional, boasts over 25 years of experience. Holding a PhD in Management from GITAM Deemed University, Hyderabad, India. Academically well-rounded, she holds dual bachelor's degrees in Commerce and Law and earned an MBA in Banking and Finance, Master of Law. She got Certified in ADR (Alternate Dispute Resolution) Methods from The Indian Law Society's Centre for Arbitration and Mediation, Pune, and Certified Corporate Director from the Institute of Directors, New Delhi. She is a qualified Independent Director in the Indian Institute of Corporate Affairs & Member of the Hyderabad Management Association. Her expertise extends beyond traditional financial roles, evidenced by her commitment to technology adoption and innovation. Dr Saroja is not only a strategic leader but also a skilled communicator and motivator. She is a dynamic director with a rich background in finance, entrepreneurship, and academia, contributing significantly to the success and growth of the organizations she leads. Dr Saroja's impactful leadership extends to diverse sectors, encompassing strategic financial management, entrepreneurship, and technology adoption. With a strong academic foundation, she continues to shape and drive success in today's dynamic business landscape.

Dayo Akindipe is an academic and researcher. He obtained his Master of Laws (LL.M) at the University of Strathclyde, Scotland and also a certification in European and International Economic Law at the University of Augsburg, Germany. He is currently a law lecturer at the Afe Babalola University, Nigeria. He has published several papers and organized seminars and lectures for all Senior Advocates of Nigeria.

Alp Cenk Arslan, Ph.D. is a scholar specializing in security and intelligence studies and currently works as an assistant professor at the Turkish National Police Academy. His research focuses on the intersection of techno-politics, intelligence, and communication studies, providing insights into modern security challenges. His academic contributions explore how emerging technologies and political dynamics shape the future of intelligence and security. Arslan has also contributed to discussions on various topics such as intelligence failures and global security developments. He is the author of the book “Intelligence Analysis: Reproduction of Information”.

C. Shree Charan is an Assistant Professor of Business Analytics. He has an experience of over 11years in Corporate Training, Research and Academics. He had excelled in the industry by training eminent Data Scientists, Big Data Architects and Hadoop Developers. He received a Ph.D. from PONDICHERRY UNIVERSITY (A CENTRAL UNIVERSITY).

Mustafa Demirkol, born in Istanbul in 1989, completed his undergraduate studies in Political Science and Public Administration at Fatih University with a 100% scholarship, graduating as the top student. He earned his master’s degree, also with a 100% scholarship, as a fellow of the Turkish Prime Ministry’s Atatürk Supreme Council for Culture, Language, and History, with a thesis on constitutional reconciliation in Turkish democracy. He later completed his Ph.D. at Istanbul University, focusing on metropolitan governance models for Turkey. With support from the TÜBİTAK 2219 Postdoctoral Fellowship, Dr. Demirkol spent 12 months at Malmö University's Urban Studies Department conducting research on alternative metropolitan management models. Since 2013, he has served as a faculty member at Tekirdağ Namık Kemal University, publishing extensively in respected national and international journals in political science and public administration.

Olalekan Moyosore Lalude, is a lawyer, writer, academic, researcher and activist. He is an international environmental law and human rights expert, who has published in learned journals and presented at international conferences on human rights and environmental law issues. He is currently a Lecturer at the Faculty of Law, Wisconsin International University College, Ghana.

Arjun J Nair is working as a Professor with St. Lawrance College, Ontario, Canada. He has completed a Master of Science degree in Hospitality and Tourism Management from Madurai Kamaraj University, an MBA in Human Resources and Finance Management from the National Institute of Business Management in India, a Bachelor's Degree in Hotel Management and a Diploma in Hospitality Management from the American Hotel and Lodging Association in the United States. He holds professional memberships in several organizations, including the International Management Research and Technology Consortium in New York, the International Association of Innovation Professionals, the American Management Association, the National Human Resources Association and the Institute of Research Engineers and Doctors (Senior Member of the Universal Association of Arts and Management Professionals). With over 15 years of practical work experience in a variety of industries, such as education, exporting, hotel food and beverage, restaurant management and management training, he offers expertise in curriculum development, project management, lecturing, tutoring, general management, business administration, business development, staff management and public relations. He is a strategic thinker who has made significant contributions to training and facilitation, business development and the operations and management aspects of various organizations.

Israel Nyaburi Nyadera (PhD) is a lecturer at the National Defence College, a college of the National Defence University -Kenya. He holds the Swiss Government Excellence Postdoc fellowship at the Center for Conflict, Development and Peacebuilding, Geneva Graduate Institute, Switzerland. Additionally, he holds a fellowship with the Irregular Warfare Initiative, a collaborative project between the Modern War Institute at West Point and the Empirical Studies of Conflict Project at Princeton University. Dr. Nyadera has also served as a visiting researcher through the India-Africa Security Fellowship Program at the Manohar Parrikar Institute for Defence Studies and Analyses in New Delhi, India. He has previously been awarded the Global Africa young researchers fellowship at LASDEL, Niger and a Charles E.

Scheidt Fellow for Genocide and Mass Atrocity Prevention, at the George Manson University.

Esin Okay is a Professor of Finance, currently serving as a sessional academic staff at universities in Istanbul, Turkey. During her career Okay stayed at Istanbul Commerce University (ICU) teaching and serving in various positions for 20 years. Respectively, Okay was the Head of Banking and Finance, board member of Finance Institute, Director of the Center for Applied Research of International Creative Economy, Director of Center for Applied Research of Economics and Finance and Vice Head of Banking and Finance at ICU. She received her BA in Business Administration and completed her PhD at the Institute of Banking and Insurance, respectively from the Marmara University. Prior to commencing her PhD thesis, she worked for Global Securities Inc. in Istanbul for 5 years, as a dealer and lastly the founding Deputy of Institutional Investment Department. Okay teaches undergradute and graduate programs in the areas of finance, majorly risk management. Esin Okay has refereed papers, books and a book chapter in a widely recognized "World ESCO Outlook". In recent years, she has focused on energy finance as her papers appeared in journals of Social Science Index and received citations.Okay is a member of Professional Risk Managers' International Association (PRMIA).

Tarun Sai Raavi is currently Assistant Professor at Vishawa Vishawani institute of Systems & Management. He has a Double MBA degrees with specializations: Finance and Analytics He is Pursuing his Ph.D. from Aurora University titled "Designing and Development of Machine Learning and Artificial Intelligence (AI) Tools for Enhanced Decision-Making by Individual Investors in India for Security Analysis, and Portfolio Optimization"

Satish Rao A.B. is an Assistant Professor at the Welcomgroup Graduate School of Hotel Administration (WGSHA) at Manipal Academy of Higher Education. He specialises in Food and Beverage Service and handles practical sessions for first-year students in the Bachelor of Hotel Management (BHM) and Bachelor of Arts (Honours) programs. He holds a PhD in Tourism Management from Madurai Kamaraj University and has several years of teaching and management experience in various educational institutions. His research interests lie in service marketing.

Marieta Stefanova, Ph.D., is an academic lecturer at Nikola Vaptsarov Naval Academy in Bulgaria. She teaches bachelor's-level courses in Logistics and Quality, and master's-level courses in Quality Management, Safety, Environmental and Security Management, Logistics, Ship Agency, and Freight Forwarding. She has more than twenty-five years of professional experience as a quality manager in food manufacturing plants. Assoc. Prof. Stefanova is a member of the Expert Council of the Center for Quality of Goods and Consumer Protection (CQGCP) at the Research Institute of the University of Economics (UE) – Varna. She is also a member of the Union of Scientists Bulgaria and the IGWT International Association for Commodity Science and Technology. She has published more than forty articles in national and international scientific journals.

Index

A

P

R

S

T

V

www.ingramcontent.com/pod-product-compliance
Lightning Source LLC
LaVergne TN
LVHW080612300926
849162LV00005B/1125